EPHESIANS

RUDOLF SCHNACKENBURG

EPHESIANS

A Commentary

Translated by
Helen Heron

T&T CLARK
EDINBURGH

T&T CLARK
59 GEORGE STREET
EDINBURGH EH2 2LQ
SCOTLAND

First Published 1991

ISBN 0 567 09556 8 HB
ISBN 0 567 29556 7 PB

Typeset by Barbers Highlands Ltd, Fort William
Printed and bound in Great Britain by
Billing & Sons Ltd, Worcester

Contents

Preface   7
Abbreviations and Literature   9

A.   INTRODUCTION   21
　　1. The Literary Form   21
　　2. Author and Addressees   24
　　3. The Relationship to Colossians   30
　　4. Date and Circumstances of Composition   33

B.   COMMENTARY   39
I   Salutation, Glorification of God and Opening (1.1–2.10)   39
　　1. Salutation and Blessing (1.1–2)   39
　　2. The Great Opening Eulogy (1.3–14)   44
　　3. Thanksgiving to God and Intercession that the readers may have a
　　　　deeper understanding of the Christ-event (1.15–23)   69
　　4. Address to the Readers on their conversion to Christianity and
　　　　their new life (2.1–10)   86

II   Christian Existence in the Church of Jesus Christ as the Mystery of
　　Salvation (2.11–3.21)   102
　　1. The New Approach to God opened up in Jesus Christ in the Church
　　　　composed of Jews and Gentiles (2.11–22)   103
　　2. Paul as Preacher and Interpreter of the Mystery of Salvation
　　　　revealed in the Church (3.1–13)   127
　　3. The Apostle's Concerns in his Prayers: inner strengthening of faith,
　　　　love and knowledge (3.14–19)   144
　　4. Conclusion with a Doxology (3.20–1)   154

III   Realising Christian Existence in Church and World (4.1–6.20)   158
　　1. The Church as the Sphere of Christian Existence (4.1–16)   158
　　　　(a) The unity of the Church as an urgent concern (4.1–6)   159
　　　　(b) Unity in variety: the meaning of the ministries in the Church
　　　　　　and for the Church (4.7–16)   169
　　2. Christian Existence in a pagan Environment (4.17–5.14)   192
　　　　(a) Separation from non-Christian behaviour and accomplishment
　　　　　　of the 'new person' (4.17–24)   193
　　　　(b) Renunciation of old tendencies and striving after Christian
　　　　　　qualities, especially love (4.25–5.2)   203
　　　　(c) Avoidance of pagan vices (sexual immorality) and acting as
　　　　　　Children of the Light (5.3–14)   215

5

3. The Life of the Christian Congregation (5.15–6.9)   231
  (a) Spiritual life in the Congregation (5.15–20)   232
  (b) (*Haustafel*) The behaviour of married people with reference to Christ and his Church (5.21–33)   240
  (c) (*Haustafel*) The behaviour of children and parents, slaves and masters (6.1–9)   258
4. The Battle against the Powers of Evil in the World; continual prayerful Alertness (6.10–20)   266

IV Conclusion of the Letter (6.21–4)   286
    Excursus: The Church in the Epistle to the Ephesians   293

C. THE INFLUENCE OF THE EPISTLE THROUGHOUT HISTORY   311
1. God and Humanity. Predestination   312
2. Christ and Redemption   315
  (a) All things summed up in Christ (*Anacephalaiosis, Recapitulatio*) (Eph. 1.10)   315
  (b) The Presence of Christ in the Faithful (Eph. 3.17)   318
3. The Theology of the Church   321
  (a) From Israel to the Church: Church and Judaism (Eph. 2.11–19)   321
  (b) The Church as God's Building (Eph. 2.20–22)   325
  (c) Ministries and Offices in the Church (Eph. 4.7–16)   328
4. Ethics and Christian Life   331
  (a) Christian Marriage (Eph. 5.21–33)   331
  (b) Spiritual Military Service (Eph. 6.10–20)   337

D. Prospect: THE EPISTLE TO THE EPHESIANS IN ITS MEANING FOR OUR TIME   343

Index of Subjects   347
Index of Names   349
Important biblical passages   356

Preface

I had originally no intention of writing a Commentary on the Epistle to the Ephesians – what scholar is not frightened off by this unusual writing which is so difficult to 'grasp'? But when Eduard Schweizer approached me about the undertaking of a 'Protestant–Catholic Commentary on the NT' in which two scholars, one Catholic, the other Protestant, should work on two related writings and each comment on the other's efforts, I agreed to take part. A further incentive was that I could study the topic of 'the Church' – a subject which I have for a long time considered of extreme importance in the ecumenical field – in this document whose ecclesiological concerns are deeply marked throughout. The working-conferences in Zürich, made possible by the generosity of the two publishing-houses involved, contributed greatly to the advancement of the studies I have been involved in over the years. I am grateful to my colleagues and friends in this stimulating study-group for all that I learned from them in open discussion – frequently in the clash of different stand-points, but always in a good ecumenical climate. I am especially grateful to Eduard Schweizer who stimulated my Commentary with many valuable suggestions, critical observations and useful comments. It is quite understandable that we were not always of the same opinion; in one case – the question of office – this is documented in this volume (v. pp. 191 f.). But I am pleased that we are in agreement on many exegetical and theological questions.

The main emphasis of my endeavours compared to earlier commentaries on Éphesians (to which I owe a great deal) is easily recognisable. I started from the textual analysis and gave this greater weight when I came to examine the syntactic, semantic and pragmatic areas. What I have included in the sections headed 'Analysis' makes no claim to be a strictly methodical, linguistic procedure as is commonly practised – admittedly in quite different ways. But my understanding of this letter, commonly considered 'general', has been particularly helped by my consideration of the pragmatic dimension of the text. Whether my determination of the type and character of the letter is correct must be shown by further research.

From this also arose the attempt to make each section 'more transparent' in the way I have arranged the text in the translation. I must confess that my attempts were somewhat constrained by the long, complicated sentences and I could not arrange everything typographically to my satisfaction. Wolfgang Schenk's remarks, based on current philology, on the question of what a commentary is (BZ NF 24 [1980] 1–20) should be given serious consideration. As he sees it, the translation should come at the end of the whole process, as its fruit, the author be conscious of his own new production of the text, give careful consideration to the interlapping of various steps etc. But is it possible to realize an ideal form of commentary? The procedure chosen for the Protestant–Catholic Commentaries was that translation, analysis, exegesis and summary should form a unit and that the sequence should not necessarily reflect the process of discovery. As far as the interpretation before you is concerned, there is no denying that it reflects its author's theological views and ecumenical objectives. I was principally, though not exclusively, concerned with the theme of the Church, its rise to prominence in the post-Pauline situation of the author of Ephesians and its continuing importance for our day and age. From the very start I intended to have only one excursus in this volume, namely that on the Church. Section C contains only a limited and fragmentary outline of the influence of the letter. But it should at least draw attention to the different ways in which the text has been influential in divers historical contexts and encourage us to reflect on what effect it should have today.

I must also thank many colleagues who gave me valuable information, particularly on the historical influence of Ephesians – but beg their understanding that I do not name them here. I should like to thank my secretary, Frau Hannelore Ferner, who tirelessly and with great care attended to all the paperwork. And last but not least the Neukirchner and Benziger publishing-houses for their trouble and patience. The thanksgiving addressed to God in Eph. 5.20 applies to us all.

Abbreviations and Literature

1. Abbreviations

These generally follow S. Schwertner, *International Glossary for Theology and Related Subjects*, de Gruyter, Berlin – New York, 1974.

AHAW.PH	Abhandlungen der Heidelberger Akademie der Wissenschaften – Philosophisch-historische Klasse
AncB	Anchor Bible
Angelos	Angelos. Archiv für neutestamentliche Zeitgeschichte
AnGr	Analecta Gregoriana
ASNU	Acta seminarii neotestamentici Upsaliensis
AThANT	Abhandlungen zur Theologie des Alten und Neuen Testaments
AUL.T	Acta universitatis Lundensis – Afdeling 1. Teologi, juridik och humanistika ämnen
BBB	Bonner biblische Beiträge
BGBE	Beiträge zur Geschichte der biblischen Exegese
BHH	Biblisch-historisches Handwörterbuch
BHTh	Beiträge zur historischen Theologie
Bib.	Biblica (Rome)
Bijdr.	Bijdragen. Tijdschrift voor philosophie en theologie
BTN	Bibliotheca theologica Norvegica
BU	Biblische Untersuchungen
BVG	Beiträge zur vaterländischen Geschichte
BWANT	Beiträge zur Wissenschaft vom Alten und Neuen Testament
BZ	Biblische Zeitschrift
BZNW	Beihefte zur Zeitschrift für die neutestamentliche Wissenschaft
CB.NT	Coniectanea biblica, New Testament series
CBQ	Catholic Biblical Quarterly
CChr	Corpus Christanorum
CNEB	Cambridge Bible Commentary on the New English Bible
CNT(N)	Commentaire du Nouveau Testament (Neuchâtel)
CR	Corpus reformatorum
CSEL	Corpus scriptorum ecclesiasticorum Latinorum
DBS	Dictionnaire de la bible. Supplément
DJD	Discoveries in the Judaen desert
EKK	Evangelisch-katholischer Kommentar zum Neuen Testament
EstB	Estudios bíblicos
ET	Expository Times
EtB	Études bibliques
EtCarm	Études carmélitaines
EthSt	Erfurter theologische Studien
EvTh	Evangelische Theologie

EWNT	Exegetisches Wörterbuch zum Neuen Testament (Stuttgart, 1980ff.)
FLB	Franziskanische Lebensbilder
FRLANT	Forschungen zur Religion und Literatur des Alten und Neuen Testaments
FS	Fetschrift
FThST	Freiburger theologische Studien
FTS	Frankfurter theologische Studien
FzB	Forschung zur Bibel (Wurzburg, 1972ff.)
GCS	Griechischen christlichen Schriftsteller ersten drei Jahrhunderte
Gr	Gregorianum (Rome)
HAW	Handbuch der Altertumswissenschaft
HC	Hand-Commentar zum Neuen Testament
HNT	Handbuch zum Neuen Testament
HSNT	Die Heilige Schrift des Neuen Testament (Bonn)
HThK	Herders theologischer Kommentar zum Neuen Testament
ICC	International Critical Commentary
IntB	Interpreter's Bible
JAC	Jahrbuch für Antike und Christentum
JBL	Journal of Biblical Literature
JETS	Journal of the Evangelical Theological Society
JLW	Jahrbuch für Liturgiewissenschaft
JThs	Journal of Theological Studies
Kairos	Kairos. Zeitschrift für Religionswissenschaft und Theologie (Salzburg)
KEK	Kritisch-exegetischer Kommentar über das Neue Testament (Meyer)
KNT	Kommentar zum Neuen Testament
Laur.	Laurentianum (Rome)
LeDiv	Lectio divina
LJ	Liturgisches Jahrbuch
LQF	Liturgiesgeschichtliche Quellen und Forschungen
LThK	Lexikon für Theologie und Kirche
MNTC	Moffat New Testament Commentary
MPG	J. Migne, *Patrologia Graeca*
MPL	J. Migne, *Patrologia Latina*
MSSNTS	Monograph Series. Society for New Testament Studies
MThS	Münchener theologische Studien
MThSt	Marburger theologische Studien
NCB	New Clarendon Bible
NedThT	Nederlandsche theologisch tijdschrift
Nestle-Aland	Nestle-Aland, *Novum Testamentum graece*, 26th newly-revised edition, Stuttgart, 1979
NF	neue Folge
NHC	Nag Hammadi Codices, v. list in Troger, *Gnosis und NT*, pp. 20f. The editions used are given in the appropriate footnotes.
NRTh	Nouvelle revue théologique
NT	Novum Testamentum (Leiden)
NT.S	Novum Testamentum Supplements
NTA	Neutestamentliche Abhandlungen
NTD	Das Neue Testament Deutsch
NTF	Neutestamentliche Forschung
NTS	New Testament Studies
QD	Quaestiones disputatae

RAC	Reallexikon für Antike und Christentum
RE	Realencyklopädie für protestantliche Theologie und Kirche
RechBib	Recherches bibliques
RGG	Religion in Geschichte und Gegenwart
RivBib	Rivista biblica
RNT	Regensburger Neues Testament
RRef	Revue réformée
Salm.	Salmanticensis (Salamanca)
SBFLA	Studii biblici Franciscani liber annuus
SBL	Svenkst biografiskt lexikon
SBS	Stuttgarter Bibelstudien
SC	Sources chrétiennes
ScC	Scuola cattolica
ScEc	Sciences ecclésiastiques
SHAW.PH	Sitzungsberichte der Heidelberger Akademie der Wissenschaften – Philosophisch-historische Klasse
SPCIC	Studiorum Paulinorum congressus internationalis catholicus
StANT	Studien zum Alten und Neuen Testament
StAnt	Studia Antoniana
StEv	Studia evangelica
StNT	Studien zum Neuen Testament
StPat	Studia Patavina
StTh	Studia theologica (Lund)
StUNT	Studien zur Umwelt des Neuen Testaments
SyBU	Symbolae biblicae Upsalienses
TBLNT	Theologisches Begriffslexikon zum NT
TDNT	Theological Dictionary of the New Testament, translation of Theologische Wörterbuch zum Neuen Testament (ThWNT)
TDOT	Theological Dictionary of the Old Testament, translation of Theologische Wörterbuch zum Alten Testament (ThWAT)
TEH	Theologische Existenz heute
THAT	Theologisches Handwörterbuch zum Alten Testament
ThBl	Theologisches Blätter
Theol.	Theology
ThLZ	Theologische Literaturzeitung
ThRv	Theologische Revue
ThStKr	Theologische Studien und Kritiken
ThZ	Theologisches Zeitschrift (Basel)
TNTC	Tyndale New Testament Commentaries
TRE	Theologische Realenzyklopädie
TThSt	Trierer theologische Studien
TU	Texte und Untersuchungen zur Geschichte der altchristlichen Literatur
UUA	Uppsala universitets årsskrift
VF	Verkündigung und Forschung
VSal	Verbum salutis
WA	Weimar edition, Luther's Works
WdF	Wege der Forschung
WMANT	Wissenschaftliche Monographien zum Alten und Neuen Testament
WuD	Wort und Dienst
WUNT	Wissenchaftliche Untersuchungen zum Neuen Testament
ZEE	Zeitschrift für evangelische Ethik
ZKTh	Zeitschrift für catholische Theologie

ZM   Zeitschrift für Missionswissenschaft
ZNW   Zeitschrift für die neutestamentliche Wissenchaft
ZThK   Zeitschrift für Theologie und Kirche

2. Commentaries which are only cited with the name of the author

Abbott, T. K., *A Critical and Exegtical Commentary on the Epistles to the Ephesians and to the Colossians*, 1897 (repr. 1974), (ICC 8).

Allan, J. A., *The Epistle to the Ephesians*, London 1959.

Ambrosiaster, *In Epistolam ad Ephesios*, in MPL 17, 393–426 or CSEL 81/3, 69–126.

Barth, M., *Ephesians*, 2 vols., 1974 (AncB 34 and 34A).

Beare, F. W. – Wedel, Th. O., *The Epistle to the Ephesians*, in IntB X (1953) 595–749.

Belser, J., *Der Epheserbrief des Apostles Paulus*, Freiburg i. Br. 1908.

Bengel, J. A., *Gnomon Novi Testamenti* (Tübingen 1773), Stuttgart [8]1887, 753–78.

Billerbeck, P. (and Strack, H. L.), *Kommentar zum Neuen Testament aus Talmud und Midrasch* III, München 1926, 579–618.

Bisping, A., *Die Briefe an die Epheser, Philipper, Kolosser*, Münster i. W. [3]1866.

Bouwman, G., *De Brief aan de Efeziërs: Het NT vertaald en toegelicht*, Bussum 1974.

Brenz, Johannes (†1570), *Komm. zum Briefe des Apostels Paulus an die Epheser*, ed. by W. Köhler, 1935, (AHAW.PH 10).

Bruce., F. F., *The Epistle to the Ephesians*, London 1961, repr. 1974.

Caird., G. B., *Paul's Letters from Prison*, 1976 (NCB).

Calvin, John, *Comm. in Ep. Pauli ad Ephesios*, in CR 79 (1895), Calvini opera 51, col. 141–240.

Conzelmann, H., *Der Brief an die Epheser*, in NTD 8, [14]1976, 86–124.

Dahl, N. A., 'Bibelstudie über den Epheserbrief', in id. et al., *Kurze Auslegung des Epheserbriefs*, Göttingen 1965, 7–83.

De Wette, W. M. L., *Kurze Erklärung der Briefe an die Colosser, an Philemon, an die Ephesier und Philipper*, Leipzig [2]1847.

Dibelius, M., *An die Kolosser, Epheser an Philemon*, new edition by H. Greeven, [3]1953 (HNT 12).

Ephräm the Syrian, *Commentarii in ep. D. Pauli*, Venedig 1893, 140–56.

Erasmus, Desiderius, of Rotterdam, *In Epistolam ad Ephesios*, in Opera VI, Leiden 1705, republ. London 1962, 831–60.

Ernst, J., *Die Briefe an die Philipper, an Philemon, an die Kolosser, an die Epheser*, 1974 (RNT).

Estius, W., *In omnes D. Pauli epistolas, item in catholicos* (Douai 1614/16), Paris 1891, II, 344–86.

Ewald, P., *Die Briefe des Paulus an die Epheser, Kolosser und Philemon*, [2]1910 (KNT 10).

Foulkes, F., *The Epistle of Paul to the Ephesians*, 1971 (TNTC 10).

Gaugler, E., *Der Epheserbrief*, Zürich 1966.

Gnilka, J., *Der Epheserbrief*, [2]1977 (HThK X/2).

Haupt, E., *Die Gefangenschaftsbriefe*, [8]1902 (KEK 8).

Hendriksen, W., *NT Comm.: Exposition of Ephesians*, Grand Rapids 1967.

Henle, F. A. von, *Der Ephesierbrief des hl. Apostels Paulus*, Augsburg [2]1908.

Houlden, J. L., *Paul's Letters from Prison: Phil, Col, Philem, Eph*, 1970 (The Pelican NT Comm.).

Huby, J. S., *Paul. Les Epîtres de la captivité*, [19]1947 (VSal 8).

Hugedé, N., *L'Épître aux Éphésiens*, Genf 1974.

Jerome, *Comm in Epistolam ad Ephesios*, in MPL 26, 439–554.

John Chrysostom, *In Epistolam ad Ephesios*, in MPG 62, 9–176.

John of Damascus, *In Epistolam ad Ephesios*, in MPG 95, 821–56.

Klöpper, A., *Der Brief an die Epheser*, Göttingen 1891.

Marius Victorinus, *In Epistolam ad Ephesios*, in MPL 8, 1235–94.

Masson, Ch., *L'épître de Saint-Paul aux Éphésiens* 1953 (CNT[N] 9, p. 133–230).

Meinertz, M., *Der Epheserbrief*, [4]1931 (HSNT 7, S. 50–106).

Mitton, C. L., *Ephesians* (New Century Bible) 1973.

Moule, Handley C. G., *Ephesian Studies*, London 1900, repr. 1975.

Oecumenius, fragments in Staab, *Pauluskommentare* 448–52.

Origen, Greek fragments in J. A. F. Gregg, JThS 3 (1902), 233–44, 398–420, 554–6.

Pelagius, *P.'s Expositions of Thirteen Epistles of St. Paul*, ed. A. Souter, II. Cambridge 1926, 344–86.

Photius of Constantinople (†891), fragments in Staab, *Pauluskommentare* 611–21.

Rienecker, F., *Der Brief des Paulus an die Epheser* (Wuppertaler Studienbibel) [4]1975.

Rhabanus Maurus (†856), *Expositio in Ep. ad. Ephesios*, in MPL 112, 381–478.

Robinson, J. A., *St. Paul's Epistle to the Ephesians*, London [2]1922.

Schlier, H., *Der Brief an die Epheser. Ein Kommentar*, Düsseldorf [7]1971.

Scott, E. F., *The Epistles of Paul to the Colossians, to Philemon and to the Ephesians*, 1930 (MNTC 10).

Severian of Gabala, fragments in Staab, *Pauluskommentare* 304–13.

Staab, K., *Pauluskommentare aus der griechischen Kirche*, 1933 (NTA 15).

——*Die Thessalonicherbriefe und die Gefangenschaftsbriefe*, [3]1959 (RNT 7).

Theodoret of Cyrrhus, *Interpretatio Epistolae ad Ephesios*, in MPG 82, 505–58.

Theodore of Mopsuestia, *In epistolas B. Pauli Commentarii*, ed. H. B. Swete, Cambridge 1880, I, 112–96.

Theophylact (†1108), *In Epistolam ad Ephesios*, in MPG 124, 1031–1138.

Thomas Aquinas, *Super epistulas S. Pauli lectura* II, ed. R. Cai, Turin-Rome [8]1953, 1–87.

Thompson, G. H. P., *The Letters of Paul to the Ephesians, to the Colossians and to Philemon*, 1967 (CNEB).

Vaughan, C., *Ephesians. A Study Guide Commentary*, Grand Rapids 1977.

von Soden, Hermann, *Die Briefe an die Epheser, Kolosser, Philemon, die Pastoralbriefe*, [2]1893 (HC 3).

Vosté, J. M., *Commentarius in Epistolam ad Ephesios*, Rome-Paris ²1932.
Weiss, B., *Die paulinischen Briefe und der Hebräerbrief*, Leipzig ²1902, II, 371–414.
Westcott, B. F., *St. Paul's Epistle to the Ephesians*, London 1906.
Zerwick, M., *Der Brief an die Epheser* (Geistl. Schriftlesung 10), Düsseldorf ²1962.

3. Literature which is cited by means of the author's name and an abbreviated title

Allan, J. A., 'The "In Christ" Formula in Ephesians', NTS 5 (1958/59) 54–62.
Barth, M., 'Die Einheit des Galater- und Epheserbriefes', ThZ 32 (1976) 78–91.
Baulès, R., *L'insondable richese du Christ. Étude des thèmes de l'Epître aux Ephésiens*, 1971 (LeDiv 66).
Becker, J., *Das Heil Gottes. Heils-und Sündenbegriffe in den Qumrantexten und im Neuen Testament*, 1964 (StUNT 3).
Beniot, P., 'Leib, Haupt und Pleroma in den Gefangenschaftsbriefen', in id., *Exegese und Theologie. Gesammelte Aufsätze*, Düsseldorf 1965, 246–79.
——Art 'Paul. Éphésiens', DBS VII (1966) 195–211.
Best E., *One Body in Christ. A study in the Relationship of the Church to Christ in the Epistles of the Apostle Paul*, London 1955.
Biblia Patristica. *Index des citations et allusions bibliques dans la littérature patrisque*, 2 vols., Paris 1975/77.
Bieder, W., *Ekklesia und Polis im Neuen Testament und in der alten Kirche*, Zürich 1941.
——'Das Geheimnis des Christus nach dem Epheserbrief', ThZ 11 (1955) 329–43.
Bultmann, R., *Theologie des Neuen Testaments*, Tübingen ⁵1965.
Burger, C., *Schöpfung und Versöhnung. Studien zum literarischen Gut im Kolosser- und Epheserbrief*, 1975 (WMANT 46).
Cadbury, H. J., 'The Dilemma of Ephesians', NTS 5 (1958/59) 91–102.
Caragounis, C. C., *The Ephesian Mysterion. Meaning and Content*, 1977 (CB.NT 8).
Chadwick, H., 'Die Absicht des Epheserbriefes', ZNW (1960) 145–53.
Colpe C., *Die religionsgeschichtliche Schule. Darstellung der Kritik ihres Bildes vom gnostischen Erlösermythus*, 1961 (FRLANT 78).
——'Zur Leib-Christi-Vorstellung im Epheserbrief', in *Judentum, Urchistentum, Kirche* (FS J. Jeremias) ed. W. Eltester, 1964 (BZNW 26) 172–87.
Conzelmann H., *Grundriß der Theologie des Neuen Testaments*, München 1967.
Coutts, J., 'The Relationship of Ephesians and Colossians', NTS 4 (1957/58) 201–7.
Cross, F. L., (ed.), *Studies in Ephesians*, London 1956.
Dautzenberg, G., *Urchristliche Prophetie*, 1975 (BWANT 104).
Deichgräber, R., *Gotteshymnus und Christushymnus in der frühen Christenheit*, 1967 (StUNT 5).

Du Plessis, I. J., *Christus as Hoof van Kerk en Kosmos*, Groningen 1962.

Dupont, J., *Gnosis. La connaissance religieuse dans les épîtres de s. Paul*, Löwen 1949.

Ernst, J., *Pleroma und Pleroma Christi. Geschichte und Deutung eines Begriffs der paulinischen Antilegomena*, 1970 (BU 5).

Feuillet, A., *Le Christ Sagesse de Dieu d'après les épîtres pauliniennes*, 1966 (EtB).

Fischer, K. M., *Tendenz und Absicht des Epheserbriefes*, 1973 (FRLANT 111).

Foerster, W., *Die Gnosis I: Zeugnisse der Kirchenväter, II: Koptische und mandäische Quellen* (by M. Krause and K. Rudolph), Zürich-Stuttgart 1969/71.

Frede, H. J., *Epistula ad Ephesios*, 1962 (Vetus Latina 24/1).

Gärtner, B., *The Temple and the Community in Qumran and the New Testament*, 1965 (MSSNTS 1).

Gewieß, J., 'Die Begriffe πληροῦν und πλήρωμα im Kolosser- und Epheserbrief' in *Vom Wort des Lebens* (FS M. Meinertz), Münster i. W. 1951, 128–41.

Gnilka, J., 'Paränetische Traditionen im Epheserbrief', in *Mélanges Bibliques en hommage au R. P. Béda Rigaux*, Gembloux o. J. (1970), 397–410.

——'Das Kirchenmodell des Epheserbriefes', BZ NF 15 (1971) 161–84.

——'Das Paulusbild im Kolosser- und Epheserbrief', in *Kontinuität und Einheit* (FS Mußner), Freiburg i. Br. 1981, 179–93.

Goodspeed, E. J., *The Key to Ephesians*, Chicago 1956.

Hahn, F., *Christologische Hoheitstitel. Ihre Geschichte im frühen Christentum*, [4]1974 (FRLANT 83).

Halter, H., *Taufe und Ethos. Paulinische Kriterien für das Proprium christlicher Moral*, 1977 (FThSt 106).

Hanson, S., *The Unity of the Church in the New Testament. Colossians and Ephesians*, 1946 (ASNU 14).

Hegermann, H., *Die Vorstellung vom Schöpfungsmittler im hellenistischen Judentum und Urchristentum*, 1961 (TU 82).

Houlden, J. L., 'Christ and Church in Ephesians', StEv 6 (1973) 267–73.

Jeremias, G., *Der Lehrer der Gerechtigkeit*, 1963 (StUNT 2).

Jonas, H., *Gnosis und spätantiker Geist I: Die mythologische Gnosis*, 1934 (FRLANT 51).

Kamlah, E., *Die Form der katalogischen Paränese im Neuen Testament*, 1964 (WUNT 7).

Käsemann, E., Art. 'Epheserbrief', in RGG II, 517–20.

——*Leib und Leib Christi*, 1933 (BHTh 9).

——'Das Interpretationsproblem des Epheserbriefes', in *Exegetische Versuche und Besinnungen* II, Göttingen 1964, 253–61.

Kehl, N., 'Der Christushymnus im Epheserbrief' (unpublished Habilitationsschrift), Innsbruck o. J.

Kirby, J. C., *Ephesians. Baptism and Pentecost*, London 1968.

Klein, G., *Die zwölf Apostel. Ursprung und Gehalt einer Idee*, 1961 (FRLANT 77).

Klinzing, G., *Die Umdeutung des Kultus in der Qumrangemeinde und im Neuen Testament*, 1971 (StUNT 7).

Kramer, W., *Christos Kyrios Gottessohn*, 1963 (AThANT 44).

Kümmel, W. G., *Introduction to the New Testament*, London 1975.

Kuhn, H.-W., *Enderwartung und gegenwärtiges Heil. Untersuchungen zu den Gemeindeliedern von Qumran*, 1966 (StUNT 4).

Kuhn, K. G., *Konkordanz zu den Qumrantexten*, Göttingen 1960.

——'Der Epheserbrief im Lichte der Qumrantexte', NTS 7 (1960/61) 334–45.

Lincoln, A. T., 'A Re-examination of "the Heavenlies" in Ephesians', NTS 19 (1972/73) 468–83.

Lindars, B., *The New Testament Apologetic. The Doctrinal Significance of the Old Testament Quotations*, London 1961.

Lindemann, A., *Die Aufhebung der Zeit. Geschichtsverständnis und Eschatologie im Epheserbrief*, 1975 (StNT 12).

——'Bemerkungen zu den Adressaten und zum Anlaß des Epheserbriefes', ZNW 67 (1976) 235–51.

——*Paulus im ältesten Christentum. Das Bild des Apostels und die Rezeption der paulinischen Theologie in der frühchristlichen Literatur bis Marcion*, 1979 (BHTh 58).

MacGregor, G. H. C., 'Principalities and Powers; the Cosmic Background of Paul's Thought', NTS 1 (1954/55) 17–28.

Maier, J., *Die Texte vom Toten Meer*, 2 vols., München–Basel 1960.

McKelvey, R. J., *The New Temple. The Church in the New Testament*, London 1969.

Merk, O., *Handeln aus Glauben. Die Motivierungen der paulinischen Ethik*, 1968 (MThSt 5).

Merklein, H., *Das kirchliche Amt nach dem Epheserbrief*, 1973 (StANT 33).

——*Christus und die Kirche. Die theologische Grundstruktur des Epheserbriefes nach Eph 2, 11–18*, 1973 SBS 66).

——'Eph 4, 1–5, 20 als Rezeption von Kol 3, 1–17 (zugleich ein Beitrag zur Problematik des Epheserbriefes)', *Kontinuität und Einheit* (FS F. Mußner), Freiburg i. Br. 1981, 194–210.

——'Paulinische Theologie in der Rezeption des Kolosser- und Epheserbriefes', in Kertelge, K., (ed.), *Paulus in den neutestamentlichen Spätschriften*, 1981 (QD 89), 25–69.

Metzger, B. M., *A Textual Commentary on the Greek New Testament*, London–New York 1971.

Meuzelaar, J. J., *Der Leib des Messias. Eine exegetische Studie über den Gedanken vom Leib Chrisi in den Paulusbriefen*, Assen 1961.

Meyer, Regina Pacis, *Kirche und Mission im Epheserbrief*, 1977 (SBS 86).

Mitton, C. L., *The Epistle to the Ephesians. Its Authorship, Origin and Purpose*, Oxford 1951.

Moule, C. F. D., *An Idiom Book of New Testament Greek*, Cambridge 1953.

Moulton, J. H. – Turner, N., *A Grammar of New Testament Greek*, Vol. III, Edinburgh 1963.

Mußner, F., *Christus, das All und die Kirche. Studien zur Theologie des Epheserbriefes*, 1955 (²1968) (TThSt 5).

——'Beiträge aus Qumran zum Verständnis des Epheserbriefes', in *Neutestamentliche Aufsätze* (FS J. Schmid), Regensburg 1963, 185–98.

Nötscher, F., *Zur theologischen Terminologie der Qumran-Texte*, 1956 (BBB 10).

——*Gotteswege und Menschenwege in der Bibel und in Qumran*, 1958 (BBB 15).

Ochel, W., *Die Annahme einer Bearbeitung des Kolosserbriefes im Epheserbrief in einer Analyse des Epheserbriefes untersucht*, Diss. Marburg 1934

Odeburg, H., *The View of the Universe in the Epistle to the Ephesians*, 1934 (AUL.T 29, 6).

Overfield, P. D., 'The Ascension, Pleroma and Ecclesia Concepts in Ephesians', Diss. St. Andrews 1976 (not accessible to me).

——'Pleroma. A Study in Content and Context', NTS 25 (1979) 384–96.

Percy, E., *Die Probleme der Kolosser- und Epheserbriefe*, Lund 1946.

——'Zu den Problemen des Kolosser- und Epheserbriefes', ZNW 43 (1950/51) 148–94.

Pfammatter, J., *Die Kirche als Bau. Eine exegetisch-theologische Studie zur Ekklesiologie der Paulusbriefe*, 1960 (AnGr 110).

Philonenko, M., *Joseph et Aséneth. Introduction, texte critique, traduction et notes*, Leiden 1968.

Pokorný, P., 'Σῶμα Χριστοῦ im Epheserbrief', EvTh 20 (1960) 456–64.

——'Epheserbrief und gnostiche Mysterien', ZNW 53 (1962) 160–94.

——*Der Epheserbrief und die Gnosis. Die Bedeutung des Haupt-Glieder-Gedankens in der entstehenden Kirche*, Berlin 1965.

Rader, W., *The Church and Racial Hostility. A History of Interpretation of Eph. 2:11–22*, 1978 (BGBE 20).

Ramaroson, L., '"L'Eglise, corps due Christ" dans les écrits pauliniennes', ScEcc 30 (1978) 129–41.

Reitzenstein, R., *Poimandres. Studien zur griechisch-ägyptischen und frühchristlichen Literatur*, Leipzig 1904, repr. Darmstadt 1966.

Rese, M., 'Formeln und Lieder im Neuen Testament', VF 15 (1970) 75–95.

Reumann, J., 'Oikonomia = "Covenant"; Terms for Heilsgeschichte in Early Christian Usage', NT 3 (1959) 282–92.

——'Οἰκονομία- Terms in Paul in Comparison with Lukan Heilsgeschichte', NTS 13 (1966/67) 147–67.

Roller, O., *Das Formular der paulinischen Briefe*, 1933 (BWANT 58).

Roloff, J., *Apostolat – Verkündigung – Kirche. Ursprung, Inhalt und Funktion des kirchlichen Apostelamtes nach Paulus, Lukas und den Pastoralbriefen*, Gütersloh 1965.

Rudolph, K., *Gnosis*, Edinburgh 1983.

Sanders, J. T., 'Hymnic Elements in Ephesians 1–3', ZNW 56 (1965) 214–32.

——*The New Testament Christological Hymns. Their Historical Religious Background*, 1971 (MSSNTS 15).

Schenke, H.-M., *Der Gott 'Mensch' in der Gnosis. Ein religionsgeschichtlicher Beitrag zur Diskussion über die paulinische Anschauung von der Kirche als Leib Christi*, Göttingen 1962.

Schenke, H.-M – Fischer, K. M., *Einleitung in die Schriften des Neuen Testaments I: Die Briefe des Paulus und Schriften des Paulinismus*, Berlin–Gütersloh 1978.

Schille, G., 'Liturgisches Gut im Epheserbrief' (unpublished Diss. Göttingen) 1952.

——'Der Autor des Epheserbriefes', ThLZ 82 (1957) 325–34.

——*Frühchristliche Hymnen*, Berlin 1965.

Schlier, H., *Religionsgeschichtliche Untersuchungen zu den Ignatiusbriefen*, 1929 (BZNW 8).

——*Christus und die Kirche im Epheserbrief*, 1930 (BHTh 6).

——*Mächte und Gewalten im Neuen Testament*, 1958 (QD 3).

Schlier, J. – Warnach, V., *Die Kirche im Epheserbrief*, Münster i. W. 1949.

Schmid, J., Der *Epheserbrief des Apostels Paulus. Seine Adresse, Sprache und literarischen Beziehungen*, 1928 (BSt [F] 22, 3–4).

Schnackenburg, R., *Das Heilsgeschehen bei der Taufe nach dem Apostel Paulus*, 1950 (MThS.H 1).

——'Gestalt und Wesen der Kirche nach dem Epheserbrief', in id., *Schriften zum Neuen Testament*, München 1971, 268–87.

——'Christus, Geist und Gemeinde (Eph 4:1–16)', in *Christ and Spirit in the New Testament* (FS C. F. D. Moule), Cambridge 1973, 279–96.

——*The Gospel According to St John*, 3 vols., London 1968–82.

Schürmann, H., *Orientierungen am Neuen Testament*, Düsseldorf 1978.

Schweizer, E., *Church Order in the New Testament*, London 1961.

——*Neotestamentica (Gesammelte Aufsätze)*, Zürich–Stuttgart 1963.

——*Beiträge zur Theologie des Neuen Testaments*, Zürich 1970.

——*The Letter to the Colossians*, London, 1982.

Spicq, C., *Notes de lexicographie néotestamentaire*, 2 vols., 1978 (Orbis Bibl. et Orient. 22, 1–2).

Stegemann, H., 'Alt und Neu bei Paulus und in den Deuteropaulinen (Kol–Eph)', EvTh 37 (1977) 508–36.

Steinmetz, F. J., *Protoligische Heils-Zuversicht. Die Strukturen des soteriologischen und christologischen Denkens im Kolosser- und Epheserbrief*, 1969 (FTS 2).

——'Parusie-Erwartung im Epheserbrief? Ein Vergleich', Bib. 50 (1969) 328–36.

Tachau, P., *'Einst' und 'Jetzt' im Neuen Testament*, 1972 (FRLANT 105).

Tröger, K.-W. (ed.), *Gnosis und Neues Testament. Studien aus Religionswissenschaft und Theologie*, Gütersloh 1973.

van der Horst, P. W., *The Sentences of Pseudo-Phocylides*, Leiden 1978.

Vanhoye, A., 'L'Épître aux Éphésiens et l'Épître aux Hébreux', Bib. 59 (1978) 198–230.

van Roon, A., *The Authenticity of Ephesians*, 1974 (NT.S 39).

Vielhauer, Ph., *Oikodome. Das Bild vom Bau in der christlichen Literatur vom Neuen Testament bis Clemens Alexandrinus*, Karlsruhe 1939, repr. München 1979.

——*Geschichte der urchristlichen Literatur*, Berlin–New York 1975.

Vögtle, A., *Die Tugend- und Lasterkataloge exegetisch, religions- und formgeschichtlich untersucht*, 1936 (NTA 16, 4–5).

Wagenführer, M.-A., *Die Bedeutung Christi für Welt und Kirche. Studien zum Kolosser- und Epheserbrief*, Leipzig 1941.

Warnach, V., 'Kirch und Kosmos', in E. Emonds (ed.), *Enkainia*, Düsseldorf 1956, 170–205.

Wegenast, K., *Das Verständnis der Tradition bei Paulus und in den Deuteropaulinen*, 1962 (WMANT 8).

Weiß, H.-F., 'Gnostische Motive und antignostische Polemik im Kolosser- und Epheserbrief', in Tröger, K.-W. (ed.), *Gnosis und NT* 311–24.

Wengst, K., *Christologische Formeln und Lieder des Urchristentums*, 1972 (StNT 7).

Wibbing, S., *Die Tugend- und Lasterkataloge im Neuen Testament und ihre Traditionsgeschichte*, 1959 (BZNW 25).

Wikenhauser, A., *Die Kirche als der mystische Leib Christi nach dem Apostel Paulus*, Münster i. W. ²1940.

Wikenhauser, A. – Schmid, J., *Einleitung in das Neue Testament*, Freiburg i. Br. ⁶1973.

Williamson, L., Jr., *God's Work of Art. Images of the Church in Ephesians*, Richmond, Va. 1971 (not accessible to me).

Zerwick, M., *Biblical Greek illustrated by examples*, Rome 1963.

4. *Special literature* for each particular section can be found preceding the biblical text. In the notes these are quoted with the author's name followed by.*

A Bibliography which follows the verses of Ephesians: G. Wagner (ed.), *An Exegetical Bibliography on the Letters to the Ephesians, to the Colossians and to Philemon*, Rüschlikon–Zürich, Baptist Theological Seminary 1977.

A. Introduction

When we attempt to give a credible explanation of the origin of the Epistle to the Ephesians and what its author intended, we are faced with a difficult task in that we have virtually no other source to draw upon. There is a scarcity of concrete details and inferences – the very address is doubtful – and the language, flow of thought and the theological ideas which emerge in it are strange. The interpreter finds himself even more than usual in a hermeneutic circle. From the interpretation of individual texts and their context he must reach a general view which in its turn is subject to control by these individual interpretations. Hence this introduction can only be read in conjunction with the following exegesis which will provide the reasoning for the opinions represented here. This difficulty also explains the choice of the topics discussed in this section. This introduction is intended to lead the readers into the exegesis rather than to instruct them in all the problems treated in the standard introductory studies. I have abstained in particular from giving a consecutive account of the religio-historical problem. This will be discussed in the relevant verses but cannot be discussed *in extenso*, particularly as research is always still in progress. Our starting-point is the question of the literary form or 'character' of this early Christian document, for here already there are areas which raise questions for its overall understanding.

1. THE LITERARY FORM

We cannot fail to notice the epistolary form of the document: prescript (epistolary beginning) 1.1–2 and epistolary conclusion with a short message to the addressees (6.21 f.) and blessing (6.23 f.) make up the framework, and the bulk of the letter almost entirely in its use of the form of address is directed at the recipients with evocative instruction and admonishing advice. Certainly the form of a letter to a congregation used previously by Paul, which is also preserved in Col., is interrupted at the beginning by the Great Eulogy (1.3–14); only subsequently comes the customary thanksgiving to God for the faithful conduct of the addressees (often called the 'Prooemium') (1.15–17). There is no list of persons to be greeted at the end; in Rom. 16[1] such a list is sent to a congregation as yet totally unknown

[1] Even today there is no agreement on whether the list of greetings in Rom. 16 originally belonged with this letter or whether it was perhaps addressed to Ephesus. But the assumption that Paul with these greetings was seeking contact with the Roman congregation is gaining increased support. Cf. Kümmel, *Introduction* 317–20; Wikenhauser-Schmid, *Einleitung* 460–2;

to the Apostle, and in Col. 4.10–17 another occupies a considerable space. Even though the main part is divided according to the Pauline pattern (cf. Gal. Rom. and Col.) into a theological section (2.11–3.21) and a 'paraclesis' section (4.1–6.20), the epistolary form seems rather contrived, in the manner of an imitation, because at no point are particular congregational affairs or problems mentioned.

This unique form has led to different definitions of the real 'character' of the document under its epistolary cover as a 'theological tract'[2] a 'wisdom speech'[3] or as a liturgically-stamped address – this admittedly in a variety of ways. G. Schille thinks he discerns an underlying early Christian baptismal liturgy which is this epistolary form betrays the intention of reminding the congregation of the obligations brought by baptism.[4] J. C. Kirby considers Eph. 1–3 to be a praise- and thanksgiving based on a Jewish model (*berakhah*) and shaped especially by Pentecost: This was intended for use in public worship, possibly at the celebration of the Eucharist – a mirror of the liturgy celebrated at Ephesus (where he locates the document). Out of this liturgical part and the long exhortatory section grew a document which could be read during worship in other congregations.[5] Other scholars think it is a sermon: P. Pokorny considers it a baptismal sermon which to some extent follows a gnostic mystery-initiation and then departs from it;[6] J. Gnilka thinks more generally of a liturgical homily which is clothed in the form of a letter.[7]

All these attempts to discern a liturgical background can be put down to the fact that it is written to a large extent in the elevated style of a hymn and includes liturgical language; in 5.14 there is possibly a fragment of the baptismal liturgy. The frequently-held opinion that Eph. 1.3–3.21 – a coherent sequence of praise (eulogy), intercession and concluding thanksgiving (doxology) – makes up a 'liturgical pattern',[8] can, it is true, be supported on the corner-posts of the Eulogy (1.3–14) and the Doxology (3.20 f.) and the intervening intercessions (1.17 ff.; 3.14–19). But it can also be questioned because of other sections which have a more kerygmatic content (1.20–3; 2.4–10, 11–22) and because of the Paul-anamnesis which likewise includes an element of preaching (3.1–13). On the other hand it can be clearly demonstrated that at least the section 1.15–2.10 is a

---

H. Schlier, *Der Römerbrief*, 1977 (HThK VI) 10–12; U. Wilckens, *Der Brief an die Römer*, 1978 (EKK VI/I), 24–7; and finally, with strong arguments, W. H. Ollrog, 'Die Abfassungsver-hältnisse von Röm 16', in *Kirche* (Festschrift für G. Bornkamm) ed. D. Lührmann and G. Strecker, Tübingen 1980, 221–44.

[2] Thus Käsemann RGG[3] II, 517 and 520; Conzelmann 86; Lindemann ZNW 67, 240; Vielhauer, *Literatur* 212 f.; Schenke-Fischer, *Einleitung* I, 174.

[3] Schlier 21. He also talks of a 'Mystery Speech'.

[4] 'Liturgisches Gut im Epheserbrief' (unpublished dissertation, Göttingen 1952) 135–45; cf. id. *Frühchristliche Hymnen* 104–7.

[5] *Ephesians* 138, 149, 165–72.

[6] ZNW 53, 160–94.

[7] *Kommentar* 33. He only continues to speak of the 'Letter' to the Ephesians for the sake of simplicity (ibid., n. 7). Cf. also Schenke-Fischer, *Einleitung* I, 174: 'not a letter in the real sense'.

[8] Thus Gnilka 27 with reference to analogies in the Jewish and early Christian literature on prayer. Kirby, *Ephesians* 129 f. (with other Anglicans) sees the original continuation from 2.22 on.

development of the epistolary form (cf. the Exegesis) and that the Paul-section performed a specific function for the recipients of the letter. The borrowing from songs or hymns (the Eulogy 1.3–12 or 14; a song 'Christ, our Peace', 2.14–18; a baptismal hymn, 2.18–22) which has often been conjectured does not stand up to re-examination.[9] We cannot deny the influence of the liturgy, but along with other kerygmatic, catechetical and exhortatory traditions which enrich the language of Eph., but which cannot be seen in isolation as its constitutive material. The epistolary pattern is not an assumed cloak but a literary form deliberately chosen by the author because it was probably in keeping with the objective or aim of his writing.

The principal objection to the view that we are here dealing with a theological tract or a wisdom speech is the extremely long paraclesis section (Chs. 4–6). Anyone who wishes to broadcast his theological ideas might include a paraclesis, but he would scarcely construct such a long, massively tail-heavy section. Added to this is the fact that the alleged theological didactic section or wisdom-speech clearly betrays pastoral interests so that the theological expositions appear rather to be meant to provoke particular concerns on the part of the recipients. The basic theme in 2.11–22 (cf. 3.4–10), the Mystery of Christ which reveals itself in the unity of former Jews and Gentiles, is oriented ecclesiologically, and this ecclesial interest emerges also in the paraclesis section under other aspects (unity in variety, offices and ministries (4.7–16); worship and encounter with the world (5.15–20; 6.10–20)), with more emphasis on its practical application. The author, who is disposed to speculation and has a tendency to theological contemplation and temperate advice, pursues in his own way the practical, pastoral concerns of his time,[10] which are, to be sure, not easy to determine! But the 'character' of the document is consequently so shaped that we must take the epistolary form seriously and look upon Eph. as a theologically-based, pastorally-oriented letter.

Can we include Eph. among the 'catholic letters' since it so obviously is intended for a larger circle than one single congregation?[11] This concept is not precisely defined nor do we have a clear description of the genre of the seven writings traditionally ascribed to this category in the NT canon. If we understand 'catholic' to mean a general writing to the whole of Christendom, this is only true to a very limited extent of any of the canonical Epistles because they are directed to certain regions or groups of Christians. If, however, it means a writing addressed to a particular area of the Church but in awareness of the whole Church, Eph. may be described as such since the author's conception of the Church shows us the one Church bound to Christ, founded on the apostles and prophets, which

---

[9] On the methodical formation cf. Deichgräber, *Gottes-hymnus*, especially 65–72; 165–7; Merklein BZ NF 17, 80–95.

[10] Most Commentaries pay too little attention to the letter's pragmatic dimension. Almost all proceed from the idea that it has no concrete background; but this would be unique in the whole of the NT literature. Fischer shows awareness of the problem, *Tendenz* 13–20; but how he defines the actual historical situation of the church can be contested (v. infra 4). There has not been enough research done on the situation of the congregations in Asia Minor – including the sociological aspect – at the end of the First Century.

[11] Thus Vielhauer, *Literatur* 213.

contains all the baptized – the *una sancta catholica et apostolica ecclesia* (cf. the excursus on the Church). And the ideas and advice put before the recipients are certainly of significance for other areas. The closest resemblance to Eph. is to be found in 1 Peter, with which it is also similar in individual details.[12] Here, too, we cannot extract a liturgical scheme or baptismal liturgy from this writing to Christians in the Diaspora of Asia Minor, and its epistolary form cannot be disputed.[13] In 1 Pet., too, Pauline tradition and theology is used and a definite historical situation taken for granted. But Eph. preserves its individuality both in its theology and as regards its situation; some details will become more precise through further examination.

2. AUTHOR AND ADDRESSEES

The question to which scholars since the beginning of the 18th century have given most attention is that of 'authenticity' – i.e. whether the apostle Paul was the author. Theodore of Mopsuestia and Jerome recognised at an early date the difficulty of its being addressed to Ephesus, and Erasmus saw its style as deviating from that of Paul; but it was not until E. Evanson (1792), L. Usteri (1824), De Wette (1826) and especially F. C. Baur and his school that Paul's authorship was disputed. The to-and-fro debate of the 19th century and the increasing denial of its authenticity in our century have been adequately dealt with,[14] We shall limit ourselves here to the present state of research which still recognises divers positions.[15] Noteworthy is the change of position taken among Roman Catholic exegetes, who in the past partly defended its authenticity but who now are of the view that its origin is post-Pauline.[16] The most recent works on

[12]The main points of contact lie in the Eulogy in 1 Pet. 1.3–5, the Baptismal Paraclesis 1, 14–22 f.; 2.1 f.; the metaphor of God's Temple 2.4–6, the calling of the Gentiles to God's people 2.9f, the *Haustafel* 2.18–3, 7. But these similarities do not point to a literary dependence (according to Mitton, *Epistle* 176–97) but go back to a common stock in the catechetical, liturgical and paraenetical tradition of that period of Early Christianity. cf. P. Carrington, *The Primitive Christian Catechism*, Cambridge, 1940; Percy, *Probleme* 433–40; E. G. Selwyn, *The First Epistle of St Peter*, London 1952, 384–439; K. H. Schelkle, *Die Petrusbriefe, der Judasbrief*[4] 1976 (HThK XIII/2), 5–7; Gnilka 22 f.

[13]Cf. the list of research done contained in N. Brox, *Der erste Petrusbrief*, 1979 (EKK XXI), 19–24. His own classification of the character of 1 Pet. comes very close to my view of Eph.: We are here concerned with a 'circular' in the sense that 1 Pet. would have fulfilled its purpose from the start much better through numerous copies than simply in the form of the one original (23).

[14]Cf. Schmid, *Epheserbrief* 1–15; van Roon, *Authenticity* 3–36; Wikenhauser-Schmid, *Einleitung* 486–9; Barth 36 f.

[15]Cf. the comparison of those who hold that it is authentic and those who oppose this view in Kümmel, *Introducion* 357, n. 25 and 26; Barth 38.

[16]Cf. J. Schmid, *Epheserbrief* (1928) with his revision of Wikenhauser's *Einleitung* (1973); R. Schnackenburg, *Taufe* (1950) 3 f., n. 9 with EKK *Vorarbeiten* I, 41; F. Mußner, *Christus* (1955) with *Petrus und Paulus – Pole der Einheit* 1976 (QD 76) 91 and 94 ('Paulusschule'); H. Schlier also in the end, in a verbal communication, had doubts of the Pauline origin. Cf. also B. Rigaux, *Paulus und seine Briefe*, Munich 1964, 145–50 (from one of Paul's 'school'); P. Benoit, 'Rapports littéraires entre les épîtres aux Colossiens et aux Éphésiens', in

pseudepigrapha are also contributing to a change. Since the Pastorals are now recognised almost without exception as pseudepigraphal writings and not a few scholars include with them 1 Pet. and 2 Thess., earlier reservations are being abandoned as to Eph. also being recognised as belonging to this group.[17]

To be sure, each individual writing demands its own particular research with regard to the question of authorship. Among researchers on Eph. in particular E. Percy (1946) sought to prove Pauline authorship; but very soon afterwards C. L. Mitton (1951) presented persuasive grounds for its inauthenticity. The last major work devoted to this subject by A. van Roon (1974) returns to the conclusion that Paul, along with another man from his circle, could be the author. The number of commentators who consider the work pseudepigraphal is growing; but in his large commentary of 1974 M. Barth still pleads for Pauline authorship.

This being the state of research, where the grounds pro and contra are continually changing, we must draw attention to a hermeneutic aspect. If the consideration of style, language and theological content cannot give a completely unambiguous picture, we must ask whether an exegesis on the assumption of a Pauline or 'deuteropauline' origin would lead to a better hypothesis. Would the Epistle *as a whole* be more comprehensible if it stemmed from the lifetime of the Apostle and went back to Paul himself (or his circle of co-workers) or if it is placed only at the beginning of the 'post-apostolic' period (around AD 90)? As my exegesis progressed the second assumption imposed itself on me and simultaneously proved to be the hermeneutic key for the interpretation of the whole. Certainly this opinion must stand up to examination in detail. Only a few remarks must be made on the many topics of discussion which cannot all be presented.

(a) When we examine the language, the *statistics of words* used are of decisive significance. The fact that Eph. contains 49 words used only once in the NT (*hapaxlegomena*) and 51 not found in the recognised Pauline corpus is no conclusive evidence that this must stem from another author since we find similar numerical relationships in other NT writings.[18] It is

Neutestamentliche Aufsätze (Festschrift für J. Schmid), Regensburg 1963, 11–22 (ditto). For those who hold that it comes from a non-Pauline background v. J. Blank, *Paulus und Jesus*, 1968 (St ANT XVIII), 20–22; Gnilka 13–18; Ernst 266 ('a theologian from the circle of Paul's pupils').

[17]Various judgements are still made with regard to Pseudepigraphy. Cf. W. Speyer, 'Religiöse Pseudepigraphie und literarische Fälschung in Altertum', JAC 8/9 (1965/66) 88–125; id. *Die religiöse Fälschung im Altertum*, 1971 (HAW I/2); K. Aland, *Das Problem der Anonymität und Pseudonymität in der christlichen Literatur der ersten beiden Jahrhunderte*, 1967 (ANTT 2), 24–34; H. R. Balz, 'Anonymität und Pseudepigraphie im Urchristentum', ZThK 66 (1969) 403–36; N. Brox, *Falsche Verfasserangaben. Zur Erklärung der frühchristlichen Pseudepigraphie*, 1975 (SBS 79); id., 'Tendenz und Pseudepigraphie im ersten Petrusbrief', Kairos NF 20 (1978) 110–20; On 2 Thess. cf. W. Trilling, *Untersuchungen zum 2 Thessalonicherbrief*, 1972 (ETh St 27); id., 'Literarische Paulusimitation im 2 Thessalonicherbrief', in *Paulus in den neutestamentlichen Spätschriften. Zur Paulusrezeption im Neuen Testament*, ed. K. Kertelge, 1981 (QD 89), 146–56. On the history of research v N. Brox (ed.), *Pseudepigraphie in der heidnischen und jüdisch-christlichen Antike*, 1977 (WdF 144).

[18]Cf. Schmid, *Epheserbrief* 131–40; Percy, *Probleme* 17 f. The list in Mitton, *Epistle* 109, is also instructive.

of greater significance that we encounter many of these *hapaxlegomena* in subsequent early Christian literature; hence the vocabulary shows a closer affinity to the post-apostolic literature.[19] Among the 15 *hapaxlegomena* which, apart from in Col. and Eph. are not found in the Pauline but in other NT writings, we come up against the type which predominate in the late writings, such as ἀπάτη, διάνοια, κράτος, κυριότης, κατοικεῖν. Even more important is the use of expressions other than those normally encountered in Paul for the same thing, especially ἐν τοῖς ἐπουρανίοις (Eph. 1.3, 20; 2.6; 3.10; 6.12) instead of ἐν οὐρανοῖς (2 Cor. 5.1; cf. Phil. 3.20; Col., 5.16, 20), διάβολος (Eph. 4.27; 6.11) instead of σατανᾶς (seven times in Paul) and the formula used before a quotation διὸ λέγει (Eph. 4.8; 5.14) which does not appear in Paul.

(b) The linguistic *style* – which is characterized by pleonastic accumulation and clustering of synonyms, connective genitives, lengthy sentences, repeated use of particular phrases, lack of conjunctions and particles – likewise gives no adequate criterion for another author but is conspicuous enough, even in comparison with Col. The calm, eirenic manner of explanation, the liturgical influence, the impression of a 'wisdom speech', the sphere of influence reaching beyond the single congregation – all these are not sufficient to explain the marked difference in style. The unusually long sentences (1.3–14; 1.15–23; 2.1–7; 3.1–7, 14–19; 4.11–16; 5.7–13; 6.14–20) certainly have many parallels in the Pauline letters, but not to this extent. Consequently van Roon presumes as author a man who belongs to the Pauline circle.[20] After the discovery of the Qumran texts the relationship of these writings in their hebraicizing style was noted, as were certain affinities of conception.[21] But since the author of Eph. shows himself little bound by the theology of Qumran we must, with regard to the style and mode of expression, presume an influence of this Jewish literature which was in some way bound up with his career or personal connections. Apart from the non-Pauline section in 2 Cor. 6.14–7.1[22] there is scarcely anything comparable in Paul.

(c) Most significant are the *theological divergences* and the changes in perspective. If one considers justification not as resulting from the working of the Law but through Grace alone, from faith in Jesus Christ, as the core of Pauline theology, then only at Eph. 2.8 f. do we find an echo of this. The Pauline antithesis 'not by works, but rather (only) through faith' (cf. Gal. 2.16; Rom. 3.21–4), and likewise the exclusion of 'boasting' (Rom. 3.27) are unmistakeably included but curiously weakened (v. under this passage). The expression 'good works' (2.10) is revealing; this never appears

---

[19] Cf. ἄθεος, ἄσοφος, ἑνότης, εὔνοια, εὐσπλαγχνος, κληροῦν, μέγεθος, ὁσιότης, συνοικοδομεῖν with their occurrence in the Apostolic Fathers in H. Kraft, *Clavis Patrum Apostolicorum*, Darmstadt 1963. Further cf. P. N. Harrison, *Paulines and Pastorals*, London 1964, 48 f.

[20] *Authenticity* 105–11 and 206.

[21] Cf. K. G. Kuhn, NTS 7, 334–46; Mußner, *Beiträge*; Gnilka, *Mél. Rigaux* 397–407.

[22] Cf. J. A. Fitzmyer, 'Qumrân and the Interpolated Paragraph in 2 Cor. 6.14–7. 1', CBQ 23 (1961) 271–80; J. Gnilka, '2 Kor. 6.14–7, 1 im Lichte der Qumranschriften und der Zwölf-Patriarchen-Testamente', in *Ntl. Aufsätze* (FS J. Schmid) Regensburg 1963, 86–99; F. J. Collange, *Énigmes de la deuxième Épître de Paul aux Corinthiens*, 1972 (MSSNTS 18), 302–17; M. E. Thrall, 'The Problem of II Cor. VI.14–VII.1 in some recent discussion', NTS 24 (1978) 231–50.

in the plural of Paul (cf. 2 Cor. 9.8) but is found frequently in the Pastoral Epistles. The 'works' are not placed alongside faith as in Jam. 2.14–26, but are firmly claimed as those which God has 'prepared in advance'. The Pauline thrust against the Jewish idea of the way to salvation through works of the Law is gone without trace. The Law (the νόμος) is only mentioned once (at 2.15), and there as a power whose overthrowal puts an end to the old enmity between Jew and Gentile. The Law was the partition between the two groups but not the curse from which the Jews in particular must be freed (cf. Col. 3.13). The whole perspective has changed. This is corroborated by the fact that a Theology of the Cross, as developed especially in Gal, has completely faded from the picture. The Cross is only mentioned once in the same connection as the place of reconciliation of the two groups with God (2.16) – clearly dependent on Col. 1.20. Elsewhere Christ's Lordship over world and Church, revealed by God in the raising from the dead, elevation and heavenly enthronement of Jesus Christ, stands at the centre of the theological thinking (cf. 1.20–3; 2.4–7). The omission of the Pauline teaching on justification, which the Apostle expounds so insistently to a Roman congregation as yet unknown to him, can scarcely be explained by the theory that it is not the centre of his theological endeavours.[23]

The changes in perspective are not only caused by the theme of the bringing together of former Jews and Gentiles in the one Church of Jesus Christ, but reach beyond this, include the whole theology of Eph. and taken together correspond to a later stage of theological reflection. Worthy of special mention is the change in the eschatological outlook. The expectation of the Parousia, which for Paul and his circle was established between the present and future in the course of salvation, and whose theology is so important for its suspenseful character, fades into the background even more in Eph. than in Col. (cf. 3.4). It is touched upon only once in the section on the Holy Spirit (4.30) as a passing motif which probably is derived from the Baptismal Spirit. For the most part the view is turned upwards, to the heavenly regions, where the 'inheritance' (κληρονομία) awaits (1.14, 18; 5.5). Paul favours the verb and applies the 'entering into the inheritance' to the expected share in God's Kingdom perfected with Christ's Parousia (cf. Gal. 5.21; 1 Cor. 6.9 f.; 15.50; cf. Gal. 4.7; Rom. 8.17).[24] The 'Mystery of Christ' (Eph. 3.4) taken over from Col. 1.26 f. certainly finds a Pauline base in 1 Cor 2.7–10, but is filled up and accentuated differently. Already in Col. 1.26 it is no longer connected to the foolishness of the message of the Cross but to the opening-up of the Gospel to the heathen, and the related 'pattern of revelation' is witnessed to more strongly in the post-Pauline period (Rom. 16.25 f.; 1 Tim. 3.16; 2 Tim. 1.9; Tit. 1.2 f.; 1 Pet. 1.20; cf. Schweizer on Col. 1.26). There is hardly any trace of a missionary impulse in Eph.; the Mystery now revealed is the unity of Jews and Gentiles in the Church of Christ.

[23]Thus Barth 47–9. He holds that the opinion that the Doctrine of Justification is the essence, climax and 'breath of life' of the Pauline theologian is a prejudgement on the part of extreme Paulinists.

[24]Cf. P. L. Hammer, 'A Comparison of κληρονομία in Paul and Ephesians', JBL 79 (1960) 267–72; Steinmetz, *Heils-Zuversicht* 33 f.; Lindemann, *Aufhebung der Zeit* 199–201.

The view throughout of the Church as an entity is typical of its ecclesiology (cf. the Excursus on the Church, pp. 293 f.), and even if the idea of the Body of Christ goes back to Paul, the conception of Christ as the Head of this Body is first put forward in Col. and brought in dominatingly in Eph. The like is true of the idea of the Fullness (*pleroma*) of Christ, which is used in an ecclesiological sense in Eph. The 'syzygy' (yoking together) of Christ and the Church which becomes in Eph. 5.22–33 the archetype and model for the matrimonial tie between man and woman is also developed far beyond its first formulation in 2 Cor. 11.2, quite apart from the fact that the high opinion of marriage over against 1 Cor. 7 is surprising. Finally, the picture of the Church as God's Building and Temple is characteristically altered in comparison with 1 Cor. 3.10–17. In Eph. 2.20 the Apostles and Prophets make up the foundation and Christ is the Corner-stone – a thought which finds its closest parallel in 1 Pet. 2.4 ff. Paul himself now belongs to the 'holy Apostles and Prophets in the Spirit' (Eph. 3.5), an expression which it is difficult to conceive as coming from Paul's lips. All this would be far more comprehensible if the author is looking back to the founding years of the Church, wants to emphasise Paul as the guarantee of 'apostolic' tradition and builds on his ecclesiology.

Various other details could be cited such as the altered use of the formula 'in Christ Jesus', the establishment of the ungodly 'forces and powers' in the region of the air (2.2), the 'sons of disobedience' (2.2; 5.6; certainly not original in Col. 3.6), the 'exposure' of those outsiders through the Sons of Light (5.11, 13). But the above-mentioned may be enough to show that an interpretation which understands Ephesians as a post-Pauline pseudepigraphal writing is not only justified hermeneutically but is actually demanded. This becomes even clearer when Col. is already considered as not being genuinely Pauline; since much that differentiates Eph. from works accepted as Pauline goes back to Col. (especially the *Haustafel*). But because this question cannot be decided with any certainty[25] we shall abstain from such arguments. The Epistle to the Ephesians contains many other details peculiar to itself which are not in Col. and which move it even farther away from Paul. We must deal later in more detail with the relationship of our document to the Epistle to the Colossians (see below, 3).

Insofar as every document aims to establish communication between its author and its recipients, we must now say something about the addressees to whom the author is speaking. If he is a man of the second or third generation (after the apostles and their time) we must consider the addressees predominantly as Christians who have been observing their faith for some time already. This is confirmed by the tenor and content of the document. They are no more neophytes than the addressees of 1 Pet.; the reflection on their Baptism (cf. 1.13; 2.5 f.; 4.4 f.; 5.8, 14) is part of the instruction and paraclesis common to early Christianity (cf. as well as 1 Pet., Heb. 6.1 f.; 1 John 3.1–10). There is also the leading pastoral theme of warning those Christians addressed against assimilation to their non-Christian environment and encouraging them to a special way of life in keeping with their calling (cf. 4.17–24; 5.3–14, 15–18;

[25]Cf. Schweizer, *Colossians* 15–24.

6.10–20). In their domestic environment they are in danger of 'becoming like the masses', adapting themselves to pagan immorality and losing their Christian identity. In accordance with the way of life existing at that time in cities, we must be dealing here with city-congregations. Since Ephesus does not come into consideration as the congregation addressed (cf. under Prescript) and the Laodicean hypothesis is rightly for the most part refuted by present-day scholars,[26] the letter cannot be identified as a writing to a specific congregation. We must think rather of a circle of congregations who are addressed jointly. It can scarcely be a circular letter with an interchangeable address; this would be a practice for which there is no proof in writings of this period. But it might be a circular which had *no* designation in the prescript (see under 1.1) and was meant for several congregations. This might also explain why we never obtain any very clear picture of concrete circumstances in the congregation. The problems addressed – the relationship between Jewish and Gentile Christians, office-bearers, the danger of corrupt teaching, the influence of the non-Christian environment, Christian congregational and family life – were everywhere alike in these congregations, while the particular difficulties of the individual congregations (cf. the letters in Rev. 2–3) could not be discussed in a circular.

Can we define the circle of these congregations more closely? This is possible because of the close relationship with the Epistle to the Colossians. If the author knew Col. and used it – at least from memory and perhaps also as a literary document (cf. under 3) it seems reasonable to think of neighbouring congregations in the Lycus Valley (Laodicea, Hierapolis) and thence to further congregations in Asia. The statement taken over almost verbatim from Col. 4.7 f. in 6.21 f. about the sending of Tychicus is, of course, on the hypothesis of pseudonymity a fiction which fulfils an epistolary function (cf. exegesis of this verse) and consequently cannot carry much weight as evidence. But it strengthens the proximity to the Epistle to the Colossians which was also to be read in Laodicea (Col. 4.16). There is no serious difficulty in assuming that Eph. could also reach congregations who already knew Col., especially if we presume a later date. Noteworthy is also the impersonal style of the concluding greeting (6.23 f.) where the second person is not used. But this, too, speaks for a writing to a circle of congregations with whom the author had no immediate contact. He may send the wish for peace 'to the brothers'; but, as in Col., he nowhere *addresses* them as brothers.[27] For further details of the circumstances of its writing see under 4.

[26]Cf. Kümmel, *Introduction* 353 f.; Wikenhauser – Schmid, *Einleitung* 483–5. The hypothesis that it was meant for Laodicea still has a supporter in Masson 140 f.
[27]Cf. E. Schweizer, 'Zur Frage der Echtheit des Kolosser-und Epheserbriefes', in *Neotestamentica* 429.

3. THE RELATIONSHIP TO COLOSSIANS

The close connection between Eph. and Col. has long been noted but has found various explanations. Those scholars who assume Pauline authorship of both letters consider the dates of their writing to be close. The frequent correspondences in language and reminiscences, as they see it, lead us back to the Apostle or one of his fellow-workers. They delivered similar lectures and warnings – naturally without reference to the 'philosophy' rife in Colossae which was weakening the Christian faith – to another congregation (usually assumed to be Laodicea) or in a circular to several congregations. But this simple assumption founders when we make a closer comparison between Eph. and Col. Is it like the Apostle to repeat himself in such a way and constantly quote his own words? Gal. and Rom. contain the same theme of justification through faith but diverge from one another in the development of thought and the choice of words. There is no parallel in the recognised Pauline corpus for the close correspondences in the paraclesis section in Col. (3.1–4.6) and Eph. (4.1–6.20). The uniqueness of the relationship between Col. and Eph. is revealed, if we make a synoptic comparison,[28] in the following points:

(a) Eph. to a large extent follows the course of Col. in parallel thoughts and language, but it does not do so slavishly. Roughly parallel are:

Prescript	Eph. 1.1 f.	Col. 1.1 f.
Thanksgiving and Intercession	Eph. 1.15–17	Col. 1.3 f., 9 f.
Coming alive with Christ again (through Baptism)	Eph. 2.5 f.	Col. 2.12 f.
Parts of the Paraclesis	Eph. 4.17–32	Col. 3.5–14
Spiritual Worship	Eph. 5.19 f.	Col. 3.16 f.
Family Life	Eph. 5.22–6.9	Col. 3.18–4.1
Steadfast Prayer	Eph. 6.18–20	Col. 4.2–4
The sending of Tychicus	Eph. 6.21 f.	Col. 4.7
Concluding salutation	Eph. 6.24	Col. 4.18

(b) Re-arrangements and insertions of thought and language from Col. in different contexts in Eph. are consequently all the more conspicuous. Only a few examples need to be cited. In the Great Eulogy, which is only in Eph. (1.3–14) there are numerous words and phrases which correspond in language to passages in Col.; cf. Eph. 1.4 and Col. 1.22; Eph. 1.7–Col. 1.13; Eph. 1.8–Col. 1.9; Eph. 1.10–Col. 1.20; Eph. 1.13–Col. 1.5. Christ's victory over the powers, forces etc. in Eph. 1.21 has clear echoes of Col. 1.16; 2.10, 15, Christ as Head of the Church Eph. 1.22; 4.15; 5.23 of Col. 1.18; 2.19. Christ 'our peace' in Eph. 2.14–17 develops an idea the seeds of which are already to be found in Col. 1.20: 3.15. In Eph. 2.16 the idea of reconciliation stemming from Col. 1.20, 22 (only there ἀποκαταλάσσειν) is incorporated with a new application (to Jews and Gentiles). Paul's case-

---

[28]Cf. the useful survey in Mitton, *Epistle* 279–315.

history at Eph. 3.1–10, 13 is oriented (along with the idea of the Mystery of Christ) on Col. 1.24–9. Eph. 4.16 takes up Col. 2.19 in a verbally reminiscent fashion although in a new connection. The exhortation to humility, gentleness, patience etc. in Eph. 4.2–4 is taken from Col. 3.12–14 and remodelled in context. Even considering all the similarities in detail, the paraclesis is generally remodelled and takes on a new character.[29]

(c) We must not overlook the new sections created by the author of Ephesians and which nevertheless are still reminiscent of Col. This is true of the Great Eulogy (1.3–14), the description of the divine work of salvation on the Christians elect in Christ Jesus (2.5–10), the reconciliation of the two groups, Jews and Gentiles (2.11–8), the picture of the building of the Church of the foundation of apostles and prophets (2.19–22), the excursus on the 'gifts' of Christ to his Church (4.8–16), the paraclesis on the Children of Light (5.8–14), the extension of the marriage-paraclesis according to the model of Christ and Church (5.22–3) and finally the picture of the armour of God (6.11–7). These passages prevent our considering Eph. simply as being towed along by Col. We must rather look at it as a deliberate re-working which is reminiscent of Col. but also of undisputed Pauline epistles (cf. the Synopsis in Mitton) and simultaneously contains ideas of its own which do not yet appear in Paul.

(d) The differences in theological outlook and change in pastoral objectives revealed by a comparison with Col. are very significant. To a large extent these can be traced back to two alterations in perspective: In its theological concern we have a shift of emphasis from Christology to Ecclesiology; and in the paraclesis the concern is here for the confrontation with the non-Christian environment rather than for the Christian demand for a 'heavenly' conversion on earth. The first of these, the change to a concern for ecclesiology rather than the emphasis on Christology which predominates in Col. has for some time received due emphasis.[30] The Mystery of Christ (Col. 1.26 f.) becomes the mystery of the one Church of Jesus Christ made up of Jews and Gentiles (Eph. 3.4 ff.). The concept of the *pleroma* (fullness) which in Col. is still understood christologically (1.19; 2.9; only in the wording of 2.10 is it applied to Christians) is taken over in Eph. 1.23 for the Church and is of greater importance in the whole letter (cf. 3.19; 4.13; also 4.10). The emphasis on ecclesiology is also revealed in the role which the 'Body of Christ' concept plays in Eph.[31] as well as in the inclusion of the descriptions of God's building (2.20–2), the perfect man and the Church as the Bride and Wife of Christ (5.25 ff.), all of which are missing in Col. Without abandoning the theocentric and christological

[29]Cf. Merklein, FS. F. Mußner.

[30]Cf. Bultmann, *Theologie* 539 f.; Käsemann, *Interpretationsproblem* 253–61; Schweizer, *Church Order* 107–9; Conzelmann 87; Ernst, *Pleroma* 149–97; Wikenhauser – Schmid, *Einleitung* 494 f.; Merklein, *Christus und die Kirche* 66 ff. 69 f. 88 f. Yet the shift in ecclesiological emphasis as compared with Paul and Col. is seen differently, either as being more a continuation or as a radical change.

[31]Cf. Schlier, *Christus und die Kirche* 37–48; Käsemann, *Leib und Leib Christi*; id., 'The Theological Problem presented by the Motif of the Body of Christ' in *Perspectives on Paul*, London 1971, 102–21; Mußner, *Christus* 118–60; Schweizer, 'Die Kirche als Leib Christi in den paulinischen Antilegomena', in *Neotestamentica* 293–316. See further in the excursus on the Church (pp. 293–370).

view, the author of Eph. makes ecclesiology the focus of his theological interest (cf. the excursus on the Church). The change in perspective in the paraclesis is obvious if we compare the formulation at Col. 3,1f, 5 ('Seek that which is above...', 'Deaden the limbs which are earthly') with the exhortations in Eph. not to live like the heathen far from God and entangled in works of darkness (4.17–9; 5, 3–14).[32] From these observations (which will be considered in greater detail in the exegesis) we can reach the following conclusions about the relationship between Col. and Eph.: a) the assumption that Eph. is pseudonymous is strengthened. Even if Col. might have been written by Paul (or by Timothy on his instructions[33]), the considerably greater gap between Eph. and Paul, as revealed in the development and re-interpretation of Pauline thought and in the extensive taking over of liturgical, catechetical and paraenetical traditions, leaves room for doubt about a Pauline origin. b) It is certain that the author of Eph. knew Col. It is not so certain whether he had it before him while writing and could refer to it as a written document. In spite of 6,21 f. it is enough to assume that he had it 'in his head' and was so familiar with it that words and phrases from Col. constantly flow from his pen.[34] Again, the differences noted in style, theology and objective are so great that we can only with difficulty conceive of the same author.[35] c) There is no place where we can prove that Eph. influenced the writing of Col. hence we may leave out of consideration complicated theories of the relationship of the two documents.[36] (d) Since there is a clear development from Col. to Eph. and the latter's theology and paraclesis point to a later date, we must postulate a greater interval between the two writings than do those who maintain the Pauline origin of Eph. The author of Eph. does not simply want to transmit the ideas in Col. to a wider circle but uses the language and thought-structures of Col. to put forward his own – different – interests. e) The hypothesis of a secretary – which could still be possible for Col. – breaks down completely with regard to Eph. Unlike Col. no co-worker is named in the prescript. The passages in which Paul introduces himself/is introduced (3.1–9; 4.1; 6.19 f.) reveal a stylized and idealized picture of Paul: the imprisoned Apostle, the outstanding interpreter of the Mystery of Christ, the great Apostle to the Gentiles, the guarantor of apostolic tradition. It is a picture of Paul which is closer to that contained in the Pastoral Epistles than to the 'real' Paul as he must also have appeared to his co-workers in his vigour.[37] Eph. is no

[32] Cf. Merklein, FS Mußner 200–7. But is more a matter of a shift in 'pragmatic' emphasis rather than one of principle.

[33] Cf. Schweizer, *Colossians* 23 f.

[34] Cf. Mitton, *Epistle* 67 and 261.

[35] In this sense Percy, *Probleme* 240 and 418 f.; van Roon, *Authenticity* 195, 205, 439.

[36] This is the case with H. J. Holtzmann, *Kritik der Epheser- und Kolosserbriefe aufgrund einer Analyse ihrer Verwandtschaftsverhältnisse*, Leipzig 1872; Ochel, *Bearbeitung*; cf. also P. N. Harrison, 'The Author of Ephesians', 1964 (StEv II = TU 87) 595–604. These theories are now rejected almost totally. A dependence of Col. on Eph. is still represented by Coutts, NTS 4, 201–7; cf. also Schille, ThLZ 82, 332 f.

[37] On the picture of Paul in Ephesians cf. Percy, *Probleme* 342–53; Fischer, *Tendenz* 95–108; Merklein, *Kirchl. Amt.* 335–42; Lindemann, *Paulus* 40–2; E. Dassmann, *Der Stachel im*

Pauline admonitory letter but a writing which looks back to him (a Paul-anamnesis).

In a hermeneutic sense the dependence of Eph. on Col. together with the assumed pseudonymity provides a further key to the explanation of this unique writing. The author's theological views and intentions receive clearer definition by a constant comparison with Col. In this respect, too, the hermeneutic circle is completed by the interpretation of the writing as a whole.

4. DATE AND CIRCUMSTANCES OF COMPOSITION

If we opt for a late dating of Eph. around AD 90 on the aforementioned grounds, we must look for contemporary circumstances which justify such an estimate. The Letters of Ignatius (the first decade of the 2nd Century) which appear to know Eph. must form the latest terminus.[38] For lack of more concrete evidence we must look more closely at the internal situation of the congregations in Asia Minor at the end of the First Century. There has been talk of a 'widespread spiritual crisis' which characterized the general situation in those congregations.[39] But this is too vague to advance our research. Among the more precise responses we must mention the opinion held by K. M. Fischer. He considers the trouble which the author of Eph. wants to overcome as consisting of two phenomena: the transition from the Pauline missionary association to the new episcopal church order in Asia Minor; and the depressed situation of the Jewish Christians amidst the predominantly Gentile Christian congregations.[40] The thesis that there was a constitutional problem is untenable on various grounds but chiefly because such a tension between 'apostolic' and 'episcopal' Church organisation can not be detected in Eph. There may be an element of truth in the idea that there was tension in their communal life between Jewish and Gentile Christians if the section Eph. 2.11–22 indicates a situation actually existing (v. exegesis).

A. Lindemann suggests that at the time of Eph. the Church was being persecuted and was in need of consolation and encouragement. To support this view he points to the description of battle in Eph. 6.10–20 and even considers it may refer to the persecution in Asia Minor under Domitian in AD 96.[41] But this is most unlikely. The spiritual battle when one is arrayed in the armour of God is not dependent upon a situation

---

Fleisch. Paulus in der frühchristlichen Literatur bis Irenäus, Münster i.W. 1979, 51–7 (sees no essential difference from the picture of Paul in the authentic letters); Gnilka, FS Mußner, especially 187–9; G. Schille, *Das älteste Paulusbild*, Berlin 1979, 60–6.

[38] The following seem to betray knowledge of Eph.: Ign. Pol. 5, cf. Eph. 5.25; Ign. Eph. Präskript cf. Eph. 1.3–5; ibid. 9.1 cf. Eph. 2.20–2. For further possible quotations in early Christian literature cf. Schmid, *Epheserbrief* 16–36. He, however, judges somewhat optimistically on allusions in other writings (Did., 1 Clem., Barn., Herm.); much can be explained from the language characteristic of the Baptismal instruction and paraclesis.

[39] Chadwick, ZNW 51, 152; Kümmel, *Introduction* 364; Ernst 252.

[40] *Tendenz* 21–39; 79–94.

[41] ZNW 67, 242 f.

where there is external persecution. When writing to congregations in Asia Minor advice for dealing with such a contingency must be expressed quite differently as a comparison with the Book of Revelation shows. Even a milder form of oppression by Gentile fellow-citizens would certainly have left deeper traces as can be seen if we consider 1 Pet. Here there are no obvious references to state-approved persecutions because of refusals to take part in the cult of Caesar; but the author repeatedly refers to slanders and harassment in their day-to-day lives (2.15; 3.13–16; 4. 12–16), and how to endure and overcome this tribulation is one of the main concerns of this letter to the Christians in the 'Diaspora'.[42]

To see this more clearly we must begin with those conditions which can be recongnised in the pragmatic objectives of the author of Eph. We see him concerned with various things, but these can all be traced back to two basic interests: the idea of the internal unity of the congregation which is intensified by the motif of the one Church founded by Jesus Christ and inseparably bound to him; and the concept of a commitment, growing out of God's calling, to a distinctly Christian way of life which should be distinguished from and contrasted to the unchristian life-style of the environment. The problem of unity and harmony within the congregations was already a cause of concern for Paul but became even more important in the years following, especially with the advance of deviant doctrine. If we look closely at the section 4.11–16 with its emphatic reference to the offices given to the Church which should serve to strengthen Christ's Body, we might suspect a 'crisis of leadership' which is connected with the dying-out of the 'apostles and prophets' and the transition to the post-apostolic period.[43] Hence the author of Eph. gives a pre-eminent place to the 'foundation of the apostles and prophets' (2.20), unlike Paul, who describes Christ himself as the unalterable foundation (1 Cor. 3.11). These changes in perspective (discussed in more detail in the excursus on the Church) can be seen in other NT writings. It is instructive to compare Paul's farewell-speech at Miletus (Acts 20, 18–35) in which the elders from the congregation at Ephesus – according to Luke's view of his time – are reminded of their responsibility for the whole Church (v. 28) and made aware of the danger of false doctrine (v. 30).[44] Jude, 1 and 2 John and the Pastorals testify to the same danger in different ways. It is also mentioned in Eph. 4.14 with the descriptive expression πλάνη (error, deception) which gains ground in the later writings.[45] It is a common phenomenon at the beginning of the post-apostolic period which the author of Eph. only notes in a non-specific

[42]Cf. Brox, *Der erste Petrusbrief* (n. 13) 24–34, especially 31–4.

[43]Cf. W. Marxsen, *Introduction to the New Testament* Oxford, 1968, 197: 'The problem which confronts not only the author of Eph., but also ourselves, is this: How can the Church remain an apostolic Church in a period when the apostles are no longer living?'; further Merklein, *Kirchl. Amt.* 368 f.

[44]On this speech cf. J. Dupont, *Paulus an die Seelsorger*, Düsseldorf 1966; H. Schürmann, 'Das Testament des Paulus für die Kirche Apg 20. 18–35,' in *Traditionsgeschichtliche Untersuchungen zu den synoptischen Evangelien*, Düsseldorf 1968, 310–40; H.-J. Michel, *Die Abschiedsrede des Paulus an die Kirche Apg. 20, 17–38*, 1973 (StANT 35); F. Prast, *Presbyter und Evangelium in nachapostolischer Zeit*, 1979 (FzB 29).

[45]2 Thess. 2.11; Jud 11; 1 John 4.6; 2 Pet. 2.18; 3.17; cf. the verb in the same sense in 2 Tim. 3.13; 1 John 2.26; 2 Pet. 2.15; Rev. 2.20.

manner because of diverse local conditions, but which he nevertheless considers as ominous.

The other concern, to urge and encourage to a new way of life in keeping with the Christian calling, can also be found in Paul when he is addressing new converts who live in heathen cities (cf. 1 Thess. 4.1–12; 1 Cor. passim). It might be regarded simply as a traditional Christian exhortation if it were not that its length and emphasis, special motifs and new accents (cf. 5.6–14) betray an urgent, topical interest. The author looks back on an extended period of Christian instruction (cf. 4.20) and has in his mind's eye a developed Christian congregational life, as is evidenced by the liturgical echoes, the verses 5.19 f. and the *Haustafel*. This brings him closer to the awareness which developed more strongly in the 2nd and 3rd centuries that Christians constitute the 'third race' (alongside Jews and Gentiles).[46] On the one hand he stresses the bond with the old Israel throughout the history of salvation, but on the other distances himself from Judaism which retains circumcision (cf. 2.11). The attitude he demands to the non-Christian surroundings differs noticeably from 1 Pet, which is more strongly of the view that Christians should give their fellow-citizens no target for attack (2.15; 3.16) while Eph. 5.11 ff. urges the exposure of their evil deeds. This is connected with the theme of suffering and the bias of 1 Pet; but at heart this epistle, too, urges a decisively Christian way of life in the face of external suspicions and harassments (cf. 4.2–4).

The picture which the congregations in Asia Minor at the turn of the 1st century presented must have been fairly varied as can be seen from the circular letters in Rev. and the Letters of Ignatius.[47] In these there come to the fore concrete features – diverse false doctrines, schisms, a reduction in the enthusiasm to participate in the gatherings for worship (Ign. Eph. 5.3; 13.1), a cooling of the first fervour (Rev. 2.4 in the Letter to Ephesus) general half-heartedness (Rev. 3.15 f. in the Letter to Laodicea). There are constant exhortations to unity in the letters of Ignatius. The Bishop of Antioch considers this guaranteed by closer connection of the faithful to the local bishop and the presbyters and deacons associated with him. We cannot use these later writings directly to throw light on the background of Eph.; but the phenomena which became apparent twenty years later might perhaps give an inkling of the sort of abuses and dangers which threatened the Church in that area at a time of transition. To this extent we are justified in talking of a 'spiritual crisis' which is mirrored in the muted admonition of Eph.

What can we say further about the author from the findings in Eph. itself? Opinion as to whether he was a Jewish-or Gentile-Christian is not unanimous.[48] The change from 'we' to 'you' is not an attempt to contrast the recipients of the letter, addressed as former Gentiles (2.11 f.) with the author, who would then appear as the representative of the Jewish

---

[46]On this see A. v Harnack, *Die Mission und Ausbreitung des Christentums in den ersten drei Jahrhunderten*, Leipzig [4]1924, I, 259–67.

[47]Cf. H. Kraft, *Die Offenbarung des Johannes*, 1974 (HNT 16a) 87–94.

[48]The general opinion today is that the author is a Christian with his roots in (Hellenistic) Judaism. Mitton, *Epistle* 264, thinks the author was born a Gentile; Lindemann also tends to this view ZNW 67, 247.

Christians (cf. under 1.13; 2.3 and other passages). It is far more the case that when he uses 'we' the author is thinking of Christians in general, the Christian community as such (the ecclesiastical 'we') in which he emphatically desires to include the recipients. He reminds them of their calling to belong to the one Church of Jesus Christ (cf. the 'you also' in 1.13; 2.1) and to possess in one Spirit, together with the former Jewish Christians, access to the Father (2.18; 3.12). That his origins lay in Judaism can only be assumed from other pieces of circumstantial evidence, such as from his theology which is bound to a Jewish way of thinking (cf. the Great Eulogy, 1.3–14; the Doxology 3.20 f.; the picture of God's Building 2.20–2; the armour of God 6.13–17), from his language which closely corresponds to that of the Qumran documents (see above) and from his knowledge of the Bible. Certainly the epistle does not contain that many scriptural quotations; but his way of analyzing Scripture (especially 2.17; 4.8; 5.31) reveals a similarity to the Jewish Midrash although it is applied in a Christian manner, and the way the quotations from Scripture are so easily introduced (4.26; 5.2, 18; 6.3, 14–17) betrays knowledge of and familiarity in dealing with Scripture. But since these scriptural allusions for the most part follow the Septuagint, and since many concepts point to contact with Philo of Alexandria (cf. *pleroma*, head and body, macro-anthropos) and the paraclesis shows the influence of Greek stoic ethics (cf. under 4.31; 5.3–5), we should have to define him more closely as a Jewish-Christian with a Hellenistic education who was receptive to his spiritual and intellectual surroundings. In that age of syncretism all sorts of ideas could have imposed themselves on him, including concepts which were more strongly developed in Gnosticism; but he assimilated them in a genuinely Christian sense. This assumption allows us best to do justice to observations on the text which, religio-historically, are not unambiguous.[49]

It is easier to give an opinion on the author's position within the Church. It is clear from the section 3.1–13 that he knows himself committed to Paul and his theology and wants to emphasize the great Apostle to the Gentiles as the enlightened theologian and best guarantee of the apostolic tradition. In the name of Paul and in dependence on his Epistles – of which, apart from Col., he appears to know Rom. Gal., 1 and 2 Cor. and Philemon.[50] – he admittedly develops his own theology, which he works out further than Paul, particularly in the sphere of ecclesiology and also in taking into consideration the changed structures in the Church (cf. 2.20–22; 4.11). Such a theological achievement is surely only possible for a man who was himself active as a teacher in a congregation, possibly in a

[49]Cf. Colpe, *Leib-Christi-Vorstellung*; Hegermann, *Schöpfungsmittler* passim; Gnilka 33–45; Vielhauer, *Literatur* 214 f. On the Gnostic derivation of many ideas (Käsemann, Schlier, K. M. Fischer etc.) cf. the exegesis on the appropriate verse. I should not like entirely to exclude a certain knowledge of Gnostic motifs; cf. also the qualified position of H.-F. Weiß in Tröger, *Gnosis und NT* 311–24; further Schenke – Fischer, *Einleitung* I, 186 f.

[50]The theory developed by E. J. Goodspeed, *The Meaning of Ephesians*, Chicago 1933; 'Ephesians in the First Edition of Paul', JBL 70 (1951) 285–91; *The Key to Ephesians*, Chicago 1956, that the author of Eph. wants to collect together the ideas in the other Pauline Epistles with his own work as a covering letter to the 'First Edition' is improbable. For criticism of this cf. Percy, *Probleme* 445; Beare 602–4; Gnilka 45 f.; Kümmel, *Introduction* 365.

prominent position.[51] His paraclesis leads us to conclude for him an office which he held in a congregation and perhaps also performed in a larger area through visits to other congregations. He conceals his identity in this pseudonymous writing not through any lack of self-confidence but because he understands himself as 'only' a communicator and interpreter of the Pauline tradition. He deliberately sets out to claim the authority of the great Apostle as other prominent figures at that time also did (cf. the Pastorals and 1 Pet.). Consequently it is also impossible to identify any otherwise known person with the author of Eph.[52] He remains for us an unknown man from a congregation in Asia Minor (from the Valley of the Lycus?) who has left behind for us the seal of his personality only in this writing composed in the spirit of Paul.

[51]Cf. Merklein, *Kirchl. Amt.* 44 f. 215 f. 350 et al.; on the fundamental position of the 'teachers' cf. H. Schürmann '... und Lehrer', in *Orientierungen am NT* 116–56, on Eph. especially 151.

[52]It is hardly possible that it was Onesimus, as is suggested by several English scholars, most recently Harrison, *Paulines* (n. 19) 53, and in StEv. II (n. 34). The like-named Bishop of Eph. at the time of Ignatius (Ign. Eph. 1.3) is certainly not the slave Onesimus converted by Paul (Philem. and Col. 4.9). The name was a common one, cf. Pr- Bauer 1129 f.; J. Schmid, LThK VII, 1158.

I. Salutation, Glorification of God and Opening (1.1–2.10)

1. SALUTATION AND BLESSING (1.1–2)

Literature

Schmid, *Epheserbrief* 51–69.
Percy, *Probleme* 449–66.
N. A. Dahl, 'Adresse und Proömium des Eph.', ThZ 7 (1951) 241–64.
R. Batey, 'The Destination of Ephesians', JBL 82 (1963) 101.
M. Santer, 'The Text of Ephesians 1.1', NTS 15 (1968/69) 247 f.
K. Berger, 'Apostelbrief und apostolische Rede. Zum Formular frühchristlicher Briefe', ZNW 65 (1974) 190–231.
van Roon, *Authenticity* 72–85.
W. Schenk, 'Zur Entstehung und zum Verständnis des Epheserbriefes', Theol. Versuche 6 (1975) 73–8.
Lindemann, ZNW 67 (1976) 235–9.
Schenke – Fischer, *Einleitung* I, 182.

1 Paul, an apostle of Christ Jesus by the will of God. To the saints
(there) and to those who are faithful
in Christ Jesus,
2 Grace to you and peace from God our Father and the
Lord Jesus Christ.

Analysis

This written communication begins in proper style with the superscription which, according to the custom in antiquity, included the names of the sender and recipient and a greeting. Apart from the Christian phrasing (cf. the Blessing) it is not here expanded as in Rom. 1.1–7, Gal. 1.1–5; 1 Cor.

1.1–3, but keeps to the shorter Pauline form. In the details of the sender Paul is called 'An apostle of Christ Jesus'[1] without the addition of 'called (to be)', but with the supplementary 'by the will of God', exactly as in Col. 1.1. The address poses a complicated problem in which textual criticism, syntactical connection and literary questions play a part. In view of the variety and diversity of hypotheses put forward on the subject it would be advisable first to settle the text as far as it is possible.

Textual criticism

The phrase giving the location of the recipients – ἐν Ἐφέσῳ – is not certain. It is to be found in most of the MSS and also in the translations and is witnessed by many of the Fathers, but is missing in the oldest MSS P⁴⁶B ℵ*, in the important minuscule 1739 which is based on the version of Origen and in the Vienna minuscule 424. Origen and Basil did not read the location in the MSS available to them.[2] From Tertullian's evidence about Marcion – in which different elements are evaluated diversely (Adv. Marc. V, 11.17) – one thing is fairly clear and that is that he, too, did not have this detail and produced the document as a letter to Laodicea.[3] The attestation of 'at Ephesus' by the many, widely-scattered later MSS can be explained by the fact that the lack of a location was noticed at an early date and there was inserted the name of a town in which Paul had long been active. There is not sufficient evidence to support the idea of the reverse having occurred, namely that the location was deleted at an early date.[4] Hence, by all the rules of textual criticism we must recognise that ἐν Ἐφέσῳ is most probably not original. Among exegetes other considerations are often decisive; but if we work methodically we must bow to the rigidity of the text-critical argument.

Is the text *without a location* grammatically or stylistically impossible?[5] For some time researchers have pointed to comparative material in Greek papyri in which the participle of εἶναι is included in like cases, similarly without a location being given, an 'idiomatic form of expression' which gives a meaning something like 'there, present' (cf. Acts 5.17; 13.1; 14.13), but which may also be omitted in the translation.[6] This linguistic peculiarity is unfamiliar to us and unique among

---

[1]Several Mss read 'of Jesus Christ' (ℵ A F G Ψ maj. VL Vg^cl sy^P). The variant 'of Christ Jesus', attested to by B P⁴⁶ D 33 pc corresponds to the predominating usage in Eph. (a further 10 times), while the reversed word-order is always encountered after (ὁ) κύριος (ἡμῶν) (1.2, 3, 17; 5.20; 6.23, 24) and in 1.5. The author might be permitted to follow the way of speaking in Philem. (cf. v. 1 and 3, v. 9 and 25) and Col. (cf. 1.1 and 3). A reference to the Messiah, as Barth (p. 66 f.) assumes, is certainly not contained to a greater degree in the wording 'Christ Jesus'; cf. the change from 'a captive of Christ Jesus' (3.1) and 'a captive in the Lord' (4.1); 2.12 ('Christ' without the article) and 2.13 (with the article). The article in front of 'Christ' is no evidence at all for the 'Messiah' (cf. 2.5; 3.4, 8, 17; 4.7, 13; 5.14) cf. also Percy, *Probleme*, p. 187 f.

[2]Origen (Gregg JThS 3 [1902] 235); Basil, *Contra Eunom.* II 19 (MPG 29, 611). Cf. Schmid* 61–3.

[3]For a discussion on the text cf. Schmid* 52–60; Dibelius – Greeven 56.

[4]The discrepancy that Paul should have written such a general letter to the Ephesians obviously struck Theodore of Mopsuestia, who put forward the explanation that Paul wrote to the Ephesians, as to the Romans, before he visited them ('*quos necdum ante vident*'), – an unlikely explanation (though often reiterated in antiquity and the Middle Ages) since Paul was the first to bring the Christian faith to Ephesus; cf. Schmid* 49*; Schenke – Fischer* 182: The lost location was later supplied in different ways.

[5]Thus Schmid* 115: 'If the words τοῖς οὖσιν are original, then they necessarily demand a location also'; similarly Ernst 266; Lindemann* 235.

[6]Cf. K. Lake – H. J. Cadbury, *The Beginnings of Christianity* I/4, London 1933, 56;

the superscriptions in NT Epistles. Paul always adds the location after the participle of εἶναι; but the pseudonymous author may proceed differently to suit his purpose.

Syntactically the text τοῖς ἁγίοις τοῖς οὖσιν καὶ πιστοῖς ἐν Χριστῷ Ἰησοῦ does not read smoothly,[7] but can be understood as a twofold address: 'to the saints and to those who are faithful in Christ Jesus'. Doubt arises whether ἐν Χριστῷ Ἰησοῦ applies to both expressions or simply to the latter. But since τοῖς ἁγίοις already has an attribute in τοῖς οὖσιν, it is preferable for the flow of the sentence and also because it follows the style of speech usual elsewhere (οἱ ἅγιοι without expansion in Eph.; πιστοὶ ἐν Χριστῷ Ἰησοῦ cf. 1.15) to limit the latter expression to 'faithful'.

Having said this we have decided against several other hypotheses: (1) The Lacuna-Hypothesis *does* presuppose the original lack of the location 'in Ephesus', but conjectures a gap in the text which would be filled with the appropriate location in each of the examples which were intended for a specific congregation. But there is no proof for a method of procedure of this kind in ancient literature.[8] (2) The hypothesis that our Eph. was the letter to Laodicea mentioned in Col. 4.16 and originally contained this location is based on the report concerning Marcion, who, however, had thereby only expressed his own opinion (cf. supra). (3) The Copy-Hypothesis, according to which Paul had sent along with Col. a letter of similar content with different addresses to several congregations (including Laodicea),[9] is also beset by difficulties. (4) A. van Roon's opinion, that the two words joined by καί ('the saints' and 'the faithful') indicate two locations, namely Hierapolis and Laodicea, which were then left out,[10] remains pure speculation. (5) The theory which has again been recently approved (Gnilka, Lindemann)[11] – that the location 'in Ephesus' was part of the original text – is not justified by external textual criticism.

The Blessing is written in a manner stylistically pleasing: two expressions for the blessing granted (grace and peace) and two persons from whom the blessing proceeds: God, our Father and the Lord Jesus Christ. The recipients (ὑμῖν) are skilfully included in the words of comfort of the blessing after the first expression χάρις. The blessing corresponds exactly with that in Rom. 1.7; 1 Cor. 1.3; 2 Cor. 1.2; Phil. 1.2; Philem. 3 – i.e.

Dibelius – Greeven 57. On the material from the papyri v. Mayser II/1, 347 f., especially under b, β. cf. also Moulton – Turner, *Grammar* III, 151 f.

[7]The omission of τοῖς before οὖσιν in P⁴⁶ perhaps came about on grammatical grounds cf. Bl-Debr §413.4 n. 10. πᾶσιν before τοῖς ἁγίοις is a secondary extension in ℵ A P 81 326al. Vg. – Batey* essays a conjecture: instead of οὖσιν (or οὔσαις) a geographical detail Ἀσίας, Santer* (with a complicated hypothesis) a transposition of τοῖς οὖσιν after πιστοῖς. Schenk* 76 interprets it as 'to the saints who are also believers in Jesus Christ', cf. also Kümmel, *Introduction* 351.

[8]The Roman senate's 'circular' quoted in 1 Macc. 15.16–24 and the letters containing the same text with different addressees mentioned by G. Zuntz (*The Text of the Epistles*, London, 1953, 228 n. 1) do not however verify the idea of gaps for the address. cf. also Gnilka 4 f.

[9]Cf. Dahl* 241–50: The letter Paul wrote at the time of Col. to several congregations in Asia Minor exists in our Eph. The congregation at Ephesus, which was not among those addressed, made a copy of it and in so doing left out the address. Schlier (31 f.) is of a similar opinion. But why did Paul not choose, as in Gal. 1.2, the name of the district if writing a letter to several congregations? The position of the place-name would also be curious in comparison with Col. 1.2.

[10]*Authenticity* 80–5.

[11]Gnilka 5–7; Lindemann* 238 f. Both regard 'Ephesus' as the fictitious address of the pseudonymous author.

follows the stereotype form of a Pauline epistle. In Col. 1.2 the naming of Jesus Christ is missing. Unlike the Col. superscription (and most of the others in Paul's epistles) no fellow-worker of Paul is named – a fact which is significant for the character of the communication.

Exegesis

1

The communication, which is given the form of a letter through the superscription,[12] names as sender 'Paul, an apostle of Christ Jesus'. This is the preferred self-description of the great missionary to the Gentiles which is missing in the superscription of 1 Thess. (but cf. 2.7) but which he claimed emphatically after the attacks on his right to be an apostle (cf. Rom. 1.1; 1 Cor. 1.1; 2 Cor. 1.1) because he was called to be an apostle by God himself through special revelation of Christ (Gal. 1.15 f.: 1 Cor. 9.1; 15.8–10). This is mentioned again in Eph. (cf. 3.3, 7–9) but no longer with an apologetic purpose; it is now positive, from the aspect of a deeper, richer revelation graciously bestowed upon him especially who was the 'very least of all the saints' (3.8).[13] Paul's authority is built up in a unique way through the very circumstance that he appears as the chosen vessel of God's grace. Thus the expression 'by the will of God', which is also found in the superscriptions of 1 and 2 Cor. and Col., receives a new accent in the context of Eph. By the will of God Paul is *the* apostle of Jesus Christ[14] whose insight into the mystery of Christ (3.3) binds the Church permanently (cf. 3.10).

A mention of fellow-workers, as Timothy is named in Philem. 1 and Col. 1.1, would be more restrictive and spoil the effect of this picture of Paul – although Eph. seems to allude to the same position of the apostle as a prisoner. Everyone else must retreat behind his outstanding figure, and our unknown author wants to reinforce this idea in order to present his own concerns with the authority of the apostle.

The recipients are addressed first with the old Christian self-description 'the saints'[15] and then with 'those who are faithful in Christ Jesus'. We should not see in this a distinguishing of two groups ('the

---

[12]On the form of letters in antiquity cf. Roller, *Formular*; White, *Body* (vid. Lit for 1.15–23); Berger*. Compared with other letters it is striking that handwritten lines from Paul (Gal. 6.11; 1 Cor. 16.21; Philem. 19; Col. 4.18; 2 Thess 3.17) and especially the otherwise regular greetings to others are missing at the end of Eph.

[13]On the picture of Paul cf. Introduction, p. 32.

[14]On the choice of words cf. Schweizer, *Colossions* 28 f.

[15]'The saints' was already a term used by the first Christians at Rome to describe themselves, as we can see from Paul's way of speaking of them (2 Cor 8.4; 9.1, 12; Rom 15.25, 26, 31; cf. Acts 9.13; 26.10). The apostle then transferred it to the Christians of his missionary congregations. The expression, which goes back to the OT (here 'holy convocation' of God's people, Ex. 12.16; Lev. 23.2–4, 7–9 and frequently; Num. 28.25. Cf. Procksch TDNT I, 107) was taken over as a self-description by the members of the Qumran Community as we see from the Qumran texts: 1 QS 5.13, 18; 8.17, 20, 23; 9.8 and frequently; 1 QM 6.6; 10.10; 16.1 etc. Cf. H. Kosmala, *Hebräer - Essener - Christen*, Leiden 1959, 50–62. The author of Eph. takes over the Pauline expression here, but also uses it *independently* (1.15.18; 2.19; 3.8, 18; 4.12; 6.18) and evaluates it ethically (cf. 1.4; 5.3). He keeps a very firm hold on the idea of an underlying call by God to be 'saints' (cf. 1 Cor. 1.2; Rom 1.7).

saints' = the Jewish Christians, 'those who are faithful' = the Gentile Christians).[16] The common article and the usage normal in the rest of Eph., which in the majority of cases uses 'the saints' to mean all Christians (1.15; 3.8, 18; 4.12; 6.18; cf. 5.3; at the most it might apply to angels in 1.18 and 2.19) gainsays this interpretation. The double expression is probably taken over from Col. 1.1. Instead of naming the location 'at Colossae', the author inserts τοῖς οὖσιν (without a location); in the second form of address, whose meaning can scarcely be distinguished, he omits ἀδελφοῖς. Why he does so is hard to say – perhaps merely from his sense of style – because at the end he wishes 'the brothers' peace and love (6.23). Because of the omission in 1.1, there arises the unusual combination 'the faithful (πιστοί) in Christ Jesus' (although cf. 1.15), while in Col. 1.1 'in Christ Jesus' is to be taken rather with 'brothers' (cf. 1 Cor. 4.17). The connection with Col. 1.1 is the more certain as πιστός in Paul generally means 'loyal'.[17] In the author's view the expression aims to describe the religious position 'in Christ Jesus' achieved by the addressees.

2

The Blessing, which in its characteristic form (cf. in addition to Paul himself Tit. 1.4,; 1 Pet. 1.2; 2 Pet. 1.2; Rev. 1.4) sometimes expanded to a tripartite formula by the addition of ἔλεος (1 Tim. 1.2; 2 Tim. 1.2; 2 Jn. 3), is a Christian neologism. It betrays a Jewish tradition which is not simply combined with a Hellenistic form of greeting (χαίρειν)[18] We usually translate as 'grace' the significant, and in each context decisive, concept χάρις.[19] Along with εἰρήνη it performs a like function to ἔλεος (mercy) which is frequently connected with it in Jewish texts (cf. the tripartite formula!).[20] The wording of the blessing preserves the original power of the blessing promised by God and his messengers (cf. Lk. 10.5f.). 'Grace', the compassion newly shown, and 'peace', the salvation which embraces all humankind, come from God, our Father, and from the Lord Jesus Christ to the receptive readers and remain effectively with them (cf. 2 Jn. 3). The combination of God the Father and Jesus Christ is typical of the blessings in the superscriptions and is taken over here by the author although he normally prefers 'God (and Father) of our Lord Jesus Christ', in keeping with the theocentric point of view (1.3, 17; cf. 5.20). Only in the concluding blessing (6.23) do we have the same syntactic construction. The whole communication is enclosed within this promise of grace and peace.

---

[16]In this sense Pokorny, *Gnosis* 17; Kirby *Ephesians* 170; cf. Kümmel, *Introduction* 351.

[17]With reference to God 1 Thess. 5.24; 1 Cor 1.9; 10.13; cf. 2 Thess. 3.3 (the 'Lord'); of men 1 Cor 4.2, 17; 7.25; Col. 1.7; 4.7, 9. Only in Gal 3.9 does it quite clearly have the sense of 'having faith' (in relation to Abraham, an established expression); and 2 Cor 6.15 (an un-Pauline passage). Only after Paul did the adjective or noun become a term for the 'faithful' in the sense of 'Christians'. Cf. Pr-Bauer 1319; Bultmann, TDNT VI, 214.

[18]Cf. Berger* 191–207.

[19]Cf. H. Conzelmann, TDNT IX, 391 f., who considers a closer definition through its OT pre-history to be of little advantage; Berger* thinks otherwise 192, n. 12.

[20]On the combination of ἔλεος and εἰρήνη cf. Jub. 12.29; 22.8–10; Eth. Enoch 1.8; Syrian Baruch 78.2; 1 QS 2.1–4. Further see Berger* 197–201.

Summary

The author is writing under the assumed name of the apostle Paul to a larger circle of readers, to whom he turns with the authority of Paul but also in the spirit of the great Apostle to the Gentiles. Consequently he addresses them as 'saints' and 'those who are faithful in Christ Jesus' and offers them the familiar blessing. Even if they receive his writing at a later date and in changed circumstances, they should accept it as the Pauline congregations received the letters of the Apostle. What he has to say to them is the interpretation of the Gospel as vouched for and made binding by the apostle. At the same time he wishes them at the start (and at the end) 'grace' and 'peace', blessings which come only from God the Father and the Lord Jesus Christ; may they be so filled with these blessings that his writing may bear fruit in them. Look at from this point of view Eph., specifically as a pseudonymous writing, retains its 'address' character and its relevance even in the present day, especially for the congregation assembled in worship.

2. THE GREAT OPENING EULOGY (1. 3–14)

Literature

T. Innitzer, 'Der Hymnus in Eph. 1.3–14', ZKTh 28 (1904) 612–21.

E. Lohmeyer, 'Das Proömium des Epheserbriefes', ThBl 5 (1926) 120–5.

W. Ochel, *Bearbeitung* 18–32.

C. Maurer 'Der Hymnus von Epheser 1 als Schlüssel zum ganzen Briefe', EvTh 11 (1951/52) 151–72.

N. A. Dahl, ThZ 7, 250–64.

J. Coutts, 'Eph. 1.3–14 and 1 Pet. 1.3–12', NTS 3 (1956/57) 115–27.

S. Lyonnet, 'La bénédiction de Éph. 1.3–14 et son arrière-plan judaïque', in *A la Rencontre de Dieu* (Mémorial A. Gelin), Le Puy 1961, 341–52.

J. Cambier, 'La bénédiction d'Éphésiens 1.3–14', ZNW 54 (1963) 58–104.

J. M. Robinson, 'Die Hodajoth-Formel in Gebet und Hymnus des Frühchristentums', in *Apophoreta* (FS E. Haenchen = BZNW 30) 1964, 194–235.

Schille, *Frühchristliche Hymnen* 65–73.

Sanders, ZNW 56, 223–32.

J. Schattenmann, *Studien zum neutestamentlichen Prosahymnus*, Munich 1965, 1–10.

Deichgräber, *Gotteshymnus* 65–76.

H. Krämer, 'Zur sprachlichen Form der Eulogie Eph. 1.3–14', WuD NF 9 (1967) 34–46.

R. Trevijano Etcheverria, 'Estudio sobre la eulogia paulina (2 Cor. 1.3 y Ef. 1.3)', Burg. 10 (1969) 35–61.

N. Kehl, 'Der Christushymnus im Epheserbrief' (unpublished Habilitationsschrift) Innsbruck 1969.

M. Rese, 'Formeln und Lieder im NT', VF 15 (1970) 75–95.

G. Santopietro, *Il rapporto eulogico tra Dio e il suo populo*, Noci 1971.

A. Suski, *Il Salmo di lode nella Lettera agli Efesina* (Diss. Pont. Univ. Gregor.), Rome 1973.

D. Jayne, '"We" and "You" in Ephesians 1.3–14', ET 85 (1974) 151–52.
R. Schnackenburg, 'Die große Eulogie Eph. 1.3–14. Analyse unter textlinguistischen Aspekten', BZ NF 21 (1977) 67–87.
P. T. O'Brien, 'Ephesians 1: An Unusual Introduction to a New Testament Letter', NTS 25 (1979) 504–16.
Caragounis, *Mysterion* 39–52, 78–96.

I   3 Blessed (is) the God and Father of our Lord Jesus Christ who has blessed us with every spiritual blessing in the heaven(lie)s in Christ.

4 in that he chose us in him before the foundation of the world that we should be holy and blameless before him

II   5 (who) in love has pre-ordained us to sonship through Jesus Christ

according to the pleasure of his will
6 to the praise of the glory of his grace which he bestowed on us in the Beloved

III 7 in whom we have redemption through his blood, the forgiveness of sins according to the riches of his grace

8 which he lavished upon us in all wisdom and insight

IV   9 (in that he) has made known to us the mystery of his will according to his sovereign purpose which he had previously made in him

10 as a plan for the fullness of the times:
to unite all things in Christ,
things in heaven and things on earth,

V   11 in him, in whom we also received what is allotted to us predetermined according to the purpose of him who accomplishes all things,

according to the counsel of his will
12 that we might exist for the praise of his glory, we who have hope in anticipation in Christ

VI   13 in whom you, too, when you heard the word of truth the gospel of your salvation

in which you also, when you came to faith
were sealed with the promised Holy Spirit
14 who is the first instalment of our inheritance until the redemption, the acqusition (of our inheritance)
to the praise of his glory.

Analysis

The author begins his letter with a great thanks-giving to God which in this extended form is unique in th NT. It is termed a eulogy because of its opening word and, in contrast to other, shorter eulogies which from time to time appear at points in letters (Rom. 1.25; 9.5; 2 Cor. 11.31), a 'eulogistic epistolary introduction'.[1] There are only two other examples in the NT, namely 2 Cor. 1.3 f. and 1 Pet. 1.3–5. Although this proves that the use of this literary form was common in early Christianity – certainly deriving from Jewish custom (*berakoth*) and stylistic form (cf. the *hadajoth* of Qumran) – the length, richness of vocabulary and style of Eph. 1.3–14, which is a single extended complex sentence, set it far apart from the usual pattern.

The elevated, solemnly ringing language, reminiscent of liturgical texts, has frequently led scholars to suspect that the author has adopted and adapted a hymn sung in early Christian worship. Efforts have accordingly been made (as with Col. 1.15–20) to disentangle the original wording from the additions and alterations of the editor, but with very diverse results.[2] Such attempts, starting off from considerations of form and content, and then generally working out some principle for separating the material, have come in for mounting criticism in recent times and need not be rehearsed here.[3] The majority of scholars today agree that we have here 'a unified ad hoc composition, a hymnic passage in artistic, rhythmical prose'.[4] But even then the question of the author's movement of thought and of the structure of this long sentence remains open.

Without having recourse to the hypothesis of a hymn, we might still wish to distinguish separate strophes or at least a thematic division of the material, either by following the verbal affirmations (election, vv. 4–6a; pardon, vv. 6b–7; initiation into the mystery, vv. 8–10)[5] or the three participles ὁ εὐλογήσας – προορίσας – γνωρίσας[6] or other points of orientation. A certain trinitarian structure has also been thought to be traceable[7] (election by the Father, salvation through the Son and 'sealing' in the Holy Spirit); or the frequently recurring formula ἐν Χριστῷ or ἐν αὐτῷ (ἐν ᾧ) has been taken as a means of dividing the sentence so as to afford a more markedly christological perspective.[8] But if we are to avoid the danger of imposing an alien theological construction on the rich and many-sided text, we ought according to linguistic method to begin first with a syntactic/stylistic analysis, to be followed by a semantic and, finally, a pragmatic analysis.[9] Here it will be enough for us to offer a structural analysis to justify our division of the text (cf. the arrangement in our translation).

Conspicuous are certain formal similarities, frequently recurring, such as καθώς (v. 4) or κατά (vv. 5b, 7c, 9b 11bc). The conjunction καθώς introducing a subordinate clause performs the same function as the preposition κατά with a noun in the accusative case. This is frequently

[1] Cf. Dahl* 250 f.; the expression was taken over by Deichgräber* 64.
[2] First Innitzer*; then Lohmeyer*, Ochel*, Masson 148–52, Coutts* 120–4; Käsemann, RGG ²II, 519; Schille* 65–9; Schattenmann*, Kehl*; most recently Fischer, *Tendenz* 111–18; cf. also Barth 97 f.
[3] See especially Sanders* 223–7; Krämer* 34–7; Deichgräber* 67–72; Caragounis* 41–5.
[4] Schlier 41; cf. Schnackenburg* 68.
[5] Schlier 39.
[6] Maurer* 154; Kehl* 70 ff.; Gnilka 59.
[7] Innitzer*; cf. Cambier* 100 f. and 103.
[8] Krämer* 38–41.
[9] Cf. Schnackenburg* 72–87. See there also on the semantic and pragmatic dimension.

followed by an expression of purpose: in v. 4 an infinitive final clause, in vv. 6 and 10 εἰς with the accusative, in v. 12 εἰς with the infinitive. At the end of the section (v. 14) there are two final clauses in succession with εἰς and the accusative but without a previous κατα-phrase. This dynamic pattern of speech can scarcely be accidental. The expressions with καθώς and κατά announce a reflection and clarification of the foregoing statements. Our blessing by God is more closely defined in the καθώς-clause as 'election'. The κατά-phrases usually refer to God's sovereign will (vv. 5b, 9b, 11bc), once to the richness of his grace (7c). While these elements in the sentence have a retrospective orientation, the naming of the intended purpose directs the view forward. Election occurs with the aim that 'we should be holy and blameless before him' (v. 4). The revelation of the mystery leads to the realisation in the fullness of time (v. 10a) of what God had already decided. The sealing with the Holy Spirit, 'the first instalment of our inheritance' results in 'redemption, the acquisition', that is, in the final acquisition of salvation (v. 14b). Three times there is an expression for the intended praise of the glory of God (vv. 6a, 12a, 14c). We cannot indeed derive from this any clear-cut division of the text, but we can identify a definite movement of thought. The similar (not fully identical) figures of speech allow us to recognise certain breaks, pauses as it were, in the flow of rhetoric, from which the author at once takes off again to elucidate, recapitulate and unfold fresh ideas until the next pause is reached.

I. The eulogy proper, 'Blessed is God, the Father of our Lord Jesus Christ', stands as the central theme and at the same time as the title of the entire meditation, which seeks to expound this same eulogy, to substantiate it and to bring it into the purview of the readers. Then follows the participle, semantically connected with εὐλογεῖν (with a shift to the active sense) extolling God's blessing of us in Christ. Now comes the καθώς clause which traces this blessing back to our election by God in Christ before the foundation of the world. This eternal election, however, took place in order that we should be holy and blameless before him. With this the flow of rhetoric has reached its first pause. Many exegetes would incorporate here the term ἐν ἀγάπη (v. 5);[10] but the rhythm of the sentence and other grounds (v. infra) make it seem advisable to place the break before it.

II. The author now begins anew. He takes up the theme of God's election and defines it more precisely as a vocation to sonship. To do this he again employs a participle, this time without the article, so that this participle appears to be subordinate to the first (ὁ εὐλογήσας). There follows a reference (with κατά) to God's sovereign will and (with εἰς) to the purpose: 'to the praise of his glorious grace'. The latter is made even more emphatic by means of a relative clause which stresses God's gracious giving 'in the Beloved'. The reference to Jesus Christ is especially appropriate since our sonship is mediated through him – only here is the formula διὰ Ἰησοῦ Χριστοῦ used. He is named 'the Beloved' because in him God poured out all his love and through him included us in that love;

---

[10]Calvin, Grotius, Westcott, Robinson, Huby, Dibelius – Greeven, Gaugler, Krämer* 40; Conzelmann, Ernst et al.

hence ἐν ἀγάπῃ must belong with προορίσας, i.e. to God. The whole unit thus presented to us is contained as if in brackets by 'in love' at the beginning and 'in the Beloved' at the end.

III. Jesus Christ has thus become the focus of attention, and a description of our debt to him follows. In a closely connected relative clause we are told that in him we have redemption by his blood, and an apposition interprets this as the forgiveness of sins. Here again comes a κατά-expression; according to the riches of his grace. On this occasion there is no development with an immediately following εἰς; instead, this grace is described in a relative clause as that which he richly lavished upon us (εἰς ἡμᾶς) in all wisdom and insight (v. 8). As in II, it would be possible here to link this last expression to the following participle γνωρίσας.[11] But as it stands it gives a good rhythmic flow and allows this unit of text to end similarly to the previous one; the relative clause in both concludes with a prepositional phrase with ἐν, which also foreshadows the theme of the following unit.

IV. God's abundant grace, granted to us 'in all wisdom and insight', has revealed itself, as the author explains in what follows, in that God has made known to us the mystery of his will. He connects these thoughts with a participle; thus γνωρίσας (v. 9) in a way continues προ-ορίσας (v. 5), though not directly, as the textual unit III comes between. The thematic development runs from predestination to sonship (II) through salvation in the blood of Christ (III) to the revelation of the mystery in vv. 9–10 (IV). Again there follows a phrase with κατά, which makes renewed reference to God's sovereign purpose which he had previously determined in Christ (v. 9b). This is a resumption of earlier statements (cf. vv. 4a, 5). Corresponding to 'previously' is 'as a plan for the fullness of time' (v. 10a); this expression, important for the revelation of the mystery, is once more clothed in the linguistic form εἰς . . . . This time, however, there follows yet another definition of the content, namely wherein the mystery consists. This is presented in the infinitive clause 'to unite all things in Christ', and 'all things' is then explained in the appositional 'things in heaven and things on earth' (v. 10bc). With this we reach an unmistakeable climax, a greatly heightened statement of God's saving activity 'in Christ'. Should ἐν αὐτῷ in v. 11a be taken in here so that 'in Christ' appears deliberately duplicated at the end of each of the two lines?[12] This is not impossible in view of the author's style, but it is improbable here. The progression of thought up to this point comes to a certain conclusion with its cosmic horizon, while the following section adds an application for the readers. The transition from v. 10 to v. 11 shows a clear shift and the author stresses the fresh beginning with ἐν αὐτῷ. Many exegetes feel that the words 'things in heaven and things on earth' provide such an effective conclusion that they want to end the original eulogy at this point and understand what comes after as a prosaic addition.[13] However, this too is not justified: the aim of the

[11]Dahl* 259, n. 23; Kehl* 70–2; Gnilka 77.
[12]Dahl* 257; Dibelius – Greeven 61; Krämer* 40 (emphatically).
[13]Cf. Schlier 40. Others extend the 'hymn' to v. 12: Schille, 'Liturgisches Gut' 68; Deichgräber* 65. Barth 98 considers vv. 11–3 as a prose insertion.

eulogy is not the cosmic glorification of God or of Christ but the fulfilling of salvation for Christians on the basis of God's global plan of salvation.

V. The next textual unit corresponds in a certain sense to vv. 7–8 (III), which likewise lay stress on Christ, the mediator of salvation (ἐν ᾧ. Yet after the cosmic consideration of v. 10 the author recalls attention with far greater emphasis to the level of the recipients of salvation: 'in him, in whom we also have been destined and appointed' (v. 11a). There again follows a retrospective reference to our predestination (cf. v. 5) by means of a participial extension with the typical κατά-expression, which on this occasion is actually doubled. The second κατά can hardly be dependent on ἐνεργοῦντος, but represents a thoroughly comprehensive parallel affirmation: 'according to the purpose of him who accomplishes all things, according to the counsel of his will' (βουλή and θελήμα are synonymous). Thereafter the statement of intended purpose with εἰς appears yet again: 'that we may live for the praise of his glory'. This would be a suitable conclusion; but the author adds (by means of a participle) 'we who have hope in anticipation in Christ'. Only with difficulty can τοὺς προηλπικότας be linked as predicative to εἶναι;[14] it is a participle associated with ἡμᾶς and gives a more detailed reason why we are destined for the praise of his glory. The 'tacked-on' addition can be explained from the hope of the future full redemption if it is appropriately interpreted (cf. Exegesis).[15] With the words 'in Christ' we are once more referred back to the beginning of the section.

VI. The last two verses are an application for the readers, whose way to the achievement of salvation is briefly outlined: there are two steps, indicated by the two participles ἀκούσαντες and πιστεύσαντες. But these lead us to the main statement, 'you were sealed with the promised Holy Spirit', by which is meant the gracious saving event vouchsafed to them, namely baptism. The Holy Spirit is described in a relative clause as the 'first instalment of our inheritance', and thereby we return significantly to the 'we' of common Christian usage. It is quite possible that the author originally intended to continue after ἐκληρώθημεν κτλ in v. 11 with ἐν ᾧ καὶ ἐσφραγίσθημεν, but in consideration for his readers inserted v. 13ab and so changed the form of the verb to ἐσφραγίσθητε. For the thought of the κληρονομία makes a good continuation of ἐκληρώθημεν: we share in salvation and through the Spirit aspire to be full heirs. The expectation which is already directed towards the consummation is strengthened by the expression of what it should achieve 'until the redemption, the acquisition (of our inheritance)', and then there is attached a further phrase using εἰς – the formula 'to the praise of his glory' which has already been frequently used. This is the fitting crown and conclusion of the entire eulogy.

---

[14] Cf. Exegesis on the passage (pp. 63 f).

[15] In contrast, some take it as reflexive (we = Jewish Christians), among them Chrysostom, Ambrosiaster, Abbott, Beare, Meinertz, Schlier, Scott, Barth, R. Bultmann, TDNT II, 535 ('less likely' that it refers to all Christians); Lyonnet* 339; cf. also Mitton, *Epistle* 227 f.

Exegesis

3

God is praised by the Christian community following the old Jewish tradition of honouring God in short eulogies introduced by ברִיך (LXX usually εὐλογητός).[16] In Israel this is the response to God's beneficent action, often experienced as miraculous, which is accordingly forthwith specified (in a causal clause or by a participle) as the warrant ('explanatory eulogy').[17] The missing copula should be understood as indicative ('is praised'). The later, more frequent eulogy in the second person is supplied in the LXX with εἶ ('you are') , and in the NT comparison with other passages (Rom. 1.25; 2 Cor. 11.31; 1 Pet. 4.11) leads to the same conclusion.[18] Through his mighty act of blessing God has devoted himself to mankind and is consequently 'blessed' by those who have received his blessing in the way open to them, i.e. he is praised. It is a 'confession of solidarity' with the God of grace (J. Scharbert), a response to all they owe him (cf. Eph. 5.20) just as in the hymns of praise in Revelation God and the Lamb are assigned the honour due to them (cf. 4.11; 5.12, 13; 7.12; 15.3 f.). It is questionable whether the formula originally had its place in cultic worship, but it was wholly taken over into it.[19] A Christian overtone can be heard in 'God and Father of our Lord Jesus Christ'. While there is no polemic against the God of Israel (cf. 2.12 f.) the Christian community is aware that it has gained access to the Father (2.18) solely through Jesus Christ, God's beloved son (1.5 f.; 4.13) and through him possesses for all time an assured communion with God (3.12).

God is praised because (causal participle) he has blessed us with every spiritual blessing. With inimitable compactness (three terms from the same stem) God's beneficent act is emphatically described as 'spiritual', transcending every earthly blessing. It is also 'spiritual' in that it is mediated by the Holy Spirit (cf. 1.13) and experienced in him (cf. too the 'spiritual' hymns in 5.19). The expression thus points forward at this early point to the last clause of the eulogy. In this way an arch is spanned from the opening to the ending, and beneath it everything which is mentioned is understood as blessing and included in the praise. It is not necessary to take the aorist as referring especially to the divine act of salvation in baptism;[20] God's predestination (v. 5) and revelation of the mystery (v. 9)

---

[16]Cf. H. W. Beyer, TDNT II, 759 f.; Deichgräber* 40–3; J. Scharbert, TDOT 2, 284–6; 300 f. (Qumran); G. Wehmeier, THAT I, 374 f.

[17]Cf. C. Westermann, *Das Loben Gottes in den Psalmen*, Göttingen ³1963, 61–7 (the people); 76–84 (the individual).

[18]Cf. Bl – Debr §128, 5 with n. 8; W. S. Towner, '"Blessed be YHWH" and "Blessed art Thou, YHWH": The Modulation of a Biblical Formula', CBQ 30 (1968) 386–99, shows the shift in OT and Judaism.

[19]For a non-cultic origin, see J. P. Audet, 'Esquisse historique du genre littéraire de la "bénédiction" juive et de l' "eucharistie" chrétienne', RB 65 (1958) 371–99, here 376–8; Towner 388 f.; Deichgräber* 40; G. Wehmeier, THAT I, 374; more for a cultic *Sitz im Leben* H. W. Beyer, TDNT II, 757 f.; J. Scharbert, TDOT 2, 285 f. – Cf. also Kirby, *Ephesians* 84–9.

[20]Cf. Gnilka 61; Cambier* 63 f. is closer to the truth: Christ's death and glorification are included in the same way as the beginning of the Christian life.

and his gracious work in Jesus Christ's act of salvation (v. 6) which affects us (v. 8) are all reported in aorist forms. In the planning, execution and realisation of his design there is evident a continous line which is recognisable as blessing – blessing for us.

With such a blessing God has blessed us 'in the heavenlies'. The expression ἐν τοῖς ἐπουρανίοις is exclusive to Eph. where it appears five times (1.3, 20; 2.6; 3.10; 6.12), and has a local sense, whether completed with τόποις or read as neuter (τὰ ἐπουράνια).[21] Difficulties of interpretation arise especially in that the expression is used both for the sphere of God or Christ (1.3, 20; 2.6) and for the location of the ungodly 'principalities and powers' (3.10; 6.12) in a manner foreign to our way of thinking. Behind it lies a distinctive conception of the world which knows several 'heavens' (cf. 4.10) and attaches a deeper (metaphysical or transcendental) meaning to them.[22] Since Christ has ascended above all the heavens (4.10) and sits at God's right hand in the heavenly places 'above all authority and power' (1.20), the 'principalities and powers' can only be located in the 'lower heavens', in the realm of the air (cf. 2.2), in the darkness of our world (6.12). But the expression does not serve any 'heavenly topography' – a third or seventh heaven is not mentioned, and certainly no Ogdoas.[23] In the present context it is, rather, a spiritual sense which is conveyed by the local imagery: the area and effectiveness of God's activity or of that of the ungodly 'powers'. In 1.3 the expression, which already has the ring of a formula, does not confine itself to indicating the place of God's blessing or the treasury of his blessings, but refers to the whole course of events – that God has blessed us with every spiritual blessing 'in Christ'. The following statement which explains this divine blessing (cf. our analysis) – that God 'chose us in him before the foundation of the world' – confims this. We were blessed with the fullness of the divine blessing 'in the heavenlies' already in God's act of election before all time 'in Christ'. All that God resolved and performed for our salvation took place 'in Christ' and every blessing which comes upon us is bestowed 'in Christ'.

The extension of Christ's sphere back before the creation hangs together with the idea of his pre-existence which the author has taken from Col. (cf. the hymn of 1.15–20) and integrated with his own view. Unlike Col., however, he is not directly and pressingly interested in this christology in itself, but makes use of it for his ecclesiological concerns. The faithful, the members of Christ's body, the Church, are included in

---

[21]Cf. H. Traub, ThWNT V, 539 f.; Dibelius – Greeven 58; Schlier 45–8; Lincoln, *Re-examination*, esp. 476; Caragounis, *Mysterion* 146–52 (excursus).

[22]According to Lincoln, *Re-examination* 479, the expression has a cosmic, transcendental reference as in the OT, but now this has a wider content. On Ephs.'s conception of the world, cf. further Mußner, *Christus* 9–28; Gnilka 63–6.

[23]On the three or seven heavens in Judaism cf. H. Bietenhard, *Die himmlische Welt im Urchristentum und Spätjudentum*, Tübingen 1951, esp. 8–18; H. Traub. TDNT V, 511 f. The Ogdoas (the Eighth) plays a part in Gnostic systems (cf. CHerm I.26; XIII, 15; the Eugnostos Letter 85, 87 [Foerster, *Gnosis* II, 43 f.]; The Being of the Archons 95, 34 [ibid. 60]; Valentinian et al.) and is related to the gnostic Pleroma; but Eph. knows nothing of such speculation.

God's all-embracing plan for and accomplishment of salvation by means of that cosmic christology including Christ's pre-existence.[24]

They are chosen from eternity 'in Christ' and blessed with every spiritual blessing. Seen thus, the constantly repeated formula ἐν Χριστῷ (ἐν αὐτῷ, ἐν ᾧ) has an indispensable function in this eulogy which surveys the whole of God's redemptive action. It is neither merely a well-worn formula nor used simply in an instrumental sense.[25] But a strictly 'local' interpretation can easily lead to misconceptions: no real-personal pre-existence is ascribed to the faithful nor yet any heavenly rapture in the course of their earthly existence, but simply a heavenly existence 'in Christ Jesus' (cf. 2.6)[26] which does not cancel their life on earth with all its worldly implications and obligations. From this we can see that to interpret the phrase 'in the heavenlies'[27] existentially is correct but also has its limitations; for it is concerned, to be sure, with the understanding of the Christian existence suspended 'between heaven and earth', but not at all with that human condition in which man is challenged by transcendence, 'that overwhelming depth of human existence', and called to make his decision. Throughout the author of Eph. has in sight the existence opened up and bestowed upon us by God 'in Christ Jesus', the life of the 'new man' created by God 'in Christ Jesus' and called to righteousness and holiness (cf. 2.19; 4.24).

4

Our election by God 'before the foundation of the world'[28] which is then explained in v. 5 as preordination (προορίσας) would still remain within the framework of Jewish ideas of predestination[29] were it not for the reference to Christ[30] in ἐν αὐτῷ. The concept is taken up again in v. 11 by means of

---

[24]Thus Barth 79.

[25]Bultmann (*Theologie* 528) considers the formula in Eph. to be a set phrase only with difficulty determinable from its liturgical use. Allan, NTS 5, 59 and Gnilka 66–9 interpret it in an instrumental sense. Ernst 270 on the other hand denies that this formula has a special theological significance and attributes to it merely the function of a 'sign' (283). Caragounis, *Mysterion* 152–7 (excursus) speaks of a 'sphere' in which the divine decisions are made and put into effect.

[26]The author connects to this view a paraclesis which deals with this world (Chs. 4–6) – i.e. he understands 'existence in Christ Jesus' basically in the same way as Paul in Gal. 3.28 though in different categories (vertical – spatial) and with a stronger visualising of salvation which is also connected with his understanding of Baptism, cf. the 'raised with him' in Col. 2.12; Eph. 2.6 with Rom. 6.5, 8. See further under 2.6.

[27]Schlier 47 f.

[28]A phrase already existing in this form which also appears in other NT writings, v. Mt. 13.35; 25.34; Lk. 11.50; Jn. 17.24; Heb. 4.3; 9.26; 1 Pet. 1.20; Rev. 13.8; 17.8. It is also to be found in connection with predestination in Rabbinism, cf. Bill. I, 982; F. Hauck, TDNT III, 621, n. 3. On early Judaism v. O. Hofius, '"Erwählt vor Grundlegung der Welt" (Eph. 1.4)', ZNW 62 (1971) 123–8.

[29]Cf. J. Wochenmark, *Die Schicksalsidee im Judentum*, Stuttgart 1933; G. Maier, *Mensch und freier Wille. Nach den jüdischen Religionsparteien zwischen Ben-Sira und Paulus*, Tübingen 1971. On the idea of predestination in Qumran which is emphasized in a similar way as in Eph., cf. F. Nötscher, 'Schicksalsglaube in Qumran und Umwelt', BZ NF 3 (1959) 205–34; 4 (1960) 98–121; J. Becker, *Heil Gottes* 85–96; H.–W. Kuhn, *Enderwartung* 120–30; H. Braun, *Qumran und das NT* II, Tübingen 1966, 243–50.

[30]The reading in G ἑαυτῷ testifies to a connection with God; but the formula without exception refers to Christ as is generally recognised today. The comparable passage in Gn. r

the participle – 'destined ... according to the purpose of him who accomplishes all things' – and here too it is included in the sphere of Christ by the introductory relative pronoun ἐν ᾧ. The semantic field 'election', 'pre-recognition', 'predestination', (divine) 'intention' (πρόθεσις) is also to be found in Paul (cf. especially Rom. 8.28c–9; 9.11; 1 Cor. 2.7) but never connected with the thought that we are chosen and predestined 'in Christ'. In this statement, peculiar to Eph., what is under discussion is not simply our predestination in God's thought but rather our election in the pre-existent Christ; for we can assume that the 'pre-existence' christology of Col. (cf. 1.15; 'in him all things were created') was known to our author.[31] But how then are we to understand our election effected 'in Christ'? On no account in such a way that our souls are conceived as pre-existent – a Platonic conception which made its way into Rabbinic Judaism[32] but which was not taken over by the early Christians. The idea also that we were really and physically (thinking in a mythological way) 'present' in the pre-existent Christ is not the author's mind.[33] For this meaning we must go to gnostic texts which posit a pre-existence of the 'pneumatics' (through their 'seed') in the pleroma[34] – a view which cannot be detected in Eph. The characteristic concerns of Eph. can only be understood from its own view of a Christian existence grounded totally and completely 'in Christ'. 'If we are in him, then we were always so' (Schlier). If God made his plan of salvation in (the pre-existent) Christ, he also included us 'in Christ' in his plan. Christ and those saved in him cannot be separated from one another. As a result of our real calling, our 'participation' in Christ (cf. v. 11) we are also assured of our eternal election 'in Christ' before the creation of the world. This certainty of election, however, does not give Christians any reason for elitist arrogance. Reflections on the 'rejected' are totally lacking in Ephesians. The beneficence of our election is an impetus to the praise of God and to moral endeavour; out of our calling grows the obligation to live godly, Christ-like lives in this world (4.1, the basic theme of the exhortation).

Also present in 1.4 is the thought that because of our election in Christ from all eternity we have a duty in our time 'to be holy and blameless before him (God)'. This mode of expression depends on Col. 1.22 where the same rare κατενώπιον (elsewhere only found in Jude 24) is used and a further synonymous predicate added. But while in Col. the goal of Christ's atoning act is to present the Christians holy, blameless and irreproachable before God, in Eph. 1.4 it is God himself who had this intention (final

44 (27a), where Israel's election 'in Abraham' is discussed, (Bill. III 579; Gaugler 30) is materially different because in Eph. the author is thinking of the pre-existent Christ.

[31] The formula in 1.10 – 'things in heaven and things on earth' – is evidence of this. It can be connected with the style of expression in Col. 1.16–20.

[32] Cf. Bill. II, 340 ff.

[33] Cf. Schlier 49 f. with n. 4.

[34] Cf. e.g. for the Valentinians Iren Haer I, 1.12 (Harvey I, 58): 'For it is not deeds which lead to the Pleroma, but the seed which is sent out unripe and brought to maturity here'; or Ev Veritatis (NHC I.2): 'He (Jesus) brought many back from the πλάνη and went before them to those places whence they had come. . . . It was a great wonder that they were in the Father and knew him not and that they could come out of themselves. . . .' (From the translation by H.–M. Schenke. *Die Herkunft des sogenannten Evangeliums Veritatis,* Göttingen 1959, 39). The idea of an origin in the Pleroma runs through Gnosis in many ways, cf. also the 'Exegesis on the Soul' (NHC II, 6); and on this Fischer, *Tendenz* 186–9.

infinative) in the very act of election. This corresponds to the author's theocentric outlook, and we must also notice that the elect are qualified for this by God through all he has done for them in Christ (cf. 2.10). There is also in this expression, however, an unmistakeable moral call to Christians to behave according to the divine intention (cf. 4.24 with the related double expression 'in righteousness and holiness'). For the two words 'holy' and 'blameless', originally indigenous to the language of the cult and sacrifice, are already in the OT made to bear on the moral behaviour of mankind 'before God'.[35] In Eph. the application of this idea to the Church is significant; Christ willed to make it without spot or wrinkle so that it might be 'holy and blameless' (5.27). The elect are gathered together in the Church; but this idea remains in the background in the eulogy.

5–6

If the perspective is thus opened up to the present and future, the author now returns anew (cf. the analysis) to his starting-point of the divine election before all time. It is not God's claim and demand which stand at the outset, but his freely-given love. In so far as he deliberately stresses this (ἐν ἀγάπῃ is to be taken with what comes after; cf. the Analysis) he clearly shows God's election as a preordination freely given in love (modal). This manner of describing our predestination, which is also encountered in the main Pauline epistles (Rom. 8.29 f.; 1 Cor. 2.7) always refers to God's positive, salvific act. This of itself prohibits the conclusion that there is also a divine decree concerning the non-elect of humanity by which they have been predestined, without any guilt of their own, to destruction and damnation (Determinism). Such a speculation has no place in this eulogy of thanks and praise.[36] God's loving predestination has as its goal our sonship (υἱοθεσία) which lies in the horizon of our election 'in Christ'. For Christ is 'the Beloved' (cf. n. 114), the son of God (cf. 4.13) through whom we are adopted as sons of God. Paul develops this idea more clearly in Gal. 4.4b. In this passage the originally juridical concept of adoptive sonship (υἱοθεσία)[37] is more clearly illuminated; we shall become sons of God in reality through the Spirit of the Son who is present in us. For Eph., too, sonship is a blessing mediated in the Holy Spirit (cf. 1.3, 12); through the love experienced in Christ we have become beloved children of God (5.1 f.). In this way the author takes up a topos which was current in the early Christian catechesis influenced by Paul, but also elsewhere (cf. 1 John 3.1). This best explains the formula 'through (διά) Jesus Christ' which in Eph. appears only here. The mediating function of Jesus Christ is fundamental; through the Son we become sons of God. The order 'Jesus Christ', which elsewhere comes only after ὁ κύριος (1.2, 3, 17; 5.20; 6.23, 24) will then also have its ground therein.[38]

[35] On ἄμωμος v. F. Hauck, TDNT IV, 830f.; there is also further material on this point in the Qumran texts: 1QS. 1.8; 2.2; 3.9 f.; 4.22; 8.22 (along with 'holy') etc., cf. K. G. Kuhn, *Konkordanz* 234.

[36] Cf. Barth 105 ff. (6 reasons against). Cf. also the history of influence, pp. 312 f.).

[37] Cf. W. v. Martitz/E. Schweizer, TDNT VIII, 397–9; commentary on Gal. 4.5; Rom. 8.15; A. Drago, 'La nostra adozione a figli di Dio in Ef. 1.5', RivBib 19 (1971) 203–19.

[38] The author prefers 'Christ Jesus' in his own formulations, cf. p. 40 n. 1.

To whom εἰς αὐτόν refers is a matter of controversy:[39] is God or Christ intended? Although in 10b Christ appears as the culmination of the divine activity of salvation, in v. 5 the reference to God is to be preferred for the following reasons: (a) The entire eulogy has an unmistakeable theocentric character. God is praised because every blessing proceeds from him, because everything happens according to his will and purpose and is directed to his glorification. (b) This theocentric view is prominent in the immediate context, namely in the κατά-phrase in 5b: 'according to the pleasure of his will'. (c) εἰς αὐτόν stands in a quite close connexion with εἰς ἔπαινον κτλ in 6a. It appears that this 'to the praise of his glorious grace' takes up and clarifies the preceding 'towards him'. (d) In v. 6 Christ's distinctive function is emphasized: God has bestowed his grace on us 'in the Beloved' – so that the latter can scarcely be seen as the goal of our elevation as sons.

This passage, rich in synonyms for God's sovereign decision, calls to mind a similar use of such expressions in the Qumran writings.[40] εὐδοκία stands in close connexion with election (cf. 1QS 8.6: 'the elect of his purpose'; 1QH 4.32 f.; 11.9: 'sons of his purpose') so that the thought of v. 4 is taken up again. Corresponding to God's freely-determined action is the expression of its intended goal: 'to the praise of his glory', which appears again in almost identical form in vv. 12 and 14. If the doxological character of the eulogy is thereby evident, the addition of 'of his grace' characterizes God's action as graciously merciful. God's freedom in all that he does is shown over against men in the sovereignty with which he forgives sin and guilt (cf. 2.4 f., 7 f.). God has already mercifully decided to redeem us through the blood of Jesus Christ in his eternal election and predestination (χαρις is used differently in Eph. 3.2, 7, 8; 4.7, q.v.). The understanding of 'grace' as God's generous forgiving action again comes close to the Qumran texts (cf. especially 1QS 11.12–4; 1QH 16.12 f.). Yet the idea of grace in Qumran never breaks out of the framework of the Law – is, by contrast , bound up with the intensification of the Torah:[41] God displays grace and faithfulness, forgives sin and has pity on those who keep his commandments and return to him (cf. 1QH 16.13, 16 f.). According to Eph., however, God has 'graced us with his grace' (a similar Greek figure of speech as in 1.3) namely 'in the Beloved'[42] in whom we have salvation

[39] Among those who take the pronoun as referring to God are Haupt 11, Cambier* 75 f., Krämer* 42, Gaugler 34, Conzelmann 91; those who think it means Christ, v. Soden 107, Schlier 54 (hesitantly), Gnilka 73 (decidedly), Ernst 272. Dibelius – Greeven and Barth pass over the expression. – Schlier interprets it from Rom. 8.29 (to be conformed to the 'image' of his son), Gnilka from Col. 1.16; but here Eph. has his own perspective (the praise of God).

[40] Cf. K. G. Kuhn NTS 7, 335 f. For Eph. 1.5 and 1.11 he points to The Damascus Rule 3.15 'the expressions of his will'.

[41] Cf. H. Braun, *Spätjüdisch-häretischer und früh-christlicher Radikalismus* I, ²1969 (BHTh 24.1), 46 f.; S. Schulz, 'Zur Rechtfertigung aus Gnaden in Qumran und bei Paulus', ZThK 56 (1959) 155–85, especially 163–5; H. Conzelmann, TDNT IX, 387.

[42] Some Mss add υἱῷ αὐτοῦ D*FG 629 VL Vg^cl sy^h sa Marcion Ambrosiaster. But the absolute ὁ ἠγαπημένος has a ring of its own as a title; cf. Robinson 229–33; Caragounis, Mysterion 90. In the LXX we find it four times (Deut. 32.15; 33.5, 26; Is. 44.2) as the translation of the honorary title 'Jeshurun' for Israel. Individual patriarchs of Israel were also called 'God's beloved' (Abraham, Moses, Samuel, Solomon). The title transferred to Jesus Christ as God's Beloved *per se* is often to be found in Christian writings of the Second Century and perhaps had its place in the early liturgy, cf. Schlier's evidence 56 f. On various other interpretations which have been proposed cf. Gnilka, 74.

through his blood. It is God's love, anticipating us and embracing us in spite of our sin, which has revealed itself in the sending of his Son.

7–8

Now our historical redemption in Jesus Christ is described within the framework of the divine plan of salvation: the greatest stress is placed on this Mediator of salvation by the introductory ἐν ᾧ. But Jesus Christ has not only brought us redemption in a single historical event: he remains the continuing source of our redemption (present ἔχομεν), the present means of access and 'location' (ἐν ᾧ) of our reconciliation with God (cf. 2.16). The 'blood' of Christ (cf. 2.13) has become, like his 'Cross' (2.16) a graphic abbreviation, a 'symbol pregnant with the truth' (P. Seidensticker) of the redemption which took place in history but which remains effective and final, as Paul expressed it with 'once for all' (ἐφάπαξ Rom. 6.10) and the author of Heb. expounded theologically. The mention of Christ's blood in this sense is to be found widely throughout early Christian documents[43] and may be counted as a topos in the early Christian catechesis, particularly for the atoning, expiating, sanctifying death of Jesus on the Cross.[44] To this group of words belongs also ἀπολύτρωσις = redemption (cf. Rom. 3.24; 1 Cor. 1.30; Col. 1.14; Heb. 9.15) howsoever the history of its meaning may have developed[45]. It is possible that here the author of Eph. followed Col. 1.14 where (following on 'his beloved Son') almost the same wording is present. For 'sins' (ἁμαρτίαι) Eph. uses the synonymous expression 'trespasses' (παραπτώματα, cf. 2.1, 5) which is familiar to him from Paul (nine times in Rom.). We are concerned here with the relationship to God, destroyed by mankind's sin but restored through Christ's act of redemption.[46]

The expression 'according to the riches of his grace' is nothing other than a resumption and intensification of the thought in v. 6. Corresponding to the 'riches' is 'to lavish' (περισσεύειν) in the following relative clause (ἧς stands for ἥν by attraction). This verb, which Paul also frequently uses, indicates the plenteousness 'present and proclaimed in the age of Salvation as compared with the old aeon'.[47] The author of Eph., who is filled with his experience of salvation already bestowed and the ongoing revelation of the mystery of salvation (cf. 3.8–10), speaks readily of the 'riches' of grace (1.7; 2.7) and glory (1.18; 3.16). He prays that God may open in his readers the eyes of their hearts so that they may realise what are the riches of his glorious inheritance (1.18). Hence the modal phase 'in all wisdom and insight' at the end of 1.8 is connected with

---

[43]A pre-Pauline formula in Rom. 3.25; Paul Rom. 5.9; also Col. 1.20; Heb 9.14, 22; 10, 19; 1 Pet. 1.2, 19; 1 Jn. 1.7; 5.6, 8: Rev. 1.5; 5.9; 12.11; 19.13.

[44]Cf. P. Seidensticker, *Lebendiges Opfer (Röm. 12.1)*, 1954 (NTA XX, 1–3) 152–62; A. Vögtle, LThK I, 539 ff.; E. Lohse, *Märtyrer und Gottesknecht*, 1955 (FRLANT 64) 138–41; F. Laubach, TBLNT I, 133 f.

[45]There is no direct connection with λύτρον = ransom, cf. F. Büchsel, TDNT IV, 354 f.; rather the term should be classified in the wider connection of 'redemption', cf. D. M. Stanley, 'The Conception of Salvation in Primitive Christian Preaching', CBQ 18 (1956) 231–54; B. Reicke, BHH I, 430 ff.

[46]W. Michaelis, TDNT VI, 172 f.

[47]F. Hauck, TDNT VI, 59.

the insight bestowed upon the elect and not with God's wisdom. It is that 'spirit of wisdom and revelation' which the author pleads may be given to his readers in 1.17.

Only if we combine this phrase with the following would we be compelled to take it as referring to God's own wisdom and insight; but there is no cogent ground compelling us so to do (cf. Analysis). For God's wisdom and insight (φρόνησις) we could certainly refer to Jer. 10.12 (repeated in 51.15); but this idea of the creation of the world by God's wisdom lies outside the horizons of Eph. 1.9, and far more frequently in the LXX the numerous uses of the word refer to the wisdom which God bestows on mankind (especially in the Wisdom Literature). In the Qumran texts, it is true, we read that 'God in the secrets of his insight and in his glorious wisdom has appointed an end to the existence of iniquity (1QS 4.18) but also that he will 'instruct the upright in the knowledge of the highest' and 'make wise those perfected through the ages' (1QS 4.22) [48]

In Eph. 1.9 we are concerned not with the establishment but with the proclamation of the divine will, and for this 'wisdom and insight' are neccessary for people rather than for God (cf. also 3.4 f.). If God willed thereby to bestow of the riches of his grace (v. 8), this is certainly stated in view of the revelation of the secret of his will; in this respect the phrase constitutes a good transition to the next step in the development of thought.[49]

9

In his description of the divine blessing the author has already advanced from our eternal election (v. 4) and preordination to sonship (v. 5) to our historical redemption through the blood of Christ (v. 7). In the process he mentioned the salvific meaning of the Cross of Jesus, in harmony with the early Christian catechesis, as forgiveness of sins. Now he is concerned to reveal yet a further dimension of the accomplished Christ-event; its universal-cosmic significance. God's total plan, conceived in eternity, has as its final goal the subordination of the universe in Christ under his rule once again. This divine plan of salvation, in which our redemption is included, is now named 'the mystery of his will' and a new reason for praising God exists in that he has 'made known' this mytery to us (γνωρίσας). The author favours this verb (cf. 3.3, 5, 10; 6.19) which is an established one in the vocabulary of revelation. The proclamation of the mystery, the 'mystery of Christ' (3.3) or also the 'mystery of the gospel' (6.19) belongs to the core of his theology, and his personal theological contribution lies in the closer understanding of this mystery. How the proclamation is effected is not yet stated in the Eulogy (Aorist of Confirmation) but becomes ever clearer in the course of the letter: God had revealed it to his holy apostles and prophets by the Spirit (3.5) and granted Paul a special insight (3.3). This apostle preaches the inexhaustible riches of Christ to the heathen and hence brings into the open wherein the mystery of God, hidden before the ages, consists (3.9). The 'manifold wisdom of God' (3.10) is revealed in the

---

[48]Cf. Nötscher, *Terminologie* 52–63 (Synonyma für Wissen und Erkenntnis auf Gott und auf Menschen angewendet); id. *Gotteswege und Menschenwege*; G. Bertram, TDNT IX, 226 f.

[49]Cf. Schlier 59 f.; Ernst 274 f.; G. Bertram, TDNT IX, 233.

apostolic preaching and through the Church in which the preaching is effective.

The conception of the divine 'mystery' has a pre-history. Although at that time there was so much talk of mysteries – in the heathen mystery-cults and in Gnosticism, in Jewish apocalyptic and in the Qumran Community[50] there emerges in Eph. a special, unusual understanding which is based on a particular tradition and its interpretation. The more general background can be seen in apocalyptic which knows of mysteries hidden in God, revealed already in visions, heavenly journeys etc. to specially-blessed individuals, but only really to 'become visible', to emerge in their actuality at the end of time.[51] In closer proximity stand the ideas of Qumran, where the gift of knowledge and recognition is granted to the members of the Community so that they may understand God's mysteries relating to the End Time and his decisions which are already being put into effect.[52]

The author of Eph. never speaks of mysteries in the plural; what is more, he identifies the mystery he has in mind as the 'mystery of Christ' (3.4) and understands it as a reality which is currently revealing itself in a cosmic dimension (cf. 1.10; 3.9 f.). In holding this opinion he stands unmistakeably in the Pauline tradition (cf. 1 Cor. 2.7–10) and perhaps is more closely dependent on Col., where the mystery of God/Christ is spoken of in a similar manner (2.2; 4.3): It was 'hidden for ages and generations, but (is) now made manifest to his saints' (1.26). But over and above this he offers a personal interpretation of that mystery, supplies it with a new content, namely by making it refer to the Church (as the Body of Christ) and its particular character (composed of former Jews and Gentiles – cf. under 3.6).

Once again the author (as in v. 5) makes reference to God's sovereign will, his purpose (εὐδοκία) and intensifies the statement in such a way that it is a matter of a mystery of God's will, a plan drawn up in divine freedom. As in v. 5 God's decision is transposed into pre-history by the 'pre-ordination', so here the author adds that God had already set forth his purpose in him (Christ) (προέθετο). But here it is the starting-point for defining the implementation of the plan when the fullness of time has come (v. 10).

10

The word οἰκονομία, which is not always used in the same way (cf. under 3.2), has, in conjunction with God's long-since planned intention, the sense of implementation or fulfilment.[53] It is this 'fulfilment' appropriate to the

[50]Survey in G. Bornkamm, TDNT IV, 803–17; Caragounis, *Mysterion* 1–26.

[51]One old view is that of the Mysteries which are written on heavenly tables (Eth. Enoch 106.19) and revealed to the writers of apocalyptic (cf. ibid. 103.2). They have to do not only with the fate of the good and the evil but also with 'time and the end of the times' (2 Esdras 14.5; Syr Baruch 81.4). On the 'becoming visible' of future things which will then be 'seen' by all, v. Syr Baruch 51 f. 6 f. (8: 'For they see the world, which is now invisible to them and they will see the time which is now hidden from them') Cf. further G. Bornkamm, TDNT IV, 821–3; H.–W. Kuhn, *Enderwartung* 148–54; Caragounis, *Mysterion* 24–6.

[52]On Qumran cf. J. Coppens, 'Le "mystère" dans la théologie paulinienne et ses parallèles qumrâniens', in *Littérature et théologie pauliniennes*, 1960 (RechBib V), 142–65; O. Betz, *Offenbarung und Schriftforschung in der Qumransekte*, 1960 (WUNT 6), 82–8; Mußner, *Beiträge* 185–8.

[53]Cf. O. Michel, TDNT V, 152. Schlier 63 understands the three passages in Eph. (1.10;

plan for salvation intended, which is important for the author. But for this God's appointed times (καιροί), which have now reached their 'fullness', are also significant. The expression 'fullness of the times' brings to mind Gal 4.4, where Paul talks of the 'fullness of time' (τ. χρόνου) when God sent his Son; but Paul is contrasting the time before Christ (under the Law) with the time fulfilled with Christ (the time of freedom). The author of Eph. sees the times having passed according to God's purpose and having now reached their 'fullness'. The idea that 'the times are counted according to their number' (2 Esdras 4.37) and that 'the appropriate times' must 'be accomplished' (Syrian Baruch 40.3 cf. also 81.4) is derived from apocalyptic. More sharply focussed is the Qumran idea that 'all the times of God come in their proper order as he has appointed for them in the secrets of his wisdom' (1QpHab 7.13 f.). But Eph. has no interest in the succession and extension of the ages (or even their self-prolonging – cf. 1QpHab 7.7). In contrast to Qumran, where the 'fulfilment of time' is considered as not proclaimed (ibid 7.2) Eph. states clearly that God has proclaimed the mystery of his will when the times have reached their 'fullness'.[54] Here the use of the Genitive construction in the Greek is also significant: it is no incident within the course of time but the consummation of the earthly passage of time which as such will never again be repeated. On the other hand the attribute καιρῶν is a warning to qualify πλήρωμα, which in 1.23 has the concise meaning of the 'place of the fullness of God' – 'as it is brought about in the times'.[55] The 'fullness of the times' indicates the climax of all earthly times, the (eschatological) time of Christ, in which God's mystery in Christ is revealed, realised and developed.

But in what does the mystery of the divine will consist? This is impressively formulated in an explanatory infinitive clause: 'to unite all things in Christ, things in heaven and things on earth'. The spatial – cosmic picture, in which there is also an echo of the old Hebrew description of the universe in 'heaven and earth', thus combines with the eschatological perspective 'fullness of time' and shows the Christ-event, which now reveals itself, as the culmination of God's eternally-planned event of salvation. This *recapitulatio mundi* (the Vulgate translation *instaurare omnia in Christo* does not achieve the terse sense of the Greek) has had considerable influence in the history of theology (cf. esp. Irenaeus);[56] but how can we define it more exactly in accordance with the meaning of the words and the larger context of Eph?

The   verb   ἀνακεφαλαιοῦσθαι,   derived   from   κεφάλαιον =

3.2, 9) together as 'administration', 'care'; in the context of Eph. 1.9 f. we must emphasize the implementation and realisation of the plan of salvation.

[54]Lindemann, *Aufhebung der Zeit* 95, carries it too far with 'the end of all time'.

[55]Schlier 64. Ernst, *Pleroma* 70, tries to clarify this.

[56]Irenaeus connects his more developed theory of recapitulation to the Incarnation of the Logos and relates the re-establishment and renewal of the unvierse to the Fall of Adam. cf., Haer III, 19.1 (Harvey II 95); further V. 14.2 (Harvey II, 361 f.); 21.2 (Harvey II, 381–3). See also E. Scharl, *Recapitulatio mundi. Der Rekapitulatsionsbegriff des hl. Irenäus und seine Anwendung auf die Körperwelt*, Freiburg/Br. 1941; G. Wingren, *Man and the Incarnation. A Study in the Biblical Theology of Irenaeus*, Edinburgh-London 1959. Further in the history of the effect of the Epistle below.

completion (not from κεφαλή = head), has several nuances but chiefly means 'to summarise, sum up'.[57] In the context of the passage here it is not the temporal aspect (assumption and summation of earlier things) which is dominant but the spatial aspect, the relation and integration of (till now) separated spheres. 'Things in heaven and things on earth' will (again) be united into one whole. When we compare this with Col. 1.20 where 'things in heaven and things on earth' are likewise mentioned we see an association with the idea of reconciliation which Eph. takes up in another connection (in considering the two groups of humankind, Jews and Gentiles) (2.16). When the author speaks in 1.10 instead about the 'unification' in Christ of a universe till now strife-torn, he elevates the idea to a cosmic level; in the view of Eph. the supernatural, spiritual 'principalities and powers' which live and work 'in the heavenlies' (cf. 3.10; 6.12) are also part of the universe. But this is also the meaning in Col. 1.20 cf. 16: the Eph. author would have chosen that expression because it brings to mind κεφαλή. Christ is not only the unifying power for the universe but is also the reigning Head over the universe cf. 1.22 f.). Consequently in the context of Eph. we must understand 'in Christ the Head' along with this 'to unite the universe'. The unification of the universe takes place in its subordination under the Head.'[58]

The strange conception of the universe which underlies this has a long pre-history. Already for the Old Stoics the universe is a unity ruled over by God (as the Cosmic Soul), yes, (in a pantheistic understanding) God himself.[59] Then in the Orphic Fragments the idea arises that the universe is a divine body of which Zeus is the head and centre, gathering everything to himself then letting it go out from him again.[60] Eph. (and Col.) differ from this Greek view of the world in that they require a disruption of the cosmic order, a destruction of its unity so that a 'reconciliation' (Col.) or a 'unification' (Eph.), a restoration of the original order is necessary.[61] The gnostic myth of the collapse of the lower, material world, the Fall of Sophia or however that dualistic split is expressed, has been called upon to explain this pessimistic view of the world as it existed up till then, torn apart and subject to destructive powers. The old picture of the God of the Universe as Makro-Anthropos underwent a gnostic-dualistic transformation through its association with the myth of the fallen Sophia.[62] It is a matter of controversy whether and how far this myth had a direct influence on Col. and Eph.: neither in the Hymn in Col. 1 nor in Eph. 1 is there a description of the

---

[57]Cf. Moulton – Milligan 442; H. Schlier, TDNT III, 681.

[58]H. Schlier, TDNT III, 682; id., *Kommentar* 65; Steinmetz, *Heils-Zuversicht* 79 f.; Ernst, *Pleroma* 190–7 (where he talks of '*Aufhauptung*'). Lindemann on the other hand, in *Aufhebung der Zeit* 96–9 interprets the 'union' as the 'representation' of the universe in Christ (cf. Hanson, *Unity* 125 f.); but this is not strong enough when we consider the further passages on the relationship Christ-Universe-Church.

[59]See the evidence brought by H. Sasse, TDNT III, 876 f.

[60]Cf. the evidence in E. Schweizer, TDNT VII, 1037; cf. id. *Colossians* 58, n. 9.

[61]When Lindemann, *Aufhebung der Zeit* 97, inveighs against all the interpretations which presume a disruption of the original order and thinks that v. 10 has an 'exclusively cosmological meaning' (n. 53), he underestimates not only the connection of the Christian doctrine of salvation (v. 7) with this cosmological conception but also Gnostic cosmology which always presupposes the 'Fall' of the Aeons. In this respect Fischer, *Tendenz* 117 f., comes closer to the mark.

[62]Cf. Fischer, *Tendenz* 74 f.; he tries to prove a direct influence of the Sophia-myth on the author of Eph., for Eph. 5.22–3. See below, however, on this section.

drama of the cosmic disorder. Both writings are interested only in the redemption through Christ which has cosmic relevance. Already in Col. 1.18 the *Weltleib*, which is originally taken for granted in the hymn, is understood as referring to the Church as 'the Body of Christ'.[63] Only in Eph. is the expression 'body' reserved consistently for the Church; but this the author considers as the cosmically-extended Body of Christ through which Christ, its Head, actualizes his control of the universe and will continue so to do (cf. 1.22 f.). This relationship between Church and cosmos is the new factor which Eph. brings to light in contrast to Col. Christ's control of the cosmos is first mentioned in the Eulogy, but how it is to be realized is not yet apparent there.

One thing is clear from 1.10: the unification of the universe in Christ, the restoration of the divine rule of the universe has already taken place. If this were not so, talk of the 'fulfilment of the fullness of the times' would be meaningless. The universe will not be unified in Christ sometime-or-other – e.g. when we take possession of our inheritance (1.14) or on the 'day of redemption' (4.30): it should already be so through what took place in Christ. This is borne out in 1.20–2: the resurrected Christ is already enthroned 'above all authority and power ...', God *has already* put all things under his feet, *has already* given him to the Church as her Head. But is this present eschatology 'radically concluded, even pushed in the direction of an "aorist eschatology"'?[64] Other passages prohibit such a view: the Christian battle against the principalities and powers still continues (6.12); the Church as the sphere of blessing, the fullness of Christ (1.23), is an entity which is still increasing (2.21; 4.16). We must interpret it thus: the universe has been unified in Christ and put under his rule finally and incontestably, and yet it will continue to be subjugated ever to a greater degree, in the earthly-historical space, to Christ's rule which is already established. In this Christ serves the Church in which his beneficent rule grows and through which their own impotence will be revealed to the ill-fated principalities and powers (cf. 3.10). What is already reality in God's world, which is beyond time, will be revealed and realised through the Church in the earthly-historical world which is bound by time. The curious idea that the goal of the divine salvation-event has been reached 'in Christ' 'in the heavenlies' and that we, too, insofar as we are 'in Christ' have reached it (cf. 2.5 f.) brings us very close to the borders of an enthusiastic existentialism (cf. 1 Cor. 4.8; 2 Tim. 2.18), but this is rectified when we look at the Christian existence in the world which still has to defend itself in moral struggle and in battle against the powers of evil (Ch. 4–6). For Eph., too, fulfilment for Christians, the final redemption (1.14) is still to come.[65]

---

[63]Cf. Schweizer. *Colossians* 58 f.

[64]Thus Lindemann, *Aufhebung der Zeit* 99.

[65]It is a shift in category from the statements about time to those about space which, however, does not exclude a future fulfilment. Steinmetz, *Heils-Zuversicht*, tries to understand this change in the outlook in Col. and Eph. from the taking-up of protology (cf. 80 f.). But protology (which hardly emerges in Eph. 1) could not be the only ground for this unusual present-eschatological view. For Eph. the Church as a present reality connected with the heavenly Christ is also an influential factor.

11

God's plan of salvation which includes the whole universe is devised and executed 'in Christ' and thus shows to advantage his cosmic significance and position as Head of the universe. Nevertheless his whole activity is directed towards 'us', the people whom he has redeemed (v. 7) and this direction dominates throughout the Eulogy (note the constant use of 'us'). The extension to the cosmic dimension of the salvation-event took place because of our involvement in the cosmos and history: the redemption of the 'world' takes place for our sake and on our account (cf. Rom. 8.19–23). Hence the continuation of the Eulogy in vv. 11–4 is both meaningful and necessary.

The re-use of 'in Christ' effects the change to bring us under consideration. If we realise what the author has in mind, we would take ἐν αὐτῷ (in him) from the end of v. 10 and connect it with what follows (cf. Analysis). If we wish to consider it as a stylistic repetition of the phrase 'things in heaven and things on earth', parallel to 'all things in Christ',[66] then we increase the importance of the cosmic consideration. But the author firmly directs attention to the fact that we have also received 'what is allotted to us' within this universal event. This verb, which only occurs here in the NT, is well-chosen to emphasize the salvation allotted to us by God and already bestowed on us in Christ. We are chosen by God and designated for the purpose that we 'exist for his praise' (v. 12a).[67] The word is possibly suggested by Col. 1.12 where, in a call to give thanks to the Father the subject is 'that which is allotted to us', which we have attained among 'the saints in light'.[68] This might well be a topos from the Baptismal Catechesis which thereby describes conversion as a calling from darkness into light (cf. Acts 26.18; further Eph. 5.8; 1 Thess. 5.4 f.; 1 Pet. 2.9). The verb is, however, also connected in root and sense with the noun 'inheritance' (κληρονομία) which appears soon afterwards in v. 14. The concept of 'that which is allotted', derived from the division of the land among the tribes of Israel, has a close connection with the 'portion of the inheritance' which God has promised (cf. Heb. 11.8) and in the opinion of the NT writers, has laid up for us in heaven (cf. 1 Pet. 1.4; Heb. 9.15).[69] God has graciously bestowed on us (passive) our share and this is further underlined by the fact that we were already destined for this 'according to the purpose of him who accomplishes all things', 'according to the counsel of his will'. 'All things' (τὰ πάντα)[70] also includes the cosmic event

---

[66]Thus Dahl* 258; Dibelius – Greeven, Gnilka etc., Krämer*40 with emphasis.

[67]Cf. W. Foerster, TDNT III, 765. Barth 92 ff. considers three translations: (a) 'We had the good fortune to be chosen by God so that. . . .', (b) 'we were given a part' (c) 'we were dedicated to God'. He leans towards the last in the sense of the idea of God's People. But it is questionable whether we can refer to περιποίησις in v. 14 in this sense (v. under v. 14). An interpretation in the sense of Col. 1.12 is better. – The v.l. ἐκλήθημεν in A D G 635 VL^pt is a *lectio facilior* although it rightly emphasizes the effective calling in becoming Christian.

[68]Cf. Schweizer, *Colossians*, on this passage.

[69]Cf. W. Foerster, TDNT III, 759–61 on the relationship of the two concepts in the LXX.

[70]With Krämer* 44 against many commentaries and newer translations. Cf. the similar parataxis in 2.2 (κατά twice) 5.13 (εἰς three times) 4.18 (διά twice) 5.12 (πρός four times). On this style cf. also Percy, *Probleme* 186 f.

(indicated here but not the cosmos itself): the same power of God which led to the unification of the universe in Christ has grasped us, too, and given us an effective share in the salvation brought about in Christ. To take the second κατά-phrase as depending on 'accomplished' is awkward: rather it once again emphasizes in other words God's sovereign decision. The decision of his will was already taken in eternity and now is realized in us.

12

The fact that we have gratefully received acceptance by God and participation in salvation through Christ should make us the sort of people who exist to praise God. This stating of the purpose builds a parallel to v. 4 'that we should be holy and blameless before him'. Hence it does not mean merely liturgical worship but implies also a way of life appropriate to what God wills. In this sense the whole of Christian existence is oriented to the glorification of God.

If we take the participle τοὺς προηλπικότας as predicative with 'us', we have a different interpretation. The sense would then be: 'we *should* be the kind of people who "hope for the future" in Christ' – i.e. hope already for the completion of salvation now.[71] But this interpretation is hampered by considerable difficulties: (a) The article before the participle is certainly possible in a predicative connection, but then it has a governing function. We cannot simply translate 'that we should hope now in Christ to the praise of his glory' (Dibelius-Greeven et al.) but must translate precisely: 'that we ... should be those who have a future hope in Christ'.[72] The meaning which results from taking this as having a governing function is not reasonable. (b) The phrase is separated from its connecting word by 'to the praise of his glory', and furthermore 'to the praise of his glory' belongs much better at the end of the sentence. To interpret this phrase as a parenthesis (Gnilka) is simply a way out of a difficult situation. (c) It is conspicuous that the author immediately afterwards (the beginning of v. 13) turns to the readers with 'you, too', Hence it is reasonable to conclude that he added this phrase appositionally to give an anticipatory indication of the thought of v. 14 ('our inheritance'). There are other instances of the custom of addressing the recipients at the end of a Eulogy.[73] But if the author returns to the use of the first person plural in v. 14, v. 13 can be shown to be a deliberate insertion with regard to the readers.

The first compound προελπίζειν causes difficulty in that it is hard to decide whether here it has a strong temporal sense – 'to hope for before' or a general 'to hope in anticipation'. Since 'to hope' always has a future sense, the prefix in the second case would only have the effect of intensifying the meaning. This is perfectly possible in Koine Greek.[74] Hence two different interpretations can be made: The 'Jewish Christians', by whom are to be

---

[71]Haupt, v. Soden, Abbott, Dibelius – Greeven, Gnilka take it as a predicative connection. On the other hand Schlier, 67, rightly says '. . . not as predicate but because of the article in apposition to ἡμᾶς'.

[72]Bl – Debr §273.

[73]Cf. Dahl* 250–2. He points to the letter of King Huram which not only appears in 2 Chron. 2.10 f. but is transmitted in a somewhat altered form by Eupolemus (in Eus. Praep. Ev IX, 34) and in Josephus (Ant VIII, 53). On Eupolemus cf. B. Z. Wacholder, *Eupolemus* (Mon. of the Hebrew Union College III), Cincinnati 1974, 156–60 and 170 (correspondence with the rules for the Jewish berakhoth).

understood – under 'we' – the Christians coming from a Jewish background, who already hoped for Christ in the time before him; and 'Christians in general', a category which makes the phrase refer to the Christians addressed throughout the Eulogy, those who hope 'in Christ' for the final redemption (v. 14).

The interpretation which takes it as meaning 'Jewish Christians' has had considerable support since early times (v. p. 49 n. 15). Initially it seems a reasonable assumption in view of the distinction in v. 13 ('you also') but it runs up against serious reservations:(1) Up till now the 'we' in the Eulogy always meant all Christians chosen 'in Christ' and there is no indication of a different interpretation in v. 12. If the author now suddenly wished to confine this 'we' to Jewish Christians he would have had to indicate this (at the very least with a new ἡμᾶς). (2) To interpret 'the Christ' as 'the Messiah'[75] so that it would address the Jewish messianic hope cannot be justified from the other findings in Eph. (cf. p. 40 n. 1). (3) The construction ἐλπίζειν ἐν in the sense of 'hope for' is very rare (LXX Regn. IV 18.5; perhaps also 1 Cor. 15.19). 'In Christ' is rather to be understood in the same sense as in every other instance in the Eulogy (also with the article in v. 10). (4) In line with the linguistic usage elsewhere the perfect participle is rather to be taken to refer to Christians in their present state of hope (cf. 1 Cor. 15.19; 2 Cor. 1.10; 1 Tim. 4.10; 5.5; 6.17).

To interpret it as meaning all Christians – which in any case is more obvious apart from v. 13 – is also supported by Col. 1.5. There the subject is the hope 'laid up for you in heaven' and about which those addressed 'have heard before in the word of truth'. The author of Eph. seems to have this passage in mind since in v. 13 he uses the same expression 'word of truth'. Certainly the prefix προ applies in Col. to 'hear'; but the sense of the whole remains the same if one includes v. 6.[76]

Thus the interpretation which has had a greater following in more recent times, that we (= all Christians) are those who have hope in Christ, deserves preference. The transition from v. 12 to v. 13 emphasized by 'you also' is therefore not to be considered as making a distinction between Jewish and Gentile Christians but as a specification between Christians in general and those addressed in particular,[77] a recognition which is also important for other passages (especially 2.1–10 and 2.11–22).

13

In his endeavours to make the readers aware of their own experience of salvation, the author gives a brief description of their route into the Christian community: they have heard the word of truth, the gospel of their salvation, and have come to faith. The emphatic turning to the

---

[74]Cf. Bl – Debr §484.4; Rademacher 31 f. – R. Bultmann, TDNT II, 535 thinks that the standpoint of the present in view of the eschatological fulfilment would be 'less likely'. To the single piece of evidence he gives from a pre-Christian date for the word (Posidippus) there can be added others from the Christian era which, according to Liddell and Scott II 1477 give the meaning: generally, anticipate, expect.

[75]Thus Barth 94; cf. 130–3.

[76]Haupt, Ewald on the passage; Percy, *Probleme* 266 f. in n. 16; Dahl* 259 f.; Dibelius – Greeven, Gnilka, Conzelmann.

[77]Cf. also Jayne* 151 f. who interprets the 'we' as the growing Church with whom the addressees ('you') should unite.

[78]Some MSS mistakenly read ἡμεῖς ℵ' A K L Ψ 326 al. or ἡμῶν ΛΨ 323 630 945 al., possibly beause of ἡμᾶς in v. 12.

addressees is expressed in the two personal pronouns ὑμεῖς and ὑμῶν[78] and further by the resumption of ἐν ᾧ which disturbs the syntax between the two participles. It is a lively manner of speaking (cf. the duplication of ὅτι in 2.11 f.) which betrays the author's concern: they, too, the recipients of the letter, have achieved a part in Christ's act of salvation; they should remind themselves gratefully that it was bestowed on them 'in Christ', The author probably took over the two expressions 'word of truth' and 'gospel' from Col. 1.5. The 'gospel' he clarifies for his context as 'the gospel of your salvation' (cf. 2.8 'by grace you have been saved through faith'). While in Col. there may stand behind the expression 'word of truth of the gospel ...' a concern for the true faith in defence against heresy, the author of Eph. is concerned solely with the fruitful reception of the salvation-bringing gospel (cf. 3.6) and with the deeper understanding of the 'mystery of the gospel' (6.19). This is, incidentally, the language of evangelization: through the gospel, which is in truth not man's word but God's word, the Gentile Christians have received God's offer of salvation and now God's word is effective in them (1 Thess. 2.13; cf. 1.6, 8; 2 Cor. 6.7). Reception of the gospel results in faith which mediates salvation (Eph. 2.8; 3.12) and is a living power in their hearts (cf. 3.17; 6.16). In this respect the Pauline concern is retained (cf. Gal. 2.16; Rom. 1.16; 3.22 etc.), admittedly without the antithesis of justification by works of the Law (cf. under 2.9 f.). The main statement to which both participles lead to the 'sealing' with the Holy Spirit. It is the 'Spirit of the promise' i.e. the promised Holy Spirit: for the genitive is merely a (semitising) paraphrase (cf. Gal. 3.14; Acts 2.33). The author is concerned with the 'promise' because it belongs to the mystery of Christ which is now revealed that the heathen are made partakers of the promise in Christ (3.6; cf. 2.12).[79] If the reception of the Spirit, of which the whole early Church was convinced, is here described as 'sealing', this is language which already has content, a metaphor Paul used earlier in 2 Cor. 1.22. This passage has another similarity with Eph. 1.13 f. in that the Holy Spirit is at the conclusion called the 'guarantee' (ἀρραβών). The metaphor of a seal does not imply that the Holy Spirit has stamped us with a seal (in 2 Cor. 1.22 God has sealed us) but that he himself is this seal, a sign characterizing our Christian existence. The seal-motif was used in various ways in antiquity: the Christian use follows the OT and Judaism, be it in Ezek 9.4 ff. where the Tau on the forehead is a sign of election, belonging and protection (cf. Rev. 7.2–8), or in the significance of circumcision (acc. to Gen. 17.11 'sign of the covenant') as 'seal'[80] which Paul has taken over in Rom. 4.11. Hence Baptism, which according to Col. 2.11 is a 'circumcision of Christ' might also be considered as a Christian 'seal' analogous to Jewish circumcision: but this derivation is not certain. The noun 'seal' (σφραγίς) has no symbolic value for Baptism in the NT, although it does come to have

[79] Cf. G. Fitzer, TDNT VII, 939–43.

[80] On circumcision as a 'seal' cf. Bill. IV, 32 f. under f.; G. Fitzer, TDNT VII, 947 f. On the meaning of Ezek. 9.4 cf. E. Dinkler, 'Jesu Wort vom Kreuztragen', in *Ntl. Studien für R. Bultmann*, Berlin 1954, 110–29; O. Betz, TDNT VII, 662 f.; F. J. Dölger, JAC 2 (1959) 15–20.

later.[81] The author of Eph. has taken over the pictorial expression from the Pauline tradition or from the Baptism Catechesis. We might suspect that the expression concerning the sealing with the Holy Spirit which is here applied to the recipients originally read '*we* have been sealed'. The author has rendered it in the second person because he is addressing the recipients.

14

The continuation of the thought from the reception of the Spirit in Baptism to the attainment of the 'inheritance' is significant. There is an internal connection in the Holy Spirit between our present state of salvation and the total redemption which we shall achieve with our coming into our 'inheritance'. The Spirit is bestowed upon us as a 'guarantee' which allows us to expect God's full 'payment' of our inheritance, the riches of his glory (cf. 1.18). The Greek expression (ἀρραβών) which is a loan-word from the Semitic, is borrowed from the language of commerce in which it means 'security, guarantee, deposit'.[82] The translation as 'security' or 'pledge' is unsuitable because these raise the idea of a legal right on the part of the one who holds the pledge. This is completely the opposite of what the expression in connection with the Holy Spirit wants to imply: rather, the Spirit is bestowed on us in plentiful abundance out of God's uncompelled loving-kindness, but not yet in the fullness which this divine gift contains. God himself reveals in this present 'guarantee' his intention to bestow the full 'inheritance' on us. Paul states clearly that God has *given* us the Spirit as a guarantee (in our hearts) (2 Cor. 1.22; 5.5) just as in Rom. 8.23 he describes the Spirit (as primal offering (ἀπαρχή) of our future complete redemption.

The perspective of our heavenly inheritance opened up with the Spirit is derived from the Baptismal Catechesis, as emerges especially from 1 Pet. 1.3–5. It should also be the *Sitz im Leben* for Eph. 1.13 f.; but the author has inwardly adopted the idea as his own. In 1.18 he returns to it for his own purpose and in 2.7 also we can take no other view. The hope which God's calling raises continues to exist (4.4) and only comes to its fulfilment when we achieve our 'inheritance'. This, too, is an old motif, widely-used in the early Church[83] and already taken over by Paul in the formulation 'to inherit the Kingdom of God' (Gal. 5.21; 1 Cor. 6.9 f.; 15.50). Our author does not take it up unthinkingly but modifies it in characteristic fashion in 5.5: no immoral person *has* any inheritance in the Kingdom of Christ and of God. The emphasis remains for him on the present possession of salvation which, however, contains as it were a change in the future or, better, in heaven, where the consummation is already deposited.

The author's position of being filled with anticipation is finally

---

[81] 2 Clem. 7.6; 8.6; Herm s VIII, 6.3; IX, 16.3 ff.; 17.4. Cf. F. J. Dölger, *Sphragis*, Paderborn 1911; id. in further articles in AuC 1930–2; W. Heitmüller, 'Σφραγίς', in FS G. Heinrici 1914 (UNT 6), 40–9. Further R. Schnackenburg, *Taufe* 81 ff.; Schlier 70 f.; G. Fitzer, TDNT VII, 952.

[82] Cf. J. Behm, TDNT I, 475. Hence the Vulgate 'pignus' misses the mark. In the Vetus Latina we also find the loan-words *arra* and *arrabon* (ed. Frede 28).

[83] As well as 1 Pet. 1.4 cf. Mk. 10.17; Mt. 5.5; 19.29; 25.34; Gal. 3.29; 4.7; Rom. 8.17; Tit. 3.7; Heb. 1.14; 6.17; 9.15; Jas. 2.5. Cf. also W. Foerster, TDNT III, 781–5.

confirmed by the statement 'for the redemption of the possession'. The 'redemption' (ἀπολύτρωσις) has in his view already taken place through the blood of Christ (v. 7) and yet can be seen by the individuals redeemed as still to be expected. A future redemption is also meant in 4.30, where the 'day of redemption' points to the Parousia (cf. Lk. 21.28; Rom. 8.23), yet not in an emphatic sense; for the idea of the Parousia does not occur elsewhere in Eph. The *date* of the (complete) redemption does not concern him. But what does he mean by 'possession'? According to the morphology it is a *nomen actionis* (the 'possessing', but it can also mean what is possessed, the property. Since the expression is used in the LXX Mal. 3.17 to describe the OT people of God and in 1 Pet. 2.9 to describe the NT people of God as God's 'property' (cf. also Acts 20.28), many exegetes would like to understand it thus in Eph. 1.14 also.[84] But the idea of the people of God or even a reference to the primary passage in Ex. 19.6 is to be found nowhere else in Eph., and the abbreviation 'property' would scarcely be understandable to the readers. Since the word signifies the acquisition of salvation or glory in 1 Thess. 5.9; 2 Thess. 2.14 too we must understand it in our passage also thus: the redemption, i.e. the taking-possession (of the inheritance).[85] It is that full and final achievement of salvation, to which the addressees are called through the 'gospel of salvation' and in which they have already received a share. After this outlook the Eulogy concludes, in keeping with its style (cf. vv. 6 and 12), with the restating of the purpose 'to the praise of his glory'.

Summary

The great introductory Eulogy includes everything that God in Jesus Christ has planned, undertaken and fulfilled for us for our salvation. The author, who is not using handed-down hymns but takes up ideas current in the catechesis and liturgy, quite deliberately begins with God's eternal election and predestination (v. 4). God's aim in salvation to adopt us as his sons (v. 5) leads to the historical Redemption which he granted to us in his 'Beloved' (v. 6), more precisely in the Blood of Christ for the forgiveness of sins (v. 7). This act of redemption has, however, a further, global meaning, namely to reveal the plan of God's wisdom which consists in the unification of the universe in Christ. It is that plan which God had already made before the foundation of the world but which he would only undertake and reveal in the 'fullness of the times' (vv. 9–10). The redeemed are included in the cosmic act of redemption: they have received their portion from God (v. 11). Hence their existence is arranged for the glorification of God and they (are also those who) hope in Christ (v. 12). this is true also for the addressees, whose way through grace to the community of the baptized the author specially stresses (v. 13). All believers are sealed with the Holy Spirit and through him who is the 'guarantee of our inheritance' possess

[84]Haupt 32; Pr – Bauer 1289 (cf. also ibid. 191 ἀπολύτρωσις 2a: 'for redemption through which you become God's property'); Percy, *Probleme* 188 f.; n. 15; Cambier* 96 f.; Gnilka 87, Barth 97, Ernst 281 (undecided). – C. Kruse, 'Il significato de περιποίησις in Eph. 1.14', RivBib 16 (1968) 465–93, interprets the word as a *nomen actionis* but with God as the agent: God chooses a new people for himself. But can this also refer to the future redemption?
[85]Cf. Abbott 23 f.; Dibelius – Greeven 62 f.; Masson 148; Schlier 71 f.; Gaugler 55.

God's confirmation of our complete redemption (v. 14). In this way the arch extends from the eternal election to the awaited consummation, one single blessing of God which he has fulfilled for us in Jesus Christ.

The praise of God, which is continually being developed in new formulations, with its frequent repetitions and synonymous expressions raises the impression of richly-wrought, liturgical language. It seems as if the author revels in enthusiastic paeans of praise to God, soars up to another world, to the 'heavenly regions' and thereby loses contact with the earthly ground under his feet. But there are considerable linguistic differences to the liturgical style which readily makes use of an abundance of predicates for God and Christ, repeats the same ideas in ever-new images and uses repetitive or refrain-style lists etc. such as can be studied e.g. in the hymns of the Heavenly Household of the Redeemed in Rev. (cf. 4.8; 7.12; 15.3; 19.1 f., 5, 6–8 et al.), in the Passah-Homily of Melito of Sardis and in the later great liturgies, especially of the East. The variety of changing pictures and symbols which are typical of an enthusiastic mysticism (cf. the Odes of Solomon) is also missing in the Eph. Eulogy. In spite of its rich phraseology it remains a theological statement which develops certain ideas in turn, although in so doing it continually goes back or looks ahead in order to emphasize forcefully God's total plan for salvation and the execution of this plan. The oft-repeated 'in Christ' is also a stylistic device deliberately inserted to express the salvation bestowed by and available through him alone. Everything is directed towards the readers addressed, to impress upon them their understanding of life which is based on the fundamental statement: 'through grace you have been saved' (cf. 2.5, 8). Hence the author, even in praising God, has a practical goal to reach among his addressees: in looking up to the God and Father of our Lord Jesus Christ, who has blessed us with every spiritual blessing in Christ, he establishes them on the basis fundamental for their self-understanding and for their consequent behaviour in the world.

We might ask whether this type of personal devotion to God does not alienate one from the toilsome earthly duties. The danger cannot be denied. The man who lifts his heart to God in this way can easily lose sight of the darknesses and difficulties of the earthly-historical empirical world. It can also make light of theological problems such as lead on to question God's very existence when we look at the continuing poverty and suffering of humankind and still more in the face of the power of evil, the increasing occurrence of terrible injustices and acts of violence: is God's desire to save and the plan of salvation which is extolled here still credible in view of these realities? Where in our world is God's blessing visible or perceptible? It would indeed be an unrealistic view and an utopian outlook if this were the author's only and final word; but this is only the beginning of and prelude to the letter, which, as it proceeds, tears open the dark depths of evil. This evil is not only seen as something which has been overcome for Christians (2.1–3; 4.17–9) but also as something still with the power to tempt (5.3–5) and extremely threatening, which we can only resist in the armour of God (6.11–20). The Great Eulogy is intended to create a prevailing mood of thankfulness and humility, of joy and trust. The author, who sets the tone from his own feeling, is convinced that, from the depths and fullness of a faith which is properly reasoned and lived courageously, we can recognise even in an indifferent or hostile environment the hidden powers of God which are working towards the unification of the universe in Christ. In the praise of God the author introduces the readers to this living faith in order then to lead them to a wider consciousness and inner renewal (cf. 4.23 f.).

3. THANKSGIVING TO GOD AND INTERCESSION THAT THE READERS MAY HAVE A DEEPER UNDERSTANDING OF THE CHRIST-EVENT (1.15–23)

Literature

K. Berger, *Apostelbrief* (v. under 1.1–2).

J. M. Robinson, Hodajoth – Formel (v. under 1.3–14).

P. Schubert, *Form and Function of the Pauline Thanksgivings*, 1939 (BZNW 20).

J. T. Sanders, 'The Transition from Opening Epistolary Thanksgiving to Body in the Letters of the Pauline Corpus', JBL 81 (1962) 348–62.

J. L. White, 'Introductory Formulae in the Body of the Pauline Letter', JBL 90 (1971) 91–7; id., *The Form and Function of the Body of the Greek Letter: A Study of the Letter-Body in the non-literary Papyri and in Paul the Apostle* (SBL Diss. Ser. 2), Missoula 1972.

G. P. Wiles, *Paul's Intercessory Prayers*, 1974 (MSSNTS 24).

P. T. O'Brien, 'Thanksgiving and the Gospel of Paul', NTS 21 (1975) 144–55; id., *Introductory Thanksgivings in the Letters of Paul*, 1977 (NTS 49).

On 1.23: A. Feuillet, 'L'Église plérôme du Christ d'après Éphés. 1.23', NRTh 78 (1956) 449–72. 593–610.

R. Hermans – L. Geysels, 'Efesiërs 1.23: het pleroma van Gods heilswerk', Bijdr. 28 (1967) 279–92.

R. Yates, 'A Re-examination of Ephesians 1.23', ET 83 (1971/72) 146–51.

G. Howard, 'The Head/Body Metaphors of Ephesians', NTS 20 (1974) 350–6.

I. de la Potterie, 'Le Christ, Plérôme de l'Église (Ep. 1.22–3)' Bib. 58 (1977) 500–24; Overfield, NTS 25, 393 f.

15 Therefore I also give thanks
   since I have heard of your faith in the Lord Jesus and of your
   love toward all the saints
16 unceasingly for you
   when I remember you in my prayers:
17 May the God of our Lord Jesus Christ, the Father of glory,
   give you the Spirit of wisdom and revelation to gain
   knowledge of him,
18 enlighten the eyes of your hearts, so that you know
   to what hope you have been called,
   how rich is the glory of his inheritance among the holy ones
19 and how immeasurably great is his power
   (which he reveals) for us, the faithful
   according to the might of his tremendous strength

20 which he accomplished in Christ:
    He raised him from the dead
    and set him at his right hand in heaven
21 high above every rule and authority and power and
    dominion
    and over every name that is named,
    not only in this age but also in that which is to come.
22 Yes, 'He has put all things under his feet'
    and gave him as Head over the whole of the Church
23 which is his Body, the fullness of him
    who fills all in all.

Analysis

Only now (after the Great Eulogy) does the author commence that part of the letter which would normally come after the introduction and before the real body of the letter – i.e. the thanksgiving for the proven character of the addressees. Such a transition, introduced by εὐχαριστῶ or sim. has an informative function: to win over the recipients through praise and recognition and make them receptive for the writer's concerns. Two forms can be distinguished in the Pauline Corpus: after εὐχαριστῶ may come either (a) one or more participles on which depend further phrases (1 Thess. 1.3–5; Phil. 1.3–6; Col. 1.3–6) or (b) a ὅτι -clause which may be extended by further dependent clauses (1 Cor. 1.4 f., 7; Rom. 1.8; Philem. 4–6; cf. 2 Thess. 1.3–5).[1] The thanks, however, are not directed to the recipients of the letter but rather to God – a custom for which we have evidence also in private letters of the Hellenistic period (the προσκύνημα Formula).[2] In Paul's letters the thanksgiving frequently passes over into intercession through which he makes clear that the recipients' present condition in faith and love still needs to grow and mature (cf. Phil. 1.4.9; Philem. 4.6; Col. 1.3.9; deutero-Pauline 2 Thess. 1.11; 2 Tim. 1.3). In 2 Cor. 1.3 we have a eulogy *in place of* the thanksgiving, a procedure which can be explained here from the situation in which the letter was written (the saving of the apostle from personal affliction) and, incidentally, from the relationship between the Jewish berakhah (blessing) and hodajah (song of thanksgiving).[3] There is a further important element in this Pauline transition to the main body of the letter: the eschatological outlook. This is to be found in 1 Cor. 1.7 f.; Phil. 1.10; cf. 1 Thess. 1.10; 2 Thess. 1.7, and in a similar manner, with characteristic modification, in Col. 1.5.

If we compare this (unpretentious, rather flexible) practice of the apostle (apart from Gal where he omits the thanksgiving because of the addressees' critical situation and replaces it with a stern 'I am astonished') with how the author of Eph. proceeds, we become aware of the following:

(a) Our author is the only one who includes in addition to a long

---

[1]Schubert* 35 f.; cf. Sanders* 348; White, JBL distinguishes six forms according to motive and function; O'Brien NTS* names three different contents of motive.

[2]White, *Body** 8; examples on p. 32 and p. 35. He attributes the expression to H. Koskenniemi, *Studien zur Idee und Phraseologie des griechischen Briefes*, Helsinki 1956, 139 ff.

[3]Cf. Robinson,* especially 208–10.

eulogy this further epistolary element of thanksgiving (and intercession) although the eulogy already performs a similar function (cf. 2 Cor. 1.3).[4] It is probable that he wished to address the recipients personally, in keeping with Paul's practice, after the long eulogy which he himself considered of great importance.

(b) With regard to its content, it displays an unmistakeable closeness to Col. and Philem.[5] To the 'thanksgiving' is connected syntactically by an aorist participle the theme that the author had 'heard' of the faith and love of the recipients (Eph. 1.15, cf. Col. 1.4; Philem. 5); furthermore a remembering in prayer (Eph. 1.16) or an intercessional prayer (Col. 1.3, cf. 9) is attached by means of a present participle.

(c) Hence the content of the intercession indicates an acquaintance with Col. Here as there we are concerned with 'recognition' of God (Eph. 1.17) or of his will (Col. 1.9), with the 'spirit of wisdom' or 'spiritual wisdom', and finally there is mention of the 'hope' which is laid up in heaven (Col. 1.5) or follows upon their calling (Eph. 1.18). It is not simply a case of appropriation; for while in Col. the intercession which is at first only touched upon is later taken up and developed (1.3, 9), Eph. is more concentrated and makes use of phraseology taken from the whole Col. context – although with the author's own stamp (cf. πατὴρ τῆς δόξης, ἀποκάλυψις, κληρονομία etc.). From this we may conclude that the author of Eph. had this section of Col. before him and that he used it as a basis for his own creation, especially in the intercession.

(d) The intercession broadens out into a christological-ecclesiological digression (vv. 19b–23), a procedure which corresponds to the author's manner of reflection and recapitulation which we have already observed in the eulogy.

In the expanded intercession of Eph. 1.17–19, an explanation is attached to the actual intercession for the 'spirit of wisdom and of revelation in the recognition of God': first, (dependent on δῷη) with the plea that 'the eyes of your hearts may be enlightened' then (dependent on that) with the goal that they may know what their calling to final salvation means. For this purpose the author, in keeping with his pleonastic style, begins three times with the interrogative pronoun τίς, τί (vv. 18b, c; 19a). Why is he concerned to develop this idea, and what lies behind his choice of expressions? It is clear that he wants to bring even more vividly before the eyes of the recipients that salvation mediated and promised by the Holy Spirit which he mentioned in v. 13 f. One only has to compare the expressions common to the two places – πίστις (or πιστεύω), πνεῦμα, δόξα, κληρονομία – and especially the perspective oriented to the completion of salvation. What emerged in the praising of God in the Eulogy is confirmed in the intercession: it is the God who elects and calls who himself guarantees for the faithful the attainment of their heavenly inheritance through the gift of the Spirit.

---

[4]On 2 Cor. 1.2–11 cf. O'Brien, Intr. *Thanksgivings* 233–58.

[5]Philem. 4–6 has strong connections with Col. 1.4–9 but is not necessarily a direct model for Eph. 1.15–16; cf. the sequence on love and faith: in Eph. 1.15 and Col. 1.4 they are in the reverse order and practically word for word the same. Schubert* 34 thinks otherwise. Cf. the three texts as they are placed alongside one another in Mitton, *Epistle* 282 f.

Frequent attempts have been made to discern an underlying hymn in verses 20–3.[6] This remains very dubious. I would prefer to speak of a christological-ecclesiological digression which the author, perhaps prompted by kerygmatic and catechetic formulations, allowed himself to make. The transition is achieved – as frequently in the Eulogy – by a κατά -phrase in v. 19c which is attached to the train of thought already completed. In this way the author recapitulates and underlines God's mighty, effective salvation-act, again (as in 1.5, 9, 11) with a similar expression ('according to the might of his tremendous strength') God has given proof of his sovereign power to save in Christ, namely in his resurrection from the dead and his enthronement at God's right hand (two participles in v. 20). Christ's investiture in power and dominion is then described impressively through his superiority over the principalities and powers which previously seemed invincible. His all-embracing dominion is described in a quotation from scripture: 'He has put all things under his feet' (v. 22a). Since the author, with this quotation, has now moved over to an independent clause (in the indicative), it is easy for him to continue this line of thought and demonstrate Christ's position for the salvation of the Church (v. 22b) after the suppression of the powers of evil. The cosmic- embracing significance of the Church as the sphere of Christ's salvific activity, as his 'body', as the 'fullness' of Christ who fills the whole universe (v. 23) – a theme which will engage him further in the body of the letter – is so important for him that he mentions it already here in a tightly-knit, theologically-laden, exegetically controversial clause (cf. the Exegesis). It is a clause which is made resonant by the (τὰ) πάντα formula – a counterpart to the culminating clause of the Eulogy in 1.10.

Exegesis

15

After the general praise Paul is introduced as praying personally (κἀγώ). Because of God's abundant blessing (διὰ τοῦτο refers to the whole Eulogy) Paul constantly gives thanks to God, and does this especially with regard to the addressees. The grounds for this special thanksgiving follow closely Col. 1.4; but instead of 'in Christ Jesus' he says 'in the Lord Jesus'. This is perhaps an echo of Philem. 5, since the short formula κύριος ᾽Ιησοῦς appears only here in Eph.[7] In accordance with Philem. 5 (πίστις ... πρός) faith toward Jesus the Lord may be meant; but if we consider 1.1 (cf. also 3.17) it is more natural to translate it as an established faith and life 'in the Lord' (cf. Schlier 76). The 'love toward all the saints' – i.e. toward all believers – is likewise taken from the aforementioned passage. Faith and

---

[6]Dibelius – Greeven 64 ('A type of hymn'), Ochel, *Bearbeitung* 37–42; Schille, *Liturgisches Gut* 114–16; Deichgräber, *Gotteshymnus* 161–65 tries to reconstruct this (but it is 'laden with many uncertainties' 164).

[7]Cf. 1 Thess. 2.15; 4.1, 2; 1 Cor. 11.23; 12.3; 2 Cor. 11.31; Rom 10.9; Phil. 2.11 etc. Kramer, *Christos* 61–7 considers the formula as a (pre-Pauline) cry of acclamation in the sense of a confession which resounded first at Baptism and then ever again in the service of worship. Cf. also Hahn, *Hoheitstitel* 119 f.

love[8] already in Paul form a connected pair (cf. Gal. 5.6; faith which is effective through love) to which hope is joined (1 Thess. 1.3; Gal. 5.5). Our author, for whom hope is especially important, follows this tradition; for him hope is focussed on the inheritance already prepared (v. 18) and intensifies the consciousness of redemption to a certainty of salvation (cf. 1.12, 14). The wording adopted speaks against concrete information about the addressees (through the use of 'hear'); the author is more concerned to make them inclined to hear what he has to say.

16

The adoption and blending of Pauline expressions is further revealed in the style. Paul assures his readers in most of the epistles to congregations of his constant intercession on their behalf. The formulation with οὐ παύομαι is only to be found in Col. 1.9, μνείαν ποιεῖσθαι also in undisputed Pauline epistles (1 Thess. 1.2; Rom. 1.9; Philem. 4). Yet in Paul this incessant remembrance is connected with his care and intercession for his congregations; in Eph. 1.16 the author *gives thanks* unceasingly for his readers,[9] and grammatically the remembrance in his prayers is dependent on this (with a participle). Admittedly in what follows (vv. 17–19) he also expresses prayerful wishes for them; but the emphasis which he puts on the thanksgiving shows his desire to win over the readers upon whom he wishes cautiously to impress his pastoral concerns.

17

The prayer (introduced by ἵνα), addressed directly to God, has a strong 'doxological' ring. The God of our Lord Jesus Christ is the 'Father of glory', a unique expression with a liturgical character, which brings to mind other laudatory divine titles such as Jas. 1.17 ('Father of the stars'); 1 Tim. 6.15 f. (with a doxology); Rev. 4.11 ('Worthy art thou . . .'). 'God of glory' is already a title for the God who reveals himself in the OT (Ps. 28.3 LXX; cf. Acts 7.2); but '*Father* of glory' in conjunction with the 'God of our Lord Jesus Christ' has a strange sound. All 'glory' proceeds from him and is seen most notably in Jesus Christ (v. 20). God's special glory, the transmission of his being, becomes in the salvation-event an effective power of the father (cf. Rom. 6.4), which leads us, too, to heavenly glory through the resurrected and 'glorified' Christ (cf. 2.5–7). This is a Pauline view (cf. Phil. 3.21) except that Paul is thinking of the eschatological resurrection of the dead which is nowhere mentioned in Eph.[10] God the Father is the origin of everything; in him all power and might is gathered (cf. 3.15 f.;

---

[8]τὴν ἀγάπην to ἁγίους is omitted by P[46]א*ABP 33 1739 al. This abbreviated form might have been influenced by Philem. 5 or could be explained by an oversight (not noticing the second expression with τὴν). The longer form corresponds to Col. 1.4 and is more probable from its content.

[9]ὑπὲρ ὑμῶν can hardly be taken with what follows ('remembering'); cf. Col. 1.9 where it stands in a similar position in relation to 'asking'. The thanking 'for you' is expressed elsewhere by περὶ ὑμῶν (1 Thess. 1.2; 1 Cor. 1.4; Rom 1.8; Col. 1.3 etc.).

[10]On the pushing back of the future eschatology cf. Steinmetz, *Heils-Zuversicht*, but with hope kept open (132–8); Lindemann, *Aufhebung der Zeit*, goes further; he denies any future aspect whatever to the concept of 'hope' in Eph. (194–6).

4.6) and he attains his goal over all opposition according to what he has planned in his wisdom (cf. 3.9–11, 20). The idea of the Father which comes so strongly to the fore in Eph. serves in the end the author's theology of election and salvation: this God and Father is the guarantee of Christian hope. To grasp this hope in all its richness we need the 'Spirit of wisdom and of revelation' which leads us to a deeper knowledge of God. The wish of the prayer draws its inspiration from Col. 1.9, but departs from it in the wording and point. That which modifies in Col. 1.9 ('in all wisdom . . .') becomes in Eph. the object of the request. The syntactic construction 'Spirit of wisdom and of revelation' for which there is no evidence elsewhere (although we have 'wisdom and understanding' cf. Schweizer on Col. 1.9) is explained in connection with the following 'to gain knowledge of him (God)'.[11] The wisdom and revelation bestowed by the Spirit affects the 'knowledge of God', which in Eph. includes the fullness of depth of the divine mystery revealed in Christ and the Church (cf. 3.9 f., 18) and in the end the love of Christ which surpasses all human knowledge (3.19), and this bestows a beneficient experience of salvation. Hence we are not concerned here with the Spirit of prophecy with special 'revelations' (cf. 1 Cor. 14.6, 26, 30), or a charismatic talent (cf. 1 Cor. 1.5, 7) but with a spiritual experience possible for all believers. Paul mentions this aspect in 1 Cor. 2.10–12 when he considers the mystery of God's wisdom concealed from the 'rulers of this age' – which for Paul reaches its climax in the Crucifixion-event – and establishes that 'God has revealed it to us through the Spirit' (2.10). We need the Spirit which proceeds from God 'that we might understand the gifts bestowed on us by God' (2.12).[12] From this experience of salvation which is bestowed on all believers through the Spirit we must distinguish that special revelation granted to Paul of the 'holy apostles and prophets in the Spirit' (Eph. 3.3, 5) to preach the riches of Christ and reveal clearly the mystery of Christ (3.8).[13]

18

The spiritual experience which all believers should achieve is described further through the request 'enlighten the eyes of your hearts' (still dependent on δώη). The heart as the location of inner perception points to a Jewish way of thinking, and 'to enlighten the eyes' is likewise found already in the OT (Ps. 12.4; 18.9 LXX; Bar. 1.12; Ezra. 9.8). The metaphor is also to be found in extra-biblical (gnostic) literature[14] and is used in a similar way in 1 Cl. 36.2; 59.3. We may suspect it comes out of a liturgical tradition, but do not have to (as Schlier) think it refers to Baptism. Such a

[11] ἐν ἐπιγνώσει should be taken modally: 'existing in', cf. Schmid, *Epheserbrief* 210. In content it is the same idea as in Col. 1.9 in the reverse word-order. On the semitizing co-ordination (with ⅂) cf. Lk. 1.77; Eph. 1.8 (ἐν πάσῃ σοφίᾳ κτλ); 2.15 (ἐν δόγμασιν); it is frequent in the Qumran texts, cf. e.g. 1 QH 5.3; 8.11; 11.20; 16.6, 10.
[12] The closeness to 1 Cor. 2.6–16 also emerges from the use of the same words – cf. σοφία, γνῶναι, εἰδέναι, ἀποκαλύπτειν, πνεῦμα. To be sure some exegetes take the passage to refer to special revelations, cf. H. Conzelmann, *1 Corinthians*, 1975, Dautzenberg, *Urchristliche Prophetie* 138–40. In Eph. clearly all believers are meant.
[13] Cf. Merklein, *Kirchl. Amt* 220.
[14] Cf. the texts named by Schlier 80, n. 1, especially the Odes of Solomon. We must admittedly observe that other metaphors of sensory perception are connected with it.

recognition, knowledge and becoming cognisant is only possible for people who have been enlightened by the divine Spirit which enables them to see with the 'eyes of the heart'. It is a contrasting picture to the 'ignorance' (ἄγνοια) of the heathen whose cognitive capacity is darkened (4.18). Behind the intercession lies the author's fear that the addressees, because their faith is not deep enough, may once more decline into an empty life-style bound to this earthly world (cf. 4.17).

In three clauses similarly constructed, co-ordinated and yet each developing the idea further the author indicates wherein their 'knowledge', the enlightenment which comes from faith, should consist: hope which springs from God's call (cf. 4.4b); richness in the majesty which is prepared in the heavenly inheritance and in which this hope is fulfilled; certainty of achieving this inheritance through God's overwhelming power which has already been shown, and which he wishes to bring about in us, the believers (v. 19). Hence hope has substance based as it is on God's previous actions: it is itself a part of salvation which, even more strongly than in Paul (cf. Gal. 5.5; Rom. 8.24; 15.4) is experienced as already present (cf. 1.12; 4.4; more clearly Col. 1.5, 27). A typical indication of this is how the noun 'hope' is more prominent than the verb in Col. and Eph.

In Paul, too, hope focusses on the glory, the perfect, infinite participation in God's majesty (cf. Rom. 5.2; 8.17 f., 21); but in Eph. it is already a present participation in the kingdom of Christ and of God (5.5; cf. Col. 1.13). We can and should become inwardly stronger 'in accordance with the riches of the glory of God' through his Spirit (3.16; cf. Col. 1.11). Nevertheless the acquisition of the full inheritance is still to come (1.14) and that inheritance remains a heavenly quantity in God's safekeeping. Since 'among the holy ones' is certainly a more detailed description of 'inheritance', these words refer to the divine-heavenly sphere. Already in the OT the angels who surround and accompany God are called 'holy ones' (Deut. 33.2 f.; Ps. 89.6, 8; Sir. 42.17; Dan. 8.13), and this way of speaking occurs increasingly in the LXX (Am. 4.2; Is. 57.15; cf. Tob. 11.14; 12.15 et al.) and in the Pseudepigrapha.[15] The Qumran Community believed that it was united with the 'holy ones' in heaven,[16] and Eph., too, clearly takes over this view (cf. also 2.19). Thus to name the faithful on earth as 'saints' (v. 15) and look up to the 'holy ones' in heaven (v. 18) can stand side by side without causing any problem (cf. also Col. 1.12 f.).

19

While the heavenly world as the goal of our hope or, in other words, the transcendent goal of the Christian existence, shines before the eyes of the readers, they are now also told that they, too, can achieve it through the power of God. By means of expressions piled upon one another for God's

[15] Jub. 31.14 (= Angel of Sanctification 2.18; 15.27); Eth. Enoch 1.9; 12.2; 14.23; 39.5; 47.2; 57.2; 61.10, 12.

[16] Cf. 1 QS 11.7 f.; 1 QSa 2.8 f.; 1 QH 3.22 f.; 1 QM 12.1, 4. In other passages it remains unclear whether heavenly beings or members of the Community are meant. Cf. F. Nötscher, 'Heiligkeit in den Qumranschriften', RdQ 2 (1959/60) 315–44, here 321–6. How the connection with heaven and the angels was visualized is assessed in various ways, cf. H. Hübner, 'Anthropologischer Dualismus in den Hodayoth', NTS 18 (1971/72) 268–284, here 272 f.

superior power, the author tries to make the readers aware that God wills that they attain full salvation and that he is capable of bestowing it on them. 'For us,[17] the faithful' God summons up his mighty power which he has made known in his salvation-act. In this 'for us', which emphasizes the essentially soteriological character of all the divine planning (cf. 1.3–5) are included all believers, among them the recipients of the letter (cf. 1.13). The theological reflection and argumentation begins with κατα κτλ, that retrospective construction which was already dominant in the Eulogy. The act of God which brings full salvation and sets us free lies in the Resurrection of Christ (v. 20). From the 'might of his strength' grows the operative force (ἐνέργεια) which he has already demonstrated in Christ (ἐνήργησεν) (v. 20). In this connection it is obvious that God will lead the faithful too, to their goal with the same sovereign power: with Christ and in Christ the way to heavenly glory is opened for them too. (cf. 2.5–7).

20

The following section on the raising of Christ from the dead and his investiture with power is therefore a persuasive continuation, added so that the readers may understand their state of salvation, consolidate their hope and live out of it. In order to describe God's action in Christ, the author makes use of early Christian theological writings (there are two indirect quotations in v. 20 and v. 22) and develops the theological perspective in a particular direction (subjugation of the ungodly powers, the Church as the sphere of blessing).

The resurrection of Jesus Christ from the dead and his investiture at God's right hand (after Ps. 110.1) belong to the fundamental sermon on Christ. It is conspicuous that the death of Jesus on the Cross, contrasted to which as a sinister background God's powerful intervention would stand out even more strongly (cf. 1 Cor. 2.8; Rom. 4.25; 6.3 f.; Col. 2.14 f. et al.), is not mentioned. The author is concerned above all with Christ's investiture 'at God's right hand'. This is what for him as for the whole of early Christianity establishes Christ's position as ruler and his lasting rule:[18] i.e. Christ rules out of the power of God who rules through his Christ. But the addition 'in the heavenly places' (cf. under 1.3) is characteristic. For the author this is important for our heavenly inheritance (v. 18) and the subjugation of the 'lower' powers (v. 21). This spatial picture governs his thinking (cf. Col. 3.1; Heb. 1.3; 8.1); it becomes understandable if we see, as the author intends, that it is meant to show the superiority of the

---

[17]Here D*FGP 33 al. VL[pr] read ὑμᾶς, a variant reading clearly rising from the intercession (cf. v. 18).

[18]Cf. Hahn, *Hoheitstitel* 126–32. Yet the idea of his elevation did not only arise in Hellenistic Jewish Christianity through the use of Ps. 110.1 but was already brought into connection with the raising of Jesus from the dead; cf. P. Vielhauer, 'Ein Weg zur neutestamentlichen Christologie?', EvTh 25 (1965) 24–72, here 45–52; Conzelmann, *Theologie* 87; W. Thüsing, *Erhöhungsvorstellung und Parusieerwartung in der ältesten nachösterlichen Christologie o.J.* (SBS 42); Lindemann, *Aufhebung der Zeit* 82–4; 206–8. – On the use of Ps. 110.1 cf. also Lindars, *NT Apologetic* 45–51; D. M. Hay, *Glory at the Right Hand: Psalm 110 in Early Christianity*, Nashville 1973 (Society of Biblical Literature Mon. Ser. 18); M. Gourgues, *A la Droite de Dieu. Résurrection de Jésus et actualisation du Psaume 110.1 dans le Nouveau Testament*, 1978 (EtB).

divine power over that which is dark and debilitating in our earthly existence.

21

As in an illustration Christ sits enthroned since his Resurrection 'above every rule and authority . . .' This spatial reflection, which sees each of the 'higher' locations as also having great power and dominion is in the Jewish apocalyptic conception of the world closely connected with the superiority of Heaven or the heavens over the earth; but in the NT, through Christ's 'elevation' or his 'ascension' to God's throne, it achieves a special character which is already present in early hymns about Christ as Phil. 2.9 f. and 1 Pet. 3.22. This happens most clearly in Eph.: the Christ who descended into the 'lower' spheres (= to earth) has since his Resurrection 'ascended over all the heavens' (4.10) and in so doing has overthrown and put under his authority the 'powers' which operate in the lower heavenly regions (in the 'realm of the air' cf. 2.12; 6.12). These 'powers and authorities' are mentioned in several places in Col. also (1.16 2.10, 15), even in the consideration of Creation: they owe their existence to Christ as the sole mediator in Creation (1.16). Through the Crucifixion-event they have been deprived of their power (2.15), and Christ is their 'head', their ruler (2.10). Eph. gives this even greater emphasis and uses Col.'s christological viewpoint ecclesiologically: The victory Christ achieved over every dark power guarantees victory for his Church also.

What are these 'rules and authorities and powers and dominions' which are enumerated here? The diverse terms, which all imply a spiritual, superhuman influence, are not intended to give any gradation or specification but to indicate in their profusion the abundance and development of power. Already in Paul we find manifold, variable expressions (cf. 1 Cor. 3.22; 15.24; Rom. 8.38 f.). In the pseudepigrapha, especially in apocalyptic writings, we come across a host of names which point to a connection with speculation about angels.[19] Most frequently named in Paul and his school are 'rules and authorities' (ἀρχαὶ καὶ ἐξουσ-ίαι). If in Eph. 1.21 two further terms appear – namely 'powers' (δυνάμεις) and 'dominions' (κυριότητες) – δυνάμεις is also found in Rom. 8.38 and 1 Pet. 3.22 and κυριότητες in Col. 1.16; cf. Jude 8; 2 Pet. 2.10 (meaning unclear), but also in extra-biblical literature.[20] It may also depend on a memory of Col. 1.16 because of the four terms; in the many lists with angels' names, numbers play a part, especially three, seven and

[19]Cf. Eth Enoch 61.10 (alongside other angel names) 'all angels of power, all angels of authority'; similarly Slav Enoch 20.1 (Res A); Asc Is. 2.2 'Satan, his angels and powers'; Test Lev. 3.8 'Thrones, powers' etc. Cf. further W. Foerster, TDNT II, 571–3; G. B. Caird, *Principalities and Powers*, Oxford 1956; Schlier, *Mächte und Gewalten*; J. Y. Lee, 'Interpreting the Demonic Powers in Pauline Thought', NT 12 (1970) 54–69; O. Böcher, *Das Neue Testament und die dämonischen Mächte*, Stuttgart 1973. P. Benoit, 'Angélologie et Démonologie pauliniennes', in *Fede e cultura alla luce della Bibbia. Atti della Sessione plenaria 1979 della Pontificia Commissione Biblica*, Turin 1981, 217–33, distinguishes more sharply between angels and cosmic powers.
[20]Cf. W. Foerster, TDNT III, 1097, who traces the abstracta back to the tendency to use them for concreta.

ten.[21] The number four may in general express completeness, but is also frequently used for the expanse of the earth or of heaven ('four corners of the earth', four points of the compass)[22] and is consequently a kind of 'cosmic' symbolic number for the extent as well as for the limitedness of the created world.[23] The world which is ruled by spiritual powers working against God will be transferred under Christ's rule in which God's plan for salvation is fulfilled. Behind this view, which describes a power-activity in spatial terms, stands the conviction that powers incomprehensible to humankind are at work in the enigmaticness of earthly-cosmic events, but through God's superior might in Christ these will be kept in check, overcome and compelled to God's service. In the end it is one single power of evil working against God which is revealed in the concentration of these multifarious 'rules and authorities' in a single form (2.2: the ruler of the sphere of the air, the spirit who effects destruction; 6.11: the devil). The way of thinking which for us is foreign, 'mythical', which takes for granted the myth of the Fall of the Angels,[24] still faces us with the question of what the secret of evil in human history and in the world is.

The addition 'and every name that is named' enlarges upon the group of four, not with a new expression for power, but in a generalising combination. The new extension is marked by the reversion to 'every': all the powers named and whatever else may have a 'name' – i.e. might and influence – all are subjected to Christ. In the pre-Pauline Christ-hymn in Phil. 2.9. Christ receives the 'name above every name' and as a result all 'in heaven, on earth and under the earth' must bow the knee before him. The 'name' signifies for the Bible and all the ancient world (cf. the Magic Papyri) the power to dispose; in it are gathered being and power, and from it proceed effect and influence.[25] If we combine ὀνομαζομένου with the following modifier 'not only in this age but also in that which is to come' as is usually done, this early Jewish time-scheme indicates the range of the efficacy inherent in a 'name'. But as attribute to the powerfully effective 'name' this time-scheme plays only a supporting role to its characterization – i.e. it has no real temporal significance.[26] In no way does it infer that in

[21] Cf. the material in J. Michl, RAC V (1962) 89–91 (Jewish); 97–100 (Gnostic); 169–75 (Christian).

[22] Cf. H. Balz, TDNT VIII, 127–35.

[23] Cf. the four creatures in Rev. (4.6, 8; 5.6, 8, 14 et al.); the four horses (6.1–8), the four angels at the 'corners of the earth' (7.1 f.), the four avenging angels (20.8) and the foursquare plan of the heavenly Jerusalem (21.16).

[24] In Judaism the link is Gen 6.1–4 (sexual intercourse between the 'sons of God' and the daughters of men) cf. especially Eth. Enoch 6–9; 15 and elsewhere (further in J. Michl, RAC V 80 ff.); this was taken over by early Christianity (Jude 6; 2 Pet. 2.4). The fall of Satan is presupposed but interpreted with reference to Christ in Lk. 10.18; Rev. 12.7 ff.; cf. Jn. 12.32.

[25] Negative powers are characterized through their 'name', especially in Revelation: Death (6.8), the star 'Wormwood' (8.11), the angel of the bottomless pit (9.11), blasphemous names on the heads of the animal (13.1), the great harlot (17.5). Yet the names need not be mentioned; the 'name' as such is an expression of power. Cf. Epiph Haer 26.9; 'I am the one who has descended from above through the names of the 365 archons'. v. Reitzenstein, *Poim* 17, n. 6. On the Magic Papyri cf. Bietenhard TDNT V 250 f. – The 'Father' from whom every race has its name (ὀνομάζεται) 3.15 builds a contrast to the powers which exert an evil influence through their 'name'.

[26] Schlier 88 and Lindemann, *Aufhebung der Zeit* 210 f. also emphasize this.

the coming age they might be able to exert an influence contrary to the dominion of God or Christ; Paul (cf. 1 Cor. 15.24–8) and the personal view of the author of Eph. (cf. 1.10: 22 f.; 3.10; 4.10) would contradict this. But perhaps one should put a comma after ὀνομαζομένου so that 'in this age and in the age that is to come' refers to Christ's position high above every force, power etc. Even then it remains a strange form of expression which does not correspond to the author's way of thinking elsewhere.[27] In his thinking we cannot say there is a true expectation of an age to come after 'this age', one still outstanding (as in the Jewish hope) because the 'transition of the aeons' has already begun in his view with the 'fullness of the times' (1.10), the coming of Christ (2.11 f.) and the reality of the Church (cf. 3.9 f.). For Eph. there are only 'approaching ages' in which the riches of the divine grace will be demonstrated (2.7). Hence the double expression is simply a stereotyped, more detailed definition, be it for the might of the 'name' or the boundless continuing lordship of Christ.

22

The total subjugation of the powers of darkness to Christ is further emphasized by the quotation from Ps. 8.6. Unlike Ps. 110.1 (in v. 20) this Psalm is not initially concerned with the messianic king but with 'man' or 'son of man' within the created world; but it was interpreted christologically in the early Christian Church (cf. 1 Cor. 15.27; Phil. 3.21; Heb. 2.6–9; 1 Pet. 3.22), in 1 Cor. 15.24–8 just as in our passage in conjunction with Ps. 110.1.[28] In this way the author takes up the Pauline tradition as is also shown in the wording which deviates from the LXX (for its form v. Heb. 2.8). The spatial view is further strengthened by the expression 'under his feet'; 'all' continues the line 'above *every* rule' – '*every* name' and thus describes Christ's rule which is superior to all other powers and embraces the whole universe (cf. 1.10).

The conjunction καί at the beginning may be understood as explicative-causal ('and in fact') but can also correspond to the second καί so that a deliberate double statement results: God has on the one hand subjected 'everything', all cosmic powers and therewith the cosmos itself, to Christ (cf. 1.10 and 4.10) and on the other hand has given this omnipotent ruler to the Church.[29] The lack of the article does not stand in the way of this interpretation, because the article is also missing in the quotation (in Heb. 2.8 the author annotates the παντα in the quotation with τὰ παντα). At all events the movement of thought, after the glance at the subjugated powers of darkness, pushes on quite decidedly to the statement about the Church in v. 23. The conjunction of the two in a way contrary thoughts – that God forces the powers of evil under Christ's feet and gives him to the Church as the one who fills her with his power to bless – becomes even closer if we presume an abbreviated form of expression

---

[27]Cf. Barth 155: The two-age schema seems like a relic of a futuristic eschatology which does not fit the 'realized eschatology' of Eph. Barth seeks to explain this through the adoption of a hymn (v. 21 from ἐγείρας to the end of 23). But does the age-schema fit in a Christian hymn?

[28]Cf. Lindars, *NT Apologetic* 50 f.; E. Schweizer, TDNT VIII, 371.

[29]Cf. Bl – Debr. §444.3.

in v. 22b: as Head 'over all things' i.e. over the cosmos, he at the same time gave him to the Church as Head.[30] The other view which is grammatically possible – that of taking ὑπερ πάντα as a modal attribute to κεφαλήν ('the Head which surpasses all things')[31] is unsatisfactory because such an emphasis is pointless here for the Church. With respect to the Church it is not so much the difference, the superiority of her 'Head' which should be emphasized but far more the effect of this upon her, the filling with mercy. Finally, it would be possible to understand Christ merely as a 'gift' for the Church: God *gave* him to her as the one who is 'Head over all things'. But what would such a predicative modifier signify for the Church? In view of the later passages where Christ is named as the Head of the Church (4.15 f.; 5.23) and of the statement which immediately follows – that she is his Body – we must recognize as the main emphasis the fact that Christ is given to the Church as Head.

23

The Church is first described (in a relative clause) as the Body of Christ and then as the pleroma of him who fills the cosmos. The whole movement of thought finds its climax here; the cosmic reflection, the subjugation of the powers of evil, serves the ecclesiological view that the called are incorporated in the redeemed community of the Church.

When the author describes the Church as 'the Body of Christ', the reason for this no doubt lies in the predicate 'Head'. Christ, the Head, and the Church, his Body, are constitutive for the author's conception of the Church (cf. 4.15 f.; 5.23). As in Col. (cf. 1.18; 2.19) we have here a theological development of the Pauline 'Body-of-Christ' concept.[32] When the author mentions this conception here without enlarging upon the picture or thought-process, he is clearly taking for granted that it is known at least in its essential features. What he has to say in addition (especially 2.16; 4.4, 12–16; 5.23–32) serves to deepen this view and helps make it beneficial for the life of the congregation.

In the context the emphasis is on the more detailed description of the Body of Christ as the fullness of him who fills everything in the cosmos.[33] The extremely compact, terse form of expression has led to the most varied interpretations which I shall not expound here in detail.[34]

[30]Cf. Hegermann, *Schöpfungsmittler* 152; Schlier 89; Gnilka 97; Barth 156; Lindemann, *Aufhebung der Zeit* 212.

[31]Older Commentaries; Hanson, *Unity* 127; Mußner, *Christus* 30 f.

[32]This is seen particularly in the new view of Christ as the 'Head' in his differentiation from the 'Body'. This is recognisable in the hymn in Col. 1.18a but is interpreted by the author to mean the Church (v. Schweizer, *Colossians* at this point). In Eph., too, we still catch a glimpse of the cosmic understanding behind the ecclesiological conception, cf. 1.10, 22 f.; 4.10; also in 2.14–18. See further in the Excursus on the Church in Eph.

[33]Here τὸ πλήρωμα is to be understood in apposition to τὸ σῶμα, the article supplying further evidence. There is another grammatical possibility: we could make πλήρωμα again dependent on ἔδωκεν after the relative clause, putting it on an equal footing with κεφαλήν, so that 'the fullness' refers to Christ. This interpretation has already been made occasionally (Moule, ET 60 (1948/49) 53; id., *Idiom Book* 25 etc.) and Hermans – Geysels* and de la Potterie* have attempted to give it a more solid basis (v. infra).

[34]Cf. Ernst, *Pleroma* 105–20; further, the history of the interpretation of the Pleroma which he offers on pp. 198–290.

Taken purely etymologically, τὸ πλήρωμα can take on either an active or a passive sense: that which fills (the filling) the supplement, the completion; or what is filled (the fullness, what is completed, the full measure).[35] The author of Eph. is not bound semantically to a single meaning as is shown by 'the fullness of the times' (1.10) its becoming full, in comparison with 'the total fullness of God' (3.19) which cannot be interpreted as becoming full, or with the 'measure of the fullness of Christ' (4.13). If we turn to the verb πληροῦν for guidance (1.23; 3.19; 4.10; 5.18) we find that the sense is clearly active in 4.10 and passive in 3.19; 5.18. But one thing is important: only Christ (4.10) and the Spirit (5.18) are attested as being active powers of 'filling'. Hence we must exclude the interpretation of τὸ πλήρωμα in 1.23 as 'filling-up, completing' which would refer to the Church in relationship to Christ. This interpretation, which has been influential in the history of exegesis from early times up till the present[36] can neither depend on Col. 1.24 (q.v.) nor does it find support in the ecclesiological thinking of Eph. As members of Christ's Body Christians should *be filled* into the total fullness of God (3.19), *attain* the fullness of Christ (4.13) *be filled* with the Spirit (5.18); but they make no contribution to the 'fulfilling' of Christ.

Is it possible to achieve an unambiguous interpretation of πληρουμένου? This present participle in the Middle Voice could have an active or passive sense. De la Potterie proceeds from the observation that there is no Middle form to be found in the whole of the NT, and consequently supports a passive interpretation. Attempts to achieve such an interpretation were repeatedly made in divers ways: the Church is the fullness which (increasingly) is filled by Christ in every respect;[37] or the Church is filled by God's activity (in his work of salvation) (Hermans – Geysels*); or Christ, the Head of the Church, is the fullness of God, filled by him increasingly in everything (W. L. Knox).[38] De la Potterie* (512–20) understands the genitive (with Hermans – Geysels) as a neuter and makes it refer to the Church: Christ is the fullness of that which is fulfilled in everything and in every way, namely the Church, his Body. But the transition from ἐκκλησία to this neuter would be extremely harsh and the content of the statement, although conceivable for the Church as a progressive process (cf. 3.19; 4.15) seems to refer more appropriately to Christ in so far as we can take the verb in an active sense. But this is in no way impossible as J. Schmid has already established.[39] The interchanging of Active and Middle can be observed in many places in Koiné Greek.[40] De la Potterie's construction that τὸ πλήρωμα refers to αὐτόν (= Christ) in v. 22 is certainly possible but is not easily understandable. The interpretation which predominates in more recent exegesis – that the Church is the fullness of him who fills all in all, namely of Christ – correctly grasps the point of the meaning which in v. 23 no longer focusses primarily on Christ but on the Church (cf. v. 19).

Through the last words in v. 23 (τὰ πάντα ἐν πᾶσιν) the Church is included in the scope of the cosmic vision that Christ rules over the universe. In Eph.

---

[35]Cf. Pr-Bauer 1333 f.; Liddell and Scott 1420; G. Delling TDNT VI, 298.

[36]Chrysostom, Oecumenius, Theophylactus, Ambrosiaster, Aquinas, Calvin, Beza, Estius, H. J. Holtzmann, Ewald, B. Weiß and others, mostly recently Overfield* 393 interpret it in the sense of 'completion'. Cf. Schmid, *Epheserbrief* 187 ff.; on the Latin Fathers, see the apparatus in Frede, *Ep ad Eph.* 46–8; also the discussion in Ernst, *Pleroma* 108–11.

[37]Cf. Benoit, *Leib* 277 f., Feuillet,* Yates.*

[38]Cf. the discussion by de la Potterie* 507–12; W. L. Knox, *St Paul and the Church of the Gentiles*, Cambridge 1939, 164 and 186.

[39]*Epheserbrief* 190–2. Most old translations and interpreters take the verb-form as passive; exceptions are Peschitta, Theodoret (MPG 82, 517), Oecumenius (MPG 118,1185B), Fulgentius of Ruspe. Cf. de la Potterie* 504 f.

[40]Cf. Rademacher 148; Bl-Debr §316 (under 2, Eph. 1.23 is interpreted as active); Moulton – Turner, *Grammar* III, 54–6.

4.10 we have another relation between 'to fill' and the 'universe', this time with an unambiguous meaning: Christ who ascends on high should 'fill the universe'. The spatial category also, the 'ascending over all the heavens' corresponds with our passage (ὑπεράνω only in 1.21 and 4.10). Hence this interpretation of the Genitive combination seems reasonable: the Church is the pleroma of the Christ who fills the universe in everything. Perhaps there is in the Middle form a hint of a deeper concern and effort on the part of the one who acts: it is an emphatic, deliberate action.[41] Christ, who fills the universe in everything (probably neuter) and desires to fill it more intensely, fills the Church in a special way so that it becomes his pleroma. The apparently 'spatial' filling is in reality a dynamic one, in a majestic activity over against the principalities and powers (1.21) and in a merciful manner with regard to the Church (1.23; cf. 4.13, 15 f.).[42] But what does it mean to describe the Church as the pleroma of Christ? Nowhere is the universe called pleroma, just as vice versa the Church is never identified with the universe. The *'whole* fullness' of divine reality dwells in Christ (Col. 1.19; 2.9) and we should be so 'filled' that we achieve the 'total fullness of God' (Eph. 3.19). Hence it is too little to ascribe only a representative function to the Church as the 'fullness of Christ'.[43] As she, as Christ's Body, grows up into Christ, her Head (4.15 f.), so she strives towards the full measure of the fullness of Christ (4.13). It is therefore a dynamic process: God's fullness has established itself in Christ in all its density and power, and through our connection with Christ we are drawn into this fullness so that we, too, are 'filled' with God's fullness and taken up in it. Seen thus, the Church is that place of Christ's 'filling' in which his power to bless becomes effective and mighty, that place where 'the fullness of Christ has established itself and is present' (Schlier 99).

Only if we proceed from this interpretation taken from Eph. itself can we give a meaningful answer to the question, which has often been discussed, as to where the background and base for this pleroma-concept is to be found. In fact there are many different types of literature and philosophic movements in which this concept plays a part, especially Gnosticism, Jewish Hellenism and Stoic philosophy.

(a)   The concept is to be found particularly in Valentinian Gnosis. Pleroma is the totality of the aeons, the higher, spiritual world from which the lower, earthly world has descended through the fall of the aeons. Ascent into the Pleroma, which is only possible for the Gnostics (Spirituals), means redemption and perfection.[44] The descent-ascent scheme is significant for Eph. as a categorical framework (cf. 4.8–10); but the Gnostic concept of the Pleroma differs substantially from the deutero-Pauline. It appears that in the Gnostic view God himself is not included in the Pleroma but as 'Father of the Universe' or 'Founding Father' has sent forth the Pleroma from himself.[45] The Gnostic concept of the Pleroma serves the redemption of the individual, which takes place through the ascent into the Pleroma. In *Ev Veritatis* the

---

[41]Cf. Mayser II/I.107–9: the 'dynamic medium'. On Eph. 1.23 cf. also Howard* 351 f.

[42]On the two aspects v. Gewieß, FS M. Meinertz 137–99; cf. also Hegermann, *Schöpfungsmittler* 152.

[43]Thus Lindemann, *Aufhebung der Zeit* 217, with an emphatic rejection of the wider interpretation.

[44]Cf. e.g. in Ptolemy's system: 'The Pneumatics discard the soul, become intelligible pneumata and enter into the Pleroma without being detained or seen . . .' (Irenaeus, Haeres I, 7.1 – Harvey 1.59).

[45]Cf. G. Delling, TDNT VI, 300.

Pleroma descends upon the Gnostic as a Word to complete what he lacks (35.1–36.10). In mythical form the aeons are Pleromata or have each their own Pleroma, the 'pair-members'.[46] There is no trace of any such mythicizing in Eph. There is a closer relationship with the Odes of Solomon, in which the Redeemer is called 'the Pleroma of the aeons and their Father' (7.11), appears in the 'fullness' of his Father (41.13) and makes it possible for the redeemed to find their way into the Pleroma through gnosis (7.13; 35.6; 36.6).[47] But the major idea in Gnosticism of a heavenly Pleroma of the aeons into which the Gnostic returns[48] has left no trace in Eph.

(b) The position is different in Hellenistic Judaism which, proceeding from Jewish Wisdom-speculation, sees the world totally filled by God, his being and action. Hence Philo states: 'God has filled and pervaded everything, he has left nothing empty and unfilled by himself' (Leg All III.4; cf. I.44; Det. Pot. Ins. 153). But the Logos, too, is totally 'filled with incorporeal powers', 'completely filled' by God (Somn I, 62.75), and if we consider its function in the Philonic system as a bridge between God and the world, between the transcendence and immanence of God, there emerges an analogy with the activity of Christ who fills the universe out of the power of God. In Eph, to be sure, such statements relate not to Creation but to the redeemed world. Hence this, too, does not fully explain the terse expression.[49]

(c) Stoic philosophy regarded the cosmos as being completely pervaded and filled by God as is expressed in the formula: the One (God) is everything, and everything is the One.[50] Its texts seem to have a close terminological relationship to the linguistic usage of (Col. and) Eph.; but the stoic pantheism is in its thought far removed from Eph. The universe does *not* become identical with him who fills it, but remains subject to him as its Head. The Church, too, as the 'Fullness of Christ' remains differentiated from him in spite of her close connection with Christ, her Head. Only perhaps for Philo can we assume an influence of stoic cosmology, and he refined it through the biblical views on God and the Creation. A connecting of the Stoic Universe/One view and the Gnostic Pleroma-concept is also scarcely conceivable because in Gnosticism the one cosmos is dualistically broken apart.[51] Hence it is scarcely possible to posit a single derivation for the language.

Wherever the linguistic key to the strange style of expression in Eph. 1.23 may lie, in its thinking the conception arises that Christ as ruler penetrates every part of the universe (ἐν πᾶσιν)[52] and at the same time finds in the Church his 'fullness', the beneficent sphere of his rule. How then are we to see the relationship between Church and cosmos? Certainly not as existing alongside one another in an unrelated way since the Church *is* in the

---

[46]Apocryphon of John (*Die Drei Versionen des Apokryphon des Johannes im Koptischen Museum zu Alt-Kairo*, ed. by M. Krause and P. Labib, Wiesbaden 1962), II, 9.19–21 (p. 134); 20.19–24 (p. 164); 22.7 (p. 169) and others; Ev Veritatis 41.15 ff.; cf. Cl Al Exc Theod. 32.1; 33.1.

[47]Cf. Schlier 98 f.

[48]Cf. also Apocryphon of John II, 9.19–21; 20.19–24; 22.7 etc.; Rheg (NHC I.3) 46.35 f.

[49]Cf. G. Delling TDNT VI, 288 f.; Colpe, *Leib-Christi-Vorstellung* 179–82; Ernst, *Pleroma* 30–6.

[50]Cf. the texts from Hermetic literature and Stoic philosophy in Dupont, *Gnosis* 454–68; Benoit, *Leib* 272. On the concept ἐν τὸ πᾶν and its history cf. V. van Zutphen, *Studies on the Hymn in Romans 11.33†6* (Diss Würzburg 1972) 87–121. – A propinquity to Stoic philosophy is postulated by Dupont, *Gnosis* 453–76; Benoit, *Leib* 271 ff.; cf. also Ernst, *Pleroma* 117 and 119.

[51]Ernst, *Pleroma* 117 and 120 (final opinion) seems to incline to this view.

[52]Schlier 99 would like to understand ἐν πᾶσιν as masculine and interpret it as meaning the individual members of the Church (as in 4.6). But this interpretation is not indicated for 1.23. Cf. Ernst, *Pleroma* 112–14.

world, wrestles in the world with the powers hostile to God (6.12 f.) and grows out of it to Christ, her Head (4.15 f.). We can describe them metaphorically as two concentric circles of which the inner represents the Church and the outer the cosmos, both ruled by Christ even if in different ways. The border between cosmos and Church is not solid and rigid but is dynamic: the Church should increasingly expand and take possession of the cosmos in an intensive rather than extensive manner.[53] For her growth takes place in inner strengthening, especially in love (4.15) which is the divine principle working against the powers of the ungodly. To the extent that the Church through the Gospel inwardly wins back humanity alienated from God and formerly enslaved by the 'powers', she reveals to the ungodly powers God's manifold wisdom (cf. 3.10) and deprivation of their own power. Hence the Church is the representative of the non-violent and yet powerful rule of Christ, but still more: she is a power which pervades and transforms the world – if she convincingly communicates to the world the effective healing-power of Christ within her – i.e. convinces by her own unity and love (cf. 4.12–14). Does the Church thereby become the organ or instrument of Christ's cosmic rule? Only if and only so far as her influence in love is effective (cf. 4.15). In the context of 1.17–23 the view of the Church as the Body and Fullness of Christ is intended only to make one thing clear to the addressees that, through their incorporation into the Church they have been put under the total beneficent rule of Christ whose victory over the powers of darkness is certain.

Summary

In the epistolary thanksgiving which the author adds to the great Eulogy, he praises the recipients for their faith and love 'toward all the saints' (1.15–16), but also gives them to understand, in the form of an intercession, that they must achieve greater insight and a deeper faith (1.17–19). To lead them to a Christian understanding of themselves as bound to God and with a home in heaven he holds up before their eyes the salvation and hope God has bestowed upon them in his work of redemption. Therewith he picks up again the line of thought brought home to the addressees in 1.13 f. and clarifies it in a twofold respect: In Jesus Christ, in his Resurrection and heavenly Enthronement, God has overcome the powers of evil and also guaranteed Christians victory in their earthly battle (1.20–22a). Christians participate in Christ's rule through their membership of the Church; for God has given Jesus Christ, to whom the universe is subjugated, to be Head of the Church. As his 'Body' she is bound up with Christ in a special way; his powers to bless and save pour into her (1.22b–3). God's mighty works are of benefit to believers (v. 19). The state of belief is described as a state of hope, but not (as in Paul) in the sense of a tense, eschatological expectation but as a looking upward, to where the heavenly inheritance lies ready ('among the saints'). This lends these (and also the further) remarks an 'other-worldly' tension, which makes us

---

[53]Cf. Wagenführer, *Bedeutung Christi* 75–7, 117 f. (makes too sharp a distinction); Warnach, *Kirche und Kosmos*; Schnackenburg, *Gestalt und Wesen* 281–6; Ernst, *Pleroma* 152–4; 169–72.

uncomfortable today in our understanding of the world and our existence. But the picture of heavens one above the other and Christ's throne 'above' the powers of evil is simply an attempt to express in a mythical way of speaking the transcendence of God and the superiority of his might. God's world expressed in spatial categories can also be experienced and understood by contemporary humanity who reflect upon their existence as 'depths' and 'source' of being. Christ's superiority over the powers of evil is, to be sure, certain only to the believing Christian who accepts the early Christian confession: God has raised the Crucified from the dead and set him at his right hand. This early Christian creed is here taken for granted and made to serve the Christian understanding of existence. The Pauline theology of the Cross, however, in which we are made continually aware of the unsolved earthly afflictions and sufferings, fades into the background. But the author wishes first to strengthen the certainty that in Christ we are superior to all that is dark, evil and degrading.

The powers of evil which appear massively in the enumeration at 1.21 belong likewise to mythical thinking. Under the depressing experience of evil and suffering in the world, all that is threatening, sinister or inexplicable is understood as an effective power and named in its various forms with different names. In comparison with Jewish apocalyptic, however, Eph. displays notable material differences in spite of a strong apparent resemblance. The enumeration is only illustrative; the dualistic differentiation between 'this present' and the 'coming' age is certainly retained rhetorically, but in reality it has been overtaken; through Christ the transition of the ages has been accomplished and the power of evil broken. Although the mythical way of speaking is no longer acceptable to us, it can still warn against a playing-down of evil and sharpen our view for this unsolved problem of human existence.

The 'all things' which comes into sight at the end as already in 1.10 is not to be equated with our universe as the visible, ascertainable, explorable world. It also includes the metaphysical area which is disclosed and imposes itself on the human spirit in the contemplation of the world and its history. Christ, who 'fills the universe in everything' is no external world-ruler, but he who, hidden in the power of God, leads what happens in the world to its goal. Hence the 'principalities and powers' also belong to the universe because they symbolize and represent the spiritual forces secretly active in the world. In so far as they are capable of bringing disaster and destruction upon humankind, when seen from the standpoint of faith they are stripped of their power by Christ, the resurrected one, and must be repelled by the Church in the world. The tension between Christ's victory 'in heaven' and the continuing struggle on earth is made clear impressively in the final section 6.10–17 which to a certain degree corresponds to our section 1.20–23.

From this point of view the Church is the sphere of the beneficent activity of Jesus Christ and of his influence upon the world. In her Christ can and will exercise his 'lordship' – which is nothing other than liberation from the power of evil and the introduction of unity, love and peace – and through her extend over the world. For the moment this has a purely programmatic ring but it will become clearer as the letter continues. If the

Church is the community of the saved which God intended, Christian existence is bound to her in the closest possible way. The Church is more than a worldly manifestation and earthly institution. She achieves her standing as significant for salvation through her relationship with Christ, but even then only if she 'witness to the truth in love' (4.15). Only in this way will she become an instrument of Christ's saving activity in the world.

4. ADDRESS TO THE READERS ON THEIR CONVERSION TO CHRISTIANITY AND THEIR NEW LIFE (2.1–10)

Literature

Tachau, *'Einst' und 'Jetzt'* 134–43.

M. Legido López, 'La Iglesia entre la communión y la tentación. Análisis exégetico en torno a Ef. 2.5–7', Salm. 18 (1971) 205–32.

D. M. Lloyd-Jones, *God's Way of Reconciliation: Studies in Eph. 2*, London 1972.

F. Mußner, 'Eph. 2 als ökumenisches Modell', in *NT und Kirche* (FS R. Schnackenburg), Freiburg i. Breisgau, 1974, 325–36.

Halter, *Taufe* 233–42.

L. Ramaroson, 'Une lecture de Éph. 1.15–2.10 (en lisant ἠλέησεν en Eph. 2.4c)', Bib. 58 (1977) 388–410.

U. Luz, 'Rechtfertigung bei den Paulusschülern', in *Rechtfertigung* (FS E. Käsemann), Tübingen-Göttingen 1976, 365–83, particularly 369–75.

1   You, too, who were dead through your trespasses and sins
2   in which you lived according to the age of this world,
    according to the ruler who exerts his might in the
        sphere of the air,
    that spirit which is active now in the Sons of
        Disobedience,
3 – among them we, too, all once lived in carnal lusts and
        the desire of the flesh
        and mind filled us.
    Thus we were by nature Children of Wrath like the rest.
4 But God, who is rich in mercy,
    because of the great love
    with which he loved us
5 even us, who were dead through our trespasses,
    made alive together with Christ
    – you are saved by grace –
6   and he raised us from the dead
    and set us in heaven in Christ Jesus,
7 that in the ages to come he may show the overflowing
    richness of his grace in goodness towards us
    in Jesus Christ.
8 For you are saved by Grace through faith;
    and this does not arise from you but is God's gift,
9   not from works, that no one should praise himself.

10 For we are his creatures, created in Christ Jesus
    for good works, which God has prepared before
        so that we should live our lives in them.

Analysis

The section 2.1–10 could be said to be the start of the main corpus of the letter after the conventional section of 'thanksgiving' for the recipients (1.15–23). The fact that the theme of the 'Church', which is the author's main theological concern, has been touched upon in v. 23 makes this seem even more obvious. But this theme is not followed up in 2.1–10, and a closer examination reveals that this section is very closely connected with the preceding one – indeed provides a necessary expansion.[1] This can be seen from the following:

(a) Just as in the Great Eulogy the salvation event (1.10 f.) was shown to apply to the addressees (1.13 f.) so the section 2.1–10 signifies an 'application' and making relevant for the readers of the rule of Christ described in the preceding section. The two corresponding passages are introduced by καὶ ὑμεῖς (1.13) – καὶ ὑμᾶς (2.1).

(b) Syntactically the opening of 2.1 – 'you, who were dead through your trespasses and sins' – is continued in v. 5 after an anacoluthon, where ὄντας ἡμᾶς νεκρούς might be a resumption, albeit in the first person.[2] The long intervening section expounds on the 'deadly' situation the Gentile Christians are in because of their sins under the rule of the ungodly ruler of the world (v. 2) and on the similar situation in which 'we all' were once to be found (v. 3). This explains the change from the second to the first person plural.

(c) The key-phrases in vv. 5–6, which describe the change from adversity to salvation, are connected in the closest way possible to what God has done in Christ (1.20): He has 'made us alive with Christ' (v. 5) and more explicitly 'raised us from the dead and set us in heaven in Christ Jesus' (v. 6). The formulations using composite verbs with συν – take up the statements about Christ in a way which is unmistakeable.

(d) It is also possible that the expression 'in the ages to come' (v. 7) is influenced by the formulation 'not only in this age but also in that which is to come' (1.21). Although we recognised this as a formula, it is possible that the author was led thereby to use this unique form of expression for the future which is still to come.

(e) If we compare this with the Thanksgiving-sections in the Pauline epistles where frequently towards the end there is a looking forward to the eschaton,[3] it is possible that the ἵνα – clause in v. 7 takes on this function

---

[1] Most interpreters separate 2.1–10 from 1.15–23 according to theme. Ramaroson* is right in seeing that they belong together, but his exegesis does not do much to support this view (cf. on 2.5).

[2] Ramaroson* 391 thinks differently: the two objects in v. 1 and v. 5 are 'strictly parallel' i.e. 'you, too' (the Gentile Christians) is to be taken with 'even us' (the Jewish Christians) as the objects of ἠλέησεν in v. 4 (he considers this reading to be the correct one).

[3] Cf. 1 Thess. 1.10; 1 Cor. 1.8; Phil. 1.10; on this see Sanders, 'The Transition from Opening Epistolary Thanksgiving to Body in the Letters of the Pauline Corpus', JBL 81 (1962) 348–62, here 355–7.

here. The out-look of the author of Eph. is characteristically directed to the heavenly sphere: If we interpret v. 7 thus, the 'eschatological' motif would then come to bear at least in a weakened form.

Even if the last two points remain uncertain, the close connection between this passage and the preceding one cannot be doubted. But let us attempt a closer analysis! The syntactical analysis of this passage is made more difficult by the repeated change in the personal pronouns in the second and first person plural (ὑμεῖς – ἡμεῖς). The author begins by addressing the readers ('You, too, who were dead . . .') and clearly wants to proceed: 'You God has made alive with Christ' (v. 5). But in between the thought of the 'trespasses and sins' causes a digression, a look back (ποτέ) to the time when the readers were still completely caught up in an iniquitous lifestyle. Their heathenish way of life under the rule of ungodly powers – represented by 'age of this world' and 'leader of the might of the sphere of the air' – is connected by a relative clause (v. 2). This is a thing of the past for the addressees, but for unbelievers, the 'Sons of Disobedience', it is still present (νῦν). Diverted by this idea from how he intended to continue – to contrast their earlier way of life with their present status of being saved (cf. 2.11, 13; 5.8: ποτέ – νῦν) – the author expounds at greater length in v. 3 on the disastrous situation in which 'we all' once passed our lives in sinful desires and acts. Behind this stands the schema, so significant for the early Christian proclamation and (baptismal) paraclesis, of 'then and now'[4] which strongly defined the change which came into being for Christians through God's merciful intervention in their conversion and baptism. Thus we understand the new beginning at v. 4 which compares human error and their lost state (δε) pointedly with God's mercy and love. Because of the change to the first person, the author continues with 'we': God has made alive with Christ 'us, who were dead through our trespasses' (v. 5). In so doing he has come back to the line of thought begun in v. 1, but because of the thoughts which intervene he includes the recipients in the general Christian 'we'. But the parenthetically inserted cry 'you are saved by grace!' shows that he is still thinking of them especially.

This could bring this particular line of thought to a conclusion; but the author continues immediately on the subject of Christ (cf. 1.20), co-ordinating the next statements by using καί twice: 'and he has raised (us) from the dead and set us in heaven in Christ Jesus' (v. 6). The co-ordination of the two indicatives with συνεζωοποίησεν signifies a clarification and continuation of the idea under another aspect. The ἐν Χριστῷ 'Ιησοῦ which comes at the end raises the whole series of events – as in the Eulogy – into the sphere of the salvation in Christ planned and inaugurated by God. This event has not only become real for Christians at the present time but should prove itself ever more effective in its overflowing richness 'in the ages to come' (v. 7). This extended perspective is pointedly included in the divine plan for and execution of salvation by the final clause (ἵνα): God himself will reveal his abundant grace and goodness

---

[4]Cf. Tachau; *further Steinmetz, *Heils-Zuversicht* 53–9 which establishes at the end: 'νῦν – ποτέ in the end indicate human ways of living. Behind this is a schema in which spheres of influence are compared' (59).

towards us 'in Christ Jesus' – as is again added at the conclusion. The event brought about in Christ through God's power, detailed in 1.20 f., thus finds its fulfilment in us, the believers (cf. 1.19). It is now easier to see why the author went over from 'you' to 'we': it is the common experience of all who have espoused the Christian faith.

But the author has not forgotten his original intention in this section – i.e. to show how this applies to the addressees (2.1). In v. 8 he returns to the use of the second person. There he takes up the interruption in v. 5, where the stress was on the merciful initiative taken in salvation by God. Now he repeats the assertion but adds 'through faith' and thereby confirms that his gaze is again directed at the recipients (cf. 1.13). Nevertheless it is not his intention to acknowledge their efforts but to insist on the unmerited mercy of the whole event. Hence with καὶ τοῦτο ('and even this')[5] he stresses that it is God's gift, and adds in a negative sense, with an echo of the Pauline antithesis, 'not from works, that no one should praise himself' (v. 9). God's absolute pre-eminence is so important for him that he once again explains: 'for we are *his* creatures . . .'. The recent transition to the First Person Plural thereby is seen as emphatic. It is as if he wants to re-introduce the recipients to the common Christian conviction and experience, which certainly knows 'good works' (cf. Col. 1.10) but recognizes them as only made possible and ensured by God's action. With a Past Participle connected to ποίημα he adds that we are 'created' (by God) in Christ Jesus 'for good works'. These he describes in a Relative Clause as those which God has 'prepared' for us to perform in our lives (v. 10) – an unusual outlook which in its basic tendency reminds us of Paul and yet which differs from him linguistically ('good works') and conceptually ('prepared' works).

What does the author hope to achieve in his readers by this? Two objectives emerge more clearly than in the Great Eulogy. In the first place he wants to make them even more conscious of their merciful election by God from the vile background of their heathen past (vv. 1–2) as is underlined in the double use of 'you are saved by grace'. They should beware of false pride (in 'good works') and vain praise (v. 9). Therewith they are already prepared for an examination of their relationship to the Jewish-Christians (cf. 2.11–18). Second, he wants to bind them more closely in the fellowship of the Church through the change from 'you' to 'we'. All that they are in their present Christians existence they owe to their acceptance into the Church which God has planned and created as the sphere of salvation filled with Christ's power to bless (1.23). This also leads in to the following section in which the Church (made up of Jews and Gentiles) is recognisable as a factor in salvation (2.15–18) and is then clearly described as God's building in the Spirit (2.20–2). This section likewise prepares for the statement that the addressees are 'built' into the construction (2.20).

[5]Cf. Pr - Bauer 1183 under b, γ.

Exegesis

1

When he turns to speak to the addressees (καὶ ὑμᾶς) the author does not intend to set them apart from the people named earlier (1.19) or those Christians ('we') who later are brought to the forefront (2.3, 5) but rather deliberately to include them in the community of all believers. Since they lie so far apart and because of the clauses which lie between them we cannot consider the 'you' (v. 1) and the 'we' (v. 5) as the two groups which God has 'made alive together' through Christ and thus united.[6]

In a similar fashion as in 1.13 (καὶ ὑμεῖς), what God has achieved for humanity through the raising of Jesus from the dead, his investiture in authority over the powers and his appointment as Head of the Church, is now shown to apply to the addressees: they, too, are caught up by his merciful saving acts. God's mercy (v. 4) took hold of them in a situation where they could only be described as 'dead' because of their misdemeanours and sins. 'Trespasses' and 'sins' make up a double expression which through the use of synonymous terms makes us more forcefully aware of human error. Perhaps these words were those prevalent in the early Christian catachesis (cf. Rom. 4.25; Eph. 1.7).[7] It was an 'unregenerate' life, a 'deathly' situation, where they had no hope, were far from God (cf. 2.12) alienated from the life of God (4.18). The Pauline idea of the power of death ruling because of sin, which delivers humanity to God's condemning judgment (cf. Rom. 5.12, 17 f. 21; 7.5 et al.) is retained only in a weakened form. The 'deadness' becomes rather a characteristic of a 'heathenish' existence which has no deeper meaning, is culpably entangled and is hopelessly dismal (cf. 4.17 ff.). Such a metaphorical use of 'dead' is found elsewhere,[8] but in the NT it is always applied to an existence unregenerate before God (cf. Mt. 8.22/Lk. 15.24, 32; Rev. 3.1). The author of Eph. has taken over this expression from Col. 2.12 f. but it was also found in the liturgy (cf. 5.14).

2

The intolerable situation in which the addressees once found themselves is now more closely described by the author as a way of life exposed to and ruled by an ungodly power. Instead of listing many separate and yet combined forces of evil as in 1.21, he now speaks of a single evil 'age' or a 'ruler' who determines what humankind will do (κατά for the entity which sets the standards) and bends them to his will. This change to the singular confirms that the earlier enumeration was intended simply to depict the

---

[6] Against Ramaroson* 391 f. (v. n. 2).

[7] Cf. also Mk. 11.25 f.; Mt. 6.14 f.; Did. 4.3; Barn. 19.4. In Paul the concept (in the singular) has a more strongly theological sense as a counter-part to χάρισμα (Rom. 5.15–20). Eph. possibly chose this concept through the influence of Col. 2.13. (Cf. W. Michaelis, TDNT VI, 171 ff.

[8] Cf. R. Bultmann, TDNT IV, 892; K. G. Kuhn, NTS 7, 343 f., who points to Ps. Sal 16.1–4 and especially to 1 QH. 3.19 ff.: 'I praise you, Lord, that you have redeemed my soul from corruption to everlasting elevation . . .'.

abundance and variety of ungodly influences and here a 'mythical' language is being used to portray the constrained, powerless circumstances of unredeemed humanity bound up with the Evil One. The relevance for the addressees of what is theologically described as Christ's cosmic-universal victory, which has already taken place, is now shown more clearly: it means that their earlier state has been overcome through the merciful love of God.

Hence the closer characterization of the Evil, in whose 'atmosphere' the addressees once lived, has no great significance. The author conforms to the ideas of his time: The 'Aeon', here portrayed as a subject who acts and determines the heathen way of life – i.e. personified –[9] is characterized by the additional (explanatory) Genitive 'of this world' in his area of influence just as the 'ruler' is by the closer definition 'power (sphere) of the air'. Behind this lies a concept of the world which assigns the lower regions of heaven to the earth, the *Lebensraum* of humanity, and separates this from the 'upper' heavens, the sphere of God. In this intermediate area between earth and heaven all those powers and forces which rebel against God and tempt humanity have their abode and sphere of influence.[10] The mythical, metaphorical language in the end only points to the mysterious phenomenon of an evil fate which hangs over each individual, limiting and dominating his/her freedom of action. The whole way of looking at things is focussed on humanity's way of life (περιπατεῖν)[11] which for Christians

---

[9]Because of the parallelism with the 'ruler who exerts his might in the sphere of the air' we cannot doubt the personification or, better, demonification of the aeon-concept. The concept which in both places follows in the Genitive should be understood as the area ruled by the 'aeon'/'archon': 'this world'/'sphere of the air'. This spatial – temporal dimension of the 'aeons'/'worlds', like their personification (with additional characterizing terms) can be met frequently in very different forms in Gnosis, and this has now been confirmed by the Nag Hammadi texts. In the 'Apocalypse of Adam' (NHC V/5) it says e.g. of Adam and Eve after the Fall: 'Then God, the archon of the aeons and powers, cut us off in his anger. Then we became two aeons and the glory which was in our hearts left us. . . .' (64.20–6 [Foerster, *Gnosis* II, 21]); or in the 'Nature of the Archons' (NHC II/4) that Noah was warned by the ruler (archon) of the powers (92.8–10 ibid 57 f.). Cf. Jonas, *Gnosis* I, 98–100; H. Sasse, TDNT I, 198, 207; RAC I, 193–204; Schlier 102; Rudolph, *Gnosis* 75–7; 132–4 et al. – Objectively the expressions are to be understood much like the 'God of this aeon' (2 Cor 4.4) or 'ruler of this world' (Jn. 12.31; 14.30; 16.11).

[10]There is an abundance of material from the Greek and Jewish world in Schlier 103 f. Especially significant is the (Christian) Asc Jes (Hennecke [3]II, 454–68) because here we see how Jewish ideas were taken over and developed in a Christian way. The area of the air reaches to the first heaven (the firmament) (7.13) and is the sphere of the evil forces, cf. 7.9; 9.14 ('God of that world'); 10.10, 12 ('the prince and his angels and the gods of this world'); 11.23 ('all the angels of the firmament and Satan'). As an example from the Nag Hammadi texts: In the document 'Noēma' (perception of our great power, NHC VI/4) it is said of water: 'It blows in the air where the gods and angels are and he who is raised above all things' (37.10 ff. [K. M. Fischer, ThLZ 98, 171]). This conception of the world was at that time widespread and was not only limited to Gnosticism (with its ascent of the soul). Instead of the 'aeons', 'archons' etc. in Gnosis, in Judaism and Christianity we find angels. Cf. also Gnilka 64–6.

[11]In Paul and in the epistles influenced by him (apart from the Pastorals) περιπατεῖν is usual in the sense of an ethical way of life grounded on faith. Such a figurative way of speaking is not to be found in secular Greek and must be derived from Jewish thought (cf. LXX and other translations of the OT), cf. H. Seesemann – G. Bertram, TDNT V, 940–5. But since the Qumran material has come on the scene we are more clearly aware of the 'way'

has changed from the compulsion to sin (2.1 f.) to the freedom to do good (2.10; cf. 4.1, 17; 5.2, 8). The power of evil is active now in the 'Sons of Disobedience', a semitizing expression which characterizes such people as shut off and rejecting the 'Word of truth, the Gospel of Salvation' (cf. 1.13). The author makes use of it once again in the paraclesis (5.6) in the context of heathen fellow-citizens of the addressees who tempt the Christians with 'empty words' and immoral behaviour and draw God's wrath upon themselves. The close similarity of the expressions (cf. 'Children of Wrath' 2.3) points to the same group of people. God in his mercy has torn them from that race which has become subject to the force of evil and God's wrathful judgement, to which the addressees also once belonged (cf. 2.4 f.). It is a separation similar to that which the Qumran Essenes describe with like expressions under different premises (observation of the Torah). All who do not belong to the chosen 'Sons of Light' are 'Sons of Darkness' (1 QS. 1.10; 1 QM. 1.1, 7, 16; 3.16 et al.) 'Sons of Injustice' (1 QS 3.21; 1 QH. 5.8), 'Sons of Disaster' (1 QH. 5.25), 'Sons of Sin' (1 QH. 6.30; 7.11), 'Sons of Corruption' (Damasc 6.15; 13.14). The idea, which stems from the OT, of the 'disobedient' people of God (as in Paul, Rom. 10.21; cf. 2.8; 11.31; 15.31) is transferred in Eph. to the heathen world which declines God's offer of salvation.

3

Since this is his view it is unlikely that the author in using 'we'[12] means to refer to the Jewish-Christians (among whom he would include himself) in the congregation. Rather he wants to show the addressees that 'we *all*' who belong to the redeemed community of Jesus Christ were once in the same disastrous predicament. The 'like the rest' which comes at the end of the verse is once again a reminder of the rest of humanity, the heathen world. *All* Christians in the past had a life-style (ἀναστρέφω) shaped by the 'desires of the flesh' and in 4.22 the addressees (ὑμεις) are exhorted to discard their old personality 'which was in accordance with your earlier way of life' (ἀναστροφή). The correspondance of the two passages shows clearly that in each case, be it in the vocative or in the inclusive 'we', the same persons are meant: those who have been saved by God in Christ Jesus. The expansion of the idea in v. 2 to 'we all' simply serves the purpose of including the Gentile-Christians addressed in the larger community of the redeemed who have all experienced the same transition from a once wretched situation to the present position of redemption and hope in Christ Jesus.

     In his depiction of enslavement to sin and guilt, the author still uses Pauline expressions. The 'desires of the flesh' (cf. Gal 5.16, 24; Rom. 13.14) lead to the *performance* of sinful works which bring about death (cf. Rom. 7.5, 28; 8.5). Yet it is notable that neither 'Sin' nor 'Death' appear as

terminology, also in a figurative sense, cf. Nötscher, *Gotteswege und Menschenwege* 83 f.; (for the NT:) 112–17; Wibbing, *Tugend- und Lasterkataloge* 33–42; 61–4; G. Ebel, ThBNT II/2, 1363–1365.

   [12]The reading ὑμεῖς in A*D*81pc is secondary, since it is clearly an attempt to bring it into line with v. 1.

in Paul as a personified power. Eph. 2.1, 5 speaks like Col. 2.13 only of 'being dead' through 'trespasses'. By the desires (θελήματα) of the flesh and of the mind (διάνοιαι) the author means principally but not exclusively the unbridled sexual desires and behaviour as is put forward in the list of vices in 5.3–5, a register of typical 'heathen' sins (v. there).

Through such activity and behaviour all were 'by nature Children of Wrath', people upon whom 'the wrath of God comes' as again 5.6 makes clear. The expression which later became dominant in the Doctrine of Original Sin[13] is explained in the context for the moment by its correspondance to 'Sons of Disobedience' (v. 2). The author retains the eschatological motif of God's wrathful judgement (cf. 1 Thess. 1.10) and does not understand it as sometimes in Paul (Rom. 1.18–31) as a judgment already present and revealing itself, although he also does not emphasize that it lies in the future. It is enough for him to establish that such people are subject to God's wrath. But why are they Children of Wrath 'by nature'? The phrase does not allow any protological speculations (divine punishment because of original sin) or anthropological reflections (on the natural predisposition of such people) but refers to the natural state in which such people found or still find themselves. It is the same nature which is attributed to the heathen in Wis. 13.1 because of their inadequate recognition of God and their worship of idols: they are 'foolish by nature'. In a similar fashion the author of Eph. (without the phrase 'by nature') says of the heathen that they lead their lives 'in the triviality of their mind (νοῦς), darkened in the understanding (διάνοια)' (4.17 f.). He uses the expression in a similarly untheological way as does Paul in Rom. 2.14, where the apostle speaks – admittedly in a positive sense – of the 'natural' disposition to moral behaviour. The same semantic field in Eph. 2.3; 4.17 f.; 5.6 leaves no room for doubt that the author is thinking of a heathen life-style – i.e. with 'we all' he means the whole, for the most part Gentile-Christian, congregation, even if Jewish-Christians are included.[14]

4

After the longer digression containing the description of the ominous situation the author now introduces the positive (emphasized by δέ) main

---

[13]J. Mehlmann, *Natura Filii Irae. Historia interpretationis Eph 2.3 eiusque cum doctrina de Peccato Originali nexus*, Rome 1957, offers a detailed history of the interpretation of this verse in the patristic period in which it played an important part in the clash with the Pelagians (Augustine, 164–215) and through the Middle Ages (especially Thomas Aquinas). The interpretation of the Reformers is only dealt with briefly, then there is again a more detailed examination of the Council of Trent (503–26). Hence the perspective is an appreciation of the Doctrine of Original Sin committed to the Roman Catholic tradition which the author, in his own interpretation of the passage (607–78) finds to be proved true. But the dogmatic questioning (with all the implications of the Doctrine of Original Sin) overtaxes what the text originally wanted to say. Cf. however Lloyd-Jones* 25–35.

[14]The widespread interpretation as Jewish-Christians is still held by H. Köster TDNT IX, 274 f. He sees in it an express contradiction of the Jewish opinion (Jos Ant IV, 193) that the Jews were freed by the Law from the power of φύσις. But the author of Eph. is only concerned with the change from their former status of being subject to Judgement to their present situation of salvation which they owe to the divine mercy; ὀργή and ἔλεος are *opposita*, cf. Rom. 9.22 f.; 11.30; further G. Stählin, TDNT V, 435.

statement about God's merciful love through which he has redeemed us. God's electing love (1.4 f.) is revealed in the face of our sins as 'rich in mercy' (cf. Tit. 3.5; 1 Pet. 1.3) and makes us, from being 'Children of Wrath', into Sons of God in Jesus Christ (cf. 1.5). Hence it is a merciful redemption (v. 6 and v. 8) which the author certainly sees here in its application and effect on us (cf. v. 5) connected to Baptism, as it Tit. 3.5 and 1 Pet. 1.3. The less-well-attested variant reading – ἠλέησεν, (instead of ἦν ἠγάπησεν) – which makes v. 4 a main clause, certainly gives what is apparently a better connection for v. 5 (καί with further main verbs) but weakens the compact expression that God's love has proved itself for us precisely in our 'dead' situation.[15] God's love to us sinners thereby contains a threefold accent: it is mercy, exceedingly great (πολλή) and directed in its entirety towards us.

5

In this way the content of the clause begun in v. 4, which brings in the motif of divine action, leads to the expression that God 'has made alive together with Christ'. The additional καὶ ὄντας ἡμᾶς κτλ is to be understood against the background of the expositions in vv. 1–3 as a defining statement of contrast: even us, who were dead through our sins, God's love has raised to life. The resumption from v. 1 of καὶ ὑμᾶς ὄντας κτλ also partly explains the καί which causes some difficulty;[16] it serves to give emphasis. Yet we must take into consideration the other position of ὄντας which stresses the condition of the sinners who had declined into death. The aorist on the other hand expresses the change from death to life and possibly (like 'you are sealed' in 1.13) refers to the event of Baptism.[17] This becomes even more certain if we accept Col. 2.12–13, where Baptism is expressly mentioned, as the model for the semantic argumentation. Only in Col. 2.13 in the whole of the NT do we again encounter the composite verb συζωοποιεῖν and what is more in the same apposition to 'dead through sins'. It is true that here the horizons of Col. are crossed (cf. v. 6) but Baptism is also in Eph. the fundamental event in salvation. In Baptism the reception of the Gospel in faith (cf. 1.13a) is confessed with the mouth (cf. Rom. 10.9 f.) salvation is achieved and incorporation into the congregation is accomplished (cf. 4.4 f.). Baptism is for the whole Church the manifestation of divine love in the redemptive act of Jesus Christ (cf. 5.25 f.).

The 'making alive with' does not refer to the union of Christians with one another – be it Gentile- and Jewish-Christians[18] or all Christians

---

[15]Against Ramaroson* 388–92.

[16]Cf. Bl – Debr §153 and the exegesis. For Schlier 108 the καί is to be explained from the idea of the inclusion of the Jews which is still retained or it is comparative (almost a καίπερ)'; Abbott 47, Haupt 58 f., Barth 219 (also interpret it as having an emphatic sense). Others such as Dibelius – Greeven 67, Gaugler 91 f., think it is a re-adoption of the καί of v. 1. – Both may have something to say; for the concessive sense (= καίπερ v. Bl – Debr §425.1.

[17]Cf. Halter* 236 ff., who in n. 14 (p. 627) also mentions some authors who dispute this. The idea that baptismal tradition lies behind this is strengthened by the relationship of Eph. 2.2–8 with Tit 3.3–5 to which Luz* 370 drew attention.

[18]Bengel 759; Schlier 109 as a possible understanding; Barth 220 (with determination!); Ramaroson* 391 f.

in general who have had this experience of salvation[19] – but should be taken with Christ.[20] Paul already used a large number of variations of such verbs compounded with συν to express our joint enacting of the way of Christ in communion with him, from Baptism through the fulfilment of our earthly existence to the eschatological 'joint glorification' with Christ (Rom. 8.17). For him, too, Baptism is the place where we are 'buried' with Christ, 'die' with him in order also 'to live with him' (Rom. 6.4, 8). Col. 2.12 f. transfers the 'raised with him' to the present but keeps the eschatological outlook open (cf. Eph. 3.1–4). Eph. goes a step farther: without referring to the 'dying with him' in Baptism, he directs attention solely to the fact that God 'made (us) alive' with Christ and hence has already raised us from the dead and established us in heaven with Christ.[21] In this context the author is concerned with the salvation already achieved, as the interjected parenthesis 'you are saved by grace' confirms. But the shift in emphasis as compared with Paul, who stresses the ethical demand (Rom. 6.12–14, 15–21) and the eschatological reservation (Rom. 6.8, 22 f.; 8.17) is unmistakeable. In Eph. the presentness of salvation is given all the emphasis.

6

When the author continues 'and he raised us from the dead and set us in heaven' our first impression at least is that this adds nothing new as regards content. These are not other acts of salvation which are attached to the making-alive but simply other aspects which underline our participation in the Christ-event. Why does the author of Eph. add these two expressions to develop what has gone before (the first καί has to be understood in this way)? Because he wants to apply the statements about Christ in 1.20 to us and to communicate them to us in the extension of the divine activity. God has shown his power in Christ and in his merciful love includes us in this Christ-event. What in Col. 2.11–13 is devloped – with a strong christological accent – from the experience of salvation in Baptism appears in Eph. as inclusion in the great divine act of salvation which is channelled towards us through Christ (1.20 f.) and the Church (1.22b–23) and embraces us 'in Christ Jesus'. This theocentric way of describing the process – which again would indicate that 2.1–10 is a logical continuation of 1.19–23 – is entirely in accord with the perspective of the Great Eulogy where God's plan of salvation is also carried out 'in Christ' for our salvation. Hence the concluding 'in Christ Jesus' is not superfluous alongside that which we have experienced 'with Christ'. The formula sets a certain ecclesiological

[19]Lindemann, *Aufhebung der Zeit* 119.
[20]Admittedly this presupposes the reading τῷ Χριστῷ which deserves preference in spite of the good attestation of ἐν τῷ Χριστῷ (P⁴⁶ B 33 a co Vgᶜˡ M Vict Ambst). Lindemann, *Aufhebung der Zeit* 119, n. 80 pleads for the reading ἐν τῷ Χριστῷ. But it can possibly be explained by alignment with 1.10, 12.20 or 2.6. Cf. also Metzger, *Text Comm* 602 (Dittography after the ending –εν?)
[21]Cf. R. Schnackenburg, '"Er hat uns mitauferweckt". Zur Tauflehre des Epheserbriefes', LJ 2 (1952) 159–83, particularly 167–72; R. C. Tannehill, *Dying and Rising with Christ*, 1966 (BZNW 32) 47–54; E. Schweizer, 'Die "Mystik" des Sterbens und Auferstehens mit Christus bei Paulus', in *Beiträge* 183–203; P. Siber, *Mit Christus leben. Eine Studie zur paulinischen Auferstehungshoffnung*, 1971 (AThANT 61); Legido López* 212–15, 216–19.

accent insofar as Christ, to whom we are bound and whose way we re-enact is in 1.22b–23 given prominence as the Head of the Church which is his Body.[22] For this theologian the Church is the comprehensive area of salvation to which our becoming Christian and our existence as Christians are tied.

7

The concluding ἵνα – clause brings the train of thought begun in v. 4, which concentrates on God's mighty merciful act towards us, to its conclusion and climax. Only with difficulty can it be seen in direct connection with our being set in heaven; for 'the overflowing richness of his grace' which he desires to show 'in goodness toward us' reminds us of the expression in v. 4, except that here ἐν ἐλέει is replaced by ἐν χρηστότητι. God's mercy is a liberally dispersed philanthropic goodness.[23] Thus the Final Clause states the purpose of the whole divine salvation-act. But in what shall the 'overflowing' richness of his grace, through which we are already saved (cf. 1.7; 2.5) 'show' itself, be revealed as such? There are two contrasting explanations for the meaning of ἐν τοῖς αἰῶσιν τοῖς ἐπερχομένοις: The first understand the 'ages to come' in a temporal sense as future times; the second as personified beings (cf. 2.2; partly also 3.9).[24] The linguistic use of 'ages' leaves room for both explanations.[25] Let us begin with ἐνδείκνυσθαι.

The verb (in the Middle Voice) means 'show, prove, demonstrate' and also, with the Dative of the person, 'to do something for/to somebody'. The person or thing for whom one does something is given by εἰς or with the Dative, not with ἐν.[26] In Rom. 9.17 (a quotation from Ex. 9.16) and in 1 Tim. 1.16 it has the sense

---

[22]Gnilka 120 takes it differently. He would like to understand the formula 'in Christ Jesus' here as elsewhere simply instrumentally and rejects an ecclesiological interpretation. Legido López* 219 f. thinks it refers to the Church; factually it means the same as in 2.17 (218).

[23]On the Pauline linguistic usage cf. Rom 2.4; 11.22. In Tit 3.4 χρ stands alongside φιλανθρωπία, just as in Diogn 9.2. In Philo, Leg All III, 73; Migr 122, God's loving-kindness is extended to all living things. The manner of speaking of God's loving-kindness comes from the OT, more exactly from the LXX, cf. K. Weiß, TDNT IX, 490 f. Further cf. L. R. Stachowiak, *Chrestotes. Ihre biblisch-theologische Entstehung und Eigenart*, 1957, (SF NS 17) 63–6; Spicq, *Notes* II, 971–6.

[24]So originally R. Reitzenstein, *Das iranische Erlösungs-mysterium*, Bonn 1921, 236; then Schlier, *Christus und die Kirche* 53 f. and *Komm.* 113 f.; Dibelius – Greeven 67; Schille, *Frühchristliche Hymnen* 57 f.; Steinmetz, *Heils-Zuversicht* 62; Lindemann, *Aufhebung der Zeit* 129–32. For the other view cf. Fischer, *Tendenz* 121 f. – cf. also Legido López* who opposes the denial of an 'eschatological reservation' (220) and sees the Church still fighting the evil forces (6.10 f.).

[25]The material previously known is now increased by the Nag Hammadi texts. Thus in the 'Apocalypse of Adam' (NHC V/5; Foerster, *Gnosis* II 21–31) we find talk of the aeon 'in which we originated' (64, 10 f.). The creator-god (the demiurge) is called 'the archon of the aeons and powers' (64.20). The 'Enlightener' (Redeemer) 'has come out of a different air, a great aeon' (82.25–7) and enlightens 'those people whom he has chosen so that they enlighten the whole aeon' (83.1–3). Later it says: 'Your fruit will not die away but it will be known till the great aeons' (85.1–3). The temporal perspective is stronger in the tract 'The Perception of Our Great Power' (NHC VI/4; K. M. Fischer ThLZ 98, 169–75). In this document which has more of a Jewish-apocalyptic stamp 'the aeon of the flesh' which ended with the Flood and 'the aeon of the psyche' with Jesus Christ as the preacher of repentence and Redeemer are distinguished and after the conflagration of the world the 'aeon of beauty' or the 'bridal chamber' receives the pure souls (47.15–17).

[26]Cf. Pr – Bauer 520; Liddell and Scott 558. Against Lindemann, *Aufhebung der Zeit* 129, who refers to Bauer mistakenly. Luz* 370, n. 16 is correct.

of showing something *to* someone (to Pharaoh/Paul). We cannot therefore translate this 'that he may show *to* the ages to come . . .' (Schlier, Lindemann) only at most 'under the . . .' (Dibelius – Greeven). Since the verb is often used without a (personal) object, an associated phrase with an adverbial ἐν must be understood, be it local (Rom. 2.15), instrumental (1 Cl. 38.2) or temporal (cf. Josephus Ant VI, 305; 1 Cl. 24.3; Herm v. 4, 3, 5). A local meaning (as in Gnostic texts) would only make sense if the richness of the divine grace were shown *to* the ages to come (in heaven).

Hence we must understand the 'ages to come' in a temporal sense. In them God's abundant grace will be demonstrated and those to whom it will be revealed are, according to the context, still the 'we' who have already experienced salvation. The Final Clause refers to the completion of salvation, already determined in God's love, in Christ Jesus, i.e. the acquisition of the inheritance which lies ready in heaven (cf. 1.18; 5.5). No date is of course given: the temporal perspective emerges only as an extension into the future. Our 'setting in heaven' (v. 6) is not thereby revoked but rather confirmed. We already have our place there 'in Christ Jesus' but we do not yet participate fully in his glory because we still live in this world.

8–10

The graciousness of our salvation which was already stressed more emphatically in vv. 4–6 is now impressed upon the readers in a renewed address (Second Person Plural) and underlined with Pauline concepts ('through faith', 'not from works' but without 'law' and 'justification'). But it is noteworthy that at the conclusion of these verses it is deflected into a call to an ethical change (v. 10b–d) in an almost violent turn from the divine acts of salvation to the responsible behaviour of Christians. Clearly the author wishes to contrast their earlier way of life in sin and darkness (vv. 2 and 3) with the new Christian existence with its obligation to 'good works' made possible by God's goodness. In these emphatic clauses (cf. the opposita) the author reveals his pragmatic concern for the addressees. They should on the one hand not praise themselves but on the other make every effort to raise themselves above their heathen environment through a Christian way of life. The *Sitz im Leben* of these clauses could be a baptismal paraclesis influenced by Paul but also widely used elsewhere in early Christianity.[27]

8

The author now adds to the phrase taken up again from the parenthesis – 'you are saved by grace' – the words 'through faith'. Faith does not stand as an emphatic antithesis to works; these are contrasted for the first time in v. 9 to the divine effect of grace as achievements which bring a temptation to self-praise (sim. Tit. 3.5). In 1.13; 3.12 faith is touched upon as the way to the fulfilment of salvation. Elsewhere it appears as the effective power in the Christian life (3.17; 6.16) and as a cardinal possession which establishes (4.5) and demands unity (4.13). This theologian, like Paul, does not see

[27]Cf. Luz* 371.

himself opposed to the Jewish way of salvation through the works of the Law, but he realises the dangers of weak faith, inadequate knowledge of faith (cf. 1.17; 3.19; 4.13) and deviation from the apostolic tradition (cf. 3.3–5). Of course he does not consider faith a human achievement any more than did Paul. Hence in 2.8 he again makes it clear that the salvation achieved through faith (καὶ τοῦτο relates to the whole clause in v. 8a) does not originate in the addressees but is God's gift. Δῶρον (only here in Eph.) appears to have been chosen deliberately to denote the grace of their calling which simultaneously brings the faith which is bestowed on all Christians in contrast to special graces (cf. δωρέα in 3.7; 4.7). Even after Paul the conviction that faith is grace was not lost.[28]

In contrast to Paul, however, it is noticeable that instead of talking about 'Justification' he talks of 'Salvation' – Salvation as an event which has already taken place and which remains an effective saving event (Perfect). This points to the experience of Baptism (cf. 1 Pet. 3.21; Tit. 3.5; 2 Tim. 1.9) and should not stand in the way of the final salvation which is still expected (cf. 1.13 with 14). But in contrast to Paul for whom the eschatological salvation is the goal of Justification (cf. Rom. 5.9 f.), the accent has shifted perceptibly.[29]

9

If the author no longer needed to guard against the Jewish Way of Salvation through the Works of the Law in his congregations, we must ask why he emphasizes 'not from works, that no one should praise himself'. Is it simply a reminiscence of Pauline language? The Apostle is constantly concerned that no human being should praise her/himself *before God*; this is impossible because of the way of salvation through faith based on Christ's Cross (cf. Gal. 6.14; 1 Cor. 1.29, 31; 4.7; 2 Cor. 10.17; Rom 5.11; Phil 3.3). This exclusion of 'self-praise' (Rom 3.27; 4.2) is due to the fact that God alone justifies the sinner. The fact that this context of 'justification' is missing in Eph. and a vague someone (τις) is addressed, leads us strongly to suspect that the author also has in mind arrogance in relation to other people – for example the Gentile-Christians over against Jewish-Christians (cf. 2.11–22) or even among themselves (cf. 4.2). Salvation achieved purely from grace becomes a motif to inculcate what should be the basic Christian attitude to God (humble gratitude) and to our fellow Christians (modesty and love).

10

Human self-praise is excluded because (γάρ) we are God's creatures (ποίημα), a work which *he* (αὐτοῦ is deliberately placed in front) made. The word (in the NT only elsewhere in Rom. 1.20 where it is used of the works of Creation) reminds us of human creatureliness[30] but in what follows is immediately relocated in the light of the New Creation in Christ

[28]Cf. Schlier 115 who (in n. 1) also gives evidence from the exegesis of the Fathers.
[29]Cf. Gnilka 119 f.; D. Lührmann, 'Rechtfertigung und Versöhnung', ZThK 67 (1970) 437–52, here 446–8; Luz.* Nevertheless according to Mußner* 327 the passage reveals 'best Pauline inheritance'.
[30]Cf. the phrase which occurs frequently in the Hodajot of Qumran 'the construction from clay' according to Gen 2.7; 1 QH 1.21; 3.23; 4.29; 11.3; 12.26, 32; 18, 12.25, 31.

Jesus (cf. 4.24; 2 Cor 5.17; Gal. 6.15; Col. 3.10). God's life-giving action on us who were dead through sins (2.5) is a merciful re-creating which makes a new person from the old. This again betrays a *Sitz im Leben* in the baptismal catechesis (cf. also Jas. 1.18) which also explains the Final Clause with the call for an appropriate life-style (περιπατεῖν). The phrase 'for good works' already points in this direction: ἐπί with the Dative denotes the purpose or goal.[31] Out of God's gift (v. 8b) grows our duty to allow the newly-given life to take effect 'in good works', in a change in our life-style. What God wills for us is forcefully underlined by the double Final modifiers (ἐπί and the ἵνα-Clause). But God has done something more to achieve his goal in our re-creation in Christ: He has already provided and prepared the good works which we are to accomplish.

The expression 'good works' can be connected with Col. 1.10: The addresses should lead their lives (περιπατῆσαι) in a way worthy of the Lord, fruitful *in every good work*. Paul also speaks in this way of the provision and fruit of a Christian life (2 Cor 9.8). But the expression 'good works' (in the Plural) is first expanded in the Pastoral Epistles (1 Tim 2.10; 5.10; 6.18; Tit. 2.7, 14, et al.) and in its frank way of speaking about them Eph. indicates this later period. But in his characteristic way the author preserves the absolute priority of the divine work of grace. For Eph. the good works which the Christian should perform are 'prepared before' by God. The verb, which stands in a strongly predestinationary perspective in Rom. 9.23, is here applied to the works which we must accomplish. Does this not make God the servant of human activity? We must reply in the negative. In this context the author's intention is exactly the opposite. After the strong emphasis which he has placed on God's merciful salvation, because he is concerned with the testing of human ethics, he now wants to preserve God's prerogative. Even the good works which we should bring to fulfilment are in fact not our works but those which *God* has prepared for us (ὧν is a Connecting Relative). The 'making ready before' reminds us only superficially of Jewish ideas that certain things were made by God before the Creation of the world or that God had already prepared them before their fulfilment.[32] There the subject is appurtenances of salvation (in Mt 25.34 the Kingdom of God) over which God has supreme power of disposal and which he gives in their proper time (cf. also Mk. 10.40; 2 Pet. 1.5). Here on the other hand it is human works which God has prepared for *accomplishment* (ἵνα – Clause) and hence has made possible at all. The 'place' of such preparation must be for Eph. Baptism: Along with our re-creation God has also given us the power (his Spirit) to accomplish the

---

[31] Pr – Bauer 569 under ε; Bl - Debr §235.4.

[32] Cf. the doctrine of the seven things which were made before the Creation of the world in Pes 54a Bar and other passages (in Bill. II, 335). According to other statements 'preparation' can also mean 'determination' in a different way, v. Bill I, 981 ff. On the NT passages cf. also W. Grundmann, TDNT II, 705. – The best comparison to Eph 2.10 is to be found in the Qumran texts, as 1 QH. 1.26–8: 'By you, God of knowledge, are all works of righteousness and the counsel of truth, but by men are the service of sins and deeds of deceit. You have created the breath on their tongues and know their words and determined the fruit of their lips before they came into being. . . .'; 1 QH 4.31; 'By the almighty God are all the works of righteousness, but human life does not stand fast unless through the Spirit which God created for it'; 1 QH. 16.5. But these, too, are only distant parallels.

appropriate works (cf. 4.24). In this the author is quite close factually to the Pauline way of thinking in Rom 8.4 – without the background of the impotent Jewish Law.

It is not easy to assess the relationship of the author of Eph. to Pauline theology which imposes itself on this passage. With his strongly-marked emphasis on the mercifulness of our salvation and the priority of the divine action in our ethical endeavours he preserves the 'best Pauline legacy'.[33] As he restrains the message of justification in favour of basing the Christian state of salvation in Baptism he reduces the polemic function of the *sola gratia* 'as a crisis of every human self-pretension'.[34] How we judge the matter depends on how far we consider the development which began in the post-Pauline period into which Eph. fits as justifiable and theologically defensible. One thing at least can be said: The legacy of Paul still continues to have a powerful effect in him.

Summary

In the section 2.1–10 the author does not yet take up the theme of the union of Jews and Gentiles in the one Church of Jesus Christ (2.11–22) but includes the addressees in the act of salvation which God has shown powerfully in Christ (1.20–3). They, too, who were formerly in a comfortless, 'deadly' situation like the rest of the Gentile world because they led impotent lives in their sinful desires, have been made alive with Christ, raised with him and set in heaven through God's merciful love. Along with all Christians ('we') who have experienced this change to the Christian position in salvation they must realise what this means. It is a salvation through grace which gives no cause for self-praise but rather puts us under the obligation to lead an appropriately Christian life. Here again as in the Great Eulogy it should be clear to all the redeemed that God has carried out his plan of salvation 'in Christ Jesus'. But this event is now more clearly emphasized as a joint accomplishment of the way of Christ, as participation in his resurrection and heavenly enthronement.

Behind this encouraging explanation lies an early Christian baptismal catechesis and paraclesis as is revealed in the call 'you are saved by grace' (v. 5) and its repetition in v. 8. The salvation which has already taken place is emphatically stressed as an act of grace, a gift from God (vv. 8–10a) – but it has as its consequence the obligation to 'good works' (10b). Although this section is especially connected with early Christian ideas about Baptism (cf. Tit. 3.4–6), there are also echoes of Pauline theology (v. 9), but these are no longer in connection with the message of justification whose antithesis to the Jewish way of fulfilment of the Law is omitted. But the author has realised that all good works which we must effect are only possible through God's mighty grace and he expresses this in an unusual way, saying that God has 'prepared' these works in advance for us to fulfil them (v. 10c–d). Our ability to lead a new way of life develops solely out of the 'new creation' (in Baptism) and our works remain in the end God's works. The Pauline tension-laden union of a justification

[33]Mußner* 326 f.
[34]Luz* 375.

which has already taken place and the subsequent development of moral obligations and hope for a future final salvation has faded. The future perspective is not entirely lacking (v. 7) but it recedes in order to give more emphasis to the Christian existence in the world which should be brought to fulfilment entirely through the power of the salvation already experienced.

Christian existence in the world finds its special place in the Church as the sphere of Christ's salvation. Although the Church is not explicitly mentioned in this section, several things suggest that the author still has the Church in mind (cf. 1.22b–23) – e.g. the constant interchange of 'you' and 'we'; the reference to the baptismal catechesis; perhaps also the warning against self-praise (in which case aimed at the life in the Church). For him the Church is the agent of salvation bound to Christ, admittedly seen in a one-sided, glorious fashion – we miss the Pauline Theology of the Cross which also reveals the weaknesses of the Church – but it is also the place of Christian preservation amid the world's temptations and struggles.

II. Christian Existence in the Church of Jesus Christ as the Mystery of Salvation (2.11–3.21)

Now there begins a new section, the theological main section, which deals with the theme of the one Church composed of Jews and Gentiles or the 'Mystery of Christ' (3.4) which the author sees realized in the Church of Jesus Christ. The section 2.11–22 is, it is true, connected with the preceding section 2.1–10 by the schema 'then – now'; but the new beginning is clearly indicated by the antithesis of the addressees – who are now expressly addressed as 'Gentiles' (v. 11) – and the 'Congregation of Israel' (v. 12) and affirmed by the appropriate new semantic phraseology. In contrast to the 'address' – style which was predominant in the earlier sections, there now begins a more markedly theological argumentation as in the view of Christ the Bringer of Peace (2.14–18), then the Church as the expanding building of God (2.19–22) and finally on the Mystery of Christ proclaimed by Paul and manifested in the Church (3.1–13). The author does not, however, introduce these ideas in a didactic fashion like a theological treatise but as a reminder and substantiation, as a theological motif for the existential concern for his readers which motivates him. This can also be seen when at the end of his theological explanations he formulates a prayer to the Father (3.14–19) in which he indirectly (as in 1.17 ff.) alludes to his wishes and admonitions. He closes this section with a doxology (3, 20 f.) in which the theme of the Church still lingers on ('in the Church' (v. 21). With 4.1 he then begins a new section which is marked by the key word παρακαλῶ ('I admonish you therefore'). In spite of the pastoral concern apparent throughout, the section 2.11–3.21 holds the whole substance of the author's theology; an ecclesiology developed from Christology which permeates the whole document theologically.

Form-critically speaking, one would best define such a theological procedure, which makes use of theology in address and admonition and in so doing also gives an exposition, as *Anamnesis*. The expression 'remember' comes right at the beginning (2.11) and stands like a watchword over the whole section. For the expositions on Christ as bringer of peace (2.14–18) and the Church as the developing building of God (2.19–22) are not intended to bring any new instruction but simply to remind the readers of the knowledge of faith already acquired and make them more aware of it. The 'Paul'-section, 3.1–13 has a similar character; for however the author intended to complete the sentence begun in 3.1, the insertion of 'you have certainly heard' in 3.2 shows that it performs the same function of an anamnesis. The 'Mystery of Christ' proclaimed by Paul, which for the author consists in the incorporation of the Gentiles in the Church of Jesus Christ and their full participation in Christ's salvation (3.6), receives, to be sure, a new interpretation but only as a deeper elucidation of the ecclesial reality which already exists (cf. vv. 9–10) and of which the readers should be made more aware (cf. v. 12). Theological anamnesis in this form has a long pre-history in the historiography, prophetic sermon and cultic practice of Israel.[1] This was taken over by the early Christians especially in their celebration of the Lord's Supper (cf. 1 Cor 11.24–5) but also in their catechesis (cf. Acts 20.35; Jn 15.20, 2 Tim 2.8). This type of theological anamnesis permeates the whole document but is especially pronounced in 2.11–3.21.

1. THE NEW APPROACH TO GOD OPENED UP IN JESUS CHRIST IN THE CHURCH COMPRISED OF JEWS AND GENTILES (2.11–22)

Literature

H. Sahlin, *Die Beschneidung Christi. Eine Interpretation von Eph. 2.11–22*, 1950 (SyBU 12), 5–22.

M. Barth, *Israel und die Kirche im Brief des Paulus an die Epheser*, 1959 (TEH 75).

id, 'Das Volk Gottes. Juden und Christen in der Botschaft des Paulus', in *Paulus – Apostat oder Apostle? Jüdische und christliche Antworten*, Regensburg 1977, 45–134, on Eph.: 98–101.

G. Giavini, 'La structure littéraire d'Éph II, 11–22', NTS 16 (1969/70) 209–21.

N. J. McEleny, 'Conversion, Circumcision and the Law', NTS 20 (1974) 319–341, particularly 337–340.

M. Rese, 'Die Vorzüge Israels in Röm 9.4 f. – Eph. 2.12', ThZ 31 (1975) 211–22.

Merklein, *Christus und die Kirche*; Rader, *Church and Racial Hostility*.

Schnackenburg, 'Zur Exegese von Eph. 2.11–22 im Hinblick auf das Verhältnis von Kirche und Israel', appeared in FS Bo Reicke, ed. D. Brownell and W. C. Weinrich.

---

[1]Cf. O. Michel, TDNT IV, 675–83; N. A. Dahl, 'Anamnesis. Mémoire et Commémoration dans le christianisme primitif', St.Th 1 (1948) 69–95; H. Groß, 'Zur Wurzel zkr', BZ NF 4 (1960) 227–37; P. A. H. de Boer, *Gedenken und Gedächtnis in der Welt des AT*, Stuttgart 1962; W. Schottroff, *'Gedenken' im alten Orient und im AT*, 1964 (WMANT 15); H. Zirker, *Die kultische Vergegenwärtigung der Vergangenheit in den Psalmen*, 1964 (BBB 20).

On verses 2.14–18.

Schille, *Frühchristliche Hymnen*, 24–31.

Sanders, ZNW 56, 216–18.

Deichgräber, *Gotteshymnus* 165–67.

E. Testa, 'Gesù pacificatore universale. Inno liturgico della Chiesa Madre (Col 1.15–20 + Ef 2.14–6)', SBFLA 19 (1969) 5–64.

González Lamadrid, 'Ipse est pax nostra. Estudio exegético-teológico de Ef 2.14–8', EstB 28 (1969) 209–61; 29 (1970) 101–36, 227–66.

J. Gnilka, 'Christus unser Friede – ein Friedenserlöserlied in Eph. 2.14–27. Erwägungen zu einer neutestamentlichen Friedenstheologie', in *Die Zeit Jesu* (FS H. Schlier), Freiburg i. Br. 1970, 190–207.

Wengst, *Formeln und Lieder* 181–194.

H. Merklein, 'Zur Tradition und Composition von Eph. 2.14–8', BZ NF 17 (1973) 79–102.

P. Stuhlmacher, '"Er ist unser Friede" (Eph 2.14). Zur Exegese und Bedeutung von Eph 2.14–8', in *NT und Kirche* (FS R. Schnackenburg), Freiburg i. Br. 1974, 337–58.

C. Burger, *Schöpfung und Versöhnung* 117–39.

On verses 2.19–22.

J. Jeremias, 'Der Eckstein', Angelos 1 (1925) 65–70; TDNT I.791 f.; ZNW 29 (1930) 264–80; ZNW 36 (1937) 154–7.

O. Michel, TDNT V, 125–8; Schlier, *Christus und die Kirche* 49–60; *Komm.* 141–5.

Vielhauer, *Oikodome* 115–36; Pfammatter, *Kirche als Bau* 73–107.

R. J. McKelvey, 'Christ the Cornerstone', NTS 8 (1961/62) 352–9; *New Temple* 195–204.

K. Schäfer, 'Zur Deutung von ἀκρογωνιαῖος Eph. 2.20', in *Neutestamentliche Aufsätze* (FS J. Schmid) Regensburg 1963, 218–24.

Mußner, *Beiträge* (ibid.) 191–4.

Merklein, *Kirchl. Amt* 125–56

R. Schnackenburg, 'Die Kirche als Bau: Eph. 2.19–22 unter ökumenischem Aspekt', in: *Paul and Paulinism* (FS C. K. Barrett, ed. M. D. Hooker and S. G. Wilson, London 1982, 258–72.

11 Remember, then, that you, the Gentiles in the flesh
called uncircumcised from the so-called circumcision
which is performed on the flesh by hands,

12 that you were at one time separated from Christ,
alien to the congregation of Israel
and far apart from the covenants with their promise,
without hope and godless in the world.

13 But now in Christ Jesus you who were once far off
have become near in the Blood of Christ.

14 For he is our peace.
He has made the two into one
and torn down the partition of the fence
the enmity
in that he in his own flesh

15 destroyed the Law of the Commandments with the statutes
that he might make the two in himself into a new, single race
bestowing peace

16 and might reconcile both with God in one single Body
through the Cross

(thus) killing the enmity by his own person.
17 And with his coming 'he preached peace
    to you who were far off and peace to those who were near'.
18 For through him we have access
    to the Father, both in the one single Spirit.
19 So you are no longer foreigners and sojourners
    but are fellow-citizens of the saints and household of God
20 built on the foundation of the apostles and prophets
    – the cornerstone is Christ Jesus himself
21 in whom the whole building grows into a holy temple
    in the Lord
22 in whom you also are built together into a dwelling-place
    of God in the Spirit.

Analysis

This section is clearly divided into three parts: The *first part* (vv. 11–3) leads from the antithesis of the former heathen and the 'congregation of Israel' (vv. 11–12) via the pattern of 'once and now' to the new situation in which the Gentiles have become 'close' through the blood of Christ (v. 13). The *second part* is pointedly connected to the naming of Christ (αὐτὸς γάρ). This part ratifies the meaning of Christ for the union of the two groups originally separated and brings the new situation of salvation more clearly to view: Through Christ 'we', the two groups, have access to the Father in one single Spirit (vv. 14–18). From this the *third part* draws the conclusion (ἄρα οὖν) for the ecclesial status of the addressees, now in a predominantly positive description: They are fellow-citizens of the saints and of the household of God in that they belong to the Church of Jesus Christ. This is depicted as a firmly-based and continually growing building or temple in its earthly/heavenly, historical/eschatological form (vv. 19–22).

The first sub-section (vv 11–3) is syntactically clear. The reminder of the former status of the Gentile Christians begins with the ὅτι-Clause which, however, only reaches its conclusion through a repetition of ὅτι and a resumption of ποτέ (at one time) with τῷ καιρῷ ἐκείνῳ (at that time). The pattern 'once – now' is filled out as regards content by the contrasting expressions 'separated from Christ' (v. 12a) – 'in Christ Jesus' (v. 13a). The earlier situation is made clearer by appositions to 'separated from Christ' which form two pairs, each introduced by a participle:

12   separated from Christ
12bα   alien to the congregation of Israel
12bβ   and far apart from the covenants with their promise
12cα   without hope
12cβ   and godless in the world.

The present state of salvation (νυνὶ δέ) which is contrasted with the past is described in a new main clause (v. 13) which echoes Is. 57.19 (far off and close), the change being marked by 'you have become' (ἐγενήθητε).

An analysis of the section about Christ is more difficult. Up to v. 16 it is a Complex Sentence whose framework is reminiscent of the phraseology of the Great Eulogy. The principal statement 'For he is our peace' (v. 14) is continued by means of participles, first by 'who has made . . . and has torn down' in v. 14, then, after several other phrases, 'who destroyed' in v. 15a. Then comes a Final Clause which contains two statements 'that he might make a new, single race . . . and might reconcile both with God') in which two participles are again interwoven. These stand in opposition to one another and explain each other: 'bestowing peace' (end of v. 15) – 'killing the enmity' (end of v. 16). In this way, with constant new extensions, he clarifies and impresses upon them the one idea that Christ, our peace, has led together to indissoluble unity the two formerly separated groups, Jews and Gentiles, in his own person through his death on the Cross and has set aside the old enmity. We might order the text as follows to make the sense clear:

I	14a	For **he himself**	is our *peace*
	14bα he has made *the two*		*to one*
	14bβ and destroyed the partition of the fence		
	14c the *enmity*	in that **he in his own flesh**	
	15a destroyed the Law of the Commandments with the statutes		
II	15bα that he *the two*	**in himself**	*might make into a new single group*
	15bβ		bestowing *peace*
	16a and *both*		reconcile with God *in one single body*
		through the Cross	
	16b killing the *enmity*	**by his own person**.	

In this arrangement we can see the two textual units (I and II) which are both characterized by the antithesis of peace – enmity. In his own person, more precisely in his own flesh (14c), through the Cross (16a), Christ has overcome the enmity and brought peace. Christ has again made one (14bα) the two groups of humanity between whom there was enmity, or, according to unit II, made them into one new, single group in his own person (15bα) and reconciled them with God in one single body (16a). In reconciling them to God he has killed the enmity which existed between them.

The end of the section about Christ leads (similarly to 1.22) into an indirect scriptural quotation (v. 17), which was almost certainly in the author's mind in v. 13. Καὶ ἐλθών ('and with his coming') – after the explanation of the event of the Cross which removed enmity and brought peace – forms the bridge to the meaning of the person of Christ as such and (with εὐηγγελίσατο) the necessary binding link to the quotation from Scripture. As in v. 14 Christ is the subject of this clause. But the second (causal) clause in v. 18, which emphasizes the effect on us of Christ's bringing of peace, is presented in the 'we' style. Thus 'in one single Spirit' corresponds to the phrase (in one single Body' in v. 16a and so makes clear the ecclesial connection. Continuing the textual arrangement of vv. 14–16 we can order vv. 17–18 as follows. Here everything negative which was previously in the left column is now erased and the positive result is recorded on the right side:

III   17   And with his coming
             he preached   *peace* to you who were far off
                                         and   *peace* to those who were near

       18   For **through him**
             we have access   *both in the one single Spirit* to the
                                                Father.

Thus the whole textual unit has one clear line of thought and the crux of it comes to the fore: Christ, the bringer of peace through the event of the Cross, in his Church.

If we analyse the unit in this way the various attempts which have been made to reconstruct an underlying hymn[2] seem superfluous and hardly convincing. If the author *did* take over curious metaphors (which will be discussed in the exegesis), both style and progression of thought point to his own hand just as in the opening Eulogy. The reflection on the scriptural quotation (from Is. 57.19) betrays a theological procedure which treats the wording very freely and brings it to bear deliberately in a Christian way just as can be shown in other passages from Eph. (cf. 1.20–2 [traditionally]; 4.8–10; 5.2; 5.32 f.). Finally, many expressions reminiscent of Col., especially the concepts of peace, reconciliation, the Blood of Christ, the Cross (cf. Col. 1.20–2) and 'the Law of the Commandments with the statutes' (cf. Col. 2.14) only show that Eph. took over these concepts after his own fashion.[3]

The third sub-section (vv. 19–22) develops the result of the section on Christ as it affects the addressees. The main statement in v. 19 takes the form of an assertion (ἐστε), emphasized by the negative/positive statement which follows – 'no longer foreigners and sojourners, but fellow-citizens of the saints and household of God'. In order to underline the new status of the Gentile-Christians addressed – i.e. that they have full rights – there follows (with an Aorist Participle) their inclusion in the holy 'building' which is founded on the apostles and prophets and whose cornerstone (Genitive Absolute) is Jesus Christ (v. 20). The fundamental and all-embracing significance of Jesus Christ is then emphasized in an added Relative Clause: In him the whole building is held together and grows into a holy temple in the Lord (v. 21). The author's great conception of the Church arises here in the metaphor of a building. He does not, however, develop it further but, in keeping with the outlook of the whole section turns once more to the addressees: 'in him you also are built together into a dwelling-place of God in the Spirit' (v. 22). In contrast to the ἦτε (you were) in v. 12 and the ἐγενήθητε (you have become) in v. 13, he is now

[2]Schille*; Sanders*; Testa* 6–24 (combines three strophes from Col. 1.15–20 and Eph. 2.14–16); Gnilka*; Wengst*; H. M. Schenke, in Tröger, *Gnosis und Neues Testament* 223 f.; Fischer, *Tendenz* 131 f.; Burger*. For criticism cf. Deichgräber*; Merklein*, BZ 17, 81–95; Stuhlmacher* 340 f. – Lindemann, *Aufhebung der Zeit* 156–8 takes as model a prose-text written in elevated language from a non-Christian sphere.
[3]Cf. Wagenführer, *Bedeutung Christi* 21 ff; Mitton, *Epistle* 289 ff.; Merklein, BZ 17, 95–8. – For another view Coutts, NTS 4, 205–7.

considering their permanent position – which is, however, not static but in keeping with the *growing* building, aspires to (εἰς . . .) participation (συν-) in the new congregation of Christ which is led dynamically to its completion by the Holy Spirit. Here, too, it is unnecessary to presume an underlying baptismal hymn.[4]

Exegesis

11

The consciousness of having been saved from an unfitting life by the grace of God and of being committed to a new life with God (2.1–10) is now deepened and steered in a particular direction. The addressees should 'remember' i.e. think about God's saving act; for in an anamnesis of this kind it is not a question of remembering human things but of recalling God's deed in the perspective of faith.[5] This 'remembering' opens one's eyes to the salvation event in which the addressees are included. This is immediately made clearer when the author addresses the readers vividly as 'Gentiles in the flesh', in accordance with their hereditary origins and nature as 'uncircumcised' (actually 'uncircumcision' – *abstractum pro concreto*) and confronts them with the Jews who are distinguished from them by the circumcision of the flesh. The author admittedly reduces the Jewish evaluation of circumcision as a sign of membership of the People of the covenant by labelling the Jews as 'so-called' circumcision and with the addition of 'which is performed on the flesh by hands'. The contrast which thereby arises to v. 12, where we find enumerated Israel's advantages in which the former heathen had no share, can be partly explained by the author's adoption of Pauline ideas; for Paul, too, relativises physical circumcision (cf. Rom. 2.25–9; 4.9–12) and yet recognizes Israel's advantages (Rom. 9.4 f.) as well as by the different linguistic intent. In his address to the readers the author is thinking of their present status for which circumcision is meaningless (v. 11). On the internal level of the text, in the theological argument, he contrasts their earlier heathen status with the then prevailing advantage held by Israel (v. 12). The reminiscent looking back is important for the judging of the old People of God but it also gains a present application for the Gentile-Christian readers.

12

The intention to illuminate the present situation of salvation through anamnesis is shown in the expression which is placed first of all the characteristics of the past: separated from Christ – which of course has as its premise the present existence 'in Christ Jesus' (v. 13). The author's thinking starts from this and everything said about 'that time' must be seen in this light. The short formula 'separated from Christ' (χωρὶς Χριστοῦ) is

---

[4]W. Nauck, 'Eph. 2.19–22 – ein Taufleid?', EvTh 12 (1953) 362–71; P. Pokorný, ZNW 53, 183 f. For criticism v Schlier 140, n. 1; Gnilka 152, n. 4; Merklein, *Kirchl. Amt* 119 f.

[5]Cf. p. 103 n. 1 – The cult especially is the Sitz im Leben for such anamnesis but it is not exclusively so. In Deut as well as the 'little creed' (26, 5–10) there are exhortations such as 7.18; 32.7. Dahl (p. 103 n. 1) 73 considers tradition responsible for this idea. The 'remember' becomes an exhortatory encouragement, cf. Jn. 15.20; Acts 20.35; 2 Tim 2.8; Rev. 2.5; 3.3.

therefore to be taken as condensed, having the same meaning as 'outside of Christ' or 'remote from Christ'. If certain advantages Israel had are now mentioned, this is done to clarify this 'being far' from Christ, and therein lies both a recognition and a restriction in the judgement of Israel. With regard to the question which is most interesting for the historical effect this passage has had and which has been most disputed and received a variety of answers up to the present day – namely the question as to the relationship between 'Church and Synagogue',[6] we must from the start establish that the author is in no way thinking of the Israel which refused to accept the Christian faith. He is concerned with the *Church* made up of former Jews and Gentiles in which earlier distinctions such as circumcision (cf. v. 11) and the Law (cf. v. 15) have lost their meaning, and he is concerned about the proper relationship, the unity of Jewish- and Gentile-Christians in the Church, perhaps especially with the understanding of the Gentile-Christians for the Jewish-Christians, but not with the relationship to Judaism outside the Church.

In fact nowhere in the whole of Eph. are the 'Jews' mentioned but here (and only here) is there a reference to 'the Congregation of Israel' who were distinguished by the merciful, promise-laden divine decrees ('Covenant contracts'). They were far apart from (ἀπηλλοτριωμένοι)[7] and alien (ξένοι) to the one-time Gentiles. Israel's advantage in the pre-Christian era was not an occasion of blame for the heathen but was simply a deficiency. The unusual combination of words can be explained as an echo of Rom. 9.4,[8] where Paul in a passionate address to his own race lists an even fuller catalogue of Israel's advantages, among them

Rom. 9.4	cf.	Eph. 2.12
Israelites		the Congregation of Israel
the (covenant-) decrees		the (covenant-) decrees
the promises		. . . the promise

Just as in Rom. 9.4 'the Israelites' is an honorary title, so in Eph. 2.12 'the Congregation of Israel' is an honourable designation for God's Chosen People. Why the author chose the singular expression ἡ πολιτεία τοῦ Ἰσραηλ can only be a matter for conjecture. In the Hellenistic world the Greek word meant the state, constitution or civil rights, but here cannot mean the Israelite state which as a long-gone political organisation is meaningless for such a religious outlook. It rather denotes in a figurative sense the community chosen by God, created by his appointment and bound to him (the *qehal Yahweh*). In the LXX this is translated by ἐκκλησία or (less frequently) συναγωγή. The author could use neither of those terms here since for him ἡ ἐκκλησία meant the Church of Jesus Christ and συναγωγή

[6]Cf. Schnackenburg* in FS Bo Reicke.

[7]Cf. H. Büchsel, TDNT I, 265 f. The word has almost the same meaning as ἀλλότριος 'foreign, distant'; he cites as a parallel Aristot Pol II 8 (1268a 40): ἀλλότριον τῆς πολιτείας. Further in R. Schnackenburg, 'Die Politeia Israels in Eph. 2.12', in *De la Tôrah au Messie* (FS H. Cazelles), ed. J. Doré, P. Grelot and M. Carrez, Paris 1981, 467–74.

[8]Cf. Rese* who, however, does not give enough consideration to the different perspectives of Rom. 9.4 f. and Eph. 2.12. See also F. Mußner, *Traktat über die Juden*, Munich 1979, 45–8.

the post-Christ synagogue community.[9] Hence a more neutral expression came to mind which takes on its special slant in its context – here the addition of τοῦ Ἰσραηλ: the Community of God which found its concrete realization in Israel. Since the expression is dependent on 'at that time', we can draw no direct conclusions about the relationship of the continuing 'Israel' (i.e. Judaism at the time Eph. was composed) to the Christian Church.

Neither the continuing religious significance of the old People of God[10] nor an equation of the 'Community of Israel' with the Church[11] can be read exegetically from the text. The backward-looking view and the general ecclesial perspective allow us to make no judgement on the evaluation of the Israel which was far from Christ – in contrast to Rom. 9.4 f. where the apostle considers the Israelites of his time to be the bearers of the promise. If we take it as meaning the Church, this breaks down with the parallel expression 'alien to the covenants of the promise' which is bound up with the old Israel. On 2.19, which has frequently been used to support the one view or the other, see below where that verse is discussed.

The 'covenant contracts' (διαθῆκαι), which it is better to understand as God's merciful decrees,[12] are certainly a reminiscence of Rom. 9.4 where they appear in connection with 'the giving of the Law and worship and promises'. Not without reason does Eph. combine the promise(s) more closely with the divine decrees through the (modal) Genitive τῆς ἐπαγγελίας. What is decisive for the present perspective is the promise which has grown from the 'covenant' given to Israel. The Singular points to a specific promise, namely that of the Messiah in whom total salvation is fulfilled. Formerly that had force for the community of Israel and only in Jesus Christ have the former gentiles also achieved their part (cf. 3.6), now in the sense of its realization.

This is confirmed by the concluding 'without hope'. Now the Gentile-Christians do have hope – no longer in the future coming of the Messiah but rather in that he has come – for the complete revelation of the salvation which has already been given and deposited (cf. 1.12.14.18). Again he is not considering whether and how far 'the congregation of Israel', the Judaism of his time, have hope after the coming of the Messiah Jesus Christ. The whole question of Israel's future fate which concerned Paul so much in Rom. 9–11 is ignored. Paul hopes that some day 'all Israel will be saved' (11.26); Eph. has nothing to say on this matter.

How much Eph. is considering the pre-Christian hopeless position

[9]Cf. H. Strathmann, TDNT VI, 534 f. (on πολιτεία); the linguistic usage in the LXX (= the community as a whole) disappears and 'synagogue' becomes the designation of the individual Jewish congregation. – On ἐκκλησία cf. the most recent discussions in W. Schrage, '"Ekklesia" und "Synagoge"' ZThK 73 (1976) 167–207; H. Merklein, 'Die Ekklesia Gottes. Der Kirchenbegriff bei Paulus und in Jerusalem', BZ NF 23 (1979) 48–70, especially 55–65.

[10]Cf. Barth's works; Mußner (p. 109 n. 8) also modifies.

[11]Hanson, *Unity* 142; cf. W. Bieder, *Ekklesia und Polis* 23 (different in ThZ 11 (1955) 334); Gnilka 135 makes more of a differentiation: the civitas Israel becomes transparent for the heavenly politeia but is now uplifted and is identical with the Church; Merklein, *Christus und die Kirche* 21, further 72–6: Insofar as the 'promise' moves towards the eschatological people of the Church grounded 'in Christ', the 'Community of Israel' is realized in the Church.

[12]Cf. E. Kutsch, *Verheißung und Gesetz. Untersuchungen zum sogenannten 'Bund' im AT*, 1973 (BZAW 131); M. Weinfeld, berith, TDOT II, 253–79; W. Eichrodt, 'Darf man heute noch von einem Gottesbund mit Israel reden?', ThZ 30 (1974) 193–206.

of the Gentiles in comparison with Israel is shown in the final statement – that they were ἄθεοι (godless) in the world. This word, which appears only here in the NT, is not to be understood in its current sense as meaning unbelievers or opponents of a religious belief, or even in the sense of classical atheism as a deliberate criticism of the prevalent religion, as resigned scepticism or rebellion against the gods.[13] It is to be understood in the sense of 4.18 to mean 'alienated from the life of God'. It was not any conscious attitude but their actual circumstances which separated the heathen from God and his life which gives a future.

13

The separation from God of the former heathen is first overcome 'in Christ Jesus' or, more exactly, through 'the blood of Christ'. Because they are now in Christ, their position before God has changed fundamentally. They who were once 'far' (from God) have now in the blood of Christ become the 'near'. The vivid expression is connected to the way of speaking of the 'far' peoples and islands (cf. Mic. 4.3; Is. 5.26; 49.1; 66.19; Jer. 31.10) which admittedly usually refers to the Israelites who return to Jerusalem from distant lands (Zech 6.15; Is. 43.6; 49.12; 60.4–9). Because of the connection with 'near' and the following statement about peace (v. 14) we already catch a glimpse of Is. 57.19 – 'Peace to the far and peace to the near, says the Lord' – a verse which is then expressly alluded to in v. 17. But while there the 'far' (Gentiles) and 'near' (Jews) are differentiated, v. 13 states that the far Gentiles have become 'near'. Hence it is a metaphorical expression which (as in Acts 2.39) is inspired by the verse from Is. but directly addresses the position of the one-time heathen. It would be difficult to complete the expression in order to have 'to be near to Israel' or 'near like Israel' for the line of thought (the isotopic axis) in vv. 11–13 is not the relationship Israel-Gentile world but the pre-Christian and Christian position of the Gentile-Christian addressees in relationship to God. Both groups have won a common way of approach to the Father through Christ (v. 18). The difference between those once 'far' and 'near' is abolished. Israel's status, too, has consequently been changed; a new way of approach to God in Christ is shown to Israel, the once 'near' People of God.

14–18

What Christ means for the two groups is now developed in a kind of christological excursus but this is done in such a way that the former relationship between Israel and the Gentile world can also be discussed. The arch extends to v. 18 as is clear not only from the clauses which relate to Christ, putting his person in the centre and emphasizing his mediatory role, but which is also shown by the 'we' which appears at the beginning and end. Christ is *our* peace (v. 14) and through him *we* have access to the Father (v. 18). It is a reflection on Christ's work of salvation from the

---

[13]E. Stauffer, TDNT III, 120 f. counts seven basic forms of 'atheism' in antiquity. There is no polemical note against the Gentiles (cf. 121) in Eph. 2.12. Cf. also W. Foerster, TDNT VII, 187 f. (the difference between ἄθεος and ἀσεβής).

standpoint of the Church in its new, saved situation. This work brought peace to the two groups formerly at enmity in that it reconciled them both together with God (v. 16). The address to the Gentile-Christians (v. 11) is inserted in v. 17 but only in v. 19 is it again taken up fully. Hence the anamnesis becomes theological reflection and argumentation based on the ecclesial self-understanding of the Gentile-Christians. The sharp antithesis to the Israel which guards and preserves the Law is striking. This is a gulf which is described as being at enmity. There was no mention of this in 11–13. This intensification must have its reasons for which we shall look in the author's actual concerns (cf. under v. 18).

The constant repeated attempts to reconstruct a hymn to Christ which the author used for his own purpose have already been dismissed in the analysis. It is much more likely that vv. 13–18 are a christological exegesis of Is. 9.5 f.; 52.7; 57.19.[14] The principal thought – that Christ has brought peace – is possibly borrowed from Col. 1.20 (εἰρηνοποιήσας only here) and closely bound up with that is the idea of reconciliation (ἀποκαταλλάσσω) (Col. 1.22; cf. Eph. 2.16). The cosmic bringing of God's peace in Christ is transferred in Eph. to the relationship of Israel and the Gentile world, always with the Church in view as a new unity founded in Jesus Christ. In the closer depiction of this enmity and its destruction Eph. introduces other metaphors (the tearing-down of the dividing partition, the setting-aside of the Law) for the new Great Church created in and through Christ (the one new humanity, the uniting 'in one single body'). The background and historical origin of these metaphors is very controversial. But the return to the OT quotation (v. 17) shows that the author has his deepest roots in the Christian interpretation of the OT Bible. The 'Prince of Peace' of Is. 9.5 who brings God's final peace to Israel (cf. Is. 52.7) he interprets as Christ, the Messiah; but this Messiah also includes the 'far off' (cf. Is. 57.19), now applied to the Gentiles, in his work of peace. It is an exegesis of Scripture similar to that in 4.8–10 and 5.31 f. – connected to the traditional Jewish manner of interpretation but given a Christian application.

14

The main statement and the one which affects the hearers – 'he is our peace' – has its place in a series of other attributes of Christ in the NT which express his meaning for 'us': For us he becomes God's Wisdom, Righteousness, Sanctification and Redemption (1 Cor. 1.30); he is our Life (Col. 3.4) our Hope (1 Tim 1.1 cf. Col. 1.27), the Atonement for our sins (1 Jn 2.2). In this context the emphatic 'he' (αὐτός) comes after the Blood of Christ through which the once far-off Gentiles have become close. Hence 'peace' receives a more precise interpretation: It is the divine peace of salvation which Christ has brought and which is incorporated in himself. In the OT 'peace' included both outward and inner human happiness, peace among nations and

---

[14]This is the thesis of Stuhlmacher* which in my opinion he substantiates convincingly in 367 f. The detailed study of González Lamadrid* tends in the same direction, but the author does not see the Jewish-Christian method of interpretation.

the peace of Creation,[15] and in the Prophets the Messiah appears as the Prince of Peace (cf. Is. 9.5; Mic. 5.5 'he shall be a man of peace'). In the Christian message Jesus Christ fulfils this hope for the Gentile world as well.

Peace means the overcoming of enmity, the putting-aside of differences, the bringing together of separated groups. The way in which Christ brings peace is described in an unusual metaphor: He has made the two into one and torn down the partition of the fence. The questions which spring to mind are what are the two separated parts and what is meant by the partition of the fence? These are answered as the explanation proceeds. The dividing wall, the 'fence' (Genitive of Apposition) is 'the Law of the Commandments with the statutes' and the parties at enmity are the Jews and Gentiles. We can see the progress from a general picture to the particular. The Masculine expressions 'the two' (τοὺς δύο v. 15) and 'both' (τοὺς ἀμφοτέρους v. 16) come after the Neuter 'the two' (τὰ ἀμφοτερα) and the metaphorical 'tear down the partition' before the factual 'destroy the Law'. How this took place is also treated in a more detailed way: 'in his flesh' – 'through the Cross'. But why did the author use such an unusual metaphor to begin with? Historical criticism has raised a question which has kept researchers busy to the present day.

Basically there are three answers competing for acceptance: 1. The cosmic i.e. Gnostic derivation.[16] There was originally a cosmic metaphor in which two regions, the heavenly and the earthly, were in opposition, divided from one another by a partition. According to the Gnostic view the Redeemer breaks through this wall, combines the separated parts and creates access for the redeemed to the heavenly world. It is a fact that such a metaphor of a solid wall between heaven and earth does exist in many Gnostic texts, but it also appears in Jewish Apocalyptic writings.[17] But it does not fit with the conception of the world taken for granted in Eph. which knows no separation of heaven and earth but only a rule of those 'powers and forces' in the lower heavens over humanity (2.2; 6.12) who are freed by the victorious Christ rising 'over all the heavens' (cf. 4.10). 2. That it points to the barrier in the Temple-area.[18] A stone separating-wall to prevent the Gentiles from entering the Jewish Court in the Temple is witnessed to in Josephus *Bellum Judaicum* V 193 f. and proved by archaeological findings (warning signs which were attached to the barrier).[19] But the memory of Herod's Temple, which at the time of the composition of Eph. lay in

[15] Cf. W. Caspari, *Der biblische Friedensgedanke nach dem AT*, Berlin 1916; G. von Rad, TDNT II, 402–6; H. Groß, *Die Idee des ewigen und allgemeinen Weltfriedens im alten Orient und AT*, Trier 1956; C. Westermann, 'Der Frieden (schalom) im AT', in *Studien zur Friedensforschung* I, Stuttgart 1969, 144–77. – On the NT cf. W. Foerster, TDNT II, 411–17; E. Brandenburger, *Frieden im NT*, Gütersloh 1973; E. Dinkler, *Eirene, Der urchristliche Friedensgedanke*, 1973 (SHAW.PH), on Eph. 2.13–18: 25–30.

[16] Grounded by Schlier, *Christus und die Kirche* 18–26; further developed in Schlier 124–33; taken up with assent by Dibelius – Greeven 69; Pokorný, ZNW 53, 182 f.; with references to Nag Hammadi texts Schenke (p. 107 n. 2); Fischer, *Tendenz* 133; Lindemann, *Aufhebung der Zeit* 161–6 (refers especially to the Thomas Psalms 1–2). Cf. also Conzelmann 99 f.

[17] Cf. Eth Enoch 14.9; Syr Baruch 54.5; Greek Baruch 2.1 f. Schlier tried to trace a development which runs from the Jewish idea of the Law as a fence, through the apocalyptic picture of a heavenly wall, to the Jewish-Gnostic identification of the Law- and heavenly-fence. Cf. Merklein, *Christus und die Kirche* 38–40.

[18] Thus Abbott, Scott, Beare; Mußner, *Christus* 84; Mitton, *Epistle* 231 f.; Kirby, *Ephesians* 158; González Lamadrid* EstB 28, 229 f.

[19] V. the illustration of the find of 1871 in Deißmann LO 63. In 1935 a further fragment was discovered, cf. K. Galling, *Textbuch zur Geschichte Israels*, Tübingen ²1968, Nr. 55.

ruins, lies far from the author's mind, and to connect with Jesus Christ the destruction of this barrier, even if only metaphorically, would be most strange.

3. That it points to the Torah with all its regulations as 'fence' which should protect Israel and separate it from the other nations.[20] There are various references which might support this interpretation, of which Arist 139 is especially worth mentioning: Moses surrounded (περιέφραξεν) the Israelites with an impenetrable compound and iron walls so that they had no association with any of the other nations; likewise 142 where the rules for cleanliness and diet are emphasized. For Judaism the Torah was a divine protecting-fence of cosmic relevance, but from a Christian point of view it loses its importance and is in fact shattered as the 'Law of the Commandments' by the event of the Cross.[21]

If the whole is a Christian (midrash-like) interpretation of Scripture which takes up in a positive fashion the OT ideas of peace and simultaneously, in antithesis to Judaism, destroys its understanding of the Law, we can manage with the standard model of the Torah as the dividing partition between Jews and non-Jews. The Neuter (the two parts) does not necessarily denote cosmic regions but can stand for the two groups of humanity 'estranged' by the Law. The Neuter can be used for persons or groups of persons (cf. 1 Cor 1.27 f; Gal. 3.22; Jn. 6.37, 39; 17.2; 1 Jn. 5.4). From this neutral wording the author progresses to a personal metaphor ('the two' v. 15) and then uses the first expression in its masculine form (τοὺς ἀμφοτέρους v. 16). There is no need to postulate the inclusion of a different tradition for vv. 14b–15a.[22]

The author wants to demonstrate the overcoming of the one-time difference between the 'uncircumcision' and the 'circumcision' in Jesus Christ and in the Church founded in him.[23] The final goal is peace with God, access to the Father (vv. 17 f.); but the way there runs via the union of the two previously separated groups.

15a

The expression which comes at the end of v. 14 'in his own flesh' must be taken, because of its form (cf. analysis) and content, to belong with what follows.[24] Christ has nullified the Law of the Commandments in his own flesh. The Clause is meant to explain more fully the pulling-down of the partition (Subordinate Participle) and without any attribute it would remain

---

[20]Cf. the material in Bill I, 693 f.; III, 587 f. According to this the 'fence' in rabbinic literature (v especially Abot III, 13b) was simply a protection for Israel; there is a different interpretation in the passages from Arist. mentioned above; cf. also Damasc. 1.20; 20.25–7. O. Betz, RdQ 6 (1967) 95–8 traces the protecting fence back to the 'bounds' on Mt Sinai (Ex. 19.12).

[21]Cf. Stuhlmacher* 344 f. He explains, with reference to M. Hengel, that for Hellenistic and Rabbinic Judaism the Torah was an 'ontologically and cosmologically effective power' (ibid. n. 33).

[22]Gnilka 139 thinks otherwise; Barth, too, 283–7 considers a definite derivation impossible.

[23]We cannot, like Lindemann, *Aufhebung der Zeit* 173, reduce his intention to mean simply that it is a matter 'of the situation of the Christians, of the effect of Christ's salvation-act on the cosmos and on the individual'. Already from vv. 11–13 on he is thinking of the relationship between former Gentiles and Jews. – On the enmity between Jews and non-Jews cf. Bill. III, 588–91; McEleney* (on Eph. 2.11–22: 337–40.

[24]On the other hand τὴν ἔχθραν must be left with what precedes it (otherwise Schlier: *die Feindschaft in seinem Fleisch* . . .); cf. the discussion of the syntactical possibilities in Abbott 61 f.

unclear how Christ has nullified the Law. The words used are influenced by Col. 1.22 ('in his body of flesh') and 2.14 (τοῖς δόγμασιν 'with its statutes') but given a special form for the context here. In the context of the 'enmity' between the Jews and Gentiles the Law, which with its commandments (ἐντολαί) and statutes (δόγματα) plays the dividing obstacle, must be 'nullified' (καταργέω) – a strong expression which Paul never uses directly of the Law (cf. the opposite in Rom. 3.31) but only of the effects of the Law on unredeemed humanity (cf. Rom. 6.6; 7.5 f). In Col. 2.14 it is the bond against us which God has nailed to the Cross and set aside; in Eph. 2.15 nothing is said of setting aside sins or debts, nothing about the curse of the Law from which Christ has ransomed us (Gal. 3.13). In the perspective of Eph. the Jewish Law (which is mentioned only here) has faded to a partition between Jews and Gentiles; but it has lost this function because of Christ. The Commandments, which consist of statutes, are then those dividing regulations, especially circumcision (cf. v. 11) and also the cleanliness and dietary rules, which are overcome with the death of Christ. 'In his own flesh' corresponds to 'in his blood' (v. 13) and does not refer to Christ's becoming human or the (gnostic) idea of the power of matter overcome by the redeemer.[25] The memory of the bloody event of the Cross is preserved even if the expressions have meanwhile become mere symbols for the redemption 'through the Cross' (cf. v. 16).

15b

To express the positive effect of Christ's deed the author again uses an unusual metaphor which is then continued by the familiar idea of reconciliation (v. 16a). Those previously separated appear as two partners whom Christ in his own person has made one single new 'man'. In contrast to v. 14b it is now clearer that we are dealing with a New Creation, the one Church composed of Jews and Gentiles. To effect this Christ does not perform the role of a builder who constructs a new, unified building from separate parts and as it were sets it up on view; he builds this new entity in his own person, it is he himself in a new dimension. For the Church is indissolubly linked to him as the head is to the body, as husband and wife in marriage (5.31 f.). But even these analogies are inadequate because Christ exists in his Church and the Church in him in a fashion for which there is nothing really comparable. The metaphor of a new person does not stand completely alone in Eph. but to a certain degree corresponds to the 'complete man' (ἀνήρ) to whom all members of the Church, Christ's Body, should strive (4.13) and also to the metaphor of marriage, since in the scriptural quotation 'man' (ἄνθρωπος) is named (5.31). We must reckon that the author knew of certain 'ἄνθρωπος' speculations even if here they are made to serve the Christological-ecclesiological expression.

---

[25]The incarnational interpretation is found e.g. in Calvin, who explains the removal of the division thus: siquidem filius Dei communem omnibus naturam induendo perfectam unitatem in corpore suo consecravit (on 2.14, CR 51.171). In Sermon XIII he takes up the idea of Christ the Second Adam (408 f.). – Käsemann represents the Gnostic interpretation, *Leib* 140 f. On σάρξ in Gnosticism cf. further E. Schweizer, TDNT VII 148–51; but he understands Eph. 2.14 like Col. 1.22 to be speaking of the physical corporeality of Jesus (ibid., 137).

Proof of a dependence on particular, especially Gnostic, texts is uncertain and can only be achieved by combinations. The complexity of the Anthropos-idea has meantime been proved.[26] A connection with the metaphor of the cosmic partition cannot be established. Comparable is the Gnostic notion that in the Unity bisexuality will be preserved. Hence we find in the Ev Phil (NHC II/3): 'If the woman had not become separate from the man, she would not die with the man. Her separation became the beginning of death. Therefore Christ came to put aside again the separation which was there from the beginning, to unite the two and give life to and unite those who died during the separation.[27] One single Gnostic model cannot be proved.[28] More will be said in the Excursus on the Church.

In the contrast here the newly-created unity is the Church made up of Jews and Gentiles, one eschatological New Creation (καινή) which, however, only comes into being as such in that Christ has created her 'in himself'. The new 'man' is Christ insofar as he represents and realizes the Church in himself. Christ and the Church are not thereby identical; the Church is grounded 'in him' and should grow into him (cf. 2.21; 4.13, 15) and Christ, the Head of the Body (1.22; 4.15; 5.23) remains her basis (2.30), the source of her growth (4.16) and her inner life through the Spirit (2.18, 22; 4.4a). In that he leads the two formerly separated groups of Jew and Gentiles in his own person to a new, indissoluble unity, he establishes ultimate peace between them.

16

Christ is 'our peace' but also in the still more profound sense that he reconciled those formerly separated *with God*. These are two internally connected aspects of Christ's one peace-bringing work. While by his death on the Cross he reconciled with God the two groups who were previously estranged, he reconciled them to one another. For the reconciliation with God, the author depends on Col. 1.20 f. (cf. the composite verb ἀποκαταλλάσσειν). For Paul reconciliation always proceeds from God (2 Cor. 5.18 f; Rom. 5.10 f.) and Col. too retains this theocentric view. Eph. attributes reconciliation to Christ who as bringer of peace effects reconciliation with God through the Cross. The Crucifixion-event is not described in graphic vividness (cf. by contrast Col. 2.14 f.) and certainly there are no offensive details which might make the readers embarrassed (cf. Gal. 3.13; 5.11; 6.14; 1 Cor. 1.18, 23) but it is simply the location of reconciliation, a topos of Christian proclamation. Certainly the atoning death of Christ is stressed as the source of salvation for all (cf. Eph. 5.2), but the Cross as a distinguishing symbol of Christian existence loses some of its force. On the other hand, as the place of reconciliation it can become an incentive for a deeper understanding of peace.

[26]Cf. C. Colpe, *Die religionsgeschichtliche Schule*, 1961 (FRLANT 78); E. Brandenburger, *Adam und Christus*, 1962 WMANT 7) 68–157; Schenke, *Der Gott 'Mensch'*; K.-M. Fischer, 'Adam und Christus. Überlegungen zu einem religionsgeschichtlichen Problem', in K.-W. Tröger (ed.), *Altes Testament – Frühjudentum – Gnosis*, Gütersloh 1980, 283–98.

[27]Logion 78 (ed. W. C. Till, Berlin 1963, 41 f.); cf. also Log. 79: 'Die Frau aber vereinigt sich mit ihrem Gatten im Brautgemach ...', (Till 43); further Log. 71; Ev of Thomas 22; 106. Cf. Fischer, *Tendenz* 133 f.; on the Gnostic idea of unity E. Haenchen, *Die Botschaft des Thomas-Evangeliums*, Berlin 1961, 52–3.

[28]Against Conzelmann 69; Lindemann, *Aufhebung der Zeit* 167 f.; in the reconstruction by Schenke (p. 107 n. 2) and Fischer, *Tendenz* 132, the lines about the one new race are omitted.

Christ has reconciled strife-torn humanity with God 'in one single body'. It is a matter of debate whether the author is thinking of the body of Jesus on the Cross or of the ecclesial Body (the Church as the Body of Christ) or even of both in so far as the Church is already represented and begins to be realized in the body of the Crucified. The stronger arguments give reason to assume that the author is already thinking in a terse style of the new unity of the two previously separated groups – i.e. the Church:[29] (a) When speaking of the body of Jesus put to death on the Cross, through which the Law was nullified, the author prefers 'in his flesh' (v. 14); (b) Throughout Eph. the 'Body' of Christ means the Church (1.23; 4.4, 12, 16; 5.23, 30); (c) The reality called the 'one' (Neuter and Masculine) (ἕν, εἷς) in the argumentation of vv. 14–18 is always the Church; (d) furthermore, the expression is easily connected to the aforementioned 'one new man' ; (e) this 'in one single body' corresponds to the following 'in one single Spirit' (v. 18) and with it builds a double expression for the Church which is understood as a unity (4.4a). The Church is thereby pulled into the immediate vicinity of the Cross, exists in fact in the Crucifixion-event. In that Christ dies on the Cross, the Church is born; in that he gives himself for us as a sacrifice (5.2) he proves his love for the Church (5.25), becomes in fact the redeemer of his Body, the Church (5.23). So close is the connection of the Church to Christ that she already appears in the Cross as a New Creation, the one redeemed humanity.

Hence we should take the concluding participial phrase 'ἐν αὐτῷ' as referring to the person of Christ ('in him') and not to the Cross just mentioned, although that is also grammatically possible.[30] It corresponds to the αὐτός at the beginning (v. 14): He is our peace and has put an end to alienation in his own person. Here 'alienation' has a double sense; it denotes that both the rift in humanity and the gulf between humanity and God have been bridged. The alienation between human beings is removed by their common peace with God. Thereby the theme 'Christ is our peace' also achieves its full resonance for the first time.

17

Christ, 'our peace', through his work of peace, has become the herald of peace to those who were far off (the Gentiles) and those who were near (the Jews). The author now adds εὐηγγελίσατο (he preached) to the quotation from Is. 57.19, interpreted in a Christian sense. Perhaps he is also taking up Is. 52.7, the starting-point for the 'Gospel' (cf. Mk 1.14 f.): God's messenger who brings good tidings (LXX εὐαγγελιζόμενος), who proclaims ultimate 'peace' (εἰρήνη) for the people, is the Messiah Jesus (cf. Is. 9.6). In early Christian reflections on Scripture, OT passages (from Is.) were combined and given a christological interpretation. The reference to

---

[29]Cf. the discussion in Merklein, *Christus und die Kirche* 45–53. The interpretation as meaning the Church can already be found in Ambrosiaster (MPL 17, 401 B: ut homines ... membra efficerentur unius corporis novi) and Oecumenius (MPG 118, 1197C); cf. also Hanson, *Unity* 144–6.

[30]Cf. Zerwick, *Greek* para 159; most recently argued for by Gnilka 144; cf. also Barth 296 f. Some texts read ἐν ἑαυτῷ G 88 823 lat. The Latin exegesis preferred the interpretation referring to Christ in his person. cf. the quotations from the Fathers in Frede, *Ep. ad Eph.* 90 f.

Is. 52.7[31] is also backed up by Eph. 6.15 where the author alludes to the same passage. The additional 'and with his coming' (ἐλθών) serves merely as an introduction since the emphasis is on the preaching. Neither Christ's coming to earth and his earthly effectiveness, which plays no part in Eph.,[32] nor his entry into the heavenly world (cf. 4.10)[33] is meant; at most the author is thinking of the apostolic preaching (cf. 3.8; 4.11 'preachers') in which Jesus remains the preacher.[34] But probably in this explanation which concentrates on the person of Jesus Christ it is simply his world-wide effective bringing of peace which is emphasized, the peace which he has proclaimed for the far off (Gentiles) and those near (Jews). The Gentiles, who are the author's chief concern (cf. vv. 11–13), are especially addressed by 'you', while the Jews are not ('we' is missing) – a sign that the author recognises that he is not a representative of the Jewish Christians.

18

The former differences are now meaningless. 'Far' and 'near' no longer exist but only the one congregation of the saved ('we') who, united by Christ ('both') have the same access to the Father. This is the distinctly Christian view, initiated by Paul (cf. Gal. 3.18; Rom. 3.21–24; 10.12) and retained and expanded in the early Christian Church (cf. Col. 3.11; Tit. 2.14; 1 Pet. 2.4–10; Rev. 5.9; 7.9). It is part of the same idea that God, from whom the Gentiles were formerly separated (cf. v. 12c) is called 'the Father'. For Christians there is only one God and Father of all (4.6), 'our' Father (1.2), the Father of our Lord Jesus Christ (1.3). If we now have 'access' to him (cf. 3.12) this was originally a cultic metaphor which was happily taken over in the early Church. Now, however, it is used of the 'drawing near' to Christ and his congregation of the saved, the spiritual temple (1 Pet. 2.4), through Christ to God (cf. 1 Pet. 3.18) or to the heavenly shrine, God's throne of grace (Heb. 4.16; 10.22; cf. 12.22 f.)[35]

The approach to the Father which is opened for us through Christ takes place 'in one single Spirit'. Christ's ministry as Mediator is thus carried on and made effective in the ever-present Spirit which fills the Church and all her members. The doctrine of the Spirit (Pneumatology) in

---

[31]So also Mußner, *Christus* 101; Barth 267; Stuhlmacher* 347, who also refers to the Jewish interpretation of Is. 9.6 and Is. 52.7 as referring to the Messiah (cf. Bill. III, 587). Others think of Zech. 9.10 MT because 9.9 was such an important messianic testimonium for the early Church (cf. Lindars, *NT Apologetic* 111–15). But in the context of Eph. this is far from his thought.

[32]Chrysostom (MPG 62.43) understands it to mean his earthly activity as do some of the earlier exegetes, Masson. More accurate is Mußner, *Christus* 101: 'ἐλθών therefore refers simply to Christ's existence in the world without asking about any particular biographical datum. Christ's work as such means the proclamation of "peace" between Jews and Gentiles in the one Church and between humanity and God'. Similarly Haupt, Staab, Gaugler, Conzelmann; G. Friedrich, TDNT II, 718 f.

[33]Thus Schlier 137–9 in the sense of the Ascent of the Redeemer (cf. Eph. 4, 8–10; 1 Tim. 3.16; 1 Pet. 3.18–20).

[34]Cf. Klöpper, Ewald, Abbott, Scott, Gnilka.

[35]Cf. K. L. Schmidt, TDNT I, 133 f. (on the Sitz im Leben in the cult 131 f.); J. Schneider, TDNT II, 684, W. Thüsing, '"Laßt uns hinzutreten . . ." (Hebr. 10.22)', BZ NF 9 (1965) 1–17.

Eph.[36] stays with the way of thinking of Paul and the early Church and reveals several functions of the divine Pneuma (cf. 1.17; 3.5, 16; 4.23; 5.18). But his unifying power is especially emphasized (4.3 f.). Paul's basic understanding that the resurrected Lord continues to be effective through *his own* Spirit, giving life (1 Cor. 15.45) and freedom (2 Cor. 3.17 f.) is no longer so clearly defined but forms the basis for the conception of the Church, as is shown especially in 2.18. The Christ who brought peace through his Cross brings together those formerly separated into a single Body (2.16) and leads them by one single Spirit, the divine Spirit (3.16) ever closer (2.22) to the Father.

Now, at the end of the exposition of the unification of the two formerly separated groups, we must consider the pragmatic tendency of the passage. The emphasis placed on the overcoming of the alienation is not only made to make the Gentile-Christians more aware than formerly (cf. 2.1–10) of their election and redemption but perhaps also out of an immediate interest in the relationship of the Gentile- to the Jewish-Christians in the Church. Unfortunately we cannot make out the contemporary background more clearly. The most we can say is that there were tensions between Christians from different backgrounds in the then predominantly Gentile-Christian congregations. It is possible that the anamnesis is motivated by a disparagement of the Jewish-Christian members by the Gentile-Christians. Should we assume further that it was made impossible for the Jewish-Christians to pursue their own life-style according to Jewish customs – i.e. to retain their own regulations for diet and ritual?[37] It is a fact that, after the catastrophe of the Jewish War in the last decades of the First Century Jewish Christianity moved more and more to the circumference of the Church in general, was spurned and finally became a sect.[38] The text of Eph. 2.11–18, particularly v. 15 according to which Christ nullified 'the Law of the Commandments with the statutes', makes it unlikely that the author wished to plead for tolerance for the Jewish-Christians in their observation of a Jewish life-style. The Jewish-Christians in the congregations are a constant admonition to remember that God had chosen Israel and not the Gentile peoples to realize his plans for salvation. For this reason they deserve all love and respect from the Gentile-Christian majority.

The author of Eph. is certainly not considering the relationship of 'Church and Synagogue' but he is far removed from any anti-Judaism – in fact with this anamnesis he makes a practical contribution towards the overcoming of the 'antisemitism' which was at that time

[36]Cf. E. Schweizer, TDNT VI, 444; Percy, *Probleme* 299–309; 317–24; Schnackenburg, FS C.F.D. Moule.

[37]Thus Fischer, *Tendenz* 86–8.

[38]G. Hoennicke, *Das Judenchristentum im ersten und zweiten Jahrhundert*, Berlin 1908; H.-J. Schoeps, *Theologie und Geschichte des Judenchristentums*, Tübingen 1949; L. Goppelt, *Christentum und Judentum im ersten und zweiten Jahrhundert*, Gütersloh 1954; G. Strecker, *Das Judenchristentum in den Pseudo-klementinen*, 1958 (TU 70); J. Munck, 'Jewish Christianity in Post-Apostolic Times', NTS 6 (1959/60) 103–16; M. Simon, *Recherches d'histoire Judéo-Chrétienne*, Paris 1962; B. Bagatti, *L'Église de la Circoncision*, Jerusalem 1965; R. Schnackenburg, 'Das Urchristentum', in J. Maier – J. Schreiner (ed.), *Literatur und Religion des Frühjudentums*, Würzburg 1973, 284–309.

growing.[39] Christianity stands on the base of the old Israel, shares a faith with them in the one God and his economy of salvation even if for the Christian faith this has been fulfilled and realized in a new way in Christ (cf. 1.10; 3.9–12).

19

Now the author draws the conclusion (ἄρα οὖν) of these interpretations for the addressees. They are no longer foreigners and sojourners (πάροικοι) but fellow-citizens (συμπολῖται) of the saints and the household (οἰκεῖοι) of God. The four expressions correspond to a certain extent, but not entirely, to the four characteristics of their pre-Christian status in v. 12.[40] The backward-pointing 'no longer' and the second person ('you are') make the reference back to vv. 11–12 certain; it is, however, only with the positive declaration of what they now are that the point of his argument is revealed. The double expression 'fellow-citizens of the saints and household of God' leads in to the metaphor which dominates the following verses i.e. the metaphor of the building ('built together' – the 'whole building' – 'dwelling-place of God') which describes the *Church* as the place where the former Gentiles have achieved full communion with God. Their alienation from *Israel* is not thereby stressed – that they have been *added* to the old People of God[41] – but rather in that Israel and the Gentiles have one new *common* access to the Father (v. 18), namely in the *Church* which is built on a different foundation (v. 20). The bridge created through Christ from the Congregation of Israel to the new universal entity, the ultimate House of God for the whole of humanity, also makes necessary a transformation of the concepts, a new understanding. If we interpret v. 12 at the level of the 'at one time' from Israel's advantages from which the Gentiles were excluded, the concepts taken up now have a new 'ecclesial' ring because – so we must conclude – the Church has stepped into the *place* of Israel, of course in the unbrokenness of the divine plan of salvation.

    The double expression 'foreigners and sojourners', which can scarcely be differentiated, reminds us first of those people who did not belong to God's people Israel in the full sense: foreigners who only lived temporarily in the land or others who settled permanently and who had certain recognised rights.[42]

---

[39]On anti-Semitism in antiquity, which we should perhaps rather name anti-Judaism, cf. I. Heinemann, Art. 'Antisemitismus', Pauly – W. Suppl. V, 3–43; J. Leipoldt, Art. 'Antisemitismus', RAC I, 469–76; W. Foerster, *Neutestamentliche Zeitgeschichte* II, Hamburg 1956, 235–8; J. N. Sevenster, *The Roots of Pagan Anti-Semitism in the Ancient World*, Leiden 1975; J. L. Daniel, 'Anti-Semitism in the Hellenistic-Roman Period', JBL 98 (1979) 45–65.

[40]Notice the syntagma ξένοι καὶ πάροικοι, and συμπολῖται ... καὶ ὀικεῖοι ..., as well as the order of the expressions. While v. 12 is influenced by Rom. 9.4, we can no longer say that about v. 19. Merklein, *Kirchliches Amt* 121 f. sees the basic ideas in Col. 1.22b–23 handed on.

[41]Thus Barth 269 f. and his n. 71.

[42]Cf. G. Stählin, TDNT V, 8 ff. (ξένος); K. L. and M. A. Schmidt TDNT V, 844–6 (πάροικος); M. de Jonge, 'Vreemdelingen en bijwoners', NedThT 11 (1956/57) 18–36; Spicq, *Notes* II, 592–6. The question whether foreigners have a share in the salvation promised to Israel was controversial in Judaism. Cf. Bill. I 353–63; II 721–3; R. Meyer, TDNT V, 850 f.; K. L. Schmidt, 'Israels Stellung zu den Fremdlingen und Beisassen', Jud. 1 (1946) 269–96. In 4Qflor I, 4 'a foreigner and a stranger' among others were excluded from God's eschatological House. Cf. Gärtner, *Temple* 62–4; Merklein, *Kirchl. Amt* 127.

But here we are not concerned with Israel's changing attitude to aliens in the course of history. The expression 'foreigners and sojourners', which could be understood by the Gentile-Christians even without any very detailed knowledge of the Jewish background,[43] points to their separation from God which was only overcome by their reception into the Church. Hence after the negative description of their former status there immediately follows a positive assertion that they are 'fellow-citizens of the saints' and the 'household of God'. Here, too, the perspective of v. 12 is clearly transcended. Semantically 'fellow-citizens' (συμπολῖται) may contain an echo of the 'community' (πολιτεία) of Israel; but the 'saints' are not the Israelites and can hardly be the Jewish-Christians[44] but, as in the rest of the document (cf. under 1.1), all the members of the Church[45] or – a possibility which must be taken seriously – the angels as representatives of the heavenly congregation (cf. 1.18). This last possibility is suggested not only from parallels in the Qumran writings[46] but also from the connection with 'household of God'. All in the earthly congregation, whether formerly Jews or Gentiles, have already a part in the heavenly world where their 'inheritance' lies ready (1.14, 18; cf. 5.5). The baptized are raised with Christ and already installed with him in heaven (2.5 f.). 'Fellow-citizens of the saints' are then the Christians as such who belong to the divine heavenly Kingdom through their incorporation in the Church (cf. Phil 3.20) and are linked with the congregation of the angels and those who have achieved the accomplishment of their faith (cf. Heb. 12.2 f.; also Rev. 7.1–10; 4.1–5). The spatial outlook, which no longer makes such an impression on us with our secular, worldly senses, is expanded by the idea of God's family. For οἰκεῖος (member of the household)[47] also brings into consideration this metaphor which likewise has a tradition in early Christianity (cf. Gal. 6.10; Mk. 3.33–35; 10.30; Heb. 3.2–6). The metaphorical expressions which emerge here are not very clearly defined and cannot be derived uniformly from traditional views be it in Judaism or Hellenism. The 'metaphorical sphere' of town, house, family and temple[48] illustrates on the whole the fellowship with God which all Christians without distinction have achieved through Christ's act of reconciliation and will continue to achieve in Christ's Church. The idea of a 'fellowship of the saints' which is later developed in various ways in the theology of the Church

[43] Cf. Dibelius – Greeven 71; Gnilka 153.

[44] Thus Schmid, *Epheserbrief* 226; Vielhauer, *Oikodome* 123 f.; Dibelius – Greeven 71; H. Strathmann, TDNT VI, 535; Bieder, *Ekklesia* 24.

[45] Cf. Abbott, Haupt, Staab, Masson, Ernst; Pfammatter, *Kirche als Bau* 77; Merklein, *Kirchl. Amt* 131 f. – With 'fellow-citizen' he is not necessarily thinking of particular groups 'with' whom one is a citizen; it can also mean membership of the community as a whole.

[46] Cf. p. 43 n. 16. On Eph. cf. Mußner, *Beiträge* 188–91; Klinzing, *Kultus* 185–7. The interpretation of the 'saints' as angels is also represented by Schlier 140 f., Gnilka 154; Lindemann, *Aufhebung* der Zeit 183.

[47] οἰκεῖος = belonging to the household was the usual meaning in the Hellenistic sphere. It is also used in the LXX for various Hebrew equivalents, in Prov. 17.9 alongside φίλοι; cf. also Job 19.15; Amos 6.10; Is. 3.6; 31.9; 58.7. Cf. Pr-Bauer 1102; O. Michel, TDNT V, 136; Spicq, Notes I, 216 f.

[48] O. Michel, TDNT V, 134.

Fathers and was taken over into the Apostles Creed comes to the fore.[49]

20

The universal Congregation of God which currently exists has also a historical component; it already has a history. The Gentile-Christians who now belong to it (ἐστε) are already built (Aorist ἐποικοδομηθέντες) on the foundation of the Apostles and Prophets. 'Foundation' makes it clear from the start that it is not merely a recollection of the beginning and development of the Church. Rather it means that those influential personalities of the early period have a 'fundamental' function and a continuing meaning for the structure of the Church. The Church is recognizable in all her dimensions in the metaphor of a growing building (v. 21). She is a present entity, held together by Christ, the 'cornerstone', and filled with the Spirit (v. 22). She is raised on an historical foundation and strives towards her perfection. This metaphor raises several questions which are important for ecclesiology and ecumenical theology.[50]

Who are the 'apostles and prophets' upon whom the Church is raised? They are mentioned again after a few verses (3.5) as those to whom the Mystery of Christ was revealed and who – as we must conclude from 3.6 f. – preached the Gospel. Hence for Eph. the Apostles are those people in the early years who first preached the Gospel and vouched for it, whose names (apart from Paul) and number seem unimportant, whose qualification and authorisation are no longer a matter of interest but whose authority is established because they were 'given' by the Lord to the Church (cf. 4.11). Some light is also shed on the 'Prophets' who are always named after them and once expressly differentiated from them (4.11). In spite of a long tradition in interpretation, this cannot mean the OT prophets according to these passages.[51] It must relate to inspired people (cf. 3.5) in the early Church who, along with the Apostles,[52] contributed to the elucidation and proclamation of the Gospel. Again we must be cautious in particularising this and comparing it with prophets mentioned elsewhere (Acts, 1 Cor., Rev. etc.) since nowhere else does Eph. make any

---

[49]The concept was originally understood in the East in the material sense (participation in the benefits of salvation, especially in the Lord's Supper); later, particularly in the West, it was taken to apply to the solidarity of saved people on earth among themselves but also with the Fathers and the righteous deceased and angels. Cf. W. Elert, *Abendmahl und Kirchengemeinschaft in der alten Kirche, hauptsächlich des Ostens*, Berlin 1954; A. Piolanti, *Il mistero della communione dei Santi nella rivelazione e nella teologia*, Rome 1957; K. Rahner, 'Gemeinschaft der Heiligen', in W. Sandfuchs (ed.), *Ich glaube*, Würzburg ²1975, 129–38.

[50]Cf. Schnackenburg* in FS Barrett.

[51]In the old Church Chrysostom, Theodoret, Ambrosiaster, Jerome, then Aquinas, Estius; F. Prat, *La théologie de s. Paul* II, Paris ³⁸1949, 340 f.; K. H. Rengstorf, TDNT I, 441, n. 212; G. Fridrichsen, *The Apostle and his Message*, Uppsala-Leipzig 1947, 19, n. 12; Mußner, *Christus* 108. Cf. the survey and discussion in Pfammatter* 87–91. In the meantime the interpretation as meaning the NT prophets has won through, cf. apart from the commentaries G. Friedrich, TDNT VI, 848–51 passim; Pfammatter* 91–7; Merklein, *Kirchl. Amt* 140–3.

[52]The opinion that in 'apostles and prophets' the same group of people in different aspects is meant is held by Sahlin* 18, n. 1; Pfammatter* 93–7, but this founders on Eph. 4.11.

[53]The phenomenon of early Christian prophecy is complex and disputed among scholars, cf. G. Friedrich, TDNT VI, 848–55. 859 ff.; U. B. Müller, *Prophetie und Predigt im NT*,

'foundation' function. Here it is more a matter of a theological principle than of an historical verification. If the 'apostolicity' of the Church is considered as an element of ecclesiology, we must not overlook the fact that for Eph. the prophetic-pneumatic is also part of the foundation of the Church.

A further question which goes beyond the exegetical problem into the area of controversial theology is raised by the concluding Genitive Absolute: In what relationship does the 'foundation' of the Apostles and Prophets stand to the 'Cornerstone' or – as others translate – to the 'keystone' (ἀκρογωνιαῖος) which is Christ? The existence of this stone is deliberately emphasized by the ὄντος which precedes it.

Exegetically the relation of the pronoun αὐτοῦ is dubious. Must we translate it as: 'Christ Jesus is *its* (the foundation's) cornerstone' or 'Christ Jesus *himself* is the corner- (or key-)stone'? Both are possible from its position in the sentence. In the first case it would mean that Christ would be seen as the cornerstone inserted into the foundation. In the second, his person, in contrast to the Apostles and Prophets, would be emphasized in its special function, possibly even as a keystone. At this point we can add no further clarification.

In what position are we to think of this stone which is the most important for the whole building, the one which holds it together (v. 21)? While formerly only a few scholars thought of the keystone – especially in the construction of a portal – which secures the whole edifice from above,[54] this view has found many supporters since the work of J. Jeremias.[55] Now, however, we can discern a counter-movement.[56] Let us consider the most important arguments!

For the interpretation as 'key-stone' we can in particular cite: (a) There are many instances in the literature of the 2nd–4th centuries which confirm this meaning; (b) a series of archaeological facts and findings (ornamented key-stones) lends support to these examples; (c) since the 'foundation' is already occupied by the Apostles and Prophets, Christ can only with difficulty be included as the cornerstone; (d) Christ as the upper key-stone which crowns and dominates the building fits better with the idea of Christ as the Head of the Church, especially according to Eph. 4.16. The representatives of the other thesis, namely that it relates to the *cornerstone*, object that the literary witnesses are in part very questionable;[57] further, that in 'foundation' we are thinking of the lowest part of the building (not the stoney basis) and the cornerstone inserted at that point has an important function; and finally that the keystone which is inserted only at the end does not fit the picture of a *growing* building. They then bring in historico-traditional and theological grounds; (a) the only place in the LXX where the word appears is Is. 28.16 which clearly indicates a (valuable) cornerstone inserted into the foundation. This passage, which is already in the Targum on Is. 28.16 interpreted as referring to the Messiah, became for the early Church, along with other 'stone' words, an important messianic evidence for Jesus

The phenomenon of early Christian prophecy is complex and disputed among scholars, cf. G. Friedrich, TDNT VI, 848–55. 859ff.; U.B. Müller, *Prophetie und Predigt in NT*,
[55]J. Jeremias*. Among those who agree with him are Vielhauer, *Oikodome* 126; Wikenhauser, *Kirche* 161; Dibelius – Greeven, Conzelmann, Gnilka.
[56]An early dissenter was Percy, *Probleme* 329–32 and 485–8; after him Mußner, *Christus* 108–110. Further critical voices are K. T. Schäfer*; Pfammatter* 143–51; McKelvey*; Merklein, *Kirchl. Amt* 144–52.
[57]V. most recently Merklein, *Kirchl. Amt* 147–9.

(cf. especially 1 Pet. 2.4–8). (b) Since in 1 Cor. 3.10 f. Christ is the foundation laid by 'master-builder' Paul, it seems reasonable to suppose that Christ also has a foundation-function in Eph. 2.20. (c) If Christ is seen as the keystone, the relationship of Apostles and Prophets to Christ remains unclear.[58]

If we weigh all the grounds pro and contra, the arguments for Christ as cornerstone carry greater weight. The unusual expression can be explained from the early Christian tradition which connected the only available passage, Is. 28.16, to refer to Christ in the sense of cornerstone. Metaphorically this can easily be combined with the foundation of Apostles and Prophets. The crucial cornerstone was the first laid for the foundation, the lowest stable part of a building (cf. 1 Cor. 3.10) and the position of all the other stones in the foundation was determined by this cornerstone.[59] Jesus Christ is still the foundation-stone in this understructure also for the author of Eph., who wants to stress the Apostles and Prophets because of their significance for later times (his own day and age). Upon him rises the whole structure of the Church, including the Apostles and Prophets. This self-consistent metaphor does not exclude Christ's being seen in other aspects, e.g. in the metaphor of the Body, which Christ as the ruling Head and the goal of the Church's growth (cf. 4.11, 13, 15 f.).

The interpretation of Eph. 2.20 played a part in the Reformation period in the controversy about papal primacy (cf. under Historical Influence).

21–22

Just as the Church is firmly established on its cornerstone, Jesus Christ, so the whole building[60] is 'joined together' (συναρμολογουμένη) in him and grows up into one holy temple. The central rôle played by Christ in the present construction of the Church (ἐν ᾧ) corresponds to his function as Mediator in the bringing of peace (ἐν αὐτῷ v. 16) and in the common access to the Father (δι' αὐτοῦ v. 18) and confirms the indissoluble connection of the Church to Christ. In the context, however, we are considering the Christians addressed who are 'built together' in him so that they themselves are living stones (cf. 1 Pet. 2.5) in God's growing building. The two Relative Clauses in v. 21 and v. 22 are closely joined together. Only in v. 22 does the line of thought reach its conclusion: they are *fellow-*citizens of the saints because, built *on* the foundation of the Apostles and Prophets they are also built *together* in Christ. At the same time the 'dwelling-place of God' reminds them that they have thus become members of God's household (v. 19). Hence it is no longer a question with which *group* the Gentile-Christians are built together; in Christ they are built up

---

[58]Merklein, *Kirchl. Amt.* 151: One could regard the foundation of the Apostles and Prophets as an isolated entity; but in reality they are totally dependent on Christ. Cf. also Masson 170 n. 1; Gaugler 121.

[59]Pfammatter* 149; Schäfer* 221; McKelvey* NTS 8, 354.

[60]According to the classical rule πᾶσα οἰκοδομή must be translated 'each building'. But this makes no sense in the context. Some MSS (among them A C P) include the article. But in the NT (under a Semitic influence) when the article is missing it can mean 'all of the building', cf. Mt. 2.3; 3.15; Acts 2.36; Rom. 11.26; on this see Zerwick, *Greek* para 143; Bl-Debr § 275.4; Moulton – Turner, *Grammar* III, 199 f.

together in the Church with *all* who belong to it. It is the same view as in
1.13 and 2.1 where the addressees are included in the community of the
Church and merely addressed separately.

The metaphor of the Church as a growing building takes up
various early Christian traditions and yet becomes a concept in its own
right. There are strong points of contact with 1 Cor. 3.9–12.16 but it is not
necessary to posit a literary dependence. In Paul's metaphors, too, the
picture of a building merges into that of a holy temple of God, and God's
Spirit 'lives' in those who belong to it (v. 16). Perhaps this explains the
expression about the 'dwelling-place of God in the Spirit' (v. 22) which
corresponds to the 'holy temple in the Lord' in the preceding verse. The
ἐν κυρίῳ, which as always in Eph. can only refer to Christ, appears
superfluous after ἐν ᾧ; but this identifies the Church founded on Christ as
a sacred building belonging to Christ. Christ reigns over it with the Holy
Spirit and so makes the Church a dwelling-place of God.

There are also points of contact with the Epistle to the Colossians:
Christians are 'rooted and *built up* in Christ' (2.7). But what is there stated
as a motif of the paraclesis (cf. Eph. 3.17) Eph. uses in our passage for its
ecclesiology. There are also connections with Col. 2.19 in the idea of
growth, although this passage first finds a stronger echo in Eph. 4.16. The
growth of the building is to be understood intensively from there.[61] The
Church grows through greater unity (cf. 4.3 f.) and love (4.15 f.) in its
'internal' form and so becomes ever more increasingly a dwelling-place of
God in the Spirit.

Finally, we cannot overlook the relationship with 1 Pet. 2.3–6 to
which our attention has already been drawn by the 'cornerstone'. Here,
too, different metaphors are blended and fused (the Christians appear also
as priests in the temple, the 'spiritual house'). Both authors take up from
the Pauline tradition the rich illustrative material which already existed in
Judaism, and, each in his own fashion, creatively form their own
conception.

Summary

This section, which is emphatically addressed to the Gentile-Christians in
the form of an anamnesis, also mentions their relationship to the former
Congregation of Israel, the old People of God. Far from Israel, the Gentiles
were at that time alienated from God and without hope in the world. Now,
however, the two groups formerly estranged have in Christ a common
access to the Father. In his death on the Cross Christ has torn down the
separating partition (the Law) and reconciled both with God and also with
one another. The reflection on Christ, 'our peace' (vv. 14–18) is in the
situation of Eph. certainly intended to help overcome current difficulties in
the congregations. The peace brought by Christ and embodied in his own
person is no abstract entity but should be concretised historically and be
realized in their community life.

---

[61]Cf. G. Delling, TDNT VIII, 518. The idea of growth is developed differently,
predominantly extensively, cf. P. Zingg, *Das Wachsen der Kirche*, 1974 (Orbis Bibl. et Orient,
3).

We must never lose sight of the reminder of God's way of salvation in humanity, especially of his covenant of mercy with Israel in the time before Christ. Without the history of Israel we should know nothing of the God who, hidden and yet mighty in history, allowing individuals and nations their freedom, punishing and pardoning, pursues his plans for salvation. Without the 'pre-history' in the OT we could not understand the Gospel of Jesus Christ through which this same God is revealed to us in a new and conclusive fashion. The Christian exegesis of the Isaiah passages on the Messiah as bringer of peace for the 'far off' and the 'near' shows very clearly how the Christian understanding of Redemption is built on the promises of the Prophets. Jesus Christ, 'our peace', has not only emerged from the People of Israel but binds us permanently to them. If Eph. does not touch upon the relationship with the Israel closed to Christ's message, this is because his whole outlook is concentrated on the Church made up of Jews and Gentiles. But Christ's cosmic act of Redemption still includes the old People of God in an unmistakeable way and today gives occasion for a re-thinking on the relationship between 'Church and synagogue'.[62] After centuries of increasing Christian culpability in relation to the Jews it is a pressing Christian responsibility to strive for reconciliation with the Jewish people for the sake of the Blood of Christ.

But Christ's bringing of peace, which has reconciled the whole of humanity to God, also requires that other walls which separate individuals and nations should be torn down, that tensions which today exist between races and castes, nations and religions should be put aside. The specifically Christian contribution to the overcoming of all enmity consists in witnessing to the whole of mankind the peace given by God. Only where in the knowledge of common guilt the will arises to accept the reconciliation offered by God and to be appropriately ready for reconciliation with one another have strivings for peace any real chance. The Church can give evidence for this if she builds in herself the model of a reconciled and united humanity under the call of divine reconciliation.

Hence as the irrefutable consequence there is finally the ecumenical concern to overcome the fragmentation into denominational churches and countless Christian groups. The one building of God, based on the foundation of the Apostles and Prophets, brought together and held together in Christ is the *una sancta, catholica et apostolica Ecclesia*. The emphasis placed on the first generation of preachers (Apostles and Prophets), whose continuing importance the author wants to underline at the beginning of the post-apostolic period ('foundation'), has today increased importance after a far longer historical separation from the origin. In the end it is Christ himself who, through his Spirit, is working towards the unity of all Christians. The more all Christians and Christian communities remember him and his Gospel witnessed to by the Apostles and Prophets and allow themselves to be led by the one Spirit through

[62]Cf. Vielhauer, *Oikodome* 9–11; Pfammatter* 152–164 (on the parallels in Qumran); O. Betz, 'Felsenmann und Felsengemeinde', ZNW 48 (1957) 49–77, especially 50–63; Gärtner, *Temple*; McKelvey, *New Temple*; Klinzing, *Kultus* 184–292. See further in the Excursus on the Church.

whom they have access to the Father the more they, growing inwardly, will
be built up into the holy temple in the Lord.

2. PAUL AS PREACHER AND INTERPRETER OF THE MYSTERY OF SALVATION REVEALED IN THE CHURCH (3.1–13)

Literature

Reumann NT 3; dit. NTS 13.
Lührmann, *Das Offenbarungsverständnis bei Paulus und in den paulinischen Gemeinden*, 1965 (WMANT 16).
N. Dahl, 'Das Geheimnis der Kirche nach Eph. 3.8–10', in *Zur Auferbauung des Leibes Christi* (FS P. Brunner), ed. E. Schlink and A. Peters, Kassel 1965, 63–75.
Merklein, *Kirchl. Amt* 159–224; Caragounis, *Mysterion* 55 f. 72–4, 96–112.
Lindemann, *Paulus* 40–2.

1 For this reason I, Paul, the captive of Christ Jesus
      for you, the Gentiles –
2 you have certainly heard of God's plan of grace
      which was given to me for you,
3 that under revelation the mystery was made known to me
      as I have previously described briefly.
4 So you can, if you read it, know my understanding
      of the Secret of Christ
5   which was not revealed
      in earlier generations of humankind
      as it is revealed now
      to his holy apostles and prophets in the Spirit:
6 The Gentiles are co-heirs, co-members and co-participants of the promise
      in Christ through the Gospel
7   whose servant I have become
      according to the gift of God's office
      which was granted to me through the effect of his power.
8 To me, the least of all the saints
      was this grace given
      to proclaim to the Gentiles the unfathomable riches of Christ
9   and to bring to light
         what the implementation of the mystery is
         which was hidden before the ages in God, the Creator of
         the universe.
10   that now the manifold wisdom of God may be revealed through
      the Church
      to the powers and forces in the heavens
11   according to (God's) eternal intention
               which he accomplished in Christ Jesus, our Lord.
12   In him we have openness and trusting access
         through faith in him.
13 Hence I ask you not to lose heart

in my sufferings for you
which serve your glorification

Analysis

The following section in which 'Paul' introduces himself with an emphatic ἐγώ and represents himself as a captive of Jesus Christ (v. 1) and then announces himself particularly as a servant of the Gospel (v. 7) is again syntactically (at least up to v. 7) a very complicated construction. V. 1 remains an Anacoluthon which originally was intended to be continued in v. 14 as is shown by the re-use of τουτου χάριν. The author begins an intercessory prayer by the Apostle for the addressees but then pauses to direct attention to Paul and his outstanding rôle in deciphering the 'Secret of Christ'. This Paul-anamnesis was apparently prompted by Col. 1.23–8 as the following (somewhat schematized) comparison shows:

Introduction of Paul	Col. 1.23	Eph. 3.1.
The suffering of the Apostle 'for you'	Col. 1.24	Eph. 3.1
		(cf. v. 13)
the 'Grace' granted to the Apostle	Col. 1.25	Eph. 3.2–3a
		(cf. v. 7)
the Revelation of the Mystery of Christ	Col. 1.26	Eph. 3.5.
the content of this Mystery	Col. 1.27	Eph. 3.6
preaching among the Gentiles	Col. 1.38	Eph. 3.8.

But we can also study Eph.'s own particular structure which is determined by its theme (inclusion of the Gentiles in Christ's Body), its theological outlook and its style. The connection of this section with the theme already developed in 2.11–22 is clear from the following points: (a) v. 1 – the addressees are expressly named as Gentiles (cf. 2.11): (b) v. 5 – 'the holy Apostles and Prophets in the Spirit' (cf. 2.20) are mentioned: (c) v. 3 – There are three expressions with συν- for the present state of the Gentile-Christians (cf. 2.19): (d) v. 6 – participation in the promise (cf. 2.12c): (e) v. 12 – 'access' to the Father (cf. 2.18). Thus the new section re-inforces the ideas developed earlier. With v. 13[1] the author steers back to the statement made about Paul at the beginning – that he endures his sufferings (as captive of Jesus Christ) for the addressees. In the next section (3.14–19) the influence of Col. 1.24–8 fades; on the other hand there are echoes of other passages in Col. (1.11, 23; 2.2).

The syntactical analysis of 3.1–13 reveals, after the Anacoluthon of v. 1 (cf. 2.1–3), a composite sentence which runs to the end of v. 7 if ὅτι originally belongs to the beginning of v. 3. The grace given to the Apostle (v. 2) consists in his insight into the 'mystery' (v. 3) as the addressees can see from what was previously described in brief (v. 4). This 'Mystery of Christ' is taken up in v. 5 with a Relative Clause and explained in more detail as that which was not made known in other generations of humankind in such a way as it is now revealed to his holy Apostles and Prophets in the Spirit. Finally the content of the Mystery is described in an

---

[1]Most commentaries take v. 13 as part of this section; Gnilka 179 thinks otherwise.

Infinitive Clause at v. 6 (cf. the same construction in 1.10). The complex construction which in v. 7 again returns to Paul, now as servant of the Gospel, reveals a special interest in the person and office of Paul. In v. 8 the author begins anew, initially again with Paul, to whom grace was given to proclaim to the Gentiles the unfathomable riches of Christ and to illuminate the divine plan of salvation (οἰκονομία) which was hidden before the ages (v. 9). Herewith attention again moves to the subject of the Mystery of Christ which is now described as the present revelation of the manifold wisdom of God through the Church (v. 10). Syntactically this idea is attached by a ἵνα-Clause which expresses the divine planning of salvation. Then follows once more the customary reversion with κατά to God's eternal intention which he has accomplished in Christ Jesus (v. 11). The naming of Jesus Christ is followed by a Relative Clause which emphasizes the consequence – that in him we have free access to the Father (v. 12). V. 13 is, as we have said, a flash-back to v. 1.

Thus vv. 8–12 comprise a second exposition, similar in content to vv. 2–7, which can admittedly be understood as an application and continuation of what was said in v. 2–7. Again it is possible that the author was inspired by Col. as a comparison illustrates:

to his saints/ to the least of all his saints		
	Col. 1.24	Eph 3.8a
the riches of the Mystery/of Christ		
	Col. 1.27a	Eph 3.8
in all wisdom/the manifold wisdom		
	Col. 1.28b	Eph 3.10

Thus on the semantic level several concepts are taken over from Col. 1.24–8. But we must note the semantic re-evaluation in Eph. This is important in the first place for οἰκονομία: In Col. 1.25 this is clearly used in the sense of 'office'; in the corresponding passage at Eph. 3.2 this meaning is doubtful (v. exegesis). The interpretation as 'plan for salvation' was already given in 1.10 and this sense emerges clearly in 3.9. If the concept is to be similarly understood in 3.2, then Paul's office (χάρις cf. 3.7, 8) is also included in the divine plan for salvation. A further important concept in this section which is taken over from Col., namely μυστήριον (mystery), is in Eph. brought into close connection with this οἰκονόμια of the divine salvation-acts (3.9) and thereby given a different *content* from that in Col.

Col. 1.27a already used the verb γνωρίζειν (reveal) in connection with the Mystery. Eph. takes it up as an expression for the revelation of the Mystery presently taking place through God (passivum divinum) and uses it no less than three times (vv. 3, 5, 10). This revelation, which exposes God's manifold wisdom, takes place 'through the Church' (v. 10). God's plan of salvation, till now hidden, will be revealed 'to the powers and forces in the heavens' through the Church herself (in her unity of former Jews and Gentiles) and through her proclamation. Eph. extends the perspective of the divine 'revelation' by using yet another word, namely ἀποκαλύπτειν. His preference for this expression is shown in that he replaces the φανερόω of Col. 1.26b, which belongs to the same semantic field, with ἀποκαλύπτειν (3.5). Furthermore, in his Paul-anamnesis he stresses that the Apostle was granted a revelation of the mystery κατὰ ἀποκάλυψιν (3.3), a reference which has no parallel in Col.

This also makes more concrete the author's pragmatic objective. In the self-portrayal of Paul as the Apostle to the Gentiles called according to God's plan, to whom a special insight into the Mystery of Christ was given, the addressees are made vividly aware of his God-given, irrevocable competence and authority. This emphasis is perhaps connected with the situation of the congregations after the Apostle's death or with the dying-out of the old 'apostolic' generation of preachers in general. The congregations should preserve the continuity with the apostolic tradition. The metaphor of the Apostle captive and suffering for his congregations is suited to strengthen their relationship to him.

Exegesis

1

The unusual connection τούτου χάριν ('for this reason') can hardly be described as a mere connecting phrase (Ernst 327). It unites the Pauline section with what has gone before[2] and betrays in its repetition in v. 14 the intention, in accordance with its theological explanation, of turning into an intercession which also suggests an admonition (cf. 1.17–19). The intercession gains special importance through the person of Paul ('I, Paul') whose rôle in God's plan the author then makes into a longer digression (vv. 2–13). In the context he has been led to do this through the naming of 'the Apostles and Prophets' in 2.20. Among them (v. 5) Paul has a special position (vv. 3.7–9) The author considers this positioning of the Apostle to the Gentiles (cf. 'for you, the Gentiles') important since he is aware that he himself is committed to Paul's theology and he wants to claim Paul's authority for his own doctrine and admonition. The picture of Paul with its power to motivate is made even more effective when he represents the Apostle as the 'captive of Christ Jesus' who endures his sufferings 'for you, the Gentiles'. He also expects them to recognise his hardships as those that he takes upon himself for them (cf. v. 13). The expression, 'captive of Christ Jesus' can be found already in Philem 1.9 and marks Paul as the one totally bound to Christ and simultaneously bound by him in the shackles of humanity. He bears his hardships in solidarity with his Lord (4.1) for the benefit of the congregation (cf. 2 Cor 4.12; 12.15; Phil. 2.17; Col. 1.24).

2

In the Pauline anamnesis which begins with 'you have certainly heard'[3] the author is concerned with the revelation (v. 3) and insight into the Mystery

---

[2]This connecting phrase is only found in Eph. 3.1, 14; Tit. 1.5; cf. Lk. 7.17. It is a matter of debate to what exactly it connects – to 2.20 (Haupt) 2.19–22 (Gaugler) 2.11–22 (Dibelius – Greeven), Chapter 2 (Schlier). If we observe that the assurance of access to the Father (v. 18) is echoed in the prayer to the Father (3.14, 16) and that 'built together' (2.22) also contains a call to the readers, we can take it that it refers to the last remarks in 2.18–22.

[3]εἴ γε can have different nuances: if otherwise, if really, cf. Kühner – Gerth II/2, 177 f.; Pr-Bauer 303. Here as in 4.21 it performs the function of reminding them of something already known.

of Christ (v. 4) granted to the Apostle. The 'real' Paul reminds the Galatians in that section to which Eph. is clearly referring (Gal. 1.15) in the first place of his earlier life in Judaism and his persecution of God's Church (1.13 f.). There is no longer any discussion of this – understandable in such an idealised picture of Paul. The subject is now the 'economy of the Grace of God' which was conferred on Paul to pass on to the Gentiles. The Greek word οἰκονομία can mean 'administration office' as well as 'establishment, order, plan' and in each case takes on a special connotation.[4] In Col. 1.25 it seems reasonable to think of the 'office' of preacher bestowed on Paul by God (cf. 1.28 f; 1 Cor. 9.17) although the context also brings into play the divine plan for salvation bound up with this (1.26 f.)[5] Certainly Eph. 3.2, is inspired by this but introduces a new accent in that it is now 'the Grace of God' (added in the Genitive) and not the 'economy' which is depicted as bestowed by God. If we compare the other passages where the Paul of Eph. refers to the Grace of God bestowed upon him (3.7, 8), we can assume that the author of Eph. means by this expression (χάρις) Paul's office as preacher and that the preceding οἰκονομία takes on the meaning rather of the divine plan of salvation, particularly when both the other passages with οἰκονομία (1.10; 3.9) mean God's all-embracing salvation-event brought about in Christ.[6] In this way Paul with his special vocation is incorporated in the wise plan with which God wished to achieve his plans for salvation.

3

The special gift which was bestowed upon Paul was his knowledge of the divine Mystery of Salvation as it was revealed to him. This reference is made clearer by Gal. 1.15 f.: God, who has called Paul through his grace, decided in his free will to *reveal* his Son to him. The author of Eph. here includes the recollection of the Damascus Road experience, which he assumes is known (v. 2) beyond what is said in Col. since he is particularly concerned with this revelation of Christ granted to Paul.[7] Only in v. 8 is the purpose included in Gal. 1.16 first mentioned – 'that I should *proclaim* him (the Son of God) among the Gentiles'. For the present he remains with the insight into the Mystery of Christ which was disclosed to Paul through grace (passivum divinum) (v. 4). In Eph. Paul is emphasized as the receiver of revelation even if later the Apostles and Prophets also appear as such (v. 5). Paul in his preaching is to bring to light God's plan for salvation (v. 9) precisely because of the revelation granted to him. This emphasis which is laid on Paul's reception of revelation and his deep knowledge of faith gives him prominence as the authoritative interpreter of the Gospel.

---

[4]Cf. Pr-Bauer 1107 f.; O. Michel, TDNT V, 152 f. Reumann, NT 3, 286 quotes another papyrus (BGU nr 321, from the year AD 184) in which οἰκονομία is used for testament or will. On the Hellenistic conception of a divine management of the world cf. id. NTS 13, 150–3. The Christian use in the Second and Third Centuries was possibly influenced by Eph.; on this material cf. Schlier, *Religionsgesch. Untersuchungen*, 32.

[5]Cf. Schweizer, *Colossians*, on the passage.

[6]Cf. Reumann, NTS 13, 164 f., Merklein, *Kirchl. Amt* 173 f.

[7]On the relationship between Eph. 3.3a and Gal. 1.12, 15 f. cf. Merklein, *Kirchl. Amt* 196–200; on the understanding of revelation v. further Lührmann 117–22.

Through the revelation of the Mystery Paul is not only awarded the office of preaching; the content of his preaching also receives a normative character and becomes the standard tradition.[8]

The closing comment 'as I have previously described briefly' can hardly refer to other Pauline Epistles to which 'briefly' does not fit; it refers to the present writing which is written under the Apostle's name.[9] The comment that the addressees can read it is a hidden exhortation to read the letter aloud in the congregations and reflect on it carefully. This would refer particularly to 2.11–22 where the participation of the Gentile-Christians in Christ's salvation (3.6) is traced back to Jesus Christ's act of Reconciliation and is given ecclesial status. But the divine plan of salvation (οἰκονομία) was already mentioned in the Great Eulogy (1.10) and what was meant by the 'uniting of all things in Christ' was given further consideration in 1.20–3.

4

The addressees should see from the letter Paul's 'understanding' of the Mystery of Christ. Col. 1.9; 2.2 also speaks of 'understanding' (σύνεσις), but as a wish for all Christians[10] Eph. makes Paul an intermediary: *He* brings them to spiritual understanding (Col. 1.9), to a knowledge of the Mystery of Christ (2.2). The author of Eph. has taken over this expression 'Mystery of Christ' from Col. 1.26 f; 2.2 where it is already connected with the divine plan for salvation. But he gives it a more precise meaning: It is the Church in which the Mystery of Christ is revealed and realized. In that the Gentiles belong to the Church and become full heirs of Salvation. (3.6) the powers and forces are made aware of their defeat (3.10). Precisely that Gentile world, which had been handed over to darkness (cf. 2.2), the former demesne of the ungodly powers, because the proof of the manifold wisdom of God. Such a clear-cut view of the place of the Gentiles in Christ's Church and their rôle in God's plan is an 'understanding' which is not yet found in this fashion in Paul himself in spite of certain formulations (cf. Rom. 11. 11–32; 15.16–21); but a similar view emerges in the post-Pauline addition in Rom. 16.25 f. It is a special insight which the author of Eph. has won as Paul's interpreter and here ascribes to Paul himself, the receiver of revelation. In this way his own theology achieves authority through the Apostle – a process which allows us to look deep into the self-understanding of such interpreters of Paul who probably were active in the congregations as teachers.

[8] Merklein, *Kirchl. Amt* 176.

[9] The interpretation which took this as referring to other Pauline Epistles led to the view that Eph. was a document written as an introduction to the collected letters of Paul; cf. p. 36 n. 50.

[10] In Paul the word appears only in one quotation 1 Cor. 1.19, and there in a negative sense: God destroys the understanding of the wise. – 'Understanding' of the secrets of God (Plural!) can be found in the interpretation of revelation in Qumran. It is given to the Teacher of Righteousness/(through him) disclosed to the other members of the community, cf. K. G. Kuhn, NTS 7, 336, who quotes as word-parallels 1 QH 2.13; 12.13; there may also be added 1 QS 4.4: But cf. also 1 QS 1.12; 4.6, 22; 11.3; 1 QH 2.18; 10.20, 29. The author of Eph. is more closely connected to the Qumran way of thinking than is Paul.

5

The content of the 'Mystery of Christ', a pregnant expression which points to the indissoluble connection of the divine plan for salvation with the person of Jesus Christ (a characterising Genitive[11]), is not at first described but as in Col. 1.26 it is set before us through the 'schema of revelation' (cf. Schweizer on this verse and also under v. 9) as now revealed, realized in Christ. It achieves its relevance in that it was not made known in earlier generations[12] of humankind as it is revealed now to the Apostles and Prophets. The conjunction ὡς (as) does not in context signify a difference in degree but a completely new occurence.[13] The fine distinction between 'made known' (ἐγνωρίσθη) and 'revealed' (ἀπεκαλύφθη) means that the Secret was totally inaccessible to human senses ('humankind') and could not be uncovered by any save God himself through revelation. Unlike Jewish Apocalyptic and the Qumran documents where divine secrets were uncovered at least to certain people,[14] according to the Christian schema of revelation the 'Mystery of the divine will' (Eph. 1.9) remains firmly hidden until its revelation in Christ because only then does it move into the light through its fulfilment. For Eph. even the OT prophets with their searching and meditating on the salvation to come (cf. 1 Pet. 1.10–12) have no part to play (v. under 2.20). Only now after Christ's Cross and Resurrection has God 'made it known to us' (1.9) and that through the revelation granted 'to the holy apostles and prophets in the Spirit'.

The specification of the recipients of revelation, which is conspicuous in contrast to Col. 1.26 where only 'his saints' (= the faithful) are named, is certainly connected with the 'foundation of the apostles and prophets' in 2.20. They have the irreplaceable function of proclaiming and interpreting the Christ-event because it was made known to them first and foremost through divine revelation. The singular expression 'the *holy* apostles' (which Paul himself would certainly never have used) is to be explained by a recollection of Col. 1.26; the deletion of either 'holy' or 'apostles'[15] is not justified. If the apostles are more closely defined by the word 'holy', it seems reasonable to suppose that the additional 'in the Spirit' is to be taken to refer to the prophets, as this also corresponds best to the style characteristic of the author.[16] The αὐτοῦ ('his') which is placed only with 'apostles' separates the apostles from the prophets in a particular way; but both groups are recipients of revelation, the prophets,

[11]Cf. Zerwick, *Greek* paras 25–8 (Gen. 'generaliter determinans'). Cf. also O. Schmitz, *Die Christus-Gemeinschaft des Paulus im Lichte seines Genitivgebrauches*, 1924 (NTF I, 2) 88–90, 229–37; Wikenhauser, *Christusmystik* 14–19.

[12]On the Dative alone used temporally cf. Bl-Debr §200.4; Moulton – Turner, *Grammaer* III, 243.

[13]With Schlier, 150, Gnilka 167, Barth 333 f.; Caragounis* 102.

[14]On the self-understanding of the writers of apocalyptic cf. 2 Esdras 14.37–48; on that of the Teacher of Righteousness in Qumran (especially according to 1 QpHab and 1 QH 2, 1–19) O. Betz, *Offenbarung und Schriftforschung in der Qumransekte*, 1960 (WUNT 6), 98 f.; G. Jeremias, *Lehrer der Gerechtigkeit* 140–6; 192–201.

[15]ἀποστόλοις is omitted by B b Ambst; now and again someone has suggested the deletion of ἁγίοις as a gloss (v. Soden).

[16]Schlier 150 points to Eph. 2.22 and Col. 1.8; cf. further Merklein, *Kirchl. Amt* 188 f.

however, in a different manner, as 'in the Spirit' may signify. As we already noticed in 2.20, the apostles and prophets at that time are already a significant 'theological' factor in a particular function for the Church, without there being any clear description of their specific tasks. In 3.5 we have a glimpse of an understanding that the apostles are closely connected with Christ ('his' apostles) and are sent out to proclaim the Gospel (as can be seen in Paul, cf. 3.8) and the prophets, because of their spiritual gifts, mediate special revelation from the Lord. The function of the prophets, who according to Paul contribute to the 'building' of the congregation (cf. 1 Cor. 14.2–5, 12), appears for Eph. to be only a spiritual phenomenon of the time of the foundation of the Church. The prophets who spoke and revealed 'in the Spirit' find their successors in the present to a certain extent in the teachers (cf. under 4.11).

6

As to its content, the author thinks that the Mystery of Christ consists in the inclusion of the Gentiles in the new unity created by Christ (2.16): God's holy building (2.22), the Church. Using three expressions to describe their full co-citizenship (cf. 2.19), he elucidates the change brought about by God which can be understood as the fulfilment of his plan for salvation. In the language of Eph. all three expressions have an ecclesial ring which also makes us aware of the new entity in comparison with the old covenant Congregation of Israel (2.12). When the Gentiles are named as 'co-heirs' we might at first think of the inheritance promised to Israel, in which the Gentiles now have a part;[17] but for Eph. (cf. Col. 3.24) 'inheritance' (κληρονομία) is a Christian concept of salvation, the expression for the full salvation which lies prepared in heaven (cf. 1.18; 5.5) and which is vouched for by the Holy Spirit (1.13 f.) Hence the Gentiles are 'co-heirs'[18] with all those with whom they are united in the Church. The reference in the συν- (co-) to the community of the church is even clearer in the unique expression possibly constructed here ad hoc – σύνσωμα = united in one body, co-members[19] – which can only mean the full membership of the Gentiles in the Body of Christ. The Gentiles are not added to a unit already existing but are from the outset planned in it and are such an integral part that the 'Body' does not exist without them. 'In Christ Jesus' they build together with all the other members the one Body in one Spirit (cf. 2.16, 18;

[17] Meuzelaar, *Leib des Messias* 65 f.; Schlier 151; Barth 337 take it as being a direct reference to Israel. But already in 2.19 (v. there) the horizon had been shifted to the Church.

[18] The word συγκληρονόμος is also found in Rom. 8.17; Heb. 11.9; 1 Pet. 3.7 each time in a different sense. Significant is the difference to Paul who in Rom. 8.17 speaks of us as 'co-heirs with Christ' because through Christ we have become children of God (cf. Gal. 4.6 f.). For him the 'inheritance' of the sons of God is set in the future (cf. 1 Cor. 15.50); in Eph. on the other hand the 'inheritance' is already a present heavenly entity (cf. 1.18; 5.5). Hammer (p. 27 n. 24) conceives it more the other way round but rightly stresses: 'co-heirs' is for Paul primarily a christological and soteriological expression, for Eph. an ecclesiological (271 f.). Cf. also Merklein, *Kirchl. Amt* 206.

[19] Cf. E. Schweizer, TDNT VII, 1080. –Meuzelaar, *Leib des Messias* 65 f., points to Philo, Spec Leg III, 131 and Virt 103 where the People of Israel are considered as one single body; but there it is merely a matter of an occasional comparison while in Eph. we are dealing with the important idea of the 'Body of Christ'.

4.4a). The 'co-' is the language used of the church community which elsewhere is made known in the change from 'you' and 'we' (cf. on 1.12; 2.1–10). Hence the expression 'co-participants of the promise' is to be seen in the same perspective. To be sure Israel once possessed the promise arising from the 'covenant' given to them by God (2.12); but Christ has gone beyond this horizon and altered it. Now the former promise (of the Messiah) is fulfilled in Christ and this fulfilment brings with it the new promise of the attainment of full salvation (cf. 1.13 f.). Hence the Gentiles are 'co-participants' in the promise with their fellow-Christians, be they former Jews or Gentiles.

'In Christ Jesus' could be taken with 'promise' because of the newness of the horizon of hope but it refers rather to all three expressions. This 'in Christ' has already in the Great Eulogy proclaimed the location where God's plan is fulfilled and realized (1.8 f.) and according to 2.6, 7 it is the same sphere ('in Christ Jesus') in which our salvation is carried out and completed. This place of salvation is opened to the Gentiles 'through the Gospel', the proclamation of Christ.[20] In that the Gospel is proclaimed and the Gentiles receive it in faith (1.13) the divine plan for salvation is manifest.

7

As soon as the proclamation of the Gospel is mentioned Paul again comes on to the scene. The phrase 'whose servant I have become' has been taken over from Col. 1.23, where Paul's world-wide mission is mentioned. Paul never describes himself thus in the Epistles accepted as genuine although many statements about his service are comparable (2 Cor. 3.6–10; Rom. 15.16; Phil. 2.17). Col. and similarly Eph. are thinking more of the successful (concluded) mission of the Apostle to the Gentiles. For them he has become the perfect example, the ideal figure of a preacher who even in prison remains true to his ministry as ambassador (Eph. 6.20). Certainly he can only perform this ministry in accordance with the divine grace bestowed upon him, which flows over him from God's mighty power.[21] Thus Paul is not praised as a human being with his human abilities but seen only as the tool of God's grace working in him; but this is precisely what gives him his place in the divine plan for salvation.

Now the author has steered us back to the office of Paul grounded in God's grace which was mentioned in v. 2. We might ask why he inserted the revelation to the Apostles and Prophets at all, especially since in what follows the uncovering of the Mystery of Christ is linked with the preaching of the Apostle to the Gentiles (v. 9). V. 10 supplies us with the answer: The manifold wisdom of God will be made known through the *Church* to the

---

[20]Merklein, *Kirchl. Amt* 207, thinks that the concept 'gospel' in Eph. as compared with Paul is already fairly commonplace and has become the term for Christian proclamation in general. According to Lührmann* 125 the preaching is the 'Sitz im Leben' of the schema of revelation.

[21]The second κατά does not co-ordinate with the first but emphasizes it; the gift of grace was bestowed on Paul according to God's effective power (cf. 1 Cor. 15.10). Schlier 151 f. sees an even closer connection with the power of God which was effective in the Resurrection of Jesus Christ and had an effect on Paul.

powers and forces in the heavens. The author was concerned to show that the Apostles and Prophets who made up the foundation of the Church (2.20) were also receivers and mediators of revelation in order to demonstrate the rôle of the Church in God's plan for salvation. The Church to whose totality the Gentiles belong is the place of God's eschatological revelation and in her it is the Apostles and Prophets to whom this revelation is entrusted. If Paul nevertheless appears as the leading preacher and interpreter of the Christ-event, this means that the author wishes to emphasize him as a man of the Church, as *the* Apostle and theologian of the founding- generation who was especially important for the future of the Church. For the author, Paul is not only the successful missionary to the Gentiles but also the church theologian who remains authoritative in later times because of his insight into the Secret of Christ and because of his preaching.

8

Beginning anew (cf. Analysis) Paul introduces himself, taking up and developing what has been said before (v. 7), as the Apostle called to minister to the Gentiles. He is the least of all the saints i.e. of all the faithful (cf. at 1.1 and 15), and to *him* was given 'this' grace, namely the ability to hold a preaching-office which came from God's all-powerful might (v. 7). The expression reminds us of 1 Cor. 15.9 ('I am the least of the apostles') but goes beyond any Pauline self-assessment. The adjective, itself already a superlative, is again made more emphatic with a comparative ending ἐλαχίσ-τερος[22] and instead of 'apostles' Eph. uses 'all the saints'. Why this heavy accent? It is to place yet stronger emphasis on the power of God's grace rather than on the former persecutor of God's Church (1 Cor. 15.9). The power of grace shines even more in the insignificance of Paul the human being, God's Wisdom in the wretchedness – that wisdom which allows *him* to preach Christ's unfathomable riches to the Gentiles. It is the Paul of the Pastoral Epistles who first calls himself the 'foremost of sinners' in whom, however, Jesus Christ displayed 'as the foremost . . . his perfect patience' (1 Tim. 1.15 f.). Paul does not become a prototype or example in Eph.[23]; he is the unique tool chosen by God to carry out his plan of salvation.

The 'riches of God's grace' (cf. 2.8; 1.18) are also revealed in the richness of the content of the proclamation which here is called the 'riches of Christ'. What is said about the Mystery which God has revealed to his saints ('Christ in you') in Col. 1.27 is in Eph. deliberately assigned to Paul's preaching. *He* reveals to the Gentiles[24] the unfathomable riches of Christ by virtue of the insight given to him (cf. v. 4) and remains the inspired teacher for the later Church also (in 1 Tim. 2.7; 2 Tim. 1.11 the 'preacher, apostle and teacher'). In Rom. 11.33 Paul calls the ways of God 'unfathomable' and when earlier in the same verse he cries 'O the depth of

[22]This is a not unusual occurrence in Koine Greek, cf. Bl-Debr §61.2.

[23]On the Paul of the Pastorals cf. G. Lohfink, Paulinische Theologie in der Rezeption der Pastoralbriefe, in K. Kertelge (ed.) *Paulus in den neutestamentlichen Spätschriften*, 1981 (QD 89), 70–121, especially 79–86.

[24]The variant reading ἐν τοῖς ἔθνεσιν in DFG MLatt has perhaps forced its way in from Col. 1.27.

the riches and wisdom and knowledge of God', he uses the same vocabulary as in Eph. Hence here the author is recollecting the passage in Rom. The manifold wisdom of God (cf. 3.10) corresponds to the riches of Christ which Paul was to proclaim to the Gentiles. Here he does not mean only the ideas contained in the Mystery of Christ (cf. v. 6) but also the reality of salvation mediated by the word of proclamation, the love of Christ which excedes all knowledge and which includes the Gentiles in God's fullness of life (cf. v. 19).

9

But now the author wants to bring more light on the Mystery of Christ (v. 4) included in God's plan for salvation, and he returns again to the schema of revelation which he already used in v. 5. The same basic plan is evident: not made known in earlier generations – now revealed (v. 5)/hidden in God – now made known (vv. 9–10). Jewish Apocalyptic and the Qumran texts have much to say about such secrets which are hidden in God and are revealed at a certain time to certain people.[25] This is the soil in which already Paul's thought is rooted, for the starting-point for the 'Mystery of Christ' in Col. and Eph. must be 1 Cor. 2.6–10, where the Apostle speaks of the Wisdom of God existing in the event of the Cross – the wisdom which was previously hidden but intended 'for our glorification' (v. 7) and which he has revealed to 'us' through his Spirit (v. 10).

The Mystery-concept in Apolyptic, first tangible in Daniel, is closely related to the hiddenness of the divine thoughts. These concern future events ('what must happen at the end of days' Dan. 2.29) which are inaccessible to human wisdom but which will be revealed by God to those whom he enlightens (cf. 2.30, 47). In the later Apocalypses the authors discern many different secrets of heaven and the last days; for there lie ready in heaven God's secret decisions which will be revealed at the end of time and will take place (cf. Eth Enoch 83.3–4; 90.4; 103.2–6; 106.19). What in 2 Esdras 14.5 is projected back in God's revelation to Moses on Mount Sinai fits the self-understanding of every writer of apocalyptic: 'I (God) told him (Moses) many wonderful things, showed him the secrets of the ages and revealed to him the end of the hours' (cf. Syr Baruch 81.4). In Qumran, too, God's secrets which here have to do with Creation, the course of history and the End of the Times, are only revealed to people for whom God 'opens their ear' (1 QH 1.21) gives 'illumination in their heart' (1 QS 11.5) whom he 'teaches in his wonderful secrets' (1 QH 7.26). The 'end-events' in particular are established 'in the secrets of his mind'; he has determined a time (or an end) for the existence of injustice (1 QS 4.18; cf. 3.23; 1 QM 3.9; 16.11, 16). In the so-called (fragmentary) 'Book of Secrets' (1 Q 27.1; 1.2–7) the subject is the 'secret that is to come', of which the doers of the 'secrets of malice' have no knowledge; consequently it then applies to the Judgement (lines 2–4) but also to the Reign of Righteousness which will then begin (lines 5–7).[26] God did not reveal the fulfilment of time to Habakkuk, but revealed to the Teacher of Righteousness all the secrets of the words of his servants, the Prophets (1 QpHab 7.1–5). Although the area of application of 'secrets' is much broader in Qumran (we also find Secrets in Creation,

---

[25]From the abundance of literature: G. Bornkamm, TDNT IV, 802–28; R. E. Brown, 'The Semitic Background of the NT Mysterion', Bib. 39 (1958) 426–48; 40 (1959) 70–87; J. Coppens, 'Le "mystère" dans la théologie paulinienne et ses parallèles qumrâniens', RechBib V (1960) 142–65; Lührmann* 84–7; Mußner, *Beiträge* 185–8; Caragounis* 121–35.
[26]J. T. Milik, DJD I, 102–4; Caragounis* 132 f.

in the understanding of the Torah and in the words of the Prophets) and the specific understanding of Col. and Eph. (the *one* secret which is 'now' revealed) is missing, the basic line of thought is similar, namely in the view of the 'Secret to come'. Without assuming a direct dependence on the apocalyptic or Qumran texts, the 'Mystery' in Eph. must be understood as related to these and a derivation from Hellenism or Gnosticism rejected.[27] But it is more important to see the Christian transformation of such thinking centred on Christ and to clarify the special character of the 'Mystery of Christ' in Eph. as compared with Paul and Col.

The main difference to Apocalyptic is that the eschatological revelation concentrates on *Christ* (*the* Secret per se) and is *already* fulfilled: It is not only made known to the receivers of revelation in secret but is at the same time revealed through them as a self-fulfilling event. Hence it is incumbent upon Paul 'to bring to light'[28] what is the execution (οἰκονομία) planned by God of the Mystery of Salvation, hidden before the ages. Paul then becomes the enlightened interpreter of the divine enterprise already extolled in the Great Eulogy – the enterprise which God planned 'before the foundation of the world' (1.4) and had decided to carry out in the 'fullness of the times' (1.9 f.). The author here takes up these thoughts from the Eulogy as is shown in the choice of words – 'make known' (γνωρίζω 1.9 cf. 3.10), 'execution' of the plan of salvation (οἰκονομία 1.10 cf. 3.9) and God's 'intention' (πρόθεσις 1.11 cf. 3.11). It is therefore unlikely that 'before the ages' has anything other than a temporal sense. The attempt by Schlier and others to understand the 'Ages' as personal beings cannot be grounded on the parallelism with the 'powers and forces' mentioned in 3.10 because these can only with difficulty be equated with the 'Ages' (cf. at v. 10). In 2.7 also the 'ages to come' were to be understood in a temporal sense (v. there).[29] According to Col. 1.26 the Secret was concealed 'before the ages and generations'; Eph. mentions the 'generations' in 3.5 where he is thinking of human history and the 'ages' in 3.9 because here he is looking back to Creation – back in fact to God's intention which is eternal and existed before time (v. 11). The schema of revelation contrasts the Mystery hidden since eternity (cf. 1 Cor 2.7 πρὸ τῶν αἰώνων; Rom. 16.25)[30] with the

---

[27]Caragounis* also comes to this conclusion in his monograph; he sees the closest correspondence to Eph.'s idea of the Mystery in Daniel (134 f.), perhaps too one-sidedly.

[28]Many MSS here add πάντας (v. the evidence in Nestle-Aland ²⁶1979, where πάντας is included in the text in square brackets). This would mean 'to enlighten every –'; but how can we complete the sense? 'Gentiles' (ἔθνη) is not concordant, 'saints' (at the beginning of v. 8) is too far away. It is not so much a matter of bringing enlightenment to humanity (cf. 1.18) but of elucidating the Mystery of Salvation itself – as is shown by the connection to v. 10. The text without is attested to by א*A 6 1739 1881 pc Ambst Aug. The closest material correspondence is in 2 Tim. 1.10, although here it is concerned with Christ. Cf. Schlier 152 f., whom H. Conzelmann, TDNT IX, 348 also follows.

[29]First represented by Reitzenstein, Ir Erl 235 f.; then Dibelius – Greeven 75 and especially Schlier 154–6 ('before the aeons. . ., the forces which have seized hold of history and concealed their own true identity as creatures' 156) and following him Steinmetz, *Heils-Zuversicht*. Against this view are, among other, H. Sasse, TDNT I, 207; Gnilka 172; Ernst 332; Conzelmann 104 is critical and Barth 343 f. undecided. On Col. 1.26 v. Schweizer, *Colossians*, on this verse.

[30]The preposition ἀπό in this phrase can have the sense of 'hide *from* someone' (Mt. 11.25; Lk. 18.34; 19.12; Jn. 12.36; Rev. 6.16) as well as being used in the temporal sense (Mt. 13.35; 25.34; Lk. 11.50 etc.), also with the article, cf. Mt. 9.22; 11.12; (ἀπὸ τοῦ νῦν) Lk. 1.18;

uncovering of God's manifold wisdom which has taken place 'now' (v. 10).

If God is called the Creator of the universe, this is not simply a stereotyped addition but is rather a meaningful reference to God's plan for salvation which he intended from the beginning before the Creation of the universe. For the author of Eph. the protological Creation of the 'universe' is fulfilled in the eschatological 'uniting of all things in Christ' (1.10) through which the unity and order of all things 'in Heaven and on earth' is re-established. The 'powers and forces' mentioned in v. 10, which are responsible for the disruption of the order of Creation are included in this because of the author's conception of the world (cf. under 1.21); it is not intended as a polemic against the Gnostic devaluation of Creation.[31] The Gnostic Marcion, it must be said, took exception to the positive reference to the Creator-God; he changed 'hidden in God' to 'hidden in the God who created the universe', for in his view this was the Demiurge from whom the material world stems, a separate being from the supreme ('different') God of Love.[32] For Eph. such a duality in the understanding of God is unthinkable, since he believes every race in heaven and on earth proceeds from the one God, the Father (3.15).

10

As the Final Clause shows, God's plan provided that the secret of his will which had been hidden before all time should be revealed now through the Church. A new element is that this Economy of Salvation is now moved into the area of 'God's manifold wisdom'; but already for Paul it was a plan made in God's wisdom (1 Cor 2.7). To be sure the attribute 'diverse' or 'manifold' (πολυποίκιλος) is strange. It appears only here in the NT and is rare elsewhere. We can certainly assume a knowledge of Judaeo-Hellenistic speculations on Wisdom; But there is still no agreement on how the author regards the myth of the divine wisdom which appears in many references.

A sort of cosmic history is told of the Divine Wisdom personified in the Judaeo-Hellenistic Wisdom literature. Wisdom was present at the Creation as spectator and overseer (Prov. 8.27–30; Wis. 9.9), as counsellor and artist (Wis. 8.4, 6). Wisdom is poured out over all God's works, over all humanity according to the greatness of God's gift (Ecclus. 1.9 f.; Syr Baruch 48.9). But Wisdom remains concealed from many people (Job 28.12–14). Wisdom desires to live among humankind, sets off on her search among every nation and tribe but finds no place till she settles in Israel (Ecclus. 24.7 f.). According to another version, because she can find no place where she can live Wisdom returns to heaven while injustice emerges and floods the earth (Eth Enoch; cf. 2 Esdras 5.9 f. Syr Baruch 48.36). Wisdom will only return in the messianic period: All who thirst shall drink from the Fountain of Wisdom (Eth Enoch 48.1) and Wisdom will reveal to them the Holy and Righteous One (the Messiah) who is filled with the Spirit of Wisdom (ibid 48.7; cf. 49.3), Such ideas

---

5.19 and often; it is frequent in papyri, cf. Mayser II/2, 379 f. Hence the way it is used cannot help us make a definite decision here (with Gnilka 172 against Schlier 154, n. 2). On the schema of revelation cf. Lührmann* 124–33.

[31] Thus Schlier 155, who also points to Estius on this passage.

[32] Cf. Tertullian Marc V, 18 (Kroymann 638); also A. v. Harnack, *Marcion: Das Evangelium vom fremden Gott*, Leipzig 1921, 47 (on Eph. 3.9); 89–99 (on the Creator-God).

exercised an influence from a very early period on the Christian faith. (It is already present in the Logos-sources.) Jesus himself becomes the mouthpiece of the divine Wisdom (Lk. 11.49); in him wisdom's sayings are fulfilled (Lk. 13.34 f./Mt. 23, 37–9; Lk. 7.35/Mt. 11.19).[33] Paul, in rejecting human wisdom, emphasized the Wisdom of God shown in the Crucified Christ in all the 'foolishness' of the divine action and in *this* sense calls Christ himself the 'wisdom, righteousness, sanctification and redemption of God' (1 Cor. 1.30). Such dialectic speaking of foolishness and wisdom of God is no longer present in Col. and Eph.; but the 'Mystery of Christ' is inserted into God's plan of wisdom in the schema of revelation (see above).[34]

Is it enough to explain the expression 'manifold' as rising from a (perhaps only confused) knowledge of the speculations about Wisdom, or must we, because of the unusual adjective, draw a line of thought to the literary witnesses where it in fact appears? Schlier, who introduces all the provable material, particularly in the Hellenistic Isis-theology, thinks that possibly a Jewish-Gnostic interpretation of the Hellenistic Isis-theology of the Ages not only provided the author of Eph. (in his view Paul himself) with the description πολυποίκιλος but also mediated the form of ideas which can appropriately discuss the nature and fate of the changeable yet ever only one Wisdom of God.[35] But this would lay too much importance on the word; the author was not necessarily thinking of that Isis-Sophia 'which bears in herself all powers and brings aid everywhere, changing her appearance and yet remaining *one* "goddess" or "hypostasis", of whom Jews and Gentiles dream'. According to Schlier, the author of Eph. would see the divine Wisdom in the Economy of Faith revealed in different forms and ways one after another; as the Wisdom determined in advance, as the Wisdom of Creation, then in Christ, himself Wisdom, and finally in the Church as Wisdom in many shapes and yet one – in Christ (Schlier 165). But such a change in the form of Wisdom is an idea foreign to Eph. For him there is only one single divine plan of Wisdom which was once concealed and is now revealed in and through the Church. The word is meant only to convey the character of the divine Wisdom, just as it is described in Wis. 7.22 with several words: 'In her there is a Spirit intelligent, holy, unique, of many forms (πολυμερές) . . .'

The Mystery of Christ which is brought to light by the Apostle to the Gentiles and which is shown to be the manifold Wisdom of God will be revealed 'to the powers and forces in the heavens' through the Church. Church and powers opposing God were already brought into a relationship with one another in 1.22 f. (see there). In 3.10 this connection becomes clearer in the light of the divine economy of salvation: Through the Church, through her becoming manifest, through her outward form which includes the one-time Gentiles (v. 6) the Wisdom of God which planned their subjugation will be revealed to the powers and forces. Their power over that very part of humanity over whom they thought to rule unrestrainedly, namely the Gentile world, is now taken from them. 'Now'[36] the time of the Church, the powers which are at

[33]Cf. U. Wilckens, TDNT VII, 515–17; F. Christ, *Jesus Sophia. Die Sophia-Christologie bei den Synoptikern*, Zürich 1970; M. J. Suggs, *Wisdom, Christology and Law in Matthew's Gospel*, Cambridge/Mass. – London 1970. In Matthew Jesus is even equated with Wisdom (Suggs 30–97).

[34]Cf. U. Wilckens, *Weisheit und Torheit*, 1959 (BHTh 26); TDNT VII, 519–24.

[35]Excursus on the 'manifold wisdom of God' in Schlier 159–66. For criticism of Schlier and those scholars who follow him cf. especially Dahl* 66–71.

[36]νῦν omitted in F G 629 lat sy^P Text MVict. The temporal particle is far better attested to and is certainly original as in v. 5. It's omission may possibly be explained because the emphasis was put on διὰ τῆς ἐκκλησίας (cf. the transposition in sy^P). – Dahl* 73 f. attempts a concrete interpretation: In the service of worship in the congregation, in which the angels are present,

work 'in the heavens', in the lower regions above the earth (cf. under 2.2) are no longer able to rule the 'world', the sphere of Darkness, of the Evil One (5.12). The Gentiles who were once 'darkness' are now 'light in the Lord' (5.8).

In this way the Church herself becomes the Mystery of Salvation, and this ecclesiological outlook is what is special and unique in Eph., even in comparison to Col. from which the author has taken over the expression 'Mystery of Christ' (v. 4). For him the Secret of the divine decision now revealed does not consist only in that Christ is proclaimed among the Gentiles and brings them hope of glory (Col. 1.27) but more concretely in that the Gentiles themselves belong to the Body of Christ and are recognisable as heirs of salvation in the Church (cf. v. 6).

11

That this was what God had in view is confirmed by the author's returning once again to God's 'intention' formed since eternity. In the Great Eulogy this expression was used in connection with our predestination (1.11) Just as there 'achieves' (ἐνεργεῖν) so here in 3.11 'accomplished' (ἐποίησεν) implies the implementation of the divine intention: What God had planned, he has now really carried out 'in Christ Jesus, and Lord'. For in him we have present and real access to God (v. 12). The other possibility, of taking the whole of v. 11 to refer to God's intention *taken* in eternity,[37] does not fit so well in the context. The scheme of revelation in vv. 9–10 also requires rather that the Mystery till now 'hidden in God' should be connected with the divine intention and the publication which has now resulted in its realization in Jesus Christ/in the Church. Then we can also see the sense of the Genitive τῶν αἰώνων (the ages) added to 'intention'; it reminds us of the decision taken by God before all time. Probably the Genitive is used in the Hebrew fashion instead of an adjective (cf. 3.21; also 1 Tim. 1.17; and Rom. 16.26 where we find the adjective).[38] It can hardly be taken as an Objective Genitive as this would make the (anthropomorphized) Ages the object or goal of the divine intention.[39] The arch stretches, as in 1.9 f., from God's eternal intention to its effective – although not yet final – accomplishment in Christ. It is revealed and further developed by the Church.

God's Wisdom is revealed to the 'powers and forces'. But are these then simply onlookers in the same way as the angels (cf. 1 Cor. 11.10)?

[37] Thus Calvin, Haupt, Abbott, Schmid (*Epheserbrief* 232 f.), Schlier, Gaugler, Gnilka; on the contrary, in the sense of 'implementing', Ewald, Scott, Dibelius – Greeven, Conzelmann, Barth et al. From the progress of thought it is just as possible that in Eph. it means God's pre-historic-eternal resolution (cf. 1.9); but from the wording and context we must give priority to the implementation which was effected in Christ and the Church (cf. 1.10). For ποιεῖν Barth 347, n. 108 points, among other references, to I Kings 5.8 (22) LXX; Is. 44.28; Lk. 1.72; 18.7; Jn. 8.38. The closest parallel for God's almighty, effective act must be Eph. 3.20.

[38] Cf. Bl-Debr § 165,1; Moulton – Turner, *Grammer* III, 213.

[39] Thus Schlier 157 and following him Steinmetz, *Heils-Zuversicht* 64. – Yet again differently Barth 345 f: He would like to make the Plural refer to the two aeons, the period when the Mystery was hidden before the coming of the Messiah and the period of its revelation he inaugurated. In this way the period past (the separation between Israel and the Gentiles) would also be seen as a time filled by God. But this reads too much from the Plural; Barth however also remains open to other interpretations (as those above).

12

In Christ – and that also means in the sphere of salvation of the Church opened up by him – we have free, trusting access to God. After the exposition of the divine plan of salvation this verse is intended to show the inference for our present position, as happened in 2.18. In both places the subject is the new entity created in Christ, the Church, but the point of view under which the same statement is made is different. In 2.18 it was the common access of the two groups in one Spirit, here it is the access to God no longer prevented by the powers and forces which gives confidence and trust. The word connected with the metaphor of access (v. under 2.18) – παρρησία – which can have various nuances of meaning[40] is here best translated by 'openness.' In Hellenism it is the type of behaviour with which one acts towards freemen and friends; an open, frank, confident communication; but only in Judaism is the idea carried over to the relationship with God. That the access to God is free and frank is also made clear in the additional 'with trust': The way to the Father is open. A similar attitude is expressed again almost immediately in the prayer which is presented from v. 14 on. The phrase, 'through faith in him (Jesus Christ)' reminds us of the basic requirement for the achievement of salvation (2.8) and the constant basis of Christian existence (cf. 4.5; 6.16).

13

The wish that the addresses may not 'lose heart' (cf. 1 Cor. 4.1, 16) in the Apostle's sufferings also belongs within the perspective of the free, trusting access to God. There is no reason to abandon their trusting attitude, not even (imprisoned) Paul's serious situation which the author again calls to mind, connecting up with v. 1. This is even more important because he is enduring his sufferings for the sake of these very recipients. Col. 1.24 expresses this even more strongly and we may wonder why Eph. did not take up its powerful ecclesiological motif in the same way. He reserves the 'for the Church' for Christ himself (cf. 5.23, 25) and looks upon Paul as the Apostle bound up with his Lord and serving the Church (cf. 4.1; 6.20). The Apostle's prayer for the Gentile-Christians is also part of this outlook. Firstly, however, he asks the addressees not to lose heart because of his desperate straits.[41] He desires to strengthen their confidence that they may reach their goal with God. Even the Apostle's sufferings help them on their way: the sufferings lead to their δόξα – i.e. the 'glory' of their heavenly inheritance (cf. 1.18; 2.7). The idea, which Paul initiated (cf. 2 Cor 4.12, 15), is given its clearest expression in 2 Tim 2.10: 'Therefore I endure

---

[40]Cf. H. Schlier, TDNT V, 871–86, especially 883. Schlier pleads for 'openness to God' (883). Through ἐν πεποιθήσει (with trust) there is added a subjective element: the open approach to God also makes it possible to approach him openly. This is an attitude before God such as was already illustrated in Job (22.25–7; 27.9 f.) Cf. also the texts in 1 Jn., and R. Schnackenburg, *Die Johannes-briefe*, Freiburg i. Br ⁵1975, 165 and 204 f.

[41]The sentence can also be understood to mean that Paul prays for himself that he may not lose heart. This understanding is perhaps presupposed in the variant reading δόξα ἡμῶν P⁴⁶ C P 33 81 al (v. in A. Merk, *Novum Testamentum graece et latine*, Rom ⁹1964). But the context (v. 12) speaks against this meaning.

everything for the sake of the elect, that they, too, may attain salvation in Christ Jesus with eternal glory'.

Summary

The introduction of Paul who presents himself as a captive of Christ Jesus (v. 1), the receiver of revelation to whom a special insight has been given (vv. 3–4), the servant of the Gospel (v. 7) and as the Apostle to the Gentiles chosen by God (v. 8) is not meant as a historical recollection or an external extolment of Paul but serves an internal concern of the author for his readers. He wants in this Paul-anamnesis to develop for them his understanding of the Mystery of Christ and supports himself in so doing on the authority of the Apostle. Paul consequently is elevated as the enlightened interpreter of Christ's message and the leading bearer of tradition among the other Apostles and Prophets. The congregations must continue in the future to hold to Paul and his proclamation as the author of Eph. understands it.

In this section the author develops his understanding of the Mystery of Salvation which has been hidden from eternity and is now revealed in the Church of Jesus Christ (v. 9). It shows itself as God's 'manifold Wisdom' (v. 10) in that God deprives the powers of evil of their sphere of influence in an undreamt-of way. The cosmic way of looking at the situation which stretches from the Creation of the universe (3.9) to its union in Christ (1.10) obtains its focus in the human world. While God through Christ in the Church increasingly takes hold of and draws to himself the human world, in particular the Gentiles, everything that is contrary to God is brought to light and deprived of power. In God's plan of wisdom the Gentiles called to the Church have a special part to play; precisely they who were particularly abandoned to the force of temptations have now free access to God (v. 12).

The picture of the Church which can be seen in this outlook is developed to a greater extent than in Paul and the Epistle to the Colossians. Now the Church comes to the forefront as God's great concept, the divine instrument of salvation through which the Mystery of Christ becomes a historical reality. The Church is not isolated from Christ; but bound to him she achieves a historically effective function of salvation. Their defeat is made known to the powers of evil *through* the Church (v. 10). There are no doubt dangers hidden in this for the self-understanding of the Church; the Church falls into the perspective of a *theologia gloriae*. A Christianity more strongly oriented on Paul and his Theology of the Cross would have a critical attitude to this.

Yet we must not see in the author of Eph., with his picture of Paul and his understanding of Pauline theology, a complete contrast to the great Preacher of Christ. There is much in his theology which is in keeping with the spirit of Paul, especially the mercifulness of Salvation and the rooting of faith in Christ Jesus alone. There are elements which come too short (as the *scandalum crucis*) and there are developments which go beyond Paul. This last is especially true for its ecclesiology which admittedly can only be properly judged after further sections (4.7–16; 5.21–3). In the idea of our open and trusting approach to God (v. 12) the author stays close to the Pauline Gospel (cf. Rom. 5.1 f.).

143

3. THE APOSTLE'S CONCERNS IN HIS PRAYERS; INNER STRENGTHENING OF FAITH, LOVE AND KNOWLEDGE (3.14–19)

Literature

G. Harder, *Paulus und das Gebet*, 1936 (NTF 10).
J. Nielen, *Gebet und Gottesdienst im Neuen Testament*, Freiburg i.Br. (1937) [2]1963.
A. Hamman, *La Prière I Le Nouveau Testament*, Tournai 1959.
A. Gonzalez, 'Prière', DBS VIII (1972) 555–606 (with Lit.).
E. von Severus, 'Gebet I', RAC VIII (1972) 1134–1258, esp. 1162–88.
G. P. Wiles, *Paul's Intercessory Prayers*, 1974 (MSSNTS 24).
N. Dahl, 'Cosmic Dimensions and Religious Knowledge (Eph. 3.18)', in *Jesus und Paulus* (FS W. G. Kümmel) ed. E. E. Ellis and E. Gräser, Göttingen 1975, 57–75.

14 For this reason I bow my knees before the Father
15   from whom every race in heaven
      and on earth has its name:
16 May he bestow upon you according to the riches of his glory
      that your power may become stronger
        through his Spirit in your inner being
17   that Christ may live in your hearts
      through faith
      (and) you (may be) rooted and grounded in love,
18   so that you may be mighty
        to understand with all the saints
        what is the breadth and length and height and depth
19   and to know that love of Christ
      which surpasses knowledge
    that you may enter into the total fullness of God.

Analysis

v. 14 makes a new start with τούτου χάριν and thereby takes up v. 1. Now the author turns to the prayer already in his mind then in which the Apostle asks that the recipients may be strengthened in faith, rooted in love and may have a growing knowledge. In form this whole section (3.14–21) is a prayer which can be divided into an intercession (vv. 14–19) and a doxology (vv. 20–1). The intercession is reminiscent of 1.16–19, where it was attached to a thanksgiving in a part of the letter which has the ring of a formula already established; here it stands at the climax of a theological reflection to give expression to the concerns motivating the author with regard to his addressees. The conclusion with a doxology, which is closely connected with the intercession by v. 20, is in keeping with the wide-spread custom of ending prayers with praise.

The intercession vv. 14–19 is again a long compound sentence whose structure shows all the characteristics of the unusual style of the author of Ephesians; no logical structure, no clearly structuring elements but rather a flood of thoughts which give rise to one another in turn, a gradual progression. An intensification is unmistakeable. The inner strengthening (v. 16) in faith and love (v. 17) should lead to a comprehensive understanding of the divine revelation (v. 18) and finally of the love of Christ (v. 19a) in such a way that Christians thereby themselves reach the fulfilment of salvation (in the fullness of God (v. 19b). The three ἵνα-Clauses (v. 16, 18, 19b) which mark this way have not all equal weight but follow one another in their inner consistency and intensification.

The main concern of the intercession is contained in the first ἵνα-clause: that they may through God's Spirit gain strength in their 'inner being'. The following Infinitive Clause (v. 17) is meant to explain this and make clearer that the 'inner being' corresponds to the indwelling of Christ 'in your hearts'. Here faith is named as mediating, and this may have conjured up the associated idea of love which is introduced by added Participles (in the Perfect) – rooted and firmly grounded in love. If we take this Clause (v. 17b) with the following, which is concerned with increasing knowledge, we lose the connection with faith, which, united with love, enables knowledge to progress. We can then discern a 'breathing-space' after v. 17.

The author makes a new beginning with the second ἵνα-Clause (v. 18), confirms the wish for inner strength with the emphatic verb ἐξισ-χύειν and simultaneously opens up new perspectives. He expresses why they should be enabled and strengthened in two parallel Infinitives: καταλαβέσθαι ... γνῶναι τε (to understand ... and to know). He is concerned with a deeper penetration into the reality of faith, into the Mystery of Christ now revealed which is realized in the Church. It can only be grasped in faith and love, and reaches dimensions described spatially ('breadth and length and height and depth'). Perhaps there is an echo in the first Infinitive Clause (v. 18) of the faith mentioned in 17a and in the second (v. 19a) of the love spoken of in 17b. But both are inseparable from this spiritual 'knowledge' which is fulfilled existentially. For it is not only a knowledge with the reasoning of faith but a dependence surpassing all reason on the love of Christ which goes beyond all understanding. The third ἵνα-Clause (v. 19b) then leads to the final goal. The growth and maturing should result in their being 'filled' into the total fullness of God in which they will be included – an expression for the perfection they will find in God through Christ.

In this section, too, we may ask how far the author is influenced in language and thought by Col. 'Parallel' statements are not so obvious as in the previous section, but there are noticeable echoes of Col. 2.2, 7, 9 f. If the author of Eph. read beyond the section made use of previously (Col. 1.23c–8), he could have found other stimuli in Col. 2.2–10 as is shown in the following comparison:

Col. 2.2   *their hearts* may be encouraged, held together *in love*
Eph. 3.17   Christ may live *in your hearts* ... rooted *in love*

Col. 2.2   to have all the riches of the fullness of understanding, for the *knowledge*
            of God's mystery, (namely) of Christ
Eph. 3.19   and to *know* the love of Christ which goes beyond knowledge.

Col. 2.7   *rooted* and *built up* in him
Eph. 3.17   *rooted* and *grounded* in love

Col. 2.9   in him the *whole fullness of deity dwells bodily*
   2.10   and you are *fulfilled* in him
Eph. 3.17   that Christ may *live* in your hearts through faith
   3.19   that you *may be filled* in the *total fullness of God.*

In Col., too, it is also a matter of knowledge through faith (2.2) which defends against dangerous false teaching (cf. 2.8), especially a firmness of faith (2.5) given by adherence to the teaching handed down to them (2.7), and a matter of clear knowledge of the Mystery of Christ (2.2), the meaning of Christ and his divine 'fullness' (2.9) which surpasses everything. Eph. takes up more than a few words and ideas but gives them a different emphasis. Our author shows no interest in warding off the false teaching at Colossae or in a corresponding immunisation of his addressees. He concentrates on the Father, whereas Col.'s dominating emphasis is on Christ. While Col. re-iterates admonitions, Eph. formulates a prayer.

The Apostle's pleading prayer is for that deeper knowledge and insight which the imprisoned Paul had previously claimed to possess (3.3 f.) and which he wishes to mediate to the addressees also. The understanding of faith grounded in the Pauline proclamation (3.8 ff.) should also make it possible to achieve a deep consummation of faith. Because the emphasis is on an inner strengthening, the effect of the Spirit, the dwelling of 'Christ . . . in your hearts through faith' (vv. 16–17) all tendency to superficiality, to a trivial, feeble Christianity should be overcome.

Exegesis

14

The solemn introduction gives the following prayer great weight. With τούτου χάριν (therefore) which takes up again the intention of 3.1 (see at that verse) but now enriched by all that was said in 3.2–13, the author in Paul's name lays before God himself his wishes and concerns for the addressees. Two elements make the introduction to the prayer unusual: the gesture of bowing the knee and the turning to the Father, which is emphasized by the Consecutive Clause in v. 15. There is more evidence for the custom of kneeling in prayer in the Eastern than in the Graeco-Roman world. It can have a different meaning according to what is said or how it is done (from kneeling to complete prostration): greeting, homage, submission, adoration, beseeching request.[1] The word used here (κάμπτειν) is found in Paul only in OT quotations (Rom. 11.4; 14.11; indirectly in Phil. 2.10) and in these places it expresses the submission and worship due to God or the exalted Christ. But because here it is followed by a prayer of supplication, the verb has probably the same meaning as other phrases in supplicatory prayers on bended knee (cf. τιθέναι τὰ γόνατα Acts 7.60; 9.40;

---

[1]Cf. H. Schlier, TDNT I, 738–40; on the different gestures in the OT, Gonzalez* 575 f.; von Severus* 1164; in Judaism Bill. II 260 f. On the different assessment of kneeling among the Greeks and Romans cf. von Severus* 1160 f.; further Caragounis, *Mysterion* 74 f., n. 84.

20.36; 21.5; γονυπετεῖν Mk. 1.40; 10.17; Mt. 17.14). The turning to the Father is a sign of reverence and trust. Yet the author's picture of the Father does not so much emphasize a trusting closeness to God but rather his greatness and power in bringing about salvation (cf. 'Father of Glory' in 1.17). This is in keeping with his theocentric outlook which emphasizes God's election, redemption and influence which takes precedence before all human endeavour (cf. 1.4 f.; 8.11; 2.9 f.) If God is here called upon as Father[2] this is for a special reason as the following verse shows.

15

'Every race' in heaven and on earth gets its name from God the Father. The play on words in Greek (for 'race' the Greek has πατρία from the same root as πατήρ, father) cannot be imitated in English, since 'fatherhood'[3] gives a misleading picture. The Greek word means 'race, clan, folk'[4] and in connection with 'in heaven and on earth' must be taken to refer to actual groups or communities. What the author intends here can be inferred from the verb 'be called, get a name' (ὀνομάζεται). The 'name' means influence and power (cf. under 1.21) and to have a name granted by God (ἐξ οὗ) signifies that all these races were given life and strength by God.[5] This can scarcely include the rebellious powers and forces subjugated to Christ (1.21; 3.10) which in 3.10 are still judged negatively. Those 'races in heaven and on earth' rather imply in the context of the prayer those good spirits (angels) in the heavenly area and the human races which live on earth and reproduce themselves (cf. 3.5).[6] If God is here named as the Father on whom all their power depends (Present), then he is seen as the Creator and Preserver of everything created in the same way as he was

---

[2]Several MSS (א* D F G MLatt lat sy) add 'of our Lord Jesus Christ'; but this addition (cf. 1.17) weakens the idea of God's fatherhood of all peoples (v. 15) and also disrupts the syntactical relation of the Relative Clause to God the Father. Calvin (Sp. 185), who adopted the longer text, made the Relative Clause refer to Jesus Christ and interpreted *omnis cognatio* as 'the one house', the Church.

[3]The Vulgate and part of the Vetus Latina translate this with *paternitas*; but many VL MSS (text-type I) render it with *cognatio, familia, congregatio* etc. cf. Frede, *Ep. ad Eph.* 122.

[4]Cf. Pr-Bauer 1262; G. Schrenk, TDNT V, 1015, 1019. On Judaism cf. Bill. III, 594: 'Fatherhood' is an expression used in a family clan which traces its ancestry back to a common progenitor; transferred to the world of angels it means 'the genre angel'. The author of Eph. possibly took the word over from the LXX where it was a 'favourite word' (Schrenk 1017, 34 ff.). He uses it here (instead of γενεά) almost certainly because of its reminder of πατήρ (paronomasia). Jerome (MPL 26, 487C) rightly explains it from its Hebrew origin: *cognatio vel familia*.

[5]The idea is not the same as in Plato who, in the Creation-myth in the Timaeus, speaks of God as the 'creator (ποιητής) and Father of the universe' (Tim. 28, c) and with 'Father' – admittedly metaphorically – is thinking of the begetter. The idea so influential in the Greek world of God the Father of all (cf. G. Schrenk, TDNT V, 954 f.) continues at the most to have only an indirect effect in Eph. (cf. on 4.6).

[6]In Rabbinism the world of angels was called the 'upper family' and Israel the 'lower family'; evidence in Bill. I 744 (under c); III, 594 (under b). When God is thereby not named 'Father' but 'head of the household' we must take into consideration the Jewish idea of God. For the groups of angels, Eth Enoch 69.3 is usually quoted: 'And these are the heads of their angels and the names of their leaders over 100, 50 and 10'; this, too, is not an exact parallel (fallen angels!). For various groupings of angels v. J. Michl, RAC V, 89–91. Although we have no parallel which fits exactly materially, the Jewish background is clear enough.

stressed as the Creator of the universe in 3.9 – a fact significant for the author's 'theological' thinking. It is the same God the Father who created all things, who through Christ once more subjected the broken world to his authority (cf. 1.20–2) and intends to complete his work in the Church. Christian confidence of salvation finds its most solid basis and support in this universal Father (4.6) the God of Jesus Christ (1.17) and merciful God of love (2.4).

16

The main concern of the author's supplication is for the inner strengthening of the addressees. He does not dispute their faith in Jesus Christ or their brotherly love (cf. 1.15) but sees that they are still weak. The Holy Spirit granted to them (cf. 1.13) is still not effective enough in them. The concern for strengthening is underlined in v. 18 (ἐξισχύσητε) and is revealed as the author's real intention (cf. also 6.10). He puts more trust in the effectiveness of God's mighty grace in Christians than in all admonition and moralising. In a similar way as is expressed in Col. 1.11 God should award them greater strength according to the riches of his glory (the same expression as in 1.18 but with a different application).[7] The power of God which is effective in humanity is the Holy Spirit which is mediated through the spiritual word of preaching (1 Thess. 1.5; 1 Cor. 2.4) and baptism (1 Cor. 12.13; Eph. 1.13), lives on in Christians as the 'Spirit of faith' (2 Cor. 4.13), binds them to Christ and makes them steadfast (cf. 2 Cor. 1.21 f.).[8] This prayer is not yet urgently concerned with the morally good deeds which should result (cf. 4.23 f., 30) but with the idea that it is God who makes them possible (cf. 2.9 f.).

The 'inner being' in which Christians should be strengthened is an expression taken over from Paul (2 Cor. 4.16; cf. Rom. 7.22) for the 'inner' existence of Christians. It is not used in the sense of an 'inwardness' freed from everything external and withdrawn from the world but as an inner strength which is unassailable by all external events because it is brought about by the Spirit. The anthropological modes of expression which are not detectable in Judaism but are derived from the Hellenistic world still function in Rom. 7.22;[9] but Paul gives them a new meaning for the Christian way of life. If Philo can call the human spirit (νοῦς) the 'human in human, the better in the worse, the immortal in the mortal' (Cong. 97), for Paul the Christian only achieves 'inner being' when he is caught and ruled by the

---

[7] In 1.18 he was concerned with the future glory of the heavenly 'inheritance', in 3.16 with the power which flows from God's glory. The two elements 'light, splendour' and 'might, power' are both contained in the concept of 'doxa', cf. J. Schneider, *Doxa*, Gütersloh 1932; H. Kittel, *Die Herrlichkeit Gottes*, Gießen 1934; G. Kittel, TDNT II, 247 f.: One and the same expression about the divine nature is always present. Cf. the raising of Christ from the dead 'by the doxa of the Father' (Rom. 6.4) with 'he lives by the power (δύναμις) of God' (2 Cor. 13.4). Eph. blends the two elements more powerfully, cf. 3.16 with 1.19.

[8] Cf. E. Schweizer, TDNT VI, 424–8.

[9] Cf. J. Jeremias, TDNT I, 365 f. While the ἔσω ἄνθρωπος in Rom. 7.22 concerns the 'natural', unredeemed humanity in their 'rational' side (cf. νοῦς in v. 23), the 'inner being' in Eph. 3.16 means the redeemed people filled with the divine Spirit and is ordered for the 'new person' (cf. 4.23 f.). Dahl* considers that in Eph. 3.16 it is a synonym for the biblical word 'heart'. In fact the expression does correspond to that in v. 17.

divine Spirit. The Gnostics thought of the 'essential being' as that which already contains within itself the pneumatic centre of being, the 'divine self', frees itself from the entanglements of matter and sours up through Gnosis.[10] This differs from the Christian in that the latter receives the Spirit, this power of the 'inner being', through God's grace and accepts it in faith in order to be led to him.

17

When this inner life of Christians made possible and supported by the Spirit is now described as the 'dwelling of Christ in your hearts', this is simply a clarification. Here, too, the author of Eph. remains bound to Paul's theological way of thinking, for which the Spirit is nothing other than the power of life which comes from Christ (1 Cor. 15.45), Christ's Spirit (Rom. 8.9b; cf. 1 Cor. 3.16b; 2 Cor. 3.17). The metaphor of indwelling, which Paul used for the divine Spirit through which God himself fills Christians (Rom. 8.9, 11) or the congregation (1 Cor. 3.16) with his life, is transferred to Christ. Paul already says 'Christ in you' (Rom. 8.10; cf. Gal. 2.20). How else could Christ live in their hearts except through the Spirit? The spatial metaphor thereby receives also a dynamic sense: The strengthening of the 'inner being' through the Spirit (v. 16) means that Christ is ever more effective in us. This is no transference of strength in a material way.[11] It means rather that Christ takes hold of us through his Spirit and leads us to true freedom and greater glory (cf. 2 Cor. 3.17 f.).

The way in which Christ is present in us is further explained and protected against misunderstanding in the additional 'through faith'. This διὰ- τῆς πίστεως does not in this context mean that faith was the means through which we entered into communion with Christ but relates to the present dwelling of Christ in our hearts which remains a living reality through faith. It is an existence 'in faith' as Paul aptly describes it in Gal. 2.20: 'It is no longer I who live but Christ lives in me. The life I now live in the flesh I live through faith in the Son of God who loved me and gave himself for me.' Later this presence of Christ 'through faith' gave ground for further reflection. (v. History of Influence).

The wish for their anchoring in love is added by the author[12] no doubt because for him as for Paul (Gal. 5.6) faith and love belong closely together. In the two verbs metaphors of growth and building are fused

[10]Cf. the 'essential being' in Corp Herm I, 15; IX, 5; XIII, 14; Ascl 7; on the 'inner spiritual being' (in the Marcosians) Iren Haer I 21.4 (Harvey I, 186): There is also an instructive text in the 'Threeform Protennoia' (NHC XIII, p. 36 f.): 'We alone are (those, whom you have redeemed) fro(m the v)isible (world) which we we(re saved in view of the) hidden (being in our) hearts (through the) unpronounceable and (im)measurab(le thought). And the (being) hidden in us counts among its fruits the control for the water of life' (after the German translation by G. Schenke, ThLZ 99, 736). On the alternation of expressions for the spiritual spark, the 'self' etc. cf. Jonas, Gnosis I, 210–12; on the basic idea, Rudolph, *Gnosis* 86–8.

[11]This is emphasized by E. Schweizer, TDNT VI, 427. But also in the Roman Catholic Doctrine of Grace the effect of the Holy Spirit in *gratia* is not understood thus.

[12]The two Participles are not to be taken indicatively but as a continuation of the prayerful wish just as elsewhere the Participle can express an exhortation, cf. Eph. 4.3, 21; 5.19 f.; in Paul cf. Rom. 12.9–13. Further in Moulton 284–88; Bl-Debr §468, 26; Moulton and Turner, *Grammar* III, 343 under e.

similarly to Col. 2.7 except that Eph. prefers 'solidly based' (cf. Col. 1.23) instead of 'built up' (cf. 2.20 on the building of the Church). The love in which the addressees should be embedded deep and fast is here not brotherly love – which only comes into consideration later, in the paraclesis-section (4.2; 4.32–5.1 f.) – but the love bestowed by God and mediated through the Holy Spirit (cf. Rom. 5.5). Whereas Col. places the emphasis on faith in the face of false teaching (2.7 f.) Eph. desires increased love to strengthen the 'inner being' as the supporting and driving force of Christian existence.

18

We may find it surprising that after faith and love 'understanding' (v. 18) and 'knowledge' (v. 19) are now named as the goal of this inner strengthening.[13] This Christian 'Gnosis' suggested by the verbs is, however, no intellectual process but a comprehension and awareness of that which God has bestowed on us (cf. 1 Cor. 2.11 f.) a 'knowledge' of the love of Christ which surpasses all gnosis (v. 19). If we ask why the author considers this so important, we are referred back to the previous section, 3.2–10, where this semantic field is predominant. What 'Paul' has brought to light as the great divine Economy of Salvation (3.9) should now be grasped internally by the Gentile-Christians to enable them to understand and make effectual their life in the Church. 'With all the saints'[14] reminds them again of their participation in Christ's salvation existing in the Church (cf. 3.6).

The unusual expression that Christians should comprehend 'what is the breadth and length and height and depth' has always been considered difficult. A picture arises of an area extended or measured on all four sides (a cube); but perhaps it is already a stereotyped phrase (Schlier). Paul speaks in a similar mysterious way in 1 Cor. 2.9 'what no eye has seen and no ear has heard and what has not arisen in any human heart, what God has prepared for those who love him'; this passage is also connected with the Secret hidden before the ages and now revealed.

The metaphor of the length and breadth, depth and height is found in many texts – in the OT, in Jewish Wisdom-Literature, in Apocalyptic, but also in Stoic popular philosophy, in Philo, in the Hermetic and Magic Texts. An abundance of comparable material has been collected but hardly allows of an unambiguous derivation.

We can arrange the material[15] roughly as follows:

(a) In Ps. 139.8–10, heaven, the Kingdom of the Dead and the 'outermost' sea are named to illustrate God's omnipresence. Four dimensions are presented in Job 11.7–9 to describe God's perfection and unfathomability (and his wisdom): as high as heaven, as deep as the underworld, longer than the earth and broader than

---

[13]The powerful expression ἐξισχύειν only appears here in the NT. Cf. on it Pr-Bauer 547; Liddell and Scott 545 (with pieces of evidence from classical and koine literature).

[14]'All the saints' – to interpret this here as angels as Dahl* 73 proposes is not to be recommended; cf. 1.15; 3.8; 6.18 (all the saints). The perspective is an ecclesiological one cf. v. 21.

[15]Cf. Gnilka 186–88; Dahl* 60–4 (From Wisdom to Apocalyptic) and 64–8 (From Philosophy to Gnosis).

the sea. Ecclus. 1.3 speaks of the height of heaven, the breadth of the earth and the depths of the sea which cannot be measured – a metaphor for the wisdom of God. A connection with these wisdom-texts could exist in view of the manifold wisdom of God mentioned in Eph. 3.10.[16]

(b) In the Stoic philosophy, in the Corp Herm and in Philo (who is not unaffected by such thinking) human beings are considered to have the ability spiritually to spread throughout the universe in that, in the fashion of a 'walker in heaven' (οὐρανοβατῶν) they can stride across the height and depth and (less often) the length and breadth. J. Dupont collected this material to which also belong ancient ideas of the movement of the stars.[17] It relates to the natural human ability to know, and only in Gnostic literature (Corp Herm) with a knowledge mediated through revelation.

(c) In Rev. 21.16 the heavenly Jerusalem is represented as a square area like in length, breadth and height (a cube), measured according to Ezekiel's vision (cf. Ezek. 48.16 f.). The typological metaphor of the Church in its ideal for re-appears in a vision of the Shepherd of Hermas (v. III.2, 5). It is a metaphor of perfection in spatial measures which transfers to the Church cosmic – perhaps even astrological – conceptions.[18] But within Eph. 3.18 we cannot recognise a direct ecclesiological sense; it is rather the thought of the heavenly inheritance which here, in continuation of 1.18, might be interpreted in its proportions.[19] But within the context of Eph. this also is unlikely; the love of Christ which surpasses all gnosis (v. 19) points in another direction.

(d) The formula which crops up in the Magic Texts connected with the Magic of Light 'Breadth, depth, length, height'[20] is meant to pull down the all-powerful God into our inner beings and make him serve us. This theurgic style is diametrically opposed to the prayer in Eph. 3 which asks for comprehension of the riches bestowed on us, and can at the most only show how widespread was the use of the formula.

(e) The idea, which came into being at an early period in the Church and which Schlier takes up, that it refers to the cosmic dimension of the *Cross* is also difficult to fit in with the thought of Eph. because nowhere else among the multifarious metaphors in the letter does the Cross play a part. Schlier (173) wants to connect the symbol of the Cross with the metaphor of the Cosmic Anthropos (cf. 2.15 f.): Christ as the world-embracing anthropos on the world-embracing Cross. But in 2.16, the only place where the Cross is mentioned, it has only an instrumental sense without any symbolic features. The view detectable in the apocryphal letters of the apostles[21] and in Irenaeus (Haer V, 17.4; Harvey, 372) could be an early interpretation partly influenced by the Eph. passage.

Taken as a whole we can only establish a vague background which could have provided the author with the metaphor or formula of cosmic measurements. What he intends the words and symbols to mean can be deduced from the context: The Mystery of Salvation revealed by God in its

[16]Cf. A. Feuillet, *Le Christ* 292–319. Dahl* 60–4 extends the line from Jewish Wisdom to Apocalyptic. Significant is also the text Sifre Num. 12.7 which he quotes: 'I revealed to him (Moses) everything that is above and below, everything which is in the sea and on the dry land' (63).

[17]*Gnosis* 476–89; cf. also 495–8.

[18]Cf. M. Dibelius, *Der Hirt des Hermas*, 1923 (HNT, suppl. vol. IV), 460.

[19]Thus H. Schlier, TDNT I, 518; Dibelius – Greeven 77.

[20]v. in Reitzenstein, *Poimandres* 25 f., also reprinted in Dibelius – Greeven 77.

[21]Mart Andreae 14 (Bonnet II/1 54 f.); Mart Petri 9 (Lipsius I, 94); Act Phil. 140 (Bonnet II/2, 74 f.).

immeasurable dimensions grounded in God's wisdom.[22] To comprehend this means that Christians not only penetrate into God's thinking but are taken up into the fullness of God's salvation through the love of Christ which surpasses all measurement. It is the same as Paul indicated in 1 Cor. 2.9 expressed under another aspect and in different language; it is that fullness which God has prepared for those who love him, impenetrable by all human seeking and searching but self-revealing and communicating to believing discernment and yearning.

19

This is how we interpret the closely connected Clause – deliberately formulated in a paradox – about the knowledge and love of Christ which surpasses knowledge. What previously appeared as something still measurable (the metaphor of the cube) is now described more potently as immeasurable and incomprehensible. If the Mystery of God which contains within itself the totality of salvation is now spoken of as the love of Christ, it is possible that the author has been prompted by Col. 2.3: In Christ, the 'Mystery of God', (v. 2) are hidden all the treasures of wisdom and knowledge. This in its turn reminds us of the 'unfathomable riches of Christ' which Paul proclaimed to the Gentiles (Eph. 3.8). Christians experience Christ's inexhaustible and never fully comprehensible love 'with all the saints' in the Church, but constantly have need of strengthening by the Holy Spirit in order to have an ever-increasing share in the riches of Christ's grace. In this way they are led more and more to God the Father in Christ through the Holy Spirit. Here we observe a certain trinitarian structure (as in the Great Eulogy 1.3–14). Admittedly it is not a theological reflection *about* the trinitarian God but a consideration of the Economy of Salvation in which the reality of God is opened up in its effect *on us*.

The prayer to the Father in this perspective finds its appropriate culmination in the wish that the Christians may achieve the total fullness of God. The process of inclusion in the communion and life of God which the author expresses in an unusual way as 'being filled' takes place when they gain strength in the inner person through the Spirit, allow Christ through faith to live in them, and increasingly come to understand and be penetrated by the love of Christ. The wording, which cannot be translated adequately in English, ('be filled into the total fullness of God') obviously caused difficulties for many copyists at an early date and led to several variant readings.[23] The text currently used, more dependable because compiled from the majority of MSS and old versions, has given rise to the most varied interpretations among which there are two main branches: that Pleroma refers to the

---

[22]According to Dahl* 3.18 refers to the revealed knowledge of the immeasurable dimensions of the universe (73); but it has more a rhetorical form and serves as a preparation for v. 19: The wisdom of God surpasses knowledge and reaches its climax in the love of Christ (74). – But only with difficulty can we make the dimensions of the universe the object of this knowledge (so Dahl 60); in the context they surely have a metaphorical sense.

[23]The most important variant reading is πληρωθῇ πάν τὸ πλήρωμα τοῦ θεοῦ in P[46] B 33 1179 pc sa (+ εἰς ὑμᾶς 33), perhaps to avoid the unusual personal construction πληρωθῆτε εἰς. 1881 is unique in having τοῦ Χριστοῦ instead of τοῦ θεοῦ.

Church[24] or to God – but here again in different ways. To equate it with the Church which appears in 1.23 as the Pleroma *of Christ* (v. Exegesis) is prohibited by the express addition of the Genitive 'of God', just as there was a good reason for the neologism πλήρωμα τοῦ Χριστοῦ in 4.13 (v. there). Furthermore in the context of this prayer, which is concerned with an inner strengthening, to take the 'total fullness of God' to mean the Church would be irrelevant. The readers should achieve the total fullness of God *in* the Church *with* all the saints. In the author's theocentric view this is the final goal to which even the love of Christ is devoted.

The Passive form 'be filled' indicates the merciful event and the Preposition εἰς with Accusative expresses the movement towards a goal. (We cannot take it as modal with the sense of 'with the total fullness of God'.) But what is this goal? 'The total fullness of God', which according to Col. 1.19; 2.9 has settled in Christ and discloses itself to the faithful (cf. Col. 2.10 'and you are filled in him') appears here in an anabatic view as the climax of Christian endeavour. However, as in the whole of the prayer, we are not concerned here with moral perfection[25] but on the fulfilment effected by God in him, the Fullness of all being and existence. What the consequence of this is for the Christian's moral endeavour the author will expound in the paraclesis, especially in the metaphor of putting on the *new* person (4.22 ff.). In the first place a person must be permeated by God's power to save and be aware of this. The 'total fullness of God' looked at in this way has nothing to do with the Gnostic idea of the heavenly Pleroma, the upper pneumatic world (cf. Exegesis 1.23); it is rather a linguistic construction formulated by the author of Eph. following Col.

Summary

The captive Apostle's intercessory prayer for his readers, which stands out compared to that of 1.17 ff. because of its position in the middle of the letter, pursues a particular goal. With great urgency, underlined by the prayerful gesture of falling to his knees, he beseeches God the Father, from whom everything exists and takes place, to strengthen the recipients inwardly through his Spirit (v. 16). The prayerful wishes which follow – may Christ live in their hearts through faith, and may they be fast rooted in love (v. 17) – further emphasize the living experience of the reality of salvation. Recommencing in v. 18, this strengthening is interpreted to mean especially that they should be increasingly able to comprehend with all the faithful the scope of the divine plan for salvation and the love of Christ which surpasses knowledge in order to be drawn in to the total fullness of the divine riches. On closer examination there emerges a connection between this seemingly timeless prayer and the preceding section 3.2–13 and therewith also a special intention for the readers at that time. The author is concerned that they understand and propagate the Pauline Gospel.

[24]Representative of this interpretation are, in antiquity Severian, John of Damascus; in modern times J. M. Vosté, V. Warnach, v. in Ernst, *Pleroma* 123 f., who even taking 4.13 into consideration thinks that the ecclesiological reference for the concept is characteristic in both passages (125).

[25]Cf. Wagenführer, *Bedeutung Christi* 74 f.; Dibelius – Greeven 77 (the 'perfect state of the Christian congregation'); earlier representatives in Ernst, *Pleroma* 123 n. 3.

The deficiency which the author discerns in the addressees is a condition of weakness which is connected with two little depth and fervour of faith. It is an outward Christianity which has not yet taken sufficient grasp of the 'inner being'. The author is convinced that he cannot improve this half-hearted Christianity by appeals to their moral sense but must recommend strengthening through God and his Spirit.

The Christian 'Gnosis' which appears as the concern of vv. 18–19 is something other than that doctrine of a self-redemption which was proclaimed in the historical intellectual movement which went under this name. It is based on God's historical revelation of salvation in Jesus Christ as it was revealed through the Apostles, particularly Paul, and is further witnessed to by the Church. But the external proclamation needs an internal adoption on the part of the faithful, and to this belong faithful insight and spiritual experience. Christian 'Gnosis' takes the reception of the Gospel for granted and wants to penetrate more deeply the 'riches of Christ'. This takes place in a process of understanding, made possible by the Holy Spirit, of the love of Christ which surpasses all human knowledge.

While the author prays for strengthening for his readers through the Holy Spirit he also gives them advice on how they on their part can rectify the deficit; by participating in the execution of the prayer. For in prayer God's power is called upon, not through human industry but through the cry to the Father who hears the prayer and will listen to it.

4. CONCLUSION WITH A DOXOLOGY (3.20–21)

Literature

L. G. Champion, *Benedictions and Doxologies in the Epistles of Paul*, Oxford 1934.
A. Stuiber, 'Doxologie', RAC IV (1959) 210–26.
Deichgräber, *Gotteshymnus* 2–40.

20 To him who can do far over everything that we can ask or devise
according to the power which is effective in us,
21 to him (belongs) glory in the Church and in Christ Jesus
for all generations of the age of ages.

Amen.

Analysis

According to their style these two verses are a doxology, the use of which was widespread in Judaism and early Christianity. This was a short praise of God, whose glory, might and act of salvation were recognised and extolled in the characteristic combination 'doxa'. The form, which could have wide variations, always had three fixed elements which appear, too, in Eph. 3.20 f.: the person named in the Dative (occasionally Genitive) for whom the eulogy is intended, then the word of praise (usually δόξα) and finally the 'eternity formula' which gives weight to the praise awarded (predominantly 'for ever and ever').[1] In most cases there follows an 'Amen' which would be spoken by the congregation as reinforcement.[2] Similar short eulogies, at home in the liturgy, are frequently also introduced into letters at different places where the author thought it meaningful (Gal 1.5; Rom. 1.25; 9.5; 1 Tim 1.17; 6.16; 1 Pet 4.11). A favourite place is before concluding remarks or greetings (Phil 4.20; 2 Tim 4.18; Heb. 13.21; 1 Pet 5.11) or at the very end (Jude 25; 2 Pet 3.18; Rom. 16, 25–7). They are less often used to conclude a *part* of a letter; but Rom 11.36 offers a good analogy to Eph. 3.21 since even in the great Pauline letter a break is marked in this way before the paraclesis which then begins.

What is unusual in our doxology consists in its structural connection with the preceding intercession. The express reference to 'what we can ask or devise' leads the prayer further into the doxology, from asking to praising and yet in praising still holding on to the concerns of the prayer. Because of this it is syntactically not the smoothest flow of speech. Considering God, it is said that he can act 'over everything' and 'over all degrees'; as for us, we are said to devise and wish for many things in prayer. Both aspects are connected in the thought that God far exceeds our requests and human senses. The Comparative is expressed twice, clearly intensifying (ὑπὲρ πάντα and ὑπερεκπερισσῶς). Then the author, with one of his frequent κατά-phrases, returns to the beginning, to the τῷ δὲ δυναμένῳ (to him who can) and explains God's power as that which is effective in us. This too may be a reference back to what was set out in the intercession (cf. vv. 16–17). Once again we can discern a connection with the concerns of the prayer in the eulogy itself (v. 21) which is filled out by the additional 'in the Church and in Christ Jesus'. The 'eternity formula' attains a special formulation in its linguistic originality.

The doxology 3.20 f. provides not only the conclusion to the intercessory prayer (3.14–19) but also the deliberate completion of what has previously been said. We cannot go so far as to maintain that there is a liturgical schema which extends from the Great Eulogy (1.3–14) to this doxology (cf. Introduction p. 00 and n. 8); but the main theme of the Church as the Mystery of Christ now revealed is echoed in v. 21. The author of Eph. includes his theological concern in the intercession and eulogy. He knows that all human endeavour is dependent on God's power and blessing.

Exegesis

20

God's power which is evoked in the prayer to the Father to strengthen us (v. 16) is praised in the doxology. It is already at work in us and should

---

[1]Cf. Stuiber* 210–15; Deichgräber* 25–40.

[2]Cf. H. Schlier, TDNT I, 336 f.; G. Delling, *Der Gottesdienst im NT*, Göttingen 1952, 73–6. Delling explains the 'Amen' in the letters thus: 'The scribe in writing the letter puts himself in the community service of worship as if he were present and in his thoughts he hears the 'Amen' of those gathered together' (75). Cf. also P. Glaue RAC I (1950) 378 f.; Stuiber* 211; Deichgräber* 25–7.

achieve in us more than all[3] that we are capable of conveying in our prayers. This is even more marked in the Greek in the uniform use of words based on δύναμις: The increase in strength which we ask from God will be achievable beyond conception according to his powerful acting in us[4] through the riches of his grace (cf. 1.7 f.; 2.7). The old biblical conviction that God's thoughts tower above the human senses (cf. only Is. 55.8 f.) is echoed in the added 'what we devise'.[5] Paul speaks in a similar way of the Peace of God which 'rises above all understanding (νοῦς) and keeps our hearts and thoughts (νοήματα) in Christ Jesus (Phil. 4.7). The transition from the author's personal pleas (v. 14) to the 'we'-form in 'what we can ask or devise' is significant. The silent congregation is drawn into the prayer: its concern should also be theirs.

21

The eulogy is directed to the God who is always greater. The missing copula can be completed as in the Eulogy with an Indicative or with an Optative (v. under 1.3); yet here, too, the granting of the glory due to God (ἐστίν) is more positive than a wish (cf. 1 Pet. 4.11; Did. 9.4; 10.5; 1 Clem. 58.2). Doxa entails more than 'honour', for the expressions which are often attached in number such as 'might, greatness, power and glory' (cf. 1 Tim 6.16; Jude 25; Rev. 5.13; 7.12 et al.) show that 'doxa', God's greatness and splendour, should include his mighty saving works – i.e. 'contain within itself a dynamic element' (Deichgräber). The translation 'glory' in English is only a stop-gap. We should detect in it the might, blessing and joy of his 'glory'. This is how we understand the modifier which here is deliberately added 'in the Church and in Jesus Christ'. For Eph. God's beneficent rule can already be seen as present in the Church, which is included in God's realm of might and blessing 'in Christ Jesus' (cf. 1.22b–23). As God's blessing comes to us 'in Christ Jesus' (1.3), so all the Church's praise goes to the Father via Jesus Christ. The co-ordinating[6] 'in Christ Jesus' links the Church to her Head, and all worship can only be an expression of thanks in his name (5.20).

The conclusion with the unusually formed eternity-formula is not taken from a speculation about the ages (cf. under 3.9 and 11) but is the author's stylised formulation of the otherwise variable third element of a

[3]The omission of ὑπέρ in P46 D F G lat can perhaps be explained by an attempt to avoid the pleonasm with ὑπερεκπερισσοῦ. In the VL some MSS (of text-type I) retain the *super/supra*. The author of Eph. who inclined to a plerophoristic style, surely used it.

[4]This part of the sentence does not belong with 'what we can ask ...' but with 'that, which he is capable of doing ...'. On this introduction to a doxology cf. Rom. 16.25; Jude 24; Mart Pol. 20.2; further Deichgräber* 53.

[5]νοεῖν can hardly have the meaning 'understand, conceive' (Gnilka) but in connection with the request must mean 'devise' Cf. Haupt on this passage; Pr-Bauer 1069 f. (see under 3) Phil 4.6 f. wards off anxiety and thereby goes in a different direction.

[6]καί omitted D2Ψ MLatt, perhaps because there was a desire to avoid the idea of a juxtaposition of the Church and Christ Jesus. The re-arrangement of 'Christ Jesus' and 'Church' in D* F G Ambst MVict is an attempt to preserve the priority of Jesus Christ to the Church. Deichgräber* 208 interprets it to mean that God is praised as the one who is revealed 'in Jesus Christ' (cf. also Ign. Rom. 2.2). But Eph. 3.21 by mentioning the Church first is more concerned to depict the praise of God which rises in the Church over Christ Jesus.

doxology.[7] There are already similar expressions to be found in the LXX, such as 'for all generations of the aeon' (Tob 1.4), 'God remains and lives for the generations of the generations in eternity' (Dan 6.26), he has wiped out the names of the godless 'in eternity and in the eternity of eternity' (Ps. 9.5). By 'generations' is meant the human generations still to come (cf. 3.5), and by the 'age of the ages', nothing other than the time which stretches unlimited into the future. It is, then, the same perspective as in 1.21 and 2.7 which here is opened up to the praise of God. The congregation reaffirms this, as almost always in the doxologies, with 'Amen'.[8] It is an indication that the author expected his writing to be read aloud in the congregation assembled for worship.

Summary

The doxology in which the Apostle's intercessory prayer ends is meant, like the introductory eulogy (1.3–14) to remind us insistently of the author's concerns for the congregation once more in the praise of God. That he has the congregation in mind is shown when with the Plural 'what *we* ask and devise' he now includes the congregation in the praying and adds to the eulogy 'in the Church and in Christ Jesus'. Thereby he once more reminds us of his theme of the community of the saved founded in Jesus Christ. The short doxology makes a powerful conclusion to this exposition.

It is characteristic that the author makes no summing-up but with his own unusual eulogy refers the congregation to God and their joint prayer. Christians are summoned to prayer above all for the inner strengthening which comes from God. Their joint worship contains spiritual dimensions (cf. 5.18–20) which can never be reached by theological reflection alone. Lex orandi est lex credendi (the rule of prayer is the rule of faith) is already in early Christianity a fundamental of their understanding of faith.

---

[7]Cf. Deichgräber* 27 f.

[8]Cf. the passages from the OT and other early Christian literature cited by Deichgräber* 26 f. 1 Cor 14.16 still shows the original function of the 'Amen': By this means those present make the eulogy their own. See further in A. Stuiber, 'Amen', JAC I (1958) 153–8, especially 154 f. (acclamation to doxologies).

III. Realising Christian Existence in Church and World (4.1–6.20)

1. THE CHURCH AS THE SPHERE OF CHRISTIAN EXISTENCE (4.1–16)

In 4.1 the author begins the paraclesis which extends for three long chapters (longer than Chapter 1–3) almost to the end of the document. The unusual length along with several exceptional features in this part betray the author's intensified interest in the addressees' realization of an existence as Christians. The beginning of the paraclesis is striking with its pieces of advice for the life of the congregation among themselves, for love and unity with one another (vv. 1–6) and for co-operation with those who hold office in the congregation (vv. 7–16). The closest parallel to this is in Rom. 12, where Paul begins his paraclesis with the same phrase παρακαλῶ οὖν ὑμᾶς ('I therefore advise you') and then – after some basic advice on Christian 'service' in this world (vv. 1–2) – commences with similar exhortations to the congregation to work together in harmony amid the multiplicity of charismata (vv. 3–8). Perhaps the author of Ephesians is following this pattern. But if we look closer we see a deliberate shaping of his own. He begins *immediately* with the call to humility, gentleness, patience and mutual toleration in love, and emphasizes most strongly his concern for the unity of the faithful (vv. 2–6). In the concluding long explanation of the variety and combination of offices 'for the building-up of the Body of Christ' (v. 12) he persists in this concern for unity (cf. v. 13) which is given and claimed by their relation to Christ, the Head (vv. 7–16) Only at v. 17 does the author return to the basic theme of the Christian 'way of life' (περιπατεῖν) stated at the beginning (4.1). This should be radically different from their former life-style as Gentiles and must be brought about in a completely new way (vv. 17–24). Looked at in this way the 'ecclesial' section 4.1–16 makes up a connected whole. Only in respect of the exposition on the various vocations to service 'according to the measure of Christ's gift' (v. 7) set apart from the basic call for harmony and unity is there a break, between v. 6 and v. 7. This is also marked linguistically by the sonorous ending of v. 6 and the new beginning with ἑνὶ δὲ . . . ('but to each single one of us') in v. 7.

1.a The Unity of the Church as an urgent Concern (4. 1–6).

Literature

C. J. Bjerkelund, *Parakalô. Form, Funktion und Sinn der parakalô-Sätze in den paulinischen Briefen*, 1967 (BTN 1).

H. Schlier, 'Die Eigenart der christlichen Mahnung nach dem Apostel Paulus', in Schlier, *Besinnung auf das NT*, Freiburg i. Br. [2]1967, 340–357.

R. Hasenstab, *Modelle paulinischer Ethik*, 1976 (TThSt 11); Merklein, FS Mußner.

E. Peterson, *Epigraphische, formgeschichtliche und religionsgeschichtliche Untersuchungen*, 1926 (FRLANT 41).

M. Dibelius, 'Die Christianisierung einer hellenistischen Formel', in *Botschaft und Geschichte* II, Tübingen 1956, 14–29.

Wengst, 'Formeln' 131–43.

van Zutphen, 'Studies on the Hymn in Romans 11.33–6' (cyclostyled dissertation), Würzburg 1972.

1	I admonish you now, I, the captive in the Lord,
	to live your lives in a way worthy of the call with which you have been called,
2	with all humility and gentleness, with patience.
	Bear one another in love,
3	endeavour to preserve the unity of the Spirit
	through the bond of peace –
4	*one* Body and *one* Spirit
	as you have been called through your call to *one* hope
5	*one* Lord, *one* faith, *one* baptism
6	*one* God and Father of all
	who is over all and through all
	and in all.

Analysis

The construction of Eph. 4.1–6 is clearly, although syntactically loose, in the style of an admonition. The introductory παρακαλῶ to which the emphatic 'I, the captive in the Lord' is set in apposition (a resumption of 3.1), is followed by an Infinitive Clause 'to live in a way worthy of the call with which you have been called' (v. 1). This admonition is to be more clearly explained in what follows. What kind of behaviour is appropriate to their calling? How is it recognised as such? The admonition therefore proceeds, but not with Imperatives, rather with Prepositional Phrases and Participles (vv. 2–3). First come two phrases with μετά – 'with all humility and gentleness', 'with patience' – then the author changes to using

Participles. These latter have no proper connection grammatically but are customary in the style of the paraenesis (cf. at 3.17b).

Once the idea of unity has appeared on the scene, the author wants to give them stronger motivation in what follows (vv. 4–6). The concepts 'one Body and one Spirit', which are inserted without any copula or verb are declaratory and have the force of an appeal. It is *one* Body and *one* Spirit – hence they should form a complete unity! The concluding καθώς-Clause is in keeping with the author's characteristic of returning to something already stated in order to make it more urgent. Here he connects up with the call mentioned in v. 2, but now he emphasizes the one hope which springs from this (v. 4). Then follows a further trio of elements of unity which are introduced by 'Kyrios': one Lord, one Faith, one Baptism (v. 5). Finally, again in an ascending line, he names the one God and Father of all whose all-embracing position and authority which carries an obligation to unity are underlined by a tripartite πάντα-formula (v. 6).

Can we detect a meaningful, uniform structure in the seven elements of unity which are introduced one after the other? It is not likely – at least taken as a whole – that an excerpt from the liturgy lies behind the acclamations (cf. the much-used εἷς-acclamation) because 'the καθώς-Clause in v. 4b with its address to the recipients of the letter is completely out of keeping in a liturgical acclamation.'[1]

Further, we know of εἷς-acclamations which focus on God the Father and the Lord (cf. 1 Cor. 8.6) but none which apply to the Church ('one Body and one Spirit'). The first pair are more in place in instruction in the faith (cf. 1 Cor. 12.13). Similarly the triad 'one Lord, one Faith, one Baptism' appears like a catechetical formulation which almost certainly would have had its origin in a baptismal confession (cf. Rom. 10.9, where it is particularly a matter of confessing the Lord Jesus). This is also shown effectively by the change of Gender in the Greek (εἷς-μία-ἕν). The expression which seems to have the strongest liturgical stamp is that of the one God and Father, for which similar expressions both to the εἷς-acclamations and the πάντα-formulae (cf. in Paul 1 Cor. 8.6; 12.6; 15.28; Rom. 11.36) can be found elsewhere.

Hence in this section we find both liturgical echoes and formulations stamped by catechetical instruction just as we saw in the Great Eulogy (1.3–14). It therefore seems reasonable to suppose that the author himself created the rhetorical pattern as a whole,[2] following homologetic and catechetic tradition. But how has the thought progressed? Within the ascending lines we can make out three steps: the double expression 'one Body and one Spirit', then the triad 'one Lord, one Faith, one Baptism' and finally the look upwards to the 'one God and Father'. He starts with the unity of the congregation. The 'unity of the Spirit' mentioned in v. 3

---

[1] Wengst* 141. Differently Barth 429, who considers that prose-words are possible in hymns.

[2] Ernst 346 wants to establish that there was already one group of three (Body – unity – peace) upon which then follow two further (one Body – one Spirit – one hope; one Lord – one faith – one Baptism. Barth 463 considers that the occurrence of the number 'one' seven times is symbolic and that the order Spirit – Christ – God must have a theological intention. Yet we must understand the sequence rather as a rhetorical composition by the author.

leads to the expression 'one Body and one Spirit', probably a reminder of Baptism (cf. 1 Cor. 12.13). This connects with the idea of a calling which was already heard in v. 1b. From this calling comes the one hope common to all (cf. 1.18). In this way everything is based on thoughts of Baptism. Baptism is the origin and manifestation of church unity. The triad then affixed – 'one Lord, one Faith, one Baptism' – also has its Sitz im Leben here. The final step, the look up to the one God and Father might have been suggested by a formula such as 1 Cor. 8.6, but is also in keeping with the author's own way of thinking which always proceeds from God and finds its goal in him (cf. 3.10 f.).

If this first part of the Paraclesis–section, 4.1–6, has been given a deliberate rhetorical shape by the author, and he then places it quite deliberately at the beginning of his admonitions, we can draw certain conclusions about his pragmatic objective. There is no doubt that he is very concerned about unity in the congregations and the Church in general. The admonitions to humility and patience do not come first without good reason. If the author at an earlier point wished to lead the addressees to a humble recognition of their election and calling from God alone (1.4, 11, 13; 2.6, 8, etc.) and to remind them of their acceptance into the enfolding community of salvation in the Church (2.11–22) he now draws conclusions from this for their concrete behaviour: They must adapt themselves to the congregations made up of different groups and bear with one another in love. For this reason he speaks in v. 3 of the 'bond of peace' (in Col. 3.14 'bond of perfection') which should enfold everyone in the church according to the one Spirit.

Exegesis

1

The author also takes over from Paul, in whose name he speaks, the word παρακαλῶ ('I admonish') which is characteristic of the Pauline exhortation. The term 'Paraenesis' which has recently become established (because the word has a similar meaning) is not a good choice since Paul never used this word and what is more the way the definition given to the term in Formgeschichte (M. Dibelius)[3] raises false conceptions. The Apostle uses παρακαλεῖν for his ethical requests and admonitions (1 Thess. 4.1, 10; 1 Cor. 1.10; 4.16; 2 Cor. 6.1; Rom. 12.1 et al.) not simply for the purpose 'usual' in the Christian missionary homily nor as in the customary non-Christian admonitory speech but rather to make a compelling beginning to his proclamation of salvation (cf. 2 Cor. 5.20). The paraclesis flows of necessity from the Gospel of Grace as is clear from the οὖν (therefore,

---

[3]Cf. M. Dibelius, *Die Formgeschichte des Evangeliums*, Tübingen ⁴1961, 239–41. He thinks that Paul's rules and instructions were related to current situations but had a general significance (239) and that the paraenetic sections of the Pauline letters have little to do with the Apostle's theoretical grounds for ethics (240). This can hardly be the case. Cf. among those who hold the opposite W. Schrage, *Die konkreten Einzelgebote in der paulinischen Paränese*, Gütersloh 1961, 187–271; Merk, *Handeln aus Glauben* 231–48; H.-D. Wendland, *Ethik des NT*, Göttingen ²1975, 90–5 (on Eph.); Gnilka, *Mél. Rigaux*; Halter, *Taufe* 242–86; Hasenstab* 31–66.

consequently) in Rom. 12.1. In Eph. 4.1, too, it extracts the consequence for a Christian way of life from all that has already been said about God's work of salvation. Seen in this way the παρακαλῶ-Clauses, although they at first appear to have simply an epistolary function,[4] are an expression of the 'essence of the apostolic admonition' (Schlier)[5] and characterize this as a specifically Christian paraclesis.

The idea of *vocation* with which the author justifies his paraclesis is also used in a similar way by Paul. God's call, in which our election by him becomes effective (cf. Rom. 8.30) and through which we achieve participation in the life of the Son (1 Cor. 1.9) also demands a life-style 'worthy of the call'. With this God who 'calls' in mind, Paul, according to 1 Thess. 2.12 – a passage similar in vocabulary – feels propelled 'to admonish, to encourage and to testify', expressions which reveal how important the preacher considers the paraclesis. The author of Eph. uses the last of these expressions (μαρτύρεσθαι = to testify) in 4.17 where he continues the paraclesis started in 4.1, taking consideration of the addressees' pagan environment. The whole paraclesis-section is based on the foundational opening clause which raises all that follows above the level of mere ethical appeals. Throughout the long expositions there is a recognisable reference back to the salvation granted to Christians (cf. 4.23– 50, 30; 5.2, 8, etc.). It is for the most part a baptismal paraclesis such as is also evident in other NT writings (1 Pet.; Tit. 3.4–7; Heb. 6.1–6; 1 Jn. 3). The author gives his paraclesis additional weight by the introduction of Paul as 'captive in the Lord.'[6]

2

The special admonitions which now begin (v. 2) lead in an ascending line to the goal to be aimed for – preserving unity (v. 3). For this they need humility and gentleness, patience and mutual toleration in a spirit of love. In vv. 2–3 the author again is clearly dependent on the language of Col. which enumerates the same Christian virtues (3.12) in a paraclesis somewhat differently constructed (3.5–17). If we compare the aco'uthia (the order of the text) in the two letters,[7] the author of Eph. takes up these admonitions right at the outset; for only later does he introduce the succinct metaphor of the removal of the old personality and the putting-on of the new personality appropriate before God and the consequences to be drawn from this (cf. 4.22–5 with Col. 3.8–10). This reconstruction of the paraclesis found in Col. 3 betrays something of his special objective. When thinking of the congregation he is principally concerned with unity, which is certainly

[4]Thus Bjerkelund.* For criticism cf. Hasenstab* 73–80.

[5]H. Schlier, 'Vom Wesen der apostolischen Mahnung', in *Die Zeit der Kirche*, Freiburg 1956, 74–89; further Schlier* Cf. O. Schmitz, TDNT V, 794–6; A. Grabner-Haider, *Paraklese und Eschatologie bei Paulus*, 1968 (NTA NF 4); Hasenstab* 67–94.

[6]From its sense ἐν κυρίῳ (in the Lord) is hardly to be differentiated from the Genitive in 3.1; the expression which rings more like a formula (cf. 2.21; 4.17; 6.1, 10, 21, and also already in Paul cf. Phil. 2.19, 24, 29; 3.1; 4.1, 4, 10 etc.) is placed here because of the paraclesis connection; cf. Barth 426; further Kramer, *Christos* 176–8. The same connotation of authority which grows out of participation in the sufferings of Christ, also in 1 Pet. 5.1.

[7]Cf. the graphic representation in Merklein* 198 f., on Eph. 4.1–4: 209.

given in advance by God to the Church but which becomes a constant task for all Christians. The closing verses 4–6 confirm this. If the dependence on Col. is unmistakeable in vv. 2–3, from v. 4 on (where the 'calling into one single Body' of Col. 3.15 is echoed) the author goes his own way (cf. analysis).

The five virtues in Col. 3.12 (in analogy to the five vices in Col. 3.5: cf. Schweizer on this passage) are reduced in Eph. to three, but keep the same order: humility, gentleness, patience. The Greek words can only be inadequately translated in English. ταπεινοφροσύνη (humility) is used only in a negative sense ('lowliness of mind')[8] in the Greek authors, but in Judaism, in Qumran as in Rabbinism, it was highly valued.[9] In Christian writings it gains a particularly high reputation (cf. Acts 20.19; Phil. 2.3; 1 Pet. 5.5). The basic position of knowing oneself lowly before God arises out of the Jewish devoutness of the poor (cf. Qumran) Lk 1.48, 52; also Mt. 5.3, 5) and was retained in early Christianity (cf. 1 Pet. 5.5; Jas. 4.6 after Prov. 3.34 LXX) but deepened because of Christ (cf. Mt. 11.29) and his way through humility to being enthroned at God's side (Phil. 2.6–11). In the Christian congregation (the civil community is not addressed) this attitude should result in their respecting their brethren and overcoming their egoism (Phil. 2.3) in reciprocal readiness to serve (cf. 1 Pet. 5.5). Such humility, which is saved from being human obsequiousness by its connection with God, is connected with πραΰτης (gentleness mildness). The connection of the two virtues is explained by their close relationship in the history of concepts. Unlike humility, gentleness was valued in Hellenism; but the Beatitudes (Mt. 5.3, 5) and the call by the Saviour (Mt. 11.29) betray Jewish tradition.[10] In Paul (1 Cor. 4.21; 2 Cor. 10.1; Gal. 6.1) and in the succeeding period (Tit. 3.2; 2 Tim. 2.25; 1 Pet. 3.15 f.) gentleness becomes a Christian virtue in one's attitude to unreasonable brothers and reluctant opponents. If tension in relationship with others is evident behind the exhortation to gentleness, the specifically added encouragement (again with μετά) to ματροθυμία (forbearance, patience) is significant. To wait patiently, suppressing one's own anger, demands a 'magnanimity' which finds its example in the Bible in God.[11] There is much about God's patience in the NT (Rom. 2.4; 9.22; 1 Tim. 1.16; 1 Pet. 3.20; 2 Pet. 3.10). When talking of human behaviour the term preferred is 'forbearance' (2 Cor. 6.6; Gal. 5.22; Col. 3.12; 2 Tim. 4.2). But it is not simply a moral virtue in one's relationship to others; it is rather a basic Christian attitude, namely a steadfast waiting in this world (Col. 1.11 in connection with ὑπομονή; cf. Heb. 6.12, 15; Jas. 5.7 f., 10) out of which then grows leniency and forbearance towards humanity (cf. 1 Thess. 5.14; 1 Cor. 13.4; 2 Cor. 6.6; Gal. 5.22).

---

[8]Cf. W. Grundmann, TDNT VIII, 6.

[9]Cf. W. Grundmann, TDNT VIII, 6–15; A. Dihle, RAC III, 737–78; F. Böhl, 'Die Demut (ענוה) als höchste der Tugenden. Bemerkungen zu Mt. 5.3, 5', BZ NF 20 (1976) 217–23.

[10]The Hebrew equivalent to πραΰτης is predominantly likewise ענוה, cf. F. Hauck/ S. Schulz, TDNT VI, 647–9. It is found often with other synonyms (lists of virtues) in Qumran, cf. 1 QS 2.24; 3.8; 5.3 f., 25; 11.1. Thereby the two components of humility and readiness for conciliation with God and a brotherly attitude in the community emerge evenly. 'Unity' and 'humility, gentleness' belong together, cf. 1 QS 2.24; 5.3.

[11]Cf. J. Horst, TDNT IV, 376–9.

If the three virtues 'humility, gentleness, patience' are already part of a tradition (Gnilka 197), in the context of Eph. they gain new emphasis and colour. They are given by God with the vocation and imposed upon the called because all Christians are called to hope and incorporated into the community of the Church (v. 4). They can be achieved through the power of the calling by grace, out of the love given by God (cf. 1 Cor. 13.4) and are here urgently demanded to preserve the unity of the Church. Hence the author also takes over the exhortation to bear one another (in love) from Col. 3.13. It follows well after the triad but is not to be connected directly with μετὰ μακροθυμίας (B. Weiss) because the two participles belong together. Love is the supporting ground for all Christian virtues (cf. Gal. 5.14, 22; 1 Cor. 13), itself borne by the Holy Spirit through whom God's love is poured into our hearts (Rom. 5.5). To bear one another in love is proof of the Spirit (cf. Gal. 6.1 f.) and suitable for preserving the unity of the Spirit (v. 3). The author does not explain wherein such bearing consists (as happens in Col. 3.13 f.) because he is more concerned with the idea of unity.

3

The 'unity of the Spirit' is that unity effected by the Holy Spirit, not simply an agreement on fundamental convictions or human concord. Because all have a share in the one Spirit which reigns over the one Body of Christ (cf. v. 4), unity is made possible and nurtured for them. They have only to make the effort to *preserve* the unity bestowed upon them. The very language bears witness to how much the author is concerned about this unity. In Col. 3.14 the emphasis is on love and peace; the author of Eph. makes a new, specific formulation – 'unity of the Spirit'. The noun ἑνότης (unity) which he alone uses in the NT (once more in 4.13) stands programmatically over the following series of elements of unity which drum in the idea. In this he is the predecessor of Bishop Ignatius of Antioch, who uses the word frequently in his letters and makes wider ecclesiological use of the idea.[12] If in 4.13 the 'unity of faith' in connection with the 'knowledge of the Son of God' is set before all Christians as the goal which they should achieve in the Church, we must detect already in 4.3 not only an exhortation to brotherly concord but also concern for the common faith.

Instead of love as the bond of perfection (Col. 3.14) Eph. speaks of the 'bond of peace', certainly prompted by Col. 3.15: 'Let the peace of Christ reign in your hearts!' but again characteristically altered. The peace brought by Christ, the peace which brings reconciliation with God (cf. 2.14–16) holds the Church as if surrounded by a bond[13] and serves its unity

---

[12]ἑνότης: Ign. Eph. 4.2; 5.1; 14.1; Phld. 2.2; 3.2; 5.2; 8.1; 9.1; Sm. 12.2; Pol. 8.3. Leading farther ecclesiologically is the idea of unity with the bishop (Ign. Eph. 4.1; 5.1), of the bishop with the presbytery and the deacons (Ign. Phld. 4), theologically the bringing-together into the 'unity of God' (Ign. Phld. 8.1; 9.1; cf. Ign. Sm. 12.2; Ign. Pol. 8.3). Unity in every relationship is shown in the common celebration of the Lord's Supper (Ign. Eph. 20.2). Cf. P. T. Camelot, *Ignace d'Antioche, Lettres* (SC ²1951), 20–55, who characterizes him as the 'Teacher of Unity'.

[13]On Col. 3.14 'bond of perfection' cf. Schweizer, *Colossians* 207 with n. 15. Whether behind 'bond' there were originally cosmic speculations (cf. Gnilka 199 f.) and the author of

which he also founded (2.15). The (modal) phrase closely connected with the unity of the Spirit has – in contrast to Col. 3.15 – a pronounced ecclesial sense. The peace bestowed on them by God in Christ (cf. Phil. 4.7) should also join them together with one another.

4

The ecclesial view comes completely to the foreground in the short formula '*one* Body and *one* Spirit!' There is no trace elsewhere of this catechetical-sounding formula; but it has its Pauline basis in 1 Cor. 12.13. The formulaic character is shown in the absence of the copula and in the joining with καί which leaves the relationship between 'Body' and 'Spirit' open. Perhaps the author already allowed himself to be led by the easily-remembered formula in 2.16, 18 ('in one single Body' – 'in one single Spirit). We can scarcely suppose that he himself constructed it since his ecclesiology reflects more strongly the relationship of the Church to Christ (as her Head) (cf. 1.22b–23; 2.15 f.; 4.16; 5.23).[14] 'One Body' introduces a new accent compared with the 'unity of the Spirit' mentioned earlier: the one Spirit works in the Church as the one Body of Christ. The author strives tirelessly to rouse this ecclesial consciousness of belonging to the Body of Christ, to make his readers committed to it and its increase (cf. 4.12; 5.30). If the formula comes from the baptismal catechism (cf. 1 Cor. 12.13 and the triad in v. 5) its function is even clearer in this context: it is meant to remind them of the obligation upon them which arises from the merciful event.

Along with their calling to the Church, the Body of Christ, all are given a common hope which grows directly out of God's call: participation in the future glory, the 'inheritance among the saints' (1.18). Co-citizenship with the saints (2.19) brings the fulfilment of the promise in which even the former Gentiles are included (3.6). God's call is structured towards the final salvation (cf. Rom. 8.30) and gives in the call itself the certainty of future fulfilment. Hope is so much a part of Christian existence that it is retained firmly in Eph. even though the eschatological perspective is different from that of Paul. If for the Apostle the most important eschatological element is to be 'changed' at the Parousia and achieve resurrection (1 Cor. 15.49–53; Rom. 8.11; Phil. 3.11, 21), this is fulfilled for Eph. in the heavenly kingdom of Christ and God (5.5) to which the Christians in the Church already belong (cf. 2.5 f.). The categorical displacement does not indicate an internal break, as is well illustrated in 1 Pet. 1.3–5 where both perspectives are bound up together. The author of Eph. considers the idea important and introduces it[15] to gain a further motif for unity and to reinforce the paraclesis (cf. v. 1).

5

The triad 'one Lord, one Faith, one Baptism' again sounds like a formula. It is distinguished by the 'one Lord' which stands at the beginning. Leaving

Eph. is still aware of these is doubtful. On the connection of 'Spirit' and 'peace' cf. already in Paul, Rom. 8.6; 14.17; 15.13.33; Gal. 5.22.

[14]Eph. does not take up the Pauline formula 'one single Body in Christ' (Rom. 12.5) but does use the idea of membership of one another (4.25; 5.30).

[15]The frequent use of the καθώς-phrase betrays his style cf. 1.4; 4.21; 5.2, 25, 29.

aside the question as to where the Kyrios-title for Jesus Christ originally came from,[16] it is certain that it was used in acclamation from a very early period (already pre-Pauline) (cf. Phil. 2.11; 1 Cor. 8.6; 12.3). Hence we must ask if this triad is not acclamatory. But the absence of the name 'Jesus (Christ)' is significant. This is hardly expendable in a laudatory acclamation of the Lord, especially in emphasizing him over against other cult deities (cf. 1 Cor. 8.5 f.). Here the Lord Jesus becomes a subject of the baptismal confession (Rom. 10.8), perhaps already in a liturgical form, so that a proximity to acclamation is retained. This triad is unmistakeably related to the event of Baptism in which all catechumen confess one Lord, proclaim their common faith in this one confession and then receive the one, for all alike, often joint Baptism. But was the sonorous trinity with its change of Gender (εἷς-μία-ἕν) already a component part of the baptismal ceremony, perhaps a liturgical acclamation which 'formed the conclusion of the baptismal ceremony in a Gentile-Christian congregation' (Wengst 142)? This remains a matter of conjecture. It may also stem from the baptismal catechesis and have become homologetically fixed. Faith and Baptism were very closely connected and related to one another in the earliest years of Christianity (cf. Gal. 3, 25–7; Acts 2.38; 16.31–3; 18.8; Mk. 16.16). The common faith is expressed in the baptismal confession, receives in Baptism the seal of the Holy Spirit (cf. Eph. 1.13) and binds the faithful into a new unity (cf. Gal. 3.28; 1 Cor. 12.13; Col. 3.11). Baptism 'on (or in) the name of the Lord (Jesus)' makes the faithful subject to the one Lord and bestows on them Christ's salvation.[17] This is the one Lord, the invocation of whom brings the promise of final salvation (cf. Rom. 10.12 f.). The tripartite formula which the author makes serve his idea of unity must come from this internal Christian understanding – more exactly from the baptismal catechism – for which the leaving out of the name also witnesses.

6

Only with the look up to the one God and Father[18] of all does the enumeration of unity-motifs reach its peak. Here the author goes beyond the horizon of the baptismal event and adds an idea of his own which corresponds to his theocentric way of thought (cf. 1.3–14; 2.4–10; 3.14–21). The 'God and Father of our Lord Jesus Christ' (1.3) is also the one God and Father of all, the one to whom all have gained access through Jesus Christ (2.18; 3.12). But the way in which this thought is formulated and stylized almost in the manner of a hymn with the tripartite, doxological-sounding extension 'who is over all and through all and in all' allows us to recognize a tradition from which this theologian draws and which he knew how to re-work for his Christian readers. For these 'all'-formulations have

[16] J. A. Fitzmyer, 'Der semitische Hintergrund des neutestamentlichen Kyriostitels', in *Jesus Christus in Historie und Theologie* (FS H. Conzelmann), ed. G. Strecker, Tübingen 1975, 267–98, after a review of previous opinions furnishes new material from the Qumran texts and thinks it quite possible that the 'Kyrios' has a Palestinian-Semitic religious origin (290–8).

[17] Cf. Acts 2.38; 8.16; 10.48; 19.5; 22.16; 1 Cor. 1.11, 13; 6.11. See also H. Bietenhard, TDNT V, 275; G. Delling, *Die Zueignung des Heils in der Taufe*, Berlin 1961.

[18] The καί is omitted by 51 pc Vg p[t] sy[p] sa bo[pt]; but it is in keeping with the author's style, cf. 1.3; 5.20; 6.23.

a long pre-history in Judaism and Hellenism in which they were applied cosmologically.[19] Our author, however, gives them an ecclesiological application. Paul already combined the acclamation 'one God, the Father from whom the universe exists and for whom we are (created and called)' with the other 'one Lord Jesus Christ, through whom the universe exists and through whom we exist' (1 Cor. 8.6). Another difference is that the Apostle places such 'all'-formulae at the end of his hymn of praise of God's unfathomable working in history (Rom. 11.36).[20] If the author of Eph. allows himself to be encouraged to a similar procedure, he still goes his own way as the choice of Prepositions shows. There are also comparable texts for this 'over all and through all and in all'. The closest in form is the famous fragment of Diogenes of Apollonia (? end of the Fifth Century BC) who says of the air, which he considers the original principle of all that exists, '. . . it appears as God to me, to reach over everything, to permeate everything and to be in everything' (Diels II, 61). But what here and in many other texts[21] is praised cosmologically-pantheistically as the power which rules and permeates everything is in Eph. attributed to God's activity for the Church and in the Church. We can consider whether the 'one God and Father of all' has only to do with the baptized united in the Church, and the concluding three-part formula added as it were to expand and give reason for this view, i.e. whether the three πάντα-predicates are to be taken as Neuter:[22] The one God and Father of all in the Church is the same God who stands over the universe, who is active through everything and in everything which exists and happens. But it is more natural to relate this originally cosmological formula to the members of the Church.[23] God is powerfully and mercifully at work over them all, permeates all[24] and is present in all through the beneficent influence of Christ whom he gave to the Church as her Head (1.22) or through the activity of the Spirit who unites all (cf. 2.18). The 'Father' is always named or called upon with the Christians in mind except in 3.15 where the outlook is broadened to include the reality of Creation; but the 'Father of all' to whom in v. 7 'each single one of us' corresponds can only relate to the faithful joined together in the Church. In spite of the influence of Hellenistic thought which also

[19]Cf. Dibelius;* B. Reicke, TDNT V, 892 f.; W. Pöhlmann, 'Die hymnischen All-Prädikationen in Kol. 1.15–20', ZNW 64 (1973) 53–74.

[20]Cf. van Zutphen* 127–52.

[21]V the texts in Pöhlmann (n. 19) 59–66, including excerpts from the Hymn to Zeus of Aelius Aristides, the Corp Herm, the Or Sib etc.

[22]Gnilka 204 would also like to take the πάντων after πατήρ as Neuter ('Father of all things'). Abbott 109, who likewise rejects the restriction to the members of the Church, interprets the oblique case as Masculine. Robinson 93 f. also pleads for the cosmic interpretation and Barth prefers the more restricted interpretation. – We should not call as witness the variant ἐν πᾶσιν ἡμῖν in D F G Ψ MLatt lat sy because this is a later interpretation; but the context speaks strongly for the 'ecclesial' interpretation.

[23]Cf. also 1 Cor. 12.6 where in connection with the charismata God is also named after the Spirit and the Lord as he 'who achieves everything in everybody'.

[24]Schlier wants to understand διὰ πάντων as instrumental 'in the sense that all (Christians) are means and tools of the one God'. But here the idea of activity on the part of the Christians has a more disrupting effect. Cf. Calvin on this passage (192): 'Deus enim spiritu sanctificationis diffusus est per omnia ecclesiae membra, et omnia complectitur suo imperio et in omnibus habitat.'

penetrated Judaism (Philo.), the idea of 'Father' in Eph. is most strongly oriented on the Christian tradition which understands the one God as the Father of Jesus Christ.[25]

Summary

The paraclesis which begins in Ch. 4 is connected internally with the author's theological proclamation but pursues the aim of making this directly effective and fruitful for Christian existence. Even in the exhortatory advice further theological ideas appear as basic and motivating but here applied to the readers' existential situation. Kerygma and paraclesis are simply like the two sides of the same coin. The proclamation of salvation necessarily entails a summons to the achievement of salvation and all the exhortations refer back to the salvation-event proclaimed. Hence the paraclesis is far more than what was then the 'usual' and prevailing customary 'paraenesis' (speech of exhortation). It begins where deviations or false signs can be discerned. For the Christians addressed by the author of Eph. the special concern is with Church unity and their life-style in comparison with their pagan environment. His principle concern is with the 'internal church' situation (4.1–16), and only later does he deal with their relationship to their surroundings (4.17–5, 14). They should gain the power from their internal unity and strength to rise to another way of existence and life-style in a non-Christian society.

The first section (4.1–6) is dominated by the idea of unity. It is given along with the call to be a Christian in the one Community of Salvation, the Church, and demands appropriate behaviour. As the author commences the paraclesis, he begins with exhortations to virtues which can advance the great cause of unity: humility, gentleness and patience in their mutual dealings. Then he proceeds with the request to bear one another in love, and finally advances to what really concerns him: they should take pains to preserve the unity of the Spirit. This cue then allows him to bring in a series of elements which form the basis for unity in the Church, which are characteristic of her and which bring an obligation to strive for total unity. The Church is one Body and one Spirit, subject to one Lord and dependent on the one God and Father. The concise formulations have their origin in the baptismal catechesis, which was always also, to be sure, a baptismal paraclesis, but the author has reformed them and built them into an impressive whole (with seven unity-motifs) – in fact to a manifesto of Christian unity.

The proclamation which commits to unity has an ever-relevant significance for the Church in any historical situation far above the author's pragmatic intentions at the time. For present-day Christianity, split into many denominational churches and Christian groupings it is especially relevant: Jesus Christ is the one Lord who constructs the one Church, his Church, through the one Spirit. All are subject to the one God and Father who is at work in all in accordance with the Economy of Salvation and

---

[25]Cf. G. Delling, 'Zusammengesetzte Gottes- und Christusbezeichnungen in den Paulusbriefen', in *Studien zum NT und zum hellenistischen Judentum*, Göttingen 1970, 417–24.

pervades them with his grace. If we notice that the Eucharist is missing in the elements of unity (cf. 1 Cor. 10.17) this is because the author is reaching back to the baptismal catechism which represents the foundation of Christian faith (cf. Heb. 6.1 f.). This very consciousness of the Baptism common to all with which the confession of the one Lord is connected has increased significance for the present time. The one Baptism which demands one Faith and makes subject to one Lord, is the basis upon which all efforts to achieve unity rest and by which all separating walls (Eucharist – Lord's Supper, differences in doctrine, constitution and office) can be pulled down. For total unity can only be thus: one Body and one Spirit, in such a way that the Spirit of God which is everywhere and at work in everything also brings to pass the corporate amalgamation of the separated churches and groups. Only in full and complete unity can the Church of Jesus Christ witness to the God and Father of all, who is over all and through all and in all Christians and desires to reveal himself to the world still separated from him.

1.b Unity in Variety: The Meaning of the Ministries in the Church and for the Church (4.7–16)

Literature

Wikenhauser, *Kirche* 172–87; Hanson, *Unity.*

E. Best, *One Body in Christ*, London 1955, 146–52.

H.-J. Klauck, 'Das Amt in der Kirche nach Eph. 4.1–16', WiWei 36 (1973) 81–110; Merklein, *Kirchl. Amt* 57–117.

J. Cambier, 'La signification christologique d'Eph. IV.7–10', NTS 9 (1962/63) 262–75.

G. B. Caird, 'The Descent of Christ in Ephesians 4.7–11', StEv II/1 (1964) 535–45.

R. Rubinkiewicz, 'Ps. LXVIII 19 (= Eph. IV 8) Another Textual Tradition or Targum?', NT 17 (1975) 219–24.

G. V. Smith, 'Paul's Use of Psalm 68:18 in Ephesians 4:8', JETS 18 (1975) 181–9.

H. Greeven, 'Propheten, Lehrer, Vorsteher bei Paulus', ZNW 44 (1952/53) 1–43.

Klein, *Die Zwölf Apostel, Ursprung und Gehalt einer Idee*, 1961 (FRLANT 77).

Schweizer, *Church Order.*

Kertelge, *Gemeinde und Amt im Neuen Testament*, Munich 1972.

U. Brockhaus, *Charisma und Amt. Die paulinische Charismenlehre auf dem Hintergrund der frühchristlichen Gemeindefunktion*, Wuppertal 1972.

H. Schürmann, '". . . und Lehrer". Die geistliche Eigenart des Lehrdienstes und sein Verhältnis zu anderen geistlichen Diensten im ntl Zeitalter', in id. *Orientierungen* 116–56.

Lemaire, *Les ministères aux origines de l'Eglise*, 1971 (LeDiv 68); J. Delorme (ed.), *Le ministère et les ministères selon le Nouveau Testament*, Paris 1974.

J. Herten, 'Charisma – Signal einer Gemeindetheologie des Paulus', in J. Hainz (ed.), *Kirche im Werden. Studien zum Thema Amt und Gemeinde im Neuen Testament*, Paderborn 1976, 57–89.

J. Rohde, 'Urchristliche und frühkatholische Ämter', Berlin 1976.

R. Schnackenburg, 'Ursprung und Sinn des kirchlichen Amtes', in *Maßstab des Glaubens*, Freiburg i. Br. 1978, 119–154.

A. Vögtle, 'Exegetische Reflexionen zur Apostolizität des Amtes und zur Amtssukzession', in *Die Kirche des Anfangs* (FS H. Schürmann), Freiburg i. Br. 1978, 529–82.

M. Barth, 'Die Parusie im Epheserbrief. Eph. 4.13', in *Neues Testament und Geschichte* (FS O. Cullmann), ed. H. Baltensweiler and B. Reicke, Zürich – Tübingen 1972, 239–50.

J. Peri, 'Gelangen zur Vollkommenheit. Zur lateinischen Interpretation von καταντάω in Eph. 4.13', BZ NF 23 (1979) 269–78.

P. J. du Plessis, ΤΕΛΕΙΟΣ. *The idea of Perfection in the New Testament*, Kampen 1959.

S. Tromp, '"Caput influit sensum et motum". Col. 2.19 et Eph. 4.16 in luce traditionis', Gr. 29 (1958) 353–66.

G. Howard, 'The Head/Body Metaphors of Ephesians', NTS 29 (1974) 350–6.

7 But grace has been given to each single one of us according to the measure of the gift of Christ.

8 Hence it is said:
   Ascending to the heights he carried off captives,
      he gave gifts to humanity.

9 This 'he ascended' – what else does it mean, but that he also descended into the deeper place of the earth?

10 He who descended is the one who also ascended over all the heavens that he might fill the universe.

11 And he gave apostles, prophets.
      preachers, pastors and teachers

12   to prepare the saints
      for a work of service
      for the building-up of the Body of Christ,

13 until we all achieve
            unity of faith and
                  knowledge of the Son of God,
            the complete person,
            the full measure of the fullness of Christ,

14 so that we are no longer minors
            tossed around and carried back and forth by every wind of doctrine
                  by the dicing of humankind,
                  by cunning which is malicious deception.

15   but rather witness to the truth in love and
            in everything grow into him who is
            the Head, Christ.

16 From him the whole Body is fulfilled,
      brought together and held together
      by every joint which serves to give it support,
   according to the strength which is meted out to each individual part,
   the growth of the body
      for its own upbuilding in love.

Analysis

This section introduces a new idea within the 'ecclesial' paraclesis of 4.1–6: the variety in unity or the meaning of the ministries in the Church. The unity previously so strongly underlined does not stand in the way of a variety of ministries but promotes them according to God's Economy of Salvation for the earthly Church bound to Christ as her Head. It is one of the most compact and also most difficult and problematic sections in the whole letter.

It is difficult to make out the syntactic structure through the author's terse, ornate diction, and many doubtful queries arise. Vv. 11–16 are again a single Complex Sentence – which is extended by Prepositional additions, Subordinate Clauses and Participial constructions – and single-mindedly pursues one idea. But this long exposition does not stand alone; it is connected by αὐτὸς ἔδωκεν with the scriptural quotation in v. 8 which in its turn is introduced as the reason for or explanation of (διό) the sentence in v. 7. If we take the text from the beginning, the structure in approximately as follows:

v. 7	different gifts of grace from Christ to each individual
v. 8	a scriptural quotation to elucidate this sentence.
vv. 9–10	(christological) interpretation of the first line of the scriptural quotation.
v. 11	(ecclesiological) interpretation of the second line of the scriptural quotation:
vv. 12–16	exposition of the ecclesiological meaning of this statement.

Looking in detail we must observe the following: in v. 7 the author separates by means of δέ (but) 'each single one' from the 'all' mentioned previously. We then notice that he has changed from the Vocative with 'you' in vv. 1–6 to 'we' (each single one of *us*). Because this way of speaking is found again in vv. 13–16 (v. 13 – 'we all') but between lie the Clauses in the Third Person relating to the 'gifts' (the people named in v. 11) given by Christ to his Church, our exegesis must clarify who is meant in v. 7 – those who are mentioned in reltion to the scriptural quotation or all the Church members who come to the fore from v. 13. If the Main Clause stands in such a dominant position over the whole section, there follows in v. 8 a short scriptural quotation which takes up the 'given' (ἐδόθη) cf. v. 7. But it also has a wider-reaching function; for in vv. 9–10 'ἀναβας' (ascending) is excerpted from the first line of the quotation and interpreted. The interpretation, which follows the wording, concludes from the 'ascending' a descending (v. 9) and the identifies the one who ascends (v. 10). But now it is said of him – i.e. Christ (cf. v. 7) – again depending on the scriptural word (εἰς ὕψος – to the heights) that he 'ascended over all the heavens'. The concluding Final Clause 'that he might fill the universe' may be taking into account the end of the first line of the quotation 'he carried off captives' which expresses the one majestic subjugation and seizure.

Only after this exegesis of the first part of the quotation does the author return (in a certain chiastic structure) to the theme of v. 7 in that he links the second line (v. 11) with ἔδωκεν (he gave). Closely connected by καί, this is the statement which emerges as his main concern in the long explanation which follows. The 'gifts' correspond – likewise in the Accusative – to the people enumerated in v. 11; they are the 'gifts' of the one who has ascended over all the heavens (Christ). There is no Objective Dative (to whom he gives them), but the context leaves no doubt: it is to the

Church, the Body of Christ (cf. v. 12). Instead he relates the reason for this giving of gifts, admittedly in three Prepositional Phrases whose syntactical relation is not clear:

πρὸς τὸν καταρτισμὸν τῶν ἁγίων	= for the preparation of the saints
εἰς ἔργον διακονίας	= for a work of service
εἰς οἰκοδομὴν τοῦ σώματος τοῦ Χριστοῦ	= for the building-up of the Body of Christ.

Are these Prepositional expressions co-ordinate so that all three phrases each have something to say about the purpose of those commissioned by Christ (dependent on ἔδωκεν), each under a new aspect? If so, we can then describe their function (following Schlier and Merklein) roughly thus: 'for the preparation of the saints' imparts the purpose of the giving as it affects the saints; 'for a work of service' relates the task self-imposed on those commissioned; 'for the building-up of the Body of Christ' introduces the real purpose for which those who hold office have taken up their ministry and for which they also prepare the saints.[1] A different picture emerges if we make the second and third phrases dependent with εἰς on the first part ('for the preparation of the saints'). In this case the people given to the Church by Christ were intended to prepare the saints for a work of service to carry out the building-up of the Body of Christ.[2] This would mean that all members of the congregation would be installed in a serving function. The order and change of Prepositions do not allow us to draw a definite conclusion. The next Clauses (vv. 13–15) apply to the Church as a whole. Clearly prompted by the goal 'for the building-up of the Body of Christ', there follows a Clause which, with a temporal conjunction (μέχρι – until), describes more clearly the goal given to the Church. The building-up of the Body of Christ will only be achieved when 'we all' attain unity of faith and knowledge of the Son and God. To bring this goal even more clearly before us the author selects yet another symbol for the perfect form of the Body of Christ. This time the syntax is clear: the expressions are similar and placed side by side:

εἰς τὴν ἑνότητα τῆς πίστεως κτλ	= to unity of faith, etc.
εἰς ἄνδρα τέλειον	= to the complete person
εἰς μέτρον ἡλικίας τοῦ πληρώματος τοῦ Χριστοῦ	= to the measure of the age (or the greatness) of the fullness of Christ.

This does not necessarily mean that each of these three aims denotes the same thing; rather we must definitely reckon with different aspects. To clarify the process of growth laid upon the Church, there follows a ἵνα-Clause which in a negative form depicts the still inadequate picture of the present (v. 14) and then, by means of an added Participle, describes positively the Christians' growing-into Christ (v. 15).

V. 16, syntactically connected to Χριστός by a Relative Clause, can be understood as a summary of the whole exposition. Here the

---

[1] Schlier 198 f.; Merklein* 76 f.
[2] Thus the majority of modern exegetes, among them Haupt 154, Meinertz 87, Huby 214, Gaugler 177, Conzelmann 75, Gnilka 213, Barth 480 f.; Klauck* 99 f.; Vögtle* 555.

metaphor of the 'body' is further developed by consideration of the 'supporting joints' and 'parts'. This can only happen, according to what has been explained before, through those participating in the building-up of the Body. Again however the question arises whether he is here thinking only of those who hold office ('office-bearers') or also of all the members of the Church. Syntactically the problem is as follows: The whole Body is brought and held together

διὰ πάσης ἁφῆς τῆς ἐπιχορηγίας
  = by every joint of support (i.e. which serves to give it support).
κατ' ἐνέργειαν ἐν μέτρῳ ἑνὸς ἑκάστου μέρους
  = according to the strength in the measure of each single part (i.e. which is
    effective in the measure of each single part).

Is the second line a clarification of the first i.e. is it connected to 'each supporting joint'? Or does it name yet other 'parts' which co-operate each according to the strength allotted to them? This question is of considerable importance because the phrase in the second line looks back at v. 7 and hence it can be helpful in deciding who is meant in v. 7.

If we start looking for written documents or earlier memories which the author of Eph. might have used for this section, we must at the outset exclude the scriptural quotation and its exegesis (vv. 8–11 without the list of people) since there are no comparable parallels to this. But the Main Clause in v. 7 is very similar to the exposition in Rom. 12.4 ff. as the following comparison shows:

Eph. 4.7   ἑνὶ δὲ ἑκάστῳ ἡμων
Rom. 12.5   τὸ δὲ καθ' εἷς ἀλλήλων μέλη (ἐσμέν)
Eph. 4.7   ἐδόθη ἡ χάρις κατὰ τὸ μέτρον τῆς δωρεᾶς τ. Χρ.
Rom. 12.6   κατὰ τὴν χάριν τὴν δοθεῖσαν ἡμῖν.

Since Rom. 12 may also have influenced, as we saw, the beginning of the paraclesis-section of Eph. (v. Introduction to 4.1–16) we must seriously consider that the author of Eph. also had the passage from Rom. in mind when writing 4.7. The unity in diversity which Rom. 12.4 f. describes congruently is in Eph. explained consecutively yet with a noticeable alteration. The same is true of the attached 'list of charismata' in Rom. 12.6–8 when compared with the 'list of ministries' in Eph. 4.11. There we find only weak echoes (the 'teachers' and 'presidents' cf. 'shepherds and teachers') and furthermore the list in Rom. 12 is more extensive and has only an illustrative character. The similarity with the list in 1 Cor. 12.28 'first Apostles, second prophets, third teachers' is much more significant. Linguistically 1 Cor. 12.27 μέλη ἐκ μέρους brings to mind Eph. 4.16 ἑνος ἑκάστου μέρους. But this is not sufficient to presume a direct influence of the great chapter on charismata in 1 Cor. on the composition of Eph. 4.7–16.

Col. 2.19, however, undoubtedly serves as a model for Eph. 4.16. There the same striking words appear: ἁφαί, ἐπιχορηγεῖν, συμβιβάζεσθαι, αὔξησις. The beginning of the Clause corresponds verbally with Col. 2.19 and the main thought, that the holding together and growth of the Body proceed from Christ, the Head, is taken over – certainly in another formulation but without any substantial change in sense, if the comment on the joints (Col.: and ligaments) does not have a concrete connection in the context of Eph. to those named in v. 11. The idea of 'building-up' (Eph. 4.12, 16) never appears in Col.

On the whole it is clear that our author stands in the Pauline tradition and made direct use of Col. 2.19, but goes his own way for the rest. Especially the position of the persons (who nowhere appear in Col.) whom he describes as 'gifts' of the heavenly Lord for his Church and whose service in the Church is important for him, gives the whole section an individual stamp. We shall have further to clarify in the exegesis how we must judge the relationship of these special ministries to the other Church members and what special goal the author is pursuing in these expositions.

Exegesis

7

From the direct paraclesis in the Second Person Plural the author now changes to using the First Person although still in the form of an appeal as is shown by the aims stated in vv. 12 and 13 and the Purpose form in v. 14. It is an indirect exhortation which combines theological motivation with a pragmatic objective, a model of a theologically effective address. The transition from the idea of unity to that of differentiation and variety marked by 'but to each single one of us' does not denote a move away from unity but is rather an appeal to achieve unity by means of that very variety and through the various forms of ministry (cf. v. 13).

But who are the 'we' to whom 'grace' has been given according to the measure of the gift of Christ? If it were not for the list in v. 11 of people entrusted with a special ministry as 'gifts' of the Lord who has ascended over all the heavens, we would have the same view as in Rom. 12.4 ff.: The totality of the faithful can be intended because of the variedness of the grace given to individual members even in their differentiation which actually serves to deepen unity. H. Schlier and H. Merklein give strong reasons for opposing the view which is that of most scholars. They hold that already in v. 7 the author has the 'office-bearers' in mind.[3] The strongest argument is the scriptural quotation in v. 8 – supposedly included as explanation (διό) – which in its midrash-like interpretation (vv. 9 f.) leads to an application to these people (v. 11). The inseparable connection of the statement in v. 11 with the scriptural quotation[4] forces us to interpret the 'gifts' mentioned therein as these men especially who perform an important service for the Church. But the quotation is closely bound to v. 7 by the explanatory Particle, διό, and

---

[3] Schlier 191; Merklein* 59 f. After Klauck* 91 f. E. Engelhardt, 'Der Gedankengang des Abschnittes Eph. 4.7–16', ThStKr 44 (1871) 107–45, especially 113, represented this interpretation. – Cambier* 272–5 wants to begin a new section at v. 11. But v. 11 in fact belongs to the interpretation of the passage. For criticism cf. Merklein* 60 f.

[4] Merklein* 60.

since the sense of vv. 7–11 depends on the verb 'give' the recipients of the giving ('we') must already in v. 7 be the gifts mentioned in v. 11. Hence the interpretation of 'we' for those named in v. 11 is logically demanded by the sequence. But there are important reservations against this view.[5]

(a) The transition from the generality (v. 6) to the particular gifts of grace (the 'office-bearers') would occur unexpectedly and would take the readers by surprise.

(b) There are frequent changings in Eph. from the Vocative (with 'you') to the 'we' form of address, by which the totality of believers is meant (cf. under 2.1–10). Not once in the changing from the First and Second Persons was a differentiation between Jewish- and Gentile-Christians indicated (cf. under 1.12 f.). It would be completely unique if it were the case that the author in using 'we' meant the special group of those who held office (the 'preachers, pastors and teachers').

(c) As to v. 7, we must consider the close relationship with Rom. 12.6, especially in the expression 'according to the measure of the grace given to us' which there applies to the totality of the faithful. To be sure we find in Eph. 3.7 a similar phrase applied to the special grace given to Paul (with an even stronger echo in 4.7 in δωρεά); but this exception must not be allowed to prejudice Eph. 4.7.

(d) It is questionable whether the introduction of the scriptural quotation with διὸ λέγει, has such a strong Causal character. In the second place where we find the same expression, namely in 5.14, this is not the case. The scriptural quotation explains and expands, just as διό in general rather serves to draw conclusions and connections with further ideas (cf. 2.11; 3.13; 4.25).[6]

On the positive side, the development of thought can be understood thus: After the constant repetitions of the idea of the unity of all (vv. 4–6) the author now directs his attention to the individual believers of whom each has been given grace in a different way (v. 7). This takes place in the general perspective 'diversity in unity' i.e. in consideration of the whole Church which should be built up as the Body of Christ. But the author already intends to emphasize the rôle of the people who perform a particular service in the Church. That is why he introduces at the end a scriptural quotation (v. 8) which he interprets as referring to such people as the Lord has given as 'gifts' to his Church (vv. 9–11). He does not, however, set these people whom he emphasizes apart from the rest who have each been given Christ's gift of grace (v. 7) but binds them together in their service for 'the saints' i.e. all the faithful (v. 12) in such a way that all strive together towards the goal of unity (v. 13). Hence there is a certain caesura between v. 7 and v. 8 which is also apparent in a slight shifting in the figure of speech: In v. 7 grace is given to each individual as the gift of Christ, while according to vv. 8–11 the 'office-bearers' themselves (as persons) are declared to be gifts for the Church.

What is the 'grace' (χάρις) which is given to each individual according to the measure of the gift of Christ? In this ecclesial connection it cannot mean the general grace of salvation (cf. 2.5, 8)[7] but must mean

[5]In the FS for C. F. D. Moule (1973) 290 f. I still followed the interpretation of Schlier and Merklein; the reasons mentioned below persuaded me to another interpretation.
[6]Cf. Pr-Bauer 394 'serving to connect what follows'; Bl-Debr §451.5.
[7]In Eph. (as in Paul) χάρις relates predominantly to the merciful behaviour of God (1.6 f.; 2.5, 7 f.; 3.2) and less to the grace bestowed upon and transmitted to humanity by him (3.7 f.; 4.7). Yet we can not draw absolute limits (cf. the Blessings in 1.2; 6.24). God remains the

each special grace which is given to each individual. In other passages in Eph. only the gift of grace given to Paul to preach as an apostle is mentioned (3.2, 7 f.). Hence at first glance it might seem to mean something like a special 'grace of office'[8]; but if we take Rom. 12.6 into consideration, where it is said that the charismata are different 'according to the grace given to us', it is also possible that it refers to special gifts of grace given to all Christians, only to each one differently, for the building-up of the Body of Christ. The expression 'charismata' does not appear once in the whole document and is possibly deliberately avoided because such marked pneumatic capabilities no longer existed at that time in the vicinity of Ephesus. But God's 'grace' for serving one another develops in a multiplicity of ways. It is, as is described in 1 Pet. 4.10, a 'manifold grace' which communicates itself to Christians for their respective 'administration'. The reading with the Definite Article[9] and the reference to the 'measure' of Christ's gift also makes this clear: Grace is measured out to each individual (Rom. 12.3). It may be that the author has in mind the picture of the distribution of the gifts in vv. 8–11 developed from the scriptural quotation, but in v. 7 it must not yet be limited to the people named in v. 11.

8

The scriptural quotation from Ps. 68 (67), 19, introduced by a short formula of quotation (cf. 5.14; Jas. 4.6) diverges from both the Hebrew (MT) and the Greek (LXX) text[10] and, when looked at from the point of view of the history of traditions, poses problems which were often discussed but do not allow themselves to be completely solved.[11] Two alterations in its use in Eph. are substantial: (a) Instead of the Second Person (where God is addressed) Eph. uses throughout the Third Person; (b) instead of 'you received gifts', Eph. has 'he gave gifts'. It is also not without significance that the first Finite Verb ('you ascended') is changed to a Participle (ἀναβάς)

---

giver in the grace which is given. Cf. also H. Conzelmann, TDNT IX, 395 (on Paul); 397 (on Eph.); I. de la Potterie, 'Χάρις paulinienne et χάρις johanniques', in *Jesus und Paulus* (FS W. G. Kümmel), Göttingen 1975, 256–82, here 267–8; Spicq, *Notes* II, 961–3.

[8]Cf. Merklein* 63 f. who also refers to Klein* 62 f. for the linguistic usage (he must mean 67 f.). But Klein does not come to a decision.

[9]The reading without the Article is fairly well attested to: B D* F G L P* 082 6 326 1739 al co; but it can be explained from the reflection that 'grace' without any closer definition has been given to each single one. Masson 188 n. 2 considers an accidental omission because of the same letter at the end of the preceding word. 'Grace' he interprets (188 f.) as the grace given to each Christian according to his personal individuality, as an 'individualisation' of grace. But in the passage we are concerned with the building-up of the Body of Christ. Klauck* 92 considers that χάρις in fact means the same as χάρισμα; cf. also Herten* 84 f.; Vögtle* 555–60.

[10]In the MT it says: 'You ascended on high, you carried captives with you, you took gifts among humanity (bᵉadam)'; the LXX translates this almost literally: ἀνέβης εἰς ὕψος ἠχμαλώτευσας αἰχμαλωσίαν, ἔλαβες δόματα ἐν ἀνθρώπῳ. Cf. the variant reading in Eph. ἐν τοῖς ἀνθρώποις F G 614 al. We cannot doubt that Eph. deliberately altered the text.

[11]Cf. apart from the commentaries Lindars, *NT Apologetic* 51–6; Meuzelaar, *Leib des Messias* 134–6; Cambier* 264 ff.; Caird* 541; Howard* 354–6; Rubinkiewicz* (the text already lying behind the Targum); Smith* (there is an allusion to the Levites in this verse of the Psalm and this is for Eph. an analogy for the Christian office-bearers – improbable).

so that the two following Verbs 'he carried off captives' and 'he gave' become the main statements and the two lines complement one another in a contrasting way. The one who ascends on high has accomplished a sovereign, victorious deed and then distributed gifts in a generous, providential way. the 'commentary' in v. 10 (on the first line) and v. 11 (on the second) corresponds to this.

Did the author of Eph. shape the quotation from the Psalm himself for his own purposes or did he take it over in this or a similar form from a tradition? The latter is more likely because (a) his own work lies in the interpretation (vv. 9–11) and this begins obviously with a form of the text handed down, (b) he quotes expressly also in 5.14 and in 5.31 f. offers only a special interpretation of a scriptural quotation taken over verbatim; (c) there are traces of an understanding of the text which presuppose a 'he gave' instead of 'he took'. This last is demonstrable from the Targum and rabbinic interpretation of Ps. 68.19. The Psalm of praise established in a cultic milieu which brings to mind God's majestic rule was in Judaism connected with the giving of the Torah to Moses on Sinai. The psalm belongs to the liturgy of Pentecost. 'You have received gifts *among* humanity' was understood as 'received gifts *for* humanity', so that he (Moses) might give the gifts to them.[12] It is admittedly unlikely that Eph. would have taken over this Jewish tradition of interpretation directly; but we can suppose an early Christian form of the text and interpretation based on the Jewish tradition which was known to the author of Eph. Perhaps we can even see a faint glimpse of it in Acts 2.33 (and 5.32b?) where it is applied to the gift of the Spirit.[13] It is possible that Ps. 110.1 and Ps. 68.19 were seen as complementary in the christological interpretation of the OT by the early Church. Factually the interpretation of Ps. 68, 19 in Eph. 4.8–11 fits the basic ideas of Ps. 110.1 developed in Eph. 1.20–3: Victory over the 'powers' and gifts for the Church. The second function of the raised Christ, his beneficent influence on the Church, would then be made clearer and expanded by the Christian understanding of Ps. 68.19. The expression which stands at the beginning – ἀναβάς ('ascending') makes the transition for the interpretation related to Christ as subject. Possibly the alteration to a Participle was made by the author of Eph. himself since in v. 9 he shows that he knew the reading ἀνέβη (as in the LXX except in the Third Person).

9–10

In expounding the passage from Scripture the author keeps to the wording and derives from it a different understanding from that in the OT and Judaism. Originally taken to apply to God who, coming from Sinai majestically rises to Zion, and in Judaism taken to mean Moses who climbs the Mountain of God (Sinai) and there receives the Tables of the Law, the text is now interpreted in the style of a midrash and is understood in a Christian way as referring to Christ. We do not know when that Jewish interpretation referring to Moses and the words of the Law first arose (It is not detectable in the Qumran documents); probably it already existed in

---

[12]Cf. Bill. III, 596–8; M. McNamara, *The NT and the Palestinian Targum to the Pentateuch*, Rome 1966, 78–81; Rubinkiewicz.* Many exegetes think that the reading 'you gave' (not only in the Targum explanation) was already old; Rubinkiewicz attempts to support the antiquity of the variant by referring to Test Dan V, 11, the translation of Ps 68.19 in the Vetus Latina and Peschitta and quotations in Justin and Tertullian; but it still remains uncertain.

[13]Thus Lindars, *NT Apologetic* 44 and 53–5.

the pre-Christian era. But there is no recognisable deliberate borrowing from Jewish tradition. The emphasis placed by the author is not directed against Moses (who could also be said to have 'descended') and hardly against God as the original subject of ἀνέβη, but is intended only to lead positively to Christ. From the 'ascent' he concludes a 'descent', and since it is the same person who carried out this movement (v. 19), the one meant here is clear for the author: It is Jesus Christ. If we ask what picture of Christ and his way underlies this and makes this argumentation possible, we are referred to his descent from heaven and his re-ascending. The reversed order, that the ascended Christ has again descended in glory (in the Spirit at Pentecost)[14] is prevented by the perspective which leads from the 'deeper places of the earth' to the filling of the universe'. It is the same perspective as in John's Gospel where the descent and ascent of the Redeemer is also discussed (3.12; 6.62; cf. 6.33, 38, 50 f, 58: 20.17). But there is no direct connection with the Johannine texts; 'Son of Man' as a title of Christ, which is characteristic of John, is foreign to Eph., and our author takes the vocabulary of 'ascending'/'descending' from the scriptural quotation which in its turn is never used in John. It is rather the same basic theological conception of the Way of the Redeemer which is common to both writings and which also appears, expressed differently, (abasement and glorification) in the Hymn of Christ in Phil. 2.6–11. There are even stronger links in thought with this pre-Pauline Hymn to Christ: the deep humiliation corresponds to the 'deeper places of the earth', and the 'exaltation' (Phil. 2.9 ὑπερύψωσεν) is formulated in Eph. as an ascent 'over all the heavens'; further, the victory over the powers which is linked to the ascent (Phil. 2.10) is echoed in Eph. 4.10, also in a Final Clause ('that he might fill the universe'). Eph. and John in a different way stand in the same theological tradition without being dependent on one another.

The unusual expression, 'the deeper places of the earth' is then more easily understood. The Comparative is not intended to compare the higher and lower-lying parts of the earth, surface and subterranean area, but can simply mean more intensively 'the lower' or 'the lowest'.[15] The Genitive is then added as explanation (appositional Genitive) just as we say 'the depressions of the earth'.[16] The phrase expresses the nadir of Christ's abasement on earth to compare it with the culmination of his exaltation in heaven. The way so described characterizes the Christian Redeemer; there is possibly some contact with the Gnostic Redeemer-myth but no dependence can be proved.[17] The interpretation as meaning Christ's descent into the realm of the dead (descensus ad inferos) has hardly any support

[14]So von Soden, Abbott (115 f.) on this verse; Caird* 536 f.; Meuzelaar, *Leib des Messias* 136 f.

[15]Bl-Debr §61.2; Pr-Bauer 840. Cf. Ael Arist 3.31 (ed. Dindorf) τῆς κάτω μοίρας (= the earth) see in P. W. van der Horst, *Aelius Aristides and the New Testament*, Leiden 1980, 61.

[16]Cf. Bl-Debr §167.2 μέρη omitted P[46] D* F G VL; Ir[lat] Tert Ambst, bracketed in the Nestle-Aland text.

[17]Cf. Colpe, *Leib-Christi-Vorstellung*, 180–2; *Die religionsgeschichtliche Schule* 203–8; Schenke, *Der Gott 'Mensch'* 155 f.; Schnackenburg, *John* 1, 544–53; Gnilka 33–45 H.-F. Weiß in: Tröger, *Gnosis und NT* 311–24; for Gnostic influence see Lindemann, *Aufhebung der Zeit* 218 f.; cf. 240–7.

today, but played a considerable part in the history of the letter's exegesis and influence.[18] It breaks down not only on the continuity of sense as it is described above but also on the author's conception of the world which certainly knows a lower and upper heaven (cf. at 2.2) but no underworld (cf. by contrast the 'under the earth' in Phil. 2.10). There is only one victorious ascent of Christ, one 'Ascension of the Redeemer'[19] which is, however, conceived differently from the Lucan Ascension, where the parting of the Resurrected One from his disciples is described as a material, factual departure and gives expression to the idea of 'exaltation'[20] in a special way.

The expression 'to fill the universe' has often been discussed. In the context it is connected with the first line of the scriptural quotation, with the 'ascending' and 'taking captive'. In his ascension on high, which is made more explicit by 'over all the heavens', Christ has 'made captives'. In spite of the spatial presentation, the 'filling' has more of a dynamic sense. Philo of Alexandria frequently uses πληροῦν (to fill) to describe God's omnipresence, which has a beneficent and kindly as well as a punishing effect. God fills and permeates everything with his power and might.[21] The expression is transferred from God to Christ in precisely this dynamic sense and can be easily understood of the subjugation of the powers and forces (cf. 1.21–22a). The closely-connected statement that the Church is the pleroma of Christ, the place where he is mercifully and beneficently active (1.23) finds in 4.11 its counterpart in the apportioning of gifts by the victoriously-ascending Christ. The question is whether this idea is already present, perhaps even predominant, in the 'filling of the universe', or whether the Final Clause relates only to the subjugation of the powers. According to the structure of vv. 8–10 the relation is closer to the 'making captive' of the rebellious powers.[22] 'To fill' can also denote an imperious subjugation, 'fullness' remains reserved for the area of salvation filled with God's might (cf. 1.23; 3.19; 4.13). If we consider what comes next, the leading of the Church to the 'complete person', to the 'fullness of Christ' (v. 13), their growing into Christ, the Head (v. 15), we might think that this

---

[18]On the history of interpretation cf. Haupt 141–50. This interpretation was not only widespread at the time of the Fathers and in the Middle Ages but was still predominant among exegetes in the Nineteenth Century. Most recently represented by H. Büchsel, TDNT III, 640–2; J. Schneider ibid. IV, 598, it has now been abandoned. Barth 433 f. gives six grounds which speak against it. Cf. also W. Bieder, *Die Vorstellung von der Höllenfahrt Jesu Christi*, 1949 (AThANT 19), 81–90.

[19]Schlier, *Christus und die Kirche* 1–18 understands this Ascent of the Redeemer against the background of the gnostic myth; cf. id. *Religionsgesch. Untersuchungen* 136–40 on Ignatius of Antioch. Now such opinions, especially of the 'soul's journey to heaven' were widespread in antiquity, cf. J. Kroll, *Die Himmelfahrt der Seele in der Antike*, Cologne 1931; W. Bousset, *Di Himmelsreise der Seele* (1901) (Reprint) Darmstadt 1960; A. Dietrich, *Eine Mithrasliturgie*, Leipzig-Berlin ²1910, 179–212. The gnostic version (especially in Mandaeism) represented only one particular type; on the gnostic 'Ascent of the Soul' cf. Jonas, *Gnosis* I, 205–10; Rudolph, *Gnosis* 169–93. Non-gnostic material can be found in Schweizer, *Colossians* 125 ff.

[20]Cf. G. Lohfink, *Die Himmelfahrt Jesu*, 1971 (StANT 26), 278 f., on Eph. 4.8 ff. p. 87.

[21]Leg All III, 4; Gig 47; Conf Ling 136; Poster C 14.30; Vit Mos II, 238 et al. Cf. Geweiß, FS Meinertz 129 f.; G. Delling, TDNT VI, 288 f.; 291 f.

[22]Cf. Geweiß, FS Meinertz 133; Mußner, *Christus* 58 f.

merciful 'filling' of the Church with Christ's powers of grace is already being included here.[23] What is certain is that in the context both aspects of Christ's ascension are inseparably bound together in a similar way as in 1.22 f.

11

The same Christ (καὶ αὐτός) who majestically fills the universe distributes gifts as it says in the discussion of the second line of the quotation (ἔδωκεν – he gave). It is not stated to whom this spiritual giving applies (in the quotation 'humanity'), but from the context it is to the Church as the Body of Christ (vv. 12.16). The gifts are interpreted as people who serve to build up Christ's Body and have specific functions for its life and growth. These functions emerge from the different terms which are assumed to be known. The author emphasizes the difference in the disjunctive arrangement with μέν – δέ . . . δέ. . . . Possibly in this arrangement the Article belongs with each group of persons named in turn: 'He gave (on the one hand) the Apostles (and on the other) the prophets, the preachers . . .'.[24] The usual translation 'he gave some to be apostles, other to be prophets etc.' is possible (cf. 1 Cor. 12.28) and allows the separate groups to appear more pronounced; but for the author 'the Apostles and Prophets' are more narrowly defined – they are established personalities of the early years (cf. 2.20; 3.5) and the same may be assumed of the 'pastors and teachers' in their time. The 'preachers' who come between as preachers of the Gospel distinct from the Apostles and Prophets, are also certainly to be ascribed to the time of writing. Nevertheless, those named, although their functions are different, are held together and bound to one another by the common action of the Lord who gave them all to the Church. They are similar gifts of the same Lord. The question often asked as to whether the list is complete or has only an illustrative character must be answered in the first-mentioned sense if we are here concerned with essential functions for the 'preparation of the saints'.

Hence this list has another meaning from that of the catalogue of charismata in 1 Cor. 12.8–11; Rom. 12.6–8. Neither glossolalia, powers to heal and to perform wonders (which can die out), nor posts which carry a social or charitable responsibility (which remain necessary) are mentioned; everything is concentrated on preaching, leading and teaching. Further, these functions do not appear as particularly 'spiritual gifts' (χαρίσματα 1 Cor. 12.4 etc.; Rom. 12.6; πνευματικά 1 Cor. 14.1; cf. 12.1) but as gifts which the Lord, as Head of the Body, gives to his Church, although in Eph., too, we cannot conceive of their effect as being other than mediated by the Spirit (cf. 4.4a). But the work of these people is more strongly emphasized in that the heavenly Lord guides and leads his earthly Church, holds her together and allows her to grow into him. The 'fundamental' significance of the apostles and prophets (2.20) is continued in a different

---

[23]Schlier 194 f.; Ernst, *Pleroma* 140 f. Not so firmly, but still including the Church, other exegetes, cf. most recently Barth 434.
[24]Merklein* 73–5; so also Klauck* 95.

way in the activity of the preachers, pastors and teachers. It is a debatable point how far church 'office' or even a 'succession of office' comes into the picutre.[25]

Although the apostles and prophets are differentiated from one another by the μέν – δέ, they are still a closely-connected group (2.20; 3.5). Through their missionary activity and grounding of congregations (apostles) and their spiritual message proclaiming the Lord's will and giving new heart (prophets) they have come to be indisputable authorities in the Church (cf. at 2.20). To these are added, in the same breath, three other groups. They are added in such a way that we must presume that the author had a special interest in attributing to them also an authority given and sustained by the Lord. The expression 'pastors' and the determination of purpose 'to prepare the saints' (v. 12) bring us into the early 'post-apostolic' period, the author's present. The 'preachers', too, are to be settled here. The 'evangelist' named as Philip in Acts 21.8 and the Timothy who, according to 2 Tim. 4.5, is to do the 'work of an evangelist' are not apostles but rather preachers of the Gospel in full agreement with the apostles. These pieces of evidence – the only others in the NT apart form Eph. 4.11 – which stem from a similar date to Eph. suggest that we should here think of the kind of people who take up and continue the 'apostolic' preaching. The later Church also understood them as Christian missionaries who penetrated more distant areas (cf. Euseb Hist Eccl III 37.2; v. 10.2) and appointed 'pastors' in the local congregations (ibid. III, 37.3).[26] Hence in this list they become links between the 'apostles' and the 'pastors' who must be regarded as the local leaders of the congregations. The description of their function as 'pastors' (only here in the NT) finds a wider basis in the metaphor of the shepherd which is frequently used in other NT writings to describe the work of such people (Acts 20.28; 1 Pet. 5.2; Jn. 21.15–17). They are responsible to Christ, the 'First- or Chief-shepherd' (cf. 1 Pet 5.4; 2.25; Heb. 13.20) – this also a feature which fits in with the 'christocentric' view of Eph. 4.11. It is a matter of debate whether 'teachers' represent a separate group alongside the 'pastors' or (because there is no Article) are identical with them. If we consider how important was the rôle of the teacher even in the Pauline period (especially in 1 Cor. 12.28) and further, how, according to Acts 13.1, the 'prophets and teachers' played a leading part in Antioch, we must assume an independent 'teaching ministry'.[27] On the other hand, if we remember that in the Pastorals the ministries of ruling and teaching are closely connected (cf. 1 Tim. 3.2; 5.17; 6.26; Tit. 1.9; 2.1, 7; 2 Tim. 3.10) it is possible that the second expression is only

[25]Merklein, *Kirchl. Amt* 224–31 develops the 'office'-concept in Eph. in comparison with the Pauline lists of charismata and considers that Eph. theology of office is governed by traditional ideas. 'The acknowledgement of tradition allowed the preaching charismata to be taken seriously as offices.' (230) F. Hahn in his 'Rezension' ThRv 72 (1976) 281–6, particularly 285, raises critical reservations for this concept of office (but Merklein wishes to think it was understood primarily theologically and not canonically, cf. 228). On the more far-reaching question of the succession of office cf. Vögtle* 554–62. But we cannot discuss this here.
[26]Cf. G. Friedrich, TDNT II, 736 f.
[27]Cf. Schürmann.* Alongside older writings (see those named on p. 174 n. 3) we must emphasize: K. H. Rengstorf, ThWNT II, 144–8, 160 ff.; Greeven* 16–31; further cf. Merklein, *Kirchl. Amt* 313–22; 350–65.

meant to emphasize the most important activity of the 'pastors'. At any rate the practical closeness of the two ministries is unmistakeable.[28]

If we compare this list with that of Paul in 1 Cor. 12.28 – 'first apostles, second prophets, third teachers' –whom God has appointed (ἔθετο) as such in the Church, we can discern a certain tradition of offices which, however, has been modified in the post-apostolic period (the Church 'which has come into being').[29] Of the three offices which existed at the time of Paul, the apostles and prophets certainly already belonged to the past at the time Eph. was written,[30] but they are still emphatically included in the list, while the teachers carry on their ministries further in the congregations. With the 'preachers, pastors and teachers' we have in Eph. a different picture of ecclesiastical preaching and ruling in the congregation. It is a period of transition in which the 'pastors and teachers' need to be strengthened in their position, and this process has advanced farther in the later Pastorals and the (still later) Letters of Ignatius.

12

The purpose which Christ pursued in the 'gift' of these people to the Church is expressed in three phrases which are controversial in their syntactical connection and sequence of thought.[31] The most important question for interpretation is whether the second purpose 'for a work of service' is co-ordinate with the first 'to prepare the saints' or is dependent on it. Since the three aims are concerned with the life of the Church in the present, we must first establish that according to the predicate (ἔδωκεν) all five groups are included for the achievement of the goal but in fact we must consider chiefly the pastors and teachers who are active in the congregations. What part do they play?

'To prepare the saints.' The verb (καταρτίζειν) in the language of the early Christians had already more the sense of 'make perfect',[32] be it in faith (1 Thess 3.10), in a common conviction (1 Cor. 1.10) or in 'everything good' (Heb. 13.21). Only once is it connected with εἰς, and then in a negative sense (Rom. 9.22 – 'made for destruction'). The verb does not need such addition: it expresses generally encouragement and strengthening (cf. Gal. 6.1; 1 Pet. 5.10). There is consequently no necessity

---

[28]Wikenhauser* 176 assumes with earlier authors that the congregational leaders and teachers were the same people. Today there is a stronger inclination to emphasize the independence of the teachers, cf. Schürmann* 151 ('holders of an independent office'); Klauck* 98; Merklein, *Kirchl. Amt* 362–5.

[29]Schürmann* 135, n. 90 expresses himself critically on Merklein's assumption, *Kirchl. Amt* 236–47, that the order of offices in Eph. 4.11 developed from the triad 'apostles, prophets, teachers' in 1 Cor. 12.28.

[30]Against Klein* 66–75; Fischer, *Tendenz* 33–9. Certainly Did. 11.3–5 is a witness that there was still a continuing 'open' office of apostle (travelling missionaries); but the concept of apostle in Eph. in keeping with 2.20 is a different one. Could the apostles and prophets of Did. 11, who should be examined on external criteria, be described as the 'foundation' of the Church? Here we find a 'fluid' concept of apostle which is on the same level as the false apostles in 2 Cor. 11.13 and Rev 2.2; cf. Roloff, *Apostolat* 82 and 198.

[31]For the various possibilities of interpretation v. in Merklein* 75; Klauck* 99. Cf. also the analysis above (p. 172).

[32]Pr-Bauer 826 v. under 1, b.

to think of instruction and training of the rest of the faithful for active service in the congregation. It must be admitted that the change in Preposition from πρός to the use of εἰς two times is striking. Is it only a variation in expression? Should we perhaps understand πρός in the sense of 'in view of'[33] and perceive the real purpose of the 'giving' only in the two expressions with εἰς? Then these people would have been given to the Church with a view to the encouragement of the saints in order to achieve a 'work of service'. But what this 'work of service' is is also unclear. If it relates to the activity of all the members of the congregation, this would be designated as 'service'; if it is seen as the task of the preachers, pastors and teachers, then their work appears as διακονία. In Paul the word often denotes the specific ministry of the preacher (2 Cor. 3.6–8; 4.1; 5.18; 6.3; Rom. 11.13; Col. 4.17), a linguistic usage which can also be observed in Acts 20.24; 21.19; 1 Tim 1.12; 2 Tim. 4.5. On the other hand the charismata can also be described as 'ministries' (1 Cor. 12.5), or it can mean simply any service for the congregation (cf. 1 Cor. 16.15; Rom. 12.7). But since in the whole section there is no discussion of activities other than preaching, guiding and teaching, we are bound to limit the διακονιά to the 'ministry' of the preachers, pastors and teachers.[34]

The third purpose 'for the building-up of the Body of Christ' imparts the final aim of Christ's 'giving' to the Church. He has appointed these people for the Church to achieve his goal of building-up his 'Body' (cf. v. 16). In his merciful action he takes certain people into 'service', uses them as his instruments 'according to the measure of grace which is given to each individual' in order to lead the Church through them to her perfection (cf. v. 13). To the metaphor of building is joined the idea of growth (cf. 2.21; 4.16) which proceeds from Christ, so that any misconception of individual, independent achievement on the part of the members involved is excluded. This metaphor, however, brings the whole Church into consideration again; all will be built up in her into a dwelling-place of God in the Spirit (2.22). All the saints will be caught up in the ministry of the preachers, pastors and teachers and participate in the building-up of Christ's Body. The author can therefore continue emphatically: 'that *we all* achieve unity of faith'.

Contrary to the majority of interpreters and transaltions which opt for the combination 'to prepare the saints for a work of service',[35] the preference would then deservedly be given to the interpretation that Christ entrusted the people mentioned in v. 11 – who were to prepare, to encourage the saints (perhaps even: in view of) – with a work of ministry, had in fact 'given' them to his church for the very purpose of building-up his Body with their help and in the combined activity of all the faithful. No exceptional position is thereby given to the 'office-bearers'. If in v. 7 each

[33]Cf. Pr-Bauer 1409 v. under 5; Wikenhauser* 178; Masson 192 f., Schlier 198, Merklein* 77. Masson 193 wishes to take πρὸς κ.τ.λ. especially with the pastors and teachers; cf. also Dibelius – Greeven 82.

[34]In this sense also Abbott 119; Hanson, *Unity* 157; Schlier 199; Merklein* 76.

[35]Among the translations cf. Luther, Menge, Zürcher, Kürzinger, Wilckens, Good News, Einheitsübersetzung, Jerusalem Bible, New English Bible, Bover. The Revised Standard Version has a different interpretation.

single individual in the Church is awarded a gift of grace by Christ and only in vv. 8–11 is special consideration given to the leading members, these are included in the general guarantee of grace which serves the building-up of Christ's Body. Only their special ministries in the Church and for the Church are emphasized, for reasons which are more clearly recognisable in vv. 13 f.

13

The inner concern which motivates the author in his exposition on Christ's distribution of gifts is the unity of the Church in faith and in the knowledge of the Son of God. The one faith which all confess in Baptism (4.5) must also be realized in the life of the Church and it is for this very purpose that the ministry of the local congregational leaders is intended. Their preaching and exhortation, which, along with the evangelists, they continue in the spirit of the apostles and prophets, should be an aid to increasing clarity and maturity; for there were already at that time 'windy', misleading doctrines threatening the congregations (cf. v. 14). The Church is only on the way to the goal of such unity, is constantly on her way ('until we . . .'). The verb (καταντᾶν) expresses this striving towards fulfilment ('the complete person, the full measure . . .')[36] which God makes possible, the preachers support and in which all the faithful should participate. Paul's strongly eschatological outlook (cf. Phil. 3.11) shifts to the vertical in Eph., since the author considers the Church as moving towards her heavenly Lord in whose glory she already has a part but only in a continuing process (cf. 2.6 f.) Faith must still mature to a true 'knowledge of the Son of God'.[37] The second expression 'the complete person' is strange. It reminds us of the 'new race' which Christ has created in the Church through his work of reconciliation (2.15). Is it a metaphor for the Church herself or for Christ who is described as the 'Head' in the metaphor of the body (v. 16)? Probably it is false to posit these alternatives. In Eph. Christ and the Church are so related that the Church, growing to her Head, herself matures to her 'Figure of Christ'.

Here there appears to be a relationship with the Gnostic idea that the redeemed are gathered together in the heavenly pleroma and united with the Redeemer.[38] cf. Od Sal. 17.14 f. 'and they gathered together with me and were redeemed. For they have become my members and I their Head'; further *ibid.* 10.5 f.; 22.10–12; 31.4. In the 'Song of Pearls' (Act Thom 108–110) the King's Son represents those souls who are to be redeemed and then redeemed souls. In the Nag Hammadi texts one section in the 'Tripartite Tract' (NHC I, 5) is instructive: When the Redemption was proclaimed the complete person received direct knowledge to return quickly to the place whence he came. His members, however, needed a place of

[36]Cf. O. Michel, TDNT III, 624 f.; Peri*. Differently Barth 484–7 (cf. n. 43 infra).

[37]τοῦ υἱοῦ is omitted in F G b. On 'knowledge of God' cf. Eph. 1.17; Col. 1.10; 2 Pet. 1.2; but in the context here 'son of God' makes good sense.

[38]Schlier, *Christus und die Kirche* 27–37; *Eph.* 201 f. This thesis finds hardly any agreement in the more recent commentaries; but cf. Ernst, *Pleroma* 147 f.; *Eph.* 357 f. For criticism cf. J. Schneider, TDNT II, 943; Hegemann, *Schöpfungsmittler* 155–7, where he points to 4.15: '. . . . the growth of the congregation here too does not lead them upwards to Christ but into him in his pneumatic fullness' (157).

instruction . . ., until all the members of the body of the church(!) are in one single place and achieve restoration at the same time, namely in the pleroma.[39] The idea is then developed in Manichaeism that the Redeemer gathers the parts of his soul of light which are scattered in the darkness. The metaphor is frequently used of a Head which gathers together the members of its body.[40] Although these texts stem from a post-Christian period (some from the Third Century) the ideas and metaphors could have an earlier origin; but a unified anthropos-myth cannot be proved.[41] Eph. differs from the Gnostic view in two respects particularly:

(a) Christ remains a historical figure; by his act of reconciliation on the Cross he creates the Church (the 'new race') and is more than a prototype of the soul or all the redeemed;

(b) the Church does not merge with Christ to the point of being identical with him; she remains subordinate to him as her Head (cf. 5.24) and continues to grow towards him (4.16).

Probably the 'complete person' – in Hellenism the adult, mature person[42] – is simply a metaphor for the mature state of the Church which she will achieve with complete unity in faith and love. But it is not the maturity of individuals which is under consideration (cf. 1 Cor. 14.20; Phil. 3.15; Col. 1.28) but that of the Church qua se; she herself should achieve the maturity of an adult person.[43]

The third expression elucidates the mature state for which the Church should strive by 'the measure of the fullness of Christ'. If we stay with the metaphor of the adult person to which the Church should mature, ἡλικία would appear to have the sense of 'age',[44] especially as in the next verse it is stated that we shall be 'no longer minors'. But the 'fullness' (πλήρωμα) of Christ disrupts this metaphor. If we are to 'enter into the total fullness of God' (3.19) which is opened for us in Christ, the author is thinking of the fulfilment which is granted to the Church in Christ. The spatial category (measure = 'the greatness') which is a possible meaning of the expression 'to fill the universe' (4.10; cf. 1.23)[45] is inadequate for the text here. The Church is not to reach the highest height of the pleroma where Christ is but is to be dynamically, intensively penetrated by the fullness of Christ, his powers to save and his divine being (cf. 1.23). Hence we can take

[39]The tract, which comes from the Valentinian school, is published in the Codex Jung (NHC I, 51–140). The passage quoted is in the third part (p. 123, 3–23), ed. R. Kasser. M. Malinine et al., *Tractatus Tripartitus*, Pars II et. III, Bern 1975, 123.

[40]Cf. Rudolph, *Gnosis* 139.

[41]Cf. Schenke, *Der Gott 'Mensch'*, especially 153–5.

[42]Cf. G. Delling, TDNT VIII, 68 f. Particularly instructive is Philo, Cher. 114 (the child – the youth – the adult person).

[43]Cf. Wikenhauser* 182 ff.; du Plessis* 188–93; Gnilka 215 and most of the modern commentaries. Otherwise Barth,* also in Eph. 489–96: He interprets the 'complete person' to mean Christ himself to whom we shall all attain at the Parousia. But this interpretation is already precluded by the other expressions dependent on καταντάω.

[44]In classical Greek the reference is almost always to the age in life, cf. Liddell and Scott 768; Pr-Bauer 682 f. (includes Eph. 4.13); J. Schneider, TDNT II, 941 f. But there is also evidence for the meaning 'stature, size', cf. Sir 26.17; Hld 7.8 Σ (LXX: μέγεθος); Lk 19.3 (classical evidence in Pr-Bauer v. under 2).

[45]Thus especially in the gnostic interpretation by Schlier (v. n. 38 supra), cf. also Dibelius – Greeven 82; but also without a gnostic interpretation, cf. du Plessis* 190; Gaugler 179; Gnilka 215.

μέτρον ἡλικίας in connection with 'fullness' as a pleonastic expression which is meant to express the complete measure. Factually what is meant is the perfection which Christ possesses and which the Church also should attain. The 'achievement' (καταντᾶν) is thus shown to be less an active endeavour than a merciful incorporation in the divine perfection of Christ.

14

With a new beginning the author elucidates (in a ἵνα-Clause) the goal of unity of faith to be aimed at in that he discusses the weaknesses of and dangers to the Church at the time (μηκέτι). This passage more than any other allows us an insight into the conditions prevailing in the vicinity of Ephesus and of the author's pragmatic concerns, although there is still little definite information. This much we can gather from the picturesque description, that the congregations have been made uncertain by unclear, tempting doctrines. The contrasting picture to the unity and the perfect form of the Church begins with the immaturity (νήπιοι = 'infants') of the Christians, which stands in glaring contradiction to the 'complete (mature) person' to which the Church should strive. Then the situation in which they are placed is described in the metaphor of a dangerous voyage on rolling waves. Finally factors are mentioned which lead to such uncertainty and danger: human capriciousness (the metaphor of dicing) and sly malice, behind which the author probably sees the intrigues of the devil (cf. 6.11).

Hence the Christians are 'infants' in a negative sense, in the same way as Paul used the word (1 Cor. 3.1; 13.11; cf. 14.20; Gal. 4.3.[46] They lack the maturity of judgement and the steadfastness of adult people, and consequently they are (as closely-connected Participles have it) tossed around and carried back and forth as if on billows. The metaphor was a natural one for the peoples of antiquity because of their fear of voyaging and of the omnipotence of the wind and waves. Here it is used to illustrate the vacillation of those Christians not steadfast in their doctrine, the ease with which they are led astray. This is brought about (Dative of Cause) 'by every wind of doctrine'! Probably ἡ διδασκαλία (with the article) designates Christian doctrine as we find elsewhere;[47] but this is endangered and perverted by various currents of wind. Although the metaphor is primarily intended to depict the inner condition of the Christians, we can hardly doubt that there were already false doctrines appearing in the congregations as is evidenced at that period in other NT writings (cf. Acts 20.29 f. Rev. 2.14 f.; Jade; 1 and 2 Jn.; the Pastorals). Possibly it is not (yet) a question of the doctrine of Christology (as in the Johannine letters) but of attitudes detrimental to morals since the author puts a finger on such in his paraclesis (cf. 5.6–13).

With a new metaphor – that of dicing (κυβεία) – the author emphasizes the volatility of human opinions ('empty words' 5.6): a matter

---

[46]G. Bertram, TDNT IV, 917. With this use of the word Paul and his school mean something different from the νήπιοι of whom Jesus speaks (Lk 10.21, parallel Mt. 11.25), who are contrasted positively with the 'wise and understanding'. Cf. R. Schnackenburg, *Die 'Mündigkeit' des Christen nach Paulus in Christliche Existenz nach dem NT* II, Munich 1968, 51–74.

[47]Merklein* 107.

of chance as happens in the fall of the dice. The remark is only loosely joined (a causal or modal ἐν) and must not be more closely connected with 'every wind of doctrine'.[48] The next remark denotes an intensification (again with ἐν) that behind this hides a cunning (πανουργία) which is nothing less than malicious deception. The author is probably thinking here of the incomprehensible seductive skill of devilish cunning which makes use of human weakness. The choice of words shows this too. According to 2 Cor. 11.3 the serpent deceived Eve by its cunning (πανουργία). We need God's armour to withstand the intrigues (μεθοδείας) of the devil (Eph. 6.11). Satan's machinations have 'method'; his aim is to mislead (πλάνη), an expression which came to have an ever darker and harsher sound for the tempted early Christian congregations (cf. 2 Thess. 2.11; 1 Jn. 4.6; Jude 11; 2 Pet. 3.17; πλανοί 1 Tim. 4.1; 2 Jn. 7).[49] Against the background of this gloomy picture sketched out by the author himself, his concern to encourage the preachers and teachers in the congregations is even more comprehensible. It was for this very purpose that Christ gave the Church such people with functions of guiding and teaching – in order to give them security and steadfastness in the rolling waves of human opinion and on the cunning ways of devilish temptation. The Lukan Paul (at about the same time) warned the presbyters of Ephesus in a similar manner (Acts 20.28–31).[50] The teachers (at the end of v. 11), who stand in the tradition of the apostles and prophets, preserve the unadulterated message of Christ.

15

The other, positive side of the picture (δέ) is seen when those who belong to the Church 'witness to the truth in love'. The contrast is linguistically unmistakeable (in a chiasmus):

ἐν πανουργίᾳ . . . τῆς πλάνης
ἀληθεύοντες . . . ἐν ἀγάπῃ.

The rare verb ἀληθεύειν (in the NT only elsewhere at Gal. 4.16) does not here have the sense of exhorting them to truthfulness in general but refers to the 'word of truth' (1.13) namely, to the Gospel (cf. 'the truth of the Gospel' Gal. 2.5, 14; Col. 1.5). This truth, guaranteed by God, gives the Christians steadfastness and strength like the warrior's belt (cf. 6.14). But to this is added 'in love', an expression which repulses all cunning which tries maliciously to deceive.[51] The Christian who witnesses to the truth of the Gospel cannot use the same methods as a tempter who is pursuing evil intentions; he wants to convince humanity by a revelation of the truth and win them by love (cf. 2 Cor. 4.2; 6.7). It is significant that this 'to speak the truth in love' applies to the whole Church ('we all' v. 13)

---

[48]Otherwise Merklein* 108.

[49]Cf. the sharpened dualistic use in the apocryphal and particularly apocalyptic literature; on this v. H. Braun, TDNT VI, 238–42; on the texts mentioned above, 245–7.

[50]See also p.185 n. 44 sup.

[51]ἐν ἀγάπῃ should not be taken with the αὐξήσωμεν which follows but belongs to ἀληθεύοντες; cf. the chiastic arrangement in the text given above. In 2 Cor. 4.2 we also find the contrast between πανουργία and a phrase with ἀλήθεια ('disclosure of the truth').

and not only to the preachers. The whole Church witnesses to the truth in the manner and power of love. The truth should not be spoken of simply in a gentle, gracious way; rather the Church should make real the word of truth it has been given in love and consequently make it recognisable in the life of the Church.[52] For this statement (in a Participle) points to the other, that in everything we grow into him who is the Head, Christ. But from him the whole Body is built up in love (v. 16 end).

As in 2.21 the growth is to be understood dynamically since it is achieved in love, a constant process which is oriented on Christ whose love bears and stimulates everything (cf. 3.19). A transitive causal interpretation 'to let the universe grow into Christ'[53] is improbable. Nowhere else is there mention of the Church having an active influence on the universe (not even in 3.10). There is no talk of a 'growth' of the universe into Christ. 'Growth' is an expression for the maturing of the Christians in faith (2 Cor. 10.15), in knowledge (Col. 1.10), in moral productiveness (cf. 1 Pet. 2.2) – always through the power of God (cf. Col. 2.19). In its transitive use, especially for the Gospel and the congregations founded on it, God is emphatically the only one who grants growth (1 Cor. 3.6 f.). With τὰ πάντα as with ἐν πᾶσιν in 1.23 the comprehensive dimension is indicated (Accusative of Relationship 'in every respect').[54] The Church should grow into her Head in everything – in faith and knowledge, in unity and especially in love.

16

With 'Christ, the Head' comes a cue which not only joins up with the thoughts of the Body but also, with this expression which has already been introduced for the Church (v. 12c, cf. 1.23), provides the chance to summarize once more the main ideas of the section in concentrated form. The explanation begins with Christ the victor over the powers and the giver of gifts to the Church (vv. 8–11); his ruling position which supports the total life of the Church is now emphasized once more. The Church which is striving towards and growing into him receives from him all her growth. The author is thinking of the leadership, care, love, the transmission of life which proceeds from Christ and which he provides for the Church.[55] Here he is using Col. 2.19, a passage which provides him with the material for the idea of the Body – which, however, he utilizes in a different way to suit his own purpose.

Initially we can extract the main statement from the Complex

---

[52]The variant ἀλήθειαν δὲ ποιοῦντες F G agrees with the Latin translation of the text – *veritatem facientes* VL (text-type D and J in Frede, Ep ad Eph. 171) Vg latt as also with bo cf. J.-D. Dubois, 'Ephesians IV, 15', NT 16 (1974) 30–4 (he pleads for an independent textual tradition) Cf. also Abbott on this passage (123); Merklein* 110.

[53]Thus Schlier 206 f. But in interpreting τὰ πάντα to mean the universe, this cosmic observation would be brought back again to the ecclesial in v. 16; the whole section, however, from v. 11 is oriented solely on the ecclesial. Steinmetz, *Heils-Zuversicht* 120, followed Schlier's interpretation. Cf. on the other hand Gnilka 218.

[54]Cf. Bl-Debr §160.1 n. 2. Pr-Bauer 1255, s.v. 2, b, β.

[55]On κεφαλή (Head) cf. H. Schlier, TDNT III, 680 ff.; Wikenhauser* 197–209; Benoit, *Leib* 261–8; Tromp*; Meuzelaar, *Leib des Messias* 117–26; du Plessis, *Christus as Hoof*, esp. 74–83; E. Schweizer, TDNT VII, 1054 (on Philo, Som I, 144 and Quaest in Ex 2.117); 1076 f..

Sentence – that the whole Body achieves its growth for its own building-up in love from Christ.[56] The two Participles closely linked with πᾶν τὸ σῶμα (the whole Body), 'brought together and held together', still remain completely within this christocentric outlook: For it is Christ who effects this and thus promotes the unity of the Body. But then in further statements which characteristically depart from Col. 2.19 the ideas developed in Eph. 4.11 f. are taken up and shown to advantage. Even in the positioning of διὰ κτλ – in Col. 2.19 before the Participles, in Eph. 4.16 after them – there is in Eph. a stronger emphasis on 'by every joint which serves to give it support' because this Clause consequently leads more closely to the growth of the Body. Further, the mediating function of 'every joint' is more strongly stressed by the noun τῆς ἐπιχορηγίας (in Col. a Participle). Finally, the author of Eph. has added 'according to the strength[57] which is meted out to each individual part'.[58] In that this expression clearly echoes v. 7, we cannot doubt but that the author has inserted it deliberately. But what is he trying to say? If we consider his exposition in v. 11, it is natural to take 'every joint which serves to give it support' as referring to these people.[59] In the ancient body-metaphors the joints have a particular function (in Col. 'ligaments' are added): they make up the connection between the individual parts of the body but also provide (ἐπιχορηγεῖν) the organism from the head with the necessary powers to move and grow.[60] Since the growth proceeds from Christ, the ἐπιχορηγία is in the end bound up with Christ who uses the joints for this purpose. The energy to promote growth which proceeds from him is assigned to each individual part in a determined measure. Can we identify 'each individual part' with 'each joint'? It is reasonable to suppose this but not necessary. Since the author is thinking more of the reality than of the metaphor, he can introduce the idea that each individual who belongs to the Body of the Church receives the power allotted to him in grace from Christ (v. 7). Then the joints would certainly be given special emphasis, but still classified in the total framework of the Body guided and nourished by Christ. Consequently, although we cannot be absolutely certain because of the concise metaphorical language, we would like to think that both the leading people from v. 11 ('every joint') and also the rest of the faithful ('each individual part' = leaders and all the others) are included in the depiction.

This corresponds exactly to the development of thought in the whole section: Proceeding from the grace which is allotted to each Christian (v. 7), the outlook narrows to the special 'gifts' of Christ with their

---

[56]The repetition of 'Body' (τοῦ σώματος) is awkward but can be perhaps explained by the long distance from the subject.

[57]P[46] reads καὶ ἐνεργείας which would fit as a supplement to τῆς ἐπιχορηγίας, but is perhaps only a misreading of κατ'.

[58]The variant μέλους A C Ψ 365 pc a Vg sy[p] bo can be explained a reminiscence of 1 Cor. 12.12–27; Rom. 12.4 f. or generally from the metaphor of the Body.

[59]Thus Schlier 208; Hegermann, Schöpfungsmittler 155 f.; Merklein* 115; Klauck* 103; also assumed by Gnilka 220. On ἐπιχορηγία cf. Pr-Bauer 603; Haupt, Abbott, Masson on this.

[60]Cf. F. W. Bayer, RAC I, 434; Tromp* 356–8.

functions of ministry (v. 8–12b) then widens out under the heading of 'building-up of Christ's Body' (v. 12c), then again to 'us all' (v. 13), to the whole Church in which the leaders co-operate with the faithful. In the final, summarising sentence of v. 16 the decisive, conclusive rôle of Christ for the life and growth of the Church is once more to be emphasized. What is said in Col. 2.19 in an undifferentiated way abut the whole Body of the Church[61] is in Eph. deliberately attributed with new emphases to those who perform a special ministry – but in such a way that Christ's outstanding position is preserved and the whole Body is drawn in to the process of growth. It achieves its growth for its own development 'in love' from Christ. The development can only be successful to the extent in which all parts, the leaders and the rest of the faithful, peaceably work together in love (cf. 4.2 f.).

Summary

After talking of the unity of the Church which concerns the author greatly (vv. 1–6) he turns to speak of individual talents and activities which are found in the Church. But these, too, are included in a plan 'given' to the Church, each according to the measure of the gift of Christ. The nature and strength of its effect is assigned to them through grace (v. 7). Christ himself takes over in Eph. that function which in 1 Cor. 12.7–11 is ascribed to the divine Spirit. In fact the same thing is meant here because for Eph., too, the Spirit is the principle which rules over Christ's 'Body' (cf. v. 4a); but in keeping with Eph.'s view of the Church Christ is to be emphasized as the omnipotent Head of the Church (cf. 1.20–3). In his beneficent 'filling' of the Church (1.23) he takes individual people into his service, each for a particular task, arranges them in the whole with the goal of unity and thus himself provides for the development of his Body (v. 12 and v. 16). In a scriptural quotation, which is re-interpreted in the manner of a midrash to refer to Christ, Christ enters the scene as the victor (who has defeated the powers of evil) ascending over all the heavens and as the beneficent giver of gifts to his Church (vv. 8–11). The 'gifts' which he distributed are interpreted as being those people who perform a special ministry for and in the Church. Initially these are the 'apostles and prophets' who founded the congregations by their preaching and spiritual words, secured them in the word of Christ and thus themselves represent the foundation of the Church (cf. 2.20). But then the 'preachers, pastors and teachers' who subsequently develop at the present time the activity of the apostles and prophets also carry on the preaching, careful guidance and teaching. They are intended – as is shown by the use of the Present – for the 'preparation of the saints' i.e. the faithful, and consequently perform a continuing service which is meant to benefit the development of Christ's Body (v. 12).

The activity of these people can also be understood to have a pneumatic or charismatic effect since they occur in the power of Christ and his Spirit. But it is not mere chance that no other charismata are mentioned as in 1 Cor. 12.8–10; Rom. 12.6–8. The function of leading and teaching to preserve the apostolic tradition, as is shown in the following (vv. 13–14),

---

[61]Cf. Schweizer, *Colossians* at this verse.

gained at that period an outstanding importance because the unity of faith was being threatened by uncertainty and arbitrary human beliefs. So such people who are appointed in the Church and in individual congregations as preachers, pastors and teachers – although nothing is said about the manner of their appointment – perform an important, even necessary service for the unity of the Church. With the ascertainment that they are gifts of the Lord for his Church, in a direct line with the apostles and prophets, they are confirmed and strengthened in their position. They have a firmly outlined task and can consequently be named 'office-bearers' if we take into account the specific sense which their 'office' achieves through their connection with Christ, his word and his instruction and through their orientation to the congregations and the whole Church.

These people are so introduced into the total organism of the Church that only in co-operation with all the faithful do they contribute to the building-up of the Body of Christ. All together (v. 13a) must achieve unity of faith and that completeness of the Church bound to Christ which is indicated in the metaphor of the 'complete person' and in the 'full measure of the fullness of Christ' (v. 13b–c). The swaying and being tossed about by human opinions and devilish deception can only be overcome when all witness to the truth in love and make it real (vv. 14–15). This is a process of inner growth which refers all members of the Church to the drive and life-giving power which proceed from Christ, the Head (v. 16). The Church can only grow up to Christ, grow into him if, overcome and filled with his love (3.19), she herself grows in love. How this actually happens or can happen, in a dissociation from the life-style of the pagan environment and in the cultivation of a brotherly, Christian life, is described in more detail in the paraclesis (cf. 4.2 f.; 5.2; Haustafel).

The author's pragmatic aim, to strengthen the position of the preachers, pastors and teachers in the congregations in the face of the danger to unity, permits him to make theological expositions of great consequence. The naming of these people side-by-side with the old authorities 'apostles and prophets' and their description as Christ's gifts gives them a solid standing, a function in the post-apostolic Church willed by Christ himself. They do not as a consequence stand above the Church or the rest of the faithful; rather their 'office' alone can bind the members of the Church to Christ, the Head, and to one another to serve the building-up of Christ's Body. But in this sense it is an essential, constitutive component part of the Church. It is an 'office of unity' which should ward off deviation and disintegration, unite the Christians through preaching and doctrine, care and exhortation, and lead them to Christ, the Head. In this view of the Church which came into being and grew in history, it is also of necessity a continuing office which must preserve its connection with its apostolic origin. Further-reaching questions such as emerge in the present problems connected with office can hardly be answered from the text.

Comment by the Protestant partner: Unity exists further in that in v. 7 and again in v. 13 all members of the congregation are meant, and in that the offices named in v. 11 seem to the author to be specially important, no doubt because they have imposed themselves as necessary in the development of the Church, in a similar way as already holds true for the three named first in 1 Cor. 12.28. Further, unity also exists in that in both places the ministry of the word described is central for the life of the Church. The discussion between the Roman Catholic author and his Protestant partner centres on whether one can therefore distinguish these 'offices' from the ministries given to each of the believers and, if so, in what way. Certainly as a rule particular ministries must be prescribed – by election and appointment – and one can then call them 'offices'. But must they always be the same, apart from the fact that the Word must be proclaimed and the Sacraments distributed in some way? Must this always continue to be so or can not this central ministry also be managed by the congregation as a whole somewhat after the fashion of the Quakers? Can it not also in a congregation in which it is prescribed be performed by a member of the congregation who has not been appointed for that purpose in emergency situations (not only *in extremis*)? Is the ministry of proclamation, of distributing the Sacrament or even diaconia – which must be organized for external reasons because the congregation must know upon whom they can call if necessary – different in a spiritually relevant way from that of intercession, whose upholder is known to God alone? Or is it not so that 'office' is only to be differentiated from other 'ministries' because of a necessary institutional organization which arises from practical rather than theological grounds? On the answer to this question depends whether the ministries mentioned in v. 11 are introduced as examples because they were particularly important at that time and place in Eph., or to make a distinction over against other ministries. On this also depends the question whether ordination or installation is theologically necessary – this is not presupposed in Eph. but is in the Pastorals – or whether a congregation which, at least in certain situations, is of the opinion that it has no need of special teachers because the Holy Spirit can speak through all members of the congregation and perhaps also through outsiders (1 Jn. 2.27) is just as much 'Church' in the full sense. We have not yet reached agreement on this question, which naturally needs a much fuller and more differentiated consideration, although I am grateful for many of the author's statements, especially on this problem (cf. also my Commentary on Colossians, p. 165, n. 43).

Eduard Schweizer.

2. CHRISTIAN EXISTENCE IN A PAGAN ENVIRONMENT (4.17–5.14)

With 4.17 the author turns his attention from the Church and her internal life to Christian existence in a pagan environment ('how the gentiles lead their lives'). Christian existence in this world can be distinguished from a way of life alienated from God and wrapped up in worldly matters. After this negative dissociation from the environment there then emerges a new turning-point in 5.15, where attention is once more directed to existence and life in the Church, again under the same catchword (πῶς περιπατεῖτε). After the transition in 5.15–17 he first discusses briefly Christian spiritual worship of God (5.18–20) then follow longer expositions on the earthly life of Christians (Haustafel 5.21–6.9).

The sub-division of this long section cannot be made exclusively from the formal indications of division. The Participle οὖν which we encountered at the beginning of the paraclesis (4.1) and which occurs again in 4.17 serves in 5.1 and 7 merely to denote the logical progress. Likewise περιπατεῖν in 5.2 and 8 does not indicate a new beginning. Although the progression of thought is developed without any very definite attempt to divide into sections, we can nevertheless discern smaller textual units. In 4.25 an exhortation containing concrete instructions is introduced by διό. This warns throughout against the aberrant behaviour of the heathen and only at the end calls for the central Christian attitude of love based on the example of Christ (4.25–5.2). In 5.3 there is again a warning against pagan vices, namely sexual immorality, which merges in 5.8 into the positive exhortation to change to become the Children of Light. The expositions up to 5.14 are still closely connected to what has gone before, so that we can take 5.3–14 as a textual unit. In all three sections (4.17–24; 4.25–5.2; 5.3–14) there is a recognisable progression from the negative depiction of the early Christian environment to a positive description of a Christian existence and life-style.

We have already been made aware in recording the characteristic traits of Eph. of certain differences in the paraclesis from those in other NT writings. In Eph. we find no guidelines for our relationship with the state and its representatives such as are found in Rom. 13.1–7; 1 Pet. 2.13–17; Tit. 3.1. Further, there are no exhortations to Christian 'good conduct' in the civic society as are emphasized in 1 Pet. and the Pastorals. In comparison with Col., where similar exhortations are also lacking, we find that Eph. alone makes the comparison between the Children of Light and the Children of Darkness (5.8–14). The author calls for a radical distinction from the non-Christian ('pagan') environment and for battle with the still-operating powers of evil. His positive concern is with the inner strengthening and sanctification of all the faithful who belong to Christ's Church.

2.a Separation from non-Christian behaviour and Accomplishment of the 'new person' (4.17–24)

Literature

R. A. Harrisville, 'The Concept of Newness in the New Testament', JBL 74 (1955) 69–79; also *The Concept of Newness in the New Testament*, Minneapolis 1960.

E. Larsson, *Christus als Vorbild. Eine Untersuchung zu den paulinischen Tauf- und Eikontexten* 1962 (ASNU 23), 223–30.

K. Wegenast, *Das Verständnis der Tradition bei Paulus und in den Deuteropaulinen*, 1962 (WMANT 8).

de la Potterie, 'Jésus et la vérité d'après Eph. 4.21'; in SPCIC (1961) 1963 (AnBib 17–18) 45–57.

Gnilka, *Mél. Rigaux* 399–405; Halter, *Taufe* 248–56.
R. Cavedo, 'Non vivere più come i pagani (Ef. 4–6)', ScC 106 (1978) 343–57.
Merklein, FS Mußner.

17 Hence I remind and profess in the Lord:
   You must no longer live your lives as do the pagans
   in the triviality of their desires
18   darkened in their understanding,
   alienated from the life of God
      because of the ignorance which dwells in them,
      because of the hardening of their hearts,
19   such as, their sensibilities blunted, have given themselves up to dissipation
   to practise any kind of uncleanliness in their greed.
20 But you did not learn Christ thus,
21 if you have heard differently about him and have been
   taught in him, as the truth is in Jesus,
22 that you put off the old personality
   which, in accordance with your earlier way of life was corrupted
   by the desires of deceit.
23 Let yourselves be renewed in the spirit of your minds
24 and put on the new person
   which is created according to God
   in righteousness and holiness of truth.

Analysis

The exhortation to a Christian way of life (περιπατεῖν) which begins at 4.17 is emphasized by the introductory expression 'hence I remind and profess in the Lord' and immediately delivers a warning against the pagan life-style. This contrast is important for the writer since he digresses into a lengthy characterization of such un-Christian states of mind and behaviour (vv. 18–19). Only in v. 20 does he change to a positive instruction with 'but you did not thus . . .'. The 'pagans', who lead their lives 'in the triviality of their desires' (v. 17b) are further described with various syntactical variations (vv. 18–19). The connectives (Participles, Prepositional Phrases, Relative Clause) are not intended to make a logical sub-division but serve the progress and intensification of thought. The author allows himself to be driven on by the association of ideas, varies the thoughts, penetrates the reason (διά plus Acc) and turns (with the Relative Clause) from the attitude of mind to its effect in everyday life. In so doing he takes over certain ideas about the moral state of the pagan world which already have a long tradition and were also expressed in Rom. 1.18–32. There are echoes of Rom. 1.21 (the triviality of their desires, the darkening of their understanding) but also of other passages in the Pauline corpus (cf. 1 Thess. 4.3–7; Gal. 5.19). These are topoi of the early Christian paraclesis which the author of Eph. introduces in a terse, concentrated manner.

The instruction laid down about the 'differentiation of the christlike' begins with a reminder of what the Christians have 'heard and been taught'. The formulation with 'Christ' as the direct object of the doctrine handed down is striking: 'You did not learn Christ thus'. All

Christian proclamation has its centre in him. The following formulations in v. 21 reveal the author's understanding of tradition. 'Learning' results from the way of 'hearing' (initially in the missionary sermon) and in 'instruction' (catechesis in the Church). It is the same line which we recognized before: The proclamation of Jesus, the Lord Christ, mediated initially by the apostles and prophets (cf. 2.20; 3.5) is transmitted by the preachers, pastors and teachers (4.11).

Only after the reminder of the doctrine and instruction which have been handed down does the author express his exhortation in form (Accusative and Infinitive) exactly as in v. 17. Again this takes place in that the addressees put off their former life-style (v. 22) and only then comes a positive formulation (v. 23 f.). They must put off the 'old personality' which is corrupted by the 'desires of deceit' and then put on the 'new person'. The linguistic presentation strives after this comparison but develops it in stages. The idea of the 'old personality' first brings 'renewal' on to the scene. Only then is the new person contrasted with the old. It is, in contrast to the earlier 'alienation from the life of God' (v. 18) once more 'created according to God' (v. 24a). The blunted life of dissipation (v. 19) is in v. 22 described as a corrupted way of life 'according to the desires of *deceit*' (v. 22). To this now corresponds a renewed being and existence 'in righteousness and holiness of *truth*' (v. 24).

The author has taken the central motif of the old and new person from Col. 3.9 f. where it is more clearly introduced in a baptismal paraclesis. Admittedly there are some stylistic differences (cf. exegesis). Possibly a topos from the early Christian baptismal catechism and paraclesis lies behind it (cf. for 'put on' Gal. 3.27; Rom. 13.12b–14; for 'old–new' 1 Cor. 5.7; Rom. 6.6; 2 Cor. 5.17); but it is possible that Eph. 4.22–4 draws directly from Col. 3.9 f. because the following exhortations are also taken from the context of Col. 3. But there is not so sharp a confrontation with an un-Christian, pagan way of life in Col. as there is in Eph. 4.17–24. If we include the other observation that the author of Eph. reminds his readers emphatically in this very connection (other than in Col.) of the doctrine which has been taken over, we can recognise his special objective and pragmatic intention. The addressees are in danger of forgetting their salvation and re-creation by God (cf. 2.4–6; 8–10) and again becoming assimilated to the style of life prevalent in their environment. In the instruction in the Church they must ever again be constantly made aware of their conversion, baptismal experience and the responsibility this entails.

Exegesis

17

The author turns to the addressees with great urgency, 'reminding' (μαρτύρ-ομαι)[1] them to keep their distance from the 'pagan' way of life. The additional 'in the Lord' reminds us of the 'captive of the Lord' in 4.1 but

---

[1] In this sense also 1 Thess. 2.12; cf. Judith 7.28; Jos. Ant. X, 104. On the secular use of the word where its meaning stretches from 'swear' (before someone), 'affirm', 'challenge' cf. H. Strathmann, TDNT IV, 510 f.

also aids communication with the readers who are reminded of their existence in light 'in the Lord' (5.8) and the responsibilities which arise from this (cf. 5.10, 17). The underlying baptismal paraclesis which, from the new existence 'in Christ' concludes and calls for a new life-style (5.8b) and a constant strengthening in the struggle against evil (6.10) can also be detected in the 'no longer' (cf. also 4.28). 'The pagans' (τὰ ἔθνη), originally 'the peoples', in the language of the Greek bible and Judaeo-Hellenistic literature signifies all the peoples other than Israel and in the Christian area also applied to the Gentile-Christians (Eph. 2.11; 3.1). Here the expression takes on an extremely negative note for those who are outside the Christian congregation. What is in fact meant is the deep gulf which exists between an understanding of life grounded on God and a rootless way of living. But in English where 'the pagans' sounds even more strongly contemptuous, we should avoid the expression wherever possible.

In principle the author calls the attitude of mind of the outsiders 'triviality of desires'. The expression frequently used in the LXX to translate various Hebrew equivalents, 'triviality' (ματαιότης)[2] characterizes a person both in his/her transitory, contingent existence and in her/his deceitful, vain striving. 'The Lord knows the thoughts of humankind, (and knows) that they are vain' (Ps. 94 (93).11; cf. 1 Cor. 3.20). People who lack knowledge of God sink in their thoughts into foolishness, miss the way in their search for meaning and go astray with self-made idols. The Wisdom of Solomon 13, where this is set out in more detail, begins 'All people were naturally trivial (μάταιοι) in whom ignorance (ἀγνωσία) of God reigned' (v. 1) and Paul takes this up in Rom. 1.19–21 with the same vocabulary. The close relationship to this passage, which makes use of a topos common elsewhere in Judaeo-Hellenistic thinking,[3] becomes even clearer in what follows. 'The triviality of their desires' is more than a noetic ignorance; it is existential unresponsiveness.

18

A darkening of the understanding (διάνοια) and alienation from the life of God go hand in hand as is expressed in the co-ordinated Participles. Paul speaks of the darkening of their 'hearts which lacked understanding' (Rom. 1.21) so that they turned away in their foolishness from the immortal God and exchanged for this the service of mortal creatures (v. 23). The process of human estrangement from God and self has effect on the capacity for knowledge, resulting in inadequate, 'darkened'

[2]On the translation in the LXX, which uses the word especially to denote the emptiness and futility of idol-worship but also of human endeavour (Is. 28.29; 30.15; 33.11 all only in the LXX) cf. O. Bauernfeind, TDNT IV, 521 in n. 4. According to Paul (Rom. 1.21) people become 'trivial', foolish in their thinking; but the (whole) creation was subjected to triviality, transitoriness (Rom. 8.20); 1 Pet. 1.18 speaks of their earlier 'futile way of living'; it appears frequently in early Christian literature: cf. Did. 5.2; Barn. 4.10; 20.2; 1 Clem. 7.2; 2 Clem. 9.2; Pol. 7.2; Herm. 9.4; 11.8; 12.6, 5 ('futile desires of this aeon') etc.

[3]Cf. Wis. Sol. 16.16; Arist. 132–8; Test R 3.8; L 14.4; N 3.3; Sib. III, 8–45, 276–9 et al.; also Syr Baruch 54.17 f. Further in U. Wilckens, *Der Brief an die Römer* I, 1978 (EKK VI/1), 96–100. But Paul uses this topos in the horizon of apocalyptic thought, cf. S. Schulz, 'Die Anklage in Röm 1.18–32', ThZ 14 (1958) 161–73; E. Käsemann, *Romans*, 1980 40–2; Wilckens (above) 99 f.

reasoning,[4] permeates a person's spiritual marrow with its ability to make decisions (the 'heart') and leads to complete disorientation and abnormal behaviour. In contrast, the Spirit of wisdom and revelation 'enlightens the eyes of the heart' (Eph. 1.17 f.) of the Christian. The person 'alienated' from the life which comes from God – in this sense 'atheistic' – (cf. 2.12) moves in a world he cannot cope with spiritually, one which is bereft of content, and consequently he suffers greater self-alienation. The current question of 'alienation' on the grounds of economic and societal relationships does not come near the depth of this existential self-understanding.

The two subsequent phrases serve to clarify and intensify this view and, like the two Participles, are to be taken together as a connected, unified statement.[5] The ignorance (ἄγνοια) in them is based on (διά plus Accusative) the darkening of their understanding but also comes about because of their alienation from God, and the 'hardening of their hearts' describes the general situation and disposition of humanity alienated from God. Both concepts are already found in the language of Judaism. 'Ignorance' – which can only with difficulty be derived from a gnostic-dualistic view[6] – is that 'not knowing' of God which becomes a sin because humanity, 'although they knew God, they did not honour him as God' (Rom. 1.21). In the 'Wisdom' thinking of Hellenistic Judaism this was a characteristic of the gentiles.[7] If this condition becomes fixed, it leads to a 'hardening of the heart'. This is often spoken of in the OT,[8] then in Judaism, especially in the Qumran Community.[9] The choice of the Greek word, πώρωσις (only twice in the LXX) points to early Christian linguistic usage (cf. Mk. 3.5; 6.52; 8.17; Jn. 12.40; Rom. 11.7, 25; 2 Cor. 3.14); but only here is such 'petrification of the heart' made to refer to the spiritual state of the non-Christians. Hence they are considered even more guilty, just as in 2.2 they were called 'Sons of disobedience'.

[4]Cf. Rom. 11.10; 1 Clem. 36.2; 2 Clem. 19.2. Frequent in the Test XII, cf. R 3.8; L 14.4; 18.9; G 6.2; more intensively dualistic (the darkness as a power) in the Qumran texts, cf. 1 QS 3.3 f.; 1 QM 11.10; 15.9 f.

[5]Earlier exegetes and Schlier 213 n. 4 want to subordinate the second phase (hardening of the heart) to the first (ignorance); but this is clumsy (Haupt 180) and does not correspond to the author's style of adding on and supplementing. He develops his ideas rhetorically rather than logically.

[6]Against R. Bultmann, TDNT I, 118 f. Cf. the criticism by Wilckens (n. 3 supra) 104, n. 169 on Bultmann's interpretation of ἀλήθεια in Rom. 1.18.

[7]Cf. Wis. Sol. 13.1, 7 f., 9; 14.22; Philo, Decal 8; Spec Leg I, 15; Fug. 8; Jos. Ant. X, 142; Test G 5.7: 'Real repentance appropriate before God destroys ignorance, dispels the darkness, lights up the eyes, increases the knowledge of the soul and leads the mind to Salvation'. In the NT cf. Acts 17.30; 1 Pet. 1.14.

[8]It is said of Pharaoh Ex. 4.21; 7.3; 9.12 and elsewhere; of the People of Israel Ps. 95 (94), 8; Is. 6.10; 63.17; cf. Jer. 7.26; 17.23; 19.15. The LXX usually translates this with σκληροῦν; related is the 'making blind' (τυφλόω) which can also be translated by πηροῦν. This frequently led copyists to change πώρωσις to πήρωσις. Cf. Schmidt, TDNT V, 1025, 1028.

[9]1 QS 1.6; 2.14–26; 3.3; 5.4 et al.; Damasc 2.17 f.; 3.5, 11; 8.8 etc. Further cf. Test L 13.7: 'Acquire for yourselves wisdom ... No-one can take away the wisdom of the wise except the blindness of sin and the paralysis (πήρωσις) of transgression'.

197

From this follows immoral actions and behaviour which are sketched starkly in only a few strokes. Paul concludes from the darkening of the heart that as punishment God delivered the heathen to their own desires, especially to unnatural vices (Rom. 1.24–32); the author of Eph. ascribes this 'handing-over' to the heathen themselves. It is the same idea: In human activity there takes place a divine judgement, which is at the same time a self-judgement. The connection with the (generalizing) Relative Pronoun merely denotes the continuation and does not give the reason.[10] The concept of 'uncleanliness' (ἀκαθαρσία) is also related to Paul's view to characterize the immoral, especially sexually dissipated way of living, only here again there is more emphasis on the human activity (εἰς ἐργασί αν). This self-abandonment to a depraved life grows out of the inner emptiness or weariness as is hinted at by the inserted 'blunted' (ἀπηλγηκότες). This hapaxlegomenon in the NT, which in a number of MSS is replaced by the similar-looking ἀπηλπικότες (=despairing),[11] expresses a state of spiritual weariness[12] – a consequence of a petrified heart. It is well-observed that a lack of purpose and aimlessness leads to an unrestrained life-style. The effort which lies in a striving for God and what is good 'has given way to a weary insufficiency' (Schlier). If 'dissipation' means sexual sins in particular (cf. Gal. 5.19; Rom. 13.13; 2 Cor. 12.21) it also signifies a 'luxurious', immoderate life-style given up to pleasure.[13] Hence it is not surprising that – as frequently in the lists of vices (cf. Schweizer, Col. 143) – 'greed' (πλεονεξία) is added. The Prepositional connection (ἐν) is intended to show a further root of excess alongside 'any kind of uncleanliness',[14] namely insatiable covetousness, that 'corrupting, hard-to-cure passion' (Philo, Vit. Mos. II, 186). This also crops up time and again in the lists of vices (Mk. 7.22; 1 Cor. 5.10 f; Col. 3.5 alongside sexual sins; also Rom. 1.29; 2 Pet. 2.3).[15] In a brief expression we have the same picture as is drawn of the gentiles in 1 Pet.

[10]Cf. Bl-Debr §293.2c; ὅστις as substitute for ὅς is 'very popular in Koine Greek'; cf. Mayser II/1.76 f.; Moulton and Turner, *Grammar* III, 47.

[11]D F G P 1241 pc latt syᵖ; perhaps an early reading-failure or else a reminiscence of 2.12 ('without hope').

[12]Cf. Polyb 1, 35, 5 (ἀ. ψυχάς). Haupt 181 interprets it as 'no longer to have the ability to distinguish between good and evil'; similarly Gaugler 187 'insensitive to any pangs of conscience'. But Polyb 9, 40, 4 (ταῖς ἐλπίσιν); Dio C 48, 37 (προς ἐλπίδα) show that it is more a question of the reduction of anticipation, of insufficient striving towards a goal. Cf. Liddell and Scott 176 s.v.

[13]The word comes from a Hellenistic background; in the LXX only in Sap 14.26; III Macc. 2.26; further Jos. Ant. IV, 151; VIII, 252.318; XX 112; Test Jud. 23.1; cf. L 17.11. The passage here is close to 1 Pet. 4.3; on the immoral lives of the false teachers Jude 4; 2 Pet. 2.2, 7, 18; then Herm. v 2.2, 2; 3,7, 2; m 12,4,6; s 9,15,3. Cf. Pr-Bauer 227 f.; O. Bauernfeind, TDNT I, 490, H. Goldstein EWNT I, 407 f.

[14]On the coordination with ἐν instead of καί (as D F G lat read). a semitizing style to be seen in the Qumran documents, cf. K. G. Kuhn, NTS 7.337; Gnilka 225. n. 4.

[15]Cf. further Vögtle, *Tugend- und Lasterkataloge* 38 f. and Index; G. Delling, TDNT VI, 266–74; Spicq, *Notes* II, 704–6. According to the lexical findings, a restriction to sexual lust as E. Klaar suggests, Πλεονεξία – ἐκτης, – εκτεῖν. ThZ 10 (1954) 395–7 is improbable (perhaps otherwise in the context of 1 Thess. 4.6).

4.3 and of the false teachers in 2 Pet. 2.13 f.: Insatiable passion and boundless covetousness plunge humanity into misery.

20–21

The addressees are strongly contrasted ('But not so ... you') with those thus alienated from God. There does not follow immediately an illuminating portrayal of their way of life appropriate before God (v. 24); first there is a reminder of what they have learned about Christ. 'To learn Christ' is a unique formulation, which corresponds to the unmediated significance of Christ for the forming of the Christian life. The closest correspondence is the exhortation in Col. 2.6: 'As you have received Christ Jesus, the Lord, so lead your lives in him!'; but in the context of Col. this is intended especially to encourage the repulsion of false teachers. What connects them is the looking back to what the Christians have been 'taught' (Col. 2.7). The missionary sermon in which the addressees heard about Christ[16] has been reinforced in catechetical instruction. This must also have included teaching about the person of the earthly Jesus if the rider 'as the truth is in Jesus' is to have any sense. 'Jesus' without any addition is not found anywhere else in Eph. and is also rare in Paul.[17] There it usually refers to the suffering, crucified Jesus with whom Paul knows himself linked. Here the person of Jesus Christ as a subject of the baptismal catechesis is meant, and then the experience of Christ in Baptism itself. In their becoming Christian, 'Christ himself has come to meet them' (Halter), has been 'illuminated' for them (5.14). The 'truth' which is 'in Jesus' means that truth which lies in the person of Christ, based on Jesus. Some have seen a polemical dig here at the gnostic separation of (the heavenly) Christ from the earthly Jesus.[18] But what is the point of such a dig in this writing which shows no other signs of combating gnostic heresy? The author probably is taking up a formulation from the catechesis which was concerned with the identity of the risen Lord with the earthly Jesus. It is a witness to the early Christian understanding of tradition.[19] In its context this expression achieves a concrete, practical meaning: The Christian life is not oriented on the 'idea' of some Christ but on the person of the one Christ, who, as the one who came in history is the trustworthy guide for the ordering of a Christian way of life.

22–23

For the baptismal paraclesis the author keeps to Col. 3.9 f. The Infinitive might be made syntactically dependent on the instruction (ἐδιδάχθητε) but

[16]On ἀκούειν with Accusative cf. Bl-Debr §173.1; Mayser II/1.207. A term from the speech of mission in Rom. 10.14; 15.21; Col. 1.6, 23; Eph. 1.13.

[17]1 Thess. 1.10; 4.14; Gal. 6.17; 1 Cor. 12.3; 2 Cor. 4.5, 10 f., 14; 11.4; Rom. 8.11.

[18]Cf. Schlier who also refers to Estius and von Soden. Otherwise Dibelius – Greeven 86, who go back to mystic formulations. Both views should be rejected; de la Potterie* 55 hits on the correct answer: 'Jesus, dead and resurrected, who thereby has become in the full sense "Christ", Messiah and Lord' (thus already Pelagius). Cf. also Larsson* 223–6; Halter* 252 f. – Barth 505 and 533–6 wants to take καθώς as a formula of quotation: 'Truth is in Jesus'. This is hardly tenable; cf. de la Potterie* 48 f.: καθώς further refers indirectly to οὕτως. 'You are instructed in him (Christ) in the way which is the truth, namely in Jesus.'

[19]Cf. Wegenast*.

have the function of an Imperative (cf. 3.8). The 'old' person, which is to be laid aside like a garment (cf. Acts 7.58; Mart. Pol. 13.2) is the personality ruined by sinful desires. The author of Eph. has contracted Col. 3.8 f. because he omits the list of sins but inserts in its place 'desires of deceit'.[20] He reminds them once again (cf. 2.3) of the 'earlier way of life' of the Gentile-Christians, which in a similar way in 2.3 he characterized as 'the desires of our flesh'. That way of life, by which the gentiles, among whom the addressees live, are still ruled, must be put off by the Christians – the total 'old personality', an expression which Paul used already in Rom. 6.6. Instead, they must 'be renewed (ἀνανεοῦσθαι)[21] in the spirit of your minds'. This is an expression supplementary to Col., inserted to emphasize the present demand (cf. also Rom. 12.2). The triviality of the gentile mind (v. 17) is contrasted with the newness of the Christian spirit. The double expression 'spirit of your minds' could pleonastically mean the human spirit according to the style of Eph.; but since pneuma is nowhere else in Eph. used this way, what must be meant is the Christian mind guided by the divine Spirit (cf. 3.16; 4.3; 5.18; 6.18).[22] The interchange of the two Greek words for 'new' (νέος and καινός) is also perhaps deliberate. The καινὸς ἄνθρωπος is contrasted with the παλαιὸς ἄνθρωπος. The former is in nature and being completely different: It is a new person created by God for life with him (v. 24). This, however, demands a constant renewal (refreshing, νέος = young, fresh) which includes human effort.[23] The Christian who lives in the world with its dangers must be constantly filled, moved and led by the divine Spirit to his/her innermost thinking, meditating and feeling (cf. 5.15–18; 6.10–12). The order is explained by the context of the exhortation which only at the end more clearly alludes to the merciful occurrence in Baptism. Paul already uses the unusual expression of 'putting on Christ' for Baptism (Gal. 3.27) as for the paraclesis (Rom. 13.14) and Col. developed it further with the analogy of the putting-off of the old personality.[24] Eph. uses it in his own way for the Gentile-Christians he is

---

[20]ἀπάτη = deception, in the LXX frequent in the story of Judith (9.3, 10, 13; 16.8) for seductive women in Test R 5.2, 5 (v. 1.); Test Jos. 9.5; also Philo, Jos. 56 etc, only appears in Christian literature for the deceit of wealth (Mk. 4.19/Mt. 13.22 and wicked desires, cf. 2 Thess. 2.10; Heb. 3.13; 2 Pet. 2.13; 2 Clem. 6.4; often in the 'Shepherd of Hermas': m 8,5; 11,12; s 6,2,1 f.4; 6,3,3 (v. 1.); 6,4,4 etc. The language betrays the proximity of Eph. to the developing early Christian tradition. Cf. Spicq, *Notes* I, 116–18.

[21]Only proved with a passive sense, cf. Pr-Bauer 115; J. Behn, TDNT IV, 899. Paul says ἀνακαινοῦσθαι 2 Cor. 4.16 (also Col. 3.10); cf. Rom. 12.2. On this v H. Büchsel, TDNT III, 452 f.; Harrisville* JBL 74.75 f. ('dynamic aspect').

[22]Differently Bengel 769: Spiritus est intimum mentis, with reference to 1 Cor. 14.14; following him Abbott, Klöpper, Ewald, Dibelius – Greeven, Gaugler. But 1 Cor. 14.14 (talking of glossolalia) shows how the divine Spirit takes hold of the human spirit (cf. J. Weiss, *Der Erste Korintherbrief*, 1910 (KEK), 327–9). Eph. admittedly is not speaking of ecstasy but has a similar opinion of the divine Spirit in relation to the human, cf. under 3.16. – The v. 1. ἐν τῷ πνεύματι p⁴⁹ B 33 1175 1739 pc makes no difference to the sense; cf. 1 Cor. 14.15 with 16 where the readings also fluctuate.

[23]Cf. Trench 133–9, especially 138; J. Behm, TDNT IV, 901. Harrisville* is unwilling to suppose any continuing difference in that time. The Infinitive has an Imperative sense as is expressed in the reading ἀνανεοῦσθε in P⁴⁶ D¹ K 33; but Behn rightly stresses: 'The change which must constantly be brought about in the life of the Christians occurs when all is said and done not through them but in them.'

[24]Cf. Schweizer, *Colossians* 145 f.

addressing; Pauline tradition and baptismal paraclesis leave their mark in ever new contexts.

24

The 'new person' is based on an actual new-creating by God which, however, brings with it an obligation to live life in an appropriate way (cf. also 2.9 f.). The insoluble connection between merciful event (Indicative) and moral duty (Imperative) is expressed in the compact formulation: We must put on the new person which has already been created (Aorist Participle Passive) according to his plan by God. The idea of the image of God which Col. 3.10 connects with the new humanity renewed according to the original plan of Creation has only the slightest echo in Eph. in the phrase 'according to God' (κατὰ θεόν). Eph. is agitating for a life 'according to God' in 'righteousness and holiness of truth'. This resonant final expression (missing in Col.) is so closely connected with 'created' that we must primarily hear God's action in it: From him proceed the righteousness and holiness granted to the new person. But the expression is also governed by the call to put on the new person, and hence becomes an exhortation. 'Righteousness and holiness' is a double expression (Wisdom of Sol. 9.3; Lk. 1.75 in the reversed order) which includes God's acting (cf. Ps. 145 (144) 17) as well as the human existence made possible by him (Lk. 1.75). 'Righteousness' in Eph. still retains the same sense as was usual in biblical language (cf. 6.14) although with a far more neutral sense than in Paul. It is difficult to connect it to the 'righteous' attitude of giving what is due to each of one's fellow beings.[25] It means, rather, taken together with 'holiness', the attitude which is in keeping with God, which corresponds to God's goodness and mercy (cf. also 4.8). 'Holiness' (ὁσιότης), which was originally the grateful behaviour of the 'pious' (חסיד)[26] in response to God's merciful grace (חסד) combines with 'righteousness' to become the basic attitude of the person made one with God. In the Pastoral Epistles 'righteous' and 'holy' fade to being mere Christian virtues (cf. Tit.. 1.8; 1 Tim. 6.11; 2 Tim. 2.22; 3.16). Eph. stands closer to the Pauline tradition (cf. also 1 Thess. 2.10). The attribute 'of truth' (which should be taken with both nouns), linguistically in opposition to 'of deceit' (v. 22), once more shows to advantage the new creation of humanity which comes from God and is characterized by his nature. This had its origin in the 'Word of Truth', the Gospel (1.23). But here, too, we must also hear the Imperative – to remain in this truth and bring it to its fruits which consist of 'goodness, righteousness and truth' (5.9).[27] 'Truth' becomes the

[25]Schlier 221 f., following Hellenistic usage, would like to interpret δικαιοσύνη as being just in relationship to other people and the world and ὁσιότης as being just in relationship to God and the saints – i.e. devoutness. – Against this also Halter* 255 f.

[26]Cf. F. Hauck, TDNT V, 490 f. The Hasidean is the one who fulfils the obligations of the Covenant; in the Maccabean period it was the special name for the organized groups of those loyal to the Law, cf. 1 Macc. 14.6. In the Qumran documents we do not find this self-description; instead they use the 'saints'.

[27]Cf. the variant in 4.24 καὶ ἀληθείᾳ D* F G Lat. But with this the Genitive lying in opposition to ἀπατης loses force.

comprehensive expression for the nature transmitted by God to the new person which differentiates him/her fundamentally from the people 'of deceit'.[28]

Summary

The exhortation to Christians in the world focusses on the recovery of the Christian identity which is in danger of being lost in the midst of a non-Christian environment. The trenchant description of a 'pagan' way of thinking and life-style (vv. 17–19) is striking compared to other early Christian paracleses and betrays an immediate concern. Only 1 Pet. 4.3–5 casts a sidelong glance in a similar fashion at the 'dissolute' life of non-Christian fellow-citizens, but with a different background: The Christians in the Diaspora there were being 'abused' by their fellows who were entangled in their mundane desires, and also suffered in other ways under their attacks (cf. 2.12, 15; 3.15 ff.).

The addressees of Eph. are in danger of the opposite, namely of being led astray into sinful activity by their fellow-citizens, of adapting to their way of life and forgetting what they have become through their divine vocation and new creation.

Christian existence and life-style is oriented solely on Jesus Christ who lived in this world as a human being and laid down per se the norm for Christian behaviour. Christ who lives in the hearts of Christians through faith (3.17) demands also a life with God as was revealed authentically in Jesus. The Christian gets support in the dynamic connection with the church community to withstand both the deceitful expressions of human opinion (cf. 4.14) and the temptations of a dissipated yet innerly empty life. Deception (4.14 πλάνη) and deceit (4.22 ἀπάτη) contribute to the destruction of the Christian person. Hence there is need of a constant 'renewal' (4.23) in order to realize in this world the 'new person' created by God.

The sharp, disparaging portrayal of the non-Christian outsiders is determined by time and circumstances. In the present pluralistic society we must distinguish between people who are morally of high standing who put many Christians to shame in their humanitarian attitude and others who are wrapped up in worldly matters and egoism. The judgement 'alienation from God' is also not applicable to many people who belong by origin and upbringing to another religion or philosophical school. Nevertheless the description of the 'alienated' person retains its meaning as a warning to all, Christians included. Christians have the possibility of constantly testing themselves by looking at Jesus Christ and in contemplating what God has bestowed upon them to see whether they remain true and come closer to the goal of the 'new person'.

---

[28]In the Qumran documents 'emet (truth, constancy) often stands in opposition to 'sin, deceit,' frequently in connection with 'righteousness', cf. 1 QS 4.17, 24; 5.10; 1 QH 1.26 f., 30; 4.10; 7.14, 28–30; 1 QM 4.6. Further Test Jud. 14.1; 20.1–3; D 5.2; A 5.3; Jos. 1.3; B 10.3. But the separation from Eph. 4.24 still remains considerable. Cf. (on the Two-Spirit Doctrine) Becker, *Heil Gottes* 88–91; H. Lichtenberger, *Studien zum Menschenbild in Texten der Qumrangemeinde*, 1980 (STUNT 15), 123–42, especially 140.

2.b Renunciation of old tendencies and striving after Christian qualities, especially love (4.25–5.2)

Literature

Dahl 59–62; Gnilka, *Mél. Rigaux* 402–5.

J. P. Sampley, 'Scripture and Tradition in the Community as Seen in Eph. 4.25 ff.', StTh 26 (1972) 101–9.

Halter, *Taufe* 256–69.

E. Schweizer,'Gottesgerechtigkeit und Lasterkataloge bei Paulus (inc. Col. and Eph.)', in *Rechtfertigung* (FS E. Käsemann), ed. J. Friedrich, W. Pöhlmann and P. Stuhlmacher, Tübingen-Göttingen 1976, 461–77.

A. Schulz, *Nachfolgen und Nachahmen*, 1962 (StANT VI).

H. D. Betz, *Nachfolge und Nachahmung Jesu Christi im Neuen Testament*, 1967 (BHTh 37).

B. Lindars, 'Imitation of God and Imitation of Christ', Theol. 76 (1973) 394–402.

4.25 Therefore put aside falsehood and speak the truth.
    each one with his neighbour
        because we are members for one another.
26 Do not sin in anger. Do not let the sun set
    on your wrath.
27   And do not give the devil scope!
28 He who is a thief, let him no longer steal; let him rather work hard
    and create with his own hands
        so that he may have (something) to give away to the needy.
29 Let no idle word come from your mouth, but
    only good which may uplift where it is necessary,
        that it may give grace to the hearers.
30   And do not grieve the Holy Spirit
        of God with which you have been sealed
        for the day of redemption!
31 Let all bitterness, rage, wrath, screaming and invective
    depart from you along with every wickedness.
32 Rather be generous to one another, merciful,
    forgive one another,
        as God has also forgiven you in Christ.
5.1 Therefore be imitators of God as beloved children
2   and live in love.
        as Christ also has loved you
        and given himself for us
        as an offering and sacrifice for God
        for a pleasing fragrance.

Analysis

At the end of the basic paraclesis with its motif of the 'new person' the author attaches concrete exhortations to illustrate the way of life 'in righteousness and holiness of truth'. First he mentions negative ways of behaving from which the addressees would refrain: Lies, anger, theft, idle gossip. But positive motifs are also bound up in these. The exhortation only becomes truly positive in v. 32 where the author urges to mutual generosity, to mercy and forgiveness 'as God has also forgiven you in Christ'. With this he progresses to the central Christian call for love, as also happens in Col. 3.12–14 subsequent to the description of the 'new person' and the unity of all in Christ. This is also a hint for the *delimitation* of the section. In spite of γίνεσθε οὖν (5.1) where a new unit might possibly begin (cf. Gnilka), there are stronger grounds for extending the section to 5.2, (1). The demand γίνεσθε δέ of 4.32 is taken up and continued with the γίνεσθε οὖν in 5.1. Now God's pardoning love which was already mentioned in 4.32 becomes the example for the behaviour of Christians to one another: They are to become imitators of God. Hence the οὖν serves to denote purpose rather than to introduce a new theme. (2) The addition of 'as beloved children' also belongs in this perspective. God is the Father, rich in mercy and love (cf. 2.4), to whom the Gentile-Christians (together with those who were earlier Jews) have achieved access through Jesus Christ (2.18; 3.12). Thus the address to the 'beloved children' makes good sense. The expression which crops up a few verses later, 'Children of Light' (5.8) stands in another connection. (3) The thought of Christ who 'loved you and gave himself for us' (5.2) is likewise hinted at in 4.32; for God has forgiven us 'in Christ'. (4) The added expression about Christ's self-offering which is derived from an OT passage 'as an offering and sacrifice, as a pleasing odour for God' gives the passage about the love of Christ a harmonious ending. (5) In 5.3 the author turns to another area of moral instruction, namely the sexual sphere, which has not yet been mentioned in 4.25–31. Hence we must begin a new paragraph after 5.2 – as the δέ in 5.3 also shows.

The *structure* of the section, which should already have been made clear by the arrangement of the text as printed above, is recognisable from the moral imperatives, the added motives and the new beginning in v. 31, which also shows a somewhat different formal structure. The first unit, 4.25–30 falls into four sections which warn against negative ways of behaving: lying, attacks of anger, stealing and gossiping. For most of these warnings (apart from anger) positive pieces of evidence are added which all apply to the Christian, brotherly community: we are members one with the other (v. 25); we should give away some of our possessions to the needy (v. 28); a good work should contribute to another's 'edification' (v. 29). If we look closely at these pieces of evidence, we notice something else: When talking about rage he adds the prohibition: 'And do not give the devil scope!' (v. 27). And at the end of the whole list there is the command, expressed in the negative but introducing a positive idea: 'And do not grieve the Holy Spirit of God . . .' (v. 30). Both exhortations are connected in a similar manner with what precedes them: μηδέ (v. 27) and καὶ μή (v. 30). In the content there is a counter-positioning of God's adversary (the devil) and God's Holy Spirit (cf. 5.11) – possibly a reminiscence of Baptism. Hence there are to a certain extent two stages in this unit: lies and rage (vv. 25–7) – theft and gossip (vv. 28–30) with an intensification towards positive behaviour. Although these particular sins seem to have been chosen arbitrarily to illustrate behaviour unfitting for Christians – according to the 'usual paraclesis' – the author is perhaps pursuing his own particular purpose.

This becomes more certain in a further observation. In v. 31 there follows a list of five negative attitudes which do not represent a catalogue of vices in the usual sense (with different vices, cf. 5.3–5) but are rather all connected with anger in its different aspects (cf. exegesis). Now they have already been warned against anger in v. 26; why, then, this stronger reversion to the theme? Clearly the author wants to stress something which he thinks is particularly important for the life of the congregation and for the realization of the Christian commandment of love. If the motif on the Holy Spirit is mentioned immediately prior to this (v. 30), it is in the best Pauline tradition: as people filled with the Spirit Christians should lead a sinful brother into the right way 'in a spirit of gentleness' (Gal. 6.1). To the question frequently asked as to whether Eph. 4.30 is to be taken as the conclusion of what goes before or as a new beginning for what follows[1] we must answer, in view of the observations made above regarding the structure, that this verse with the importance of its motif forms the conclusion of the unit preceding. But it is also particularly suitable as a basis for the exhortation which urges the Christian commandment of love.

We must also not overlook the fact that this more illustrative exhortation, which follows the fundamental baptismal paraclesis of the 'new person', takes over the traditional topoi and motifs (cf. the motifs arranged to the right in the text). But there are several observations added which allow us a glimpse of the manner in which the author of Eph. took up but also enriched the early Christian tradition. The first thing we notice is his predilection for scriptural allusions. Hence, instead of the simple command 'do not lie to one another' (Col. 3.9), he says 'put aside falsehood and speak the truth, each one with his neighbour!' (4.25). The positive formulation corresponds almost word for word with Zech. 8.16 LXX. In the very next verse he takes up Ps. 4.4: 'Do not be wrathful and sin!', and the continuation 'Do not let the sun set on your wrath' may likewise have been suggested by the second part of the same verse of that Psalm. There is also a play on scripture behind the warning 'do not grieve the Holy Spirit of God!' (4.30), namely on Is. 63.10. Finally the concluding phrase in 5.2 'as an offering and sacrifice, as a pleasing odour for God' is possibly a reminiscence of Ps. 39.6 LXX (Ps. 40.6); the syntactic construction 'odour and fragrance' (ὀσμὴ εὐωδίας) often appears in the Greek Bible. Perhaps in this knowledge of Scripture we can recognise that the author is himself a teacher in a Christian congregation.

A further characteristic of the author is the way in which he takes up and consequently emphasizes ideas and expressions which he himself has already used at an earlier point. There are two examples of this in this section. In v. 25 he interweaves 'because we are members for one another'. He had already used the metaphor of the body in 4.12, 16 (admittedly without the expression 'members'). In v. 30 he adds to 'God's Holy Spirit': 'in whom you have been sealed for the day of redemption', a reversion to

---

[1] Ewald, Haupt, Dibelius – Greeven, Gaugler, Gnilka and others take v. 30 with the preceding verses. Schlier on the other hand considers whether perhaps the sentence does not introduce a new kind of paraenesis (227) and sees a connection between the Spirit's grief and rage (228).

1.13 f. The exhortation: 'Do not give the devil scope' is also part of the author's own contribution. Only in 6.11 does the devil come more sharply into the foreground as a dangerous enemy of Christian existence.

A comparison of the contents with Col. 3.8 f. shows a close correspondence of the two writings. The only thing new is the attack on the thief with the command that he work with his own hands in order to be able to give to the needy from his honest earnings. Is there here a reminiscence of 1 Thess. 4.11 (cf. also 2 Thess. 3.11–13), or does this belong to the topos of such an exhortatory speech (cf. 1 Cor. 6.10 and 1 Pet. 4.15)? V.29 ('Let nothing come from your mouth') echoes Col. 3.8, and from the five vices named there four re-appear in Eph. 4.31. Likewise v. 32 is clearly influenced by Col. 3.12 f.; for the expressions χριστοί, εὔσπλαγχνοι and χαριζόμενοι ἑαυτοῖς all have their counterpart in that passage in Col.

In view of these observations we must be wary of drawing-up a concrete picture of conditions in the congregation from these exhortations which appear to apply to the conditions there. But we cannot fail to recognize a particular tendency in Eph.'s own contribution to the formation. The deficient condition of the Gentile-Christian congregations at that time is brought to light under cover of a conventional Christian exhortation.

Exegesis

25

In the address beginning here, which merges into specific admonitions, the author employs certain rhetorical tools. He uses as a key-word the 'truth' mentioned at the end of the previous verse and begins (in a different way from Col. 3.8) with the command to put aside falsehood and speak the truth with one's neighbour. The 'putting aside' also links up with 'put aside the old personality' and the 'falsehood' brings to mind the 'deceit' of the desires in their former way of life (v. 22). Hence the meaning of the concepts is changed, applied to positive action and thereby narrowed down. It is no mere trick but rather a profile of the 'new person' in his/her historical existence. The consequence of the merciful new creation (διό) is appropriate moral action. That is why the Aorist Participle ἀποθέμενοι (cf. 1 Pet. 2.1) must be taken to have an Imperative sense and not be regarded merely as a reversion ('after putting aside falsehood') to the event brought about by God[2] as Col. 3.9 also suggests. But the avoidance of falsehood and speaking the truth in this context gains connotations with a deeper substance: From God proceeds *only* truth, truth which was reality in Jesus and which should be spread in the Christian congregations even in their mutual conversation. The scriptural quotation used (Zech. 8.16) speaks of one's 'neighbour' and is thinking of the community of Israel from whom God, after a new, benevolent turning to her (8.11–15), demands honest speaking and fair judgement. Eph. makes the exhortation to the new community which has been created in Jesus Christ: We are all members

---

[2]Gaugler translates differently; Haupt 190 was already against this. On the connection of the catalogue with Baptism cf. Kamlah, *Form* 34–8, with justification, Schweizer.*

with one another. The idea of the Body of Christ is already so familiar to the author that he introduces as self-evident, both here and in 5.30, the motif of members who are bound to one another (cf. 1 Cor. 12.12–27).

26

The warning against anger which now follows (at the beginning in Col. 3.8) is also clothed in a scriptural form (Ps. 4.4), which in its original context desires to prevent sinning against God through ill-humour. The co-ordination of the Imperative is to be understood according to the semitic feeling for language: If you work yourself into a rage, do not sin! or better: Do not sin by getting worked up in anger! We can not derive from this any trace of a justified or 'holy' rage.[3] A certain concession to a natural outburst of rage might possibly be glimpsed in the Consecutive Clause: Do not let the sun set on your wrath. This is perhaps the incorporation of a folk-saying[4] but should in no way weaken the warning against rage (cf. 31). Rage is a dangerous temptation to sin. It destroys the brotherly communion.[5]

27

If the devil now appears upon the scene this is not a warning against new sins but gives a motivation as it is still closely connected with v. 26 (οὐδέ). Rage leaves one an easy prey for the devil's snares (cf. 1 Tim. 3.7; 6.9). The reference to the 'devil' (διάβολος, used frequently in the LXX while Paul talks only of 'Satan') betrays a closeness to other late NT writings (cf. 1 Tim. 3.6 f.' 2 Tim. 2.26; Jas. 4.7; 1 Pet. 5.8) which likewise see in him the dangerous tempter. He is God's adversary (cf. Eph. 6.11; Jas. 4.7) who desires to draw the Christians bound to God (back) into his sphere of influence. We must allow him no 'scope', no opportunity for cunning activity (6.11). Recollections of Satan as the 'prosecutor' before God fade into the background as in the early Christian literature which followed.[6] Christians in their Baptism have renounced the 'dark' or 'black' one.[7] For Eph. he is the representative of the 'lords of the world of this darkness' (cf. 6.12 with 17). The metaphorical – mythical style underlines how full of

---

[3]On the interpretation of Ps. 4.4 by the Rabbis who also recognize a righteous anger, cf. Bill. III, 602 f. According to Jas. 1.20, where Jewish tradition is taken up, (cf. F. Mußner, *Der Jakobusbrief*, Freiburg i.Br. 1964, 100) human anger is considered reprehensible. Cf. further G. Stählin, TDNT V, 420 f.

[4]Reference can be made to the custom among the Pythagoreans mentioned by Plutarch (II 488c): If they allow themselves in their anger to abuse someone, before sunset they shake hands and leave one another with a salutation.

[5]Gnilka 235 f., in consideration of the Qumran texts (Damasc.9.6; cf. 7.2 f.; 1 QS 5.26–6.1) thinks of a concrete situation; if a brother has sinned, one should not allow him in rage to become hardened in his situation but attempt to win him over. But such a situation would need to be addressed more directly; cf. compared with this Mt. 18.15; Gal. 6.1.

[6]On the warning against the devil as tempter and cause of evil cf. Jas. 4.7; Ign Eph. 10.3; Trall 8.1 (in connection with exhortations to leniency and gentleness); Herm m IV, 3.4, 6; V, 1.3 ('in patience dwells the Lord, but in violent rage the devil'); VII, 3 and often. But in these texts it often also says that the Christian should not fear the devil because God is stronger: m VII, 2; XII, 4.6; 5.1 f.; 6,1. 2. 4.

[7]Cf. F. J. Dölger, *Die Sonne der Gerechtigkeit und der Schwarze*, Münster i W. 1918; Kamlah, *Form* 185–8, who, however, emphasizes the difference between 'renounce' ἀπο-τάσσεσθαι and 'cast off' ἀποτίθεσθαι.

temptation is the situation in which every Christian still exists and how she/he can only be saved in it by the power of God, his Holy Spirit (cf. v. 30). The picture, which is tied to its own time, cannot support a true personification of evil ('person' would be a caricature) and certainly not something abhorrent which instils fear.

28

Surprisingly, there now follows a warning against stealing which only takes up by way of illustration another tendency of the old personality. But according to 1 Thess. 4.11 f.; 2 Thess. 3.6–12 there were grounds in the early Christian congregations for demanding that people live by the work of their own hands, and Paul is the unforgotten example. There is no such concrete background recognisable in Eph. What matters to the author is the change in attitude and action: Anyone who formerly was inclined to steal (ὁ κλέπτων)[8] should do so no longer. Theft was already considered a cardinal sin in the OT (Ex. 20.15; Deut. 5.19; Is. 1.23; Jer. 7.9) and in Lev. 19.11 rated as a violation of social behaviour. In contrast one's own work is emphasized (Ex. 20.9) and praised (Prov. 28.19; Ecclus. 7.15; Jos Ap II, 291). The high regard for work has a religious base in Judaism but can also be found in Hellenistic ethics.[9] A contemporary witness (around the First Century AD) is the Judaeo-Hellenistic didactic poem of Pseudo-Phocylides, where in a fairly long passage (153–74) we find: 'Work hard so that you can live from your own income; for the one who is work-shy lives from what his hands steal . . .'.[10] But Eph. connects this to the Christian idea of achieving the means for charity through work (cf. also Did. 4.5–8). To give to the needy from one's own belongings is a concrete expression of Christian brotherly love (cf. Rom. 12.13; Acts 2.45; 4.35). In this way a common paraenesis (cf. also in the list of vices in 1 Cor. 6.10) is deepened in a Christian sense.

29

The fourth command is concerned with useless, fruitless talk (σαπρός really means 'causing decay'). The semitising style[11] as well as the idea itself

---

[8] The Present Participle expresses the continuing, habitual action but because of the context ('no longer') is assigned to the past, cf. Bl-Debr §339, 2b with n. 9; K. Beyer, *Semitische Syntax im Neuen Testament* I/1, Göttingen ²1968, 224, n. 4; Moulton – Turner, *Grammar* III, 81.

[9] Epictet, Diss I, 16.16 f.: One should also praise God for work; admittedly there is no more profound reason given. The wide-spread opinion that to work with one's hands was at that time considered undignified for a free person needs to be considerably qualified. Cf. the material collected from the gnomological tradition in van der Horst, *Ps. – Phocylides* 217. On the assessment of manual work in antiquity, which varied according to the social conditions at any particular time cf. F. Hauck, RAC I, 585–8; on the biblical opinion W. Bienert, *Die Arbeit nach der Lehre der Bibel*, Stuttgart ²1956.

[10] V. in van der Horst, *Ps. – Phocylides* 216 f. He comes out against the one-sided interpretation of Bienert (v. n. 9) 159–64, where only Jewish opinion is reiterated, but also declares that the atmosphere of the whole section is Jewish rather than Greek (217).

[11] πᾶς–μή: the expression 'come from the mouth' (Mt. 4.4; Lk. 4.22; Jas. 3.10); ἀλλα = but only; cf. Gnilka 237. But such semitizing language can be found elsewhere in the NT, cf. Lk. 1.37; Jn. 3.16; 6.39; 12.46; Acts 10.14; Rom. 3.20 etc., cf. Moulton – Turner, *Grammar* III,

(especially in Qumran, cf. 1 QS 7, 9; Damasc. 10.17 f.) again point to Jewish tradition. But here a Christian motif is added: a good word should 4.12). The following Genitive – τῆς χρείας (of necessity), probably occasioned by the same word in v. 28 – is hard to classify grammatically.[12] It draws attention to what is necessary and useful for the congregation in which there are not only material but also spiritual needs.[13] The two ἵνα-Clauses in v. 28 and v. 29 correspond to one another linguistically and also complement one another in their content. As Christians should give away some of their earthly possessions to the needy, so they should bestow 'grace' on the listeners, give a spiritual gift, with every good word spoken. 'Grace', which elsewhere stems only from God and is bound to him, does not have a strongly theological tone at this point but rather the overtone that exchange among the members of the congregation contributes to the divinely-realized construction (cf. Rom. 14.19; 1 Cor. 14.3, 5). Possibly we have here a memory of Col. 4.6, but in that passage the speech is thought of as being addressed to outsiders (cf. Schweizer on this verse). If we look carefully at the ethical motifs in vv. 25b, 28c, 29c we can see the deliberate orientation to the Christian community.

30

Hence we are not surprised by the introduction of the motif of the Holy Spirit; for the Spirit is the divine strength and the unifying bond in the Christian congregations (4.3). Again there is possibly a play on Scripture, namely on Is. 63.10: 'They (the Israelites), however, rebelled against him and *grieved his holy spirit*'. Only so can we explain the unusual phraseology of 'grieving' (λυπεῖν)[14] the 'Holy Spirit of God' – a rich expression not usual elsewhere (but cf. 1 Thess. 4.8). What was a reproach for the old People of God has become a command for the Christian congregation (cf. Paul in 1 Cor. 10.5–11). The words of encouragement can hardly be seen merely as intended to strengthen the exhortation to guard against any hard word (v. 29);[15] this is a command that they feel under an obligation to God's Spirit which is operative in the church community. As

196 f. – Sampley* 105 f. refers to the opposition of σαπρός/ἀγαθός in the OT and NT; on this C. Lindhagen, 'Die Wurzel ΣΑΠ im NT und AT', UUA 40 (1950) 27–69.

[12] Explanations fluctuate between an Objective Genitive (something like = for the building-up of that which is necessary) and a Genitive of Quality (– for the building-up which is characterized by necessity). The free use of the Genitive is comprehensible in the context for edification where it is necessary (thus Pr-Bauer 1750, s.v. 3).

[13] The easier reading τῆς πίστεως (of faith) (instead of τῆς χρείας) in D* F G pc VL^pt Vg^cl interprets this as a stengthening of faith and thereby certainly hits an important aspect (cf. 4.13) but does not take into account the other aspect of moral strengthening. Jerome, Eph. 2 (MPL 26.513A) was struck by the alteration compared with the Greek text and explained 'docet virtutes sequendas'.

[14] Pr-Bauer 952, s.v. 1 cites 2 Cor. 2.2, 5; 7.8, but in the context there the meaning is rather 'sadden'. The two meanings now and then merge into one another, cf. also Mt 18.31. 'Sadden' would be too weak to use for the Holy Spirit; otherwise Schlier 227. Cf. also R. Bultmann, TDNT IV, 322; Spicq, *Notes* I, 517–19 who cites 2 Sam 13.21 LXX for Eph. 4.30.

[15] Thus Haupt 174 f., Robinson 113, Dibelius – Greeven 88; Gaugler 196; R. Bultmann, TDNT IV, 322. The exhortation overlaps the one before it in a similar way as the warning about the devil overlapped that against anger (v. 26).

in 1.13 f. and 4.3–5 the reminder of their Baptism and the baptismal paraclesis shows through; 'sealing' and 'redemption' have been taken up again from 1.13 f. (see there). What is new is the '*Day* of redemption' which makes us think of the 'Day of the Lord', the Parousia (cf. 1 Thess. 5.2; 2 Thess. 2.2; 1 Cor. 1.8; 5.3; 2 Cor. 1.14). But if we leave this well-known expression out of consideration, 'day' can also open up the perspective of hope generally to mean the achievement of the inheritance which lies already prepared in heaven and is guaranteed by the Spirit (cf. 1.14, 18; 5.5). The idea of judgment retreats completely into the background with the attribute, 'redemption'. The motif, which is only here taken up and which only here is touched upon, demands no basic correction of the author of Eph.'s eschatological view: It shows that he has not given up the temporal anticipation of the fulfilment still to come.[16] But his gaze is fixed earnestly on the presence of the Spirit, who, as the Holy Spirit, places us under an obligation to be holy. The expression 'to grieve the Holy Spirit' is also taken up in an agraphon, an unrecorded Saying attributed to Jesus: 'Do not grieve the Holy Spirit who dwells in you, and do not extinguish the light which shines in you',[17] and again in a different form in the 'Shepherd of Hermas' which urges the overcoming of all sadness, which distresses and drives away the Holy Spirit which dwells in Christians (m X, 2.1–6; 3.2).[18] Possibly at the back of this lies a topos of the early Christian admonitory speeches which Eph. reflects in his own way, applying it more forcefully to the congregation.

31

In a new paragraph (cf. analysis) the author once again takes up the subject of wrath (cf. v. 26) which he describes with five expressions for the different forms in which it appears. Everything that belongs to wrath and originates in it (ὀργή is in the central position) must fall off the readers like an old piece of clothing; there is an echo of the idea of 'putting off the old personality' (cf. Col. 3.8). The origin of the use of a five-fold partition already seen in Col. 3.5 and 8 cannot be fully explained.[19] It is also found here, because 'with every wickedness' is then added only in a generalised way. The Greeks had many expressions for wrath which were a source of discussion particularly in the Stoic ethic.[20] The author of Eph. uses these (not entirely uniform) characteristic and differentiating words for wrathful

[16]Cf. Steinmetz, *Heils-Zuversicht* 33; on the contrary Lindemann, *Aufhebung der Zeit* 230–2 would like to eliminate the future perspective completely.

[17]Handed down in Ps.-Cyprian, De aleatoribus 3, v. in A. Resch, *Agrapha*, Leipzig ²1906, 134 f. J. Jeremias, *Unbekannte Jesusworte*, Gütersloh ³1963, and also in Hennecke ³I, 52–5, does not accept this as an authentic saying of Jesus.

[18]The perspective in Hermas is a different one: Grief appears 'worse than all other spirits' and arises from involvement in earthly affairs. This is confronted by the Holy Spirit who 'endures neither grief nor restriction' (2.6). It is a praise of Christian joy which equips us for all that is good, cf. Dib Herm 533–5. Sampley* 104 f. also quotes Test Isaac 5.4 and recognizes in it old Jewish tradition.

[19]Cf. Schweizer, *Colossians* on this passage.

[20]Cf. the material in G. Stählin, TDNT V, 384, n. 6; further in van der Horst, *Ps.-Phocylides* 156 f. Vögtle, *Tugend- und Lasterkataloge* 218 f., also emphasizes the difference between NT and Stoic ethics.

passion to depict the pernicious, destructive effect of wrath on the community. In so doing he clearly wants to advance from a gentle simmer to a mighty explosion: bitterness (πικρία) – ire (θυμός) – outbreak of wrath (ὀργή) – screaming (κραυγή) – abusing and defaming of others (βλασφημία).[21] This brings with it all kinds of wickedness (πᾶσα κακία). Clearly the author sees in bitterness and wrath a root of division and conflict in the congregations.

32

After this depressing picture there now follows the positive exhortation, created out of the Christian commandment of love, to generosity, mercy and forgiveness. The words used are taken from Col. 3.12 f. with small changes. But the list of virtues is shortened and concentrates on generous behaviour and forgiveness – although again with a deliberate intensification: From generosity (χρηστότης)[22] grows a merciful disposition (εὔσπλαγχνοι) and from this the will to forgive. The addition of 'one another' underlines the obligation to the community. The Greek expression 'to forgive' (χαρίζεσθαι) is reminiscent of 'grace' in v. 29 which they should show to one another as God has mercifully forgiven us in Christ. This characteristic Christian motif is here pressed into service of the paraclesis intended for the congregation; In Col. 3.13 the exhortation is directed more to the individual ('if one has a complaint against another'). Gentleness and mercy were already highly esteemed in Jewish exhortation,[23] but the Christian encouragement is oriented on God's mercifulness already proved. 'In Christ' points to the event of redemption on the Cross (cf. 1.6 f.; 5.2).

5.1

Bound up with God's benevolent forgiveness in Christ but now broadened fundamentally there follows a command to be imitators of God. Since this is the only place in the NT which speaks directly of an 'imitation' of God and since the idea of mimesis played no small part in antiquity,[24] this expression demands consideration. Fairly similar is the Jewish idea of a

---

[21]Cf. Herm m V, 2.4; 'Out of folly rises bitterness (πικρία), from bitterness, wrath (θυμός), from wrath, rage (ὀργή) and from rage, fury (μῆνις).' Elsewhere, too, there is evidence for the intensification θυμός – ὀργή – μῆνις, cf. Dib Herm 517. In the Jewish sphere rage was seen in a similar way – in Test Dan it is thematically treated with falsehood (especially 2–4) but without the *differentiae irarum*. Eph. (like Herm) also takes up Stoic tradition here; but peculiar to him is the extension to 'screaming and invective'.

[22]This attitude, which was also highly thought of in the Gentile world at that time (on many inscriptions, cf. Spicq, *Notes* II, 974), is here introduced into a Christian context. Cf. further L. R. Stachowiak, *Chrestotès. Ihre biblisch-theologische Entwicklung und Eigenart*, Freiburg/Schw. 1957; K. Weiß, TDNT IX, 489–92; Spicq, *Notes* II, 971–6.

[23]Cf. Test Seb, which deals thematically with compassion and mercy (εὐσπλαγχνία and ἔλεος). Compassion is not only called for towards human beings but also towards animals (5.1). Characteristic of the Jewish motivation is the sentence: 'Have compassion in mercy for every person, so that the Lord will also have mercy on you compassionately!' (8.1). According to Test S 4.4 Joseph was considered a 'good man who had in him God's Spirit, compassionate and merciful'. In Test Seb 9.7 these qualities are attributed to God himself.

[24]The idea can be found in philosophy as well as in literature and the fine arts, cf. W. Michaelis, TDNT IV, 659–63; Betz* 48–84 (the cultic origin of the concept of mimesis).

paradoxical imitation of the holiness of God.[25] But the context reveals the author's connection with the early Christian paraclesis. The exhortation 'therefore be imitators of God' is a linguistic continuation of the other 'rather be generous to one another . . .' (4.32) and draws the concrete conclusion (οὖν) from God's merciful love shown in Christ. This 'in Christ' leads to the further motif in v. 2, so to live in love as Christ also loved us. The 'formula of self-offering' which is also added (cf. at v. 2) is here applied to Christ but in other places, possibly its original meaning, it is said of God (Rom. 8.32; cf. 4.25). This application to Christ makes the connection even closer: God does not become in a general manner the paradigm of Christian behaviour but in the way in which he has shown his love in the offering of his Son. The addition 'as beloved children' is not to be explained from a comparison between father and children but is intended to emphasize the love his children owe God which answers to and befits his own love. This, however, points to the Pauline idea that we have become children of God through the Spirit (Rom. 8.15; cf. Gal. 4.5 f.) and the love of God has been poured into our hearts (Rom. 5.5). The exhortation is tied up with the baptismal paraclesis which concludes that they must pursue an appropriate life-style having experienced God's mercy. As children who have experienced God's love to the highest degree, now live your lives also in love.

The unusual expression 'be imitators of God' may have come to the author from the contemporary linguistic canon available to him. The ancient example-ethic which can also be seen in Judaism[26] may have played a part and also Paul's repeated exhortation to imitate him as he imitates the Lord, obedient to the Gospel.[27] Objectively closest lies Jesus' call to be merciful as the heavenly Father is merciful (Luke 6.36) because here too God's action becomes the binding norm for humanity. But what the preacher of the Beatitudes promises as an eschatological reward – namely that they will become 'sons of the most high' (Lk. 6.35) – has in a certain way been fulfilled for the post-Easter Church in the gift of their becoming God's children, but again with a new moral challenge. In 1 Pet. 2.21 the idea of following Jesus has become fused with that of imitating.[28] Basically

---

[25]Cf. Bill. I, 372 f.; H. J. Schoeps, 'Von der Imitatio Dei zur Nachfolge Christi', in *Aus frühchristlicher Zeit, Religionsgeschichtliche Untersuchungen*, Tübingen 1950, 286–301. The interpretation of Ex. 15.2 by R. Abba Schaul is significant: 'This is my God, I wish to be like him . . . as he is merciful and gracious, so may you also be merciful and forgive' (j Pea; Mekh 37a; Schabb 133b), v. in Schoeps (above) 286 f. Further cf. F. Böhl, 'Das rabbinische Verständnis des Handelns in der Nachahmung Gottes', ZM 58 (1975) 134–41.

[26]Cf. Test B 3.1; 'You, my children, love the Lord, the God of heaven and keep his commandments in that you imitate the good and devout Joseph!'; ibid., 4.1: 'See, children, the end of the good man! Imitate his mercy in a good attitude!' Further 4 Macc. 9.23; 13.9; Ps.-Phocylides 77, Arist 188, 210, 280 f. (here referred to God); Philo Vit Mos I, 158; Spec Leg IV, 173, 182 and often, cf. W. Michaelis, TDNT IV, 665.

[27]The element of obedience is emphasized too one-sidedly, even for Eph. 5.1 (671) by W. Michaelis, TDNT IV, 667–72. Cf. the passages which are connected with τύπος: 1 Thess. 1.7; 2 Thess. 3.9; Phil. 3.17; certainly it does not mean imitation of an ideal but orientation on an influential example, cf. L. Goppelt, TDNT VIII, 249 f.; Lindars*. On the advance of the idea of imitation in the NT see Schulz* 302–31; Betz* 186–89 (influence of syncretistic ideas from the Mysteries).

[28]Cf. N. Brox, *Der erste Petrusbrief*, 1979 (EKK XXI) on this passage.

the exhortation in Eph. 5.1 has been created from the early Christian proclamation and baptismal paraclesis.

2

The Christian way of living, totally determined by love, is further motivated by considering Christ. It is a development of the motif which appeared already in 4.32 ('in Christ') as is also shown grammatically by the two corresponding καθώς-clauses. God and Christ are both ground and measure (καθώς reason and comparison) of the love demanded. Eph. clearly takes up the Pauline formulations (cf. Gal. 1.4; 2.20) which, however, in their turn have their roots in an early 'self-giving formula' of the early Church.[29] The original forensic 'surrendering' of Jesus to death came to be understood at an early date as a divine decision to bring about salvation (cf. Mk. 9.31; 10.33; 14.41) and after Easter was understood as a voluntary self-offering by Jesus in ultimate love for the salvation of humankind. The love of God, the Father, for the world (cf. Jn. 3.16) and the love of the Son meet in this act of offering to death. Jesus' 'life for others', his existence lived totally in love and concern for humanity, is fulfilled on the Cross. The change from 'you' (5.2b, still in the address to the readers) to 'us' (5.2c in the formula of self-offering)[30] is probably most easily explained by the fact that it was taken over from tradition. This 'for us' originally implied 'for our benefit' but already in Paul there is an overtone of representation (cf. Gal. 3.13; 2 Cor. 5.14, 21).[31] Eph.'s own contribution is the combination with the idea of sacrifice which in Paul is once suggested by the paschal typology (1 Cor. 5.7) but is here taken from Ps. 39 (40), 7. It is the same verse which Heb. 10, 5–10 develops christologically to make the readers aware of Christ's self-offering which surpasses and 'abolishes' all the OT sacrifices and offerings. In the ecclesiological application of the formula of self-offering in Eph. 5.25–7, the 'for us' as the caring love of Christ which wants what is best for us is defined even more sharply. The addition 'for a pleasing fragrance' – a plerophonic expression often used in the LXX – is rhetorical padding. What Christ has done for us in his self-giving in perfect love is at the same time the highest glorification of God. With this phrase the passage ends in a doxological fashion.

Summary

The section 4.25–5.1 is intended in the general structure of the paraclesis to illustrate with several examples and bring to concrete realization in the reader' situation the life-style of the 'new person' demanded by God's new-

---

[29]Cf. Kramer, *Christos* 112–16; W. Popkes, *Christus Traditus*, 1967 (AThANT 49), especially 246–351; Wengst, *Formeln* 55–77.

[30]There are traces in the MSS of attempts to align the personal pronouns to one another – i.e. to read either the First Person or the Second Person Plural in both places. A considerable group (earlier 'western' text) read instead of ὑμᾶς (in the first place) ἡμᾶς: P⁴⁶ℵ² D F G Ψ MLatt lat sy. This reading was taken up in the Nestle-Aland²⁶ text. But the change remains the more difficult reading, in the editor's opinion admittedly too difficult. Cf. Metzger, *Text Comm* 606.

[31]Cf. H. Riesenfeld, TDNT VIII, 508 f., especially 509.

creating (v. 24). For this purpose exhortations apparently selected arbitrarily are included as was usual elsewhere at that period in moral addresses (both Jewish and Hellenistic). Lies, anger, theft and evil speech are ways of behaving which are often castigated, but for the Christians they are forbidden because of a new motivation. Fundamental remains the opportunity to live a new life created by God in his gracious benevolence, to 'put aside' the old sinful vices (v. 25), 'no longer' to continue in old habits (v. 26) and especially to contribute positively to the building of a new community. What is new are the Christian motives which arise from the perspectives of the paraclesis aimed at the congregation: we are members with one another (v. 25b), obliged to one another and should enrich the congregation both in material (v. 28c) and spiritual (v. 29c) respects. The motives culminate in the love experienced from God which calls for a like benevolence and readiness to forgive (v. 32). As beloved children we should be imitators of God (5.1), not as if we could imitate the transcendent God in his being but in our trying to emulate the love he has shown to us. God's love was revealed to us in Christ, and now we should so orient our lives on love as Christ has loved us in his self-offering in death (5.2). Embedded in this section are the motifs, which possibly came from the baptismal paraclesis, of denying the devil (v. 27) and the sealing by the Holy Spirit whom we should not grieve (v. 30).

The author stands in the tradition of the early Christian admonitory address which continues to educate; yet the accents he places and particular observations he makes justify a consideration of special concerns which he pursues with regard to his readership. The most conspicuous is the re-adoption of the warning against wrath which is depicted in its various manifestations – admittedly after an established pattern (v. 31). If we remember the earlier exposition on Christ, our peace, (2.11–18), the urgent exhortation to unity and peace at the beginning of the paraclesis (4.1–6) and the metaphor, which is laid out at length, of the Church as Christ's Body in which all members should co-operate according to the measure of grace allotted to them in order to strive for the goal of complete unity (4.1–16), we also sense in the concrete paraclesis of this section the concern that the special character of the Christian community impressed upon it by God might be destroyed by squabbles in the congregation, tension between individual groups and violent arguments. That would be a relapse into their earlier mentality, a break away from the new ethic of love which is laid upon all Christians because of God's re-creation. In this the author reveals a great and constant danger to Christian existence, namely that 'all remains as it was', that the breakthrough to a new attitude to life changed by love and to a new community life does not really take place. If a Christian congregation is not distinguished by this 'group-specific' ethic of love, it remains colourless and bears no fruit.

2.c Avoidance of pagan vices (sexual immorality) and acting as Children of the Light (5.3–14)

Literature

L. Nieder, *Die Motive der religiös-sittlichen Paränese in den paulinischen Gemeindebriefen*, 1956 (MThS I/12), 58–60.

Wibbing, *Tugend- und Lasterkataloge* 111–13.

E. Schweizer, 'Gottesgerechtigkeit und Lasterkataloge bei Paulus (inkl Kol und Eph.)', in *Rechtfertigung* (FS E. Käsemann), ed J. Friedrich, W. Pöhlmann and P. Stuhlmacher, Tübingen-Göttingen 1976, 461–77.

Dahl 62–6.

F. Dölger, *Sol Salutis. Gebet und Gesang im christlichen Altertum* ²1925 (LQF 16/17), 364–74.

B. Noack, 'Das Zitat in Eph. 5.14', StTh 5 (1952) 52–64.

Schnackenburg, '"Er hat uns mitauferweckt". Zur Tauflehre des Epheserbriefes', LJ 2 (1952) 159–83, especially 160–6.

Fischer, *Tendenz* 140–6.

Halter, *Taufe* 269–81.

3 But fornication and shamelessness of every kind and covetousness
should not even be mentioned among you,
as is fitting among saints,
4 nor indecent conversation or foolish chatter or ribaldry (take
place),
that is not fitting.
but rather thanksgiving.
5 For you should be aware of and consider this:
No immoral or shameless or greedy person
–such is an idolator –
has an inheritance in the Kingdom of Christ and of God.
6 Let no one beguile you with empty words:
for because of such things the wrath of God comes
upon the sons of disobedience.
7 Therefore do not make common cause with them!
8 For once you were darkness but now (you are) light in the Lord.
Live as children of light!
9 For the fruit of the light (consists) in pure
goodness, righteousness and fidelity.
10 Test what is pleasing to the Lord!
11 And do not participate in the unfruitful works
of darkness, but rather expose them, convict them!
12 For what they do in secret,
even only to talk of it
is shameful.
13 But all that, if it is exposed,
is made visible by the light
14 For everything that is visible is light.
Hence it is said:
'Awake, sleeper,
and arise from the dead,
and Christ will shine upon you'

Analysis

After the insistent exhortation of Christian love the author begins a new section with a catalogue of unchristian vices, chiefly of the sexual variety. The stimulus for this came from Col. 3.5–7 where fornication, shamelessness and covetousness are likewise named, admittedly with two other expressions so that there is a quintet.[1] The author of Eph. prefers a trinitarian arrangement since in v. 4 he again uses three (indecency, foolish chatter, ribaldry) and there is a resumption of the first triad in v. 5. In the following section, too, in a description of the life in light he depicts a positive triad (goodness, righteousness and truth v. 9. If he displays a different feeling for style from Col. other differences are also apparent, especially in the motivation. After the warning against fornication, shamelessness and covetousness he adds the motive 'as is fitting among saints' (v. 3) and after the further list in v. 4 there is a similar motive 'that is not fitting'. For the silly, witty talk which is forbidden to Christians he poses the alternative of thanksgiving (εὐχαριστία), here only mentioned briefly but later expanded more fully (5.20): arising out of worship it should permeate the whole life of the Christian. V. 5 brings a new motive: the wrongdoers named have no part in the Kingdom of Christ and of God; rather the wrath of God comes upon the 'sons of disobedience'. Out of the total unified warning directed against those pagan vices he draws the conclusion: Do not make common cause with them (v. 7).

In comparison with the paraclesis in Col. 3, Eph. reveals in this individual structuring the special intention of shielding the Christians from the destructive life-style of their pagan environment. Whereas Col. recalled the Christians' earlier way of life (Col. 3.7) here the author is considering the depraved life of outsiders. For this purpose the author introduces the motive also used by Paul that such depraved people are excluded from God's Kingdom (cf. 1 Cor. 6.9 f.; Gal. 5.19–21). But he changes the Pauline command 'Do not be deceived!' (1 Cor. 6.9) into another warning against the outsiders: 'Let no one beguile you with empty words!' (v. 6). His aim is revealed particularly in the closing admonition in v. 7.

In the following section, vv. 8–14, which has no parallel in Col. the author reinforces the difference between a Christian and a pagan way of life in the contrast of light and darkness. This pictorial motif dominates the exhortation up to v. 14, where the quotation of an otherwise unknown text reaches a climax in the words 'and Christ will shine upon you'. In spite of this uniformity, which gives the section emphasis as a special exposition, it is still closely connected with the unit of vv. 3–7. It is closely joined by γάρ, contains the central demand that they should not participate in the 'unfruitful works of darkness' (v. 11), makes us think in talking of 'what they do in secret' (v. 12) of the same vices as in v. 3 and clearly throughout still has in mind the same people (in the model of communication, the 'opponents').

---

[1] Cf. Schweizer, *Colossians* on this part.

If we look at the structure more closely, the two Imperatives 'live as children of light!' (v. 8) and 'Do not participate in the unfruitful works of darkness!' (v. 11) appear at first to stand over against one another. What is in English translated as an Imperative between these two – 'Test what is pleasing to the Lord!' (v. 10) is in Greek a Participle which is more closely connected with the living in the light. Vv. 9–10 are therefore an intermediate explanation meant to illustrate life in the light with three positive expressions, incidentally with only the bare comment 'what is pleasing to the Lord'. The command to keep their distance from the works of darkness is then immediately followed in a countermove by the exhortation (likewise in an Imperative) to 'expose', i.e. bring to light how things stand with the works of darkness. The interest of the following verses (12–14a) has to do with this 'exposing', 'making known' in a characteristic argumentation which is not easy to comprehend (cf. the Conjunctions γάρ v. 12 – δέ v. 13 – γάρ v. 14a). This can only be explained in the exegesis. The function of the concluding quotation, introduced by the formula already met with the 4.8 (v. there) can only be understood through the interpretation of the preceding sentences. At any rate it forms a bracket with v. 8: 'Now you are light in the Lord'.

From this structure it follows that the author is pursuing his intention of separating the Christians from the immoral, pagan way of life. But now he wants to achieve more (cf. μᾶλλον δέ v. 11b): Instead of the seduction by which the Christians are threatened, it must come to a 'traduction', a conviction of the realm of darkness with which they are confronted. He desires to lead the Christians as it were from the defensive to the offensive.

If we compare 5.3–14 with 4.17–24, the first section of the paraclesis for Christian existence in the world, we cannot fail to note that the author proceeds in a similar fashion. There, too, the exhortation passed over from a gloomy description of the pagan way of life to a bright picture of the Christian existence founded on God. There are even certain parallel features: the 'depiction of the milieu' in 4.19 spoke of dissipation 'to practise any kind of impurity in their greed' and in 5.3 'any kind of impurity and greed' resurfaces. For the confrontation of the new, Christian existence with the old pagan one the author in 4.22–4 used the motif of the 'old and new person': now, in 5.8–14 he introduces another, yet related motif: the people who have succumbed to darkness and the Sons of Light. We shall only discuss the historico-traditional background in the exegesis.

Exegesis

3

Separated from the foregoing section by δέ there now begins a new warning against an unchristian life-style. First sexual sins are mentioned and in what follows he seems to have such particularly, though not exclusively, in mind (cf. vv. 4, 5, 11 f.). Since there was as yet no mention of these in 4.25–5.2, we can see a deliberate progression and intensification. Fornication (πορνεία), especially intercourse with prostitutes and adultery,[2] was denounced in Judaism as in Christianity as a serious sin. The Jews considered all gentiles as suspect of committing fornication.[3] Paul takes pains, with many motives, to restrain the Christians in Corinth from intercourse with prostitutes (πόρνη) since in their city they were especially exposed to this temptation and moreover were confused by libertine catchwords in their own ranks (1 Cor. 6.12–20). There is no such concrete background visible in Eph. The view broadens immediately to 'every kind of shamelessness', sexual impurity (ἀκαθαρσία of every type. It is possible that he means unnatural depravation which already in Judaism was held to be a typical gentile aberration.[4] But the combination of 'fornication' and 'impurity' is already traditional in the lists of vices,[5] and Eph. contents himself with hints (cf. v. 12). Alongside sexual immorality covetousness (πλεονεξία) is singled out (ἤ as a further typical characteristic of a pagan way of life. This has been taken over from Col. 3.5 as the similar characterizing of this as 'idolatry' in Eph. 5.5 shows. Lack of moderation in sexual activity and greed is typical of a dissipated, unbridled life (cf. at 4.19) and the author wants to dam this flood at the spring. They should not even talk of it; and they should certainly not – so we must add – become involved in such activity[6] It is a radical denial of what dominates the thoughts and speech of many people and embroils them in insatiable desires.

The added motive 'as is fitting among saints' appeals to the Christian consciousness of having been chosen by God and called to a life-style beyond reproach (1.4) so that they are cut off from the life of the pagan, which is foreign to God and at the mercy of their own desires (cf. 2.3; 4.17–19). The whole of early Christianity was sustained by this consciousness. Especially close is the exhortation to holiness in 1 Thess. 4.3–7, where in like manner the sexual desires of the gentiles 'who do not know God' are contrasted with the divine call to holiness. The motive (in spite of 'it is not fitting') has not yet paled through convention. The fact that the article is missing gives 'saints' a qualitative note and points to the new, different reality of life which has opened up for the Christians. The paraclesis on marriage in Eph. 5.22–33 allows us to recognise a profound reflection on the sanctification which proceeds from Christ and permeates even married life.

[2]Cf. F. Hauck/ S. Schulz, TDNT VI, 587–90. In Sir. 23.16–27 sexual offence is condemned both on the part of the man and of the woman. In the Test XII there are many warnings against sexual offence, in the Test Jud. in the very title (along with avarice); in Test S 5.3 it is called the 'mother of every evil'; 'it separates from God and leads to Belial'. In Philo, Joseph, who is extolled as a model, stresses that the Israelites are not permitted like others to use common prostitutes; he does not want to begin to sin with adultery, 'the greatest of all offences' (Philo: Jos. 43 f.). The use of the word πορνεία was then extended to other sexual sins.

[3]Cf. M. Aboda Zara II.1: 'A (Jewish) woman should not be alone with them (non-Jews) because they are suspected of sexual offence.' Further in Bill. IV, 363 f.

[4]Cf. the material in Bill. III, 70 f.; if such sexual offence also occurred among Jews it was

[5]Cf. Gal. 5.19; 2 Cor. 12.21; Col. 3.5; also in the list of vices in 1 QS. 4.10; Wibbing* 111–13. threatened with severe punishment, cf. ibid. 72 ff. For the NT cf. 1 Cor. 6.9; Rom. 1.24 (ἀκαθαρσία 26 f. Gnilka 246 thinks it refers to every kind of sexual perversion and transgression.

[6]Schlier 233 thinks that μηδὲ ὀνομαζέσθω is not to be literally; what is meant is that it should not exist in the Christian congregation. Cf. otherwise Haupt 199 f. ('not once the subject of conversation'); Gaugler 199 ('the danger of sexual gossip is obvious').

4

Loosely connected (καί) and clearly considering conversation among Christians there is now mention of further things which they should avoid. We can hardly supplement the verb from the previous Clause since the subject is now the manner of speaking itself, hence we must presume it is an abbreviated style of expression: You should also not talk of it. The intensification consists in that the Christians, as well as not committing sins such as fornication and greed should also not talk of anything 'indecent' (αἰσχρότης). Since 'foolish chatter' (μωρολογία) and 'ribaldry' (εὐτραπελία)[7] are mentioned, the first expression must mean indecent coversation (cf. αἰσχρολογία Col. 3.8). The admonition to refrain from stupid, lewd talk is reminiscent of the strict instructions in Qumran where even uncontrolled laughter over an improper joke is punished with thirty days suspension (1 QS. 7.14 f.). The pious person is resolved 'not to hear foolishness from his/her mouth' and 'that nothing repulsive should be found on her/his tongue'; rather they will open their mouths 'to give thanks' (1 QS. 10.21–3). The close correspondance with this text does not necessarily imply dependence.[8] For Eph. unseemly talk and jokes are not a matter for punishment but something which is not proper for Christian (ἃ οὐκ ἀνῆκεν)[9] because as 'saints' they are called to praise God. This thought of what they owe God appears in the positive expression 'rather thanksgiving'. It is not a matter of a prudish, humourless Christianity but of a consistent rejection of promiscuity and equivocalness.

5

The motive of exclusion from the Kingdom of God is found in the Pauline tradition (1 Cor. 6.9 f.; Gal. 5.21) and is here firmly stressed but in another formulation. The same sins/sinners are mentioned as in v. 3 except that here is added 'that is an idolator'[10] This characterization need not be

---

[7]In secular Greek literature the word is used with more of a positive sense cf. Liddell – Scott 735 s,v. G. Bertram, TDNT IV, 844 f. with n. 99. But also the related 'witty' talk is corrupted by a smutty intention. Dibelius – Greeven 89 think that, because εὐτραπελία did not count as nearly so reprehensible the author added emphatically: That is not fitting. – On αἰσχρότης a rare word found only here in the NT, cf. Pr-Bauer 49 ('ugliness'); R. Bultmann, TDNT I, 191. He is not thinking of futile squabbles; against this G. Bertram, TDNT IV, 844, who reminds us of the 'senseless controversies' of 2 Tim. 2.23; Tit. 3.9 and elsewhere.

[8]Clearly K. G. Kuhn, NTS 7, 338 f. tends to this view. He was the first to furnish these parallels. On the metaphor contrasting light and darkness which also has contract with the Qumran texts, cf. at v. 8.

[9]The motif 'what is fitting' comes from the Greek, especially Stoic, ethics and was taken over by Hellenistic Judaism, cf. Nieder* 59; Schweizer on Col. 3.18. In Eph. 5.4 it corresponds with καθὼς πρέπει ἁγίοις in v. 3; thus there is note of 'what is proper for Christians', cf. H. Schlier, TDNT I, 360. The Imperfect expresses duty or obligation, but here was occasioned by Col. 3.18; cf. Bl-Debr §358,2; Moulton – Turner, *Grammar* III, 90 f. The variant reading τα οὐκ ἀνήκοντα in Ψ D G 177 326 al pl (not taken up by Nestle – Aland) is later; on negation with the Participle cf. Bl-Debr §430.

[10]ὅ as opposed to ὅς in A D and the majority of the later MSS is the better reading. Perhaps the author applies the Relative Pronoun to all three expressions connected to πᾶς (cf. v. 4 ἃ οὐκ ἀνῆκεν); but in Col. 3.5 greed is clearly described as idolatry.

limited to the 'greedy' although that is syntactically reasonable (as is also the case in Col. 3.5). In Jewish texts more often than not fornication is connected with idolatry (cf. Wis. Sol. 14.12; Test R 4.6; Test Jud. 23.1; Test B 10.10); but in Test Jud. 19.1 it also says: 'Avarice leads to idols; seduced by money they name as gods those who are not'. In Rabbinism the cardinal sins, among them greed, are *compared* with idolatry to indicate the gravity of the sins.[11] Jesus contrasts serving Mammon with serving God (Mt. 6.24/Lk. 16.13). Philo accuses the avaricious of guarding their riches like an idol in secret chambers and of honouring their riches like gods.[12] Fornication and covetousness not only blind the eyes to worship of the true God but are themselves idolatry. Pol 11.1 f. combines the two ideas: anyone who does not abstain from covetousness will be stained by idolatry, counted among the heathen and judged with them. The author of Eph. also desires to stamp these vices with the hallmark of the unchristian-pagan. The Christians are called as saints (v. 3) to participation in the Kingdom of Christ and of God. The formulation which departs from Paul – 'he has no inheritance' – and the double expression 'Kingdom of Christ and of God'[13] are informative for the theological thinking of Eph. In spite of the redemption still to come, which consists in the 'appropriation' of the inheritance, (1.14, v. there) this already lies prepared in heaven (cf. 1.18) and the Christians even now have a part in the power of the heavenly Christ (cf. 2.6). They have been, as it says in the related passage in Col. 1.13, snatched by God the Father from the power of darkness and transferred to the Kingdom of his beloved Son. Such depraved people are now excluded from this and await God's wrathful judgement (cf. v. 6b). Perhaps the double expression 'Kingdom of Christ and of God' has also been chosen because of its curious combining of present and future (cf. 1 Cor 15.25–8).

6

The people who might beguile the Christians with 'empty', meaningless words[14] can scarcely be teachers of false doctrine or tempters who appear in the congregation (cf. 4.14)[15] but in this context are the same people against whose vices the warning is given and who are then called 'Sons of disobedience'. The line of battle in this paraclesis is a unified one, and the Greek verb for 'beguile' (ἀπατᾶν) or the noun (ἀπάτη) signifies the temptation

[11]Cf. Bill. III, 606 f.

[12]Spec Leg I, 23.25. Avarice was also considered (as in other texts sexual offences) the mother of all evil: Ps-Phocylides 42; cf. 1 Tim. 6.10; (Col. 3.5–4.1) Further in G. Delling, TDNT VI, 268–70; van der Horst, *Ps-Phocyl.* 142 f.; Spicq, *Notes* II, 704–6. Cf. also Schweizer* 462 f.

[13]Some scribes attempted to improve the unfamiliar double expression τοῦ θεοῦ κὰι Χριστοῦ F G bo^{ms} Ambst; τοῦ Χριστοῦ τοῦ θεοῦ 1739* Vg^{ms}.

[14]'Empty' words could be useless chatter (Ex. 5.9), without significance in contrast to the instruction of the Torah (Deut. 32.47), gossip which brought no profit (cf. Job 15.3). Closer is the Test N 3.1: 'Endeavour not to spoil your deeds or deceive (ἀπατᾶν) your souls by empty words.' Cf. also Corp Herm XVI, 2: The Greeks have only empty words which produce evidence, their philosophy is verbiage.

[15]Against Bertram (v. n. 7), Schlier 236 (thinks of circles of indifferent or even libertine gnosis as in Corinth), Gaugler 201 (lay opinions even among Christians), Barth 565 f. Ernst 373 is rightly cautious.

to sin (cf. Eph. 4.22; Mk. 4.19; 2 Thess. 2.10; Heb. 3.13). Vice wants to justify itself and, glossing things over, draw others in the same direction. But God cannot be deceived and consequently brings his wrathful judgement to bear on the 'Sons of disobedience' – because of all these deeds which cannot be veiled by empty words. The expression is probably the author's own composition[16] and chosen here, as in 2.2, to emphasize how such people are subject to divine judgement (2.3 'by nature Children of Wrath').

Whether the judgement 'comes upon them' in the present or is still outstanding cannot be decided from the wording since the Present can have a Future meaning.[17] Rom. 1.18–32 depicts the wrath of God on godless humanity being revealed already in the present which has effect in that their minds are changed for the worse; but it is not certain that Eph. has this in mind[18] because such a self-alienation of humanity, which he also knows (4.18 f.), is not depicted as clearly as is divine punishment. It would be best to take both together like the present and future reference of the 'Kingdom of Christ and of God': The wrath of God comes already now upon people who defy him; but it is yet to come upon them in its entirety. The traditional motif of the 'wrath to come' (1 Thess. 1.10; cf. 5.9; Col. 3.6; Rev. 11.18) is taken up and made topical (cf. also 1 Thess. 2.16) so that a present experience of it cannot be excluded.

7

The conclusion the author draws for his readers from these warnings he expresses forcefully in his own words (συμμέτοχοι = co-participants appears only here and in Eph. 3.6). The sharp distinction which he thereby advances has only one parallel – admittedly a conspicuous one – in 2 Cor. 6.14 which is possibly a non-Pauline insertion (v. p. 26 n. 22). It is a matter of debate whether the Personal Pronoun at the end (αὐτῶν) refers to the evil deeds or to the people. Although we would expect the Dative of Person, and in the similar warning in v. 11 the 'unfruitful works of darkness' are named, a connection with the 'Sons of disobedience' mentioned immediately prior deserves preference[19] The διὰ ταῦτα is separated and too vague and must rather be taken with τούτων. Above all the 'axis' of the whole address

---

[16]υἱοὶ τῆς ἀπειθείας only in Eph. 2.2; 5.6 further in the majority of MSS at Col. 3.6. But the phrase is missing there in P⁴⁶ B D*ᵛⁱᵈb sa, so that the suspicion arises that it only later found its way here from Eph. (so also Schweizer, *Colossians* 191, n. 34). It is taken up in brackets in the Nestle-Aland ²⁶ text. On the idea cf. 1 Pet. 3.20; 4.17 f.; 1 Clem. 58.1; R. Bultmann, TDNT VI, 118.

[17]The Present of ἔρχεσθαι often has a Future sense, cf. Mt. 17.11; Lk. 23.29; Jn. 5.28; 9.4; 16.2, 25; 1 Thess. 5.2; Heb. 8.8; Rev. 1.7; 2.5, 16 and often; cf. Bl-Debr §323. On ἔρχομαι ἐπί of tragic fate coming upon someone, cf. Mt. 23.35; Lk. 14.31; Jn. 18.4; Acts 7.11; Rev. 3.10; Jos. Ant. IV, 128; Ign R 5.3.

[18]Cf. Calvin 216: God shows often enough in frequent examples of punishment that he justly repays such evil, be it privately for individuals or publicly in that he shows his wrath against citites, realms and nations. Ernst 374 thinks that this eschatological wrathful judegment is already realized in the hostages of the heathen sins; Lindemann *Aufhebung der Zeit*, 144: The once-for-all Judgement in the sense of Rom. 1.18. The majority of modern exegetes combine both views with variations. Abbott 152: The Wrath of God will one day be revealed, but it already exists; Barth 566: God's Judgement or 'wrath' is not only a future threat but is already experienced in the present time; similarly Schlier 236; cf. also Stählin, TDNT V, 430–3.

from v. 6 on is oriented to the people: The sinners stand over against the addressees who are now required not to become 'participators' with them.

8

This separation of the Christians from their unchristian environment is now given basis in a return to the decisive change in their life. It must be noted that 'darkness' and 'light' are not only realms *in which* humanity at any one time move, but *they themselves* are darkness or light. Dominated by the might of darkness or light they themselves represent the dark or light sphere. The progression of the statements is thought out exactly; they start with the already-known schema of then – now (cf. 2.2 f.,11–13) and develop for the Christians who belong to the sphere of light a consistent reasoning:

> Now (you are) light in the Lord
> live as children of the light!
> The fruit of the light consists in . . .
> Do not participate in the unfruitful works of darkness!

The former Gentiles have become 'light' in that they have entered Christ's sphere of influence ('in the Lord')[20] From this merciful event (Indicative of salvation) emerges the obligation (moral Imperative) with inner consequence to live as 'children of the light' (cf. the same reasoning in 2.8–10). Paul more than anyone else emphasized this insoluable interlocking of salvation and moral challenge (cf. 1 Cor. 5.7 f.; 6.9–11; 2 Cor. 5.17–20; Rom. 6) and it remained effective in the early Christian baptismal paraclesis (especially 1 Pet. 1.3–5, 22 f.; 2.1–5; in a different way also in 1 Jn. 3.1–10). What is special here is the connection with the motif of light and darkness which rings in a similar manner – with reference to the call and conversion of the gentiles – in Acts 26.18; Col. 1.12 f.; 1 Pet. 2.9 and in the picture of enlightenment in Heb. 6.4; 10.32.[21] Paul, too, used this metaphor but mainly in an eschatological connection, under a qualification of near expectation (1 Thess. 5.5 f.; Rom. 13.12 f.). This concern with the eschaton is missing in our passage, and the Pauline texts

[19]With Dibelius – Greeven (who also quote Theodoret), Schlier, against Ewald, Haupt, Gnilka. Undecided Ernst, Barth (566 f. thinks of erring members of the congregation and their deeds).

[20]Already a somewhat polished formula, cf. at 2.21; also 4.1, 17; 6.1. But in 5.8 its original sense shines through: faith and Baptism make the Christians subordinate to the Kyrious Jesus Christ, to his power which brings salvation and makes demands (cf. Col. 1.10). The power of Christ is effective in the Christian life but it also demands 'be strong in the Lord' (Eph. 6.10). Cf. F. Neugebauer, *In Christus*, Göttingen 1961, 175–81 (but he considers Eph. 5.8 'hard'; the expression should only express the Christian existence of those addressed); M. Bauttier, *En Christ*, 1962 (EHPhR 54) 54–61 (the formula belongs especially to the apostolic paraenesis in which, however, it refers to the mighty, effective intervention of the Lord).

[21]As an expression for Baptism φωτισμός is encountered clearly in Just Apol 61.12 f.; 65.1; Dial 39.2; 122.1, 3–5; 123.2. Cf. Y. Ysebaert, *Greek Baptismal Terminology*, Nimwegen, 1962, 158–78; H. Conzelmann, TDNT IX, 355 (on Heb.); 357 f. (on Justin). Halter* 273 f. thinks that this understanding of Baptism was already established in the Hellenistic congregations.

utilize the metaphor in a different way (to wake, be sober). Hence we must presume still other historico-traditional influences for Eph.

The sharp distinction between light and darkness in the 'Children of Light' and – unnamed – people of darkness (cf. 'works of darkness' v. 11) has led, after the discovery of the Qumran texts, to an assumption of a close connection with these writings[22] Indeed not only the War Scroll (1 QM) treats of the 'Battle between the Sons of Light and the Sons of Darkness', but this dualistic separation and confrontation is also found in the Rule of the Community (1 QS 1.9 f.; 2.1–10; 3.13, 20 f., 24 f.). Added to this is the passage in 2 Cor 6.14–7.1 – probably interpolated – which has an even stronger echo of Qumran ('Belial', no 'participation' of one of the faithful with an unbeliever) and on the other hand closely coincides with Eph. 5.8–11 in its distinction between light and darkness and its demand for a decision. Hence a connection with the Qumran way of thinking and speaking can be assumed. But the historico-traditional way need not run directly or exclusively from Qumran to Eph. Perhaps at a relatively early date converted Qumran Essenes already influenced the Christian baptismal paraclesis; but we cannot say anything more definite. A similar dualism of light and darkness, though with a more markedly ethical application, is also encountered in the Testament of the Twelve Patriarchs:[23] and in the Judaeo-Hellenistic propaganda-document 'Joseph and Aseneth' conversion is extolled as a transition from darkness into light.[24] What differentiates the Christian faith is the close connection to Christ, the Resurrected One from whom light and life proceed (cf. v. 14), the forcing open of particularistic exclusiveness (as opposed to Qumran) and the relinquishment of a life-style according to the Torah (as opposed to Diaspora Judaism). The expression 'Sons of Light' is found frequently elsewhere in early Christian literature to describe the people belonging to God (cf. Lk. 16.8; Jn. 12.36).[25]

9

The life appropriate to the Children of Light must reveal what proceeds from the power of light. The author names it 'fruit of the light', as Paul in Gal. 5.22 speaks of the 'fruit of the Spirit'.[26] If 'the unfruitful works of darkness' in v. 11 (cf. Gal. 5.19 'the works of the flesh') are set over against

[22]Cf. G. Molin, *Die Söhne des Lichts*, Vienna-Munich 1954, 179; K. G. Kuhn, NTS 7.339 ff.; Wibbing* 111 f.; Gnilka 251–3.

[23]Cf. Test L 19; 'Choose light or darkness, the Law of the Lord or the works of Belial!'; further Test B 5.3; G 5.7; L 14.4.

[24]15.13: 'Praised be the Lord, God, who has sent you to save me from darkness and lead me into the light'; cf. 8.10; 14,2 f. Philonenko, *Joseph et Asénath* 158, believes he recognizes in 8.10 the traces of a liturgy for the admission of proselytes, which Philo might also have known.

[25]On the other hand the same expression in the Mandaean writings often means the heavenly light-beings (Uthras), once also 'people of proven righteousness' (Lidz Liturg 36). The Gnostic conception is quite different: The light-soul (the pneumatic self) has its origin in the heavenly world to which it also returns. The light is thought of as having substance – an idea foreign to Eph. Cf. H. Conzelmann, TDNT IX, 333 f.; 335 f.

[26]A reminiscence of this passage certainly led to the variant reading πνεύματος in P[46] D[2] Ψ MLatt sy[h]. For Eph. too, the divine Spirit is at work.

this fruit of the light, we can recognise the Pauline influence. Fruit of righteousness grows from the work of Jesus Christ (Phil. 1.11) and matures for all who want to serve God for their salvation and eternal life (Rom. 6.22). 'Fruit' as the successful outcome of the Christian life is a permanent reminder of the divine vitality planted in us.[27] The Singular also points to this divine origin while the many 'unfruitful works' reflect the divers desires of human beings which miss their goal (as in Gal. 5.19, 22).

Hence the three expressions which explain the fruit of the light – goodness, righteousness and fidelity – are also more than mere moral virtues which are contrasted with the triad of vices in vv. 3–5. The 'goodness' (ἀγαθωσύνη)[28] mentioned in the first place here (other than in Gal. 5.22 where it has more the sense of 'kindness') focusses on the basic position of the people caught by the light of the Lord: they desire to do what is good and fitting before God, as the basic rule for the pious in Israel says: 'It has been said to you what is good, what the Lord requires from you (Mic. 6.8; cf. also 2 Chron. 31.20). The following expressions 'righteousness and fidelity', clarify this goodness in a biblical sense in a similar way to that prophetic saying: '. . . to love doing what is just, goodness and faithfulness' or as in Qumran: 'Faithfulness, righteousness and doing what is just'. (1 QS. 1.5; cf. 8.2). 'Righteousness' signifies in a comprehensive sense uprightness before God and behaving justly towards other people, 'truth' according to the basic Hebrew meaning (*'emet*) – steadfastness in the order appointed by God – hence rather 'fidelity'. This description of the 'fruit of light' differs from the philosophical ethic which proceeds from a person's being[29] but also differs from the Jewish instruction oriented on the way of life laid down in the Torah. To be sure 'righteousness' and 'truth' (in the sense of fidelity) are primary, closely-connected concepts which demand from humanity what God contains in perfection in himself;[30] but in the New Creation by God a new basis of life accrues to the Christian which

[27]The metaphor is used in a similar way to the metaphor of the vine and its branches in Jn. 15, 1–8, cf. Schnackenburg, *John* III, 99. It is significant that in Qumran 'fruit' does not refer to morally good works but stands for 'fruit of praise' or something similar, cf. 1 QS. 10.8, 22; 1 QH 1.28 (differently in 1 QH 8.11, 13.20; see on this G. Jeremias, *Lehrer der Gerechtigkeit* 256–8). In the Od Sol the metaphor expresses the fruits of gnosis (cf. 4.4; 7.1; 8.2; 11.1. 12.23; 14.6 f.; 17.13; 38.17) which are extolled in praise (cf. 10.2; 11.12; 12.2; 16.2). Certainly they are also revealed in a 'holy life' (8.2; cf. 14.5 f.); but the idea of the happiness and joy of salvation achieved through gnosis predominates. – On 'fruit' in Paul cf. also Kamlah, *Form* 181 f.; Schweizer* 467.

[28]As has often been established the word is not to be found in secular Greek or in the papyri, but is witnessed to in the Greek Bible (cf. Hatch-Redp s.v.), in the NT again in Gal. 5.22; Rom. 15.14; 2 Thess. 1.11. In any particular context it takes on a different nuance, cf. Spicq, *Notes* I, 13 f.

[29]Philo combines Hellenistic and biblical concepts. He starts from the ἀγαθότης (= goodness, kindness) of the being from which the world was created (Imm 108), the goodness of God (cf. All III, 78; Cher 127), and then names the virtue of ἀ, the 'general virtue' from which the other virtues are derived. He compares it with the Tree of Life in Paradise (Migr Abr 37) and with the River of Paradise, from which the other four rivers of Paradise – the four cardinal virtues – flow (Leg All I, 63.65). Cf. also Gnilka 253 f.

[30]Cf. on the OT G. Quell, TDNT I, 235 ff.; on Qumran F. Nötscher, 'Die "Wahrheit" als theologischer Terminus in den Qumran-Schriften', in FS V. Christian, Vienna 1956, 83–92; also *Gotteswege und Menschenwege* 77 f., 83; J. Murphy O'Connor, 'La 'vérité' chez s. Paul et à Qumran', RB72 (1965) 29–76, on Eph. 5.9, especially 51–3.

puts him under an obligation solely to the will of the Lord (cf. v. 10). Hence the echo of 4.24 'in righteousness and holiness of truth' is also significant although the concepts do not exactly correspond.

10

The new element in the Christian ethic lies, aside from its new creation by God, in its orientation on Jesus Christ the Lord. Because the Christians have become 'light in the Lord' (v. 8) they should also test what is pleasing to the Lord. This means nothing other than the Pauline exhortation to prove what is God's will, what is good, pleasing to him and perfect (Rom. 12.2). Only here are they commanded to look to the 'Lord' (= Christ) to whom the Christians have been subordinated in Baptism (cf.4.5). The author takes up this motif again in the following section, again in a contrast between the gentile-foolish and the Christian-wise way of life: They must understand what the will of the Lord is (5.17). This 'testing' (δοκιμάζειν) has a rich tradition in the Pauline instruction, stronger in consideration of the responsibility before the Lord who is to come (cf. 1 Cor. 11.28, 31 f.; Phil. 1.10 f.) but also for the protection of the Christian in the world.[31] The testing before the Lord, the questioning as to what is his will, draws our attention to what makes the distinction and keeps us from a false assimilation.

11

The life-style of the 'children of light' cannot be reconciled to the works of 'darkness'. 'Unfruitful', as the works here are named in contrast to the fruit of light, has a Casual sense: they contribute nothing to the goal of human existence. The Adjective is often used elsewhere in early Christian literature for the frustration and futility of a life which does not achieve its purpose (cf. Mk. 4.19; Tit. 3.14; 2 Pet. 1.8; Jude 12).'Darkness' means not only the dark sphere in which the works take place ('what takes place in secret' v. 12) but also the people themselves who carry out the actions.[32] This is of some import since the Christians, too, in their former condition were named 'darkness' (v. 8) and in v. 12 the present evil-doers emerge behind their works ('what is done in secret *by them*'). People's actions reveal their condition and make them representatives of the sphere in which they are caught up.

Light is superior to darkness; hence the children of light should repel and break the power of darkness. How can they do this? In that they 'convict' (ἐλέγχειν), expound openly and expose the situation of the works of darkness and those who perform them. This verb can have quite varied meanings but in biblical and Jewish usuage it has a special reference to the conviction of the sinner.[33] A brother should reprimand another by

---

[31]Cf. W. Grundmann, TDNT II, 258–9.

[32]This is not clear in most commentaries; but cf. Gnilka 256, n. 3.

[33]Pr-Bauer 494 names four meanings (1) to bring to light; (2) to find someone guilty of something; (3) to rebuke, reprimand; (4) punish; to Eph. 5.11, 13 he gives the first meeting. H. Büchsel, TDNT V, 474 explains for Eph. 5.11: To hold up their sins before people and challenge them to change their ways; H. G. Link, TBLNT III, 1095: convicting exposure of sin. The commentaries are correspondingly varied.

holding up his sins before his eyes.[34] More frequently it is God who reprimands, punishes and instructs,[35] but also convicts the sinner at the Last Judgement.[36] We can hardly think that a verbal reprimand is meant, which already in the Book of Proverbs was considered to be pointless for godless people (Prov. 9.7; 15.12.[37] Rather the exposure and conviction takes place through their witness to another way of life guided by the light of the Lord. A purpose is not mentioned; but in that they reveal the works of darkness to be such through their own behaviour, they also unmask and convict the people who perform such deeds. In a similar way, though with even more effect, Paul describes the 'conviction' of an unbeliever who becomes involved in a Christian congregational meeting with prophetic voices (1 Cor. 14.24 f.). Even the convicting activity of the Paraclete on the unbelieving world of which Jn. 16.8–11 speaks presumes the existential witness of the believing congregation.

12–13

The next two verses can only be understood as a unit. The author desires to give his exhortation a reason (γάρ) and demonstrate the force of this 'conviction'. Hence he intensifies the reprehensibility of the works of darkness (v.12) and contrasts them even more strongly with the power of light (δέ). With deeds 'done in secret' he is thinking of sexual sins, perhaps perversions, but not necessarily of sexual excesses as they occured in the Mystery Cults.[38] Philo, too, characterized 'immoderate and sinful desires' as such which one should 'not even express' (Op Mund 80). 'All that', including the list of vices, which takes place in secret is exposed by the light in the process of conviction[39] and revealed as a work of darkness. It is controversial where we should connect the phrase 'by the light' – with 'conviction' or 'exposure'.[40] At all events there is a stronger accent on the power of the light. If we leave the expression with 'convict', we can then understand under light the Christians who have previously been challenged to this conviction. But perhaps the light (in this case attached to 'exposing') is seen as the power of light effective in Christians, so that in the end Christ himself is the light which brings to view through the children of

---

[34]Lev. 19.17; Sir 19.13 ff.; 1 QS 5.24, 26; Damasc 7.2; 9.8; 20.4. On Qumran cf. K. G. Kuhn NTS 7, 340 f.; from these and other NT texts Gnilka 255 interprets: to rebuke the sinner in the congregation. But till now only outsiders were under discussion ('the Sons of Disobedience'). Halter* 276 interprets: It is a matter of the continuing conversion of Christians with regard to their way of life, not of the *correctio fraterna*.

[35]Ps. 6.2; Prov. 3.11 f.; Wis. 12.2; Job. 5.17; Sir 18.13; 1 QH 9.23; 18.12.

[36]Wis. 4.20; Syr Baruch 83.3; 2 Esdras 12, 32 f.; cf. Jud. 15.

[37]In Qumran, too, a reprimand of outsiders was expressly rejected (1 QS 9.16).

[38]This was repeatedly assumed, cf. Schlier 239. Some even thought of Christian sectarian circles (cf. Beare 710); rightly against this is Gnilka 256.

[39]It does not say πάντα δὲ τὰ ἐλεγχόμενα = everything revealed, found guilty, but τὰ δὲ πάντα, and this summarizes what 'is done by them in secret'. The Participle is connected to this as a new statement (predicative) (cf. de Wette, Haupt on this passage).

[40]Klöpper, Scott, Staab and Gnilka connect the phrase to ἐλεγχόμενα, Bengel, Haupt, Abbott, Dibelius – Greeven, Schlier, Conzelmann and others to φανεροῦται. Barth 572, n. 74 thinks that the position of ὑπο τοῦ φωτός would allow it to be connected either with what precedes it or with what follows; but the examples he quotes (ἐν ἀγάπῃ Eph. 1.4 f.; ἐν Χριστῷ Gal. 2.17) are not convincing.

light everything wicked and shameful. This fits better with what follows where, in the quotation, Christ himself appears as the source of the light. We can compare the passage in Jn. 3.19, 21 which is related in its metaphorical character and language. Here Christ himself is the 'light' whom people who do wrong do not want to approach so that their deeds may not be 'exposed' (ἐλεγχθῇ) while those who 'do what is true' come to him that their works may 'be made manifest' (φανερωθῇ) as achieved in God. The light has an unveiling function: What is dark is recognisable in its darkness, what is light in its lightness.

14a

Possibly the connected sentence 'for everything that is visible is light' (v. 14a) – whose meaning is puzzling – is intended to explain the function of the light (explanatory γάρ): for all which is exposed by the light stands in the light. If we take 'light' in the succinct sense as the area of salvation (cf. v. 8) and 'exposing' as 'illuminating' or bringing into the light, then it means that Christians should make missionary efforts for their fellow-citizens entangled in their vices: Through 'conviction' Christians realize what their works are and find their way to the light so that they themselves are light.[41] But to be made visible' (φανεροῦσθαι) is not the same as 'to be illuminated' (φωτίζεσθαι) and instead of 'is light' it must rather mean '*becomes* light'. This idea otherwise has no connection with the context. With this interpretation we impose on the parenthesis of v. 14a a burden of proof which it is unable to bear. It is a general statement which illustrates the function of light[42] and steers us back to the self-understanding of the children of light (v. 8).

14b

The closing quotation, a fragment of a song of unknown origin, rounds off the exhoratation to the children of light. The formula of quotation 'hence it is said' (cf. 4.8) provides a loose connection which has no real logical (causal) sense between the three lines of song and the discussion of light, the metaphorical character of which it corresponds to at the end ('and Christ will shine upon you'). The first two lines make up a synthetic parallelism synonymous in content, a call to wake followed by a promise. If the purpose of the paraclesis is that the Christians should reflect on their own personalities, achieve the life in the light made possible by their becoming Christian and keep away from the sinful life of their pagan fellow-citizens which is in the clutches of darkness, the call to waken makes good sense in an address to them. They are in danger of losing the vigilance demanded from Christians (cf. 1 Thess. 5.5 f.; Rom. 13.11–3). But we must

---

[41]Cf. Haupt 211 f.; Schlier 240; K. G. Kuhn, NTS 7 also reaches this view from his understanding of v. 14; the ἐλέγχειν as a call to the sinner to change his ways should lead him to Baptism (345).

[42]Calvin (218 f.) recognized this but understood τὸ φανερούμενον wrongly in the Active sense. ('it is the light which reveals everything'). On the different interpretation cf. Barth 573, who himself makes it refer to Christ's victory over darkness (574, cf. 602). Halter* 639, n. 22: Each person as a new being must constantly allow him/herself to be renewed (4.23). Fischer* 145 suspects textual corruption.

not conclude from this that a sleep of death is meant, from which people called must first be awakened (cf. Haupt 213), because it is a quotation which might originally demand a different situation – even before their becoming Christian. Being incorporated in a letter it gains a new character: Reflect on what was then (before Baptism) called to you! The sleeping in the second line, which was originally understood as the sleep of death,[43] is now seen as a condition of forgetfulness and intoxication (cf. 1 Thess. 5.7) subject to the sphere of night and 'darkness' (ibid. v. 5). In Rom. 13.12 f. Paul commands them to put away the 'works of darkness' which he perceives in a dissipated life. The 'arising from sleep' is, to be sure, in Paul eschatologically motivated, with a view to the approaching Day of the Lord. In Eph. it is otherwise: Christ will 'illuminate' those who shake off (deathlike) sleep, shine out like a star,[44] fill them with new light and lustre. Then the 'rising from the dead' is not to be referred to those who are still spiritually dead but refers to the metaphor of the sleeper who rises to new life. Hence it is still the best explanation that here a fragment from the baptismal liturgy is applied to the situation of those already baptized to remind them of the radiant life which has been granted to them in Baptism.

The question of the quotation's origin has been debated since early times. Some of the Church Fathers thought it came from the OT (e.g. Is. 60.1)) and some from an apocryphal writing:[45] but these were only vague conjectures to justify the character of the quotation. Clement of Alexandria thought it was a Saying about Jesus, and after 'Christ will shine upon you' he also adds: 'the Lord, the sun of the Resurrection who was born before the Morning Star, who has given life through his own rays'.[46] In more recent times the view of R. Reitzenstein has had a large following. He thinks that the call to awaken goes back to a gnostic, ultimately Iranian idea. In a Turfan fragment, two verses of a Zarathustra hymn read: 'Shake off the drunkenness in which you have fallen asleep, awaken and look at me. Salvation upon you from the world of joy from which I have been sent for your sake'.[47] In another text from an alchemistic writing it says: 'Awake out of Hades, come up out of the grave and be awakened from darkness . . .'[48] There are many

---

[43]For the true 'sleepers', i.e. the deceased, κοιμᾶσθαι is normally used (Jn. 11.11 f.; Acts 7.60; 13.36; 1 Thess. 4.13–15; 1 Cor. 7.39; 11.30; 15.6 and often); but cf. also καθεύδειν in Mk. 5.39 and parallels. On the idea of the sleep of death, cf. P. Hoffmann, *Die Toten in Christus*, 1966 (NTA NF 2), 186–206; H. Balz, TDNT VIII, 548 f.

[44]Cf. Job 25.5; 31.26; in the Orph Hymn 50.9 of Bacchus: 'shining on mortals and immortals'; in Act Thom 34 the Apostle says of the young man who has been revived that he has been shone upon (by light). Cf. Pr-Bauer 602. – The early but weakly attested variant ἐπιψαύσεις τοῦ Χριστοῦ (= you will have a share in Christ) D* b MVict Ambst can be explained from its similar sound in Greek, but it does not fit so well in the talk about light.

[45]Epiph Haer 42, 12, 3 (GCS Holl II, 179 f.) attributes the quotation to 'Elijah' (the Apoc El), other Fathers to an Apocryphon of Jeremiah. Cf. on this Resch (p. 210 n. 17) 32–4; A.-M. Denis, *Introduction aux pseudépigraphes grecs d'Ancien Testament*, Leiden 1970, 76 f., 165 f., 284.

[46]Prot IX, 84 (I, 63). In his view the Lord therewith admonishes those who have gone astray (τοὺς πεπλανημένους). Probably this is an extension which goes back to him; cf. Dölger* 368: 'Clement expands the sentence in the Letter to the Ephesians (where from we do not know) . . . '; Schille, *Frühchristliche Hymnen* 95 f.; Gnilka 260, n. 4 – Dibelius – Greeven 91 think it not impossible, even though it cannot be proved, that Clement restores the real continuation of the saying.

[47]Quoted according to Reitzenstein, *Hell Myst* 58.

[48]Ibid 314; cf. Reitzenstein, *Ir Erl* 135–7. Called into play by Fischer* 143 along with other texts to lead back to the call to wake in the Mystery Cults.

gnostic texts which might be used here, from Hermetic and Mandaean literature but also from Christian Gnosis (Act Thom. 110; Od Sol. 8.3–5; 11.13 f.; 15.1–3).[49] They relate to the gnostic myth according to which the soul is snatched by the call to wake from sleep and drunkenness and summoned back to its heavenly home. But the gnostic derivation, which still has its supporters,[50] might at the most be an analogous articulation to provide documentation since the content is different, for nowhere does Eph. recognize the pre-existence of souls, a pneumatic core in humanity, an ascent of the soul. The same holds for the Mystery Cults in which the call to awaken was given to the members of the cult at their initiation.[51] Another perspective opens up in early Judaism. After the discovery of the Qumran documents K. G. Kuhn drew attention, along with Ps Sol. 16, 1–4, to comparable texts from Qumran (1 QH. 3.19–21; in relation to 'shine upon', Damasc 20.25 f.; 1 QH 4.5 f., 23; 9.31) in which the same metaphors are used for the conversion of the sinner and the battle against sins.[52] These texts are indeed closer to the Christian ideas bound up with Baptism even if Christian Baptism has no parallel in Qumran as a part of salvation.

Some of the Church Fathers already asserted that the origin of the three lines lay in a Christian hymn.[53] It seems reasonable to suppose that it would have been from a *baptismal* hymn, and this idea is strengthened by the baptismal text from the syr. Didascalia 21 to which F. J. Dölger drew attention.[54] Here the Jewish-Christians are told: 'You have seen the great Light, our Lord, Jesus Christ' and the Gentiles: 'A great light has arisen over you'. Christ as a 'dawning from on high' (cf. Luke 1.78 f.), 'Sun of the Resurrection' etc. was a popular symbol in the early Church.[55] The use of baptismal concepts in a modal admonition which is already to be found in Paul (cf. Rom. 6.3 f.) (without this metaphor) with a deep theological insight which Eph. does not reach, occurs in this passage in a liturgical reminiscence – which, however, had the same goal in mind.[56]

Summary

The two parts of the paraclesis 5.3–14 which can be recognized in vv. 3–7 and 8–14 are related to one another, dove-tailed by v. 7 and arranged in an intensification from a description of dark things to a bright perspective. In

[49]Cf. Jonas, *Gnosis* I, 126–33; Schlier 241. Dölger* 369 f. also quotes Od Sol 15 as a baptismal text. It is close to the text in Clem Al.

[50]Cf. Lindemann, *Aufhebung der Zeit* 234 f.; H. Conzelmann TDNT IX, 347 f.

[51]Cf. already E. Norden, *Agnostos Theos. Untersuchungen zur Formengeschichte religiöser Rede*, Stuttgart [4]1956, 258 n. 1; Dibelius – Greeven 91 and other Commentaries; Fischer* 142 f. For criticism cf. G. Wagner, *Das religionsgeschichtliche Problem von Römer 6.1–11*, 1962 (AThANT 39). Yet the relationship of Christian Baptism and the Mystery Cults is still assessed variedly.

[52]NTS 7, 341–5. On earlier attempts to compare Qumran texts with Eph. 5.3–11, cf. H. Braun, 'Qumran und das NT', ThT 29 (1963) 239–42.

[53]Theodoret of Cyrrhus, who referred to other expositors (MPG 82, 544 f.); Severian of Gabala in Staab 311.

[54]Dölger 366 f. with a reprint of the full text.

[55]To this also belongs a fragment of Melito of Sardis 'On the Baptismal Bath', German translation and explanation in Dölger* 342–5; Greek text with English translation in St. G. Hall, *Melito of Sardis, On Pascha and Fragments*, Oxford 1979, 70–3. Here (under §4) Christ is described as 'the sun of the ascent which also appeared to those in Hades and to mortals on earth, and as sole sun he rose from heaven'. On Christ as sun in the Morning Hymn v Dölger* 379–410.

[56]The opinion of Noack that the last line refers to Christ's Parousia rightly found no approval.

this respect this paraclesis corresponds to the two preceding in 4.17–24 and 4.25–5,2. As in 4.17–19 there is a confrontation with the pagan immorality by which the Christians are surrounded and it is a matter of extreme importance to strengthen the Christian congregations in their new way of life made possible and demanded by God's New Creation (4,24) and preserve them from a relapse into that pernicious way of life. The quotation which Paul once declaimed to the Corinthians: 'Bad company ruins good morals' (1 Cor. 15.33) gains greater significance at a time when the Christian congregations (probably in the wider surroundings of Ephesus) have already gained an established position in the bourgeois society which has still to a great extent an un-Christian character. The author is not concerned with the trial of the depraved, blaspheming pagans (cf. 1 Pet. 4.3–6) and is also not simply delivering a homily for his Christian readers. More important for him is to remind the Christians of the novelty and different quality of their existence as Christians based on their Baptism, and to warn them of the danger of being dazzled by the glitter of a life of pleasure, giving heed to empty words (v. 6) and participating in 'unfruitful works' (v. 11) caused by passion.

In the first part he defines more precisely the behaviour and deeds he has in mind. Above all he is thinking of sexual promiscuity and indecency, and then of avarice and acquisitiveness which are considered typically pagan vices. As a defence against such behaviour the author does use the customary Hellenistic motif of the impertinent and improper (v. 4) but he favours the Christian motif ('as is fitting among saints', participation in the Kingdom of Christ and of God.) The motivation reaches deeper in the second part in the comparison between light and darkness (vv. 8–14). Although the metaphor is frequently used elsewhere –in Hellenistic, Jewish and early Christian writings – here it attains a particular meaningfulness. The addressees were themselves once darkness but now they are 'light in the Lord' and accordingly should live as 'Children of light!' They should make every attempt to test and decide in favour of 'what is pleasing to the Lord'. Mastered by the power of the light which proceeds from Christ and permeates them they should also produce the 'fruit of light'. Behind this idea lies the experience of Baptism as the closing quotation (v. 14) – probably stemming from the Baptismal Liturgy – also bears out. Baptism is not simply a single act, but constantly bathes the whole life of the baptized in light. Anyone who has once experienced this novel experience, the different quality of Christian life (even if realisation only comes after Baptism) will continually reject the temptations of a sinful life.

The call in the last verses to 'expose' or 'convict' – i.e. to show the works of darkness for what they are (v. 11b) is not intended to encourage the Christians to attempt directly to convert the people who have fallen into shameless vices. Its intention is rather to strengthen their faith in the power of light: In their witness to another way of life filled by the light of Christ – which also includes an exposure of evil and a charge against those who do it – the realm of light presses forward, Christ himself becomes effective and darkness loses its menacing influence. The living witness of a Christian existence is more important than all talking and persuading.

Again, as in the preceding sections, the question is raised whether such a black/white depiction and withdrawal from the non-Christian environment is still possible in today's pluralistic society. Christians who themselves are frequently far removed from a decidedly Christian, different way of life often encounter people who, though not believers in Jesus Christ lead morally high-standing lives and are called to co-operate with all those concerned for the true good of humankind. Yet the task of preserving the Christian proprium and of introducing it into the struggle for ethical norms in the moral sphere of a society which has become wavering continues to be necessary. This can only take place successfully if Christians put the Christian values into practice in a convincing way and thus communicate to their environment the light which comes from Christ.

3. THE LIFE OF THE CHRISTIAN CONGREGATION (5.15–6.9)

After making the distinction from the non-Christian environment, the author now considers the life of Christians among themselves. He clearly distinguishes this new chapter on Christian existence in this world by the introductory exhortation: 'Therefore pay careful attention to how you lead your lives . . .'. The main line of thought in the paraclesis is once again evident: 4.1 – live lives appropriate to the Christian calling, as members of Christ's Church; 4.17 – no longer lead lives like the pagans; 5.15 – consider carefully how to realize the Christian way of life in your own community of fellow-Christians. To this extent *these* passages which use περιπατεῖν (to lead life) represent a real scheme for dividing into sections. The third part on the realization of a Christian existence extends to 6.9 because with 6.10, emphasized by 'as for the rest' (τοῦ λοιποῦ), there begins a final exhortation to stand fast, resist and fight with God's weapons in this age which is still embroiled in evil (6.10–20).

Within this part of the paraclesis the section 5.15–20 is separated from the following 'Haustafel' (5.21–6.9) which itself can also be divided into two according to its emphases: the attitude of married couples in relation to Christ and his Church (5.21–33) and the behaviour of children and parents, slaves and masters (6.1–9). The end of the section devoted to life in the congregation – 5.15–20 – is not immediately clear because v. 21, a Participial Phrase, appears outwardly to belong to the structure which precedes it. Consequently many editions of the text take 5.21 with the preceding section;[1] but technical aspects and content demand that we make the division before this verse. The doxological phrase in 5.20 builds a natural rhetorical conclusion; then the command to wives (v. 22) needs the verb in v. 21; v. 21 and v. 22 also belong together with regard to content, while v. 21 introduces a new idea different from the preceding remarks. After the fundamental demand for mutual subordination in reverence of

---

[1]So also the 3rd Edition of 'The Greek New Testament' of the United Bible Societies; Nestle-Aland, however, now ends the section after v. 20. Commentaries and the more recent translations have been doing this for some time.

Christ – v. 21 – (which can be expressed in a Participle) the author passes over immediately under this 'title' to discuss rules for the household.

In spite of 5.15–17, it is only with difficulty that we can conceive the paraclesis so divided as an instruction on 'Christian wisdom' (Gnilka). This idea does not surface again in what follows; rather these verses form a bridge from the section 5.3–14, in which separation from the immoral environment is called for, to the exhortations for the common life of Christians in the congregation. This is made clear in the continued opposition to the heathen: 'not as fools, but as wise men' (v. 15), 'not lacking understanding, but understanding ...' (v. 17). Both sections are joined by consideration of the will of the Lord (cf. v. 17 with v. 10). The final section 6.10–20 with its call to battle against the powers of evil can later be connected with v. 16 ('Redeem time, for the days are evil'). In 5.18–20 attention is given principally to the worshipping life of the congregation but not so exclusively that we must consider this the subject matter. The cultic eulogy which is alluded to in v. 19 is simply the expression of that basic Christian mood which can be nothing other than 'sober intoxication in the Spirit' (cf. v. 18) and continual thanksgiving (v. 20). Hence for the section 5.15–20 we prefer the title 'Spiritual life in the Congregation'. The author steers our attention from the common life of the congregation to the Christian households in which the Christians day by day must give proof of their calling.

3.a Spiritual Life in the Congregation (5.15–20)

Literature

H. Lewy, *Sobria ebrietas*, 1929 (BZNW 9).

J. M. Nielen, *Gebet und Gottesdienst im Neuen Testament*, Freiburg i. Br. 1934.

G. Delling, *Der Gottesdienst im Neuen Testament*, Göttingen 1952.

A. Hamman, *La prière, I Le Nouveau Testament*, Tournai 1959.

F. Hahn, *Der urchristliche Gottesdienst*, 1970 (SBS 41).

15 Therefore pay careful attention to how you lead your lives,
    not like fools, but as wise men!
16 Redeem time; for the days are evil.
17 Hence do not become lacking in understanding,
    but understand what is the Lord's will.
18 Do not become intoxicated with wine – that is dissolute – but let
    yourselves be filled with (the) Spirit.
19 Speak to one another with psalms and hymns and spiritual songs.
    sing with your hearts and praise the Lord.
20 Give thanks continually to God the Father for everything
    in the name of our Lord, Jesus Christ!

Analysis

Syntactically this unit is constructed in the style usual for a paraclesis, mainly with Imperatives and connected Participles which explain and continue the commands. The main exhortation in v. 15 – to pay careful attention as to how they conduct their lives – is followed first by the contrast 'not like fools but as wise men' which is explained by a Participial Clause (v. 16). Hence 'redeem time' does not introduce a new instruction but illustrates what is the essence of Christian wisdom and v. 16b, a Causal Clause, (ὅτι) gives the reason why we must make the most of time. The conclusion in v. 17 (διὰ τοῦτο) reinforces with a new Imperative the same command which we found already in v. 15. Hence the three verses represent a unit in itself which is governed by the contrast 'foolish – wise'. This way of contrasting connects the small unit with the preceding section 5.3–14, to which it is also joined by οὖν (therefore).

With v. 18 a new command is introduced. This too is in the form of an antithesis (μὴ -ἀλλά): intoxication with wine is contrasted with being filled with the (Holy) Spirit, both in the Imperative. That a real (and not merely a rhetorical) contrast lies behind this is made clear by the emphatic Relative Clause which is added to the warning against intoxication by wine: therein lies dissoluteness. But from here on antitheses disappear and everything comes under the command to be filled with the Spirit. Three Participial Clauses reveal what is expected and demanded from Christians filled with the Spirit: they should speak to one another (λαλοῦντες) with psalms, hymns and spiritual songs (v. 19a), sing with their hearts and praise the Lord (ἄδοντες καὶ ψάλλοντες) (v. 19b) and give thanks continually (εὐχαριστοῦντες) for everything (v. 20). If, then, v. 18 in its contrast between intoxication with wine and being filled with the Spirit still stands under the influence of vv. 15–17, it nevertheless builds a bridge to a positive description. The three Participles which are arranged in a similar way and are similar in content reveal the desire for a real description of activity filled with the Spirit which is offered to the members of the congregation. This is the centre of the positive command which is concluded with a melodious, almost liturgical stylized formulation ('to God the Father in the name of our Lord, Jesus Christ').

On the semantic level (cf. 1.8–17) the idea of Christian wisdom and understanding is not new but here it is emphasized by the comparison with foolishness and lack of judgement. The 'evil days' recall the rule of the powers opposed to God, the 'spirit which is active now in the Sons of Disobedience' (2.2) and the 'wrath of God' which comes upon such people (5.6). There has also already been mention of spiritual blessing (1.3) and the effect of the Spirit on Christians (3.16); but the description of spiritual intoxication which makes itself known outwardly in song and praise (v. 19a) and is impressed upon the heart (v. 19b) is new and is clearly a particular concern in this section.

The author has taken over individual constituents of this paraclesis from Col. Verses. 15–16 make use of Col. 4.5: 'Conduct your lives with wisdom towards outsiders, redeem time!' – which, however, in Col. comes after the rules for the household, among various other exhortations. The giving of priority to and emphasis of this command can be explained by its connection with the paraclesis of 5.3–14. Only after this does the author turn to the description of the spiritual life in the congregation which he has taken over from Col. 3.16 with slight variation.

He also did this in the composition of the paraclesis as a whole; for after the call to Christian love (Col. 3.12–14) which our author took into account in 4.32–5.2 there follows in Col. 3.15–17 encouragement for congregational life, which Eph. takes over – admittedly only in part. It is significant that the author omits the principal exhortation which gives the paraclesis in Col. its particular character[2] 'Let the Word of Christ dwell among you richly' – and instead introduces the warning 'Do not become intoxicated with wine' which for its part is missing in Col. Hence there arises a different perspective. Attention is directed less to the richness of the Word of Christ – which should be communicated to the congregation in teaching and instruction (Col. 3.16b) and find response in praise and thankfulness (16c) – than to the behaviour of Christians, who should be enabled to serve their Lord amid a different environment and be filled and led in their fellowship by the joy of the Holy Spirit. In this way the whole section moves more forcefully under the practical reference of a Christian way of coping with life.

Exegesis

15

Out of the previous expositions, especially on living in the light in view of the surrounding darkness (5.8–14) there arises (οὖν) the command to order their lives not as fools (ἄσοφοι = not wise) but as wise men. The call to heightened attention,[3] emphasized by ἀκριβῶς (= exactly, carefully) is directed at how they actually lead their lives. After his gloomy description of how the heathen live the author now wants to cross to a positive instruction for the realization of a Christian existence which he now provides for their life in the congregation (vv. 18–20) and everyday life as Christians ('Haustafel'). In the transition he again confronts the Christians with the depraved people in their surroundings; otherwise the comparison between foolish/wise, not understanding/understanding the will of the Lord and also the characterizing of the present time as 'evil' would scarcely be justified. The choice of expression 'wise' is influenced by Col. 4.5, where the characteristic phrase 'redeem time' (Eph. 5.16) is also found. The 'outsiders' named there whom the Christians should meet 'with wisdom' are for Eph. the foolish and those who do not understand. Already in the OT Wisdom-tradition this means those foolish people who do not know God and deny him by the way they behave.[4] If the Christians are to stand

---

[2] Cf. Schweizer, *Colossians* on this passage.

[3] The Imperative βλέπετε (take heed!) is particularly characteristic of the Marcan speech about the Last Days (Mk 13.5, 9, 23, 33) but also Acts 13.40; 1 Cor. 8.9; Gal. 5.13, Heb. 3.12; 2 Jn. 8. In Eph. 5.15 the motif of the Evil Days has no effect. -ἀκριβῶς (carefully), used in a similar way in 1 Thess. 5.2 is to be taken with βλέπετε as in the majority of the MSS and not with περιπατεῖτε (D F G Ψ MLatt b m* sy).

[4] Cf. Deut. 32.6 LXX: you foolish (μωρός) and senseless (οὐχὶ σοφος) people; Jer. 4.22; Prov. 1.22; 6.12; it occurs often in Eccles, Wis Sol., Sir. In the Greek Bible as well as μωρός we often find ἄφρων. Cf. further G. Bertram, TDNT IV, 833–6; ibid. IX, 224–6. This group of words is also met with in Qumran, cf. especially 1 QS 4.24 for the two types of people: 'They live in wisdom and in foolishness . . .'; 1 QH 13.3 f.; Damasc. 15.15. A 'Teacher of Wisdom' is appointed for the Community 1 QS 3.13; 9.12–21; Damasc. 12.21. Cf. Nötscher, *Terminologie* 46.51 f.

out from such people as 'wise', what is here meant is that wisdom which for devout Jews is shown in living according to God's instruction (the Torah);[5] for Christians the 'will of the Lord' is decisive (v. 17).

16

The exhortation is made more urgent by the motive of the 'redemption of time', for making the best use of everything that belongs to the present time.[6] If what is said in Col. 4.5 is perhaps to be understood as trying to win over the outsiders,[7] the addition here of 'for the days are evil' lends a different perspective. Just because the days are overshadowed by the power of evil Christians should exhaust every possibility of the 'appropriate time' (καιρός).[8] But is there not a contradiction here that opportunities for doing good desired by the Lord should arise from the 'evil days'? For Christians it is the same time which, outwardly ruled by evil, is the 'acceptable time, the Day of Salvation' (2 Cor. 6.2), the time which is available for and demands good works (cf. Gal. 6.10). It is just because the readers are surrounded by sin and darkness that they should recognize the call of time which places them under an obligation as the Children of Light to live a different kind of life. Hence the 'evil days' stress the gloomy horizon torn open in 5.8–10 and summon Christians in the midst of this world to lead their lives 'wisely' in the light of the Lord.

17

That is confirmed by this exhortation, which picks up that of v. 15. 'Lacking in understanding' is simply another expression for the foolishness of those people who disregard God. In the Greek Bible it is even more common (cf. n. 4). We can vacillate as to how we are to understand the Greek Imperative γίνεσθε: 'become!' or 'be!' or 'prove yourselves!'[9] Even if the verb frequently in a command need mean nothing more than 'be!',[10] in the context it may also contain a warning: Christians should not accommodate themselves to the ignorance, the foolishness which is manifest in the sinful

[5]Wisdom is clearly equated with the Torah in Sir, e.g. 19.20: All wisdom is fear of the Lord, and all wisdom is the fulfilling of the Law; 32.14–33, 6; 39.6–11 (the scribes), then also in apocalyptic and Rabbinic literature. There is an abundance of material in U. Wilckens, TDNT VII, 503–7.

[6]According to Pr-Bauer 537 the oldest evidence for this is the Verbum Herakleides (third Century BC): to repay the claims of a victim – similarly Mart Pol. 2.3. F. Büchsel, TDNT I, 128 explains the word – which can have other meanings (cf. Gal. 3.13; 4.5) – in its context more correctly as an intensive purchasing, a purchasing which exhausts the possibilities available.

[7]Cf. Schweizer, *Colossians* on the passage.

[8]Frequently with this sense in Classical literature; in the NT it means the time of salvation brought in by God which also, however, makes demands upon humanity, cf. Mk. 1.15; Lk. 12.56; 19.44; 21.36; Rom. 13.11; 1 Cor. 7.29; 2 Cor. 6.2; Gal. 6.10. In Eph. the element of tension in καιρός has otherwise faded (cf. 1.10; 2.12; 6.18), a sign that in 5.16 the author is using a phrase already formed. G. Delling, TDNT III, 460 is right in seeing that in the situation of the Christian as opposed to the non-Christian there is a special compulsion for this (to use every opportunity).

[9]Cf. Pr-Bauer 317 f. (s.v. II.1); Schnackenburg, *John* III, 419–20, n. 38 (on 15.8) and 475, n. 103 (on 20.27).

[10]Cf. Mt. 10.16; Lk. 12.40 par; Jn. 20.27; Rom. 12.16; 1 Cor. 4.16 and often; Col. 3.15.

lives of other people. The antithetical 'understand what is the Lord's will!' brings to mind v. 10 where there is sharp emphasis on the Christian way of life determined by the will of Christ, their Lord[11] with the 'unfruitful works of darkness'. Christian 'wisdom' is therefore a way of behaving oriented on the instruction of the heavenly Lord in the midst of a world which has dissociated itself from God by its own foolishness.

18

Suddenly and unexpectedly there follows the command 'Do not become intoxicated with wine!' The connecting καί ('and') marks the transition from the general to the particular.[12] The author steers towards the spiritual fulfilment and emotion which should be specially noticeable in the congregations assembled for worship. If in this context he warns against intoxication, we need not assume that behind this warning lie abuses in the celebration of the Lord's Supper as in Corinth (cf. 1 Cor. 11.21 f.); the motive ('that is dissolute' would be far too weak for this. The interjection is still part of the consideration of the behaviour of those around them; the negative formulation (καὶ μή) continues the Clauses with μή in v. 15 and v. 16. The identification of drunkenness as 'dissoluteness'[13] fits with the rejection of pagan immorality in similar general ethical motives in the previous section (5.3 f.,12). We need not even think of cultic orgies, bacchanaliae, or the cult of the wine-god Dionysus which flourished in Asia Minor. It is enough to assume the same opposition to a life given over to gluttony and drunkenness to which Paul also alludes in Rom. 13.13 (cf. also in 1 Thess. 5.7b). What *is* peculiar to Eph. is the comparison between being filled with drink and being filled with the Spirit. Something similar can be found in the reaction of one group of people who experienced the spiritual preaching of the Apostles at Pentecost: 'They are full of sweet wine' (Acts 2.13); but it is improbable that the author of Eph. knew this Lucan description.[14] It is also completely unnecessary since there are traces of a long tradition for such a comparison. Philo takes up the story of Hannah, whose beseeching prayers in the temple at Shiloh were attributed by the High Priest, Eli, to drunkenness (1 Sam 1.12–14). Out of this the Jewish philosopher of religion develops his conception of another kind of drunkenness. 'For those who are carried away by God (θεοφορήτοις), not only is the soul wont to be roused and worked up into a frenzy but even the body becomes red and is flushed. Many ignorant people are misled and suppose the sober to be drunk because they have absorbed all that is good at one time like pure wine and perfect virtue has congenially

---

[11]The v. 1. τοῦ θεοῦ A81 365 al a d Vg^cl sy^p is influenced by the phrase 'will of God' which predominates in Paul (cf. 1 Thess. 4.3; 5.18; Rom. 12.2; 15.32; 2 Cor. 8.5 et al). In Eph. the κύριος is always Christ who is deliberately named here as in 5.10.

[12]Cf. Abbott 160 f., who points to Mk 16.7; 1.5.

[13]The expression is frequently used in connection with the enjoyment of wine and an extravagant life. Cf. Aristot Eth. Nic. IV.1: 'We name the immoderate and those who are too unrestrained ἀσώτους (dissolute)'; Athen 11 (485;): 'Those who are too much given to inebriation and dissoluteness'. 1 Pet. 4.4 also alludes to the wild drinking-sessions of the heathen (v. 3) with this expression. Test Jud. 16.1 warns against this in a similar way. Further in Pr-Bauer 237; W. Foerster, TDNT I, 506 f.; Spicq, *Notes* I, 154–6.

[14]Cf. Dibelius – Greeven who come out against Mitton, *Ephesians* 205 f.

drunk their health' (Ebr. 147 f.). This is the idea of the 'sober inebriation' (sobria ebrietas) which Philo develops in many other places and which had a considerable after-effect in the Church Fathers.[15] But there are also differences between Philo and Eph. 5.18 which we must not overlook: What in Philo is described as a condition of the soul (more precisely of the νοῦς, the human reason) is in Eph. the effect of the divine Spirit.[16] There is also no mention in Eph. of effects upon the body or ecstatic phenomena. The comparison with drunkenness has its clear limits for being filled with the Spirit. The change from the Dative (οἴνῳ – with wine) to the Preposition ἐν is not unimportant: Christians should allow themselves to be filled *by* the Spirit (Instrumental use of ἐν) and at the same time *with* him.[17] The challenge cannot mean that they have the Spirit at their disposal – an idea contradictory to every other similar statement (cf. 3.16) – but rather that they should keep themselves ready for him, open their hearts to him. The Spirit is seen in an active, dynamic rôle, as is shown in what follows; he has an 'inspiring' effect but does not impart any special charismata as in Corinth (glossolalia, prophecy).[18]

19

The effect of the Spirit with which the author is concerned is the congregational worship produced by the Spirit. It we keep in view the wild orgies of other people as a contrasting background, we can recognize the intention of emphasizing the community of Christians enflamed by the divine Spirit gathered together to give praise and thanks to God.[19] The three Participles which describe and encourage this event, which is filled with the Spirit and bursts forth in songs and hymns, should be taken as a unit, albeit one with a certain intensification: speaking to one another – singing from the heart – giving thanks. The singing 'to one another' (ἑαυτοῖς) (not necessarily antiphonally)[20] underlines the communal character. 'Psalms, hymns and spiritual songs' can only with difficulty be differentiated: here we have an example – as with the three Verbs – of the author's stylistic preference for the triplicate. He is not talking of OT psalms and praises, but about Christian ones – perhaps in part songs composed and performed by individual members (cf. 1 Cor. 14.26), but on the whole about hymns they know in common. Such already belonged at this period to the congregations' liturgical treasury, especially Hymns of

---

[15]Cf. Lewy* 3–41 (Philo); 108–64 (Patristic).

[16]The occasional interpretation of ἐν πνεύματι as meaning in their human spirits is erroneous. If we take the expression as local, we then need an indication of with what the spirit is to be filled.

[17]The use of ἐν with πληροῦσθαι remains conspicuous because Gal. 5.14; Rom. 8.4; Col. 2.10 are not really parallel. On 'to fill with' cf. Bl-Debr §172.3; G. Delling, TDNT VI, 291, n. 27. Ernst, *Pleroma* 103, translates it as 'be filled by the Spirit' (differently 128 'in the Spirit'). Possibly the author wanted to emphasize the difference to being filled with wine.

[18]Cf. Dibelius – Greeven 92; E. Schweizer, TDNT VI, 423.

[19]Cf. Philo, Vit Cont. 88 f. on the gatherings of the Therapeutae in Egypt: 'Their thoughts are good, the assemblies splendid, the dancers dignified; the goal of thoughts, readings and dancers is devoutness. Intoxicated (μεθυσθέντες) till morning by this splendid inebriation, they neither let their heads nod nor close their eyes . . .'

[20]Cf. eg: Pliny the Younger X, 96.7; Delling, *Gottesdienst* 84 f.

Christ. We get an idea of these from Phil. 2.6–11; Col. 1.15–20 (making allowance for editorial additions); 1 Tim. 3.16 and the Logos-Hymn which can be extracted from Jn. 1.1–16.[21] The addition 'spiritual',[22] which initially belongs with 'songs' (ᾠδαί) can be applied to all three expressions;[23] it characterizes all that the congregation sings as being inspired and produced by the Spirit.

The second line with its 'sing and praise' (ᾄδοντες καὶ ψάλλοντες) is connected to the afore-mentioned 'psalms . . . and songs' (ψαλμοῖς . . . καὶ ᾠδαῖς) in a characteristic chiasmus, and heightens what is said by the reference to the heart. 'With your hearts' does not mean that their mouths should remain silent, but has the meaning of 'from the heart', 'from the bottom of your heart'[24] – naturally not simply in the psychological sense. It means rather that the Spirit with his power should take hold of the 'inner person' (cf. 3.16 f.) and the outward song should be produced by the inner dynamic. In contrast to Col. 3.16 the praise is directed to the 'Lord', that is, to Christ, and only in the third line (v. 20) is thanks then given to God the Father 'in the name of our Lord, Jesus Christ'. The concentration on worship filled by the Spirit as a contrast to the non-Chritian world with its false intoxication means that we do not have a complete picture of worship at Ephesus. Certainly preaching and teaching must have formed a part of worship there too (cf. Col. 3.16; Eph. 4.20).[25]

20

Already in the OT psalms and in the Hodajoth (songs of Praise and Thanksgiving) of Qumran thanksgiving is closely connected with praise. We cannot discern from the wording a 'eucharistic' interpretation in the narrower sense – i.e. with relation to the celebration of the Lord's Supper.[26] The verb (εὐχαριστεῖν) does not yet necessarily have the special overtone which it has in the Didache, Ignatius of Antioch and Justin.[27] In Col.

[21]On the predomination of Hymns of Christ in contrast to Hymns of God cf. Deichgräber, *Gotteshymnus* 106 and the whole of the following section. On Psalmody and Hymnody cf. also Nielen* 212–18; Delling* 84 f.

[22]The attribute is omitted in several important MSS (p[46] B b d) but makes good sense as a counterpart to ἐν πνεύματι. For the Greeks ᾠδαί are songs of all kinds, in the LXX it is usually the translation of שִׁיר, often connected in the psalm-title with ψαλμός (Song of a Psalm). On the character of the ᾠδή as an inspired liturgical song cf. H. Schlier, TDNT I, 164 f.

[23]Cf. Bl-Debr § 135.3; Attributes which are connected with several nouns habitually follow the noun closest to them, thus Lk. 10.1; 1 Thess. 5.23; Heb. 9.9; Jas. 1.17.

[24]The variants with ἐν (Singular or Plural) which in fact denotes the same as the Dative are probably influenced by Col. 3.16. G. Delling, TDNT VIII, 498 n. 66 thinks that ἐν corresponds to the Hebrew ב in Ps. 9.2; 85.12; 110.1; 137.1 LXX.

[25]It is difficult to establish how the spoken service in the congregations was carried out. It is still controversial whether there were readings from the OT; cf. W. Bauer, *Der Wortgottesdienst der ältesten Christen* (1930), printed in *Aufsätze und kleine Schriften*, Tübingen 1967, 155–209, especially 188–93 (negative); Delling* 89–98; Hahn* 49 f. (positive).

[26]Differently Schlier 248 f. He also sees the third Participle as being subordinate to the first two ('in that you give thanks'); this is the offering of the prayer of thanksgiving at the Lord's Supper. Gnilka 373 leaves the question open. E. Lohse is critical in *Die Briefe an die Kolosser und an Philemon*, 1968 (KEK [14]IX/2), 219 n. 1; H. Conzelmann, TDNT IX, 414, n. 78.

[27]Did. 9.1–3; 10.1–4.7; 14.1; Just Apol. 65.5; 66.2; 67.5; cf. the noun εὐχαριστία in Did. 9.1–5; Ign. Eph. 13.1; Phld. 4.1; Sm. 7.1; 8.1; Just Apol. 65.3; 66.1; Dial. 41.1, 3; 117.1. Cf. Hamman* 292–4; Schnackenburg, *John* II, 16 f.; H. Conzelmann, TDNT IX, 411–15.

3.15–17 the thanksgiving (at the beginning and end of this small unit) is also the most important element; here the Christians should do in the name of the Lord Jesus all that 'they do in word and deed' while they give thanks to God the Father. In Eph. 5.20 the command to give thanks is the crowning thought for the spiritually inspired worship of the congregation. Since everything comes under the aspect of the community moved by the Spirit, we might admittedly ask what form of early Christian worship is pre-supposed. We do not know a great deal about its precise order in the early post-apostolic period. We can assume a form of the liturgy from the hymnic elements in Eph. itself but also from traces in other writings (1 Pet.; Heb.; Rev.). Hence it is possible, even if it cannot be provable for the early period, that the celebration of the Lord's Supper followed the service of preaching as Justin later describes (Apol. 67).[28] Even if it does not say so in words, from the content it is possible that the author has in his mind's eye a celebration connected with the Eucharist. As the prayers in the Didache 10.1–4 show, thanks were given also for the Creator's earthly gifts and for God's mighty works. In our passage the horizon is wide open: give thanks continually, for everything 'in the name of our Lord, Jesus Christ'. This old early-Christian formulation[29] has already here a liturgical ring, but still indicates 'the fullness of Jesus' being and achievement' (Bietenhard). The praise given to the Lord (v. 19) becomes an inclusive thanksgiving to God the Father in view of and in reference to the work of Jesus. The awareness of God's election, redemption and gracious guidance, which gives the Christian understanding of existence its distinguishing character, lives on in thanksgiving. In giving thanks to God Christians acknowledge the inner riches bestowed upon them (cf. 2.7) before which all external lustre of a life taken up with this world pales into insignificance.

Summary

After the negative dissociation from the un-Christian-pagan life-style and the general suggestions for an alternative way of life for the Christians as 'children of the light' (5.8–10) the author proceeds to give positive advice, especially for life in the Christian community. Still opposing the ignorant way of life blinded by foolishness which outsiders follow, he exhorts them to Christian wisdom (v. 15). Because the present age is still surrounded by evil, Christians should seize every possibility God gives them to use the time for good as the Lord directed (vv. 16–17). As the place for reflection and composure, source of the Christian life and manifestation of its prevailing mood, he looks to the common service of worship. In contrast to the intoxication which comes from drunkenness, which characterizes the behaviour of other people, it is necessary to achieve another kind of

[28]O. Cullmann, *Urchristentum und Gottesdienst*, ²1950 (AThANT 3), 29–34, maintains that even in the earliest period there was a regular connection of spoken service and Supper. L. Goppelt, *Die Apostolische und Nachapostolische Zeit*, Göttingen 1962, 143–5 follows him to a certain extent. Hahn* 61 comes out against Cullmann on the basis of a comparison between 1 Cor. 11.17–19 and 1 Cor. 14.

[29]Cf. Nielen* 159–62. – W. Heitmüller, *Im Namen Jesu*, 1903 (FRLANT 2) wished to limit the formula closely to the calling of the name of Jesus; cf. opposing this G. Delling, *Die Zueignung des Heils in der Taufe*, Berlin 1961, especially 53; H. Bietenhard, TDNT V, 272 f.

intoxication, the 'sober inebriation' which is generated by God's Spirit (v. 18). This becomes apparent in the service of worship when those assembled, their hearts enflamed, sing songs of praise and thanksgiving to the Lord and, conscious of how they have been blessed, give thanks continually to God the Father for everything in the name of Jesus Christ (v. 20).

However clearly we see here depicted a congregation enflamed by God's Spirit assembled to praise him in the cult, what the author intends – as is shown by the wide-open horizon in v. 20 – goes farther. The explicit picture forms a counterpart to the powers, aspirations and pleasures which hold sway in the world. The Christian congregation lives from the deeper awareness that they are filled and moved by God's Spirit, that they serve a Lord to whom they owe their liberation from sin, a meaningless existence and fear of death. They know that they may look up to God the Father who remains ever the Giver and discloses to them his riches. In giving thanks they find the true meaning of their existence which proves to be able to bear up even in dark times.

One might question critically whether such a disassociation from the environment and the turning to the internal life of the congregation as it is stressed here does not imply a flight from the world, a retreat into the ghetto. We cannot deny the danger of such a misunderstanding – Paul already had to guard against this (cf. 1 Cor. 5.9–11). But in the situation which this letter presupposes and its author judges, it is of ultimate importance that the congregation then and there should reflect on what is its own special characteristic. The dynamic of the Spirit which is communicated in the service of worship need not lead to rapture and unworldliness but can make everyday life rational and pervade it in a productive way.

3.b ('Haustafel') The Behaviour of Married People with Reference to Christ and his Church (5.21–33)

Literature

On the 'Haustafeln' v. most recently:

J. E. Crouch, *The Origin and Intention of the Colossian Haustafel*, 1972 (FRLANT 109).

W. Schrage, 'Zur Ethik der neutestamentlichen Haustafeln', NTS 21 (1975) 1–22.

E. Schweizer, 'Die Weltlichkeit des Neuen Testaments: die Haustafeln', in *Beiträge zur alttestamentlichen Theologie* (FS W. Zimmerli), ed. R. Smend, Göttingen 1977, 397–413; also *Colossians* Excursus 213–20.

J. Gnilka, *Der Kolosserbrief*, 1980 (HThK X/i), Exk 205–16.

K. Thraede, 'Zum historischen Hintergrund der "Haustafeln" im Neuen Testament', in *Pietas* (FS B. Kötting), Münster i. W. 1980, 359–68.

Literature on 5.21–33:

R. A. Batey, 'Jewish Gnosticism and the "Hieros Gamos" of Eph. V, 21–33', NTS 10

(1963/64) 121–27; and 'The MIA ΣΑΡΞ. Union of Christ and the Church', NTS 13 (1966/67) 270–81.

E. Kähler, *Die Frau in den paulinischen Briefen*, Zürich-Frankfurt 1960, 88–140.

J. Cambier, 'Le grand mystère concernant le Christ et son Eglise. Eph. 5.22–33', Bib. 47 (1966) 43–90; Baltensweiler, *Die Ehe im Neuen Testament*, 1967 (AThANT 52), 218–35.

E. Kamlah, 'Ὑποτάσσεσθαι in den neutestamentlichen "Haustafeln"', in *Verborum Veritas* (FS G. Stählin), Wuppertal 1970, 237–43.

J. P. Sampley, *'And the Two shall become One Flesh'*, 1971 (MSSNTS 16).

Fischer, *Tendenz* 176–200.

A. di Marco, '"Misterium hoc magnum est . . ." (Ef. 5.32)', Laur. 14 (1973) 43–80.

D. M. Lloyd-Jones, *Life in the Spirit – in Marriage, Home and Work. An Exposition of Eph. 5:18 to 6:9*, Edinburgh 1974.

A. Feuillet, 'La dignité et le rôle de la femme d'après quelques textes pauliniennes: comparaison avec l'Ancien Testament', NTS 21 (1975) 157–91.

Halter, *Taufe* 281–86.

F. Hahn, 'Die christologische Begründung urchristlicher Paränese', ZNW 72 (1981) 88–99, more specifically 96–9.

The following so-called 'Haustafel' (5.21–6.9) which is directed in paired exhortations to the individual members of the household (married couples 5.21–33; children and parents 6.1–4; slaves and masters 6.5–9) raises many questions, particularly about the origin and individuality of this literary form. Here we can neither enter into the turbulent history of research[1] nor extend our view to the other Haustafeln in the NT.[2] For Eph. it is clear that the author knows the Haustafel in Col. 3.18–4.1 and takes them as his basis; we find the same restriction to three times two groups, the same order and the same intention.[3] But it is just as clear that the author has developed and deepened the instruction. We wish to concentrate our attention on the unusual features, the introduction of scriptural quotations (5.31; 6.2 f.) and even more on the theological enrichment of the paraclesis on marriage. The motif of seeing a model for Christian marriage in the relationship between Christ and his Church suggests itself to the author from his own ecclesiological thinking, but also allows us to look more deeply into this. The 'theology' of marriage has for him its roots in the Mystery of Christ – Church and the ecclesiology which rules his thinking leads to practical consequences for Christian couples. Hence in the development of the marriage-paraclesis there emerge, not altogether by chance, special curious statements about Christ and the Church. Only in the exegesis can we discuss the questions frequently asked about the origin or background of these views which have been answered in very different ways up to the present time. After the previous section on life in the Christian congregation and how it is revealed especially and in exemplary fashion in a spiritual service of worship, the transition to the Haustafel is not simply to be understood as a turning to the 'domestic' life of Christians. The inherited schema represents rather an instruction which is intended to illustrate what is important for the realization of Christian existence as a

---

[1] Cf. Crouch* 9–31; Gnilka* 207–10.
[2] Cf. Schrage, Schweizer*, FS Zimmerli and *Col* 162–4.
[3] Cf. Schweizer, *Colossians* Excursus: The Household Rules 213–20.

whole. Christian life in the everyday world is oriented on Christ who desires to establish his rule of mercy and love in the Church, in the respective congregation, in the concrete situation of the individual Christian. Marriage, the normal and at the same time exemplary case of the closest co-existence of Christians, presents itself especially as a representation of a Christian life lived according to the will and instruction of the Lord (cf. v. 17) in the light of the Mystery of Christ and his Church.

The lay-out of the text in the translation takes into account the following analysis, especially in separating the exhortations from the motives.[4]

21 Subordinate yourselves to one another in reverence to Christ,
22 wives (subordinate) to their husbands as to the Lord,
23 for the husband is the head of the wife
    as Christ is also the Head of the Church,
    he, the saviour of the body.
24   So then, as the Church is subordinate to Christ
  wives (should be subject) to their husbands
  in everything.
25 Husbands, love your wives
    as Christ loved the Church
    and gave himself for her
26   to make her holy, in that he purified her
    by the cleansing with the waterbath in the Word
27   to prepare the Church in splendour for himself,
    without spot or wrinkle or any such thing
    but rather that she might be holy and blameless.
28 In the same way ought husbands (also) to
  love their wives like their own body.
  He who loves his wife loves himself.
29 For no one ever hates his own flesh
  but nourishes it and tends it
    as Christ (does) his Church;
30   because we are members of his body.
31 'For this reason a man will leave father and mother
  and be joined to his wife,
  and the two shall become *one* flesh'.
32 This is a great mystery; but I interpret it to mean
    Christ and the Church.
33 At any rate you, too, each individual one of you
  should love his wife as himself, but the wife
  should revere her husband.

Analysis

The exhortation to subordinate themselves to one another in reverence to Christ (v. 21) is directed at all members of the congregation (cf. 5.15–20), as is shown by the Masculine form of the Participle. Although the command to be subordinate was originally addressed to the women (cf. Col. 3.18), the author of Eph. has extended it to everyone in the congregation and made it a Leitsatz for the whole section of the Haustafel. Since the motive

[4] Similarly also Sampley* 104.

'fear' (in the sense of reverence) comes up again at the end of the instructions for married couples – at this point addressed to the wives – (v. 33) it entails a certain *inclusio* (comprehensiveness).

The general exhortation, however, passes over immediately, without a new Verb (but cf. the variant readings) to the command to the wives. It is striking that in the whole Haustafel the 'weaker' group are always mentioned first: wives compared with husbands, children – parents/fathers (6.1–4), slaves – masters (6.5–9). If this corresponds to a traditional form then the introductory exhortation is even more remarkable. The structure of the instruction for married people is on the whole patently clear. A longer exhortation to the husbands (vv. 25–30) follows upon that to the wives (vv. 22–4). Then the author inserts the quotation from Gen. 2.24, with a short note on his interpretation of it (vv. 31–2) and concludes by repeating his command to both marriage-partners, this time in the reverse order (v. 33).

The paraclesis only achieves its individual character through the motive arising out of the relationship Christ-Church. On three occasions a ὡς or καθὼς καὶ ὁ Χριστός (as Christ also) signals the insertion of such a Clause relating to the Church: once for wives (v. 23), twice for husbands (v. 25 and v. 29). At these places Christ is mentioned first so that his pre-eminence to the Church is emphasized. He is the Head of the Church (v. 23) but gives himself in love for her (v. 25) and tends her with care (v. 29). The insertions, however, do not stand in isolation but are connected in an unusual fashion to the exhortations to wives and husbands. In the case of the wives, who according to this outlook represent the Church, the relationship of the Church to Christ (again with a comparison ὡς – οὕτως) is mentioned in order to motivate them (v. 24). For the husbands what Christ has done and intended for the Church is described in a longer exposition (vv. 25b–7) to move the husbands to true love in the Christian sense (ἀγαπᾶν) (v. 25a). What Christ wished to achieve in his loving self-giving for the Church is developed in three Final Clauses which do not have equal emphasis but as they proceed make it ever more clear the form Christ wished his Church to take: He wanted 'to make her holy' (v. 26a) – how that took place is developed in a Participial Clause (καθαρίσας κτλ) – to prepare her 'in splendour' (v. 27a) – and that is explained further at first negatively: without spot or wrinkle or any such thing, then positively (in a ἵνα-Clause: that she might be holy and blameless (v. 27b, c). The whole explanation is made a rounded unit by the idea of 'making holy' (at the beginning and end). Based on the 'cleansing with the waterbath' there arises the picture of a beautiful, radiant woman whose physical beauty is merely the expression of her inner purity and blamelessness. Then such loving care is again spoken of in a new paragraph, this time initially with a natural-sounding motive: husbands should love their wives as their own bodies, nourish and tend them as they do their own flesh (vv. 28–9a, b). But this motive is at one and the same time raised to a higher level by a consideration of Christ and his Church (v. 29c): Christ also loves the Church through which we are 'members of his Body' (v. 30) in like manner.

Suddenly, but prepared for by the cue 'flesh', there follows in v. 31

the quotation from Gen. 2.24, whose purpose in the text can only be explained in the exegesis. Important for this is the author's commentating note in v. 32. In the construction of the section as a whole the quotation goes beyond the advice to wives and husbands. It represents rather a theological reflection which, nevertheless, has an important connection with the whole speech oriented on the Christ-Church relationship. That the two verses form a kind of expansion or even a conclusion to the explanations is confirmed in that the author gathers up his commands to husbands and wives (v. 33) in a πλήν (which at the end of a speech = at any rate) which once again brings out attention back to what has been said before.

On the semantic level, apart from the conceptual areas already mentioned (Head and Body; purity, holiness; nourishing, tending) we can find in this section further conspicuous expressions and phrases such as 'saviour of the body' (v. 23c); cleansing with the waterbath in the Word (v. 26b); their own body, to love themselves (v. 28). These express particular conceptions or material motives which were already available for the author. What kind they are and where he took them from is highly controversial; from Gnosticism, Judaism, a mixture from the Judaeo-Hellenistic or Christian field which had already come into being. Is it a uniform idea (something like the Sophia-myth) or is it made up of a cycle of separate ideas or traditions (Sampley names six) which have been coalesced? We can only try to answer this in the exegesis. But one thing is certain: In his enrichment of the existent exhortation for husband and wife in their marriage by the ecclesiological motif, and his inclusion of Christian spouses in the relationship between Christ and Church, he has created instruction on Christian marriage which, in spite of possible external influences, must be regarded as his own work and consequently must first be declared to be such and appreciated as such.

Exegesis

21

The exhortation to mutual subordination in reverence to (fear of) Christ which now stands like a title over the following commands (cf. analysis) is a composition by the author himself to form a transition from the address to the whole congregation (vv. 15–20) to the paraclesis for individual Christians (cf. v. 33 'each individual one'). The choice of a Participle instead of an Imperative[5] makes a connection with 5.20. The command 'subordinate yourselves' otherwise remains for the most part limited to individual groups[6] or is concerned with the subordination of the Christians to the governing powers (Rom. 13.1, 5; 1 Pet. 2.13; Tit. 3.1). There are already in Paul exhortations materially comparable – though without the

[5]Cf. p. 149 n. 12. On Eph. 5.21 Schmid, *Epheserbrief* 355, who points to Col. 3.16. Good examples are Rom. 12.9–13.16; 1 Pet. 2.18; 3.1, 7; 4.8. – A number of MSS transpose vv. 20 and 21: P⁴⁶ D* F G 1175 2464 pc VL MVict Ambst. But v. 21 does not fit in the context of v. 20 and the new beginning in v. 21 then goes unrecognized.

[6]Especially the women – 1 Cor. 14.34 (Pauline? Probably a later interpolation); Col. 3.18; Tit. 2.5; 1 Tim. 2.11 (with a noun); 1 Pet. 3.1, 5; Slaves – Tit 2.9; 1 Pet. 2.18; Children – cf. 1 Tim. 3.4; younger people – 1 Pet. 5.5.

verb ὑποτάσσεσθαι (Rom. 12.16; Phil. 2.3; Gal. 6.2) – to the command to all to subordinate themselves *to one another*. In 1 Pet. 5.5 there is added to the instruction for younger people: 'Clothe yourselves with humility in your dealings with one another!' What is meant is that obliging behaviour towards one another in 'humility' (ταπεινοφροσύνη) which Eph. 4.2 also demanded. 'Subordination' in this sense becomes an embracing expression for the behaviour of the Christians in community, it might be said a 'specificum of the early Christian Haustafel'.[7] For the author it is not an external legal category but an attitude demanded by love, urging to service ('humility') for which every Christian must be willing. Hence if certain anthropological-social ideas of that time creep in in the exhortation to wives (cf. vv. 22 f.), this is a contemporary limitation which does not question the fundamental claim on all Christians to be subordinate to one another.

The motive 'in reverence to Christ' must also be included in this view. If we compare for instance Phil. 2.1–5 where Paul urgently admonishes the Christians to respect one another highly in humility, each considering the other better than himself, and places before them the example of Christ, we not only understand the unique phrasing 'fear of *Christ*'[8] but also interpret 'fear' properly. The word which already in classical literature can take on various shades of meaning (fear of something, anxiety, but also reverence, respect) and then in Jewish literature received a special character in the sense 'fear of God',[9] here tends strongly to the meaning 'reverence'. In this context we can only with difficulty think he has in mind Christ the Judge.[10] Nowhere in Eph. are the Christians threatened with the future judgement (in 5.5 f. the threat is to depraved people, in context the heathen) but at the most their responsibility before the Lord is held up before them (cf. 6.8 f.). On the contrary Christ as Head of the Church who always remains superior to his Body is owed conscious reverence, they ought to give him thanks for everything and be committed to him.

22

Initially the command to be subordinate is addressed to the wives,[11] and in a particular sense, since children and slaves are to be concerned with obedience rather than subordination (6.15). 'Subordination' is the more inclusive concept (in Tit. 2.9; 1 Pet. 2.18 it is also used of slaves); if in Eph. its use is restricted to members of the congregation among themselves (v. 21) and to wives (v. 22), it certainly does not mean a total 'subjection'

[7]Kamlah* 238.

[8]The v. 1. θεοῦ 6 81 614 1881 pm can be explained from the expression 'fear of God' frequent especially in the Wisdom literature. There is talk of the fear of the Lord (v. 1. K bo^ms in Acts 9.31; 2 Cor. 5.11; cf. (with the verb) Col. 3.22.

[9]On the Greek linguistic usage cf. H. Balz, TDNT IX, 189–97; on fear of God in the OT, G. Wanke, ibid., 201–3.

[10]Against Schlier 252, who refers to 2 Cor. 5.10 f.; Barth 662–8 who finds in it an eschatological aspect which places 'all the ethical commands in the Haustafel under the mark of eschatological promise and hope' (666 f.). But this is not obvious in 5.21–33.

[11]Failing to appreciate the syntactical connection with v. 21 (cf. n. 5) ℵ A I P Ψ 6 3381 al lat sy co expressly add ὑποτάσσεσθωσαν; D F G MLatt ὑποτάσσεσθε. V 22 stands without the verb in P^46 B Cl Alex.

as if wives should obey their husbands like a child or slave. Only the motive 'as to the Lord' makes a connection with the command to slaves ('as to Christ' 6.5). But how then are we to understand this 'subordination to one another' more precisely? In Greek the word has a considerable range of meaning according to whether it is applied to subjects, slaves or members of the family. In general it can be understood as a term for order[12] which presumes a particular social structure with its resulting responsibilities. These, however, are not necessarily of a legal sort but might also be moral duties such as are befitting (πρέπον) and advisable so that it is a voluntary subjection.[13] Yet we cannot deny that behind it lies a conception of society which reserves the first place for the man.[14]

23–24

The contemporary view appears even more forcibly in the Clause 'the husband is the head of the wife'. The same expression is to be found in Paul (1 Cor. 11.3) with a reason given in the context which goes back to the order of Creation (11.8 f.). The author of Eph. also belongs to this tradition; it provides him with the bridge for the introduction of the analogy Christ–Church. But we must realise that the idea he takes over is simply a means of support for the progression of his argumentation. The command proceeds farther (v. 24), that the wife should be subordinate to her husband *in the same way* as the Church is to Christ – namely voluntarily, willingly, in response to his love. Because of the introduction of the model 'Christ–Church', the behaviour of the wife is from the start correlated to the behaviour of the husband who, according to the model of Christ, should provide his wife with the utmost love, care and attention. Strangely enough he does not talk of the *loving* subordination of the wife to the husband; but this is connected with the fact that he always talks only of the love of Christ for his Church, not vice versa (cf. also 4.16; 5.2). The Church is the grateful recipient and thereby also the reciprocator of Christ's love. Because of the way in which Christ exercises his position as 'head' in relationship to the Church any unworthy 'subordination' is excluded. But by this very token the argument taken from the order of Creation (which is no longer a convincing one for us) loses its status (cf. Paul in 1 Cor. 11.11 f.).[15] More important than 'subordination' is the mutual ordering to each other. This

[12]Cf. G. Delling, TDNT VIII, 40 f.; Kähler*; Kamlah* 239 f.

[13]Cf. the word of Alexander to his mother who was hurt by her husband, Philipp: 'It is fitting for a wife to be subordinate to her husband' (Pseud-Callisth I, 22.4) in G. Delling, TDNT VIII, 40, 40–2. Ep Ar 257: 'For God adopts those who by nature humble themselves and loves the type of people who subordinate themselves (τους ὑποτασσομένους)'.

[14]On the situation in the (Hellenistic-Roman) society at that time cf. among other J. Leipoldt, *Die Frau in der antiken Welt und im Urchristentum*, Leipzig ³1965; K. Thraede, RAC 8, 197–224; 224–7 (Judaism); Barth 655–9; J. Pairman Brown, 'The Role of Women and the Treaty in the Ancient World', BZ 25 (1981) 1–8 (with further literature). – ἰδίοις ('own') is not emphatic; in Koine Greek it often takes the place of the Personal Pronoun (αὐτῶν), cf. Pr-Bauer 731, s.v. 2; Mayser II/2, 73 f.; Moulton–Turner, *Grammar* III, 191 f.

[15]On this cf. M. Boucher, 'Some unexplored Parallels to 1 Cor. 11.11–12 and Gal. 3.28: the NT on the Role of Women', CBQ 31 (1969) 50–8; J. Kürzinger, 'Frau und Mann nach 1 Kor. 11.11 f.', BZ NF 22 (1978) 270–5.

view, that a corresponding attitude on the part of the husband is to be expected, is emphasized by the additional remark which comes in the middle 'he himself the saviour of the body' (v. 23c). The strange expression, which has contributed not a little to the presumption of the influence of a gnostic Redeemer-myth behind the conception of the 'marriage' between Christ and the Church,[16] lays stress upon Christ (αὐτό ς) in his capacity as Saviour, which is then described in v. 25 as a loving self-offering for the Church. A one-sided 'domineering' understanding of the 'Head' is excluded by this attribute. Christ as Head of the Church has far greater significance for his Body, the Church, and therewith admittedly also shatters the analogy to an earthly husband and his wife.[17] Only after this does the author return to his exhortation (v. 24). The abbreviated Consecutive Clause (Ellipse), since as it stands it is grammatically imprecise, must surely be filled out to have the sense of an Imperative. The analogy of Church–Christ put before the wives is not added later but confronts them from the very start in 'as to the Lord' (v. 22). The connecting αλλά[18] challenges them more strongly to subordinate themselves to their husbands 'in everything' just as the Church subordinates herself to Christ as her Head and Saviour to whom she owes everything. If we bear in mind that the same loving self-giving is demanded from the husband as Christ has shown for the Church (except that he does not become 'saviour' as did Christ), we are prevented from misunderstanding the subordination 'in everything'. In the correlation of the behaviour of husband and wife, the utmost is required from *both*, always in the perspective which is provided by Christ and the Church.

With the expression 'saviour of the body' the author interrupts the metaphor of the 'marriage' between Christ and the Church. Prompted by the expression 'Head of the Church' – which can be interpreted in the first place as 'ruling head',[19] although already in 1.22 f. connected with 'body' (then also in 4.15) – he uses 'Body' for Church in this unusual syntactic construction. This mixing of metaphors used for the Church, although each throws light upon the reality of the Church in a particular aspect, is in the main to be ascribed to the author himself, regardless of a possible religio-historical background. The conception of the Church as a Body breaks through once again in v. 30 ('because we are members of his Body') although it has already had an influence on vv. 28–9. The most obvious explanation is that the author brings in the familiar idea in the middle of another metaphor of marriage at a point where he thinks it appropriate. Whether we can trace the change in the metaphors of marriage/

---

[16]Cf. Schlier, *Christus und die Kirche* 72 f.; also *Eph.* 254 f. 266; Fischer, *Tendenz* 176, 194.

[17]Chrysostom, Theophylactus and Oecumenius transferred the function of saviour to the earthly husband. But this interpolation which with modification has survived till recent times (cf. Robinson, Scott, Huby) is objectively improbable and ignores the emphatic αὐτός which stresses Christ in his exceptional character.

[18]Cf. Pr-Bauer 76 f., s.v. 6.

[19]From the Semitic meaning of 'head' as 'leader', in which one need not think of the body, many scholars wanted to derive the further development of the Pauline body-concept, cf. especially Benoit, *Leib* 262–4. But we must consider the inclusion of 'head' in the body-concept with which it is not yet connected in the OT. Here we take into consideration influence from the idea of the 'Universal God', cf. Schweizer, *Colossians* 58 with n. 9.

matrimony and Head-Body back to the gnostic redeemer-myth is doubtful, in spite of the wealth of material for the 'holy marriage'. It is certain that the expressions only appear together in 2 Cl. 14[20] where we find the Clause 'the living Church is the Body of Christ', but this could also have been influenced by the NT. In the coptic-gnostic writing 'Exegesis of the Soul' which K. M. Fischer now brings as a comparison, in which the redemption in the bridal chamber of the soul which has fallen into sin (whoring) is described, there is no suggestion that it is 'the Body' of the Redeemer.[21] Even the expression σωτήρ (redeemer) can only be established with certainty in post-Christian Gnosis.[22] In particular the idea fundamental to that myth of the *pre-existent* Church cannot be confirmed in Eph.[23] According to Eph. 2.15 f. Christ 'creates' in his person the one new human being and reconciles the two groups of humankind in one single body with God through the Cross; in this act the Church is constituted for the very first time and called to life (cf. further under 5.25 f.).

25

The command to husbands, considerably expanded compared with Col. 3.19 and also much more detailed than that to wives, draws an emotive picture of Christ's care for the Church. The two stages of the paraclesis (vv. 25–7 and 28–30, cf. analysis) are held together by the requirement to love. The Verb ἀγαπᾶν, already to be found in Col. 3.19, which is used without exception for Christian love, directs attention from the outset to the personal, integral love in which every natural, sexual love, even if it is spiritually sublimated (Eros) finds its true fulfilment. Agape does not necessarily conflict with Eros; it also includes friendly relationships (Philia); but it surpasses all other love in the way it considers the other's good and subordinates its own interests, in its self-offering and concern for the other.[24] Agape finds its highest example in Christ who 'loved the Church

[20]The passage is called into play especially by Schlier, *Religionsgeschichtliche Untersuchungen* 91 f.; *Eph.* 268 f. But for this document from the Second Century AD we must reckon with various ideas running together.

[21]Fischer, *Tendenz* 186–91, discusses this document and finds in it very strong similarities to Eph. 5.22–3 (194 f.) but notices himself: 'The only divergence which can be established concerns the connection of this thought-structure with the σῶμα – κεφαλή cycle, which according to our analysis comes from the "Universal God" concept and not from Gnosis' (194); M. Krause–P. Labib, *Gnostische und hermetische Schriften aus Codex II und VI*, Glückstadt 1971, 68–87; further Foerster, *Gnosis* II, 127–35. But Fischer fails to notice that the idea of the Church's pre-existence in Eph. (v. infra) is missing. How different the conception is is shown by the following passages: 'But the cleansing of the soul is when they again achieve the simplicity of their original nature and return again; this is their Baptism' (131, 34–6); 'but because she is a woman who cannot bring forth children alone, the Father sent her from heaven her husband, who is her brother, the first-born' (132, 6–8).

[22]Cf. W. Foerster, TDNT VII, 1019. This does not rule out the idea that the title σωτήρ, which has its deepest roots in the OT and Judaism is not also influenced by Hellenism (cf. Philo); cf. Dib Past ³75–7; Foerster loc. cit. 1005/12; 1014 f. Here it is only a matter of the derivation from Gnosis.

[23]Against Schlier 255 f.; Fischer, *Tendenz* 176. The idea of the Church's pre-existence is rejected by Percy, *Probleme* 328; E. Schweizer, TDNT VII, 1080, n. 513; Gnilka 279.

[24]Cf. E. Stauffer, TDNT I, 35–8; V. Warnach, *Agape*, Düsseldorf 1951; also 'Liebe', in *Bibeltheologisches Wörterbuch*, Graz ³1967, II, 927–65 (with literature); C. Spicq, *Agapè. Prolégomènes à une étude de théologie néo-testamentaire*, Louvain-Leiden 1955; also *Agapè dans le NT*, four volumes, Paris 1957/61; *Notes* I, 15–30 (with literature). Cf. also Barth 715–

and gave himself for her'. With this the author reminds us of Christ's sacrificial death of which he has already spoken in a similar manner in 5.2. The way of speaking of Christ's self-offering (v. under 5.2), taken over from the early Christian tradition, is here applied to the 'church' as if she already existed at his death. But in 5.2 it is also said that Christ loved 'you' (according to the better readings) – i.e. the addressees were already being taken into consideration. The Church as the Community of the redeemed is constituted in the Blood of Christ (cf. 2.13) and consequently is for all subsequent believers an existing entity in which they are taken up and incorporated by their Baptism (cf. v. 26). This way of looking at things in Eph. has a decisive theological significance in so far as the Church is presented to the individual believer as an objective entity. 'Just because for the author the Church is the objectively given place of salvation, he must ground her in Christ's act on the Cross if he is not to make her absolute as an institution of salvation on her own authority'.[25] There is no analogy in the gnostic Sophia-myth for this solidarity of Christ and Church based on the *death* of Christ.

26

Already in his death on the Cross Christ intended (ἵνα) to sanctify the Church. This is a comprehensive expression for Christ's work of salvation through which Christians are 'sanctified' in Christ Jesus (cf. 1 Cor. 1.2; 6.11), but here it has a special reference to the Church as a whole, which should be 'holy and blameless' (v. 27). If the exposition in vv. 26–7 is a unified description complete in itself, the picture arises of a radiantly pure and beautiful bride whom Christ desires to prepare or lead to himself. But we can hardly restrict 'make holy' in the sense of a rabbinical usage to the special meaning of 'select a woman (as bride), betroth oneself to her'.[26] This would not only be incomprehensible to the Gentile-Christian addressees but would also have little meaning for the men already married to whom the paraclesis is addressed. The sanctification which Christ strives after for his Church is immediately explained in a Participial Clause as a cleansing 'with the waterbath in the Word'. The Aorist form is chosen because of the preceding verbs in the Aorist. In principle the cleansing takes place already in the death of Christ on the Cross; all subsequent 'cleansing' takes place in the continuing power of his death. The author is clearly thinking of Baptism through which believers are incorporated into the Church; we cannot doubt this because of the unmistakeable expression 'waterbath'.[27] But the outward event is not what is decisive for the

---

20. Schrage* 12 f. especially emphasizes the meaning of the idea of love in Eph. 5: Against the background of the conception of marriage at that time the exhortation to agape towards a woman is 'something not at all self-evident but something absolutely incredible.' But cf. Ps.-Phocylides 195–8 (van der Horst, *Ps.-Phocyl* 100): 'Love (στέργε) your wife ...'; on this van der Horst, *Ps.-Phocyl* 241 f.

[25] Merklein, *Christus und die Kirche* 68.

[26] Cf. Sampley* 42 f. who bases his theory on K. G. Kuhn, TDNT I, 97 f. (Kuhn however does not apply this 'profane' meaning to Eph. 5.26).

[27] Against Barth 695 f., who takes the 'cleansing with the waterbath' simply as a metaphor for 'Baptism with the Spirit'. Cf. the criticism in Halter* 283.

occurrence of salvation; the additional 'in the word' (ἐν ῥήματι) stresses the effective factor (Instrumental use of ἐν). It is a matter of debate whether we should take the phrase with 'make holy' or 'cleansing with the waterbath'. If we leave it closely connected with the waterbath, then it can be said that Baptism only receives its power to cleanse through the word,[28] and then it seems reasonable to assume that 'word' here means the baptismal formula.[29] If we give the preference to the connection with 'make holy' – which is syntactically just as possible – then it is the power of sanctifying as such, proceeding from the word of Christ (which is also effective in Baptism) which is emphasized.[30] Whichever way we take it all the emphasis is on Christ's action which is carried out on his Church and further in her. The cleansing which takes place in Baptism, which is connected with the metaphor of the waterbath but is founded in the blood of Christ (cf. Heb 10.19–21; 1 Jn 1.7, 9) names only one special aspect of the whole process of sanctification (cf. 1 Cor 6.11), as making holy and cleansing correspond closely anyway.[31] The metaphor of the bath passes over in v. 27 to a description of how Christ wishes to make his Church splendidly beautiful. Because the wife is represented by the Church and the husband by Christ, it is not apposite to reflect that the husbands, as members of the Church and receivers of Baptism, have also experienced that attention from Christ.

27

The metaphor of the Bride cleansed by the bath is extended in a new (continuing) Final Clause. Christ wished to make the Church 'splendid' (ἔνδοξος), endow her, as it were, himself. The metaphor of the person who gives away the bride (in fact it was two older men of good repute)[32] is applied in Jn 3.29 to John the Baptist and in 2 Cor 11.2 Paul sees himself in a similar rôle, probably, however, more as the father of the bride.[33] The Apostle wants to lead the congregation to Christ (at his Parousia) as an unblemished virgin. Although the same verb is used here as in Eph 5.27 (παρίστημι), the objective alteration of the metaphor is unmistakeable. In Eph. no other person appears to lead the bride or as her father, and the

---

[28]In the sense of Augustine's word, In Joh Ev Tract 80.3 (C Chr. 36, 529): 'Detrahe verbum, et quid est aqua nisi aqua? Accedit verbum ad elementum, et fit sacramentum, etiam ipsum tamquam visibile verbum.' Thomas Aquinas on this passage (Cai nr. 323) says with reference to Rom. 6.3 that this bath draws its power from the suffering of Christ. Calvin (223) also points to the Sacrament: God testifies to our washing which 'simul efficit quod figurat'. The power for this only comes in the blood of Christ.

[29]Thus among the more recent exegetes Abbott, Huby, Masson, Schlier, Gaugler, Gnilka. Cf. also Halter* 284.

[30]Jerome (MPL 26.532D) points to the 'word of teaching', similarly Estius*, Bisping; Cambier* 75–7 'the divine Word which is taken up in faith', Caird: the Gospel. But for this ὁ λόγος (of God, of Christ) is usually preferred or additional remarks are made (cf. Rom. 10.17; Eph. 6.17; Heb. 1.3; 6.5; 11.3; 1 Pet. 1.25). In spite of Rom. 10.9 (where ῥῆμα is qualified by its context) we should not connect the phrase with the confession of the one being baptized because the subject is the effectiveness of Christ (against Scott on this verse, Kirby; *Ephesians* 152).

[31]Cf. Gnilka 281 who also refers to parallels in Qumran: 1 QS 3.4; 1 QH 11.10–12.

[32]Cf. Bill. I, 500–4; J. Jeremias, TDNT IV, 1101; Schnackenburg, *John* I, 416 f.

[33]Cf. Wnd 2K 319 f.; J. Schmid, RAC II, 546.

'wedding' of Christ and the Church does not lie in the future. We can not accept the interpretation which in the past has often been represented that it refers to the Parousia which is never mentioned in Eph.[34] Christ himself makes his Bride, the Church, ready and brings her before himself in her youthful, fresh beauty. But because Baptism continually incorporates new people into the Church, this making splendid is also a present and continuing event – the metaphor of the Bride's bath as a unique event is shattered. This makes good sense in the command to husbands: They should continue to love their wives and care for them as Christ does. This alteration in the metaphor with an eye on reality is confirmed by the additional attribute which is ascribed to the Church: She should be 'without spot or wrinkle or any such thing'. 'Wrinkle' (ῥυτίς) at least is a sign of old age which no bridal bath can erase.[35] The positive contrast, that the Church should be 'holy and blameless' points to the ethical beauty and unimpeachablility which is a distinguishing feature of the Church under Christ's care (cf. 1.4; Col 1.22).

If the exegesis produces such an idiosyncratic mixture of metaphor and reality, we must seek for the origin of this conception. The *bridal bath* is admittedly a custom wide-spread in antiquity, but it does not explain everything. Why is it connected with Baptism,[36] and does the description reach beyond this? Nowhere in the texts which are chiefly referred to on it is the motif of the 'holy marriage' connected with any bath, either in Gnosticism[37] or in the Hellenistic Mystery Cults.[38] Hence we have no explanation for the strange connection between the bridal bath and the holy marriage. Sampley points to Ezek. 16.8–14 where the motif of washing also appears in the metaphor of the marriage between Yahweh and his hitherto faithless wife, Israel: 'Then I bathed you, washed off your blood from you and anointed you with oil' (v. 9). Thereafter God clothes and adorns his bride so that she becomes radiantly beautiful.[39] In word and thought this text is considerably closer to Eph. 5 than is the gnostic redemption in the nuptial chamber. Certainly the washing is only a part of the whole description and has no such fundamental significance as the baptismal bath in Eph. Even with this background we must assume a transformation of the metaphor because of the reality of Christ and Church. Possibly the author has fused different ideas.

---

[34]Older Commentaries, Wnd 2K 321 f.; J. Jeremias, TDNT IV, 1104 f.; J. Schmid, RAC II, 546 f.

[35]It is simply a part in the general description (cf. 'or any such thing') but it shows that he is looking to the future. Cf. W. Straub, *Die Bildersprache des Apostel Paulus*, Tübingen 1937, 62. – On ἄμωμος (blameless) Feuillet* 186 refers to Song 4.7 (LXX: μῶμος οὐκ ἔστιν ἐν σοί) because only here is the attribute attributed to a bride.

[36]Cf. O. Casel, 'Die Taufe als Brautbad der Kirche', JLW 5 (1925) 144–7. For criticism cf. Schnackenburg, *Taufe* 4 n. 10; Halter* 281 f.

[37]Cf. J. Schmid, RAC II, 530–47 (critical on the adoption in Eph. 5); excursus in Schlier 264–76; Fischer, *Tendenz* 176–200. Among those who speak for the adoption of the myth of the 'holy marriage' are Dibelius–Greeven 93, Conzelmann 119 ('. . . appears to have an effect through the mediation of Hellenistic Judaism'). In the Gnostic document 'Exegesis of the Soul' the soul is cleansed not by a bath but through her union with the redeemer in the bridal chamber (v. n. 21).

[38]Cf. E. Stauffer, TDNT I, 653 f.; J. Schmid, RAC II, 537 f.; Schnackenburg, *Taufe* 12 ff. (the washings belong only to the introductory lustrations); Wagner, *Römer 6.1–11* (p. 229 n. 51) 109–12.

[39]Sampley* 38–43. Cf. also Feuillet* 127 f.; Barth 679.

28–29

A new paragraph begins with the renewed exhortation to the husbands to love their wives, even more strongly formulated ('they ought'). The address in the Third Person sounds almost categorical. If the καί (here = also) was part of the original letter,[40] οὕτως (in the same way) must refer to what goes before: In the same way as Christ does the husbands *also* should love their wives, and we are tempted to proceed: *as* their own bodies.[41] But as in v. 24 the Particles οὕτως-ὡς are intended to carry the comparison through except that οὕτως at the beginning is more strongly accentuated. We find the same sequence in v. 33, and this revision to the theme confirms the reading without καί. But does this not mean that a banal, unworthy motif is introduced after the lofty motif of Christ's concern for the Church? Does not the husband's self-love (v. 28b) which is expressed in the care of his flesh (v. 29) compare very badly with the selfless love demanded by the model of Christ, a love which goes to the limits? Yet at the latest in v. 29c ('as Christ his Church') the reader should be aware that this motif of love for one's own body is not meant to be interpreted in this fashion. The idea that Christ loves, nourishes and cares for his Church, which is his Body (cf. v. 23c) is in the author's mind from the very beginning of this exposition. Just as previously he used the metaphor of the bridal bath by way of comparison, he now uses the natural, understandable love of one's own body. The *argumentum ad hominem* is introduced in a comprehensive argumentation which teaches us to regard the wife as the 'body' of the husband, as it were a second ego – even to take husband and wife together as *'one* flesh' according to the analogy of Christ-Church. The author confirms this in referring the quotation from Genesis in v. 31 expressly to Christ and the Church; this is the perspective upon which vv. 28–30 are already oriented.

When after the categorical statement that husbands ought to love their wives as their own bodies there then follows the sentence 'who loves his wife, loves himself' (v. 28b), this could easily be misunderstood as if the husband had the right of disposal over his wife as over his own body. In fact the husband is called to loving concern for his wife as is shown in what follows. The comparison often made with Plutarch's saying – 'The husband should rule his wife not as a lord rules over his property but as the soul rules the body, sympathizing with her and fostering their growing together by a good attitude'[42] – reveals what is special in the Christian exhortation: no 'ruling' at all, but 'loving'! Further, we can ask whether, behind the formulation, 'himself', which is taken up in v. 33 in 'as himself', does not lie the commandment from Lev 19.18 to love one's neighbour 'as one's self'. Sampley detects a Jewish tradition of applying 'neighbour' to

---

[40]καί is found in P[46] A B D F G P Ψ 048 33 81 1175 al latt sy co. Hence although the older MSS (Alexandrine text) include καί, it is questionable whether it was original because its addition would also suggest itself to early copyists; besides it is suspect because of its various positions. Nestle-Aland[26] puts it in brackets; Tisch NT omits it (according to א).

[41]Cf. Haupt 228 f.

[42]Praec Conjug 142 E, Greek text in Dibelius–Greeven 95.

'wife'.[43] But it is neither necessary nor reasonable to assume such a resemblance: for the formulation 'himself' springs to mind already with 'body' or 'flesh'.

The love of the body is described in v. 29 as to 'nourish and tend' one's own flesh. Again we must prevent any misunderstanding as if it were simply a matter of the care of one's own body. Behind the obvious meaning of the Clause formulated from experience it is already noticeable from the wording that what is intended is the care for the wives. 'Flesh' is chosen instead of 'body' because the author is already thinking of the quotation in v. 31. The Greek expression for 'nourish' (ἐκτρέφειν, elsewhere τρέφειν) is used in various connections, including in the figurative sense of spiritual nourishment with spiritual gifts which God grants to humanity;[44] but Gnilka rightly goes back to the language of the marriage contract in which the same words occur.[45] If no express application to the wife as the husband's 'flesh' follows, that is because the Clause is connected to what goes before as a clarification (γάρ): He who loves his wife, loves himself. The description of how the husband nourishes and tends his own flesh is also relevant for his wife for whom he should care in a similar fashion. Only so is the reference which follows immediately to Christ and his Church understandable. The body or flesh which Christ nourishes and cares for is the Church. With this attention is drawn back to the great paradigm with which the command to husbands began (v. 25). The whole paraclesis for husbands is rounded off.

30

But what is also remarkable is the reason given for Christ's nourishment and care of the Church. It is not because she is his Body (or flesh), but because *we* are members of his Body. The metaphor of the body provides the opportunity of interchanging body, flesh or members. Does the author prefer 'members' here because it is familiar to him from the Pauline tradition (cf. 4.25; 1 Cor 6.15; 12.12–27; Rom 12.4 f.)? Does he wish to emphasize the obligation for his wife placed upon each individual husband (cf. v. 33)? The use of 'we' which interrupts the style of the rest suggests yet another meaning: The relationship Christ-Church is not only an ideal model for husband and wife in their marriage but is also a reality in which Christian spouses are included as are all Christians. By using 'we' he reminds the readers that they themselves participate in this care. It is not appropriate here to consider in detail wherein this 'nourishing' and 'caring' for the Church or her members by Christ consists. The use of 'nourish'

[43]Sampley* 30–4. He refers to Song 1.9, 15; 2.2, 10, 13; 4.1, 7; 5.2; 6.4, where the beloved is addressed or described as 'my companion' (ra^{e}jati, the Feminine form of re^{e}a, a neighbour) and further to the use of Lev. 19.18 on questions of marriage.

[44]Schlier, *Christus und die Kirche* 59, n. 2 and 71; also *Eph.* 260 f. n. 4 has gathered a large number of texts from Gnosis in which τρέφειν is encountered as a cosmological and soteriological concept. But is it necessary to give this background? Cf. the 'simple' parallels in Vita Aesopi I, c. 9 (p. 250, 13 Eberhard) τρέφει καί θάλπει, which Pr-Bauer cites.

[45]Gnilka 285; in such a marriage-contract (*Preisigke Wört* I, 665) it was imposed upon a husband θάλπειν καί τρέφειν καί ἱματίζειν (care for, nourish and clothe) his wife. Cf. also P. Rainer 30.20 (with θάλπειν) in Pr-Bauer 693.

might raise the idea of the Eucharist which would then come onto the scene after Baptism (v. 26);[46] but the use of 'care' in conjunction with 'nourish' leaves the expression in the realm of metaphor. It is rather a reminder of the power to grow and develop which comes from Christ, the Head, as in 4.16. A further early reflection is clear in the reading found in several MSS which supplements the Clause about the members in accordance with Gen 2.23 – 'from his own flesh and bones'.[47] This provides a transition to the following quotation from Gen 2.24 and allows us to think of the Church emerging from Christ in a similar manner as Eve was taken from Adam's side (a well-loved patristic interpretation of Jn 19.34). But it can scarcely be original since this idea is nowhere else connected with the 'body'-ecclesiology.[48]

31–32

The way for the quotation which follows without an introductory formula has already been prepared by the preceding exposition (especially 'flesh'). It is indeed the climax of the whole line of thought. If v. 32 had not been added by way of interpretation we might think of the love of the husband for his 'flesh', i.e. his wife, and in fact the passage is frequently applied directly to the marriage between man and woman.[49] But it would contradict the structure of the whole paraclesis on marriage if the relationship between husband and wife were now interpreted according to the order of Creation and not as hitherto according to the model of Christ and Church. V. 32 is not a belated re-interpretation of the quotation which originally related to the creation of man and woman so that marriage is only in retrospect interpreted according to the relationship of Christ and Church. Rather it must be seen from the outset as a key to the understanding which the author wishes to give to the quotation. Because he interprets the 'man' as Christ and the wife to whom he is joined as the Church and the two together in their insoluble connection as 'one flesh' as the unity of Christ and Church, the 'marriage' of Christ and Church remains here too the great example for Christian marriage. This view is also corroborated by the order of the text; for immediately prior (vv. 29–30) the subject was not a human person but Christ and his 'Body'.

    The quotation itself apart from minor deviations[50] corresponds to the text of the LXX. The Genesis passage, significant for the 'establishment' by God of marriage, played a not unimportant part in Judaism, in the NT (Mk 10.7 f./Mt 19.4; 1 Cor. 6.16) but also in gnostic

---

[46]Cf. V. Warnach in: Schlier–Warnach, *Kirche* 27; Mußner, *Christus* 154 ('perhaps'); Schlier 261 ('certain probability'); Cambier* 79.

[47]Heb. A² D F G (K) M Latt lat sy⁽ᴾ⁾Ir

[48]An Eve-typology only appears on the fringe in 2 Cor 11.3 and 1 Tim 2.13f.

[49]Earlier exegetes such as Henle, Belser, Meinertz, Ewald, Westcott, Haupt and also Schmid, *Epheserbrief* 166; 330 f. In more recent exegesis the direct reference of the quotation to Christ and the Church has fairly well asserted itself although with various modifications.

[50]Instead of the ἕνεκεν of the LXX we have here ἀντί; further the LXX text says 'his father and his mother'. Perhaps the author of Eph. deliberately omits the possessive pronouns because he is thinking of Christ. The articles with father and mother are textually uncertain. On the whole it makes no difference to the sense.

speculations. It was used in legal interpretation in Judaism (Halakha) on marital questions, and in the question of divorce in Mk/Mt it is the basis for the indissolubility of marriage according to the order of Creation. Only in Jewish Hellenism, in Philo, do we find an allegorical interpretation as well (Leg All II 49) but in a different way from that in Eph. – for the striving after what is better, for human yearning for God.[51] For the gnostic myth, the 'Exegesis of the Soul' is now informative. This also enlists Gen 2.24 for the union of the soul in the bridal chamber.[52] But in the gnostic syzygy-doctrine the soul (= wisdom) is seen as a pre-existent entity who yearns for the heavenly bridegroom with whom she was originally united in the Father and with whom she again unites in the bridal chamber.[53] In Eph. the passage is intended solely to form the basis of the unity of Christ and Church (the two are *one* flesh); there is no *re*-uniting. The first part of the quotation – that a man should leave his father and mother – cannot be explained allegorically, however, father and mother might be interpreted.[54]

The 'great mystery' therefore lies for the author, according to his understanding of the scriptural quotation, not in marriage as such but in the relationship between Christ and Church.[55] To be sure marriage is seen in the light of the unity between Christ and Church; it illustrates this relationship pictorially and from this arise the commands to both partners in the marriage. 'The mystery' is called 'great' not because of its obscurity but because of its meaningfulness (cf. 1 Tim 3.16). The concept of mysterion as used here is connected with God's revealed desire for salvation (1.9) which is still far off, but does not achieve the specific meaning of the Economy of Salvation hidden before the ages and now revealed (the schema of revelation cf. 3.2 f. 9). The author stresses the interpretation of the quotation as referring to Christ and the Church as his own (cf. the similar formula in Acts 2.25),[56] because he knows of other ways of interpreting it. This does not necessarily mean that he is standing out polemically against another (in particular, gnostic)

---

[51]Cf. Sampley* 53; the passages referred to from apocryphal literature (Sampley* 57–61) are less productive for Eph. Further cf. Batey* NTS 13.271–3; Barth 725–9. Baltensweiler* 231 f., with reference to a dissertation by J. B. Schaller) also quotes a passage from Ps-Philo Liber Antiqu. Bibl. (32.15; Kisch 206 f.) according to which the creation of Eve from Adam's rib represents God's election of Israel.

[52]V n. 21; reference to Gen 2.24; 132.20–133.5.

[53]Ibid 133 in connection with the Genesis passage: 'They were initially united in the Father before the woman forsook the man who is her brother. This marriage again re-united them.'

[54]Jerome (MPL 26.535): God the Father and the heavenly Jerusalem the mother. In Gnosis the mother is sometimes interpreted as the Holy Spirit; cf. also G. Quispel, *Makarius, das Thomasevangelium und das Lied von der Perle*, 1967 (NT. S 15), 9 f. (Jewish-Christian inheritance).

[55]Cf. G. Bornkamm, TDNT IV, 823. Dibelius–Greeven 95. Schlier 262 differentiates: The 'Mystery' does not mean the scriptural passage as such but the event indicated in the passage: similarly Gnilka 287 f.: The unifying connection of Church and Christ grounded by love.

[56]di Marco* 44–55 would like to understand εἰς in a Final sense: 'This mystery is great but I declare it to the extent it has Christ and the Church as its goal'. Marriage comes into this mystery (67.79). But this interpretation which connects εἰς κτλ directly with μυστήριον (69) remains difficult.

understanding;[57] though we cannot say with any clarity how he himself came to this interpretation.[58]

The Latin translation *sacramentum* (in one part of the Vetus Latina and in the Vulgate, while a wide-spread family of the VL retains *mysterium*) has played a part in the question whether marriage is to be regarded as a 'sacrament' (in the later sense). The understanding of what is a sacrament is still problematical today for the conception of marriage between the confessions. If the 'great mystery' has to do with the connection of Christ and Church, a direct sacramental interpretation of marriage is prohibited. But how can we judge Christian marriage if it is analogous to the relationship between Christ and the Church, when it has been taken up into the merciful activity of Christ through the membership of the spouses in the Body of Christ (cf. v. 30)? Roman Catholic authors conclude that marriage is thereby given a dignity and holiness which might be called 'sacrament'.[59] Protestant theologians emphasize the 'worldliness' of marriage; Christian marriage according to Eph. is not elevated to a sacral plane but remains a marriage like any other. But partners in a Christian marriage are called by the model of Christ and his Church as well as by their belonging to Christ's Body to live a truly Christian life.[60] Perhaps the idea of the 'contract' – analogous to the 'marriage-contract' between God and Israel in which the earthly-historical existence of Israel remains untouched and now carried over to Christ and the Church/Christian marriage – might bring the viewpoints closer.[61] Just as the Church is not freed from her existence in the world, so is the worldliness of marriage not called into question; and yet if the Christian marriage is lived in the manner required, as a meeting of love and subordination in love, it is also constantly summoned from a compulsive connection with the world in its limitations and referred to the area of salvation in Christ – Church. See further under the History of the Influence of Eph.

33

After this consideration of Christ and Church in which the relationship of Christian spouses is given a prototype, the author brings this paraclesis to a forceful end. The connecting Particle πλήν which is elsewhere used adversatively ('however, but') can also conclude a discussion and emphasize

[57]Against Bornkamm, TDNT IV, 823; Dibelius–Greeven 95 ('perhaps'); Schlier 262. On criticism of the Gnostic interpretation in the sense of the doctrine of syzygy cf. Barth 740–4.

[58]Even the derivation from the 'marriage' between God and Israel still does not elucidate this understanding of the Genesis-passage. The passage from Ps-Philo Liber Antiqu. Bibl. 32.15 mentioned in n 51 does not refer to Gen 2.24 but 2.23 (the formation of Eve).

[59]Cf. M. Schmaus, *Katholische Dogmatik* IV/1, Munich 1952, 622; 'Marriage is to a certain extent an epiphany of the bond between Christ and Church. The fellowship of Christ with the Church has an effect on the fellowship between man and woman. This is filled with the life exchanged between Christ and the Church ...'; Schlier 263, n. l; J. Ratzinger, 'Zur Theologie der Ehe', in H. Greeven et al, *Theologie der Ehe*. Regensburg – Göttingen 1969, 81–115, especially 85–8; Gnilka 289.

[60]Cf. Baltensweiler* 234 f.; H.-D. Wendland, 'Zur Theologie der Sexualität und der Ehe', in *Theologie der Ehe* (v n 59) 117–42, especially 136–8; Barth 744–9.

[61]Cf. Barth's deliberations in 749–53 with J. Ratzinger, loc cit (n 59) 86 f.; 91–4.

what is essential (now, at any rate').[62] Thus both partners are now addressed again, first the husbands, then, looking back to the beginning, the wives. The husbands should also – as Christ does the Church – each for himself love their wives as themselves (a reference back to v. 28b) and each wife should 'fear' her husband, treat him with reverence, as the Church does in her 'subordination' to Christ (v. 24) and as all members of the Church should do (cf. v. 21). In addressing the husbands and wives separately we see the desire to call both marriage-partners to a positive realization of the exhortations. Although the concept was an elevated one, it should not remain merely an ideal. It is a matter of how they carry out their married fellowship in their daily lives.

Summary

The paraclesis on marriage with which the Haustafel begins (as in Col.) receives its individuality and exceptional character from the fact that the relationship between Christ and the Church is held up before married people as the prototype of a perfect marriage and as a model for their behaviour. Christian marriage urges the partners to complete unity and a deeper relationship with one another. It demands on the wife's part a 'subordination', on the husband's utmost love and care as in the conduct of Christ and Church. The 'allocation of rôles' for husband and wife is seen according to the social conditions and views which pertained at that time, but in a reciprocal relation which relativizes the differences and raises to a higher unity. The misleading 'subordination' of the wife to the husband as her 'head' has the thorn removed in that, in the transition to the Haustafel, (v. 21) all members of the congregation are told that they should subordinate themselves to one another in reverence to Christ. Because in the sort of marriage typified by Christ and the Church the wife represents the Church, she should subordinate herself to her husband as the Church does to Christ (vv. 22–24). But the considerably longer command to husbands (vv. 25–30) shows that devoted love and care on the part of the husbands after Christ's example is a prerequisite of this. Thereby 'subordination' loses all sense of the oppressive or degrading. In the horizon of our time with its changed view of the position of women and the conviction of the equal partnership of husband and wife in marriage the question arises whether the 'model marriage of Christ–Church' has not been superceded. But even today the basic intention of the paraclesis can be retained under the aspect of mutual exchange according to the manner and ability of the 'partner': To receive and give love in its fullest sense of Agape.

The exhortation to husbands consists basically only in the one command to love (cf. vv. 25, 28, 33a). But how far this should extend and how they are to do it is explained in the exemplary behaviour of Christ with regard to the Church (vv. 25b–27) and then, in a new paragraph, in the love a man has for his own 'body' or 'flesh' (vv. 28–29b) – an exposition which at first seems strange but behind which the model is again recognisable of how Christ loves and cares for the Church as his 'Body' (vv. 29c–30). The depiction of how Christ has given himself for the Church (in his death) and

---

[62]Pr-Bauer 1828, s.v. 1.c; Bl-Debr § 449.2

cleansed her through the 'waterbath in the Word' (Baptism) is significant for the ecclesiological thinking of the Eph. theologian. The Church is not seen as in the gnostic Sophia-myth as a pre-existent figure which must be and is redeemed in the bridal chamber, but rather as an entity, constituted by Christ's sacrifical death, which from that time forth and forever has a share in salvation (cf. v. 23c – Christ 'himself the saviour of the Body') and ever anew incorporates people through Baptism. It is – with reference to the marriage-model – an unusual personified view in which the Church appears on one hand as the Bride of Christ for whom Baptism is prepared like a bridal bath and on the other as the wife of Christ who is the object of his far-reaching care and attention. Christ who has cleansed the Church and made her holy wishes to continue to make her splendidly beautiful and blameless and in this view becomes the example for Christian husbands in relationship to their wives. True love is concerned with the bodily, mental and spiritual welfare of the marriage-partner.

To support and round off this idea the author takes up the Genesis passage according to which a man should leave his father and mother and cling to his wife so that they become *one* flesh (v. 31). He sees a plan drawn up here for the great mystery which has been fulfilled in Christ and the Church. According to the author's express interpretation (v. 32) the mystery in his view lies in the unity of Christ and Church, which becomes the prototype of and model for Christian marriage. The consequences for the Christian understanding of marriage are not developed further. Returning to the paraclesis the author once more impresses upon each individual one of the husbands the obligation to love their wives, and upon the wives to revere their husbands (v. 33).

The question whether, in the light of the mystery of the 'marriage' of Christ and Church Christian marriage receives a higher, 'sacramental' dignity goes beyond what is actually said and has been answered in various ways up to the present time. Christian marriage contains within itself – like the Church – a connection with the earthly world (as any married connection among human beings) and also with God's world (through the Christian vocation of the partners in the marriage.) To preserve the 'wordliness' of the marriage which also guides Christians in their earthly duties is a concern as much justified as that of seeing marriage as the place where Christians, borne by their Lord's gracious power, should concretely realize their heavenly vocation. If we keep sight of both it should not be impossible to reach a greater agreement in the theologically controversial question of the understanding of Christian marriage.

3.c (Haustafel) The Behaviour of Children and Parents, Slaves and Masters (6.1–9)

The two following sets of instructions for the relationship of children and parents (6.1–4) and slaves and masters (6.5–9) can be treated together since they are similar to one another structurally and in the manner of their exhortation and motivation. After the longer paraclesis on marriage, they consider in shorter form, each in pairs, the other groupings which normally co-existed in a Christian household.

Literature

v. under 5.21–33.
Merk, *Handeln aus Glauben* 214–24.
Stuhlmacher, *Der Brief an Philemon*, 1975 (EKK XVIII), especially 44–8.

> 6.1 You children, obey your parents in the Lord;
>   for this is right.
>   2   'Honour your father and mother'
>   – that is the first commandment with a promise:
>   3   'that it may go well with you
>   and you may have a long life on earth'
>   4 And you, fathers, do not rouse your children to rage, but bring them up
>   in the discipline and instruction of the Lord.
>   5 You slaves, obey your earthly master
>   with fear and trembling
>   in purity of heart
>   as to Christ,
>   6   not in eye-service, to please people
>   but as slaves of Christ
>   who do the will of God from the heart.
>   7   who serve with joy and love
>   as if they served the Lord and not men,
>   8   knowing that each, if he performs some good action
>   will receive his reward from the Lord
>   be he slave or free.
>   9 And you, masters, treat them in the same way,
>   forbear to threaten,
>   know that your Lord and theirs is in heaven
>   and that he does not consider a person's reputation.

Analysis

The structure of the two sets of commands is clearly visible. As in the instructions to married people each group is addressed in the Vocative. Yet in the process a καί joins the fathers (v. 4) more closely with the slaves. After the address follows an Imperative, and in the case of the children (v. 1) and the slaves (v. 5) it is the same command – 'Obey!' In the case of the fathers or masters there is not the same harmony. A further common structural feature is the negative-positive formulation with μή – ἀλλά which appears in the exhortations to fathers (v. 4) and slaves (v. 6). Finally there is a substantiating εἰδότες ('for we know') both in the instruction for the slaves (v. 8) and also for the masters (v. 9c). In these characteristics we recognise the author's sense of style and desire for structure. Incidentally, each individual exhortation is formed differently according to the motives which are offered for the individual groups. We ought to pay special attention to the motives (separated from the exhortations in the text printed above). The command to children to obey their parents is initially grounded on the general ethical motive 'for this is right'. Without a formula of introduction (cf. 5.31) the author then quotes the fourth Commandment, almost word-for-word from the LXX although without the last part. In a parenthesis he explicitly draws attention to the promise. The addition of the quotation without a connection acts as a second motive, whose main emphasis lies in the promise. The command to fathers not to provoke their children to rage is likewise enriched by a motive in the positive continuation, but only in the modal expression 'in the discipline and instruction of the Lord'.

The command to slaves, the longest in this section (vv. 5–8) because it most of all has to overcome difficulties and resistance, is composed in a more complicated way. The principle injunction 'obey' is strengthened by two Prepositional expressions: 'with fear and trembling' and 'in purity of heart' which together lead to the emphatic conclusion 'as to Christ'. This is the dominating motive which is developed further in what follows. The antithetical formulation in v. 6 emphasizes 'slaves of Christ'. V. 7 underlines the same idea in a different way. But the Participle εἰδότες (v. 8), which remains in the flow of rhetoric, introduces and gives grounds for a new motive: repayment by the Lord. The fundamental formulated Clause gives the author the opportunity of adding 'be he slave or free'. With this he simultaneously creates the transition to the command for the masters.

This last instruction in the Haustafel (v. 9) calls in the Imperative for the masters to treat the slaves in the same way – a somewhat general formulation which, however, is immediately expanded by a concrete command attached by a Participle: 'Forbear to threaten!' Then the motive is introduced with the same Participle as for the slaves (εἰδότες): This is that the slaves as well as their earthly masters have the same Lord in heaven who does not take a person's status into consideration. In the whole section the author endeavours to give each group a grammatically complete exhortation and at the same time to bind the 'partners' to one another and refer them to one another by the use of corresponding formulations.

The structure of thought (the semantic level) shows his endeavour to make the Christian life subject to Christ, the Lord. To be sure we can find corresponding motives in the Haustafel in Col.; but in Eph. they are strengthened and multiplied: by the priority given to 'in the Lord' in the command for obedience on the part of the children (v. 1); by the introduction of the motive 'in the discipline and instruction of the Lord' in the exhortation to fathers as to how they should bring up their children; by a stronger accent in the instruction to slaves ('slaves of Christ' v. 6) and masters (the *common* Lord in heaven, no consideration of a person's standing v. 9). Only the introduction of the quotation in vv. 2–3 is completely new, and this has no special connection with the orientation of life on Christ, the Lord. It can be explained simply from the author's fondness for such quotations. On the whole the Haustafel from Col. 3.20–4.1 has clearly been used as a basis. The author of Eph. has taken this over, altered it linguistically to fit his own style and enriched it with motives – though only to a moderate extent.

Exegesis

1

That children should obey their parents was self-evident throughout antiquity, and we can explain the adoption of this command from the tradition of Haustafeln, more precisely from Col. 3.20. The variations in wording do not call for us to assume a literary independence on the part of the author of Eph.[1] but rather allow us to recognize his special concern for form. He does not want necessarily to call for children's obedience 'in everything', but instead he substitutes obedience 'in the Lord'. Admittedly this addition is dubious according to the MSS evidence;[2] but we can well imagine that the author deliberately gave more emphasis to the general Causal Clause in Col. ('that is pleasing to the Lord'). In this way the formulation gains the same sense as the command to the slaves to be obedient to their masters 'as to Christ' (v. 5). Even the children, who are full members of the congregation, should let their behaviour be determined by the will of the Lord. The Christian understanding of the congregation, which includes in like manner all members, even the 'weaker', can be seen in the address to the children and slaves. In Hellenism, by contrast, only the masculine, free, adult person was addressed.[3] In giving his reasons the author uses, instead of the 'pleasing' in Col. 3.20b, 'right' – an expression which has its home both in the Greek doctrine of virtue (cf. Epict. Diss. I, 22.1; II, 17.6) and in the biblical area. Here it means obedience to God's Commandments (cf. Josephus Ant. VI, 165; VIII, 208). Philo can combine the Greek ideal of virtue with the fulfilment of God's Commandments.[4] When the author of Eph. then immediately introduces the Commandment from the Decalogue, he remains true to the Jewish tradition.

2–3

The wording of the Commandment is taken over from the LXX (Ex. 20.10) except for the addition of τῆς γῆς (in the OT = 'land', in Eph. = 'earth') which related to the promised possession of the land in Canaan and must be dropped for Hellenistic-Christian readers. Yet the author emphasizes the promise: it is the 'first Commandment' to which a promise is added. The Jewish interpretation that it is the 'most difficult' Commandment which corresponds to the 'easiest' in Deut. 22.7 (that one should let the mother-bird go when one takes the young from the nest) – which has the same promise of a long life[5] – can hardly be the background for this. It means rather that after the four 'cardinal statements' which

[1]Thus Schlier 280 f., who finds this 'clearly and in an exemplary fashion' shown at this very point.

[2]It is missing in B D* F G b; Mcion Cl Cyp Ambst. The Greek NT[3] of the United Bible Societies and Nestle-Aland[26] put ἐν κυρίῳ in brackets. Cf. Metzger, *Textual Comm.* 609.

[3]Cf. Schweizer, *Colossians* 217.

[4]Cf. G. Schrenk, TDNT II, 183.

[5]This interpretation can be found repeatedly in rabbinic texts, cf. Bill. III, 614 f. Dibelius – Greeven 95 use it as an argument; Schlier 281, n. 3 (with reservations); Ernst 393. Differently (as in the text above) Gnilka 296 f.

relate to God it is the first and most important which regulates human dealings with one another to which consequently there is also added a 'comforting promise' (Philo, Spec. Leg. II, 261). But it is not necessary to spiritualize the promise as Philo does.[6] It is unlikely that 'it may go well with you and you may have a long life' is meant to conjure up thoughts of eternal life or the heavenly inheritance as Thomas Aquinas and some modern scholars think,[7] because the author would then have omitted 'on earth'. What is more, other than in 4.8–10 and 5.31 f. he gives no indication of a re-interpretation of the quotation. The reality of the promise qua se is important for him because it underlines the significance of this divine Commandment. He is not concerned with whether or how the promise is fulfilled.

4

The command to fathers also follows the Haustafel in Col. 3.21, but changes it in a characteristic fashion. Perhaps he has both parents in mind.[8] According to Philo[9] upbringing is the responsibility of both father and mother, but the father is especially responsible for discipline: to scold the child, rebuke him, and, should he not obey cautionary words, to beat him. The exhortation not to 'rouse' the children (cf. 4.2b; Col. 3.21 used another word: 'provoke') is directed against such severity, against which contemporary Hellenistic literature also warns.[10] For the human motive 'lest they become discouraged', the author of Eph. substitutes the positive command 'bring them up in the discipline and instruction of the Lord'. With this an important expression is pronounced which in the OT tradition[11] and also in Paul (1 Cor. 11.32; cf. 10.11) and in Heb. 12.5–11 denotes especially God's punitive intervention for the purification of the people. In the context of Eph., however, it gains a somewhat different note. For because it is set in opposition to a kind of hard behaviour which rouses

[6]Philo suggests in the passage mentioned the promise of a double reward: one which lies in the possession of the virtue, and the other of the immortality to which the long lifespan points (262).

[7]Thomas Aquinas: sensus spiritualis according to Ps. 143.10 f. (Cai nr 341); Schlier 282 (refers to 1.18); Barth 756 (sees in the whole section an 'eschatological perspective'); Ernst 393 ('not with certainty').

[8]Cf. Schweizer, *Colossians* on this passage.

[9]Spec. Leg. II, 229–32. In discussing Deut. 21.18–21 (the killing of a rebellious son) Philo claims that the punishment is imposed not only by one spouse but by both in agreement. (§232). The following expositions (§§233–6) are also instructive.

[10]Cf. Schweizer, *Colossians* 224 n. 50–1.

[11]Cf. G. Bertram, TDNT V, 603–7. In the OT there is 'no broad vocabulary of education' (604); yet all upbringing and discipline proceeds from God. In Deut. there is also positive reference to proof of God's grace (cf. 4.32–6; 8.2–5; 11.2–7); in the preaching of the prophets, however, the discipline and punishment of God for the education of his people stand in the foreground (cf. Hos. 10.10; Zeph. 3.2, 7; Jer. 2.30; 5.3; 7.28; 17.23; Is. 53.5). The picture only changes in the Wisdom literature in which παιδεία and σοφία are associated (cf. Prov. 1.2 f., 7; 3.11 f. (discipline of the Lord); 5.12; 6.23 and often) but now the wise upbringing by human beings is recognised and recommended – clearly under the influence of the Greek educational ideal (cf. Wis. Sol. 3.11; 6.17; 7.14; everywhere in Sir). But still the fear of God is the starting-point and epitome of 'wisdom and upbringing' (Sir preface; 1.27; 4.17; 6.18; 8.8 et al.). Faith in God, the religiousness of the Torah and Greek striving after education run together in Hellenistic Judaism.

to rage, the 'discipline and instruction of the Lord' must surely in all its firmness include kindness and leniency. Paul as father of the congregation wishes to reprimand (νουθέτων) the Corinthians 'as beloved children', and according to Rom. 15.14 Christians ought to treat one another in this way. Christ's Lordship gives to every necessary command and reprimand the spirit of love. The two concepts connected here – 'education' (παιδεία) and 'admonition' (νουθεσία) have each in themselves a different emphasis. The first has more the sense of a (strict) total education, the second more a verbal reprimanding, a more lenient way as is more appropriate for dealing with older children.[12] But by the addition of 'of the Lord' both concepts are made subordinate to a higher principle in which the clear, firm and yet kindly instruction of the Lord is the decisive factor.

5

The command to slaves takes into account the subordinate social position of the slaves: in the Roman Empire they were not considered as persons with rights but as objects over which their master had the right of disposal. But in practice there were various humane alleviations and there were frequent instances of their being set free.[13] The early Church did not make any attempt at a fundamental change in their social status but tried to alter their position in the Christian household so that they recognised slaves as full brothers in the Lord and an appropriate attitude was then required on the part of the masters.[14] In the Haustafeln both sides in their different social positions are advised to strive appropriately according to the 'virtues of their rank' which gain a higher motivation from Christ. Hence the command to slaves to obey their earthly masters is obvious, but it takes on a different appearance if they recognize in it a service to their heavenly Lord. 'With fear and trembling' underlines the obedience owed but as a familiar double expression[15] is not intended to arouse quivering anxiety but salutary fear (cf. Phil. 2.12 for the achievement of our salvation). The positive expression 'in purity of heart' presses for inner acceptance and the honest, sincere execution of what is required.[16] The deeper reason for this is the understanding of the service of slaves as a service to Christ; for this Lord is at one and the same time the model of service (cf. 1 Pet. 2.18–21) and the 'shepherd and guardian' of those who follow him (ibid. v. 25). The

---

[12]Cf. Trench 66–9 with evidence from Classical literature.

[13]On the position and situation of slaves cf. W. L. Westermann, RE Suppl VI, 894–1068 especially 994–1063 (the Empire); also *The Slave Systems of Greek and Roman Antiquity*, Philadelphia ³1964; H. Gülzow, *Christentum und Sklaverei in den ersten drei Jahrhunderten*, Bonn 1969; J. Vogt, *Sklaverei und Humanität*, ²1972 (Historia-Einzelschriften 8); Stuhlmacher* 46; H. Volkmann, KPV, 230–4.

[14]Cf. Philem.; on the interpretation of Philem. 16 especially Stuhlmacher* 42–9.

[15]Cf. Gen. 9.2; Ex. 15.16; Deut. 2.25; Ps. 2.11; Is. 19.16; 1 Cor. 2.3; 2 Cor. 7.15; Phil. 2.12. The slant, of course, is different according to each context.

[16]Cf. 1 Chron. 29.17; Wis. 1.1; 1 Macc. 2.37; often in Test XII where the whole speech of Issachar stands under the title ἁπλότης, further R 4, 1; S 4, 5; L 13, 1; B 6, 7; also in Qumran texts: 1 QS 11.2; Damasc. 8.14; 19.27; further Philo, Op. Mund. 156. 170; Vit. Mos. I, 172. In the different contexts the word has not unimportant nuances of meaning, cf. J. Amstutz, *ΑΠΛΟΤΗΣ. Eine begriffsgeschichtliche Studie zum jüdisch-christlichen Griechisch*, Bonn 1968; Spicq, *Notes* I, 125–9.

earthly masters do not stand in Christ's place, but to serve them is understood as a service for Christ (ὡς Χριστῷ) – a motive which is not given without consideration.[17]

6–7

Purity of heart prevents all hypocrisy and grovelling with which slaves might buy their masters' favour. Such behaviour is aptly named 'eye-service' and the striving thereby 'to please people' (both expressions already in Col. 3.22) is contrasted with the will to serve Christ/God from the inner compulsion (ἐκ ψυχῆς). In contrast to Col. the author of Eph. has placed yet another strong emphasis. As 'slaves of Christ' those who are addressed should do God's will from the heart. The change of synonyms from καρδίας (heart) to ἐκ ψυχῆς (from the soul) might be a reminder of the principal commandment to love God (Deut. 6.5) but it is a general Hebrew and also Hellenistic expression. More significant is the neologism 'slaves of Christ' which intensifies the thought of v. 5 ('as to Christ'). The social status of slaves is raised to the higher level of being bound to Christ. This is not to be compared with Paul's self-designation as a 'slave of Christ' (Rom. 1.1; Gal. 1.10; cf. Phil. 1.1) – Paul was a free man – but rather with his instruction in 1 Cor. 7.20–2 in which he relativises the social position of a slave and a free man in view of their 'being in Christ'. Yet in that passage the one who is socially free is paradoxically called a 'slave of Christ' (v. 22b).[18] The author of Eph. recommends slaves to accept their 'existence as slave' not thinking of an inner freedom but of a different understanding of their service. As 'slaves of Christ' they should be prepared to serve eagerly,[19] because this service is regarded as being not for humans but for the Lord (v. 7). The Pauline motive doubtless deserves to be more highly estimated.

8

The willingness to serve is strengthened by the motive of reward: Christ, the Lord, will reward everyone for the good he does. It might surprise us that the author does not take over the definition of the reward contained in Col. 3.24, i.e. the 'inheritance' (cf. Eph. 1.14, 18; 5.5). But in the motive of reward he also puts the accent somewhat differently. He leaves out the threat to those who do wrong (Col. 3.25). In their connection as 'slaves of Christ' they should be assured that their Master will leave no good deed (ἐάν τι)[20] unrewarded. Perhaps behind this lies the consideration that slaves often received no recognition from their masters for their good efforts. The heavenly Lord overlooks nothing and nobody and treats slaves no

[17]Cf. Schweizer, *Colossians* 219.

[18]The Christian life, in spite of being freed from the enslaving Law, from sin and death, is a new service for God and Christ, cf. Rom. 6.16 f.; 7.6; 12.11; 14.18; 16.18. In this respect Christian masters and slaves are treated as equal. But this view appears already to have been submerged in the Haustafel.

[19]εὔνοια is good intention, enthusiasm (connected with σπουδή: Ditt Syll,³ 799, 27; PGeiss 56.14) and counts as a virtue in slaves. Cf. Pr-Bauer 639 s.v. 2; Gnilka 301, n. 4.

[20]In the variants to the text (v. in Nestle-Aland²⁶) we should take special note of the position of ἕκαστος (each). The text which later came to be accepted puts the emphasis on the Object 'whatever good'; that followed here, (with Nestle-Aland) upon 'each'. To this there corresponds as the end 'be he slave or free'.

differently from free people. Thus the addition 'be he slave or free', which is at first surprising, makes sense: the heavenly Lord does not differentiate.

9

In keeping with this is the command to masters to treat their slaves in the same manner, aware that a person's standing does not matter to their common Lord in heaven. The fairly colourless expression 'do the same' – which does not refer back to the 'do good' of v. 8 (change in number!) but demands a corresponding behaviour on the part of the masters – is explained by the equality before Christ. What was recommended for the slaves also holds true *mutatis mutandis* for their masters. Having the power to command they should not misuse it in harshness or threats but exercise it according to the will of their common Lord i.e. with leniency and kindness. In Col. 4.1 the demand is more concrete ('do what is just and fair'); but the author of Eph. is more concerned with the appropriate mutual behaviour in responsibility to the common Lord. Hence he formulates it even more clearly: your Lord and theirs is in heaven. The motive that he does not show partiality is now related to both groups, other than in Col. where is stands in the command to slaves (3.25). The author suppresses a threat of judgement (as there is in Col.); at any rate he does not mention the eschatological retributary judgement (cf. Rom. 2.5–11; 2 Cor. 5.10). Although the conventional motive can be glimpsed, he promises the slaves only the reward for their good actions and he refers the masters generally to their responsibility before their heavenly Lord.

Summary

In his instruction to children and fathers, slaves and masters the author moves in conventional lines. And yet, in comparison with the Haustafel in Col., which he almost certainly used as a basis, he makes us aware of certain emphases which were important for him for motivation. In a similar way to that in which marriage-partners should be in harmony with one another after the pattern of Christ and the Church in partnership, the corresponding groups of children and fathers (or parents) and slaves and masters are referred to one another. Although the author does not want to remove the natural and social differences, he sees a way to reconcile opposites and avoid conflict in the care of one group for the other in the Spirit of Christ. He recommends each individual group to do what is required of them looking to Christ, the Lord. Children will find obedience easier if they perform it 'in the Lord', in accordance with God's Commandment which is accompanied by a promise. Upbringing by parents complies with this if it is understood and practised as the 'discipline and instruction of the Lord'. For slaves, their earthly service becomes an opportunity to show their willingness to serve Christ, the Lord, as 'slaves of Christ'. Conversely it is expected of masters that they should lighten their slaves' service by the manner in which they give orders and commands, responsible to the Lord in heaven. The idea of the common Lord is emphasized as a constant, dominating motive. He lays obligations upon all, each in his particular place, and this binds the 'conflict-laden' groups to one another. Thereby the basic motive of 5.21 once more comes into play:

'Subordinate yourselves to one another in reverence to Christ!' One might ask whether in a Christian congregation which knew itself subject to Christ alone as its 'Head' changes in the social order, particularly with reference to slaves, might not have suggested themselves. In this respect Eph. remains, together with the whole Early Church, a child of its time. The Early Church sought another way of coping with the social problem as is shown particularly in the Epistle to Philemon.[21] Deep as are the theological motives and effective as they could be in a living congregation truly caught by faith in Christ, it appears for us even today that there are consequences irrefutable for the social structure which are demanded by the message of Jesus and the fundamental Christian understanding (cf. Gal. 3.28). But the directive to overcome social tensions by their personal behaviour in the spirit of Jesus Christ retains its significance even in a society which has outwardly broken down social and class distinctions.

4. THE BATTLE AGAINST THE POWERS OF EVIL IN THE WORLD; CONTINUAL PRAYERFUL ALERTNESS (6.10–20)

After the Haustafel the author begins a final paraclesis which is dominated by the metaphor of the battle against the cosmic powers of evil. In contrast to the previously established longer sections of the paraclesis – namely the 'ecclesial' exhortation related directly to the congregation as the Church of Christ (4.1–16), the instructions for the realization of a Christian existence in pagan surroundings (4.17–5.14) and the instructions for the fashioning of life within the congregation, in home and family (5.15–6.10), this section depicts something new. The horizon widens on a universal, cosmic level to the situation of Christians in this age of the world which is still surrounded and darkened by the forces of evil.

Literature

D. E. H. Whiteley, 'Expository Problems: Eph. VI:12 – Evil Powers', ET 68 (1957) 100–3.
Kamlah, *Form* 189–196.
R. M. Trevijano Etcheverria, *En lucha contra las Potestades. Exégesis primitiva de Ef 6.11–17 hasta Origenes*, Vitoria 1968.
J. Y. Lee, 'Interpreting the Demonic Powers in Pauline Thought', NT 12 (1970) 54–69.
P. Beatrice, 'Il combattimento spirituale secondo san Paolo, Interpretazione di Ef 6.10–17', StPat 19 (1972) 359–422.
D. M. Lloyd-Jones, *The Christian Warfare. An Exposition of Eph 6.10 to 13*, Edinburgh 1976.
A. Hamman, *La prière, I Le Nouveau Testament*, Tournai 1959.
E. Lövestam, *Spiritual Wakefulness in the New Testament*, Lund 1963.
P. R. Jones, 'La Prière par l'Esprit. Ephésiens 6:18', RRef. 27 (1976) 128–39.

---

[21] Cf. Stuhlmacher* 48 f.

10 Finally be strong in the Lord and in the power of his strength!
11 Put on the full armour of God
    so that you can stand fast against the devil's intrigues.
12 For our battle is not against blood and flesh
    but against the forces, against the powers,
    against the world-rulers of this darkness,
    against the spirits of wickedness in the heavenly places.
13 Therefore don the full armour of God
    that you may withstand in the evil day
    and, when you have done everything, you may be able to stand
    fast.
14 Stand then,
    your waist girded with truth,
    attired with the breastplate of righteousness,
15   under your feet bound preparedness for the Gospel of peace,
16   to all this grasp the shield of faith
      with which you may be able to quench all the fiery
        arrows of the evil one.
17   And take the helmet of salvation
    and the sword of the Spirit, which is the word of God.
18 (Stand then) with every prayer and supplication,
    praying at every opportunity in the Spirit,
    and to that end stay alert
    with all perseverance and intercession for all the saints
19   also for me,
    that the Word may be given to me,
    when I open my mouth,
    to proclaim freely and openly the mystery of the Gospel
20   for which I may fulfill my service as an ambassador in
    chains,
    that I may speak freely and openly in it
      as I must speak.

Analysis

Where does this last section of the paraclesis end and how is it structured? If we work from the contents, which speak of battle and armour we might be tempted to end this exhortation at v. 17 and assume a new one beginning at v. 18, namely a call to prayer and vigilance (cf. Gnilka). But if we begin the analysis by looking at its syntactic structure, we must consider the section 6.10–20 as a unit. For after the fitting-out with Christ's weapons the author calls the readers in the same breath – with a Prepositional Phrase – (modal διὰ πάσης προσευχῆς κτλ) and two Participles (προσευχό-μενοι ... ἀγρυπνοῦντες) – to urgent prayer and incessant watchfulness (v. 18). The last two verses are then a special request to pray for the Apostle, the (fictitious) writer of the letter, that he may be allowed to proclaim the mystery of the Gospel openly (vv. 19 f.) – a reference back to the situation at the beginning of the letter and a bridge to the post-script to the letter. The transition to this special intercession takes place easily in connection with the intercession 'for all the saints' so that here, too, there is no sign of a new paragraph. Thus the section 6.10–20 appears to be a unified whole and we must understand the call to battle and resistance, to prayer and vigilance as a command bound together internally. The battle of the Christians against the powers of evil is not possible without prayer and constant alertness, prayerful vigilance impossible without God's armour and constant battle. All this is necessary in the world's gloomy situation to strengthen them 'in the Lord', in his mighty power (v. 10). But we can distinguish the following sub-divisions:

    (a) The necessity to fight with God's weapons (vv. 10–13)

    (b) The donning of God's armour (vv. 14–17)

    (c) Vigilant prayer and intercession for the preacher (vv. 18–20).

(a) With the connecting set-phrase τοῦ λοιποῦ ('finally') the author indicates that he wishes to give his readers a last important exhortation. It is initially formulated in a general way with an Imperative – 'be strong in the Lord!' – which is emphasized by a Prepositional Phrase with synonymous words ('in the power of his strength') (v. 10). Then follows, again in the Imperative, the command to put on God's armour in order (πρός with Infinitive) to be able to resist the intrigues of the devil (v. 11). He justifies this necessary arming with the (still continuing) battle against the superhumanly ('not against blood and flesh') strong powers of evil (v. 12). In the course of this we are aware of the four designations of these foes, each marked by πρός. These do not imply different groups but mean the same ungodly forces described differently. They come ever more clearly and more menacingly into view – a rhetoric device to indicate their power and dangerousness. From this the author again concludes (διὰ τοῦτο) the necessity of grasping God's armour. V. 13 is a stronger repetition of the call in v. 11, again with an Imperative but now with a more detailed expression of Purpose (ἵνα-Clause). In this way the Christians will be able to resist 'in the evil day' and, when they have accomplished everything, to 'stand'. With this the first basic command is rounded off.

(b) In connection with the 'standing' (οὖν) the author now gives a description of the armour of God. There are, if we check them, six parts of the armour or, better, 'armoury', since some of the weapons or garments are not named at all. They are also not meant to describe a complete 'armour' but only to illustrate how resourcefully and comprehensively the Christian must be armed for this battle. The construction, which is not syntactically exact, betrays the fact that here we are concerned with a loose enumeration. To the main command 'Stand, then' there are added three closely connected (by καί) Participles: (like those who) have their waist girded with truth (he has the belt in mind), who have put on the breast-plate of righteousness and bound under their feet the preparedness (literally: with the readiness) for the Gospel of peace (vv. 14–15). To this is added, somewhat emphasized by ἐν πᾶσιν ('to all this') a further Participle: who have grasped the shield of faith. The reason for this is explained in a Relative Clause: with which they will be able to quench 'the fiery arrows of the evil one' (v. 16). After this description the author begins anew with an Imperative (omitted in some MSS): 'And take (δέξασθε) the helmet of salvation and the sword of the Spirit, which is the word of God . . .' (v. 17). From here he moves on, still in the same Complex Sentence, to discuss prayer and vigilance. Hence the syntactic structure provides us with no logical division; the connections are chosen according to what is needed and possible for the continuation of the description. Only one thing is emphasized as a principle concern and recognisable in the verbal structure: the command placed above the whole description – 'Stand, then!'

(c) The call to prayer which is closely connected to this (v. 18) has a parallel in the Epistle to the Col. (4.2 f.) and a comparison leaves no doubt that the author of Eph. followed this pattern. Syntactically the exhortation is so closely connected to v. 17 by the double expression 'with every prayer and supplication' that such prayer appears as an accompanying condition (διά plus Genitive) to the arming for battle. It is true we could also take the expression with the following Participle προσευχόμενοι; then the call to take the helmet of salvation and the sword of the Spirit would be continued in this Participle. But this would mean that the call to prayer in v. 18 would be heavily overburdened, for there then follows 'at every opportunity in the Spirit'. To the intercession for the saints 'Paul' immediately adds the wish that they should pray for him, too, that 'the word be given' to him, when he opens his mouth, and what he is thinking of here is explained in further additions. The connected Infinitive Clause puts the emphasis on 'openly' (v. 19) and a subsequent ἵνα-Clause (v. 20) says it even more clearly: so that he – in spite of the chains he bears – may be able to speak as freely and openly as he must. Hence the first ἵνα-Clause names the content of the intercession, the second the purpose.

On the *semantic level*, the perspective of the world which is at present under the domination of evil is significant at the beginning (v. under a). It is not a completely new perspective; in the paraclesis up till now it has also formed the background but was concealed by the central commands to the congregation that they should represent and realize the area of Christ's salvation in the world, a pagan environment. Now the author appears once more to take up the statement: 'The days are evil' (5.16). The depiction of the superhumanly strong forces of evil which dominate the world's stage reminds us of the first part of the document in which these personified spiritual powers are named initially in the description of the divine demonstration of power in the Christ-event (1.20 f.) and then in a look back at the wretched pre-Christian situation of the addressees (2.2). Finally the 'powers and forces' surface once again in the revelation of the mystery of Christ through the Church (3.10). At the end the author clearly wishes to include the Christians he addresses in that wide cosmic perspective which is in his view important for the understanding of Christian existence in the present.

The semantic field which comes to the fore in the description of God's armour (under b) includes as leading concepts: truth, righteousness, peace, faith, salvation, spirit, word of God. For the readers these are well-known symbols for that which has been given to them and which gives them strength to win the inevitable battle against the evil in the world. The command to 'stand' (vv. 11, 13, 14), once to 'withstand' (v. 13b) corresponds exactly to the task laid upon the Christians. They already have their 'place to stand' in God; God's weapons also lie ready for them, they need only to grasp them and will then be able to stand fast and resist.

In the concluding part the language of prayer is significant:
with every prayer and supplication
in that you pray at every opportunity in the Spirit
and to that end stay alert
with all perseverance and intercession for all the saints . . .

The theme is indicated in the first line, in two expressions: προσευχή and δέησις, which can be used synonymously but here are differentiated by what comes after. The προσευχή as speech and solidarity with God is taken up in the second line by προσευχόμενοι and stressed in more detail as continual praying in the Spirit. For this very reason it is necessary to be vigilant, and this mentioned in the second Participle ἀγρυπνοῦντες (third line). In order to underline the 'at every opportunity' yet again, the author adds 'with all perseverance' but then returns to the δέησις which he now classifies rather as intercession for all the saints. In this way prayer and vigilance are interwoven with one another. It is a matter of a continual vigilant praying or a tireless prayerful vigilance.

If we look at the order of the text in Col. we can see clearly that the author of Eph. has inserted the metaphor of the battle and the armour after the Haustafel and then returned to the schema of Col. with the call to prayer. In Col. 4.3 f. after the call to prayer and vigilance in thanksgiving comes the wish that the Colossians should also pray for Paul. Eph. takes this up in 6.19 f., with clear dependence on the formulations in Col. and yet again with characteristic alterations (cf. exegesis).

Finally we must ask what *pragmatic intentions* the author is pursuing with these amendments, alterations and accentulations over against Col. The insertion of the battle-metaphor is in keeping with his endeavour in immunize his Christian readers against the influences of their pagan environment and to activate them to a more determined realization of a Christian existence. For this it is necessary to hold before their eyes the ever-present danger to their salvation but also to remind them of God's power effective in them. They cannot wage the necessary battle depending on their own strength, but it is possible for them with God's weapons, through the power of the divine Spirit and in constant vigilant prayer. The call to intercede for the captive Apostle must have a special meaning in this pseudonymous document. It can scarcely be that the author simply wishes to strengthen the fiction that the letter comes from Paul himself. The emphasis which falls on the open preaching and the proclamation of the mystery of the Gospel leads us to suspect that the author is speaking on his own account; he himself is endeavouring to reveal through his writing the hidden mystery of the divine will (cf. 3.4–10), thereby announcing their defeat to the 'powers and forces in the heavens' (3.10) but also making the congregation aware of their task of salvation as the Church of Christ and impressing upon them the obligations which emerge from this for them in the world.

Exegesis

10

In a concluding speech of exhortation which is marked as such by the Adverbial Phrase τοῦ λοιποῦ (= henceforth, finally)[1] the Christians are called to stand fast and resist in the midst of a world dominated by evil. The horizon has again broadened out from the congregational service of worship (5.18–20) through the domestic responsibilities of Christians (Haustafel 5.21–6.9) to the world. The command to make the most of the right time for action, for the days are evil, (5.15 f.) is taken up and continued. Thereby the dismal view of the powers of evil in this world – which the Christians have rejected (2.2) and to which the Church has revealed God's triumph (cf. 3.10) – shows through anew, just as the consideration of the environment estranged from God and fallen into an immoral life-style formed the horizon of the paraclesis on Christian existence (4.17–5.14). For the idea of the Church this represents a consideration amendment to an apparent triumphalistic view which concluded from the certainty of Christ's victory that Christians have a part in his dominion. (cf. 2.6). In reality that 'all-becoming-one' in Christ which is the goal of the divine plan of salvation (1.10) consists for the moment only in the transcendent world of God which discloses itself to faith, while the earthly world, unchanged for the Christian too, offers the picture of a battleground between light and darkness, good and evil. And yet something *has* changed, for God's powers which have been released by Christ give promise of the prospect of victory for the Christians in the battle.

Hence the exhortation set over the whole exposition reads that they should become stronger powerfully in the Lord. A similar encouragement comes early in the Epistle to the Colossians (1.11), and at the end of 1 Cor. there is combined to it the call to be vigilant and stand fast in faith (16.13). The following picture of God's armour can also be connected with similar metaphorical motifs in Paul's letters (cf. 1 Thess. 5.8; 2 Cor. 6.7; 10.3 f.; Rom. 13.12). But the author of Eph. has developed from the tradition he took over a larger, self-made and, in its unity, more impressive description of God's soldier[2] which betrays a special interest in this battle situation. His own hand gives itself away in v. 10 in the accumulation of concepts (for 'power of his strength' cf. 1.19). 'In the Lord' here also (as in 6.1–9) relates to Christ who provides God's weapons for the Christian.

---

[1] According to Classical Greek usage the Genitive should be understood as Temporal, cf. Bl-Debr §186, 4. in the NT Gal. 6.17; Schlier 289 takes this meaning ('in future'). But since paracleses are all meant for the future, the meaning 'finally', in the same sense as the frequent (τὸ) λοιπόν is to be preferred; cf. Pr-Bauer 949 and the majority of the commentaries. Beatrice* 339 n. 75 favours the variant τὸ λοιπόν.

[2] 2 Tim. 2.3 f. only briefly takes up the motif of military service along with that of the athlete and the hard-working farmer (similarly Paul in 1 Cor. 9.7, 24–6), cf. N. Brox, *Die Pastoralbriefe*, 1969 (RNT 7/2⁴) 241. In Ign. Pol. 6.2 the description is also shorter.

11

The command to put on the full armour (πανοπλία) of God follows immediately. It is the equipment of a fully-armed foot-soldier[3] which is then described in detail in vv. 13–17 and metaphorically transferred to God's warrior. Has he the picture of a Roman legionary in mind as Oepke thinks? Even if the individual weapons correspond to the armour of a warrior of that period, the expression 'full armour' which is taken up in v. 13 and even more the addition 'of God' indicates that here what he wants to describe in metaphorical language is simply the hardness of the battle which can only be won in the strength of the Lord. Hence God's adversary, the devil, is immediately named as the enemy who must be resisted. In the choice of these expressions the author shows that he is bound to the early Christian tradition which prefers the Greek name for the devil to the 'Satan' which is prominent in Paul.[4] God's adversary directs his furious assaults on the Christian congregations after Christ's victory on the Cross (cf. Rev. 12; 1 Pet. 5.8 '*your* adversary') but apart from outward persecutions (Rev.) he does this not in open battle but in insidious attacks. The 'intrigues' or machinations (μεθοδεῖαι) mark the cunning of his temptation for which he makes use of insecure people (cf. 4.14).[5] In the traditional view he is the leader of the angels who are allied to him (Rev. 12.7–9), for Eph. the inspirer of the 'powers and forces' hostile to God who are named immediately after this (v. 12). The adoption by the author of the belief in the devil, which at that time had asserted itself in varied forms of development and manifold shapes,[6] and his own adaption of it in his own ideas, is instructive. The 'devil' is an expression for the ungodly power of evil which on the one hand manifests itself in human dealings (cf. 2.2; 4.14) and on the other conceals within itself an inscrutability which transcends a purely human explanation (5.12). A personal, concrete pre-objectivising interpretation is therefore ruled out just as is a resolution into internal human-social conditions. Behind every inexplicable, unaccountable human malice there is visible a spiritual power of evil which disastrously envelops human will and human history.[7] More will be said at v. 13 on 'stand' which as standing fast and resisting is the appropriate attitude promising victory in this spiritual battle.

[3]Cf. A. Oepke, TDNT V, 295–8.

[4]In Paul never διάβολος; on the other hand cf. the advance of διάβολος in Luke's two works, in the Pastorals, in Jas. 4.7; 1 Pet. 5.8; 1 Jn. 3.8, 10; Jude 9; in the Apostolic Fathers.

[5]Beatrice developed the thesis that the enemies to be resisted are specifically the judaising teachers of false doctrine as already in Gal. and 2 Cor. But this is erroneous on various grounds (non-Pauline authorship, another perspective, cf. 2, 11–18 etc.)

[6]Cf. A. Frank-Duqesne, 'En marge de la tradition judéochrétienne', in *Satan*, Et Carm 27 (1948) 181–311; W. Foerster, TDNT VII, 151–63; Whiteley*; H. Haag, *Teufelsglaube* (with various contributions), Tübingen 1974; H. Kruse, 'Das Reich Satans', Bib. 58 (1977) 29–61; K. Kertelge, 'Teufel, Dämonen, Exorzismen in biblischer Sicht', in W. Kasper – K. Lehmann (ed.), *Teufel – Dämonen – Besessenheit*, Mainz 1978, 9–39; R. Schnackenburg, 'Das Problem des Bösen in der Bibel', in: *Die Macht des Bösen und der Glaube der Kirche*, Düsseldorf 1979, 11–32.

[7]In the face of attempts to explain evil (a) merely as resulting from the misdirected aggressive impulse (K. Lorenz, *On Aggression*, London 1966) (b) from depth psychology (following C. G. Jung) or (c) as arising from social constraints, cf. P. Ricoeur, *Phänomenologie der*

Christians ('for us', v. 1 'for you') are concerned not with human battles but with a spiritual struggle against opponents who are not of 'blood and flesh',[8] i.e. who cannot be wounded or vanquished like human beings. The Greek expression πάλη originally means wrestling-match but can also stand for 'fight' in general.[9] If Philo uses the word for the struggle of the ascetic who combats his passions and evil inclinations,[10] we must not limit the battle here to asceticism, severance from the bonds of matter, struggling free from sin etc. The picture of battle unrolled in Eph. has cosmic dimensions and rather calls for 'endurance of the world's situation' (Greeven). The following enumeration of the evil powers brings to view the spiritual world subordinate to the devil, inspired and directed by him, which darkens and threatens the whole of the human Lebensraum, including that of the Christians. 'Powers' and 'forces' were already mentioned in 1.21. There they are those over which Christ has been put in a dominating position 'not only in this age but also in that which is to come'. But 'this age' still exists and puts pressure on Christians, too, in their earthly existence. According to 2.2 'the age of this world' is still effective as a spiritual power (πνεῦμα) in the 'Sons of Disobedience'. The Christians are still surrounded by this disastrous influence. The local idea, too, that the ungoldly ruler exercises his power in the sphere of the air (2.2) is again to be found in 6.12 in the attribute 'in the heavenly places'.[11] This can only mean the 'lower heavens' which overlie the earth in contrast to the transcendent heaven of God to which Christ has ascended ('over all the heavens' 4.10). Most indicative however is the new reference, only met with here, to the 'world-rulers (of this darkness)', an expression which cannot deny its astrological origin. The planets which are thereby indicated[12] in astrology not only exercise functions of ordering in space but also exert a

Schuld, Freiburg-Munich 1971; E. Drewermann, *Strukturen des Bösen*, 3 volumes, Paderborn 1977/78. Cf. also Lloyd-Jones*, who in his sermons argues for the existence of the Devil and evil spiritual powers (especially 53–65).

[8]Usually in the reverse order 'flesh and blood'; Sir 14.18; 17.31; Mt. 16.17; Gal. 1.16; 1 Cor. 15.50, a semitism for human weakness and transitoriness. But cf. Heb. 2.14; again different in Jn. 1.13. On the Jewish mode of expression cf. R. Meyer, TDNT VII, 116, on the NT E. Schweizer ibid. 124; 137. The idea of the incorporeality of the angels and 'evil spirits' corresponds to the development in early Judaism, cf. Eth. Enoch 15.4–12; Jub. 10.3, 5–11; 11.5; 15.31 f.; Apoc. Abr. 19; Test. Hiob. 27 (ed. Brock, Leiden 1967, p. 38 f.); Test D 6, 1; Qumran texts. Admittedly the teaching on the spirits is stamped in a different way.

[9]Cf. H. Greeven, TDNT V, 721.

[10]Philo, Mut. Nom.; Leg. All. III, 190; '. . . by Jacob who was skilled in wrestling, admittedly not in physical wrestling but in the fight which the soul conducts against her adversary where she struggles with passions and vices'. – The early Christian understanding of spiritual military service went a different road, cf. the work of Trevijano Etcheverria*. Further in the History of the effect of the Epistle.

[11]This phrase is missing in P⁴⁶; but it corresponds to the author's conception elsewhere (cf. at 2.2). C. J. A. Lash, 'Where Do Devils Live? A Problem of Textual Criticism of Ephesians 6.12', VigChr 30 (1976) 161–174, would like to trace an early Syrian variant ἐν τοῖς ὑπουρανίοις. The sense would then be even clearer.

[12]Cf. the material in F. Cumont, *Mithra ou Sarapis* κοσμοκράτωρ Acad. des Inscriptions et Belles Lettres, Paris 1919, 313–28; Schmid, *Epheserbrief*, 145; W. Michaelis, TDNT III, 914; Lee* 59 f.

power over humanity which determines their fate. In the Magic Papyri the sun is frequently named as such, but also gods such as Serapis and Hermes. In Gnosis the 'world-rulers' still clearly betray their connection with the planetary sphere.[13] In the Jewish area, too, where the Greek expression appears as a loan-word but signifies Satan,[14] the astral background can still be recognized in connection with other speculations about angels. The 'darkness' is that of the lower world, the earth, which thereby sinks into bondage, oppression and invalidity. In the Qumran texts humanity is caught amidst the battle which has flared up between the 'Angel of Darkness' and his horde and the 'Angel of Light' and his army.[15] Since the contrast of light and darkness can be found in an appropriate form in all the philosophies of that time (cf. also John's Gospel)[16] we need not determine a concrete point of reference, be it in Gnosis, in Qumran or other texts. What the author is trying to say in his enumeration of these powers and forces, the world-rulers of this darkness and also in the 'spirits of wickedness'[17] is explained by the accumulation of concepts: the whole of human existence comes under the pressure of powers which act disastrously or a concentrated power of evil (personified in the 'devil') against which human beings seem powerless in their earthly state. He thereby takes up the sense of existence predominant at the time, that worldly fear which, beaten down by a paralyzing belief in fate and fear of demons, looks for ways of escape in resorting to sorcerers, in yearning for initiation into the Mysteries or for gnostic reconciliation to the self.[18]

13

The oppressive weight of such fear of the world which imposed itself on people bound to the contemporary conception of the world is basically removed from the readers of this letter, from the introductory Eulogy to

---

[13]For the Mandaeans the planets are controlled by the Rūhā ruler of the world, cf. Ginza 99, 15–32; 104.5 f.; 105, 24–33 etc. Cf. Lidz Ginza Regist s.v. Planeten. Cf. Jonas, *Gnosis* I, 272–4. The ideas have their roots in Babylonian and Iranian notions which were debased by the Mandaeans. cf. K. Rudolph, *Die Mandäer* I, 1960 (FRLANT 74) 147–9; 207–9.

[14]Cf. Bill. II, 552.

[15]Cf. the Doctrine of the Two Spirits in 1 QS 3.18–25; then again the document about the 'Battle of the Sons of Light against the Sons of Darkness' (1 QM). According to this depiction Belial arms himself to help the Sons of Darkness but God sends eternal help for the situation of his elect through Michael (1 QM 16, 11–16; 17, 5–9).

[16]Cf. S. Aalen, *Die Begriffe 'Licht' und 'Finsternis' im Alten Testament, im Spätjudentum und im Rabbinismus*, Oslo 1951; H. W. Huppenbauer, *Der Mensch zwischen zwei Welten*, 1959 (AThANT 34) (on Qumran); R. Schnackenburg, *John* I 245–9; O. Böcher, *der johanneische Dualismus im Zusammenhang des nachbiblischen Judentums*, Gütersloh 1965, 96–108; H. Conzelmann, TDNT VII, 423–5; IX, 310–58.

[17]Cf. the 'evil spirits' in Jub. 10.3, 5, 13; 11.4 f.; 12.20; Eth. Enoch 15.8 f; 11 f.; Test L 5.6; B 3.3 et al. The Genitive τῆς πονηρίας characterizes the spirits in general as wicked and leading astray to evil, cf. similar semitizing Genitives in 1.13; 2.2, 3, 12, 15: 4.24; 5.6. On the seat of the evil spirits in the sphere of the air cf. also Test B 3, 4; Slav. Enoch 29.4 f.

[18]Cf. E. Schweizer, 'Das hellenistische Weltbild als Produkt der Weltangst', in *Neotestamentica* 15–27. Schlier 291 speaks of the 'atmosphere' of existence which those evil powers spread around themselves.

the instructions for a Christian existence ('Be children of the Light'). As the elect of God, as the redeemed who are included in Christ's all-embracing dominion in the saving area of the Church, they need no longer fear the menacing powers of evil. Yet in view of the continuing situation of the world the author warns them against carelessness and self-confidence. He deliberately puts at the end the demand that they should face up to this gloomy situation and avoids new pressures of anxiety by means of the metaphor of God's armour with which the Christians may be enabled to withstand the overwhelming forces.

The reference to the 'evil day' is conspicuous. This appears still to be in the future. The expression is interpreted in very different ways according to the assessment of the whole. Alongside an interpretation of the time of the battle as being decidedly at the end of history, immediately preceding the coming of the Lord,[19] there are others; an individualizing one, which understands it to mean a critical time which comes once or frequently to every person or even the day of their death;[20] a purely present one which believes that the concept which arises from Apocalyptic is made present in Eph. and the Christians, already moved to heaven with Christ, fight from there against the hostile powers;[21] finally, one which combines present and future: The Christians are already now in the eschatological decisive situation but must reckon with a climax or several still to come.[22] If we orient ourselves on the broader context of Eph., according to 4.16 'the days are evil' already, and the exhortation given in the present (6.10–12) to take up God's armour forbids our thinking simply of a preparation for the situation of need and battle intensified at the end, since there is no longer a trace of the idea that the 'Day' is immanently expected. The expression 'the evil (or wicked) day' certainly reminds us of many similar statements in Jewish-apocalyptic literature,[23] but it is no firmly marked terminus for the last, evil time. The author of Eph. uses eschatological – apocalyptic concepts in a hazy way[24] so that it is not certain whether he really was thinking of a last date when the situation becomes intensified before the end. We can exclude the individualizing interpretation – that it means the lifetime of individual Christians with their trials and temptations – because of the cosmic horizon and the general

---

[19]von Soden, Dibelius – Greeven; Grabner-Haider, *Paraklese* (p. 162 n. 5) 104; Schlier 293 (the time of terror which precedes the end which has already begun but which will be completely revealed on an indefinite 'day'). Gaugler.

[20]Bengel: ubi malus vos invadit; Ewald 250; Haupt 247; G. Harder, TDNT VI, 554.

[21]Lindemann, *Aufhebung der Zeit* 64 and 235 f.

[22]Gnilka 308; cf. Barth 804 f.; Beatrice* 395–7.

[23]The starting-point for apocalyptic is Dan. 12.1 'time of suffering' (Hebrew '*eth zarath*, LXX ἡ ἡμέρα θλίψεως, ὁ καιρός θλίψεως) 'such as has never been as long as nations have existed up to that time'. The idea of the final, evil time is widespread, cf. Volz. Esch. 147–63 and is expressed in various ways, cf. Grabner–Haider, *Paraklese* (p. 162, n. 5) 104, n. 278; Schlier 292 f. But for Eph. 6.13 it is doubtful whether this apocalyptic description is intended in its original sense (the evil immediately before the end). G. Delling, TDNT II, 953 applies the expressions to the time of the devil's intrigues (v. 11), similarly Lindemann, *Aufhebung der Zeit* 235 f. (already present).

[24]Cf. the Wrath of God 2.3; the age to come 1.21; the ages to come 2.7; the inheritance 1.14, 18; 5.5; the Day of Redemption 4.30.

address to all Christians. But a purely present interpretation is also inadequate when we consider the passages in Eph. which are open to the future and the wording in 6.13 where another serious threat comes upon the readers with the 'evil day'. We must therefore, as at other places, combine present and (an indefinite) future: The days are already evil now, and they will remain so – in fact they will become darker still. The 'evil day' is a linguistic sharpening, in dependence on the language of apocalyptic, from which no further conclusions can be drawn for a concrete expectation of the end.

The 'stand' which comes after 'resist' – which is again taken up in v. 14 in the command to stand (cf. οὖν) – can therefore not be explained as the standing before the Judge, the withstanding in Judgement or the eternal standing before God.[25] Such standing (cf. Eth. Enoch 62, -H; 1 QS 11.16 f.; 1 QH 4.21; Lk. 21.36; also Rom. 14.4) cannot do without a supplementary 'before God', 'before the Son of Man' or something similar. We must also interpret the controversial ἅπαντα κατεργασάμενοι in a corresponding way. The verb can mean 'accomplish, carry out' as well as 'vanquish, overcome'; does it relate to the putting on of the complete armour or to the conquest of the enemies?[26] Because the verb in the NT, especially in Paul, only occurs in the first sense (21 times), it seems reasonable to interpret it here also in this way: After carrying out all their preparations for battle the Christians, fully armed with God's weapons, should stand fast however much the situation deteriorates.

14

Now there begins the description of God's soldier by means of the individual weapons he has put on or should put on. The whole is an illustration because what is fundamental has already been said. Conclusive is the standing (vv. 11 and 13c) or withstanding (v. 13b) as is shown by the resumption of this command. But why does he offer this portrayal of God's armour? The following is important for our understanding: (1) The author takes pains to describe *all-round* equipment which protects the fighter on all sides and makes him able for battle. He begins in the middle of the body (loins, breast), takes the feet into account, goes on to the shield which protects the whole body, turns to the head (the helmet of salvation) and finally mentions the sword as a sharp offensive weapon. Does he intend to name the most important weapons? The belt and shoes are not weapons in the real sense but simply belong to the warrior's clothing. If the weapons do correspond to the picture of a Roman legionary, other interests are revealed in features which interrupt the picture (readiness for the Gospel of peace, the 'fiery' arrows). (2) The author is less concerned with the weapons or articles of clothing themselves than with the function which is indicated for each of them: the belt ('the truth') surrounds and stiffens the

---

[25] Against Schlier 293.

[26] Opinions are divided up to the present time. A compromise solution 'after the victory over everything to maintain their stand' (Pr-Bauer 834 s.v. 4 as alternative), 'maintain their ground' (M. Zerwick, *Analysis philologica Novi Testamenti graeci*, Rome 1953, 437) does not fit in the context; for what remains to be done after the enemy has been completely defeated? The question is left open by G. Bertram, TDNT III, 653.

body; the breastplate protects the warrior; the shoes indicate the readiness to spread peace etc. It is a symbolic representation of the battle of the Christians against the evil in the world. (3) The whole description is marked by allusions to scriptural passages or reminiscences of biblical expressions. This is not only an enrichment from the language of the Bible with which the author is familiar but above all a description of how the Christian is equipped by *God*. The power of God, which is superior to all the forces of evil, must be shown to advantage under symbols which are testified to by the OT. The old picture of the 'Warrior of Yahweh' lies at the most far in the background[27] since to speak up for the Gospel of Christ is a prerequisite of God's soldier (cf. vv. 15 and 19). What the metaphor means is: The Christian does not have just any indeterminate weapons at his disposal but the weapons *of God* revealed in the Scriptures. It is the same line of thought as in Paul's saying: 'The weapons of our campaign are not human (σαρκικά) but are powerful through God . . .' 2 Cor. 10.4).

The act of girding oneself was metaphorically used in different ways in Judaism and early Christianity[28] but only here in the NT for the arming of a warrior. By the addition of ἐν ἀληθείᾳ (with truth) it can be seen that the author has in mind Is. 11.5 LXX, where it is said of the expected Messiah that his waist will be girded with righteousness and his loins with truth. The 'truth' has still the OT echo of constancy, fidelity. In the context of Eph. the word takes on a new shading: the uprightness and holiness (cf. 4.24; 5.9) given and demanded by God to the 'new' humanity created in Christ. We hardly need to look for a closer definition of 'truth';[29] together with 'righteousness' it is the expression for the equipment given to the Christian through grace. The 'breast-plate of righteousness' is to be found in Is. 59., 17 and Wis. Sol. 5.18 in the picture of the 'warrior' of Yahweh who creates justice and holds judgement. In Eph. it becomes the expression for the protection provided by God in the fight against evil. In 1 Thess. 5.8 Paul makes the breastplate mean faith and love, and the helmet hope – i.e. the basic attitudes of Christians which have their roots in God's election and blessing (cf. 1.3 f.). Underlying the picture in Eph. is the same fundamental philosophy of the Christian stance made possible and required by God.

[27]Cf. Is. 42.13; 59.17; Hab. 3.8 f.; Ps. 35.1 ff.; Wis. Sol. 5, 17–22 et al. The features which describe God's wrath and retaliation (cf. Is. 59, 17 f.) which could not be taken over for the portrayal of the Christian soldier are significant. But for the OT, too, it holds true that the portrayal of Jahweh the Warrior is 'already spiritual' (A. Oepke, TDNT V, 297); cf. also Fischer, *Tendenz* 166.

[28]In Judaism: cf. Ber. 16[b]: God girds himself with his grace; Num. R 2 (138a): Moses girds his loins with prayer (Bill. III 617); In the NT: the disciples should gird their loins for watchful readiness to serve (Lk. 12.35 cf. 37; 17.8); the symbolism is different in Jn. 21.18. Cf. A. Oepke, TDNT V, 302–8.

[29]Cf. the attempts at interpretation mentioned in A. Oepke, TDNT V, 307. There is little thought given especially to the truth of the Gospel because preparedness for the Gospel was already specifically mentioned in v. 15. Beatrice* 363 f. points to the truth of God realized in Christ.

15

Attention is now directed to the feet. For Roman soldiers the short boots (caliga) were a necessary part of their equipment for long marches and so were a characteristic feature.[30] Our author, however, does not mention footwear directly but immediately picks up metaphorically the 'preparedness for the Gospel of peace', clearly following Is 52.7: 'How welcome upon the mountains are the steps of the messenger of joy, who proclaims peace . . .' In Rom. 10.15 Paul makes the passage refer to the messengers of the Gospel. The author of Eph. is concerned in this exhortation to stand fast in the battle against evil not so much with the spreading of the Gospel as with the preparedness for peace. In a paradoxical way this is part of the equipment of God's soldier. Prompted by Is. 52.7, the 'Gospel of peace' does not mean the readiness for peace lent by the Gospel (Ewald) but the content of the Gospel which proclaims peace and salvation, peace which is realized in Christ (cf. 2.17). Christ, our peace (2.14), becomes the demand to God's soldiers to preserve the peace which has been presented to them. Compared with the descriptions of battle in Qumran which are focussed on victory and vengeance on God's enemies[31] we see here the exceptional character of the Christian congregation who know that they are already victors in Christ and with their battles in the world have simply to fulfil a task of peace in a comprehensive sense: to proclaim God's peace and spread it abroad. To this belongs also the striving to promote peace among humankind, to deny and resist all the powers of evil which break out in human conflicts and wars.

16

After the first three preparations we now see God's soldier taking up other weapons ('to all this'[32]). The long shield (θυρεός) was a defensive weapon which protected the warrior's whole body and was already in the OT a favourite metaphor for God's protection of the devout person. God says to Moses: 'I am your shield, your reward will be very great' (Gen. 15.1), and in the Psalms the motif that God himself is a shield for those who worship him occurs repeatedly (5.12; 18.2, 30; 28.7; 33.20 et al.) But God also gives the devout person the shield of his help (Ps 18.35) just as he girded him with strength (ibid. v. 32). If here the shield is interpreted as faith, faith appears as a weapon proferred by God. Faith is the basic power provided by God (cf. Col. 1.23) to enable us to resist the assaults of the devil (cf. 1 Pet. 5.9). The assaults of 'evil' (= of the devil) are compared to fiery arrows which in the way in which war was waged at that time, especially in

---

[30]A. Oepke, TDNT V, 301: 6: the caliga according to the evidence of statues 'is part of the equipment only from the Roman period, when long marches were required'.

[31]Cf. already 1 QS 1, 10 f.: 'but to hate all the Sons of Darkness, each according to his blame in God's vengeance', further 4.12–14; 1 QM 3.6 'the order of God's units for the vengeance of his wrath on all the Sons of Darkness'. 4.12 'God's war, the vengeance of God, God's battle, God's retribution . . . God's annihilation against every vain people'; Damasc. 8.12; 19.24.

[32]The v 1 ἐπὶ πᾶσιν A D F G Ψ MLatt Ambst. From the sense what would be most appropriate here is 'in all this' or 'besides all this' (cf. Lk. 16.26 with the same v. 1).

sieges, were extremely dangerous.[33] Firebrands are also mentioned occasionally in the OT (Ps. 2.7; Prov. 26.18; Is 50.11), more frequently in the Qumran documents.[34] In the description of Eph. they become a metaphor for the devil's unstoppable temptations which are like an unquenchable fire gaining ground. The metaphor of battle (*'all* the fiery arrows') forbids our thinking merely of the inner temptations to sin;[35] above and beyond these it means disruptions of faith, enticements of any kind (hence 'shield of faith'). What is inconceivable in the conduct of earthly warfare, the shield of God is capable of doing: not only of blocking the threatening arrows but even of putting them out. The metaphorical language breaks through reality.

17

Alongside the shield the helmet is a necessary protection for the warrior who is exposed to violent assaults. Again the helmet is immediately interpreted metaphorically as 'salvation' or 'deliverance', in connection with Is 59.17, a description of the 'warrior' of Yahweh from which the 'breastplate of righteousness' (v. 14b) was also taken. It is simply another metaphor for the all-round protection which God provides: As the breastplate covers the chest, so the helmet surrounds the head. Like the other weapons God's soldier also receives this equipment from God.[36] God himself is salvation and deliverance for all those under attack (cf. Ps. 3.3 f.; 18.3, 46; 35.3; 37.39 f.; 65.5 et al.; Is. 33.2; Jer. 3.23). In 1 Thess. 5.8 the helmet is interpreted as the *hope* of salvation, in the context of a decidedly eschatological perspective. In this the author of Eph. diverges from Paul; for him it is a matter of God's protection and deliverance in the present battle against evil.[37]

As the sole offensive weapon he finally mentions the 'sword of the Spirit' and interprets it as the Word of God. The sharp short-sword (μάχαιρα in contrast to ῥομφαία, the broad-sword) the most important weapon in close combat, enabled one to kill one's opponent (cf. Rev. 13.10). Herein lies the intensification in the enumeration of the weapons. But again it is a spiritual weapon which simply illustrates God's power. 'Sword of the Spirit' – only here in this combination – does not mean that the Spirit himself is a sword; rather that is the Word of God.[38] The Spirit is that strength which is effective in God's word, which provides piercing sharpness (cf. Heb 4.12). The might of God's spiritual word is reflected in

[33]Cf. A. Oepke, TDNT V, 314 n. 10.

[34]1 QH 2.26: 'and arrows strike and no one heals . . .'; 3.16, 27: 'where all arrows of the grave fly inevitably and hopelessly destroy'; cf. 1 QH 1.12 ('fiery arrows'); 1 QM ('bloody arrows'); Damasc 5.13 (after Is. 50.11). K. G. Kuhn, TDNT V, 300 f. points to the similarity of the depiction in the Hodajoth.

[35]Thomas Aquinas (Cai nr. 365): Ignea sunt, quia adurentia pravis concupiscentiis; Estius: omnia ignita jacula variorum tentationum; similarly Ewald.

[36]δέξασθε which is missing in D* F G b m* and in Ter. Cyp. Ambst. Spec. does not ask for human activity (not even for the sword as an offensive weapon) but merely serves to describe the equipment further.

[37]Differently Schlier 297 f., Gnilka 313, who at this point are thinking of hope and future.

[38]The Relative Pronoun ὅ should not be taken with πνεῦμα but with the syntactic construction 'sword of the Spirit'.

279

many ways in the Bible (as word of Creation, word of the Prophets, word of Christ, the Gospel) and already in Judaism (related to the Torah) compared with a sword.[39] Borrowing from Is 11.4, 2 Thess 2.8 says that the Lord (at his Parousia) will destroy the Antichrist with the breath (πνεῦμα) of his mouth, and in Rev. 19.15 it is said that from the mouth of the one who is called 'the Word of God' (v. 13) there issues a sharp sword (ῥομφαία) (cf. also 1.16; 2.12, 16). Possibly the author of Eph. has in mind the passage in Is. 11.4 where 'word' and 'breath' (πνεῦμα) stand parallel in the description of the coming Messiah. Already in v. 14a (girding with truth) he has drawn from the following passage in Is. 11.5. Thus here again a statement about the Messiah is transferred to God's soldier. The 'word (ὁ ῆμα) of God' with which he fights the battle as if with a sword is not defined more closely (without an article) and in the context surely means nothing other than the Christian message, the Gospel (cf. Rom. 10.8; 1 Pet 1.25). The 'Gospel of your salvation' (1.13) held firmly in faith and held up to one's enemies in truth, proves itself in battle through the power of the divine Spirit which is inherent in it.

With this the picture of God's soldier, who arms himself with God's weapons, is brought to an end. The impressive metaphor, as the exegesis should have shown, has no moralizing tendency but is meant in the first place to show the Christians the protection provided for them by God and encourage them to stand fast amid the temptations and struggles of the world. In this respect the Christian paraclesis differs from comparable uses of the familiar metaphor in the non-Jewish environment.[40] The religio-historical comparison which has made us aware of the mythical ideas of God's weapons and the thoughts inspired by the Mysteries of the religious person as God's soldier (e.g. in the cult of Mithras)[41] can at best reveal a general background which has produced a variety of specific views. The author of Eph. is most closely tied to the OT and Jewish tradition as is proved by the constant allusions to Scripture. The Qumran texts which reveal most clearly the picture of the battle waged by God's congregation in the world, especially vivid in the description of the Holy War (1 QM), are certainly close to the sketch in Eph.[42] but do not reach the actual theological scopus that the soldiers with God's weapons have only to hold on to and

---

[39]Cf. Targ. Hld. 3.8; Midr. Ps. 45 §17 (136[a]), where the sword which the young king dons is likened to the Torah which Moses procured (Bill. III, 618).

[40]Cf. Epict. Diss. III, 24.34: 'The life of every person is a campaign, a long and varied one. You must keep hold of the rôle of the soldier and perform everything according to the commander's signal, and at the same time foresee what he wants'; Sen. ep. 107.9. Further in H. Edmonds, 'Geistlicher Kriegsdienst. Der Topos der "Militia spiritualis" in der antiken Philosophie', in *Heilige Überlieferung* (FS I. Herwegen), Münster i. W. 1938, 21–50. There is a moralising Persian text in A. Oepke, TDNT V, 298. Later the model of the Roman soldier was held up to Christ's warrior, cf. 1 Cl. 37, 1–3; Ign. Pol. 6.2 (but Baptism should remain the arming). Further A. von Harnack, *Militia Christi. Die christliche Religion und der Soldatenstand in den ersten drei Jahrhunderten*, Tübingen 1905; Trevijano-Etcheverria*.

[41]Cf. Dibelius – Greeven 97; Kamlah* 194 goes back to Babylonian-Iranian mythology (cf. 85–92) which continues to have an effect in a modified form in Hellenistic Judaism, but stresses the new way it is used in Paul. As for Eph. 6.13–17 he stresses that it is a Baptismal exhortation in which the weapons describe the new existence (cf. 189–92). Cf. also Fischer, *Tendenz* 166 f.; Barth is critical 788–790.

[42]Cf. K. G. Kuhn, TDNT V, 298–300; Fischer, *Tendenz* 167–9 – but he stresses the 'significant' differences; Barth 791–3. The closeness of the Qumran texts to the description in Eph. 6 lies in their common conviction that all strength and help come from God; but in Eph. this is more deeply grounded in the merciful provision (Baptism) given for the Christians.

defend for themselves the victory already won, while they grow stronger in the strength of God.

18

Through the close connection 'with every prayer and supplication' (διά used to indicate the manner, circumstance)[43] the following call to prayer and vigilance still belongs with the readiness of Christians for battle – which is, however, something other than a worldly battle or human struggle. Although the author picks up the independent command to pray from Col. 4.2–4, he understands it in connection with the portrayal of God's soldier as a necessary supplement to standing fast and gaining strength in the Lord.[44] Anyone who wears *God's* armour must also beg in prayer for God's help for himself and for the Church ('all the saints'). Christ's soldier stands in constant vigilant prayer. The double expression for prayer[45] is made more specific in what follows: prayer in the Spirit which must be constantly practised (προσευχόμενοι) and intercession for the Church and her preachers (δέησις). Unceasing prayer was a great concern of the early Church. It is witnessed to and demanded especially by Paul and Luke though in different ways and point of view.[46] The expressions for 'unceasing' change: always (Lk. 18.1; cf. Rom. 1.10; Phil. 1.4; Col. 1.3; 4.12; 2 Thess. 1.11), steadfastly (Rom. 12.12; Col. 4.2), unceasing (1 Thess 5.17; cf. Rom. 1.9). In Eph. 6.18 we find 'at every opportunity (καιρῷ)' and that reminds us of the command in 5.16 'Redeem time (τὸν καιρὸν) because the days are evil'. Prayer is the Christian way of coping with a time dominated by evil because in prayer God is called upon and asked to help overcome evil. The metaphor of vigilant prayer is the same as in Lk. 21.36, only the 'eschatological temperature' is different. The author of Eph. is no longer worried about the Day of the Lord which comes like a snare over humanity (Lk. 21.34 f.) suddenly overtaking them. He adds as well that we should pray at all times 'in the Spirit' – a different accent from the Lucan praying *for* the Spirit (cf. Lk. 11.13). The addition again betrays Pauline tradition. Although Paul does not put it in this way the calling and praying of the Spirit in our hearts (cf. Gal. 4.6; Rom. 8.15 f, 26 f.)

---

[43]Cf. Pr-Bauer 357 s.v. III, 1, b (translated as 'call in prayer and beseeching'); Bl-Debr § 233.4. Cf. especially Acts 15.27; 2 Cor. 2.4; Rom. 2.27; 14.20; Heb. 12.1. So also Lövestam* 71. – We should reject the combining of the phrase with what precedes it because this does not fit well with the 'sword of the Spirit'. The author begins a new line with a Prepositional Phrase, cf. 1.4 f. (ἐν ἀγάπη; 2.14 f.; 3.17; 6.7.

[44]With Schlier 300; Beatrice* 19.361 f.; otherwise Gnilka 314 f. who would like to see in the exhortation to prayer a correspondence to the intercession for the addresses at the beginning of the letter (1.15–17). – On the tradition of such connection of wakefulness and prayer cf. Löves+am* 64–70.

[45]Schlier 300 refers for the double phrase as an expression to LXX III Kings 8.45; 2 Chron. 6.19; Acts 1.14 v. 1.; Phil. 4.6; 1 Tim. 2.1; 5.5; Ign. Magn. 7.1. – On the distinction between προσευχή and δέησις v. H. Greeven, TDNT II, 86.

[46]Cf. W. Ott, *Gebet und Heil. Die Bedeutung der Gebetsparänese in der lukanischen Theologie*, 1965 (StANT 12) 139–43. According to Ott unceasing prayer is for Paul humanity's answer to their redemption, bound up with thanksgiving and perpetual joy. – Insofar as Eph. 6.18 is concerned with unceasing intercession (it is different in 5.20), the exhortation in Lk. 21.36 is closer.

objectively fits most easily what our author wants to suggest. Our human praying only achieves power and effectiveness in the strength of the divine Spirit. Hence the Epistle of Jude also warns against mockers and tempters: 'Pray in the Holy Spirit' (v. 20).[47] Continuous prayer is practised especially in times of trouble and persecution (cf. Lk. 18.7; Rom. 15.30 f.; 1 Pet 4.7; Rev. 5.8; 8.3).

Vigilance is closely connected to prayer, so that one must be vigilant to pray (εἰς αὐτό) and the vigilance serves the continuing (προσκαρτερήσει)[48] and beseeching prayer (δεήσει). It is a vigilant prayer 'for all the saints', a metaphor which fits in well with the soldier of God as the soldier, too, keeps watch. The command to pray and watch is at home in the early Christian tradition without this metaphor. The request of Jesus to his disciples in Gethsemane (Mk 14.38) should surely speak also to later congregations. The triple call to vigilance, addressed to 'all', which Mark puts at the end of the eschatological speech (Mk 13.33–37) is translated by Luke in his paraenesis (21.34–6) as a call to constant vigilant prayer (v. 36).[49] We might ask whether behind this curious combination of 'watch' and 'pray' there is not already an established practice of a nightly prayer-vigil in the old Church. Apart from the eve of Easter when the whole congregation watched and prayed, there was also a private prayer-vigil which was practised especially in monastic circles.[50] An analogy can be found in Qumran: The members of the Community should for a third of the year stay awake through the whole night, reading the Scriptures and giving praise (1 QS 6.7); cf. also Ps 119.62; 134.1 f. A similar Christian custom of prayer-vigils could have developed at an early period based on what Luke tells of Jesus in 6.12 and of the Christians in Acts 12.12; 16.25, what Paul says of himself (1 Thess. 3.10; 2 Cor. 6.5) and what he expects from the real widow in 1 Tim. 5.5. But we have no certain knowledge for the early period, and a metaphorical interpretation would be justified from the text. What is significant is that, in the intercession 'for all the saints' the whole Church is brought into consideration as also in the prayers in the Didache (9.4; 10.5).

19

The prayers of the faithful should also contain special intercessions for the Apostle and, represented by him, for the preachers of the Gospel. The formulation clearly follows Col. 4.2–4 but does not speak in the Plural of

---

[47]Jones* would like to root Eph. 6.18 even more deeply in Eph.'s theology; Eph. is concerned with the common access to the Father of Jewish- and Gentile-Christians 'in one single Spirit' just as after Is. 59.17 the outlook is directed in what follows (59, 18–60, 7) to the saving of the nations. But this is reading too much into the terse expression.

[48]The noun is rare, only here in the Bible, but cf. W. Grundmann, TDNT III, 619f.; Spicq, *Notes* II, 760 f. with reference to Jewish inscriptions in which the duty constantly to attend the synagogue and to pray is impressed upon them.

[49]Cf. Lövestam* 70–5. 135–7.

[50]In this sense Schlier 301 f. On vigils in the early Church cf. J. A. Jungmann, LThK ²X, 785–7. The first evidence for the prayer-vigil in the Easter night is found in the Ep. Apostolorum 15 (26) which stems from the second century. Hennecke ³I, 133 f. In the Coptic version there is talk of a 'night of walking' (till cock-crow) for the celebration of the Passover.

Paul and his fellow-workers. It is drawn up on Paul's account according to the picture of him which is sketched in 3.1–4, 8 f. But just as in that passage the author was talking about himself and his own concerns, here too we must listen to the way he sees himself and his interests. It is the same semantic field as in the making known (γνωρίσαι) of the Mystery which is more thoroughly revealed in the wider proclamation and must be ever more realized in the existence of the Church (cf. 3.10). This does not take place through the human abilities and efforts of the preacher who takes up and carries farther the apostkolic sermon, but through the grace of God (cf. 3.8) which gives force and effect to his Word. 'The Word shall be given' to him when he 'opens his (my) mouth'. This is an old biblical expression which is used for prayer and praising (Ps. 51.15 – LXX 50.17 –; Dan. 3, 25 LXX), proclaiming God's mysteries (Ps. 78.2), prophetic speech (Ezek. 3.27; 29.21; 33.22; Dan. 10.16). As wisdom opens the mouth of the devout person (cf. Wis Sol. 10.21; Sir. 15.5; 24.2; 39.6) so will God give to the preacher of the Gospel the 'Word'[51] which unveils the wisdom of the divine plan of salvation (cf. 3.10 f.). The metaphor of the opening of a door, which is used in Col. 4.3 for the preaching of the Gospel in spite of the Apostle's imprisonment,[52] is deliberately omitted.

A further feature which the author emphasizes is the desire to proclaim the Mystery of the Gospel[53] 'openly' (ἐν παρρησία). The Greek word can take on various meanings: frankness, openness, honesty, joyful confidence.[54] In 3.12 it means the free and open access to God. Here it is more closely defined by the verb in v. 20. It is an open and freely revealing way of speaking such as one must use in proclaiming the Gospel. It certainly does not simply mean, taking into consideration that Paul is a prisoner, that the Gospel should take its course freely (cf. 2 Tim. 2.9). But the author of Eph. is also not simply asking for frankness in his speaking in the obligation laid upon him to preach (v. 20). He understands himself at the same time as an instrument for facilitating the function of revealing the Word of God, laying open the Mystery of the Gospel. The mystery made known 'openly' is the mystery of Christ disclosed to the Gentiles, the unfathomable riches of Christ which must increasingly be recognised and grasped (cf. 3.18 f.). Thus the intercession is to serve his task of proclamation as he understands it as servant of the Word, as carrying on the Pauline Gospel (cf. 3.7).

[51] In Eph. 1.13 the 'Word of truth' is discussed in an objective sense; but here it is the Word given to the preacher which stands in the foreground. We might think of the charismata mentioned in 1 Cor. 1.5; 12.8, but these are not limited to the one proclaiming the Gospel. The closest correspondence is in 1 Thess. 2.13 (the word of proclamation through us); further Phil. 1.14; 2 Cor. 4.2. In 2 Thess. 3.1 the addressees are requested to pray for the preacher 'that the Word of the Lord may take its course and be extolled'.

[52] Cf. Schweizer, *Colossians* on this verse.

[53] The Genitive 'of the Gospel' which is missing in B F G b m; MVict Ambst must be original because the 'mystery' needs to be more closely defined. The omission can perhaps be explained in view of 3.3, 9 where, however, the mystery is obvious from the context. The Relative Clause only connects meaningfully with 'Gospel'.

[54] Cf. E. Peterson, 'Zur Bedeutungsgeschichte von παρρησία' in FS R. Seeberg I, Leipzig 1929, 283–97; H. Schlier, TDNT V, 871–86; also Eph. 303 f. (combines the unveiledness of the Gospel and the openness of the preacher).

20

The high self-understanding which fills the author in his request for their help in prayer is also revealed in the allusion to his 'service as ambassador'. This word (πρεσβεύω) only appears again in the NT in 2 Cor 5.20, so that the author certainly had his passage (or a similar remark of the Apostle's) in mind.[55] Paul realizes that he represents an important theological connection as the ambassador of Christ in the service of the reconciliation which God has granted to the world in Christ. The service of reconciliation which the Apostle transmits also requires that he should constantly command the congregation to let themselves be reconciled to God.[56] 'In chains' retains the reminder of Paul's captivity. This belongs to the author's picture of Paul (cf. 3.1; 4.1) or to the situation presupposed in Col. 4.3. The Apostle's service as ambassador is taken up and continued by the author as he just as openly preaches the Mystery of the Gospel together with the demands to the congregation which grow out of this. The expression 'as I must speak' which is taken over from Col. 4.3 is perhaps also intended in the context of the letter to justify his paracleses. He feels himself like Paul in the service of Christ obliged to proclaim and interpret the Mystery of Christ and also to exhort.

Summary

At the conclusion of his speech of exhortation to the Christian congregation the author depicts the current situation of the world as an evil, desperate and dangerous time even for those saved by God. With a glance at the gloomy present and a future like to be even more gloomy he destroys all illusions of a carefree life in the world and of a storm-free zone for the Church bound to her heavenly head. Yet he does not want to depress the addressees and cast them back into that attitude to life which tormented many people at that time: belief in fate and fear of the world. As those chosen by God and included in Christ's Church they should have overcome this. Freed from all force of evil by the might of God they should now simply grow stronger in the strength of the Lord and resist the assaults of the ungodly power of evil (vv. 10 f.) The description of a battle which cannot be won by human strength (vv. 12 f.) is simply meant to point even more insistently to the inner strength given by God. Hence they are also not called to more intensive human activity – as if they themselves could destroy all that is offensive and evil in the world – but ordered to do only one thing: stand fast and resist (vv. 11, 13, 14). What the Christian attitude should be to the phenomenon of evil in the world is summed up in this characteristic exhortation: they should recognise in a practical manner the invincible power of evil which still exists and is humanly incomprehensible

---

[55]The two passages are also similar in form because of ὑπὲρ οὗ/ὑπὲρ Χριστοῦ. Whether one can (with Schlier 303) conclude from this that τοῦ εὐαγγελίου gives the content of the mystery and is to be equated with Christ remains doubtful. What is meant is rather the Mystery of Christ revealed by the Gospel (cf. 3.6, 8 f.). It is not certain that the author of Eph. had a literary knowledge of 2 Cor.

[56]Cf. the commentaries on 2 Cor.; further O. Hofius, '"Gott hat unter uns aufgerichtet das Wort von der Versöhnung" (2 Cor. 5.19)', ZNW 71 (1980) 3–20.

but resist it in the awareness of God's superior might. Admittedly, Christians are also called in what follows to work for peace and intercede for one another.

To illustrate the power given by God to Christians, God's armour is described in a metaphor well-known in antiquity. This armour lies ready prepared for the Christians and they need only grasp it anew (vv. 14–17). The description is full of allusions to biblical passages and appeals to the readers in symbolical words which have associations: the belt of truth, breast-plate of righteousness, shield of faith, helmet of salvation, sword of the Spirit. The battle waged by Christians is God's just cause, yet at the same time related to the Gospel of peace brought by Christ (v. 15). Their offensive weapon for attack is the sword of the Spirit which is interpreted as the word of God (v. 17). The Gospel which Christians have to proclaim and bear witness to in the world carries within itself the truth and power of the divine Word, the effective and productive power of the divine Spirit. This does not exclude the Christian engagement for all efforts for peace in the world, for the elimination of unjust social structures and inhumane conditions. Rather it demands this more urgently, though always guided by the message of the Gospel and borne by the consciousness that in all human endeavour God alone guarantees the victory. The metaphor of the battle against evil can certainly be transferred to the moral struggles of the individual Christian, as happened not infrequently in the history of the exegesis of these verses. But the picture here painted still lies primarily in a cosmic perspective of the Church's battle against all the powers of evil, and its original intention should not be blurred.

The Christian's 'spiritual military service' is further illustrated by the connected command to pray and watch. It is a constant prayer-vigil which is laid upon all Christians against the assaults and temptations of evil. Here we must consider both the temptations which come from the society in which we live as well as threats to inner unity, resistance to the proclamation of the Gospel as well as the danger of a falling away, and finally also the violence and injustice in the world through which evil celebrates its triumphs. The word to watch and pray which Jesus speaks to his Disciples in his hour in Gethsemane (Mk.14.38 par) and many similar exhortations in the NT literature to soberness, vigilance and prayer (1 Thess. 5.6, 8; 1 Cor. 16.13; Col. 4.2; Mk 13.37; Lk 21.36; 1 Pet 4.7; 5.8; Rev. 3.2 f.; 8.3 f.; 16.15) show how prevalent this idea was in the early Church. If the author of Eph. combines it with the metaphor of God's armour, he is thereby explaining how he imagines the battle against he force of evil. The prayer which should be practised at every opportunity in the way inspired and borne by the Spirit (v. 18) summons the help of God. The intercession for all the saints gives support for the whole Church's battle for God's cause. The special intercession for the captive Apostle (v. 19) draws attention to the responsibility everyone has for the frank and open proclamation of the Gospel. Praying together and intercession for one another bind the Church together more closely. In this way the Church becomes God's fighting force in the world. Fighting with other than worldly weapons she counteracts the force of evil in order to overcome it in the power of God.

EPHESIANS 6.21–24

IV. Conclusion of the Letter (6.21–24)

21 But so that you also may know about my affairs, how I am, Tychicus, the beloved brother and faithful servant in the Lord will tell you everything.

22 It is for this purpose that I am sending him to you, that you may learn how we fare and that he may encourage your hearts.

23 Peace to the brothers and love with faith
from God the Father and the Lord Jesus Christ.

24 Grace be with all who love our Lord Jesus Christ in immortal (life).

Analysis

The last verses of the letter are divided into remarks about the Apostle's situation on which Tychicus will inform them in a visit (vv. 21–2) and the customary final greeting which is presented in the form of a Blessing (vv. 23–4). In the process the details on Paul's situation not enumerated in the content, which Tychicus is to deliver, give the impression of forming simply an elegant transition to the blessing which is relatively long and warm. Both epistolary elements are written in the form of the postscript used in antiquity / in the style of the Pauline Epistles. It was customary to send greetings at the end of a letter and to close with a short greeting from the sender. Further, it was a Christian custom to deliver the final greeting in the form of a blessing. In the Pauline Epistles this normally reads: 'The grace of our Lord, Jesus Christ, be with you' or something similar; cf. 1 Thess. 5.28; Gal. 6.18; 1 Cor. 16.23; 2 Cor. 13.13 (expanded); Rom. 16.20; Phil. 4.23; Col. 4.18. The way in which the author takes into account and deals with the epistolary elements bears out the pseudonymity of his writing. It is remarkable that there is no list of greetings while in Col. 4.10–17 we find a very detailed one. This is even more conspicuous because the remarks about the Apostle's situation and the sending of Tychicus correspond almost verbatim with Col. 4.7 f. If the author takes over these remarks but omits the list of greetings which in Col. follows before the final greeting and Blessing, this cannot be a mere accident. Why he does this will be discussed in the exegesis. In the verbal correspondence of Eph. 6.21 f. with Col. 4.7 f. one observation is important in a formal respect: While the Paul of Eph. elsewhere throughout speaks in the First Person Singular, he interchanges in these verses τὸ κατ' ἐμέ (what concerns me) with τὰ περὶ ἡμῶν (what concerns *us*). In Col. 4.7 the same exchange is easily explained from the fact that alongside Paul Timothy is also named in the details about the sender (1.1) and according to the list of greetings there are other co-workers present with Paul. By contrast in Eph Paul alone is considered to be the sender (v. under 1.1) and apart from Tychicus (as in Col. 4.7) there is no mention of other co-workers. The sentence-structure (v. 22 is connected as a Relative Clause about Tychicus) corresponds completely with the passage in Col. Only at the beginning there stands 'that you may know'; then the recipients of the letter and Paul are set face to face and Tychicus is introduced as bringer of the news (v. 21). The further reason for sending him, apart from the purpose of giving information, is that he should encourage their hearts (v. 22).

The structure of the individualistic Blessing is determined by the words 'peace' (v. 23) and 'grace' (v. 24), the same words as in the introductory blessing but in the reverse order. But both prayerful wishes are expanded: 'Peace' by the address to the 'brothers' and the addition of 'love and faith', the saying about grace by the address to 'all who love our Lord, Jesus Christ' and the addition of 'in immortality'. This last conspicuous expression is probably due to the author's feeling for language and his stylistic idiosyncrasy. As in v. 23 he adds 'with faith', so here he adds 'in immortality'. In the whole section he reveals a tendency to pad out the Blessing – which in Paul is usually short – and provide it with his own emphases.

Exegesis

21

In connection with the intercession for the captive Apostle to which the addressees were called (vv. 19–20), it seems reasonable that they should learn more details about Paul's situation. Taking up this silent expectation ('so that you may know'), the author still does not give them any more precise information but refers to Tychicus who shall inform them of it. Personal messages are customary at the end of Paul's Epistles especially when the Apostle promises to visit the recipients (cf. 1 Cor. 16.5–12; 2 Cor. 13.1 f.; Rom. 15.22–9). Even when he is in prison the Apostle speaks clearly about his situation (cf. Phil. 1.12–26; 4.10–16; Philem. 22). Here nothing of the like follows. Even greetings from co-workers and friends of the captive Apostle are missing and likewise there are no greetings sent to members of the congregation (cf. in comparison Philem. 23 f.; Col. 4.10–17). Even the handwritten greeting by the Apostle which is meant to authenticate a dictated letter (cf. Gal. 6.11; 1 Cor. 16.21) is omitted.[1] All this makes us

---

[1] It is possible that Paul personally wrote the letter to Philemon cf. Philem 19 (on this

suspect that the fiction that this stems from the captive Apostle should be kept up (Dibelius: 'the Pauline mark of identification').

But the remarks also fulfil an epistolary function. The author wishes to lead up to the final greeting and in so doing takes into consideration the personal news customary at this point (cf. the similar endeavour at 1.15 f.). If he omits the list of greetings, the letter cannot be intended for the congregation at Ephesus in which Paul was active over a long period and knew many Christians personally. The author must also be aware of this. The best explanation is that this document was meant for several congregations and hence greetings to specific people in individual congregations must be left out (cf. on the Address at 1.1). If he has picked up the Clauses about Tychicus in Col. 4.7 f. and taken them over practically verbatim,[2] he thereby betrays that, in contrast to other passages which he alters or expands upon to suit his theological aim, he is here pursuing no special purpose. To name Tychicus, who came from Asia Minor (perhaps from the same area in which the addressees of Eph. live) (Acts 20.4) as Paul's envoy was quite safe in a pseudonymous letter if this were to reach the recipients only at a later date.[3] We cannot exclude the possibility that Tychicus once came to Colossae (Col. 4.7 f.) and Ephesus (cf. 2 Tim 4.12). But here (as in Col.) his coming (in the Aorist according to the style of the letter) is only promised (v. 22) and it can simply be a matter of a mere fiction. At any rate the author takes over the sending of Tychicus from Col. and also characterizes him, similarly to that passage, as 'beloved brother and faithful servant in the Lord'. He omits to name him as 'fellow labourer as he elsewhere also avoids identifying fellow-workers of Paul (Timothy is not mentioned as in Col. 1.1). The Apostle has become a leading, almost solitary figure who towers above all others.

The 'you also' – interpreted by the representatives of the hypothesis that the document is authentic as showing that it points to another Pauline letter from the same situation[4] – can be explained more easily. It belongs to the sentence as a whole and simply sets the addressees face to face with the Apostle.[5] If they are to pray for Paul in his situation, they ought also to hear something about it. The τί πράσσω which is

---

Stuhlmacher [EKK 1973] 50, n. 122). In 2 Thess. 3.17 the remark is possibly made to give the appearance of authenticity, cf. W. Trilling, *Der zweite Brief an die Thessalonicher*, 1980 (EKK XIV) 158 f., perhaps also in Col. 4.18. Why does Eph. not take this over? Does he consider Col. a genuine Pauline Epistle?

[2]Mitton, *Epistle* 58 establishes that fifteen words in v. 21 correspond with Col. 4.7 and that v. 22 follows Col. 4.8 word for word. The divergences in v. 21 can be easily explained (v. supra in the text) and are not important (against Schlier 305).

[3]This is even clearer in the Pastorals, cf. Tit. 3.12; 2 Tim. 4.12; Brox *Past* (p. 271 n.2) 268 on the function of such personal notes; cf. also his 'Zu den persönlichen Notizen der Pastoralbriefe', BZ NF 13 (1969) 76–94.

[4]von Soden and Belser take 'you also' to refer to other congregations who are close to Paul; Klöpper, Haupt, Huby, Staab, Masson, Schlier and others think of the congregation at Colossae to which Tychicus was sent.

[5]The transposition in some MSS (א A D F G I P 81 326 al lat.) betrays a certain doubt. On the frequently vague position and function of καί cf. Eph. 1.13 (in the second place) 15; 2.3; 4.17; but it was already so in Paul: 1 Thess. 2.13; 3.15; Rom. 3.7; 8.11; 9.24; 15.14, 19. Cf. also Percy, *Untersuchungen* 390.

additional to Col. 4.7, can hardly mean 'what I am doing' but 'how I am'.[6]

22

This sentence corresponds verbatim to Col. 4.8. Thereby the change to the Plural (τα περὶ ἡμῶν = how we fare) is proof that the author of Eph. copied from Col. where the Apostle is in the company of other co-workers. He deliberately omits mentioning Onesimus as companion to Tychicus (Col. 4.9). He is also concerned to strengthen, encourage and comfort (παρακαλεῖν)[7] their hearts. The verb has here a more comprehensive sense than in 4.1, where the author uses it to commence his exhortation founded on faith. In Col. 4.8 it takes up 2.2 and embraces exhortation, strengthening and comfort.[8] The comforting advice is more powerfully developed in 2 Thess. 2.16 f.; cf. also 1 Cl. 59.4 'to put new heart into the fainthearted'. In the framework of Eph., in which the ethical paraclesis takes up so much space, it can be understood as meaning that the apostolic exhortation should continue to be effective and lead to strengthening and encouragement of their hearts (cf. 1.18; 3.16 f.).

23

The peace granted to the brothers is a Blessing at the end of the writing, similar to Rom. 15.33: 'The God of peace be with you all!' For peace (along with love and faith) should proceed from God the Father and the Lord Jesus Christ. Peace therefore means in the broad biblical sense the divine salvation which envelops humanity, which has been realized for Chritians in Christ and through which they themselves have been set upon the way of peace (cf. 6.15). If we consider the conception of peace developed in 2.14–18, we hear an echo again that true peace comes from the reconcilation with God brought by Christ which, however, commits us to uphold peace among ourselves. The author would also think of peace in the congregations, the resolving of tensions between individual groups (Jewish- and Gentile-Christians, cf. 2.17 f.), the peaceable, brotherly standing by each other (cf. 4.3) and co-operation (cf. 4.13).[9] A clear sign of this is that he also addresses the recipients as 'brothers' – a designation he uses only here. Again it is striking that they are not *addressed* as brothers as in Paul's Epistles, but the blessing, more strongly reserved, is presented 'to the brothers'. This too may be a sign that the letter was sent to a larger circle of Christians who were not personally known to the author. He understands all congregations to be one single Christian brotherhood (cf. 1 Pet. 5.9).

---

[6]Cf. Pr-Bauer 1386, s.v. 2.6 with Classical evidence. There is a similar use in modern languages – e.g. 'How do you do?'

[7]O. Schmitz, TDNT V, 793–9 demonstrates the breadth of meaning this verb has in the NT but classifies Col. 2.2; 4.8; Eph. 6.22 too one-sidedly under 'consoling' help (797). The author is not concerned here with the need for consolation under the 'heavy pressure of the present age'; Tychicus is also to consolidate the exhortations made by the Apostle in this letter (in accordance with the pseudepigraphical writing).

[8]Cf. Schweizer, *Colossians* on this verse.

[9]Cf. Calvin on this verse. He emphasizes the *concordia* and comments: 'Facit enim amor, ut se in pace contineant homines: amorem mutuo conciliat fides, eiusque vinculum est.' Of course faith and love, like peace, are gifts of God.

The peace requested from above is expanded by 'love with faith'. Peace among Christians is realized in concrete terms in their mutual love. Such agape in its turn has as a prerequisite the common faith as a constantly regenerating power (cf. 1.15). Hence we must understand the list peace – love – faith as a unit. The addition of 'faith' in a Prepositional Phrase ('with faith') is a stylistic peculiarity (cf. 4.2; 6.5, 7) and is intended to introduce the faith upon which in the end all Christian conduct is based.[10] In the wish for peace we must also consider the Spirit who embraces their hearts and leads all to unity (cf. 2.18, 22; 4.3 f.).

24

The real final blessing, as known from the Pauline Epistles, calls down upon the addressees the grace of our Lord, Jesus Christ, but it is again altered by the author of Eph. in a characteristic fashion. Instead of 'with you (or: with your Spirit)' he says 'with all who love our Lord Jesus Christ' – i.e. as in v. 23 he chooses the Third Person. The parallelism with 'brothers' is significant: all Christians are brothers because they receive the same love from God in Christ and are committed to practise similar love. If here the love for Jesus Christ, our Lord, is emphasized, it implies no polemic against outsiders – the Blessing is bestowed entirely on the congregations – but conceals within itself the concern to bind the Christian brothers closely to the person, teaching and instruction of Jesus Christ as they are transmitted in the apostolic paraclesis and paradosis (cf. 4.20 f.). The expression therefore does not betray 'the pathos of the old Apostle who is now falling silent' (Schlier),[11] but once again the letter-writer's pastoral concern. Even in the Blessing he leads and exhorts. Paul uses a similar formula derived from the liturgy in the anathema against anyone who 'does not love (φιλεῖ) the Lord' (1 Cor. 16.22). In contrast to this formula of exclusion[12] the positive formulation points to a different intention. The closest correspondence to this is in 1 Pet. 1.8, where the love of the addressees for the heavenly Lord whom they love without having seen him is praised, but in the final Blessing in Eph. there is also an admonitory overtone. Otherwise than in the gnostically-coloured old Christian literature[13] such love has nothing effusive about

[10]Cf. Pr-Bauer 1007 s.v. II, 6; μετά with the Genitive serves 'to combine closely two nouns, upon the first of which the main emphasis should be placed'; according to Mayser II/2, 443 μετά τινος 'frequently combines two ideas in a fashion similar to καί' (with examples from Papyri, 444.

[11]Schlier 310. He recalls the OT and Jewish name for religious people 'those who love God'. It is true that such an expression could continue to have an effect transferred to Christ, the Lord; but 'to love God' is also retained in the NT, v. 1 Cor. 2.9; 8.3; Rom. 8.28; Jas. 1.12; 2.5; 1 Jn. 4.10, 20 f.; 5.1. All 'who love our Lord Jesus Christ' appears to be a special formula, possibly stemming from the Christian liturgy.

[12]Cf. J. Behm, TDNT I, 345 f.; K. Hofmann, RAC I, 427–30; C. Spicq, 'Comment comprendre φιλεῖν dans 1 Cor. XVI, 22?', NT 1 (1956) 200–4 (not to love=to curse); G. Bornkamm, 'Das Anathema in der urchristlichen Abendmahlsliturgie', in *Das Ende des Gesetzes* (BEvTh 16) ⁵1966, 123–32.

[13]Schlier 311 mentions many passages from the Od Sol and the apocryphal Acts of the Apostles. But these very texts from the Od Sol reveal in many metaphors, including some from the sexual sphere, the other manner of such love for the redeemer felt by the redeemed who act like him, unite with him and marry him.

it; but rather something demanding. In the love of all for their common Lord the brotherhood is consolidated, and in the Blessing this love is mercifully reinforced.

The addition 'in immortality' which we would like to attribute to the author's rhetorical-stylistic idiosyncrasy (cf. Analysis) confirms how powerful he considers the Blessing. For this expression cannot be connected either with Jesus Christ – because he lives in the glory of the Father (for which ἀφθαρσία is never used) – or with 'love' which should be everlasting,[14] but explains the self-realizing power of grace. The typically Hellenistic word which means 'incorruption, immortality' and in this sense 'everlastingness'[15] here signifies the continuing effectiveness – even better, the fruit – of God's abundant grace which pours forth (cf. 2.7).[16] With the Blessing the addressees are promised immortal, everlasting life (cf. translation). The loose connection formed by ἐν plus the Dative is a similar peculiarity of style as 'with faith' at the end of v. 23a.[17] In Paul incorruption (ἀφθαρσία) denotes the future life of the resurrection, the different quality of the resurrection bodies (1 Cor. 15.42, 50, 53 f.). In Eph. there is no mention of the future resurrection; but even in his spatial-vertical oriented outlook the author looks forward to the inheritance lying ready in heaven for the readers (cf. 1.14, 18) and the fulfilment of this hope (cf. 4.4) is included in the Blessing. The more intensively Christianity was Hellenized, the more words and ideas about everlastingness and immortality also spread. In the NT cf. 1 Pet. 1.4, 23; 3.4; 1 Tim. 1.17; 2 Tim. 1.10.[18]

In retrospect the two verses 23 and 24 appear as two Blessings, except that v. 23 looks more to the present, v. 24 more to the future. But they make up a unit, since 'peace' and 'grace' belong closely together. The correspondence to the opening greeting is unmistakeable. The Blessing sought from God the Father and the Lord Jesus Christ embraces the hearers or readers and should have a still stronger effect on them because of the letter. The language which is reminiscent of the liturgy in this respect finds a 'Sitz im Leben' since the letter was certainly intended to be read aloud in the congregations. The congregation assembled for worship is included by the Blessings at the beginning and end in that which is promised to them in the letter itself with its reminders and exhortations, and at the same time they are graciously secured in it. Hence the 'Amen' added in many MSS – even if probably not original – is appropriate and meaningful.

[14]Among others Klöpper, Staab and also U. Wilckens in his translation take the expression to refer to Christ. Many earlier and some more recent exegetes combine it with 'love' – thus Ephraem, Chrysostom, Luther, Estius, Abbott, Robinson, Masson. Others, e.g. Dibelius – Greeven do not come to a decision.

[15]There is no Hebrew equivalent. In the LXX the word first appears in the Wis Sol 2.23; 6.19; 4 Macc. 9.22; 17.12. It is often found in Philo, v on this G. Harder TDNT IX, 101 f. But it also penetrates non-Christian philosophy; cf. on the whole question Harder, ibid. 93–106.

[16]With Schlier, Gnilka, Gaugler, Barth 813 f.; cf. also G. Harder, TDNT IX, 105 who, however, equates it – hardly with right – to the liturgical formula 'in eternity' (cf. against this 3.21).

[17]Cf. 2.4, 7 (in mercy, in goodness); 3.12 (in faith); 4.2, 16 (in love); 4.19 (in dissipation); 4.24 (in righteousness etc); 6.2 (with a promise). It is a semitizing style of which similar examples can be found in the Qumran documents, and has the same meaning as 'and'; cf. K. G. Kuhn, NTS 7, 337.

[18]On the early Church cf. G. Harder, TDNT IX, 105 f.

With it the congregation subordinate themselves in acknowledgement and request for the Blessing which proceeds from God the Father and Jesus Christ and which should spread itself in them (cf. 3.21).

Summary

The announcement that Tychicus will give them news of the captive Apostle's situation is only added to the letter for reasons of form, as is betrayed by the almost verbatim takeover of Col. 4.7. It has no material importance and is only interesting for the question of pseudepigraphy. From several observations, especially the lack of a list of greetings, it emerges that we are really dealing with a pseudonymous writing. The captive Apostle has already become an ideal figure.

Nevertheless the letter, which probably is directed to a circle of congregations not far from Ephesus, possibly including that town, still retains its value as a letter of the post-apostolic period because it upholds the Pauline tradition and offers it in a new interpretation. Indeed as a pseudonymous writing of instruction and exhortation it gains a heightened importance because it shows how the apostolic teaching and paraclesis is constantly to be passed on and applied in a new and different way to the prevailing situation of the congregation. The external and internal situation presupposed for the congregation in Eph. at that time is similar in many ways to ours, in spite of the changed intellectual horizon. The decreasing enthusiasm of the first years, the danger of becoming incorporated with their fellow-citizens and assimilation to a non-Christian environment, the worry about unity being broken, the threat from the powers of evil: all these are comparable with our intensified situation in a 'post-Christian' era. The paraclesis of Eph., translated into our language, today wins a new relevance.[19]

All the more then are the congregations called to renew themselves from the inner powers which accrue for them from the grace of god which is still effective and the living Spirit of Jesus Christ. The Blessing at the end of the letter is intended to remind them of this once again and at the same time make it happen. In it ring the basic attitudes of the Christian, faith and love – not as achievements which can be humanly produced but as ways of proving one's worth given and made possible by God in the darkness of time. In his faithfulness and desire to bless (cf. the Great Eulogy, 1.3–14) God takes the congregations into his peace, the peace brought by Christ, and consolidates them in their brotherly solidarity (v. 23). He further bestows his mercy on all who love Jesus Christ, the Lord, and leads them to the goal of their Christian existence, to immortal life (v. 24). In the blessing which is ever and again granted to the congregations in worship, God's peace and mercy descend ever new upon them and in exhorting, encouraging and comforting keep them steadfast in the hope to which they are called.

---

[19]Cf. R. Schnackenburg, 'Der Epheserbrief im heutigen Horizont', in *Maßstab des Glaubens*, Freiburg i. Br. 1978, 155–75.

Excursus: The Church in the Epistle to the Ephesians

In the whole of the NT literature there is nowhere an ecclesiology which is so extensively structured or which is revealed so effectively as that in the Epistle to the Ephesians. This theme so dominates the document that it deserves to be given special attention, especially in an ecumenical commentary such as this which takes into consideration the meeting of the churches and their striving toward unity. Since about the 1920s many monographs and individual studies have been written on the theme of the Church[20] and although in the process the interests of the academic literature were varied, we may still affirm a connection with the ecumenical movement in the sense of *Wirkungsgeschichte*.

Academic interest centres particularly on the religio-historical question: Where did the unusual metaphors and the overall conception of the Church which is reflected in them come from? Can we not detect a fundamentally Gnostic philosophy in the close relationship between Christ and Church – the subordination of the 'Body' to the 'Head', the growth of the Church towards Christ, her growing into him and conversely Christ's 'fulfilment' so that the Church is his 'fullness' (1.22 f.) and in him reaches the 'fullness' of God (cf. 3.19), further, the *hieros gamos* in which Christ appears to be bound with the Church to a 'syzygy' (5.22–3)? Or can we see Judaeo-Hellenistic thinking in its ideas? Is not the Jewish background clearly recognisable in various passages (cf. 2.14–18, 19–22; 4.8 f.; 5.31 f.)? Does she herself become a heavenly entity which is basically taken out of this world, or, still located on earth, move towards her heavenly prototype? Is she a pre-existent entity, bound with Christ before time in God's thought, which now in the proclamation of the Mystery of Christ through the Church comes to the fore in history as the one Church made up of Jews and Gentiles and thus reveals the Mystery of Christ in herself (cf. 3.4–12)? Does she not thereby become a cosmic entity which fulfils God's plan of salvation and in this sense an eschatological entity?

All these questions reveal how the conception of the Church is interwoven with research into the history of religion as well as the far-reaching conclusions which result from this. For is this not a one-sided, exaggerated idea of the Church carried to extremes which loses sight of the earthly form, the weakness and guilt of the empirical Church, and awards her a triumphal position and excessive greatness? Should we not distance ourselves theologically because from this point of view Christology ceases to be the centre-point and is as it were absorbed by Ecclesiology?[21]

---

[20]Those to be emphasized: F. Kattenbusch, 'Der Quellort der Kirchenidee', in *Festgabe für A. v. Harnack*, Tübingen 1921, 143–172; K. L. Schmidt, 'Die Kirche des Urchristentums', in *Festgabe für A. Deißmann*, Tübingen 1927, 258–319; also TDNT III, 501–36; Schlier, *Christus und Kirche*; Käsemann, *Leib und Leib Christi*; A. Médebielle, DBS II (1934) 487–691 (with bibliography); Wikenhauser, *Kirche*; N. A. Dahl, *Das Volk Gottes*, Oslo 1941; L. Cerfaux, *La théologie de l'Église suivant s. Paul*, Paris 1942; Hanson, *Unity*; G. Aulén et al, *Ein Buch von der Kirche* (Swedish theologians), Göttingen 1951; Best, *One Body in Christ*; Schweizer, *Church Order*; P. S. Minear, *Images of the Church in the New Testament*, Philadelphia 1960; U. Valeske, *Votum Ecclesiae*, Munich 1962 (with a full bibliography); H. Schlier 'Ekklesiologie des Neuen Testaments', in *Mysterium Salutis* IV/1 Zürich 1972, 101–221; J. Roloff, EWNT I, 998–1011. Further literature in ThWNT X, 1127–1131.

[21]Cf. Käsemann, *Interpretationsproblem* 254 f.: the Christology is interpreted almost entirely from the ecclesiology. Against Schlier's ontological interpretation he calls for a hermeneutical consciousness, that the Church should only be seen in her function, in her obedience to Christ her Head (257). This is expanded further in 'The Theological Problem presented by the Motif of the Body of Christ' in *Perspectives on Paul*, London 1971, 102–21, on Eph. 109 f. and 120 f.

Before we reach such conclusions, we must consider the historical position of Eph., what the author wanted to impress upon the recipients, the modifications of this picture of the Church which might arise in other sections – namely, the paraclesis – and the significance of the theological conception. For theology does not come about in an isolated vacuum but is embedded in historical, social reality and can only be understood out of such. Hence to achieve a proper evaluation we must consider the document in its entirety, not only particular passages which are important for its ecclesiology. We must also make a more detailed examination of the relationship between Christology and Ecclesiology which in its turn is an integral part of the author's theological understanding.

We shall use as our starting-point the striking features of the Church as they are revealed in Eph. After exploring the meaning of the metaphors and expressions used here – which might be useful for the religio-historical comparison but is not of prime importance in the context of the letter – we shall then attempt to clarify its ecclesiological conception and its significance for those to whom the letter was written. Finally, we shall discuss what effect it might have on the present-day situation.

1. The Church as a Total Entity

In contrast to the Epistles accepted as Pauline in which ἡ ἐκκλησία predominantly, perhaps even exclusively, means the local or individual congregation,[22] in Eph. this concept always signifies the Church as a total entity, as the totality of those who believe in Jesus Christ and who are taken up into this community through Baptism (cf. 4.5; 5.26). If we compare, for instance, the address in 1 Thess. 1.1 'To the church of the Thessalonians' or in the two Epistles to the Corinthians 'to the church which is at Corinth' (1 Cor. 1.2; 2 Cor. 1.1) with the heading in Eph. 1.1, the absence of such a concise expression is striking. We might point to Col. 1.2, where there is also mention only of the 'saints and brothers who believe in Christ at Colossae'; but in this document which served the author of Eph. as a model there is at least reference made in 4.15 to the house-church of Nympha and in the following verse to the congregation of the Laodiceans. In the nine places where the ecclesia is mentioned in Eph., it is always the Church in her entirety which is under consideration, especially in her close connection to Christ. In the Epistle to the Colossians there are two places (1.18, 24) in which the 'Body' of Christ is identified as the ecclesia. In the Hymn of Christ the ecclesia appears as an important addition on the part of the author,[23] whereas in 1.24 the Body of Christ is identified in a Relative Clause as the Church. For Col., too, the idea of the Church as the Body of Christ, who is her Head, was already established (cf. also 2.19) but was not yet so much in the foreground as for Eph. In Eph. God gives Christ as he triumphs over the powers to the ecclesia (as Head) (1.22) and she is then described, in her significance as the Body of Christ, as the fullness of him who fills all in all (1.23). Here the Church is included from the outset in the great divine Economy of Salvation. In 3.10 she becomes the instrument of the divine wisdom since the plan already made by the Creator for the subjugation of the evil powers is proclaimed and realized through her. In the Doxology of 3.21 God is praised 'in the

---

[22]Cf. J. Hainz, *Ekklesia. Strukturen paulinischer Gemeinde-Theologie und Gemeinde-Ordnung*, Regensburg 1972; H. Merklein, 'Die Ekklesia Gottes. Der Kirchenbegriff bei Paulus und in Jerusalem', BZ NF 23 (1979) 48–70, especially 51–55, but with reservations. There are even stronger reservations in J. Roloff, EWNT I, 1003 on 1 Cor. 1.1 f.: 'Congregations in whose existence the characteristics of the emergent world-wide Church of God become visible and which consequently may represent this Church in her totality': further 1005 on 1 Cor. 10.32 and 12.28.

[23]Cf. Schweizer, *Colossians* 82 f. (on Col. 1.18).

Church and in Christ Jesus', and such an emphatic inclusion of the ecclesia in the glorification of God is unique in the whole NT. If this theologian had not had such a vivid conception of the Church in her close connection to Christ, as a partner whom we cannot imagine him without, it would have been impossible for him to develop the profound marriage-paraclesis with Christ and the Church as the prototype of Christian marriage (5.22–33). Other than in Col. the Church has become a theologically thought-out salvation-entity which must fulfil the rôle in the Redemption-event determined for her by God – admittedly never isolated from Christ but indispensable for his further work in the world.

In what relationship, then, do the individual local congregations, the existing groups of believers down to and including the house-churches, stand to the *ecclesia* as a total entity? Do the local congregations and groups, in which the life of the Church is realized, epitomise the Church in her divine calling and historical manifestation?[24] Are they parts or bricks of the one, universal Church and do they consequently each offer only a limited picture of the Church as a whole? Are they only earthly shadows of the true ecclesia which never has been and never can be attained? Perhaps we can give some answers to this if we examine the concrete background of the text. But as has been shown in the exegesis there are limits placed upon our knowledge here. This is related to the nature of the document as a whole and perhaps also to the conditions of its drafting. If it was intended for a larger circle of congregations, it is natural that less attention is given to individual congregations. We can say only one thing with certainty: For the author all the congregations which lie within his field of vision do not yet, even taken together, constitute 'the ecclesia'. This is rather an entity which has precedence over all, in which they participate and in accordance with which they should orient their lives. It is the point of reference of the theological argumentation and of the paraclesis relating to the congregations. The theology of the Church in Eph. is not simply a free-floating speculation; it serves the motivation and a pastoral concern.

2. Symbols of the Church

How does the author of Eph. bring home to his readers linguistically and visually the Church as a total entity in her relationship to Christ and the rest of the world? We often speak of 'metaphors' for the Church, but we must note that these are not simply pictorial comparisons but modes of expression which simultaneously depict the reality of the Church. They are not chosen arbitrarily but are for the most part prompted by tradition and suggested by the subject itself. Thus the Church as 'Body of Christ', which is already found in Paul, is developed in Col. and Eph. to the conception of Christ, the Head, and the Church, his Body, but in Eph. still seen in a connection with Jesus' 'flesh' (cf. 2.14 with 16). We might call this pictorial style of expression which nevertheless contains reality 'metaphorical' if we understand therewith a style which infers reality, indeed the only one which really does so.[25] For lack of a better expression we intend to call these metaphors which point to the reality itself 'symbols'. To be distinguished from them are cryptic ways of speaking which likewise in their use of particular linguistic devices bring the Church closer to

---

[24]Cf. K. L. Schmidt, TDNT III, 506: Each congregation be it ever so small represents the whole Congregation, the Church (for Paul). For criticism of this traditional interpretation cf. Hainz (n. 22 supra).

[25]Cf. the more recent research on the Parables, especially H. J. Klauck, *Allegorie und in synoptischen Gleichnissen*, 1978 (NTA NS 22); H. Weder, *Die Gleichnisse Jesu als Metaphern*, ²1980 (FRLANT 120); further P. Ricoeur – E. Jüngel, *Metapher. Zur Hermeneutik religiöser Sprache*, Munich 1974; P. Ricoeur, *The Rule of Metaphor*, London 1978.

our understanding. To this group belong the phrases in Eph. which speak of 'filling', 'being filled' and 'fullness' (v under 3). We shall begin with the 'symbols' whose meaning we can also ascertain with the help of the history of tradition and of religio-historical comparison.

(a) The Church as a Building

This symbol is most clearly connected with the Pauline tradition and with a pictorial language widely used in the OT and Judaism.[26] Most instructive are the Qumran texts, where not only is the congregation described as a building but their 'foundation' is also discussed. 'You (God) lay down the "foundation" upon rock and the beams on the plumb-line of justice and on the r(ight) spirit-level, (to test) the "proven stones" in order to build a strong (wall)' (1 QH 6.26 after the German text of J. Maier). The congregation (sōd) is since its establishment a foundation (jesōd) on the rockbed of God[27] and the members are proven stones built up upon it. Or it can be understood as the 'precious cornerstone' laid by God (1 QS 8.7), a 'foundation of truth' for Israel (1 QS 5.5). In a song of the Teacher of Righteousness we read: 'You have placed me like a strong tower on a high wall and have established my building on rocks and fixed eternal foundations as my basis . . .' (1 QH 7.8 f. according to the translation of G. Jeremias). The 'building' probably here, too, refers to the congregation; the founder of the congregation (cf. 4 QpPs 37: 2.16 to 23 f.) is himself a strong support (a strong tower) for this building. The scriptural basis for the interpretation of the congregation as God's Building which is built upon a rock is, according to 1 QS 8.7 (the 'precious cornerstone') and 5.5 (the 'foundation of truth') Is. 28.16, the same passage which in the NT is claimed for Christ as the 'cornerstone' (1 Pet. 2.6; Eph. 2.20). The 'proven stones' and the 'wall' which God builds with them (cf. Is. 26.1) allow the picture of a fortified city (1 QH 6.25) or a temple-sanctuary 1 QS 5.6; 8.5 f.; 9.6; Damasc. 3.19) to develop. In 1 QS 8.8 the appellation 'residence of the Most High' is also used (cf. 1 QS 10.3; 1 QM 12.2; 1 QH 12.2; 1 QSb 4.25); this might well explain the change to 'dwelling-place of God in the Spirit' in Eph. 2.22.

The terminology and metaphorical elements which describe the congregation as building, temple and dwelling-place of God are so strongly represented in Qumran that there can be no doubt that this symbol arose from a Jewish background. But we must go even farther: While the New Jerusalem was in Judaism in general expected only in the future, the time of the Messiah or the 'world that is to come',[28] the Qumran Community understood itself already as a present divine foundation, as 'place of the Most Holy for Aaron' and 'house of perfection and truth in Israel' (1 QS 8.8 f.) and that had been so since its historical founding by the Teacher of Righteousness. The Christian conception borders very closely on this in the conviction of God's house already erected in the present except that Jesus Christ (1 Cor. 3.11) or the Apostles and Prophets (Eph. 2.20) are the foundation and in the Christian view the inner-judaic self-understanding of the Qumran Community is surpassed. We need

---

[26]Cf. Vielhauer, *Oikodome*; Pfammatter, *Kirche als Bau*; on the OT and Judaism (apart from Qumran): O. Michel, TDNT V, 137 f.; H. Pohlmann, RAC V, 1044–9; S. Wagner, TDOT II, 172 f.

[27]*sōd* and *jesōd* are interchangeable in the Qumran texts; cf. Jeremias, *Lehrer der Gerechtigkeit* 181 n. 4. On the metaphorical language in Qumran cf. Maier, *Texte* II, 93 f.; Jeremias, *Lehrer der Gerechtigkeit* 245–49; Gärtner, *Temple* 16–46, on Eph. 2.18–22: 60–66.

[28]Cf. Bill. IV, 883 f. and 919–927. On the 'present' aspect in Qumran, cf. the literature in the previous footnote. Gärtner, *Temple* 34 f. also points to 4 QFlor 1.6 f.: 'And he (God) said that a holy place should be built for him among humanity in which they should bring before him as burnt offerings works of the Law' (from the translation of J. Maier); Gärtner interprets this to mean 'a Temple consisting of humanity'. Cf. also H.-W. Kuhn, *Enderwartung* 184–6.

not suppose a direct traditio-historical derivation from Qumran because the analysis of Is. 28.16 and its combination with other scriptural passages (in 1 Pet. 2.4–6 with Is. 8.11 f. and Ps. 118.22; cf. Mk. 12.10 f.) also betray independent theological reflection on the part of the early Church. But to fall back on the gnostic idea of a 'heavenly building'[29] is unnecessary, indeed is forbidden if we heed the earthly, historical founding, the foundation-laying of the Church. The Apostles and Prophets who only in Eph. 2.20 are named as the foundation are the outstanding authorities of the founding-period of the Church (cf. 3.5) and our exegesis revealed that Christ was probably looked upon as the definitive cornerstone providing security in this foundation (cf. pp. 123 f.).[30] Hence the Church is no mere 'heavenly' entity even if she opens the way of approach to God's heavenly world (cf. 2.18) and is a building in the process of growing towards her heavenly goal. This very 'growing into the holy temple of the Lord' (v. 22) demonstrates her earthly location just as does her penetration by divine powers through which she fulfils her growth. The completely different gnostic conception is shown e.g. in the Nag Hammadi document 'The Second Logos of Seth' where the 'Community of the Perfect' (= the Gnostics) on earth (p. 60, 25) strives only to reach again the heavenly community which has been gathered there 'before the foundation of the world', 'above the places of the Ogdoan' in order to celebrate the 'spiritual marriage' (p. 65, 34–6).[31]

Traditio-historically Eph. 2.20–2, in spite of considerable differences, is still connected with the Pauline conception of the congregation in 1 Cor. 3.10 f., 16 f. Here Jesus Christ is the unshakeable foundation (v. 11), Paul the wise architect (v. 10) and the congregation the holy, spiritually-filled temple of God (vv. 16 f.). The shift in the picture can be explained from the post-Pauline perspective. The Apostle belongs in the meantime to the founding generation. He built up on Christ, the foundation – in Eph. 2.20 the cornerstone – and together with the other apostles and the prophets can be considered as the foundation, bound together with Christ, of the later Church. Among these men who, as the first authorized preachers, retain their 'fundamental' importance, Paul stands out for the author of Eph. as the authoritative guarantee of the apostolic tradition because the Mystery of Christ in all its riches was revealed for him to proclaim to the Gentiles (3.3 f., 8 f.). But typical of the picture of Paul in Eph. is his inclusion in the circle of the 'holy Apostles and Prophets in the Spirit' (3.5). The idea of an 'apostolic' Church including and uniting former Jews and Gentiles – consequently also 'catholic' Church – emerges. Yet for the author of Eph. Paul remains the real apostolic authority, *the* Apostle who continues to give exhortation and encouragement to the congregations (4.1 and the whole of the paraclesis-section).[32] All members are 'built up together' in this world-wide house and

---

[29]Cf. Schlier, *Christus und die Kirche* 49–60; *Eph.* 141, 143–5. On the Shepherd of Hermas, v. III and s IX (tower allegory) cf. Vielhauer, *Oikodome* 147–52; Jeremias, *Lehrer der Gerechtigkeit* 247; Old Jewish material about the building of the Heavenly City is taken over and interpreted paraenetically in an allegory.

[30]Fischer, *Tendenz* 36 thinks that θεμέλιον in Eph. 2.20 need not necessarily express a temporal priority; but after a comparison with the Qumran texts no one would think of interpreting it thus. Further, the Apostles and Prophets in 3.5 are separated from earlier generations. That they are still important entities for the author in his day as Fischer, ibid. 37, thinks is unlikely for other reasons, especially because of the time at which the document was composed. Cf. also Merklein, *Kirch. Amt* 156. Further v. supra p. 182 n. 30.

[31]Translation after that in ThLZ 100 (1975) 97–110 (Berliner Arbeitskreis under the overall control of H.-G. Bethge) here 104 and 107. Further cf. Tract. Tripartitus (NHC I, 5) 58.29 ff.: 'That is the Church, made up of many people, which existed before the aeons and which authentically bears the name "the ages of the ages"'. More in K. Koschorke, *Die Polemik der Gnostiker gegen das kirchliche Christentum*, Leiden 1978, 77–80. According to Koschorke this Ecclesia should be defined as totally other-worldly, an 'other-worldly, spiritual Church'.

[32]On the picture of Paul in Eph. cf. supra p. 32 n. 37.

temple of God which projects into the heavenly world – a thought which is not yet developed in this way in Paul but appears in a similar fashion in 1 Pet. 2.5. The idea of the Church in Eph. reveals and confirms the post-Pauline, post-apostolic location of the document.

The establishment of the Church in God's salvific action and in Jesus Christ's work as the agent of salvation must be emphasized theologically. Through Christ the two previously separated groups of Jews and Gentiles have access to God the Father 'in one single Spirit' (v. 18) since he has reconciled them both 'in one single Body' to God through the Cross (v. 16). Now the addressees are 'members of God's household' (v. 19) and God also stands behind the passive expression 'built up' (v. 19) and 'you are built up together' (v. 22). But because of his act of reconciliation Christ is the 'cornerstone' for the Apostles and Prophets who make up the foundation of the Church, their definitive 'guide-stone' (cf. exegesis on this verse). Christ's function as sole mediator is so important for the author that he inserts an emphatic phrase (Genitive Absolute v. 20b) and then stresses that the whole construction is so 'fitted together', held together in Christ Jesus that only so are the Christians as living stones built up into the heavenly temple, the dwelling-place of God. We cannot entertain the idea of detaching the ecclesiology from the Christology; the Church is only the Church insofar as she remains in Christ and allows herself to be carried, determined and led up to God by him. The questions which broke out at the time of the Reformation as to what part the Apostles and Prophets / office-bearers play in relation to Christ and their fellow church-members (cf. the history of influence) have not yet appeared. All the emphasis falls on the unique, indispensable rôle of Christ which he performs in and for the Church, for the Apostles and Prophets no less than for later believers. Without him God's building of the Church would lose all its security, would fall apart and miss its goal.

(b) The Church as the Body of Christ

No other symbol for the Church – especially here understood as a symbol related to reality and filled with reality – has received greater attention; but here research has achieved real progress.[33] The transition from the Pauline conception of the congregation as the Body of Christ, in which there is as yet no differentiation made between Christ the Head and the congregation as Body – in 1 Cor 12.12–27 it is the total Body 'of Christ' (v. 12), the 'Head' one member among others (v. 21) – to that in Col. and Eph., where the Head has a special, characteristic position with regard to the Body, is so significant that we must talk of a new beginning which changes the conception.[34] This does not lie simply in the outline of the picture but has a deeper root in the factual difference that in the main Pauline Epistles (cf. 1 Cor. 6.15; 10.11; Rom. 12.4 f.) attention is centred on the individual congregations, whereas in Col. and Eph. the Church is seen as a total entity (v. above under 1) which is brought into a special relationship to Christ, the 'Head' set by God over all the 'powers' and the universe (cf. Col. 2.10, 19; Eph. 1.20–3). This cosmic extension of the conception

---

[33]We must stress the defeat of the notion of a Gnostic derivation, v. infra. On the positive side a dependence on the idea of the god-of-the-universe, especially in Philo's shaping of it, has been accepted, cf. Colpe. FS J. Jeremias; Hegermann, *Schöpfungsmittler*; Schweizer, *Neotestamentica* 304 f. (with reference to TDNT VII, art. σῶμα); Gnilka 101–5; Fischer, *Tendenz* 68–78. But this has also consequences for the theological interpretation.

[34]Wikenhauser, *Kirche* 153 f., had already observed this although he thinks it possible that Paul himself could have developed the idea. The changed conception becomes clear in the two discourses by Schweizer on the Church as the Body of Christ in the Pauline Homologumena and Antilegomena (*Neotestamentica* 272–92; 293–316). Further cf. Merklein, *Kirch. Amt* 89; Paulinische Theologie 49–51.

produces a more comprehensive ecclesiological view insofar as the Church is seen also in her relationship to the world and in her God-given tasks in and for the world. Christ is Head of the Church and Head of the world[35] and consequently in his own person simultaneously holds them together and in tension. He desires to extend the area of his Rule of Blessing through the Church and thereby repel the influence of the powers of evil which are still at work in the world – in spite of their subjugation through Christ's victory on the Cross (cf. Col. 2.15; Eph. 1.20 f.). How can we explain this new approach?

The religio-historical research begins with the gnostic idea of 'primeval man'. According to this anthropos-myth god-'man' fell into the power of the forces of darkness which rule in the lower world. Only one part of the 'man', (namely the 'head') managed to return to its heavenly home, his other parts ('members') were all the more chained to matter, and now redemption takes place in that the heavenly head gathers together his scattered members and unites them with him in heaven.[36] But closer enquiry after such a myth (R. Reitzenstein: 'redeemed redeemer') has shown that there was no such unified, pre-Christian myth but only different ideas – of a god of the universe, of a first man or king of paradise and finally of a god-'man' – which only gradually ran together and finally led in Manichaeism to the development of the myth of the 'redeemed redeemer'.[37] Hence a researcher into gnosis concludes: 'Thereby the essential condition for a gnostic interpretation of the idea of the Body of Christ from Gnosis is inapplicable on chronological grounds'.[38] An examinhation of the concepts 'head', 'members' and 'body' (in an ecclesiological sense) in gnostic texts also confirms this conclusion.[39] On the other hand there was at an early period a wide-spread idea that the whole world is one large body, a 'great-man' (Macro-anthropos), and in the area of Greek culture Zeus was then identified with him as 'god of the universe' or the god Aion (who always remains the same).[40] Philo also took over such ideas and combined them with his logos-doctrine. According to this the universe is the 'most perfect person' (Migr. Abr. 220), the 'great man' (Rer. Div. Her. 155) or the 'most perfect living thing' (Spec. Leg. I, 210 f.). But the universe is not as in pantheistic philosophy simply God, but is connected to God by the Logos. God is the father of the Logos, his mother is wisdom, the Logos puts on the universe like a garment and holds it together as the soul builds the body (Fug. 108–13).

Today the favoured understanding of the Head-Body conception in (Col. and) Eph. is that it is derived from such widespread ideas about a 'god of the universe' and from Philo's particular formulations (v n. 33). But we must note that even the Philonic Logos was not directly named as head of the world. The Logos is 'head' among the many logoi, i.e. the immortal souls: God chooses him for himself

---

[35]Cf. Wagenführer, *Bedeutung Christi*; Mußner, *Christus*; O. Perels, 'Kirche und Welt nach dem Epheser- und Kolosserbrief', ThLZ 76 (1951) 393–400; Warnach, *Kirche und Kosmos* 170–205; H. J. Bagathuler, *Jesus Christus, Haupt der Kirche – Haupt der Welt* 1965 (AThANT 45) (on Col.); Schnackenburg, *Gestalt und Wesen* 281–6.

[36]Cf. Käsemann, *Leib* 51; Schenke, *Der Gott 'Mensch'* 1 f. On the basic idea of the Gnostic myth cf. also Schweizer, TDNT VI, 393–5; Rudolph, *Gnosis* 97–102, 86–93, 111–18.

[37]Thus Schenke, *Der Gott 'Mensch'* 153 f.; cf. also now Rudolph, *Gnosis* 88 f. He attempts to reduce the doctrine of the god 'Man' to two basic types: In one case the highest being is himself the first or original 'Man', in the other he creates a heavenly 'Man' identical in nature. Rudolph, too, recognizes that the redeemer-myth in Reitzenstein's sense is only found in Manichaean texts (120), but would like to retain the basic idea for Gnosis (121 f.) – probably rightly, only not in connection with the body – members conception.

[38]Fischer, *Tendenz* 58.

[39]Ibid. 58–68.

[40]On the ideas in Babylonian and Indian cosmogony cf. Fischer, *Tendenz* 69 f.; on the Orphic and Stoic texts, Schweizer, TDNT VII, 1037 f.; on Philo ibid. 1054 f.; Hegermann, *Schöpfungsmittler* 59–67.

'so to speak as the head of a united body and places him close to his Spirit' (Som. I, 144). Hence the Philonic Logos is not completely comparable with Christ, Head over the world and Head of the Church.[41] The power of Christ to hold down the evil forces because of the victory he has already won (cf. Col. 2.15) has no parallel in Philo. Christ's rising from the dead and heavenly enthronement (cf. Eph. 1.20 f.) give a special characterization to the Christian understanding of the Head over the universe. 'Head of the Church' is only distantly exemplified in Philo's thought. For the activity of the Logos which raises him to God is accomplished in Philo principally in the soul of the individual person which as microcosmos corresponds to the macrocosmos represented as a cosmic body. For 'the oldest Logos of being has the world as raiment . . ., the individual souls the body, the spirit of the wise the virtues' (Fug. 110). The ascent into the heavenly world is at the most connected in the 'Mystery of Sinai' with the 'people' of Israel but remains in the end related to the individual.[42] To be sure Moses is the representative of the 'divine race' and the 'servants of the king' have placed him at the front as leader (Conf. Ling. 94 f.): but the ascent into the heavenly world is only possible for one soul which is adorned with virtues (Quaest in Ex. II, 27). Correspondingly it is said of the Logos: 'If, however, a person is not yet worthy to be called God's son, he should endeavour to relate himself to the Logos, his first-born . . .'. (Conf. Ling. 146) The merciful foundation-laying in Baptism and the bond of Baptism which unites all members (cf. Eph. 4.4 f.) differentiate the Christian Church from Philo's holy race of souls searching for God. Hence the Judaeo-Hellenistic way of thinking which comes to the fore in Philo's allegorical interpretations may reveal the basis of the idea of the Body of Christ but cannot explain the concrete conception of the Church in Col. and Eph. which is oriented on the Christ-event.

According to historical tradition, the author of Eph. takes up the statements in Col. about Christ's dominant position as Head over every rule and authority (Col. 2.10) and as Head of the Body (i.e. the Church) which supports life and growth (Col. 2.19) but develops in more depth the conception of the Body of Christ (cf. 4.11–16) and combines it with other symbols of his ecclesiology (cf. 2.15 f.; 5.23, 30). His talk of 'edification' (οἰκοδομή) of the Body of Christ (4.12, 16) is striking since this metaphor is missing in Col. It is possible that the Pauline exhortation to edify the congregation continues to have an effect (cf. 1 Cor. 14.5, 12, 26). But, even without this, 'edification' is connected to the symbol of God's building (2.20–2). The idea of growth unites the two symbols of 'building' and 'body' (cf. 2.21 with 4.16) which are also related at other places.[43] Nevertheless, the two models of God's Building and of the Body of Christ do not need to harmonize in every detail (so that the 'cornerstone' would become the uppermost 'keystone'). Each can emphasize special aspects: God's Building, raised on high by God himself, rises on a foundation – i.e. grows up from below; the Body of Christ, equipped with the gifts of the Christ who has risen above all the heavens, grows from her heavenly head and builds herself from him in love.

---

[41]The clearest passage is Quaest in Ex II, 117: 'The eternal Logos of the eternal God is the Head of the universe under whom, as if it were feet or other members, lies the whole world, above which he, passing through (*transiens*), has been settled' – if this passage has not probably been interpolated in a Christian sense. The whole context is Christian, cf. R. Marcus in the Loeb edition (1953), p. 168. There is evidence of Zeus as the head and centre of the universe in Orph. Fr. 21a (cf. 168) and the ether (heaven) as highest step in the universe likened to the head of the body (E. Schweizer, TDNT VII, 1037).

[42]Cf. on this Hegermann, *Schöpfungsmittler* 26–47. In connection with Quaest in Ex II, 29 he opines: 'Hence the Mystery of Sinai is a prototype for the way of salvation for the individual members of the Congregation of Israel' (42). The emphasis on the 'people' he traces back to missionary intentions (45 f.).

[43]Cf. 1 Cor. 3.16 f. with 6.15, 19; Pfammatter, *Kirche als Bau* 25–37; Schweizer, TDNT VII, 1073, n. 462.

Christ's function of 'joining together', bestowing unity, is factually expressed in both symbols. There is yet another conception in the marriage-paraclesis: Christ has won the Church as his wife through his self-giving in death and through the bridal-bath of Baptism, and loves her as his own body (cf. 5.25 f., 29 f.). Here, too, the reality-related symbol of the 'Body of Christ' has an effect, but not in a predominant way. The metaphors merge, but give proof of the strength of the idea of the Body of Christ handed down by tradition.

Hence we must ask a more detailed question: What does the author want to say *theologically* in using the symbol of the Body of Christ? The most striking thing is the *unity* of the Church with Christ, her Head. God has given the Church Christ as her Head (1.23) and the Church is so related to this Head that she only realizes her being and activity meaningfully when she comes closer to him in everything, grows into him, reaches towards Christ in love (4.16; 5.24). Through the one Spirit which rules over her, the Church is one single Body (4.4).

Nevertheless the Church is not a form without shape, and human differences do not disappear in her. In the first place, as the author of Eph. sees her before him, there are recognisable in the Church the two earlier groups of Jews and Gentiles, who, even after their union in the one Body, through the one Spirit (2.16, 18; 4.4) retain their historical human distinctiveness. Second, the Body of Christ also, according to Eph., consists of individual 'members' (4.25; 5.30; cf. 4.16) who are related to one another. Among the various parts or members of the Body of Christ certain special 'gifts' are emphasized (4.11), namely the office-bearers given by Christ, the heavenly Head. Admittedly they are intended to advance the edification of the Body of Christ working closely together with all the other members (4.12). Unity does not abolish human variety; Christ desires variety and this is planned in his distribution of 'Gifts' (4.7). The Church is not an abstract, heavenly entity but always also shows herself in her earthly location. Finally, this holds good for the encounter of individual Christians with one another (4.25 and the exhortations which follow) and in particular for Christian spouses, for whom the relationship of Christ and Church becomes the prototype and model for their married life together (5.25, 30). The Church as an ideal entity bound to Christ is deeply imbedded in the earthly congregations with their human members, inseparable from them; in them and from them she rises, despite all human weakness, to Christ, her heavenly Head.

Christ is both origin and end of this earthly Church which is indigenous in heaven. Her origin in Christ needs to be considered more closely. If in 5.25 she appears as a pre-existent entity, like a bride for whom Christ has given himself in his death, elsewhere (2.15) it is obvious that she had her origin in that very death on the Cross. Only the symbol of the marital union raises the idea of a pre-existence of the Church; in reality she exists neither before Christ nor apart from Christ. She owes her calling and her existence to him alone. Probably this is also what is meant by the unusual expression 'he himself, the Saviour of the Body' (5.23).[44] 'Head' and 'Saviour' correspond to one another in a certain tension (cf. the emphatic 'he himself'): The Lordship of Christ is revealed precisely in his redeeming love. 'Saviour of the Body' becomes a short expression for Christ's whole work of Redemption from which the Church lives. She not only has her origin in Christ but also her continuing, saved existence. If the marriage-paraclesis keeps to this 'model' of Christ, which is more fully set out in 5.25–7, Christ's constant concern for his Church becomes apparent (cf. also 5.29 with the Present form). Again there is visible in the

---

[44] Cf. exegesis at this point with p. 247 n. 17 Fischer, *Tendenz* 76 f. comments: 'We can produce no real parallel for the expression that the god of the universe is also the saviour of the 'body', but he thinks it possible that such a text may still be found, most probably for one of the gods of the Mysteries who are described as redeemers and gods of the universe.

background the still inadequate form of the earthly Church which continues to need the purifying and redeeming power of Christ, her Head.

(c) The 'new person' and the 'complete man'

A strange symbol appears in the passage Eph. 2.14–16 which is also curious and complex in other respects. The new unity which Christ has created by his peacemaking in removing the enmity between Jews and Gentiles is described in v. 15 as 'new person' (ἄνθρωπος). The two areas (τὰ ἀμφότερα v. 14) which until then were separated by the 'fence' of the Law are now described in a personal expression as 'the two' (οἱ δύο) whom Christ has created in his own person as a new personality.[45] The Church appears thereby as an extremely compact unity, as if she existed in only one person, and at the same time as something new which did not exist previously, as Christ creates (κτίσῃ) this new human being (v. 16) in his own person – he himself is '(the) peace' (v. 14).

We cannot fit this metaphor anywhere satisfactorily in the development of religion. We have already in the exegesis made reference to a gnostic interpretation according to which only the earlier unity of the heavenly Anthropos with his separated members on earth would be re-established. But the reference to Philo's idea of the Universal-God is also incapable of supporting the burden of proof which some would like to place upon it.[46] The Philonic doctrine of the Logos, which is combined with speculation about the Macro-Anthropos, does not explain Christ's act of Redemption which creates a 'new person'. Again (as with the doctrine of the Soma) this only introduces a general way of thinking, namely the cosmic-universal one, which the Christian idea then makes its own in a new, specific manner. We might also recall the 'second person who comes from heaven' whom Paul introduces in the course of his Adam/Christ typology to those in Corinth who denied the Resurrection (1 Cor. 15.47) and behind whom stand certain speculations on Adam/Anthropos.[47] The most important link theologically is Gal. 3.28, where the new unity created in Baptism is described as 'one' (εἷς, masc) in Christ. The community of the baptized thus becomes one person, 'Christ' himself in the new dimension which he has achieved since his Resurrection through the Spirit (cf. 1 Cor. 12.12 f., 27; Rom. 12.5).

With this we come to the traditio-historical question. If the Adam/Christ typology continued to have an effect, the author of Eph. has interpreted it anew with reference to the Church. The impetus for this may have come from Col. 3.10 f. where the Pauline theology of Baptism also introduces the metaphor of the new unity (v. 11). The idea of the 'new creation' (cf. 2 Cor. 5.7) is alredy in Paul extended to a corporate view (cf. also Gal. 6.15 f.), which comes to the fore in Eph. in a new way. The overcoming of the problem of circumcised and uncircumcised, the new existence 'in Christ' (cf. Gal. 5.6) and the perspective of the 'Israel of God' (Gal. 6.16) all bring Pauline thinking close to Eph. 2.11–18; but the direct tracing back of the 'one new

---

[45]This prevents an individualizing interpretation as if what was meant was the new creation of every Christian (in Baptism); rightly against this Schlier 134; Gnilka 142. Schlier also refers to Ign. Eph. 20.1, the Economy focussed 'on the one new Man, Jesus Christ'.

[46]Against Gnilka, FS Schlier 199 f. Above all this does not explain the innovation of this one anthropos which Christ creates in himself. Lindemann, *Aufhebung der Zeit* 167 also sees the main problem in the expression, cf. his discussion 168–70. In his view, in spite of some reservations, the Gnostic anthropos-idea comes closest to Eph. 2.15.

[47]Cf. E. Brandenburger, *Adam und Christus. Exegetisch-religionsgeschichtliche Untersuchung zu Röm 5.12–21 (1 Kor 15)*, 1962 (WMANT 7) 135–9; K. M. Fischer, 'Adam und Christus. Überlegungen zu einem religionsgeschichtlichen Problem', in K.-W. Tröger (ed), *Altes Testament – Frühjudentum – Gnosis*, Gütersloh 1980, 283–298.

person' to Christ's death on the Cross and the spatial-cosmic category which is taken up in Eph. 2.44 place new theological accents. Probably the author of Eph. was prompted to this by the cosmic Christology of Colossians.[48]

As in the case of the other symbols for the Church we must reckon here, too, in the 'one new person' with influences from the Pauline tradition and the Judaeo-Hellenistic world of thought which have been fused in Eph. to his own individual conception. The theological consequences of this are considerable. The Church appears as an objective entity which arises out of Christ's act of Redemption, and at the same time one which serves her own fulfilment in the world. From this H. Merklein concludes that ecclesiology has priority over soteriology: Christ's work of salvation is realized through and in the Church. Her existence is a pre-requisite in order that the saving event of Baptism can take place.[49] The Church does not actually replace Christ, but becomes an instrument of his saving activity, a 'missionary Body of Christ'.[50]

In its metaphorical character the 'complete man' (Eph. 4.13) is related to the 'new person', but it must be differentiated in what it intends to express. In this passage, too, we are concerned with the unity of the Church as the Body of Christ, not, however, with the fundamental unity already given but as it were with the unity that is coming into being. All *should* attain unity of faith and recognition of God's Son and in this way they attain 'to the complete man'. Comprehension of this metaphor is made more difficult by the connected expression 'to the measure of the age (or: of the greatness) of the fullness of Christ' although this is in fact meant to make it clearer. Without repeating the discussion in the exegesis (cf. p. 185) we can say that the emphasis is on 'complete' which corresponds to the 'fullness' of Christ. The metaphor is intended to express the maturing to adulthood or to one's full size. But we must also see the close relationship of the 'complete man' to Christ. In that all together become the complete man, they realize the figure of Christ. The 'complete man' is not simply Christ, but also not the Church in the figure of perfection without a connection to Christ. It is the Church who has grown up to Christ, her Head, grown in him and into him and is completely united with him.

Because of this unusual relation of the Church which matures to her full measure, grows into Christ and finds in him her fullness and goal, some exegetes have again suspected gnostic ideas in the background (cf. exegesis on this point). But the concept is not necessarily specifically gnostic. It is possible that the idea of the cosmic Anthropos still has an effect on the metaphor of ἀνήρ (man): but the metaphor has its own importance which is determined by the context (growing to maturity). As passages in Paul show, it is a popular metaphor in the area of Greek culture (cf. 1 Cor. 3.1; 13.10 f.; 14.20), but we cannot draw a direct traditio-historical line from Paul to Eph. 4.13. It is difficult to understand a transference of the maturing process of the individual Christians to the growth of the Church as a whole.[51] There is also no direct bridge from Col. 1.28; 4.12b to the metaphor of the complete man which from the outset is ecclesially stamped and applied to the Church as a whole. It is easier to suppose that the christological expression of the divine fullness which dwells

---

[48]Cf. Merklein, *Christus und die Kirche* 90–7; also *Paulinische Theologie* 58–62.

[49]*Christus und die Kirche* 68.69–71; also *Paulinische Theologie* 46–51.

[50]This expression is found as the title of an article by E. Schweizer ('The Church as the Missionary Body of Christ', in *Neotestamentica* 317–29). In connection with the Hymn in Col. he thinks this is a correction aimed at a group of Hellenizing Christians who saw in Christ the World Spirit who permeates and rules the whole cosmos. – But the missionary idea is not so emphatic in Eph. as in Col; cf. infra n. 63.

[51]In this sense Mußner, *Christus* 62 f.; Percy, *Probleme* 321 f.; B. Rigaux, NTS 4 (1957/58) 251, n. 2; Hegermann, *Schöpfungsmittler* 156, who appeals to ideas from the Mysteries; Masson 194; Fischer, *Tendenz* 154. Cf. on the other hand p. 185 n. 43.

in Christ (Col. 2.9) is changed ecclesiologically in Eph. 4.13 and ecclesiologically evaluated. According to Col. 2.10a Christians are 'fulfilled' in Christ; according to Eph. 4.13 they grow up in the Church to the 'fullness of Christ' (cf. infra under 3).

(d) The Church as the Bride and Wife of Christ

This symbol for the Church is also found in the paraclesis-section (5.22–3) and is used more than any other for a concrete exhortation. This at least partly explains the metaphorical transitions, the merging with the symbol of the Body – the husband as the Head like Christ (v. 23) the woman like his Body (cf. v. 29), the spouses members of Christ's Body (v. 30). But we should not understand the metaphor of wedding and marriage simply as a symbol devised for this paraenetical purpose. It is far too 'cryptic' for this. It expresses in a new and impressive way the connection of Christ with his Church, and suggests an existing symbol which is here utilized for the marriage-paraclesis.

Again various possibilities of explanation are offered by a comparison with the history of religion and tradition. For a long time exegetes supposed gnostic influences in connection with the idea of the *hieros gamos*, the 'holy wedding' (cf. p. 251 n. 38). Most recently K. M. Fischer took up this view and sought to give it a more solid basis by referring to gnostic texts from Nag Hammadi. In the background of Eph. 5.22–33 would stand the myth of the Fall and of the Salvation of Sophia.[52] The Sophia-myth has a different emphasis (181–91); but the 'mystery of the nuptial chamber' in which Sophia is redeemed (Sophia salvanda), especially according to the 'Exegesis of the Soul' (NHC II, 6) would provide the appropriate background for the conception in Eph. 5 (186–8, 194 f.). The main objection to this attempt at explanation, apart from individual bold conjectures (e.g. 'through the word' = instruction on all things in the Pleroma) is that it would assume a real, heavenly pre-existence of the Church corresponding to that of Sophia in the gnostic myth.[53] It is improbable that this is a Christian adaptation of the gnostic myth, which would then be bent at a crucial point.

The other way of explaining it, from the metaphor common in the OT of the 'marriage' between God and Israel (cf. Hos. 1–3; Ezek. 16; Jer. 2.2; Is. 62.5 etc) which was further developed in apocalyptic and Rabbinism,[54] seems at first to do less than justice to the realism with which the married relationship of Christ and the Church is marked in Ch. 5. But we can point to the fact that this metaphor, which was originally tailored for the especial relationship of God to his faithless Covenant-people, had already experienced a considerable transformation in Paul. According to 2 Cor. 11.2 Paul, like a person giving away the bride or like the bride's father, has betrothed the congregation ('you') to a single man, in order to 'stand her in front' of Christ as a pure virgin, to lead her to him. The difference from Eph. 5 is still considerable: The individual congregation, not the Church as a whole, is bound to Christ as a bride; the marriage union has still to take place, namely at the Parousia; Paul brings himself in as bride-leader or father of the bride (cf. under Eph. 5.27). The eschatological leading home of the Bride of the Lamb adorned for her wedding – i.e. the Church – in Rev. 19.7 f.; 21.2, 9 is closer to the perspective of 2 Cor. 11.2 but is

---

[52] *Tendenz* 173–200. The page-reference is given in brackets in n. 53.

[53] Cf. p. 248 n. 21 and 23. Fischer also tends to an allegorical interpretation of v. 31: The sōter leaves father and mother in the pleroma and unites with his wife – i.e. Sophia – as a pair (194 f.). But we cannot extract from the passage anything more than a special interpretation of Gen. 2.24 by the author of Eph. (v. 32).

[54] Cf. Sampley, *And the Two* (v under 5.21–33) 34–51. He depends especially on Ezek. 16 and the allegorical interpretation of the Song of Solomon. Further cf. J. Schmid, RAC II, 544 f.; Gnilka 293.

certainly not dependent on Paul. Rather Paul and the writer of the Apocalypse drew from a common Jewish source. In Gal. 4.26 the Apostle also uses the idea of the heavenly Jerusalem 'above' in order to apply it to the congregation in a new way. The blending of the metaphors of the Bride and the New Jerusalem which descends from heaven to earth in Rev. 21 is, however, something only found here.[55] If the early Church made these symbols their own elsewhere and used each in a particular way, Eph. may be regarded as witness, along with others, for this process of adoption. Admittedly in the process we cannot entirely exclude influences from the Hellenistic environment.[56]

Theologically, apart from the characteristics already observed, what is especially emphasized in this symbol is Christ's love and concern for his Church. The Church owes her existence to Christ's self-giving to death (cf. 5.25 with 5.2); he is her Saviour (v. 23) and continues to nourish her with care (v. 29). He wants to make her pure and holy (v. 26) beautiful and glorious (v. 27). In these metaphors there is expressed in another way what is said in 4.16 about the growth of the Church from her Head. In 3.19, also, the subject is the love of Christ which surpasses all knowledge, through which the Christians are to achieve the total fullness of God. Here we can recognise a constant process of renewal which is fulfilled in the Church out of the power of Christ's act of Redemption. The building-up in love is relevant not least in the congregations and in the smaller long-term relationships which exist within them.

If we examine the various symbols for the Church in Eph. all together, they appear in part strange and difficult to comprehend, of little help for our understanding of the Church today. But it is a language of symbols which we must penetrate to the theology of the Church. The reality of the Church, as the author sees it, also gleams through everywhere. The talk of the 'heavenly Church' which people try to find in Eph. urgently needs to be corrected. In spite of her 'presence' in heaven (cf. 2.5 f.) which is bestowed upon her in Christ, her 'Head', she still remains his instrument on earth, even, if we do not shy away from the expression, the 'Sacrament of salvation' in this world.[57]

3. The Church as the 'Fullness' (Pleroma) of Christ

Even more difficult to understand than the symbols is the way of speaking about 'fulfilling' and of 'fullness' which the author of Eph. uses in connection with the

[55]On the future Jerusalem which Judaism expected cf. Bill. IV, 883 f.; Volz Esch 371–6; Lohse, TDNT VII, 325 f. 336 f., In Judaism there is no connection between the New Jerusalem and the metaphor of the bride. On the fusing of different metaphorical motifs in Rev. 21 cf. H. Strathmann, TDNT VI, 532.

[56]It is quite possible that the author of Eph. knew the motif of the *hieros qamos* which was widespread in Hellenism. Here we can also point to Philo who repeatedly uses the motif – but in a different way than in Gnosis, cf. J. Schmid, RAC II, 545 f. The Gnostic myth represents a typical form in accordance with its doctrine of salvation. In my opinion a direct derivation of the conception in Eph. 5 from the Gnostic Sophia-myth has not been proved.

[57]The expression appears several times (with modification) in the Church Constitution of the Second Vatican Council (Art 1; 9 and 48) but also in a similar form in a document of the Word Missionary Conference in Melbourne (1980). With 'Sacrament' is meant in a wider sense something like an instrument or sign of the divine Economy of Salvation, cf. the Commentary by A. Grillmeier in *Das Zweite Vatikanische Konzil I*, freiburg i. Br. 1966, 157 f. In the Report in section III of the WMC it states that 'The whole church of God in every place and time, is a sacrament of the Kingdom which came in the person of Jesus Christ and will come in its fullness when he returns in glory' (in *Your Kingdom Come. Report on the World Conference on Mission and Evangelism, Melbourne 1980*, Geneva 1980, 193. In both documents the subordination of the Church to Christ, her provisional, imperfect character as well as her obligation for structuring of life in the world is emphasized.

Church but also with the universe.[58] In interpreting the relevant texts each exegete must take up a particular position; in this excursus the commentary above is taken for granted and it must be referred to. The area which uses this idea includes four passages with the verb (1.23; 3.19; 4.10; 5.18) and four with the noun (1.10, 23; 3.19; 4.13) and is not homogeneous. The 'fullness of the times' (1.10) stands out as a concept which already has a special character (cf. Gal. 4.4). 'That you may enter into the total fullness of God' (3.19) is a different aspect from 'achieve the full measure of the fullness of Christ' (4.13) or 'be filled with the Spirit' (5.18) although the passages coincide in their objective, theological substance. The Church as the 'fullness of Christ' (1.23) is understood in a different way from the universe which Christ rising in majesty 'fills' (4.10). These observations show that the manner of speaking is rather a linguistic instrument to express divers facts and aspects and place them in relationship to one another. In comparison with the symbols it is a cryptic manner of speaking.

As we examine this area, our previous observations on the theology of the Church widen to include the relationship of the Church to the universe which was hardly mentioned in the symbols. The description of the Church as the 'fullness of him who fills all in all' (1.23) is of fundamental importance for Christ's exertion of influence on her. According to our exegesis of this verse, we understand 'the fullness' as being in apposition to the Church, 'which is his Body'. Here we have the suggestion of a spatial conception, yet with a dynamic sense: the area in which Christ's beneficent powers are effective and mighty. God himself has assigned this function to Christ when he gave Christ to the Church as her Head. If we compare this with 3.19, where the subject is the total fullness of God in which we are to be included, then the Church may be understood as the place where we are drawn ever more closely into the love and fellowship of God through the mediation of Christ. The Holy Spirit is also part of this process of leading to God those believers united in the Church. For in the one single Spirit, in the one Body (here again the idea of the Body of Christ) we have access to the Father (2.18, cf. 16). Even the passage at 5.18 which is in a paraenetic connection then gains significance: 'Let yourselves be filled with the Spirit!' The beneficent power with which Christ fills the Church, his pleroma, is nothing other than the Holy Spirit which permeates the Church and must continue ever more so to do in order to lead her to the total fullness of God (cf. also 3.16). Elsewhere, too, the ecclesiology is interwoven into the 'Economy of Salvation' view of Eph. which includes God, Christ and the Spirit (cf. 2.21; 4.3–6). The conceptual area of 'filling' performs a useful service in this.

The possible comparisons from the religio-historical field have already been discussed in the exegesis (v pp. 82 f). Neither Stoic philosophy nor Jewish Hellenism (Philo), and certainly not Gnosis with its particular view of the Pleroma, could sufficiently explain the unusual manner of speaking in Ephesians, but might possibly throw light upon the linguistic code which the author uses. Paul offers no way of approach for these texts in Eph. unless we were to consider the formulae about 'all things' (cf. 1 Cor. 8.6; 15.28; Rom. 11.36; Phil. 3.21) as a starting-point. For the Apostle 'all things' means the created powers which rebel against God, which previously ruled the world and which God has made subject to the exalted Christ (cf. Phil. 2.10) and those who believe in Christ who are taken up through him into God's protecting love (cf. Rom. 8.37–9). But in Paul's writings we hear no mention that the fullness of God or the fullness of Christ has established itself in the Church. On the other hand the Hymn of Christ in Col. 1 represents a real link in the statement that the 'total fullness' (of God) was pleased to dwell in Christ (1.19). The second

---

[58]For literature cf. G. Delling, TDNT VI, 302–6; Ernst, *Pleroma* and the articles mentioned there; A. Feuillet, 'Plérôme', DBS VIII (1972) 18–40; Fischer, *Tendenz* 59–63; I. de la Potterie, 'Le Christ, Plérôme de l'Église', Bib. 58 (1977) 500–24.

important passage in Col., namely 2.9 f., first takes up emphatically the statement in the Hymn: In him (Christ) the whole divine fullness dwells bodily,[59] and then it links up with the believers: 'and you are fulfilled in him'. The divine fullness which dwells in Christ therefore is also communicated to those united with him, and the context (v. 12) points to Baptism as the place of origin of this 'fulfilling' with God's merciful power. In the same connection Christ is further designated as Head of all rule and authority (v. 10), with the result that the curious double meaning of 'fulfill' in Eph. – the (merciful) fulfilment of the faithful (Eph. 3.19) and the (majestic) filling of all things (4.10)[60] – also finds correspondence as to the content (though not yet in the formulation).

If Col. then appears, looked at traditio-historically, as a preliminary stage in the way Eph. expresses this, the development of thought in Col. has not yet progressed to the point which is fundamental for the author of Eph. Now the *Church*, the Body of Christ, is considered as the fullness of Christ/God (but cf. what is said in Col. 2.19). The fundamental, almost programmatic expression in Eph. 1.23 indicates the decisive theological advance the author has made. The Christological viewpoint of Col. – that the total fullness of God dwells in Christ (and in him alone), and then that all who believe in him participate in it – is applied ecclesiologically in Eph. The Church in her entirety is 'the fullness of him who fills all in all' i.e. he rules totally and completely with the power of God given to him. Within Christ's realm, which includes everything, the Church in his 'fullness' – the universe is never so named – the place filled with God's powers to save and bless.

Through the same semantic level of 'filling' the Church enters a curious relationship to 'everything', and we would like to examine this further.[61] We must note that in Eph. 1.20–3 Christ's Lordship over the 'powers and authorities' is described first and only then is it said that God has given the majestic Christ, the 'Head over all things' to the Church – as her Head. The cosmic perspective is the primary one, the ecclesiological is included as an addition, albeit in an emphatic way. Christ's 'Headship' over everything brings to mind the expression in the Great Eulogy 'to unite all things in Christ, things in heaven and things on earth' (1.10). The conception of everthing (with or without the article) stands, as 'things in heaven and things on earth' shows, not simply for the visible, empirical world, for that which we call the universe, but also for the invisible, spiritual reality of the world which is hidden behind this (cf. Col. 1.16 'visible and invisible') and which was no less real to the people of the ancient world. It is presumed that the world originally ordered and led by God has been confused and is in turmoil and disorder. This made a deep impression on the people of that time and they attributed it to the influence of spiritual powers standing behind the visible events in the world – those powers and authorities etc of 1.21. But the cosmic order should be re-established by God's saving work carried out in Christ, the influence of these evil powers should be broken and everything in heaven and on earth made peaceful and reconciled. This can be seen more clearly in the Hymn in Col.,[62] which may also have been the impetus for the statement about the uniting of everything in Christ (Eph. 1.10).

The author of Eph.'s interest is fixed on the re-establishment of world order, the liberation of humanity from the force of destiny and all the powers of evil. God the Creator (3.9) already before the ages has drawn up a plan in his wisdom to regain for himself through Jesus Christ the world which had become alienated from him and to open up for humankind a new, free approach to him (3.10 f.). The victory over the

---

[59]Cf. Schweizer, *Colossians*, on this passage.

[60]V especially on this question Gewieß, FS Meinertz.

[61]Cf. the exegesis on these passages. Here we are concerned with a theological overall view; for literature cf. n. 35 supra.

[62]Cf. Schweizer, *Colossians* 83–8 (on Col. 1.20).

rebellious forces is also described in 4.8–10 in a Christian Midrash as Christ's victorious 'ascent' over all the heavens – i.e. over the 'lower' realms of existence controlled by evil – as a penetration or 'fulfilment' of everything. That has already happened on God's part through Christ's Resurrection, yet still requires progressive realization in the historical world. For that very purpose the Church united with Christ becomes the instrument chosen by God. Through her, through her existence and proclamation, God's wise plan will be revealed to the powers and authorities and their defeat declared (3.10). The 'fulfilment' of everything with divine powers is for the present beneficently fulfilled in the Church, which thereby becomes the 'fullness' of Christ in the real sense (1.23).

If we attempt to transfer Eph.'s view of 'Church and World' – which is combined with mythological ideas of the world and expressed in strange language – into our present-day horizon of understanding, we can say something like the following:

(a) The 'world' or 'everything' when mentioned in connection with the Church means not the world or universe as it is nor creation in its original order, but the reality of the world as people experience it together with its transcendent references, the historical world of experience in its involvement in disaster, malice and violence, a world from whose constrained oppression humanity wishes to be liberated.

(b) Correspondingly the 'Church' does not mean an earthly institution, an entity marked out or identifiable in individual congregations or churches but an instrument of salvation created by God in Christ, which to be sure includes and combines the empirical congregations, is realized in them and through them encounters the world.

(c) The Church in the world has the God-given task of overcoming in herself those corrupting forces which rule in the world. This takes place through the powers graciously bestowed upon her, the filling with the Holy Spirit, in concrete terms by the love received from Christ and passed on. In that she grows in love and gains strength in unity, she also has an influence outside herself on the world which is still separate from Christ and repels the influence of evil. She also achieves a task of mission to the world.[63]

(d) Church and world are not separated areas. The Church should not retreat into her internal life nor should the world remain separated from God. Through Christ, the Head, Church and World are referred to one another by God. God's power, which Christ administers, 'fills' world and Church, each in a special way; but it is the goal of its work of salvation to penetrate the world ever more deeply through the Church with the healing, liberating power of his love.

4. The Importance of Eph.'s View of the Church when it was written

and today

Many barriers separate us from the strange ecclesiology of Eph.: Its conception of the world, language, development of tradition and denominational solidifications with new questions such as have appeared since the time of the Reformation. The

[63]Meyer, *Kirche und Mission*, tries to extract a stronger missionary perspective from Eph. But the author understands 'mission' less in an extensive, active sense but rather (using ideas of K. Rahner) as a dimension of the task of bringing salvation laid upon the Church. Accordingly the Church is 'the mediator of the revelation of the Mystery once hidden to the "world in general"; she is the proclamation of God's desire for universal salvation' (80).

idea of the Church as an objectively existing entity – even if insolubly bound to Christ – is also found elsewhere in early Christian literature but already in the Apostolic Fathers and particularly in the 'Shepherd of Hermas' takes different forms.[64] Then the *sancta Ecclesia catholica* is adopted as an Article in its own right in the 'Apostles' Creed' which is taken into consideration for their self-understanding by all the church communions which recognise it. At the end of the excursus we would only ask what service Eph.'s view of the Church could provide for the congregations at the time of its writing and what it can provide anew for us today.

For the congregations addressed in Eph., we certainly cannot limit to one single particular purpose the interest which guided our author. We must eliminate a purely speculative interest, as if he intended merely to write a theological treatise on the Church. Against this speaks the 'stern-heaviness' of the long paraclesis-section (Ch. 4–6) in which we find important expositions on the Church as motivation for the concrete behaviour of believers (cf. 4.11–16; 5.22–33). But even in the first section which sounds more didactic (especially 2.11–3.21) we detected that the theological explanations had more of a motivating function. They are introduced as 'reminding' (Anamnesis) (cf. 2.11; 3.2), especially in order to show the one Church made up of Jews and Gentiles that Mystery determined by God since eternity and realized in Christ (3.4–6) but also to emphasize the 'foundation of the Apostles and Prophets' (2.20) and give prominence in particular to the great Apostle to the Gentiles, Paul, as the blessed interpreter of the Gospel and authoritative upholder of tradition (3.7–9). Even this passage leads into an address to the recipients, in the form of an impressive intercession with a clearly pastoral objective (3.14–19). The theology of the Church, which certainly dominates the author's thoughts, is immediately put to the service of the instruction and internal leadership of the congregations.

In this respect the conception of the Church in Eph. retains its significance even in today's situation and gains new, topical references. Let me emphasize some details which seem to me to be important:

(a) In the first place there is only one thing (especially) we can learn from this theologian – how to understand the Church in general as a theological entity. A purely sociological view which only heeds the empirical shape of the Church (or churches) does not achieve the believing insight into the nature of 'Church' without which it is also impossible to understand the Church as a social entity. Likewise it is true that if a church or Christian community no longer recognizes that it is bound to the all-embracing task of bringing salvation which is depicted in Eph., then it fails to understand what 'Church' is by nature and mission. The Church is more than a union of people who believe in Jesus Christ, united through Baptism, a common confession and outward organisation; it is a community bound to her Lord who lives on, who through him belongs at the same time to God's transcendent world. The author of Eph. shares this conviction (cf. 2.19) with the rest of early Christianity (cf. Phil. 3.20; Col. 3.3; Heb. 6.4 f.; 12, 22–4; Rev passim).

(b) Nevertheless the Church must not be exalted as a purely 'heavenly' or spiritual entity. She is represented and realized in the earthly congregations, in the people who belong to her and who leave their mark on her appearance. There, too, her weaknesses, failures and guilt are obvious. In Eph. this is expressed less in the total picture of the Church than in the exhortations to the addressees, in a similar way as in the circular letters in Revelation (Chs. 2–3). Insofar as the impression arises thereby of a Church translated into heaven (cf. 2.5 f.), the letter must be read critically in the context of its paraclesis. The constant exhortations to the addressees

---

[64]On this cf. F. Kattenbusch, *Festgabe v. Harnack* (p. 293 n. 20) 146–51 upon which K. L. Schmidt, TDNT III, 532 f. also relies.

to be aware of their calling and obligation need to be made topical for ecclesiastical negotiations in the present time, certainly even more strongly in the social area.

(c) The relationship of Church to world, more precisely to the human world which closes its mind to the message of Christ, becomes the focus of attention more emphatically because of Eph. Those people who are not yet members of the Church also belong to the 'everything' which has been put under Christ, the Resurrected One. They are included in Christ's work of Redemption but as Eph. sees it are still under the influence of the 'powers and authorities' which resist Christ's rule (cf. 2.2 f.; 4.17 f.; 5.6 f.). The sharp dissociation from the 'pagan' environment which is explained by the situation of the congregations at that time still contains an important warning for the present-day congregations, but also requires critical qualification. With regard to 'outsiders' we must think further theologically about the effective area of the rule of Christ which is to unite everything in heaven and on earth and can also lead to God people who for various reasons are remote from the Church as she is constituted on earth. Christ's lordship is the all-embracing figure to which the Church is also subject. Nevertheless, those statements are still valid which declare that the Church, even in her earthly form (cf. 4.11–16) is the 'fullness' of Christ, the area of his total rule of blessing (1.23) and God's instrument for announcing their defeat to the powers which work against him. The Church today, although the conditions for her mission to all peoples are different, cannot abandon this self-understanding.

(d) The idea of the Church contained in Eph. is highly relevant for the Ecumenical Movement since it imperiously demands one Church under one Head, Christ. If the Church is not a purely spiritual entity which rises like a spiritual superstructure above the fragmented churches, congregations and groups on earth but is one single House of God built on the foundation of the Apostles and Prophets and borne by Christ, the corner-stone (2.20–22), we must strive with all our might for the external unity of all those who are 'built up together' in this building. According to Eph. even the unity of the Church provided in advance by God and Christ (cf. 4.4–6) does not make human endeavour towards total unity superfluous, but demands it all the more (cf. 4.3, 13). If that was true at that time when external unity was far less splintered than it is today, then it is particularly so today. The conception of the Church in Eph., which demonstrates the true form of the Church bound to Christ, becomes a pointer for ecumenism today in the way in which the author brings it to the attention of the congregations, confronts them with it and motivates them to a new way of behaving.

C. The Influence of the Epistle throughout History

Even though relatively few commentaries on Eph. have come down to us from the old Church, this document – which was considered a true part of the Pauline corpus – was eagerly read and drawn upon as is proved by numerous quotations in early Christian literature.[1] Certainly it influenced the liturgy and piety down through the centuries and even today the Opening Eulogy is well-used among the *cantica* of the Roman canonical prayers and short readings are not infrequently taken from Eph. (especially 2.4–6; 2.19–22; 4.11–13; 4.23–6).[2] Likewise piety in prayer has also received strong impetus from this letter: the Apostle brings this before the recipients, praying and interceding (1.16–20; 3.14–21), and summons all Christians to constant prayerful vigilance (6.14–20). The spirit-filled service of worship described in it (5.19 f.), which is also reflected in the doxological and hymn-like parts (1.2–14; 3.20 f.; cf. 2.14–18; 4.4–7; 5.14), has borne fruit. But an investigation into its influence on the history of piety goes beyond the competence of this commentator and it is also not the purpose of this ecumenically-oriented commentary. What we are concerned with are theological interpretations and denominational repercussions, especially since the time of the Reformation. But in the process we must establish the fact that how they understood the Church was for the most part not directly based on this writing with its concentration on ecclesiology. An exception to this was perhaps John Calvin whose great commentary on Eph. shows that it had a considerable influence on his theology. Martin Luther wrote no commentary on Eph. and only occasionally referred to it. A heightened interest in the ecclesiology of this document is really only first perceptible in our century which has a greater interest in the question of the Church (cf. p. 293 n. 20). We must limit ourselves to thematic emphases which can be

[1] Cf. the two volumes of the *Biblia Patristica* and the apparatus in Frede, *Ep. ad Eph.*
[2] *Stundenbuch für die katholischen Bistümer des deutschen Sprachgebietes*, 3 volumes, Einsiedeln – Freiburg i. B. – Vienna et al. 1978, v Register.

proved to have been of importance in theological reflections and interpretations and by no means are connected only with ecclesiology.

1. God and Humanity. Predestination

The theocentric outlook of Eph. which already dominates the Great Eulogy and gives impetus to the ideas of Divine Election, Predetermination to sonship (1.4 f., 11) and the Economy of Salvation was noted by the ancient exegetes but Predestination was hardly considered a problem before the dispute with the Pelagians. They combined the eternal divine intention with the human efforts made possible by God's grace in such a way that salvation proceeds entirely from God but humankind is called upon to co-operate. Both Eastern and Western Fathers are in agreement on this point. On Eph. 1.4 f. Chrysostom says: 'Election is a sign both of God's love for humanity and also of human virtue; for he has only chosen the proven ones. He has made them saints, but we also must remain holy' (MPG 62.12). Election 'takes place not on the basis of our efforts and good works but through his love – though not only through his love but also on the basis of our virtue' (ibid.). Jerome remarks on the same passage: The election that we may be holy and spotless before God belongs to the divine foreknowledge (MPL 26, 446). But the clause that 'no living person is justified before you' remains; for Paul does not say that God chose us because we were holy and spotless but *in order that* we might become holy and spotless (447 f.). For the Final Judgement, however, there are still required 'services of the souls' since God had otherwise already from the foundation of the world determined some for salvation and others for everlasting punishment, and that would not redound to his honour (449). Hence they found no difficulty in the synergism (co-operation of God and humanity) and solved the problem by divine foreknowledge of human conduct. Augustine in his doctrine of Predestination, which depends especially on Rom. 9.19–24, was the first to develop consistently the sheer gracious character of Election right through to final Salvation by the power of the Grace of perseverance but avoided in the process a predestination to sin. To ask for a reason why God should save one and leave another to ruin would mean to strive for the impossible (Sermo. 26.13 [MPL 38, 177]).[3] This Augustinian view was very influential in the period following but plunged the doctrine of Predestination into considerable difficulties.[4]

Calvin went beyond Augustine and taught a double predestination to salvation and damnation and in so doing – which concerns us here – also took Eph. into consideration. He expresses his understanding of Eph. 1.4–5 succinctly (CR 51.147–9). In reply to the questions of why God has

---

[3]Cf. Altaner, *Patrologie* 404 f.; G. Nygren, *Das Prädestinationsproblem in der Theologie Augustins*, Göttingen 1956. On the development of the history of the doctrine cf. J. Auer, LThK VIII, 663–8.

[4]Cf. O. Kuss, *Der Römerbrief*, third instalment, Regensburg 1978, excursus: 'Zu der Problematik um die "Prädestination"' 828–932.

called us to participation in the Gospel and daily deems us worthy of so many favours and opens heaven, we must always return to the precept that he chose us before the Creation of the world. Calvin comes out sharply against the excuse that God had already foreseen our merit. We are rather chosen *in Christ*, and that means without our help (extra nos); the name of Christ excludes any merit on our part. Holiness and all the virtues are the fruits of our election alone: 'The efficient cause is the good pleasure of the will of God, the material cause is Christ, and the final cause is the praise of his grace' (148). He also goes into this exegesis in his systemmatic explanation of Predestination (Institutio III, 21–4) and along with the important passages from the Epistle to the Romans it makes up a constituent part of his oft-discussed and controversial doctrine of Predestination.[5]

The other Reformers rejected a double predestination; the idea of election, our election *in Christ* could be fully evaluated in a different way. According to Huldrych Zwingli our election applies expressly to the Redemption prepared by Christ; we are in Christ and chosen in Christ so that we have him to thank for our election and adoption as sons by God. Alluding to Eph. 1.4 Zwingli writes. 'God's election is certain and remains certain; for those whom he chose before the foundation of the world he so chose that he might choose them through his Son (cooptaret)'. God's goodness and mercy as well as his holiness and righteousness are made perceptible. It corresponds to his goodness that he chose whom he wished, but to his righteousness that he joined us with his Son whom he had made an offering in order to satisfy the divine righteousness.[6] Luther also in his writings after 1525 avoided concluding a double predestination from the idea of our concrete, historical election by God. We ought not to seek the predestination of the *Deus absconditus* (of the hidden God who has revealed nothing about it).[7]

In his monumental description of the Doctrine of Election Karl Barth[8] likewise decisively rejected Calvin's Doctrine of Predestination and presented his own view with a radical christological starting-point, clearly influenced by Eph. 'The knowledge of election is only a distinctive form of the knowledge of Jesus Christ' he writes with reference to Eph. 1.4 f., 11; 3.10f.; Rom 8.28 f.; Col. 1.15 (60). Because (with Calvin) he considers the election of the congregation as primary and that of individual Christians as secondary, he traces predestination back to the biblical concept of the Covenant and utilizes for this purpose Eph. 1.3–5, 9–11; 3.10 f. (102). The divine Predestination is the election of Jesus Christ, and that has a double

---

[5]Cf. P. Jacobs, *Prädestination und Verantwortlichkeit bei Calvin*, Neukirchen 1937, ³1968 (Reprinted Darmstadt 1973); H. Otten, *Prädestination in Calvins theologischer Lehre*, Neukirchen 1938, Reprinted 1968; F. H. Klooster, *Calvin's Doctrine of Predestination*, Grand Rapids ²1977, on Eph. especially 42–4.

[6]Fidei ratio under 3, CR 93, 796. Cf. also G. W. Locher, 'Die Prädestinationslehre Huldrych Zwinglis', ThZ 12 (1956) 526–48, particularly 539–41.

[7]On Luther cf. E. Brunner, *The Christian Doctrine of God* Dogmatics vol. 1, London 1949, 168–71 f.

[8]*Church Dogmatics* II/2: *The Doctrine of God*, Edinburgh T. & T. Clark 1957. Page reference in the text according to this translation.

reference: Jesus Christ is the electing God and also the elected man (103, set out in 103–16 and 116–45). Barth wishes to understand the double aspect of election and rejection from this starting-point. 'In the election of Jesus Christ, which is the eternal will of God. God has *ascribed to man the former, election*, salvation and life, and to *himself* he has ascribed *the latter, reprobation*, perdition and death'. (163) in that God in his Son 'tasted the damnation, death and hell' (164). We cannot here discuss in detail the problematic nature of this bold concept,[9] but recognize in it a speculative moulding of the 'in Christ' of Eph. 1.4 and 11. On the Roman Catholic side the problem of the Doctrine of Predestination led to the 'Grace Controversy' (1597–1607) and the different position of Thomism and Molinism.

The expression 'by nature children of wrath' (Eph. 2.3) had just as much effect on later generations. We would like to understand this in connection with and corresponding to 'Sons of Disobedience' (v. 2) in the simple sense that all people were sinners and, according to their human condition, without salvation which comes from God's mercy, were also 'Children of Wrath', subject to divine judgement. But the history of the interpretation of this expression (discussed in detail by J. Mehlmann, v. p. 93 n. 13) shows how it was drawn into the discussion on original sin, election and damnation. Here, too, Pelagianism had the effect of a catalyst. The Greek Fathers before Pelagius gave a similar natural explanation to that in this commentary. Clement of Alexandria and Basil do not even pay any attention to φύσει (by nature).[10] Origen makes use of the passage against the Gnostics with their view of the pneumatic nature (of the elect) from their origin (ἀρχῆθεν) and refers also to Gen. 8.21 and Eccles 7.20.[11] Didymus of Alexandria on the other hand emphasized against the Manichaeans – who considered the physical qua se as evil – that we *were* once Children of Wrath but have now been changed by God's love into sons of truth and virtue; the 'by nature' means 'in truth' (ἀληθείᾳ).[12] We can see how the text was continually bound up in new contexts. Even in Chrysostom there is no recognisable connection back to original sin.[13] The situation is different in Tertullian, who contemplated that nature which the higher divine nature (reason) introduces against the devil.[14] Marius Victorinus explains 'naturally (naturales) Sons of Wrath' from the fact that they 'were born in accordance with the nature of flesh and matter'.[15] These Latin scholars, then, saw corruption in the physical and material, while the spiritual part of humanity (reason) was scarcely touched by it.

[9]Cf. on this H. U. von Balthasar, *Karl Barth. Darstellung und Deutung seiner Theologie*, Köln 1951, 186–201; E. Brunner (n. 7) 346-52. Brunner objects that with the eternal pre-existence of the God-man assumed by Barth the Incarnation would no longer be a special event and he accuses Barth of departing from the basis of biblical revelation (347).

[10]Clem Alex, Protrepticus II, 27 (GCS 12a, 20); Basilius, Regulae brevius tractatae 268 (MPG 31, 1268).

[11]Text in Gregg, JThS 3, 404.

[12]Contra Manichaeos 3 (MPG 39, 1089).

[13]In Eph., on this verse (MPG 62, 32).

[14]De anima 16, 7 (C. Chr. 2, 803). In an earlier section (16.1–2) he distinguishes between the rational and irrational in humanity.

[15]In Eph., on the passage (MPL 8, 1254).

Only because of the denial of original sin by Pelagius and his followers did Eph. 2.3 becomes a definite scriptural argument for the corruptness of human nature, especially in Augustine who repeatedly quotes this passage, perhaps stimulated by Tertullian.[16] In *De Trinitate* he clearly states: 'Hence all human beings are from their origin (ab origine) under the ruler of the realm of the air who is active in the Sons of Disobedience. What I have named "from their origin" the Apostles names "by nature" . . . nature, namely, as it is ruined by sins, not fair as it was created in the beginning'[17] This Augustinian conception then entered that theological line of development – with all the further modifications and later also with denominational differences – which we have already indicated for the Doctrine of Predestination but cannot pursue further here.

2. CHRIST AND REDEMPTION

(a) All things summed up in Christ (Anacephalaiosis, Recapitulatio) (Eph. 1.10)

The line of thought in Eph. 1.10 is related to the 'reconciliation of all things' in Col. 1.20 and along with its has kept many theologians busy. But since E. Schweizer has gone over the more recent history of this Doctrine of Reconciliation in detail (Col. 193–202) we shall restrict ourselves to the curious expression of the anacephalaiosis which already caused the Latin Fathers difficulties. They translate the verb by *recapitulare*, *restaurare* or *instaurare* (cf. Frede, Ep ad Eph. 21–3). These have overtones of different meanings, such as 'combine, restore, re-new'. Origen and, following him, Jerome derive the verb from κεφάλαιον (principal part, sum total): All God's saving acts (related in the OT) up to that time which demonstrated the Christ-event typologically or in a preparatory way were 'recapitulated', gathered together and led to their goal in the Cross and Passion of the Lord.[1] But Irenaeus derives yet other nuances from the word; in addition to the 'gathering together' which looks back at what has gone before he sees also a recapitulation which points to the future, to the completion. The creation which has fallen away from God will be renewed to its original condition and led to its fulfilment under the Kyrios (cf. Haer IV, 34.2, v. infra). Perhaps the Bishop of Lyons also heard in the Greek expression the subjugation of everything under Christ, the 'Head' (κεφαλή).

It is almost exclusively a development of the idea of recapitulation which we find in this Church author who is important for the struggle against Gnosticism. Irenaeus appears to have taken over from Justin the idea that Jesus Christ restored what Adam had lost; for he quotes a passage from the lost writing of Justin against Marcion in which it is stated that the

[16]Cf. Mehlmann (p. 93 n. 13) 164–215.
[17]De Trinitate XIII, 12, 16 (C. CHR. 50a, 403).
[1]Origen, v. in Gregg, JThS 3.241; Jerome on this verse (MPG 26.453 f.). Cf. also Tertullian, Marc V, 17 (CSEL 47.632): 'recapitulare: id est ad initium redigere vel ab initio recensere.'

one Son, begotten by the one God who created this world and made us, came to us and restored (recapitulans)[2] in his own person his creation (humanity). On one occasion Irenaeus expresses his own ideas about the restoration of humanity in their original form and the gathering together of human history in the Son of God who became human: 'When he (the Son of God) took on flesh and became human, he gathered together (recapitulavit) in himself the long exposition of humanity, giving us in short (compendio, as in an abridged version) salvation so that we regained in Jesus Christ what we had lost in Adam, namely existence according to the image and likeness of God'.[3] Here the 'summing-up' seems to be thinking particularly of something related to the incarnate Word of God. Christ however also brought everything new to us in that he brought himself (Haer IV, 56.1 [Harvey II, 269 f.]). Christ is the new man in whom humanity is being renewed.

But along with the new creation of humanity the whole universe is also renewed. The heavenly spirits are included in this renewal as well as the physical world (cf. Haer V, 20.2 [Harvey II, 380]). 'Jesus Christ, our Lord is one single being who came through the cosmic order (dispositio, probably οἰκονομία) and gathered together everything in himself ... the Word became human, gathering everything together in himself so that God's Word, just as it is ruler over the heavenly, spiritual and invisible, should also have control over the visible and physical. He who grasps the primacy for himself and makes himself the Head of the Church should thus draw everything (universa) to himself at the appropriate time' (Haer III, 17.6 [Harvey II, 87 f.]). In the Logos who became man it is humanity primarily who are renewed but at the same time the physical world is also renewed. The Church, too, of whom Christ has made himself Head, is included in this outlook. But the perfection of the world is still to come; the Lord will draw all things to himself 'at the appropriate time'. For this theologian what is important is this very recapitulation of the physical world in Christ, the Logos who became flesh; only with the resurrection of the dead will the final goal be reached (cf. Haer IV, 34.2 [Harvey II, 214]). Thus Christ becomes the perfection of the world – is, indeed, himself the perfection.[4]

It is clear that Irenaeus was inspired by the ideas in Eph. but he developed them further in a speculative way and in so doing shifted the perspective in some areas. Least affected is the reference back to the reality of Creation since the author of Eph. could also have presupposed the protological statements in the Hymn in Col. (cf. 3.9, 11). More important is the change of emphasis from the theocentrism of Eph. to Christology:

[2]Haer IV, 11.2 (Harvey II, 159). On the comparison of Adam and Christ and God's corresponding action before time and at the end of time cf. W. Staerk, RAC I, 413.

[3]Haer III, 19.1 (Harvey II, 95). Scharl, Recapitulatio mundi (p. 59 n. 56) 7 f. comments thus on this 'intentional' recapitulation: Humanity was a long speech. It had its origin in the Creator's Word ... Now he has repeated and completed the explanation 'in himself': he has become flesh and human.

[4]Scharl (p. 59 n. 56) 21–31 calls this the 'real' recapitulation because the re-newal of humanity and the world has been realized in Christ. 'The whole universe is recapitulated by the Kyrios in himself (in semetipsum). He is the Head of the Church which is incorporated in him. He is the keystone in the building of the universe which is held together, unified in and crowned by him' (29).

Whereas in Eph. the whole process of salvation proceeds from God, (1.9 f., 20–3; 2.4–7) in Irenaeus Christ 'in himself' grasps the primacy (repeated: *in semetipsum*), makes himself the Head of the Church and draws everything to himself. This results finally in the most significant difference to Eph.: Irenaeus shifts the recapitulation, namely the re-newal of humanity, yet in principle of the world also, to the Incarnation even though he gives due consideration to the suffering and Cross as well as the Resurrection of Christ. The Christology of the Incarnation, admittedly connected with biblical thinking on the history of Salvation, is the starting-point of his theological reflection. As for the author of Eph. already in the relationship to Col. 1.20, then in the exposition in Eph. 1.20–3 (cf. also 2.5 f.; 2.14–16), there is no doubt that he connects the gathering-up of everything with Christ's victory on the Cross, his Resurrection and Installation at God's right hand. In the struggle against Gnosticism Irenaeus goes back to the Johannine Christology of the Incarnation. The more this became the decisive factor in the christological contests in the time that followed, the less could the view assert itself which saw the story of salvation culminating in the Cross and Resurrection of Jesus.

Akin to Irenaeus' thinking is the typological comparison of Old and New as it appears in the writing of Melito of Sardis 'On the Passover' (c. AD 170). Here it says: 'In the place of the Lamb came God, in the place of the sheep a person, but in the person (came) Christ who has included everything (κεχώρηκεν)'.[5] But there is no recognisable reference to Eph., and the typological outlook is characteristic of the whole of the early Church. Methodius of Olympus (about the end of the Third Century) seems to presume a 'recapitulation' of Christ's saving work in the Church when, in connection with Eph. 5.26 f. he writes: 'The Church could not conceive the faithful and bear them anew through the bath of rebirth if Christ had not emptied himself in order to make himself accessible through the *recapitulation of suffering* if he were not to die again, descending from heaven and uniting himself with his Bride, the Church'.[6] Marcellus of Ancyra (†c. 374), whose Christology was controversial, takes up the thought of Eph. 1.10, and Eusebius of Caesarea (†339), who wrote against him, shows in other places that he was influenced by Irenaeus' doctrine of Recapitulation.[7]

In the Commentaries on Eph. the passage is explained in its context without any further-reaching ideas. Theodore of Mopsuestia (†428) offers an apt explanation. He understands the 'instauravit' (vel potius 'recapitulavit') in Christ as 'a so to speak combining (compendiosam) renewal and reintegration (redintegrationem)' of the whole of Creation, admittedly as such that only really achieves its goal with the Resurrection and fulfilment of the world.[8]

An ecclesiological and universal application of the idea of

---

[5]S. G. Hall, *Melito of Sardis, On Pascha and Fragments*, Oxford 1979, 4.

[6]Symp. 3.8 (SChr 95.108); cf. also A. von Harnack, *Lehrbuch der Dogmengeschichte* I, Tübingen [5]1931, 785–8.

[7]Marcellus of Ancyra, Fr. 6 in Eusebius, Contra Marcellum (GCS 14 [Eusebius IV], 186, 16–20); Eusebius, Eccl. theol. III, 2 (ibid. 142.5–15).

[8]Swete I, 130.

Recapitulation still continues to have an effect in the Second Vatican Council. At the beginning (Art 3) of the Church Constitution (Lumen gentium), the aim of the sending of God's Son into the world is described by Eph. 1.4 f. and 10, and towards the end (Art 48) there is emphasis on the eschatological goal, the complete renewal (instaurare) in Christ of the whole world which is bound to humanity as closely as possible. It is more significant that the Pastoral Constitution on the Church in the present-day world (Gaudium et spes) also utilizes the idea. The Word of God entered the historical world as a real human being and while living in the human world made it his own (in se assumens) and gathered it together in himself (recapitulans). But, as such, Jesus Christ has revealed to the world that God is love and has shown them the Commandment of love as a basic law of human perfection and transformation of the world.[9] Then it might also be possible to attend to cultural values; for, freed from enslavement to the material world, a person can rise to contemplate and worship the Creator. The Word of God before he became flesh was already in the world as 'the light that enlightens every person' (Jn. 1.9).[10] Finally we have the statement '. . . it makes fruitful, as it were from within, the spiritual qualities and gifts of every people and of every age. It strengthens, perfects, and restores (restaurat) them in Christ'.[11] This interpretation of *omnia instaurare* (or *restaurare*) in Christ for the Church (in Eph. 1.10 said of God) has as its basis an understanding of the Church which gives rise to reservation in its interpretation of the relationship between Church and world. Especially dubious is the combination of this idea with worldly culture and inculturation of the Gospel among all peoples.[12]

(b) The Presence of Christ in the Faithful (Eph. 3.17)

Alongside the cosmic view, that God wished to gather everything together in Christ, there is another viewpoint focussed on the inner life, that Christ lives in our hearts through faith (3.17). There are only a few comparable statements in the early writers of the Church, for example in Ignatius of Antioch: 'Let us then do everything as if he (Jesus, the Lord) dwelt within us, so that we are his Temple and he, our God, is in us (Ign. Eph. 15.3); then in the Epistle of Barnabas 'For the dwelling in our hearts, my brothers, is a holy temple for the Lord' (6.15; cf. also 16.8 f.). The early Christian interpreters of Eph. rightly emphasize that Christ lives in our hearts through the Holy Spirit. Theodoret of Cyrrhus (†c. 466) interprets the prayerful wish of the Apostle to mean 'that your souls through the grace of the Spirit may be a dwelling-place for Christ who has saved you'. Because Theodoret combines 'through faith in your hearts' closely with 'rooted and grounded

---

[9] *The Documents of Vatican II*, W. M. Abbott, (London, 1967) Art. 38, p. 236.

[10] Art. 57, Abbott p. 263: reference is made to Irenaeus in a separate footnote.

[11] Art. 58, Abbott, 264.

[12] From the Commentary by R. Tucci (ibid. p. 465 f) we learn that Cardinal Lercaro called for emphasis on the 'poverty' of the Church in the area of culture.

in love', he concludes: 'faith and love are necessary that you may burst forth in them'.[13] For the Latin scholars let us quote Marius Victorinus († after 362): 'But how are they (the Ephesians) strengthened by God's Spirit, i.e. made strong? It says Christ should live in their inner person; for if Christ lives in the inner person, i.e. in the soul, people are strong in power through the Spirit. But as Christ dwells in people, he adds "through faith". Hence it is an easy and wonderful thing, easy because faith alone fulfils such a great service and so great a favour that Christ dwells in our hearts'.[14]

The theological relevance of the statement was only later considered in greater depth. Thomas Aquinas (†1274) only remarks briefly in his Commentary on Ephesians: 'How (does Christ dwell in our hearts)? I say not only through faith which as a gift is very powerful, but also through the love which is in the saints' (Cai nr. 172); but in another place he writes 'He who believes in Christ takes him into himself ... to wit through complete faith (*fide formata*) which includes not only the intellect but also the emotions (for a person does not strive for something believed in except in love) ... but Christ is in us in a double way; in our intellect through faith in so far as it is faith, and in our emotions through love which completes faith.'[15] Luther took exception to this scholastic distinction between *fides informis* (purely intellectual faith) and *fides formata* (complete faith which is effective in love). He rejected this from his understanding of faith as *fiducia* (trust). In his great lecture on the Epistle to the Galatians in 1535 he writes: 'Hence faith justifies because it grasps and holds this treasure, namely the present Christ. But how he (Christ) is present we cannot imagine because it is a mystery as I have said. Hence where there is a trusting heart, Christ is present, even in a misty faith, and that is the formal righteousness through which a person is justified, not through love as the Sophists say ... Hence Christ, grasped by faith and dwelling in our hearts, is Christian righteousness, for whose sake God assesses us fairly and gives us eternal life.'[16] We cannot fail to see a difference in the understanding of what faith is and how it works; but in the Roman Catholic understanding, too, the living connection with Christ is established only through the Holy Spirit through whom God's love is poured out into our hearts (Rom. 5.5).[17] The Wurtemberg reformer Johannes Brenz stands closer to the Roman Catholic view. On Eph. 3.17 he writes: 'Christ is that heavenly "inner man", but he dwells through faith which is active in deeds of love (in us). For faith has love as an inseparable companion everywhere.

---

[13]MPG 82,529/32; cf. also Chrysostom, who points to Jn. 14, 23 for the 'indwelling' (MPG 62.51 f.); John of Damascus (MPG 95.837 C).

[14]MPL 8,1268 f.; cf. further Jerome on the passage (MPL 26.490).

[15]In Jo. 6, lect., VI, 1, ed. R. Cai, Turin-Rome ⁵1952 nr. 950.

[16]WA 40, 1, 229. Cf. also G. Söhngen, 'Christi Gegenwart in uns durch den Glauben', in *Die Einheit in der Theologie*, Munich 1952, 324–41, here 335–7.

[17]Cf. Conc. Tridentinum, Decr. de iustificatione Cap. 7 (D 800). G. Söhngen is especially concerned in his article (v. previous note) to emphasize the effective presence of Christ in contrast to the intrinsic (sacramental): 'The Spirit of Christ lives in our inner person as a personal power of thinking and living through belief in Christ. It should have such an effect in love and knowledge that we are filled with the fullness of God' (332). M. Schmaus gives a similar interpretation in *Katholische Dogmatik* III/E Munich ⁶1965, 62 f.

For he who believes that Christ has transferred his possessions to him easily transfers the things he possesses to another'.[18] Calvin was especially concerned with the close connection of the Spirit and Christ. The Spirit can be found in no other place than in Christ, and Christ cannot be separated from his Spirit. The heart is rightly described as Christ's dwelling-place so that we may know that he is not in the tongue or flying around in the brain. Faith is emphasized because through it God's Son becomes our own so that he may make his dwelling-place in us.[19] The Genevan preacher goes into the passage even more strongly in his sermons. Christ is not only our Head (Chef) but we also live from his essence as a tree draws its strength from its roots. Then again: Christ performs the function of the Head as regards us, we are members of his Body and live in his essence.[20]

In our century there has been a tendency to understand the presence of Christ in believers as expressed in the Pauline formulae '(we) in Christ' and 'Christ in us' as 'Christ-mysticism'. Given strong stimulus by the works of Adolf Deissman, who depicted Paul as a mystic of deep experience,[21] a lively discussion developed. Considerable qualifications had to be made to the enigmatic concept 'mysticism' or re-define it for Paul ('faith-mysticism', 'eschatological mysticism' etc.).[22] Although Paul himself naturally was the centre of discussion in the writings accepted as his, the statements in Eph. which do take up Pauline tradition were taken into consideration. Thus O. Schmitz who investigated 'Paul's Communion-with-Christ in the light of his use of the Genitive' explains the Genitive 'of Christ' in Eph. 3.19 (ἀγάπην τοῦ Χριστοῦ) as the 'living current of "Christ-love" which flows through those ἐν Χριστῷ ὄντες (who are located in Christ) in whose depths one dives ever and again knowingly without ever reaching the bottom'. He also finds this suggested by the context which unmistakably bears the stamp of the Pauline Christ-'mysticism', especially in v. 17.[23] On the Roman Catholic side A. Wikenhauser followed him. For Wikenhauser the passage 'has a strongly mystical tone' and reveals a 'present power working in Christians'.[24] M. Dibelius discusses in several works the 'mysticism' of the Apostle Paul and circumscribes it considerably.[25] But still in the Third Edition of his Commentary on Ephesians (revised by H. Greeven) it states

[18] *Kommentar zu Eph.* ed Köhler 33.

[19] CR 51.186 f. Admittedly Calvin then separates himself from those who take from Paul's words that love is the foundation and root of our salvation. But who claims that?

[20] CR 51.489–93, especially 491.

[21] Cf. already in his article 'Die neutestamentliche Formel "In Christo Jesu"', Marburg 1892; but it was only his book *Paulus*, Tübingen 1911 which triggered off a heated debate. In the re-worked Second Edition (Tübingen 1925) Deissmann had to confront sharp objections.

[22] Cf. Schnackenburg, *Taufe* 175 f. and the literature mentioned in the note there; E. Güttgemanns, *Der leidende Apostel und sein Herr*, 1966 (FRLANT 90) 102–12; G. Bornkamm, *Paul*, London 1971, 154–6; Barth 385–8; Karl Barth C D IV/3/2, Edinburgh 1962, 539 also pleads for avoidance of the expression 'mysticism'.

[23] 1924 (NTF, i Series, 2 part) 136 f.

[24] *Christusmystik* 17; he brings the passage into closer connection with 2 Cor. 4.16; Gal. 2.20; Col. 3.4 (23 f.).

[25] Cf. 'Glaube und Mystik bei Paulus' (1931), printed in *Botschaft und Geschichte. Ges. Aufsätze* II, Tübingen 1956, 94–116; 'Paulus und die Mystik' (1941), ibid., 134–59.

at Eph. 3.17: 'πίστις (faith) is here thought of as a means for the mystical in-dwelling of Christ, is thus an expression for the pneumatic life.' Today we avoid the expression 'mysticism' almost completely; and rightly so, for that close communion-with-Christ mediated by the Spirit and experienced in faith is clearly different from a mystical experience as witnessed to elsewhere, especially from a fusion with the Godhead, a blessed participation in the union, a deification. The in-dwelling of Christ in Christians is thought of rather as an effective presence of the heavenly Lord, who through his Spirit stimulates the inner life of Christians and desires to bind them ever more closely to himself. What is here voiced as a prayerful wish for Christians is in fact nothing other than what is said in Eph. 4.16 with regard to the activity of the heavenly Christ for his Body, the Church. The ecclesial view oriented to the action is given in Eph. 3.14–19 by the context (cf. v. 18 'with all the saints'). To this extent we can exclude an experiential mysticism, although religious experience underlies it; but all Christ's 'being within' is based on a deepening of faith, growing knowledge and maturing in love (cf. v. 19). Such an understanding of the communion-with-Christ bestowed upon the Christians is today hardly a matter of dispute between the denominations.[26] With the emphasis which it places upon faith Eph. 3.17 can preserve (us) from all over-enthusiasm, from striving after irrational religious experience and from seeking an individual salvation apart from the Christian community.

3. THE THEOLOGY OF THE CHURCH

It is not possible in the framework of this Commentary to look into the development of ecclesiological thought as a whole as Eph. would certainly continue to stimulate us to do. We must limit ourselves to certain special themes which have played a part through particular passages in theological discussion and dominate the field to the present day. There is available a detailed description by W. Rader of the history of the interpretation of the important section Eph. 2.11–22, and we would refer readers to this for a more intensive study (v Literature list).

(a) From Israel to the Church; Church and Judaism (Eph. 2.11–19)

In the current situation after the terrible 'Holocaust' under the Hitler regime honest efforts are being made towards a new Christian-Jewish encounter, and in this Eph. 1.11–22 also plays a part. In this section, certainly, as was shown in the exegesis, the concern is not directly with the relationship to the Church of the Israel who had no connection with the Christian faith (the 'Synagogue') but with the relationship of the Gentile Christians to the Jewish Christians in the one Church of Jesus Christ. Nevertheless the

---

[26]Cf. K. Barth, loc. cit. (n. 22) 539–54; M. Schmaus, loc. cit. (n. 17) 60–82.

relationship of the former Gentiles to the 'Congregation of Israel' is mentioned (2.12) and since the reciprocal, for the most part painful, relationship has been a problem through the centuries, we may ask how this is reflected in the history of interpretation.

In the early Jewish-Christian 'Religious Discussion' as represented by Justin's 'Dialogue with the Jew, Trypho', the Christian partner argues from the fulfilment of the Old Testament prophecies in Christ. In so doing Justin at no point makes reference to Eph. 2.12 (or even, 3.6). But Ch. 53 of his 'Apology' is instructive for his basic position. 'All other tribes of humanity were called "nations" (ἔθνη) by the prophetic spirit, but the Jewish and Samaritan people were called Israel and the House of Jacob' (53.4). From Is. 54.1 Justin concludes that the faithful among the nations will be more than those among the Jews and Samaritans (53.5) and according to Jer. 9.26 they will be more true and trustworthy (53.10 f.). The Christian philosopher stresses the promise fulfilled with regard to the Gentiles and the superiority of Christianity to Judaism, but emphasizes the continuity between the old and new Covenant. In the 'Dialogue' Justin recognizes the Jewish-Christians who continue to observe the Jewish Law if they do not request circumcision, Sabbath-observance or similar things from the Gentile-Christians and keep fellowship with them, but he rejects the Jews who do not believe in Christ, especially those who curse the Christians in the synagogues (47.2–4). The Gentile-Christians are also circumcised in his view, admittedly with a spiritual circumcision which Justin reads typologically from Josh 5.2, a circumcision 'which cuts us off from idolatry and all kinds of misdeeds' (114.4). In a network of allusions to New Testament passages he obviously also has Eph. 2.20 in mind. In the period which followed Church writers stress the continuity with the old Israel in their struggle against Gnosticism, particularly against Marcion. In Irenaeus the symbolic interpretation of the Cross for both 'nations' emerges for the first time although already a part of the Jewish-Christian tradition. 'As one of our predecessors said, by the divine stretching-out of his hands, he led the two nations together to one God.'[1] The same symbolism is also found in Hippolytus and Athanasius.[2] Irenaeus also describes the union of Jews and Gentiles using the metaphor of the corner-stone. 'Jesus Christ, who appeared in the last times, the supreme corner-stone, has gathered in himself and united those who were far off and those who were near, that is the circumcised and the uncircumcised, enlarging Japheth and placing them in the house of Shem' (cf. Gen 9.27).[3] Tertullian expresses himself sharply against Marcion in his analysis of Eph. 2.11–22. The God of Jesus Christ can be no other than the God of the Old Testament (the Creator) because Christ has led the Gentiles precisely to this God. The two whom Christ has made one are clearly the Jewish and the Gentile peoples, those near and those far off.[4]

---

[1]Haer V. 17.4 (Harvey II, 372). Cf. also J. Daniélou, *The Theology of Jewish Christianity* London 1964, 279–80.

[2]Hippolytus Fr zu Gen (GCS 1/2, 54, 23–5); Athanasius, De Incarn 25 (MPG 25, 140; SChr 18. 254 f.).

[3]Haer III, 5.3 (Harvey II, 20).

[4]Marc V. 17 (CSEL 47. 636 f.). More details in Rader, *Church* 13–16.

The same pugnacious African admittedly also wrote a tract 'Against the Jews' and there followed other Christian writers with a similar tendency to separate Christianity from Judaism.[5] The sharpest anti-Jewish notes are heard in Chrysostom who is well-known for his aversion to the Jews (cf. his 'Homilies against the Jews'). He interprets the 'Congregation of Israel' (Eph. 2.12) as the heavenly community and excludes the Jews from this (MPG 62.38 cf. 43). He concedes that God gave the promise to the Israelites but adds: 'They were unworthy of it' (ibid). The Greek does not need to become a Jew; on the contrary 'the Jew will be united with the Greek if he becomes a believer' (ibid. 40). But there are also friendlier voices in the same school at Antioch. Severian of Gabala († after 408) concludes from the 'near' that the Apostle does not name the Law of Moses godless like idolatry; 'near' partly indicates piety, although not yet perfect.[6] For Theodore of Mopsuestia enmity and separation which stem from circumcision and all the Law are abolished because Christ through his Resurrection has made us one single new person.[7] For Theodoret of Cyrrhus the reconciliation of both groups with God has taken place in Christ's sacrifice.[8] The Commentary on the Pauline Epistles ascribed to Oecumenius (Sixth Century) which actually dates from a later period distances itself critically from the sharp verdict of Chrysostom: 'If the Jews also failed God because they were unworthy, they still had hope because of the promise' and 'if they also offended against God, they still knew him'.[9] Theophylactus (Eleventh Century) even writes 'For the Israelities were respected and praised for their worship of God'.[10] In the West the attitude of Augustine is remarkable. He often applies the metaphor of the corner-stone to the union of the separated; even in the tract 'Against the Jews' he writes 'The nations of the circumcised and the uncircumcised are like walls which come from different directions, joined together in the corner-stone as in a kiss of peace'.[11] By and large in the early period the continuity of the Church with Israel was seen more strongly, but from the beginning of the Fourth Century it was rather the discontinuity which was emphasized. Probably the Constantinian era signified a turning-point which led to a heightened anti-Judaism.[12]

[5]A. L. Williams, *Adversus Judaeos*, Cambridge 1935 offers a painstaking survey of literature of this type up to the Renaissance; on the assessment of these documents cf. M. Simon *Verus Israel*, Paris ²1964, 165–203; further v. K. H. Rengstorf – S. von Kortzfleisch (eds), *Kirche und Synagoge* I, Stuttgart 1968; K. Hruby, *Juden und Judentum bei den Kirchenvätern*, Zürich 1972. In reaction against anti-Jewish literature F. Mußner wrote a 'Traktat über die Juden', Munich 1979.

[6]Fragment in Staab, *Pauluskommentare* 308–10, here 310.

[7]Swete I, 151.

[8]MPG 82.524.

[9]MPG 118.1195. On the origin of this commentary which is only found in a few scholia of Oecumenius on the commentary of Chrysostom, cf. Staab, *Pauluskommentare* XXXVII; J. Schmid LThK VII, 1122 f. ('at the earliest towards the end of the Eighth Century').

[10]MPG 124.1060.

[11]Ch VIII (MPL 40.60); on Augustine cf. further B. Blumenkranz, *Die Judenpredigt Augustins*, Basle 1946; Rader, *Church* 46–51. – The metaphor for the uniting of the two nations ('walls') in Christ, the Corner-Stone, is also found in Jerome (MPL 26.476), Theodoret (MPG 82, 525), Aquinas (Cai nr 129) and continues to have an effect up to the time of the Reformation, cf. Calvin on the passage (CR 51.175).

[12]Cf. Rader, *Church* 51–3.

The exegesis of the Middle Ages remained on the lines of the Fathers. Unfortunately neither the Reformation nor post-Reformation period overcame the enmity to the Jews. In Spain, where the persecution of the Jews was especially severe and led to the exclusion of the Sephardim (1492), the Jesuit Alfons Salmeron (†1585) deserves special honour. In his interpretation of Eph. 2.11–22 he came out against racial discrimination: Christ has so joined to one another those formerly separated that each neighbour is for us what Christ is for us. Hence each person who abhors another nation or race is immature and has not yet put off the old personality. He expressly comes out against the ecclesiastical measures against people stemming from Islam or Judaism.[13] On the Protestant side Philip Melanchthon in his *Loci Communes* interprets Eph. 2.14 as a call to love one's enemies even with regard to Gentiles and Jews.[14] In Pietism it is especially the Swiss theologian, Christian Starke (†1744) who interprets it as the abolition of enmity not only between Jews and Gentiles in the New Testament period but also in the present – admittedly only in relation to converts.[15]

In the struggle between Church and state in the 'Third Reich' Eph. 2.11–22 played a part as a controversy developed regarding the application of the 'Aryan Paragraph' to Christians of non-Aryan descent. The representatives of the Confessing Church, among them Dietrich Bonhoeffer and Rudolf Bultmann and also the Theological Faculty at Marburg in a report could justifiably refer to this passage, and it seems to us today incomprehensible how other theologians could oppose it.[16]

The question as to whether we can learn anything from Eph. 2.11–22 for the relationship of the Church and Synagogue has come in for lively discussion in the last decades, stimulated by the situation 'after Ausschwitz'. Justified, even unavoidable, as the question is in the current horizon, it is difficult to answer from the text of Eph., as the divergent answers show. The spectrum reaches from a pre-eminence of Israel which has never been revoked to a total elimination of interest in Jewish Christians:

(1) Markus Barth in various publications maintains Israel's priority and an equal status with the Church even of the Israel which rejects Christ.[17] In the Monograph of 1959 he writes 'According to Eph. 2.15; 3.6 the Gentiles only become members of the one Body of Christ through their being joined together with Israel' (13). Under 'Israel' he understands *all* Israelites, 'the recipients of the promises and hope, and the nation which continually grumbled; those who recognize the Messiah and those others who crucify him . . . the Israel of the past and the Israel of the

---

[13]Cf. Rader, *Church* 68 f.; I have no access to the edition of Salmeron's Works (Cologne 1604).

[14]Cf. Rader, *Church* 81.

[15]Cf. Rader, *Church* 117.

[16]Cf. Rader, *Church* 213–22; K. Meier, *Kirche und Judentum und die Haltung der evangelischen Kirche zur Judenpolemik des Dritten Reiches*, Göttingen 1968.

[17]*Israel und die Kirche im Brief des Paulus an die Epheser* 1959 (TEH 75); 'Das Volk Gottes. Juden und Christen in der Botschaft des Paulus', in *Paulus – Apostat oder Apostel? Jüdische und christliche Antworten*, Regensburg 1977, 45–134, on Eph. 98–101; cf. his *Commentary* (1974).

present' (18). In 'one new race' (Eph. 2.15; 4.24) Paul is thinking of *all* the Jews and *all* the Gentiles, not only of the Jews and Gentiles *in the Church* (19). 'Fellow-citizens of the saints' (Eph. 2.19) means fellow-citizens of Israel (24).[18]

(2) F. Mußner thinks there is a continuation of Israel's advantages even after the constitution of a Church made up of former Jews and Gentiles. Undoubtedly the author of the letter was thinking of the Church in the new community consisting of Jewish- and Gentile-Christians, but he does not say that Israel has lost the privileges listed in 2.12.[19]

(3) The majority of more recent interpreters (as in this commentary) consider that Israel had priority in the history of salvation until the coming of Christ but that all are equal, whether Jew or Gentile, in the one Church of Jesus Christ.

(4) Some interpret 'the Congregation of Israel' as meaning the Church (S. Hanson) or consider it as a prefiguration of the Church (cf. H. Merklein).[20]

(5) Finally, A. Lindemann wants completely to eliminate an interest in Israel: interest focusses entirely on the existence of the Christians, on the 'now' of the Church. Reference is not even made to her origin and development.[21] Although views differ so widely, yet the salutary stimulation of the text is unmistakeable, even if the real bone of contention is the interpretation of Rom. 9–11.

(b) The Church as God's Building (Eph. 2.20–22)

The Church as Building or Temple was a favourite metaphor in the Fathers and was used under various aspects. From the context of Eph. 2, Christ the Corner-stone was readily interpreted as the crucial point through whom the two 'walls', Jews and Gentiles, were held together (cf. n. 11). Here they were thinking of the foundation of the holy building on the 'Apostles and Prophets' and their connection with Jesus Christ, the corner- or main stone. In early exegesis 'prophets' was predominantly interpreted as the prophets of the Old Testament (cf. p. 122 n. 51); but both Pelagius and Theodore of Mopsuestia recognised that the author had in mind the prophets of early Christianity.[22] Most early interpreters understood the

---

[18]M. Barth retained this basic position in his later publications, cf. *Comm* 270: 'A Gentile finds fellowship with God through his incorporation into Israel.'

[19]Loc cit (n. 5) 48. Mußner's position only becomes clear in the thesis that, according to Rom. 11.26, all Israel will achieve salvation 'solely through an initiative of the God who has mercy on all completely independent of the behaviour of Israel and the rest of humanity' v. ibid. 49–67, especially 59 f.

[20]Cf. Hanson, *Unity* 142; Merklein, *Christus und die Kirche*: We must consider the whole section in the light of the author's conception of the Church. In v. 12 Israel has an ambivalent meaning: it refers both to the Congregation of Israel in the OT sense and also to the Church as the eschatological People of God (21). 'The Congregation of Israel' is for Eph. a purely ecclesiological term and consequently is open to both meanings (74).

[21]*Aufhebung der Zeit* 145–52, 161 f.

[22]Pelagius on 2.20 (Souter II. 356); Theodore of Mopsuestia on 3.6 (Swete I, 156).

Genitive as an appositional Genitive, giving a more detailed description of the foundation: the Apostles and prophets are the foundation.[23] The question frequently asked in recent years as to whether by ἀκρογωνιαῖος he means the corner-stone built into the base or the key-stone which forms the upper end and holds the whole together (cf. supra p. 123) did not particularly concern or perturb the Church Fathers. Tertullian appears to understand the stone as the key-stone.[24] Many Church Fathers saw in Christ both the foundation and the apex – the metaphor of the Body of Christ is beginning to have an effect. Thus Clement of Alexandria writes: 'Christ is both, the foundation and the superstructure (ἐποικοδομή), in him (is) the beginning and the end'[25] or Chrysostom: Christ 'shows that he at one time holds the Body together from above, but then he also supports the building from beneath since he is also the root'.[26] Hilary of Poitiers says from Ps. 126 that the whole building is constructed by God. Built on the foundation of the Apostles and Prophets, it must be increased by living stones and held together by the corner-stone that it may be raised by mutual connection to the perfect man and the measure of the love of Christ (cf. Eph. 4.13). Hilary adds that Israel, too, will be included in this building according to the fullness of the nations.[27] Without disputing about one component part the Fathers devoted their attention to the 'fundamental' and final position of Christ.

In the Reformation period Eph. 2.20 played a part in the controversy about papal primacy. For Luther and other Reformers the passage became an argument against Mt. 16.18 and the claims of the Church of Rome derived from it.[28] Luther comes to speak of this in his writing 'Against the papacy at Rome'. If the Roman Church is not built on this stone along with all the other churches, then she is the devil's church. But if she *is* built on this stone along with all the other churches, then she cannot be ruler or head of the other churches. She should be a part or number of the holy Christian Church, not the head, which is a position reserved for Christ, the corner-stone.[29] Calvin gives a detailed explanation in his commentary on Eph.: the Ephesians, like the other Christians, are founded on the teaching of the Apostles and Prophets. He then defends the (OT) prophets against Marcion and his supporters and connects them with the Apostles who are our teachers. God speaks through all of them, but Christ is the corner-stone, the single foundation of the apostolic teaching. Hence those who

---

[23]An exception to this interpretation is found in Ambrosiaster who thinks that the Apostles and Prophets have laid the foundation (Genitive of Agent) (CSEL 81/3.86, 4 f.) Cf. Henle 153 f. who sees here a Possessive Genitive: the foundation on which the Apostles and Prophets themselves rest, namely doctrine. For this interpretation he refers to Anselm and Aquinas whom he follows.

[24]Adversus Marcionem III, 7 (CSEL 47.386): lapis summus angularis, post reprobationem adsumptus et sublimatus in consummationem templi ... Yet he also is more concerned with the significance and power of this stone since he goes on to compare it with the rock which according to Dan. 2.34 f. 44 f. will anihilate the earthly kingdoms.

[25]Stromata VII, 55.5 f. (GCS 17/2, 41.1–3).

[26]MPG 62.44; similarly Jerome (MPL 30.828 f.).

[27]In Ps. 126 under 8 (CSEL 22.618 f.)

[28]Cf. on this Rader, *Church* 70–8.

[29]WA 54.245 f.

transfer the honour of being the corner-stone to Peter and maintain that the Church is founded on him shamelessly abuse this witness as an excuse for their error. For they so represent things that Christ is named as the primary stone with regard to others; hence there are several stones upon which the Church is supported. For the interpretation of the foundation as the teaching of the Apostles and Prophets Calvin, like most of the Reformers, refers to 1 Cor 3.11, where Paul calls himself an architect who builds on Christ, the foundation once laid down, so that further building consists simply in preaching and teaching.[30] Now in this there is yet no contradiction to Roman Catholic interpretation, since Thomas Aquinas also interprets the foundation as the teaching of the Apostles and Prophets. The teaching of both groups is necessary for salvation; what the prophets foretold for the future, the Apostles preached as being fulfilled. But Christ is the main (principal) foundation, the teaching of the Apostles and Prophets secondary – likewise with reference to 1 Cor 3.11.[31] A difference arises in that Aquinas does not draw such a sharp distinction between the Apostles and Prophets and their teaching as does Calvin. At the time of the Reformation Cardinal Cajetan (†1534), who based his argument, like other Roman Catholics, on Aquinas, declares that we are built up on Christ, but indirectly, only insofar as he supports the Apostles and Prophets.[32] A. Salmeron (†1585) says that the Apostles and Prophets, who are not separate from Christ nor against him, carry on his work; hence it is possible for him to emphasize Peter in accordance with Mt. 16.18.[33]

The deeper difference without doubt lies in the interpretation of the apostolic succession. For Protestant theologians doctrine, the proper interpretation of the Gospel in accordance with apostolic tradition, came increasingly to be the criterion for the Church. Roman Catholics link apostolic tradition with the succession of office: The apostolic tradition is preserved in the succession of office. But both sides keep a firm hold on the unique, irrevocable position of Jesus Christ as the corner-stone, a position which is valid for all times and alone is definitive. Roman Catholics do not transfer the function of the corner-stone to Peter, nor do Protestants underestimate the importance of the Apostles and Prophets as mediators of the message of Jesus Christ. We must agree with Rader that in the conflict of the Reformation period there were misunderstandings and false perspectives on both sides. One person who saw the strengths and weaknesses of both positions was the Bernese Reformer, Wolfgang Musculus (†1581)[34]

Today Protestant and Roman Catholic exegetes agree that the Apostles and Prophets in Eph. 2.20 are really valid as the foundation (appositional Genitive) because that is important for the author in his post-apostolic view. But in his additional emphasis of Christ the corner-

[30]CR. 51.174–76.

[31]In Eph. 2. lect VI (Cai nr. 127–31).

[32]*Epistolae Pauli*, Paris 1540, 264, according to Rader, *Church* 72; in this work we can also find Roman Catholic voices from the Reformation period.

[33]V. in Rader, *Church* 73.

[34]Cf. Rader, *Church* 77 f.

stone (or key-stone) he keeps a firm hand on the intention which concerned Paul in 1 Cor 3.11. For all denominations Eph. 2.20 provides the essential features of the Church: Unity and holiness, apostolicity and catholicity (generality). The differences in these features only emerge in a closer qualification, namely in the understanding of office and the succession of office.

(c) Ministries and Offices in the Church (Eph. 4.7–16)

The Church Fathers, for whom the episcopal constitution was familiar and self-evident, saw no problem in the catalogue of special ministries which were emphasized in Eph. 4.11 as gifts of the heavenly Christ but partly went their own ways in interpreting individual ministries. All emphasize that it is Christ who gives and provides freely, and each should consider his ministry as a beneficent gift (frequently called a charisma) and employ it for the edification of the Church. Origen links the blessing of all the saints with the special services mentioned in 4.11, among which he stresses the charisma of teaching; all members of the Church should achieve unity and maturity of faith.[35] How strongly the idea of bishops united in faith ruled the East is shown by Chrysostom's interpretation. For 'pastors and teachers' he points to Acts 20.28, then also to 1 Cor. 12.28; 3.6, 8 (MPG 62, 82) 'Each one builds up, each prepares, each serves', all have taken over a single task, to build one unity through faith (ibid 83). V. 16 he applies principally to the office-bearers, who are, however, exhorted to be humble. It is well known that Cyprian in North Africa was a champion of Church unity and a resolute advocate of the parity of all bishops; but he does not refer to Eph. 4.11 f. Ambrosiaster puts forward his own interpretation: the Apostles are the bishops (a reference to Acts 20.28) the Prophets the exegetes of Holy Scripture, the Evangelists deacons, the pastors readers, the teachers exorcists (MPL 17.409). But this interpretation based on the structure of the *ordo* never found acceptance (cf. Estius, 363). Jerome applies the grace appointed according to the measure of the gift of Christ (v. 7 and v. 16) to all the faithful (MPL 26.497/503) and for v 11 goes back to 1 Cor. 12.28. Pastors and teachers are the same group; one who is a pastor must also be a teacher (ibid. 500). On the other hand Theophylactus says that under shepherds can be understood priests and bishops, and under teachers also deacons (MPG 124, 1085). The exegetes obviously proceed from the existing 'hierarchical' order and find this again in Eph. 4.11. Thereby it is unimportant how pastors and teachers are more exactly interpreted.[36] Aquinas differentiates the Apostles furnished with special authority by Christ from the three following 'ecclesiastical ranks' who have special tasks. To administer earthly affairs (*temporalia*) is not

---

[35]On 4.11 f. (Gregg, JThS 3.413 f.) and on 4.13–15 (ibid. 414 f.).

[36]According to Pelagius (in Souter II, 364 f.) the pastors are the priests but the teachers are all who are suitable for giving instruction. Theodore of Mopsuestia (in Swete I, 108) gives no more detailed explanation of v. 11.

part of the office of bishops who are successors of the Apostles but rather belongs to the diaconate (a reference to Acts, 6.2).[37]

It was only with the Reformers that the primacy of bishops and a hierarchical structure of offices in general became a matter of strife. Their starting-point is the priesthood of all believers (1 Pet 2.4–10) which is based on Baptism. But they do not question ecclesiastical office as such, and base it especially on Eph. 4.11 f. Luther, it is true, recognized no essential difference between bishops and priests; all who hold office are servants of the Word (1 Cor. 4.1). Nevertheless the German Reformer has a high opinion of office and its necessity for the Church. This comes more emphatically to the fore with time in the rejection of zealots.[38] In his writing 'Of Councils and Churches' (1539) he says with reference to Eph. 4.11 f. 'For we must have bishops, priests or preachers who publicly and especially are responsible for giving, distributing and practising the four above-mentioned Items or Holy Things (namely Word, Baptism, Eucharist and Interpretation) for and in the name of the Church, but even more because of their appointment by Christ'.[39] The people as a whole (the 'hauffe gantz') cannot do this but they must 'allow themselves to be ordered' and consent to it. The office of preacher, through which the Word of reconciliation is spoken to the congregation and through which she is edified, is therefore for Luther constitutive and indispensable for the Church. Melanchthon clarified the Lutheran conception of office: Any church has the authority to call, elect and ordain ecclesiastical servants (ministri). It is an authority given to the Church by God and cannot be taken away by any human authority according to what Paul says in Eph. 4.8, 11 f.[40]

Hyldrich Zwingli has similar views on office. In his essay 'On the preaching-office' (1525), in which he combats the Anabaptists, he proceeds from Eph. 4.11–14 and develops his view of office from this passage. Christ has placed the offices named there in his Body, the Church; but in the end there is only one office. The priests were already in the time of the Apostles preachers, prophets or bishops.[41] With reference to 'pastors and teachers' the Zürich Reformer remarks that the pastors are the true bishops and overseers; the teachers also are either prophets or also all who teach, apostles and preachers (ibid. 416). The election takes place either through the whole congregation or through the Apostles or one single Apostle (ibid. 426).

Calvin in his exegesis of the passage makes a sharper distinction. He interprets Apostles, preachers and prophets in an historical sense with reference to the first years of the Church; with prophets he is thinking not so much of those who foretell the future (like Agabus) as of the charismatics who appear in 1 Cor. 14. Unlike Chrysostom and Augustine,

---

[37]In Eph. 4. lect IV (Cai nr. 211–12).

[38]Cf. E. Kinder, *Der evangelische Glaube und die Kirche*, Berlin 1958, 150–59; H. Faberberg, TRE II, 559 f.

[39]WA 50. 633; quoted also in E. Kinder (n. 38) 152.

[40]Tractatus de potestate pape 67, in *Bekenntnisschriften der Evangelisch-lutherischen Kirche*, Göttingen ²1955, 491; cf. also tr. 61 (p. 489).

[41]CR 91. 382–433, especially 390 and 408.

he does not wish to apply pastors and teachers to the same group of people; although it is the task of pastors to teach, there is the special gift of interpreting Scripture so that sound doctrine may be held fast.[42] From its silence on Peter's office Calvin derives an attack on the Papacy. If Paul had recognized any primacy of any individual, would he not then have placed it at the centre?[43] In the 'Institutio' of 1559 the Genevan Reformer depicts the first three offices (Apostles, Prophets and Evangelists) as temporary, the last two (pastors and teachers) as universally valid and necessary for the continued existence of the Church.[44] He also postulates two further offices: that of leading and keeping order by the 'elders' and the care for the poor by the 'deacons'. But there is no difference in grade between these four necessary offices; all have a common task – they all serve the Word.[45]

Hence there is no denial of ecclesiastical office among the great Reformers; on the contrary, against the Anabaptists and Enthusiasts they consider office as a divine institution. Johannes Brenz even understands in the gifts named in Eph. 4.7 civil and ecclesiastical qualifications.[46] The Anglicans hold fast to the threefold office; the Ordinal of 1661 refers for this to Eph. 4.7–11.[47] A denial of office was reserved for the Anabaptists and Socinians who allowed all believers to preach and teach in the Church. It is difficult to establish how they coped with Eph. 4.11 f. while holding this view. Only with the rise of Pietism does office lose in importance. On the radical wing Gottfried Arnold († 1714) sees ecclesiastical office among Roman Catholics and Lutherans as a sign of deterioration. The border-line between office-bearers and laity is fluid, and worldly authority has no right to impose office-bearers. In his 'Unbiased History of the Church and Heretics from the Beginning of the New Testament up to AD 1688' he interprets Eph. 4.11 as follows: All are teachers but are called by different names.[48] The Free Churches which have taken up the inheritance of the 'anabaptismally-minded' of the Reformation period or emerged as a new revivalist movement have for the most part a similar attitude, as is shown particularly by their admission of lay-preachers. But it is very difficult to establish their respective interpretation of Eph. 4.11 f.; we cannot talk of its 'historical influence' because the requirements of their congregational structure are based on other principles.

In present-day exegesis the most controversial question is that of

---

[42]CR 51. 197 f.

[43]CR 51. 198, also with reference to Cyprian. Then Estius 364 opposed the *argumentum e silentio*.

[44]Inst IV, 3.4–5 (CR 30. 779 f.).

[45]Inst IV, 3.8–9 (CR 30. 782 f.). Cf. further A. Ganoczy, *Ecclesia ministrans. Dienende Kirche und kirchlicher Dienst bei Calvin*, 1968, (ÖF) 246–329; H. Faberberg, TRE II, 568–72.

[46]Ed Köhler 37; according to his view 'pastors and teachers' simply designed under another name bishops whom the Holy Spirit has appointed to lead the Church (a reference to Acts 20.28). He compares the bountifulness of the gifts with God's generosity in Creation (ibid. 38 f.).

[47]Cf. Faberberg, TRE II, 576 f.

[48]Reprint of the edition of Frankfurt 1729, Hildesheim 1967, 33–7, cf. Faberberg, TRE II, 584 f.

the relationship of the 'charismatic' order (1 Cor. 12–14; Rom. 12.4–8) and a structure of office developing from it. Certainly there is no longer a desire to make a contrast between office and charisma; but it is still a matter of debate how we should assess those preachers of the Gospel named in Eph. 4.11 as given by the Lord to his Church, especially the pastors and teachers in the congregations, when we look back at the congregational structure in the Pauline period and forward to the development which followed (the Pastoral Epistles, Ignatius of Antioch). Here we are confronted by many questions, as E. Schweizer indicated in his contribution on the passage (v. p. 192). On the Roman Catholic side, too, there are still different views on the transition from the Pauline understanding of the congregation to the post-Pauline conception of congregation and office.[49] But we can also discern attempts between the denominations towards a greater agreement on charisma and office – 'office' as a function of the proclamation and transmission of the Gospel (H. Merklein), as a service for the Church in the communion of all believers, and further for the 'immediacy of Christ in all office-bearers' (A. Vögtle) and for the connection to the 'apostolic' tradition. The current intense dialogue on ecclesiastical office cannot simply ignore Eph. 4.7–16.

4. ETHICS AND CHRISTIAN LIFE

Since E. Schweizer[1] has already made a considerable contribution to ethics in general and to individual aspects (particularly the Haustafel) in Col. which also holds true for Eph., we shall limit ourselves to the two expositions peculiar to the author of Eph. – the marriage-paraclesis in 5.21–33 according to the prototype and example of Christ and the Church, and the depiction of spiritual military service in 6.10–20.

(a) Christian Marriage (Eph. 5.21–33)

The main question which we are compelled to face today in ecumenical conversations may be formulated thus: Is marriage – which according to the biblical conception is a 'natural' institution established by God with the creation of humankind – given increased dignity by the attitude of Eph. 5 to a marriage entered into between Christians? Is it 'sanctified' through the connection with Christ? Are its ties consolidated through its character as a reflection of the unity which exists between Christ and the Church? Does it become a 'sacrament' through inclusion in the Body of Christ as Roman Catholic tradition has held since the Council of Trent (Sessio XXIV of 1563, D 969–82)? Or should we give more emphasis to the worldly context

---

[49]Cf. the contribution by A. Vögtle mentioned in the literature-list on Eph. 4.7–16 (p. 170), especially 534–40 (on J. Hainz) and 554–62) (on Eph., particularly on the work of H. Merklein).
[1]*Colossians* 277–89.

of marriage, its social responsibilities, its createdness and 'secularity'? To answer such questions, which have existed since the Reformation, the whole section to which the Haustafel belongs is certainly important; but the emphasis rests on vv. 31–2 where Gen. 2.24 is quoted, named the 'great mystery' by the author and related to Christ and the Church. The early Church gave considerable consideration to this passage and it was frequently quoted by the Church Fathers.[2] We shall concentrate our interest on their interpretation and the effect it later had.

In tracing the perspective of patristic exegesis we must at the outset make the following observations: (1) The writers of the early Church without exception took the quotation in v. 31 to refer directly to human marriage and then only in a second step referred the 'great mystery' to Christ and the Church; (2) The Fathers, who look back to the divine establishment of marriage on the morning of Creation, make no basic difference between a 'natural marriage' and Christian marriage; (3) the marriage established by God is regarded as good and holy in the repulsing of other conceptions, especially in Gnosticism; (5) considerable consideration is given to the figurative character of marriage in relationship to Christ and the Church, but it is evaluated in various ways; (6) the character of the 'great mystery' is only partly explained in more detail; (7) in the area of the Latin writers, too, where *mysterium* in one version of the *Vetus Latina* (especially in Africa) and in the Vulgate is translated as *sacramentum*, the expression in the patristic period was not specifically interpreted in the sense of the concept of Sacrament which only developed slowly.

Clement of Alexandria defends the integrity and holiness of marriage against a Gnostic devaluation and refers for support to the passage in Ephesians. In the *Paedagogos*, where we also find other exhortations for a devout married life, he states that those bound in marriage should love one another 'as their own body'.[3] The extension to both partners in comparison with Eph. 5.28 is significant. In the *Stromateis* ('Carpets') III the whole of Ch. XII (§§79–90) is devoted to the high regard for marriage. Even before this (§49.3) Clement says: 'Some even call marriage almost an obscenity and teach that it is appointed by the Devil. In their arrogance they claim that they themselves imitate the Lord ... But the Lord has his own Bride, the Church.' Then he writes: 'But if legal marriage is a sin, I do not know how anyone can say he knows God ... If the Law is holy, then marriage is also holy. The Apostle connects this mystery to Christ and the Church.'[4]

For Origen the 'great mystery' is a welcome starting-point for his typological-allegorizing interpretation in which he searches for a 'spiritual' sense alongside the literal. Hence for him the command to the progenitors at the Creation 'Be fruitful and multiply' symbolizes the spreading of the

---

[2]There is a collection and consideration of passages from the patristic period in the work by P. Colli, *La pericope paolina ad Ephesio V 32 nella interpretazione dei SS. Padri e del Concilio di Trento*, Parma 1951. Cf. also the rich collection of quotations from the Fathers in Frede, *Ep. ad Eph.* 258–62.

[3]Paedagogos III, 95.1 (GCS [3]12.298).

[4]Stromata III, 49.3 (GCS [3]52.218) and III, 84, 2 (ibid. 234).

Gospel as the Apostle's word in Eph. 5.32 suggests.[5] This passage is also important for him for other metaphorical interpretations in order to grasp the deeper sense of a scriptural passage,[6] one might say fundamental in order to follow this principle of interpretation.[7] Thus Origen recognises human marriage as in accordance to Creation (for this he refers to Mt 19.5) but keeps the Genesis passage open for further interpretations. How this affects the recommendation to virginity is illustrated by Methodius of Olympus. In his book on the 'Guest Meal' in which virginity is extolled, Theophila is an eloquent defender of holy marriage endowed by God; but then Thaleia argues that the passage in Genesis also contains a spiritual sense according to what the Apostle says in Eph. 5.29–32, and that gives virginity, too, its rights.[8]

Theodore of Mopsuestia offers a special interpretation of the Mystery: the birth of children which ensues in marriage remains extrinsic and leads to an earthly existence, while the spiritual re-birth which is shown by the connection to Christ and the Church brings about resurrection and immortality.[9] Chrysostom on the other hand, who also in other places betrays a high opinion of marriage, sees the 'great mystery' in marital love, even in the physical union; but human marriage is a *typos* of the spiritual union of Christ with his Church.[10]

In the West, Tertullian, especially in his Montanist period, battles against bigamy and uses Eph. 5.32 as an argument for this purpose: Christ, the more perfect Adam, meets us in the Spirit as one who has only one Bride, the Church, after the pattern (figura) of Adam and Eve.[11] Although he uses the Latin concept of *sacramentum* for Baptism, the Eucharist and Doctrine, in something like the sense of a 'holy thing' which makes intrinsically holy, he draws no such conclusion for marriage from the expression. Later Latin church authors, who in part kept to the rendition *mysterium* (Irenaeus, Hilary, Ambrosiaster etc.) likewise do not do so.[12] Marius Victorinus in his Commentary on Ephesians interprets the joining of man and woman, the 'great mystery' (mysterium), as a union of spirit (spiritus) and soul (anima) and accordingly Christ as Spirit and the Church as soul (MPL 8.1289). Pelagius concludes from the addition of v. 32b (the interpretation as Christ and the Church) that the physical-sexual love is thereby meant to be elevated to the higher plane of a holy, spiritual

---

[5]Hom. in Gn. IX, 2 (GCS 29.90).

[6]Thus Adam becomes a prophet of Christ and the Church: In Cant Cant II (CS 33.157 f.) the childbearing of the free woman, Sarah (Gal. 4.21–31) can thereby be understood as a pre-description of the Church: Comm. in Mt. XVII, 34 (GCS 40.695).

[7]Hom in Num. XI, 1 (GCS 30.77 f.): Even if we can derive some meaning from the actual words themselves we must also look in such passages for the figurative ('allegorical') sense; Paul gives an example of this in Eph. 5.32.

[8]Symp. 3.1 (GCS 27.26–8); cf. also Basil (of Ancyra?) De virginitate (MPG 30.769); Athanasius, De virginitate (MPG 28.253).

[9]In Eph. 5.32 (Swete I, 187).

[10]This is especially clear in his exegesis of Col. hom XII (MPG 62.387) but also on Eph., hom XX (MPG 62.140); cf. also the remarks on the assessment of women in MPG 51.229 f. It is less clear in Theodoret of Cyrrhus on this passage (MPG 82.548 f.).

[11]De Monogamia V (CChr. 2.1235).

[12]Cf. the apparatus in Frede, *Ep. ad Eph.* on the passage (259).

love.[13] But this is by no means the general interpretation; Ambrose sees the unity of Christ and the Church, the great mystery (here: *sacramentum*), exemplified in the physical union (copula) of Adam and Eve.[14] Jerome speaks of greater and lesser mysteries (*sacramenta*), reports on the opinion of Gregory of Nazianzus that this passage is full of inexpressible secrets, but remarks that he himself is down-to-earth – one dare not transfer everything about Adam and Eve to Christ and the Church (MPL 26.535 f.). Augustine saw himself forced to defend marriage on three fronts – against the Manichaeans, against the Pelagians – who accused him of making marriage the source of original sin – and against Jovinian who accused the Catholics of a contempt for marriage compared with virginity. The great teacher again and again cites Eph. 5.31 f. (according to Colli [n. 2] 35 times), admittedly to demonstrate the sanctity of marriage before the Fall in which the 'marriage' between Christ and the Church is exemplified. But he also says: 'Far be it from us to say ... that marriages which are now entered into are a foundation of the devil; for these are the marriages which God has established from the beginning. God has not retracted after the damnation of humankind this benefaction which has been established for the propagation of humankind'. Then Augustine refers to Eph. 5.31 f. and remarks: 'This was said before the Fall and if no one had sinned it could also have occurred without shameful desires.'[15]

Thus in patristic exegesis in general the marriage in Paradise is interpreted as a pre-description, a 'model' (figura) of the connection between Christ and Church. The Fathers did not reflect further that elsewhere in the section as a whole the relationship between Christ and Church is a prototype and model of Christian marriage according to which a marriage should be oriented and conducted, or they have failed to notice that the scriptural quotation can also be applied directly to Christ and the Church. That would have lent Christian marriage even more lustre and dignity. But even in their way of looking at things from the beginning in Creation to its highest fulfilment in Christ and his Church there lay, as we can see, a strong impetus to hold fast to the divine intention conceived in Creation and the benefaction of marriage against many currents from outside (Gnosticism, Manichaeism) and from within (a deep respect for virginity and reservations against concupiscence).

In the theological discussion on the concept of Sacrament which began in early Scholasticism, led to a clarification in the Twelfth Century under the influence of Peter Lombard[16] and was continued in the great Scholastics, the interpretation of Eph. 5.31 f. played a significant if not principal part. We do not have the space to go into this in detail here.[17] To help in understanding this development E. Schillebeeckx gives two grounds in particular: the concept of Sacrament itself, which, following Augustine

---

[13]ed. Souter II, 378 f.

[14]Ep. 76.4 (MPL 16.1315).

[15]De nuptiis et concupiscentia II, 54 (CSEL 42.311).

[16]Sentiarum lib IV, dist. 1, n. 2; cf. on marriage ibid. dist. 26, n. 6.

[17]Cf. R. J. Lawrence, *The Sacramental Interpretation of Eph. 5.32 from Peter Lombard to the Council of Trent*, Washington 1963; E. Schillebeeckx, *Marriage: Human Reality and Sacred Mystery*, New York 1965, 111–117.

('sign of a holy matter') was discussed more critically in a clash with Berengar of Tours (†1088) and in repulse of the Cathari and Albigensians who, in their hostility to the physical, considered marriage as an evil.[18] In Aquinas the development reached a particular conclusion. He based his argument on the passage from Eph. and says that the Sacraments cause what they indicate and that this Sacrament gives participation in grace to the people being married in that they belong to the imperishable union of Christ and the Church.[19] But it is interesting that views on the evidential value of Eph. 5.32 were still divided in the consultations at the Council of Trent.[20] That is why in the final formulation it says only that the Apostle Paul in Eph. 5.25 and 32 *indicates* (innuit) the grace which Christ earned for us through his death which completes the natural love, secures the insoluble unity and sanctifies the partners in the marriage. Because marriage in the New Covenant through the grace brought by Christ stands out above marriages of old, it is rightly considered among the Sacraments of the New Covenant.[21]

At the time of the Reformation the view of the erudite humanist, Erasmus of Rotterdam (†1536) is noteworthy. He does not actually want to dispute the seven Sacraments or that marriage is a Sacrament; but it cannot be proved from Eph. 5.32 because the Greek word does not mean 'Sacrament' but something hidden and secret. Exegetically he takes the 'great mystery' to apply not to marriage but solely to the connection between Christ and Church – a finding significant when compared with the Church Fathers and for the period that followed.[22] Luther, who interpreted the passage in a similar way, went further and rejected marriage as a Sacrament.[23] For him marriage is a 'worldly, external thing such as wife, child, house and garden etc.' and belongs to the sphere of earthly rule.[24] Calvin and the other Reformers agreed with Luther in this assessment. In his Commentary on Eph. Calvin inveighed vehemently against the Papists who wanted to make one of the seven Sacraments from the expression in Eph. 5.32 'as if they could change water into wine'. They put forward seven Sacraments although Christ only instituted two.[25] In the *Institutio Christianae Religionis* (of 1559) he expounds his view in even greater detail.[26] In order to understand the sharp polemic and the passionate debate we must not limit ourselves simply to a consideration of Luther's personal situation and the emotions of the other Reformers. E. Schillebeeckx level-headedly gives his opinion: 'The reaction of the Reformation which refused to accept the *sacramentality* of marriage was

[18]*Marriage* (n. 17) 312–27.
[19]Summa theol., Suppl. q. 42, a.1. Cf. further Schillebeeckx, *Marriage* (n. 17) 326 f.; Lawrence, *Sacr. Interpretation* (ibid.) 56–9.
[20]Cf. Colli, *La pericope* (n. 2) 125–44. On the pre-Tridentine period v. Lawrence (n. 17) 117–31.
[21]D 969–70.
[22]On this passage Opera VI, 855. Cardinal Cajetan (de Vio, †1534) held the same view, against which Estius 389 f. later turned.
[23]Über die babylonische Gefangenschaft der Kirche, WA 6.550–3, on Eph. 551 f.
[24]Predigt über die Bergpredigt, WA 32.376 f.
[25]CR 51.227.
[26]Inst. IV, 19.34–6 (CR 30, 1089–92, on Eph. especially 1090 f.).

not, if we go to the root of the matter, a denial of the holy character of married life but rather a protest against the extension of ecclesiastical jurisdiction in a matter which was held to be essentially 'worldly', although it was conceded that it must be lived 'in the Lord'. Certainly he then disputes that this was in fact the intention of the Roman Church which from the time of Pope Leo the Great had required that in this matter they should follow the conventional civil customs.[27] Hence there were false perspectives here, too, on both sides. The Tridentinum in no way desired to question the natural conception and manner of marriage after the style intended at Creation; grace does not abolish what is natural but rather presupposes it and makes it perfect. Admittedly the Council held fast to the idea of a Sacrament which had in the meantime come to predominate, which for their part the Reformers did not want to take over. Deep-lying differences are apparent in the understanding of Sacrament and grace.

These denominational differences have still not been overcome today. Even Protestant theologians who are engaged in ecumenical attempts at convergence still take exception to marriage as a 'Sacrament'. H. Baltensweiler writes on Eph. 5.22–33 that marriage is based on God's design at Creation and hence is something autonomous; but in relationship to Christ marriage is understood as a recollection of Christ and his Congregation. Christians lead a marriage in exactly the same way as everyone else, but just because they are Christians they can regard their marriage as something completely new. But even if Christian marriage is a place where salvation can really occur (cf. 1 Cor. 7.12–16) this does not take place in the sense of a Christian elevation of marriage, as if something Christian were added to the everyday marriage.[28] Similar opinions are increasing.[29] H.-D. Wendland formulates a thesis: 'The Christian ethic of marriage shows to advantage the *worldliness* of marriage which can also be respected by non-Christians as a real marriage. The "Christianness" of marriage does not consist in the removal of its worldliness but in its critical reception in the Body of Christ where the fulfilment of salvation takes place through the agency of Christ's Church. Here a new unity of *agape* and *eros* is born'.[30] If we look at the subject meant under different conceptions – i.e. at Christian marriage or the natural, human marriage 'under Christ's influence' (G. Friedrich) – I do not think the standpoints are so very far apart. The difficulty of the conception of what is a 'Sacrament' is also recognized on the Roman Catholic side. In a fundamental reflection J. Ratzinger writes: Sacramentality of marriage implies that the Creation-order of the relationship between man and woman realized in marriage does not stand neutral and merely worldly alongside

[27] *Marriage* (n. 17) 317–19.

[28] *Die Ehe im NT* (v. Literature on 5.21–33) 234 f.

[29] Cf. H. Greeven, 'Zu den Aussagen des Neuen Testaments über die Ehe', ZEE 1 (1957) 109–25, particularly 121–5; G. Friedrich, *Sexualität und Ehe. Rückfragen an das Neue Testament*, Stuttgart 1977, 85–96, particularly 94 f.; among the Commentaries on Eph. especially Barth 744–9. He reveals understanding for the expression 'sacrament' but only if thereby we mean the 'mysticism' of marriage (747). Among the systematic theologians cf. K. Barth CD III/4 Edinburgh, 1961 (69), 122–5.

[30] 'Zur Theologie der Sexualität und der Ehe' (p. 256 n.60) 136 f.

the covenant mystery of Jesus Christ but is itself taken up into the covenant-order of God's covenant people.[31]

This introduces an idea which we already referred to in the Commentary (p. 256): The inclusion of marriage into God's Covenant which is fulfilled in the New Covenant in Christ and the Church. This idea is also emphatically developed by Karl Barth. In his view, in the account of Creation (Gen. 2.24) we find ourselves 'before the mystery of the divine covenant of grace as the inner basis of the divine creation' and that is 'imperiously suggested by the explicit reference in Eph. 5.32'.[32] It is true that we cannot overlook the divergences which arise from the Roman Catholic Doctrine of Grace (the Sacrament of Marriage mediates particular grace); but Christ's Covenant of Grace with his Church which is reflected and effective in marriage appears to be a basis for agreement to set off the concerns of both sides. The idea is also echoed in the Pastoral Constitution of the Second Vatican Council: 'For as God of old made Himself present to His people through a covenant of love and fidelity, so now the Saviour of men and the Spouse of the Church comes into the lives of married Christians through the sacrament of matrimony. He abides with them thereafter so that, just as He loved the Church and handed Himself over on her behalf, the spouses may love each other with perpetual fidelity through mutual self-bestowal'.[33]

(b) Spiritual Military Service (Eph. 6.10–20)

Among the passages in the NT which use the metaphor of military service for a Christian life in the world (Paul – 1 Thess. 5.8; 2 Cor. 6.7; 10.3; Rom. 6.13 f.; 13.12; Pastorals – 1 Tim. 1.18; 2 Tim. 2.3 f.; cf. Rev.) the description of Eph. 6 is the most detailed and most strongly individual paraclesis. Its after-effects on early Christian literature were great even if it had not alone led to the development of a *topos* of the *militia Christi* (military service for Christ).[34] If we trace the development of its effect, we notice the various ways in which the military metaphor was used, be it in the confrontation with super-human 'powers and authorities' or for striving after virtue and Christian asceticism or in the conflict-situations of the world. The paraclesis continually leaves its mark on new historical contexts, reflects the Roman military scene, distances itself from Gnostic Dualism, becomes an encouragement for martyrdom, includes monasticism, influences Humanism and in yet another way affects mysticism. We can scarcely grasp all this far less describe it; we must content ourselves with several lines and examples in which we pay special attention to the influence of Eph. 6.[35]

[31]*Zur Theologie der Ehe* (p. 256 n. 59) 91 f.

[32]CD III/1 Edinburgh, (1958), 312; cf. also ibid. 332; III/2 (1960) 312–19, especially 316 f.

[33]'On the Church in the World of today' (Gaudium et spes) Art 48 (Abbott p. 251).

[34]Cf. Harnack, *Militia Christi* (p. 280 n. 40); Trevijano Etcheverria, *En Lucha* (v. literature on 6.10–20); J. Auer, LThK VII, 418 f.

[35]Only belatedly was my attention drawn to Andreas Wang's thesis 'Der "miles Christianus" im 16. und 17. Jahrhundert und seine mittelalterliche Tradition', Frankfurt-Bern 1975. Cf. the review

The military metaphor was already popular at an early date. Ignatius of Antioch writes in his letter to Polycarp: 'Let your Baptism be your arms, faith your helmet, love your spear, endurance your armour' (6.2). The symbols for the spiritual armour are different from Eph. 6; but an essential Pauline basis is unmistakeable (Baptism – Faith – Love – Patience). Clement of Rome uses the military structure as an exhortation to be subject to their leaders (1 Cl. 37). Justin illustrates the renunciation of earthly possessions in order to achieve what is everlasting with the service of soldiers who have a higher regard for the vow they have taken than for life, family and homeland (Apol. 39). But as yet there is no visible reference to Eph. 6.

Among the Christian authors who make use of our passage Clement of Alexandria is one of the first. Three features characterize his frequent quotations: the moral-ascetic interpretation of the struggle against the passions and desires, the embedding in the metaphor of the Christian 'Gnostic' and the emphasis that the Christian battle serves Christ's message of peace. The pernicious passions are as it were the stamp of the spiritual powers with whom we have to wrestle.[36] The Christian Gnostic is the real competitor who is crowned with the victor's laurels in the great arena – namely in the beautiful world – because of his victory over his passions (again an allusion to Eph. 6.12).[37] Clement combines the metaphor of the armour (Eph. 6.14–17) with the call of the Gospel: With this trumpet Christ gathers his soldiers with invulnerable armour for the battle for peace.[38] The founder of the catechetical school at Alexandria uses these warlike pictures without exception metaphorically: 'We are brought up, not in war but in peace (through the Logos).'[39]

Possibly Eph. 6.12 had already been 'discovered' by the Gnostics and exploited in their sense. In the Coptic-Gnostic writing 'On the Being of the Archons' (NHC II, 4) the verse is quoted right at the beginning, possibly by a Christian editor, to take up the theme of the 'origin' and 'being' of the evil powers (Archontes) – 'hypostasis' can mean both.[40] The passage is also quoted in the 'Exegesis of the Soul' (NHC II, 6), a writing in the same Codex which has a more Christian emphasis, and Clement of Alexandria in his 'Excerpts from Theodotius', a Gnostic of the Valentinian school, hands down a passage which contains this quotation.[41] The Gnostics found their strong dualism between the heavenly and earthly worlds, between light and darkness, confirmed in it. The Church Fathers resisted this way of thinking which is revealed in different ways in the devaluation of the created world.[42]

---

by H.-J. Klauck in ThRv 77 (1981) 41 f. The dissertation also considers minor works, book-illustrations etc.

[36]Stromata II, 109–10 (GCS 52.172 f.); cf. also Stromata III, 101.3 (ibid. 241).

[37]Stromata VII, 20.3–4 (GCS 17a, 14); cf. VII, 82.5 (ibid. 59).

[38]Protrepticus XI, 116 (GCS 12.82).

[39]Paedagogos I, 98 (GCS 12.149); cf. ibid. II, 42 (ibid. 183).

[40]According to the page-numbering in the edition of Labib 134, 23–5. Cf. L. Abramowski, 'Notizen zur "Hypostase der Archonten"' (ed. Bullard), ZNW 67 (1978) 280–5, here 280; B. Barc, *L'Hypostase des Archontes*, Quebec-Löwen 1980, 74.

[41]Exegesis of the Soul 131, v. in Foerster, *Gnosis* II, 130; Clement of Alexandria Exc. Theod. 48.2 (GCS 17a, 122).

[42]Cf. further Etcheverria, *En Lucha* (n. 34) 91–4. He also refers to the 'Gospel according to Philip' (Log 11.12 et al.' but there is no echo of Eph. 6 there.

Nevertheless the description of the battle in which Christians know they are placed also became a problem for Christian theologians. How can the real battles in the OT, ordered and led by God, be compatible with this? Is there a line of divine battle which continues on from the Old Covenant to the New? Origen constantly occupied himself with this question, especially in his homilies on the book of Joshua, because he saw Jesus, the bringer of salvation, foreshadowed in the name of this great military leader of Israel. For the great interpreter of Scripture the tension is resolved by means of the 'spiritual' sense of Scripture which he found behind the verbal sense; earthly military service points to the spiritual *militia Christi*, and in view of this the exposition in Eph. 6.12–17 is for him significant. The struggles of the Christians are against demons and vices. 'For this reason truth must be our belt ... we separate ourselves from Christ's military service by lying.'[43] 'We have often said that the Christian struggle is a double one: namely, for the perfect – as Paul and the Ephesians were – ... against the spirits of evil in heaven, and for lesser mortals and those who are not yet perfect, it is still a battle against flesh and blood.'[44] 'If those physical battles (in the OT) do not represent a type of the spiritual battles, the Books of Jewish history would not have been presented by the Apostles to the disciples of Christ, who came to teach peace, to be read in the churches. Hence the Apostle (Paul) teaches that for us there are no longer physical, earthly battles but only those of the soul against spiritual opponents, as he writes in Eph. 6.'[45] Similar quotations from the interpretation of other OT books could be piled up.[46] 'Now Jesus Christ is the leader of our host (princeps militiae nostrae) who demands from us courage and renunciation of earthly things, a spiritual courage because victory must be sought not through fiery darts but through verbal arrows. We often see in our camps women and children of a tender age suffering torments for a tyrannical martyrdom.'[47] Thus Origen, too, remains on Clement's lines: For Christians battle exists only in moral struggles, and in everything our goal is Christ's peace, a heavenly reward awaits us after our earthly suffering. Martyrdom is an outstanding way of proving the worth of Christ's soldier.[48]

In the West, Tertullian sees Christ's soldier's victory particularly in martyrdom. To Christians who are awaiting trial in prison he writes: 'The house of the devil is a prison; but you have entered the prison to trample him down in his own house. He found you fortified and armed with concord; for your peace means war for him.'[49] At the moment warfare is in the ascendancy; but 'victory consists in achieving that for which one has fought ... Hence we are the victors if we are saved.'[50] In the writing on

[43]Hom. in Jesu Nave V, 2 (SChr 71.164).
[44]Hom. in Jesu Nave XI, 4 (SChr 71.288).
[45]Hom. in Jesu Nave XV, 1 (SChr 71.330).
[46]Hom. in Judic VI, 2 (MPG 12.975 f.); ibid. IX, 1 (988); Hom. in Ex III, 3 (MPG 12.316); In Num hom VII, 5 (MPG 12.618).
[47]Hom. in Judic IX, 1 (MPG 12.987 f.); cf. also Contra Celsum VIII, 34 (SC 150.250).
[48]In great detail on Origen, Etcheverria, En lucha (n. 34) 153–373.
[49]Mart. 1 (CChr 1.3); cf. also Mart. 3 (CChr 1.5 f.).
[50]Apol. 37 (CChr 1.148 f.); cf. also Apol. 50 (CChr 1.169).

taking flight (whether one should flee or take upon oneself martyrdom) there are frequent quotations from Eph. 6. 'Can a good soldier of Christ, fully armed by the Apostle, run away from the Day of Persecution when he hears the trumpet of persecution?' (10.1). 'The weapons were not given in order that one could take flight' (9.2). 'The Lord has delivered us from the power of the angels who rule the world, the spirits of evil; will you then behave in a peaceful way?' (12.3)[51] There is no doubt that the African speaker, himself the son of a captain, is attracted by the military metaphors; but he rejects worldly military rank for Christians, and spiritual military service has the purpose of achieving the prize of heavenly victory. Cyprian of Carthage is also dominated by the idea of the *militia Christi*, so that A. v. Harnack concludes: 'In the Third Century a warlike mood, which was morally not completely harmless, had taken hold of Latin Christianity . . . The Christian was in danger of becoming the "*miles gloriosus*" (glorious soldier)'.[52]

The endeavour of the early ascetics and monks to overcome the Devil in a spiritual battle against the temptations of the flesh was more internal. Like Antony they withdrew to the desert, the place where God was near but so also were the demonic powers. 'The monk goes now to the desert to fight the devil in his very own kingdom (cf. Mt. 12.43) because he knows that he himself is mercifully included in Christ's line of battle where the fight is not against flesh and blood but "against the forces, against the powers . . ."' (Eph. 6.12).[53] Although it is hardly possible to ascertain how much influence the Eph. text had on the Hermits and Cenobites, this view would still apply. We can also not accuse the ascetics of having failed to see the strength for battle which comes from God (Eph. 6.10 f.!); for them everything is borne in God through prayer and stillness.[54] But there is no need to deny that the heavier accent falls on the ascetic efforts.

At a time which was filled with a completely different sense of the world, of a positive attitude to Creation and culture and especially of endeavour towards a spiritual education, we have evidence as to how 'spiritual military service' can be combined with this educational ideal. This is the first writing of the Humanist Erasmus of Rotterdam 'A Handbook for the Christian Soldier' dating from 1501 (first appeared in printed form in 1503).[55] The first chapter ('Life demands vigilance') describes the life of

---

[51]CChr 2.1147, 1146, 1150. The document *De corona* is about a soldier who refused the victor's laurel-wreath (as a heathen custom) and faced martyrdom; for Tertullian he is one 'totally armed by the Apostle' and 'who is better crowned with the glorious crown of Martyrdom' (1.3; CChr 2.1040).

[52]*Militia Christi* (cf. n. 34) 42 f.

[53]P. Bonifatius OSB in the Introduction to his edition of the *Sprüche der Väter*, Graz 1963, 13. Cf. the verdict on the Anchorites of Benedict of Nursia in his Rule, Ch. 1, 3–5 (B. Steidle, *Die Benediktusgregel*, Beuron 1963, 64). Benedict himself also uses the word 'military' for the service of his monks: preface 1.3, 40; Ch. 1.2; 2.20 et al.

[54]Cf. the remark of Abbas Ammonas: 'For fourteen years I prayed to God day and night in the Scetian desert that he might give me grace to conquer wrath' in Bonifatius, *Sprüche der Väter* (n. 53) 67.

[55]The translation is based on the rendering by H. Schiel in *Erasmus von Rotterdam*, Handbüchlein des christlichen Streiters, Olten – Freiburg i Br 1952. The page-numbers in the text refer to this edition.

mortals as a constant military service (Job 7.1). 'The person who lives in peace with vices has broken the alliance made with God in Baptism' (25). True peace can only come from God, the creator of peace. Through the Baptismal bath we are consecrated to Christ, the Leader, to whom we have sworn the oath of loyalty in a firmly established formula (25f.). We can see traces of the chivalrous way of thinking and are not surprised to hear in the second chapter 'Of the weapons of Christian Knighthood'. First two weapons against the 'seven tribes', the seven cardinal sins, are named: Prayer and knowledge (33), with many allusions to scriptural passages. Erasmus does not reject 'preparing oneself for this military service as in a military academy in the writings of ancient authors and the worldly-wise' (37). But the real weapons are those of the Christian wisdom named in the Bible. 'If you are pleased to enter the arsenal of our brave captain, Paul, you will certainly not find there physical weapons for our military service, but spiritually powerful ones for the destruction of the entrenchment . . .' (cf. 2 Cor. 10.4). Then he says 'You will find God's armour with which you will be able to resist on the day of evil (Eph. 6.13). You will find the weapons of righteousness upon the right and upon the left (2 Cor. 6.7). As protection for your loins you will find truth and the armour of righteousness, the shield of faith with which you can put out all the fiery darts of the evil one. You will find the helmet of salvation and the sword of the Spirit' (Eph. 6.14–17) (45). On the eve of the Reformation this booklet, which offers practical rules for the Christian soldier, shows a deep penetration of the humanistic spirit with the power of the biblical word.

The Reformer with a classical education, Zwingli, also shows a similar attitude in his little book on the instruction of young people (1523). Alongside a classical education he demands Christian discipline and a control of desires. A Christian person should as far as possible abstain from using weapons, and trust in God, who will give him the necessary arms; but he does not refer to Eph. 6.[56] Several sermons by Luther on Eph. 6.10–20 have come down to us. In strong language he calls Christians to battle against the Devil and the great lords and squires (the evil spirits) who rule in this world – not without side-swipes at the Papists and Enthusiasts.[57] Paul delivers a 'camp sermon' to us; the Word of God should rouse us from idleness and laziness like a trumpet and drum. God himself conducts the war against the cunning attacks of the devil who besets us, not simply anywhere but daily and constantly.[58] Luther sees the spiritual campaign taking place more fiercely in the world, but contrasts the 'physical' armour with the 'spiritual'; the first belongs to the worldly power and does not concern us (The Doctrine of the Two Kingdoms).[59] Later his language becomes more irenic: he defends himself against the accusation that he has kindled war and rebellion; one dare not give way

---

[56]Quo pacto ingenui adolescentes formandi sint (CR 89.536–51), especially 546 f.

[57]Cf. the sermon of 21. 10. 1531 (WA 34/2, 360–71).

[58]Second sermon from the same year, WA 34/2, 371–406. The long description of devilish machinations – in which Müntzer and his 'pack' are named – is striking.

[59]Sermon from 13. 11. 1530 (WA 32.169–77).

when on God's business.[60] Calvin, concurring exegetically with the paraclesis of Eph. 6, emphasizes the power which comes from God for our struggles with the world and its rulers. If Paul exhorts us to be brave, then we should ask God for strength because only he can give us what we ourselves do not have.[61] God is stronger than the demonic powers; Calvin emphasizes this in rejecting the Manichaeans who make a counter-god of the Devil.[62] We cannot make a Paradise out of the world so that we may enjoy the fruits of victory, but must test our faith in the fire and prove it like gold and silver.[63]

The one-time officer, Ignatius of Loyola, the founder of the Order of Jesuits, subordinated himself and his Compañia de Jesús to the king, Jesus Christ, for the peaceful conquest of the world. His military way of thinking also comes through in his booklet of spiritual exercises in the contemplation of two camps, that of Babylon (Satan and his realm) and that of Jerusalem (Christ and the Apostles and disciples sent out by him).[64] He stresses spiritual poverty and the renunciation of earthly glory but does not refer to the metaphor in Eph. 6. The religious renewal movement of the 'devotio moderna' is more strongly devoted to the internal struggle, the overcoming of sinful tendencies (cf. Thomas à Kempis, the Imitation of Christ). But here as in Pietism there is no trace of a direct influence by Eph. 6.

The metaphor of the battle against the powers which threaten Christians and that of the spiritual armoury, namely the *topos* of the *militia Christi*, has affected Christian thinking in such a way that we can establish the following main lines: the more external interpretation – which pointed to the Devil and the demons – which was influential in antiquity; the spiritualized interpretation – as the struggle against the desires and passions – which has survived to the present day;[65] and the application to the Christians' battle with suffering up to and including martyrdom; but also a view directed rather at the victory of faith in the world under the banner of Jesus Christ. The intention of the text in Eph. 6 remains most closely bound to those interpretations which place the emphasis on the strength which comes from God, Christ's task of bringing peace and the necessity of constant prayerful vigilance.

---

[60]Cf. the sermon from 25. 10. 1545 (WA 51.67–76, particularly 75).

[61]On Eph. 6.10 (CR 51.233); cf. also his sermon, ibid. 813 f.

[62]On Eph. 6.12 (CR 51.234).

[63]Sermon on Eph. 6.11–17 (CR 51.826).

[64]*Ignatius von Loyola, Geistliche Übungen*, translation and exegesis by A. Haas, Freiburg i Br. 1966, 54–7 (§§136–48).

[65]Cf. the prayer on Ash Wednesday in the Roman Catholic Liturgy: 'Let us, o Lord, enter the vigilant service of the life of Christian battle through holy fasting, that we may have support and help in the battle with the evil spirits in abstinence': A. Schott, *Das Meßbuch der heiligen Kirche*, Freiburg i Br. 1962, 91. Admittedly the prayer has not been taken over into the new liturgy.

D. Prospect: The Epistle to the Ephesians in its Meaning for our Time

If we succeed in penetrating the barriers of the curious linguistic style of the Epistle to the Ephesians – which is far different from ours today – and pay heed to what the author wanted to say about the affairs of the congregations at that time, this document can be a strong testimony even for our day and age. It confronts us with the idea of the Church, the one, holy Church, inseparably bound to Christ, which is built on the foundation of the Apostles and Prophets. Both fascination and provocation can arise from this – fascination for all ecumenically-disposed Christians who suffer under the disunity of Christianity, provocation for many who are critically and negatively disposed to the established churches. Theologically the Epistle to the Ephesians forces us to reflect on the rôle of the Church in God's plan of salvation, her mediating function in Christ's work of Reconciliation, her penetration by the Holy Spirit in spite of all the depressing experiences in the reality of this world. We cannot overcome the discontent with the existing churches, their structures and behaviour, by patching up their external appearance; we can do so only if the idea of the Church as an indispensible factor in the spreading and making productive of the Gospel once again gains a foothold and puts down roots in our hearts. For this reason it seems to me that the fundamental, pioneering thing we can learn from the Epistle to the Ephesians is theological reflection on what the Church is, should be and can be. Hence over and above what has already been said in the excursus on the Church, the following must also be stressed.

The theological uncertainty as to whether the interpolation of the Church as an 'instrument' or 'sacrament' of salvation (v. n. p. 305 n. 57) does not displace or obscure the unique rôle of Christ as Mediator of salvation, can and must be overcome in the light of the ecclesiology of this Epistle, and the legitimate place of the Church be re-discovered. This

343

disappear if only one thing was recognized – that the Church is so closely connected to Christ that without him she does not exist, and without total incorporation in him (4.12, 15) and subordination to him (4.23) her meaning is lost. Conversely Christ 'needs' the Church to reach the world with his message and power to bless, and he 'uses' her according to her presence in the world, i.e. in her combination of weak and imperfect people, whom he can only now and again fill and move with his Spirit, choose for particular tasks and lead together to work harmoniously (4.7–16). If this was true in the early years of the Church when the direct witnesses of Jesus' earthly activity and the appointed preachers of his Cross and Resurrection carried the Gospel out into the world, the more this necessity imposes itself in the time which followed in which our author took up his pen. He recognized this and in his writing gave to the Church, which continued to exist down the centuries, a reminder which to this day has lost none of its urgency. He sees the possibility of proclaiming to the nations the 'inexhaustible riches of Christ' and of realizing God's plan of salvation for humankind and the world only in the faithful transmission of the message of Christ, especially on the guidelines of the Pauline Gospel (cf. 3.8–10). But this takes place 'through the Church' which thus becomes the mouthpiece of Jesus Christ and the sign of his presence in the world.

From the perspective of our time this can be elucidated thus: the message of Jesus Christ would have been lost long ago, at least as 'the power of God for everyone who has faith' (Rom. 1.16) had it not been for the continuous proclamation of the Church – in spite of all the human inadequacy, distortion and incorrect application which were connected with it. The 'Word of Reconciliation' (2 Cor. 5.19) and that mediated by it, the work of reconciliation coming solely from God in Jesus Christ, is entrusted to the Church. Contrary to all religious individualism, behind which there is often hidden an excessive striving for autonomy, we must say with Karl Barth: 'Where there is any attempt to hear and receive the Word of God in isolation – even the Word of God in the form of Holy Scripture – there is no Church, and no real hearing and receiving of the Word of God; for the Word of God is not spoken to individuals, but to the Church of God and to individuals only in the Church.'[1] This does not exclude a critical hearing and consideration of the statements of ecclesiastical preachers; but first the believing Christian must have found his place in the Church as the community of those who place themselves under God's Word.

The acceptance of the Church as the place where 'the Gospel of Salvation' is received, where Baptism mediates the 'sealing with the Holy Spirit' and where hope of complete salvation is founded (1.13 f.; 4.4 f.) means far more, however, than keeping a firm hold on the apostolic doctrine handed down. It is also a step into the living congregation which wants to realize the Christian life in its place. For this reason the author of Eph. is very concerned about spiritual worship (5.18–20), then the structuring of married-, family- and working-life according to Christ's instructions and under his effective power (5.21–6, 9). If he draws on the vocabulary of the liturgy, includes the readers in the praise of God (1.3–

---

[1]CD I/2 Edinburgh 1963, 588.

14), lets them participate in his prayer (3.14–21) and exhorts them to constant prayer and intercession (6. 18–20), this denotes a serious question for Christianity today as to how far a congregation remains the Church of Jesus Christ if it no longer assembles regularly for the service of worship or continues in prayer as an expression of its faith and hope. The Haustafel – but also the rest of the paraclesis – are conceived as instructions for the way to live as Christians, which should take form in the congregation in the face of an environment which thinks and acts differently. In the context of the Epistle this is all borne by an ecclesial consciousness – i.e. from a living knowledge that as members of the Church of Jesus Christ the faithful are constantly called to allow themselves to be built up from their Head in love to become the Body of Christ (4.12, 16). From the theology of the Church grows the practical, ecclesiastical and social behaviour which admittedly must ever and again be re-thought.

In saying this we have already indicated limitations which arise from the historical situation and the author's personal view. We have already referred to several in the exegesis, particularly the irreconcilable withdrawal from the 'pagan' environment, the sharply dualistic confrontation with the powers of evil, the tendency to an esoteric behaviour as the Elect of God. Theologically the picture of the Church comes dangerously close to that of a glorious one situated more in heaven than on earth, a community bound to the triumphant Lord and too little considered as the Church under the Cross, emulating its suffering, expiating Lord. This is a danger for the ecclesial consciousness roused by this theologian which is clearer to us today than in earlier centuries. But that in no way changes the theological insight that the Church, the one Church of Jesus Christ, has an indispensable task for the divinely-intended re-establishment and uniting of everything in Christ (1.10), or, as we would put it today: for the saving of humankind from all want and from all threat from the power of evil. The more this consciousness grows in divided Christianity, in the churches and in all individual Christians, the nearer we shall be to the goal which the author of Ephesians set for the Church in his day. It would be the finest fruit for our time of the effect of this document.

Index of Subjects

Adam – Christ typology, 302
Age(s), aeon(s), 79, 87, 88, 91–2, 96–7, 138, 141, 157
Anacephalaiosis (gathering together of the universe), 59–61, 315–18
Anamnesis, 103, 108–9
Anthropos speculations, 116, 299, 302, 303
Apostles, 42, 122–4, 133–4, 180–2
Apostolic Fathers, 164 (n. 12), 196 (n. 2), 198 (n. 13), 200 (n. 20), 207 (n. 6), 210, 211, 238, 309

Baptism, baptismal catachesis, 62, 66, 67, 94, 95, 98, 99, 165–6, 195, 199–200, 201, 213, 223, 229, 249–50, 251
Blessing, 43, 51, 52
Body of Christ, 80, 84, 117, 134, 165, 188–90, 191, 207, 247–8, 253, 298–302
Building-symbol, 122–5, 296–8, 325–8

Church,
  passim
  excursus on, 293–310
  unity of, 34, 159–69, 184, 294–5, 298, 310
Cosmology, 77, 91, 113, 139, 178
Cosmos, universe, 60–2, 83, 167, 179, 298–9, 306, 307–8
Cross, theology of, 27, 116–17, 151

Devil, 187, 207–8, 272–3, 339
Doxology, 22, 154–7

Economy (realization of the plan of salvation), 58–9, 131, 138
Election, predestination, 52–3, 53–4, 312–15
Epistolary form, 21–2, 39–42, 70–1, 286, 287–8
Eschatological perspective, 27, 165, 184, 210, 235, 251, 275–6

Ethics, Hellenistic, 208, 211, 214, 219 (n. 9), 224 (n. 29), 246
Eulogy, 22, 44–69

Faith, 97–8, 149–50, 318–20

God the Father, 73–4, 118, 147–8, 166–8
Gospel, 64–5, 135, 283
Grace, 43, 55, 56, 97, 131, 175–6

Haustafel, 231, 240–41, 245, 262, 263
Head, headship, 80, 83, 188, 246, 247–8, 298–9, 300, 301
Heaven, 51–2, 76, 178, 273
Hope, 63–4, 75, 110, 165
Hymns, songs, 23, 46, 72, 107, 108, 229, 238

In Christ (Jesus), 52–3, 96, 108, 111, 135, 212, 320–21
Inheritance, 67, 75, 134, 220
Israel, Jews, 35, 109–10, 119–20, 321–5

Justification, 27, 98

Law, 112–15
Linguistic style, 26, 46–7, 68, 128–9, 144–5, 171–3, 188–9, 194
Liturgy, 22, 68, 160, 228–9, 237–9, 291–2
Love, 152, 164, 212, 246, 248–9, 252–3

Marriage, 240–58, 301, 304, 305, 331–7
Ministries and offices, 175–6, 180–4, 190, 191–2, 301, 328–31
Mission, 309
Mystery, 57–8, 131–4, 135, 136–8, 255, 335

Nag Hammadi texts, 91, 96, 116, 149, 184–5, 248, 255, 297, 304, 338

Name, 78–9, 147, 239

Paraclesis, 23, 158, 161–2, 271
Paul, picture of, 32, 42, 130, 135–6
Peace, 43, 112–13, 116, 117–18, 125–6, 164–5, 278, 289, 338
Pleroma (fullness) 59, 81–4, 153, 179–80, 185–6, 303, 305–6, 307
Powers and authorities, 28, 51, 77–9, 140–41, 273, 338, 339
Prayer, 72, 73, 144, 146, 269, 270, 281–2
Pre-existence, 51–2, 53, 248, 255, 304
Prophets, prophecy, 74, 122, 123, 133–4, 180–2
Pseudepigraphy, 25, 32–3

Qumran texts, 26, 55, 57, 59, 75, 92, 137, 197, 202 (n. 28), 219, 223, 224, 234, 274, 278, 279, 282, 296

Reconciliation, 30, 112, 117, 125–6
Revelation, 128–9, 131–3
   plan of, 27, 133, 138, 141

Saints, 42–3, 75, 120–2, 218, 282
Sexual vices, 216, 217–18, 220
Sin, original, doctrine of, 93, 314, 315
Sins, 56, 90
Spirit, Holy, 66, 74, 118–19, 133–4, 148–9, 164–5, 200, 209–10, 237, 281
Spiritual military service (*militia Christi*), 276–81, 284–5, 337–42

Teachers of false doctrine, 34, 186
Then – Now, 88, 102, 111, 222

Vices and virtues, catalogue of, 163–4, 198, 204–5, 216, 219–20, 223–4

Wisdom, 139–40, 232, 233, 234–5

Index of Names

The following index was compiled by Mr Mathias Hartmann, student assistant to the Chair of Reformed Theology in Erlangen. It does not include the names of authors or editors of standard reference works (e.g. Lidell and Scott, Hatch and Redpath, Bauer, Blass and Debrunner) or editors of individual works or collections of texts (e.g. Hennecke, Souter, Harvey). Patristic authors are included where they are mentioned or discussed in the text of the commentary, but not when they are merely cited as witnesses to variant readings (e.g. frequently Ambrosiaster).

Aalen, S., 274
Abbott, T. K., 49, 63, 67, 94, 113, 114, 118, 121, 141, 167, 178, 183, 188, 189, 200, 221, 226, 236, 250, 291, 318, 337
Abraham, 43, 55
Abramowski, L., 338
Adam, 254, 255, 302, 315, 316, 333, 334
Aelius Aristides, 167, 178, 212
Agabus, 329
Aland, K., 25
Allan, J. A., 52
Ambrose, 334
Ambrosiaster, 49, 81, 117, 122, 326, 328, 333
Ammonas, A., 340
Aristotle, 109, 236
Arnold, G., 330
Athanasius, 322, 333
Audet, J. P., 50
Auer, J., 312, 337
Augustine, 93, 250, 312, 315, 323, 329, 334
Aulen, G., 293

Bagathuler, H. J., 299
Bagatti, B., 119
Baltensweiler, H., 169–92, 336
Balthasar, H. U. von, 314
Balz, H. R., 25, 78, 228, 245
Barc, B., 338

Barret, C. K., 103–27
Barth, K., 313, 314, 320, 321, 336, 337, 344
Barth, M., 24, 25, 27, 40, 46, 48, 49, 52, 54, 55, 62, 64, 67, 79, 80, 94, 103–27, 133, 134, 138, 141, 160, 162, 167, 169–92, 199, 220, 221, 222, 226, 227, 245, 246, 248, 249, 251, 255, 256, 262, 275, 280, 291, 320, 324, 325, 336
Basil, 314, 333
Batey, R., 39–44, 240–58
Bauer, W., 238
Bauernfeind, O., 196, 198
Baur, F. C., 24
Bauttier, M., 222
Bayer, F. W., 189
Beare, F. W., 36, 49, 113, 226
Beatrice, P., 266–85
Becker, J., 52, 202
Behm, J., 66, 200, 290
Belser, J., 254, 288
Benedict of Nursia, 340
Bengel, J. A., 94, 200, 226, 275
Benoit, P., 24, 77, 81, 83, 188, 247
Berengar of Tours, 335
Berger, K., 39–44, 69–86
Bertram, G., 57, 91, 186, 219, 220, 234, 262, 276
Best, E., 169–92, 293

Bethge, H.-G., 297
Betz, H. D., 203–14
Betz, O., 58, 65, 126, 133
Beyer, H. W., 50
Beza, Th., 81
Bieder, W., 110, 121, 179
Bienert, W., 208
Bietenhard, H., 51, 78, 166, 239
Bisping, A., 250
Bjerkelund, C. J., 159–69
Blank, J., 25
Blumenkranz, B., 323
Böcher, O., 77, 274
Böhl, F., 163, 212
Bonhoeffer, D., 324
Bonifatius, P., 340
Bornkamm, G., 22, 58, 137, 255, 256, 290, 320
Boucher, M., 246
Bousset, W., 179
Brandenburger, E., 113, 116, 302
Braun, H., 52, 55, 187, 229
Brenz, J., 319, 330
Brockhaus, U., 169–92
Brown, R. E., 137
Brownell, D., 103–27
Brox, N., 24, 25, 34, 212, 271, 288
Brunner, E., 313, 314
Brunner, P., 127–43
Büchsel, F., 56, 235
Büchsel, H., 109, 179, 200, 225
Bultmann, R., 31, 43, 49, 52, 64, 65, 90, 197, 209, 219, 221, 324
Burger, C., 103–27

Cadbury, H. J., 41
Cai, R., 319
Caird, G. B., 77, 169–92, 250
Cajetan, 327, 335
Calvin, J., 47, 81, 115, 141, 147, 167, 221, 227, 289, 311, 312, 313, 320, 323, 326, 327, 329, 330, 335, 342
Cambier, J., 44–69, 169–92, 240–58
Camelot, P. T., 164
Caragounis, C. C., 44–69, 146
Carrez, M., 109
Carrington, P., 24
Casel, O., 251
Caspari, W., 113
Cavedo, R., 193–202
Cazelles, H., 109
Cerfaux, L., 293
Chadwick, H., 33
Champion, L. G., 154–7
Christ, F., 140
Christian, V., 224
Chrysostom, 49, 81, 118, 122, 247, 291, 312, 314, 319, 323, 326, 328, 329, 333
Clement of Alexandria, 83, 228, 229, 314,

326, 332, 338, 339
Clement of Rome, 338
Colpe, C., 36, 83, 116, 178, 298
Collange, F. J., 26
Colli, P., 332, 335
Conzelmann, H., 22, 31, 43, 47, 55, 64, 74, 76, 113, 116, 118, 123, 138, 141, 166, 172, 176, 222, 223, 226, 229, 238, 251, 274
Coppens, J., 58, 137
Coutts, J., 32, 44–69, 107
Crouch, J. E., 240–58
Cullmann, O., 169–92, 239
Cumont, F., 273
Cyprian, 328, 330, 340

Dahl, N. A., 39–44, 44–69, 103, 108, 127–43, 144–54, 203–14, 215–31, 293
Daniel, J. L., 120
Daniélou, J., 322
Dassmann, E., 32
Dautzenberg, G., 74
de Boer, P. A. H., 103
de Jonge, M., 120
de la Potterie, I., 69–86, 176, 193–202, 306
De Wette, W. M. L., 24, 226
Deichgräber, R., 23, 44–69, 72, 103–27, 154–7, 238
Deissmann, A., 113, 293, 320
Delling, G., 81, 82, 83, 125, 155, 168, 179, 185, 198, 220, 232–40, 246, 275, 306
Delorme, J., 169–92
di Marco, A., 240–58
Dibelius, M., 40, 41, 47, 48, 51, 55, 62, 63, 64, 67, 72, 94, 96, 97, 113, 121, 123, 130, 138, 141, 151, 153, 159–69, 183, 185, 199, 200, 205, 209, 219, 222, 226, 228, 229, 236, 237, 251, 252, 255, 256, 261, 275, 280, 288, 291, 320
Didymus of Alexandria, 314
Dietrich, A., 179
Dihle, A., 163
Dinkler, E., 65, 113
Diogenes of Apollonia, 167
Dölger, F. J., 65, 66, 207, 215, 229
Doré, J., 109
Drago, A., 54
Drewermann, E., 273
du Plessis, P. J., 169–92
Dubois, J.-D., 188
Dupont, J., 34, 83, 151

Ebel, G., 92
Edmonds, H., 280
Eichrodt, W., 110
Elert, W., 122
Ellis, E. E., 144–54
Engelhardt, E., 174
Ephraem, 291
Epictet, 208, 261, 280

Epiphanius, 78, 228
Erasmus, D., of Rotterdam, 24, 335, 340, 341
Ernst, J., 25, 31, 33, 40, 47, 52, 55, 57, 59, 60, 67, 80, 81, 83, 84, 121, 130, 138, 153, 160, 180, 184, 220, 221, 222, 237, 261, 262, 306
Estius, W., 81, 122, 199, 250, 291, 328, 330, 335
Etcheverria, R. M. T., 44–69, 266–85, 337, 338, 339
Eupolemus, 63
Eusebius of Caesarea, 181, 317
Evanson, E., 24
Eve, 187, 254, 255, 256, 333, 334
Ewald, P., 81, 118, 141, 200, 205, 222, 254, 275, 278, 279

Faberberg, H., 329
Ferner, H., 8
Feuillet, A., 69–86, 151, 240–58, 306
Fischer, K. M., 22, 23, 32, 33, 36, 39–44, 46, 53, 60, 91, 96, 107, 113, 116, 119, 182, 215–31, 240–58, 280, 297, 298, 299, 301, 302, 303, 304, 306
Fitzer, G., 65, 66
Fitzmyer, J. A., 26, 166
Foerster, W., 51, 62, 66, 77, 91, 96, 111, 113, 120, 236, 248, 272, 338
Frank-Duqesne, A., 272
Frede, H. J., 81, 117, 188, 311, 315, 332, 333
Fridrichsen, G., 122
Friedrich, G., 118, 122, 123, 181, 336
Friedrich, J., 203–14, 215–31

Gärtner, B., 120, 126, 296
Galling, K., 113
Ganoczy, A., 330
Gaugler, E., 47, 53, 55, 67, 94, 118, 124, 130, 141, 172, 185, 198, 200, 205, 206, 209, 218, 220, 250, 291
Gelin, A., 44–69
Gewiess, J., 82, 179, 307
Geysels, L., 69–86
Giavani, G., 103–27
Glaue, P., 155
Gnilka, J., 22, 24, 25, 26, 33, 36, 41, 46, 48, 50, 52, 55, 62, 63, 64, 67, 80, 91, 96, 98, 103–27, 128, 133, 138, 139, 141, 150, 156, 161, 164, 167, 172, 178, 185, 188, 189, 193–202, 203–14, 218, 222, 223, 224, 225, 226, 228, 238, 240–58, 261, 264, 267, 275, 279, 281, 291, 298, 302, 304
Goldstein, H., 198
Gonzales, A., 144–54
Goodspeed, E. J., 36
Goppelt, L., 119, 212, 239
Gourgues, M., 76
Grabner-Haider, A., 162, 275
Gräser, E., 144–54

Greeven, H., 40, 41, 47, 48, 51, 55, 62, 63, 64, 67, 72, 94, 96, 97, 113, 121, 123, 130, 138, 141, 151, 153, 169–92, 199, 200, 205, 209, 219, 222, 226, 228, 229, 236, 237, 251, 252, 255, 256, 261, 273, 275, 280, 281, 291, 320, 336
Gregg, 40, 315
Gregory of Nazianzus, 334
Grelot, P., 109
Grillmeier, A., 305
Gross, H., 103, 113
Grotius, H., 47
Grundmann, W., 99, 163, 225, 282
Gülzow, H., 263
Güttgemanns, E., 320

Haag, H., 272
Haas, A., 342
Habakkuk, 137
Haenchen, E., 44–69, 116
Hahn, F., 72, 76, 181, 232–40, 240–58
Hainz, J., 169–92, 294, 295, 331
Hall, S. G., 229, 317
Halter, H., 86–101, 161, 193–202, 203–14, 215–31, 240–58
Hamman, A., 144–54, 232–40, 266–85
Hammer, P. L., 27, 134
Hanson, S., 60, 80, 110, 117, 183, 293, 325
Harder, G., 144–54, 275, 291
Harnack, A. von, 35, 139, 280, 293, 309, 317, 337, 340
Harrison, P. N., 26, 32, 37
Harrisville, R. A., 193–202
Hasenstab, R., 159–69
Hauck, F., 52, 54, 56, 163, 201, 218
Haupt, E., 55, 63, 64, 67, 94, 118, 121, 130, 141, 156, 172, 179, 189, 197, 198, 205, 206, 209, 218, 222, 226, 227, 228, 252, 254, 275, 288
Hay, D. M., 76
Hegermann, H., 36, 80, 82, 184, 189, 298, 299, 300, 303
Heinemann, I., 120
Heinrici, G., 66
Heitmüller, W., 66, 239
Hengel, M., 114
Henle, F. A. von, 254
Hermans, R., 69–86
Herod, 113
Herten, J., 169–92
Herwegen, I., 280
Hilary of Poitiers, 326, 333
Hippolytus, 322
Hoennicke, G., 119
Hoffmann, P., 228
Hofius, O., 52, 284
Hofmann, K., 290
Holtzmann, H. J., 32, 81
Hooker, M. D., 103–27

Horst, J., 163
Howard, G., 69–86, 169–92
Hruby, K., 323
Huby, J. S., 47, 172, 247, 250, 288
Hübner, H., 75
Huppenbauer, H. W., 274

Irenaeus, 53, 59, 82, 149, 151, 315, 316, 317, 322, 333
Ignatius of Antioch, 33, 35, 37, 164, 179, 182, 207, 238, 271, 280, 281, 302, 318, 331, 338
Ignatius of Loyola, 342
Innitzer, T., 44–69

Jacobs, P., 313
Jayne, D., 44–69
Jeremias, G., 133, 224, 296, 297
Jeremias, J., 103–27, 148, 210, 250, 251, 298
Jerome, 24, 122, 147, 209, 250, 255, 312, 315, 319, 323, 326, 328
John of Damascus, 153, 319
Jonas, H., 91, 149, 179, 229, 274
Jones, P. R., 266–285
Joseph, 218
Josephus, 63, 93, 97, 113, 195, 197, 198, 208, 221, 261
Joshua, 339
Jovinian, 334
Jüngel, E., 295
Jung, C. G., 272
Jungmann, J. A., 282
Justin, 222, 238, 315, 322, 338

Kähler, E., 240–58
Käsemann, E., 22, 31, 36, 46, 86–101, 115, 196, 203–14, 215–31, 293, 299
Kamlah, E., 206, 207, 224, 240–58, 266–85
Kasper, W., 272
Kasser, R., 185
Kattenbusch, F., 293, 309
Kehl, N., 44–69
Kertelge, K., 25, 136, 169–92, 272
Kinder, E., 329
Kirby, J. C., 22, 43, 50, 113, 250
Kittel, G., 148
Kittel, H., 148
Klaar, E., 198
Klauck, H.-J., 169–92, 295
Klein, G., 169–92
Klinzing, G., 121, 126
Klöpper, A., 118, 200, 226, 288, 291
Klooster, F. H., 313
Knox, W. L., 81
Köhler, W., 320, 330
Kötting, B., 240–58
Krämer, H., 44–69
Kraft, H., 26, 35
Kramer, W., 72, 162, 213
Krause, M., 83, 248

Kroll, J., 179
Kruse, C., 67
Kruse, H., 272
Köster, H., 93
Kortzfleisch, S. von, 323
Koschorke, K., 297
Koskenniemi, H., 70
Kosmala, H., 42
Kümmel, W. G., 21, 24, 29, 33, 36, 41, 43, 144–54, 176
Kürzinger, J., 246
Kuhn, H.-W., 52, 58, 296
Kuhn, K. G., 26, 54, 55, 90, 132, 198, 219, 223, 226, 227, 229, 249, 279, 280, 291
Kuss, O., 312
Kutsch, E., 110

Labib, P., 83, 248
Lake, K., 41
Lamadrid, G., 103–27
Larsson, E., 193–202
Lash, C. J. A., 273
Laubach, F., 56
Lawrence, R. J., 334, 335
Lee, J. Y., 77, 266–85
Lehmann, K., 272
Leipoldt, J., 120, 246
Lemaire, 169–92
Leo the Great, 336
Lercaro, 318
Lewy, H., 232–40
Lichtenberger, H., 202
Lincoln, A. T., 51
Lindars, B., 76, 79, 118, 176, 177, 203–14
Lindemann, A., 22, 27, 32, 33, 35, 39–44, 59, 60, 61, 73, 76, 78, 80, 82, 95, 96, 97, 107, 113, 114, 116, 121, 127–43, 178, 210, 221, 229, 275, 302, 325
Lindhagen, C., 209
Link, H. G., 225
Lloyd-Jones, D. M., 86–101, 240–58, 266–85
Locher, G. W., 313
Lövestam, E., 266–85
Lohfink, G., 136, 179
Lohmeyer, E., 44–69
Lohse, E., 56, 238, 305
Lombard, P., 334
López, M. L., 86–101
Lorenz, K., 272
Lührmann, D., 22, 98, 127–43
Luther, M., 183, 291, 311, 313, 319, 326, 329, 335, 341
Luz, U., 86–101
Lyonnet, S., 44–69

Maier, G., 52
Maier, J., 119, 296
Malinine, M., 185
Marcellus of Ancyra, 317

Marcion, 41, 139, 315, 322, 326
Marcus, R., 300
Marius Victorinus, 314, 319, 333
Martitz, W.v., 54
Marxsen, W., 34
Masson, Ch., 29, 46, 67, 118, 121, 124, 176, 183, 189, 250, 288, 291, 303
Maurer, C., 44–69
McEleny, N. J., 103–27
McKelvey, R. J., 104
McNamara, M., 177
Médebielle, A., 293
Mehlmann, J., 93, 314, 315
Meier, K., 324
Meinertz, M., 49, 82, 172, 179, 254, 307
Melanchthon, Ph., 324, 329
Melito of Sardis, 68, 229, 317
Menge, H., 183
Merk, A., 142
Merk, O., 161, 258–66
Merklein, H., 23, 31, 32, 34, 37, 74, 103–27, 127–43, 169–92, 193–202, 249, 294, 297, 298, 303, 325, 331
Methodius of Olympus, 317, 333
Metzger, B. M., 95, 213
Meuzelaar, J. J., 134, 176, 178, 188
Meyer, R., 120, 273, 308
Michaelis, W., 56, 90, 211, 212, 273
Michel, H.-J., 3
Michel, O., 58, 103–27, 131, 184, 296
Michl, J., 78, 147
Milik, J. T., 137
Minear, P. S., 293
Mitton, C. L., 24, 25, 30, 31, 32, 35, 49, 71, 107, 113, 236, 288
Molin, G., 223
Moses, 55, 137, 151, 177, 178, 277, 280, 300
Moule, C. F. D., 80, 119, 175
Müller, U. B., 122, 123
Müntzer, T., 341
Munck, J., 119
Musculus, W., 327
Mussner, F., 24, 26, 31, 32, 33, 51, 58, 80, 86–101, 103–27, 137, 179, 193–202, 207, 254, 299, 303, 323, 325

Nauck, W., 108
Neugebauer, F., 222
Nieder, L., 215–31
Nielen, J. M., 114–54, 232–40
Noack, B., 215–31
Noah, 91
Nötscher, F., 52, 57, 75, 92, 224, 234
Norden, E., 229
Nygren, G., 312

O'Brien P. T., 44–69, 69–86
O'Connor, J. M., 224
Ochel, W., 32, 44–69, 72

Oecumenius, 81, 117, 247, 323
Oepke, A., 272, 277, 278, 279, 280
Ollrog, W. H., 22
Onesimus, 37, 289
Origen, 314, 315, 328, 332, 333, 339
Ott, W., 281
Otten, H., 313
Overfield, P. D., 69–86

Pairman Brown, J., 246
Pauly, W., 120
Pelagius, 199, 314, 315, 325, 328, 333
Peri, J., 169–92
Percy, E., 24, 25, 32, 36, 39–44, 62, 64, 67, 119, 123, 248, 288, 303
Perels, O., 299
Peters, A., 127–43
Peterson, E., 159–69, 283
Pfammatter, J., 103–27, 296, 300
Philemon, 287
Philip, 181
Philo of Alexandria, 36, 83, 96, 134, 150, 151, 168, 179, 185, 188, 197, 198, 200, 212, 218, 220, 223, 224, 226, 236, 237, 248, 261, 262, 263, 273, 291, 298, 299, 300, 302, 305, 306
Philonenko, 223
Piolanti, A., 122
Plato, 147
Pliny the Younger, 237
Plutarch, 207, 252
Pöhlmann, W., 167, 203–14, 215–31
Pohlmann, H., 296
Pokorný, P., 22, 43, 108, 113
Polykarp, 338
Popkes, W., 213
Prast, F., 34
Prat, F., 122
Procksch, O., 42
Ptolemy, 82

Quell, G., 224
Quispel, G., 255

Rad, G. von, 113
Rader, W., 103–27, 321, 322, 323, 324, 326, 327
Rahner, K., 122, 308
Rainer, P., 253
Ramaroson, L., 86–101
Ratzinger, J., 256, 336
Reicke, B., 56, 103–27, 167, 169–92
Reitzenstein, R., 78, 96, 138, 151, 228, 299
Rengstorf, K. H., 122, 181, 323
Resch, A., 210
Rese, M., 44–69, 103–27
Reumann, J., 127–43
Ricoeur, P., 272, 295
Riesenfeld, H., 213
Rigaux, B., 24, 303

Robinson, J. M., 44–69, 69–86, 167, 209, 247, 291
Rohde, J., 169–92
Roller, O., 42
Roloff, J., 182, 293, 294
Rubinkiewicz, R., 169–92
Rudolph, K., 91, 149, 179, 185, 274, 299

Sahlin, H., 103–27
Salmeron, A., 324, 327
Sampley, J. P., 203–14, 240–58, 304
Samuel, 55
Sanders, J. T., 44–69, 69–86, 87, 103–27
Sandfuchs, W., 122
Santer, M., 39–44
Santopietro, G., 44–69
Sarah, 333
Sasse, H., 60, 91, 138
Schäfer, K., 103–27
Schaller, J. B., 255
Scharbert, J., 50
Scharl, E., 59, 316
Schattenmann, J., 44–69
Schaul, R. A., 212
Schelkle, K. H., 24
Schenk, W., 7, 39–44
Schenke, G., 149
Schenke, H.-M., 22, 36, 39–44, 53, 107, 113, 116, 178, 185, 299
Schiel, H., 340
Schille, G., 22, 32, 33, 44–69, 72, 96, 103–27, 228
Schillebeeckx, E., 334, 335
Schlier, H., 22, 24, 31, 36, 41, 46, 48, 49, 51, 52, 53, 55, 57, 58, 59, 60, 63, 66, 67, 74, 77, 78, 80, 82, 83, 91, 94, 96, 97, 98, 103–27, 130, 131, 133, 134, 135, 138, 139, 140, 141, 142, 146, 150, 151, 155, 159–69, 172, 174, 175, 179, 180, 183, 184, 185, 188, 189, 197, 198, 199, 201, 205, 209, 218, 219, 220, 221, 222, 226, 227, 229, 238, 245, 247, 248, 250, 251, 253, 254, 255, 261, 262, 271, 274, 275, 276, 279, 281, 283, 284, 288, 290, 291, 293, 297, 302
Schlink, E., 127–43
Schmaus, M., 256, 319, 321
Schmid, J., 21, 24, 25, 26, 29, 31, 33, 37, 39–44, 74, 81, 103–27, 141, 244, 250, 251, 254, 273, 304, 305, 323
Schmidt, K. L., 118, 120, 197, 293, 295, 309
Schmidt, M. A., 120, 197
Schmitz, O., 133, 162, 289, 320
Schnackenburg, R., 24, 44–69, 84, 86–101, 103–27, 142, 169–92, 215–31, 235, 238, 250, 251, 272, 274, 292, 299, 320
Schneider, J., 118, 148, 179, 184, 185
Schoeps, H.-J., 119, 212
Schott, A., 342
Schottroff, W., 103

Schrage, W., 110, 161, 240–58
Schreiner, J., 119
Schrenk, G., 147, 261
Schubert, P., 69–86
Schürmann, H., 34, 37, 169–92
Schulz, A., 203–14
Schulz, S., 55, 163, 196, 218
Schweizer, E., 7, 27, 28, 29, 31, 32, 42, 54, 60, 61, 62, 74, 79, 80, 95, 115, 119, 131, 133, 134, 138, 148, 149, 164, 169–92, 198, 200, 203–14, 215–31, 234, 235, 237, 240–58, 261, 262, 264, 273, 274, 283, 289, 293, 294, 298, 299, 300, 303, 307, 315, 331
Scott, E. F., 49, 113, 118, 141, 226, 247, 250
Seeberg, R., 283
Seesemann, H., 91
Seidensticker, P., 56
Sevenster, J. N., 120
Severian of Gabala, 153, 229, 323
Severus, E. von, 144–54
Siber, P., 95
Simon, M., 119, 323
Smend, R., 240–58
Smith, G. V., 169–92
Soden, H. von, 55, 63, 133, 178, 199, 275, 288
Söhngen, G., 319
Solomon, 55
Speyer, W., 25
Spicq, C., 96, 120, 176, 198, 209, 211, 220, 224, 236, 248, 282, 290
Staab, K., 118, 121, 226, 229, 288, 291, 323
Stachowiak, L. R., 96, 211
Stählin, G., 93, 120, 207, 210, 221
Staerk, W., 316
Stanley, D. M., 56
Starke, Ch., 324
Stauffer, E., 111, 248, 251
Steidle, B., 340
Steinmetz, F. J., 27, 60, 61, 73, 88, 96, 138, 141, 188, 210
Strathmann, H., 110, 121, 195, 305
Straub, W., 251
Strecker, G., 22, 119, 166
Stuhlmacher, P., 103–27, 203–14, 215–31, 258–66, 288
Stuiber, A., 154, 157
Suggs, M. J., 140
Suski, A., 44–69

Tachau, P., 86–101
Tannehill, R. C., 95
Tertullian, 139, 314, 315, 322, 326, 333, 340
Testa, E., 103–127
Theodore of Mopsuestia, 24, 40, 317, 323, 325, 328, 333
Theodoret of Cyrrhus, 122, 222, 229, 318, 323, 333
Theodotius, 338

Theophylactus, 81, 247, 323, 328
Thomas Aquinas, 81, 93, 122, 250, 262, 279, 319, 323, 327, 328
Thomas à Kempis, 342
Thraede, K., 240–58
Thrall, M. E., 26
Thüsing, W., 76, 118
Till, W. C., 116
Timothy, 32, 42, 181, 287, 288
Towner, W. S., 50
Traub, H., 51
Trilling, W., 25, 288
Tröger, K.-W., 36, 107, 116, 178, 302
Tromp, S., 169–192
Tucci, R., 318
Tychicus, 29, 30, 286, 287, 288, 292

Usteri, L., 24

Valeske, U., 293
van der Horst, P. W., 178, 208, 210, 220, 249
van Roon, A., 24, 25, 26, 32, 39–44
van Zutphen, V., 83, 159–169
Vielhauer, Ph., 22, 23, 36, 76, 103–127, 296, 297
Vögtle, A., 56, 169–192, 198, 210, 331
Vogt, J., 263
Volkmann, H., 263
Vosté, J. M., 153

Wacholder, B. Z., 63
Wagenführer, M.-A., 84, 107, 153, 299
Wagner, G., 229, 251
Wagner, S., 296
Wang, A., 337
Wanke, G., 245

Warnach, V., 84, 153, 248, 254, 299
Weder, H., 295
Wegenast, K., 193–202
Wehmeier, G., 50
Weinfeld, M., 110
Weinrich, W. C., 103–27
Weiss, B., 81, 164
Weiss, H.-F., 36, 178
Weiss, J., 200
Weiss, K., 96, 211
Wendland, H.-D., 161, 256, 336
Wengst, K., 103–27, 159–69, 213
Westcott, B. F., 47, 254
Westermann, C., 50, 113
Westermann, W. L., 263
White, J. L., 42, 69–86
Whiteley, D. E. H., 266–85
Wibbing, S., 92, 215–231
Wikenhauser, A., 21, 24, 29, 31, 123, 133, 169–192, 293, 298, 320
Wilckens, U., 22, 140, 183, 196, 197, 235, 291
Wiles, G. P., 69–86, 144–54
Williams, A. L., 323
Wilson, S. G., 103–27
Wingren, G., 59
Wochenmark, J., 52

Yates, R., 69–86
Ysebaert, Y., 222

Zerwick, M., 117, 124, 133, 276
Zimmerli, W., 240–258
Zingg, P., 125
Zirker, H., 103
Zuntz, G., 41
Zwingli, H., 313, 329, 341

Important Biblical Passages outwith Eph. and Col.

Genesis
2.24   244, 254–5

Exodus
20.10   261–2

Psalms
39(40).7   213
68(67).19   176–7

Isaiah
9.5 f   112, 113, 117
11.5 (LXX)   277, 280
28.16   123
52.7   117–18, 278
57.19   107, 111, 117
59.17   277, 279

Mark
14.38   282

Luke
6.35 f.   212

Romans
1.18–32   221
1.19–21   196
8.28–9   53, 54

9.4   108, 109–110
12.1–8   158
12.4–8   174, 180
16.25 f.   132, 138

1 Corinthians
2.7–10   58, 137
2.12   74, 150
3.10 f.   124, 297
11.3   246
12.13   118, 148, 165
12.28   173, 181, 182

2 Corinthians
5.20   284
6.14–7.1   26, 223
11.2   304

Galatians
1.15 f.   131
2.20   149, 213
3.28   118, 302
4.4–6   54

Philemon
2.1–5   245

1 Peter
2.4–8   124, 125, 329